Cross-Border Insolvency

To Amarylla

Cross-Border Insolvency

Philip St J Smart LLB, LLM

of Lincoln's Inn, Barrister,
England and Wales and Hong Kong

Associate Professor, Faculty of Law
University of Hong Kong

Butterworths
London, Charlottesville, Dublin, Durban, Edinburgh,
Hong Kong, Kuala Lumpur, New Delhi, Singapore,
Sydney, Toronto, Wellington
1998

United Kingdom	Butterworths, a Division of Reed Elsevier (UK Ltd), Halsbury House, 35 Chancery Lane, LONDON WC2A 1EL and 4 Hill Street, EDINBURGH EH2 3JZ
Australia	Butterworths, a Division of Reed International Books Australia Pty Ltd, CHATSWOOD, New South Wales
Canada	Butterworths Canada Ltd, MARKHAM, Ontario
Hong Kong	Butterworths Asia (Hong Kong), HONG KONG
India	Butterworths India, NEW DELHI
Ireland	Butterworth (Ireland) Ltd, DUBLIN
Malaysia	Malayan Law Journal Sdn Bhd, KUALA LUMPUR
New Zealand	Butterworths of New Zealand Ltd, WELLINGTON
Singapore	Butterworths Asia, SINGAPORE
South Africa	Butterworths Publishers (Pty) Ltd, DURBAN
USA	Lexis Law Publishing, CHARLOTTESVILLE, Virginia

A CIP Catalogue record for this book is available from the British Library.

ISBN 0 406 08134 4

Typeset by J&L Composition Ltd, Filey, North Yorkshire
Printed by Redwood Books Ltd, Trowbridge, Wilts

Visit us at our website: http://www.butterworths.co.uk

Preface

In the seven years since the first edition of this book was published such so-called 'mega' international insolvencies as BCCI and Maxwell – not to mention Olympia & York or Barings plc – have highlighted far more clearly than could any author the importance of cross-border insolvency in international commercial law and practice. Yet the relevance of cross-border insolvency is in no way confined to these 'mega' cases. The law of cross-border insolvency comes into play whenever international elements present themselves in the course of English insolvency proceedings, or when property in England is being administered in insolvency proceedings abroad.[1]

The increasing number of international insolvencies is a consequence of the fact that more and more business activities are being conducted across national boundaries. This is, of course, true not only regionally (particularly within Europe) but also on a worldwide basis. 'Globalisation' has been one of the buzz-words of the 1990s and the connection to international insolvency, including corporate restructuring and rescue, requires no elaboration. Moreover, the judges have not been slow to point out that changing economic realities have made apparent the pressing need for an international treaty to regulate cross-border insolvency and supplement, or to a certain extent replace, the somewhat out-dated rules of private international law which almost by default currently apply.[2] This edition, accordingly, covers relevant international initiatives, particularly the (now lapsed) EC Convention on Insolvency Proceedings.[3] Nevertheless, I have sought to stick to my primary objective: that is, to offer a modern and systematic analysis of the applicable rules of English case and statute law.

At the same time it is important to appreciate the restricted role the English court has to play in many international insolvencies. For the rules of cross-border insolvency may more appropriately be regarded as providing a framework, rather than laying down rigid procedures that must invariably be applied; and within that framework an insolvency practitioner may well have considerable scope to work out (often in conjunction

---

[1] The rules may also become relevant when there are individuals in England whom a foreign insolvency representative wishes to examine, or when civil actions have been commenced in England against a defendant subject to a foreign insolvency process.

[2] For details, see pp. 2–3 *infra*.

[3] Whilst the Convention was not signed by the United Kingdom Government and accordingly lapsed, see p. 10 below, it is anticipated that similar provisions may be introduced by the Commission in the form of a Directive in the next few years.

with a foreign counterpart) the most efficient way of liquidating the debtor's assets or the rescue plan with the optimum chance of success. Certainly, recent examples – the most obvious being the Maxwell insolvency[4] – have shown that the judges will play their part in facilitating co-operation between insolvency practitioners from different jurisdictions. Similarly, this judicial spirit of co-operation has found expression recently in relation to 'ancillary' winding up. For, in what can only be regarded as the most important decision yet on the topic, Sir Richard Scott V-C in *Re BCCI S.A. (No. 10)*[5] has confirmed that, despite the absence of any specific statutory authorisation, the English court is prepared in appropriate circumstances to authorise an English liquidator to remit assets to the foreign liquidator conducting the principal winding up abroad.[6]

The expanded coverage in this edition of international co-operation and assistance also includes an analysis of the several cases decided under section 426 of the Insolvency Act 1986,[7] especially *Hughes* v *Hannover Rückversicherungs-Aktiengesellschaft*,[8] the very first case under this section to reach the Court of Appeal. Readers may also be interested to note that a major statutory reform was introduced last year. As from 1 April 1997, without any reliance upon section 426 of the Insolvency Act 1986, interim relief is available in aid of insolvency proceedings being conducted in any part of the world. The impact and apparent limitations of the Civil Jurisdiction and Judgments Act 1982 (Interim Relief) Order 1997 are fully considered in chapter 15.

Such developments have contributed to the increase in length of this edition. In addition to those decisions already mentioned, there have been significant cases dealing with, *inter alia*, the jurisdiction to wind up foreign companies,[9] the extra-territorial operation of the Insolvency Act 1986,[10] the application of the doctrine of *forum non conveniens* to insolvency proceedings,[11] the treatment of US chapter 11 reorganisations in England[12] and the consequences of the recognition of foreign insolvencies generally.[13] I have also written a new chapter 1 which, it is hoped, provides a useful introduction to the theory and practice of cross-border insolvency. Additional consideration is given to the analysis of international issues that may arise out of the operation of the administration regime and corporate rescue generally.[14]

On a personal note, I would like to acknowledge the debt I owe to my colleague Charles D. Booth, one of the leading experts on US trans-

---

[4] See p. 332, *infra*.

[5] [1997] Ch. 213 and chapter 14.

[6] The Vice-Chancellor approved a passage appearing at p. 244 of the first edition in this regard.

[7] See chapter 15.

[8] [1997] 1 B.C.L.C. 497.

[9] See chapter 4.

[10] *Re Paramount Airways Ltd. (In Administration)* [1993] Ch. 223, *Re Seagull Manufacturing Co. Ltd.* [1993] Ch. 345 and more recently *Re Howard Holdings Inc.*, Chancery Division, 6 June 1997, discussed at pp. 26–27, *infra*.

[11] Note *Re Wallace Smith & Co. Ltd.* [1992] B.C.L.C. 970 and the discussion at pp. 125–130, *infra*.

[12] *Banque Indosuez S.A.* v. *Ferromet Resources Inc.* [1993] B.C.L.C. 112, *Barclays Bank plc* v. *Homan* [1993] B.C.L.C. 680 and *Rowland* v. *Gulfpac Ltd.*, p. 238, *infra*.

[13] See, for example, *Firswood Ltd.* v. *Petra Bank* [1996] C.L.C. 608 and p. 247, *infra*.

[14] See pp. 130, 202, 296 and 335, *infra* for analysis.

national insolvency law. Our many discussions over the last seven years have prompted me, more than once, completely to re-examine my rather incomplete understanding of cross-border insolvency issues. I must, of course, accept full responsibility for any and all errors in this work. Having already mentioned globalisation, I like to think of a practical illustration as an English lawyer and a US lawyer sitting down over a cup of coffee (or at times something stronger) in the Senior Common Room at Hong Kong University discussing the pros and cons of the UNCITRAL Model Law on Cross-Border Insolvency and the IBA's Concordat.

Finally, I would like to thank my publishers for preparing the tables and index and for all their help and assistance, not to mention patience.

The law is stated as it is understood to be on 1 June 1998.

Philip Smart
Hong Kong
Dragon Boat Day
(30 May 1998)

Contents

CHAPTER 15.   INTERNATIONAL CO-OPERATION AND ASSISTANCE   391

Table of Statutes

References in this Table to *Statutes* are to Halsbury's Statutes of England (Fourth Edition) showing the volume and page number at which the annotated text of the Act may be found.

Page references printed in **bold** type indicate where the Act is set out in part or in full.

Table of Statutory Instruments

Page references printed in **bold** type indicate where the Statutory Instrument is set out in part or in full.

Table of Cases

C

H

I

J

K

Chapter 1

Theory and Practice

1. INTRODUCTION

The law of cross-border insolvency becomes relevant whenever international elements present themselves in the course of English insolvency proceedings, or property in England is the subject-matter of proceedings abroad. When writing the Introduction to the first edition of this book in 1990, the author felt it necessary to set out a number of simple (if not simplistic) fact scenarios[1] in order to convey to the reader a rough and ready idea of what was involved in cross-border insolvency. Such an approach is now quite unnecessary. One does not have to be a commercial or insolvency law expert to be aware of the international dimension to such landmark insolvencies as BCCI[2] or Maxwell,[3] or the perhaps just as well-known collapses involving Olympia & York[4] or Barings plc;[5] and it goes without saying that for every such 'mega' international insolvency there will be many smaller-scale cases, which may often be just as significant in terms of their value as legal precedents. The increasing number of international insolvencies is a consequence of the fact that more and more business activities are being conducted across national boundaries. 'Globalisation' has been one of the 'buzz-words' of the 1990s and the connection to international insolvency (including corporate restructuring and rescue) is self-evident.[6]

At the outset it is important to appreciate the necessarily restricted role the English court has to play in many international insolvency cases.[7] For

---

[1] At pp. vii–viii of the first edition.

[2] See *infra*, p. 362.

[3] See *infra*, p. 332.

[4] The restructuring of Olympia & York has not produced any significant case law in England, cf. *Re Olympia & York Developments Ltd.* (1996) 29 O.R. (3d) 626.

[5] Although there is no reported decision, see Rushworth (1995) 7: 1 Int. Insol. & Cred. Rights Rep. at pp. 13–15.

[6] As the *Guide to Enactment of the UNCITRAL Model Law on Cross-Border Insolvency,* December. 1997, A/CN9/442, puts it (at para.13): 'The increasing incidence of cross-border insolvencies reflects the continuing global expansion of trade and investment. However, national insolvency laws have by and large not kept pace with the trend, and they are often ill-equipped to deal with cases of a cross-border nature. This frequently results in inadequate and inharmonious legal approaches, which hamper the rescue of financially troubled businesses, are not conducive to fair and efficient administration of cross-border insolvencies, impede the protection of the assets of the insolvent debtor against dissipation, and hinder maximization of the value of those assets.'

[7] One is here referring particularly to concurrent insolvency proceedings, see chapter 12.

the rules of cross-border insolvency tend to provide a framework and establish boundaries, rather than lay down rigid and detailed procedures that must invariably be followed; and within those boundaries the insolvency practitioner may have considerable scope to work out, often in co-operation with a foreign counterpart, the most efficient liquidation of the debtor's assets or a restructuring plan with the optimum chance of success.[8] But it must not for one moment be thought that an underdeveloped legal framework assists the practitioner. Although it may well be true in one sense that the fewer legal boundaries there are the more room for man-oeuvre there will be, if the legal structure is out-dated or inadequate then almost every issue becomes potentially contentious and shrouded in doubt. Obviously, an up-to-date and transparent set of legal rules will promote co-operation and compromise amongst the numerous interests that are present in many international insolvency cases. Hence, in recent years, one does not have to look hard to find strong judicial support for an international treaty to regulate cross-border insolvency and supplement, if not replace, the rather out-dated rules of private international law which by default, as it were, currently apply.[9] Unfortunately, no broad-based international convention has yet been promulgated, whilst the EC Convention on Insolvency Proceedings failed at the last moment, having become hostage to the so-called 'beef war' in 1996.[10] The EC Convention does not seem likely to re-appear in the near future.[11] On a brighter note, international practitioner groups (notably INSOL and Committee J of the Section on Business Law of the IBA) have spent the last decade or so building bridges between insolvency practitioners, regulators and judges from different countries and regions. The practical benefits from increased familiarity with and confidence in foreign insolvency laws should not be underestimated.[12] Moreover, without the activities of INSOL and Committee J it is doubtful that the UNCITRAL Model Law on Cross-Border Insolvency would have come into existence in 1997, or at all. The Model Law, which is not of course a treaty, has taken a pragmatic approach and doubtless currently represents the best way forward on a truly international (rather than regional) basis.[13]

A. Private International Law

In *Re Bank of Credit and Commerce International S.A.* Sir Nicolas Browne-Wilkinson V-C (as he then was) commented:[14]

---

[8]   See the remarks of Lord Hoffmann in relation to the Maxwell insolvency, set out at p. 336, *infra*.

[9]   See, for example, *per* Browne-Wilkinson V-C in *Re Bank of Credit and Commerce International S.A.* [1992] B.C.L.C. 570 at 577 or *per* Nicholls V-C in *Re Paramount Airways Ltd. (in administration)* [1993] Ch. 223 at 239.

[10]   See p. 10, *infra*.

[11]   Although a Directive seems almost inevitable, *idem*.

[12]   One may cite as an example the joint hearing between US and Canadian judges involving a corporation named 'Solvex' (letter of 10 March 1998 from the President of INSOL to members refers).

[13]   See also p. 8, *infra*.

[14]   [1992] B.C.L.C. 570 at 577.

'It is a matter of profound regret to me that there is no international convention regulating international insolvency. This case, I hope, if it does nothing else may concentrate people's minds on the necessity for such a convention. What we do have are some rather dated rules of private international law which will regulate the disposal of the assets in the event that no rescue scheme is possible.'

Many of the rules applicable to the cross-border insolvency cases discussed in the following chapters have a basis in English private international law; and, particularly if one looks at the date of some of the leading authorities,[15] no one could seriously take issue with the suggestion that these rules are often out-dated. It is also worth noting that whereas domestic insolvency law derives, and has always derived, from statutory sources, the rules of private international law referred to by the Vice-Chancellor stem in most part from the judges' inherent common law jurisdiction.[16] In addition, the legislature has largely ignored this area of English law – indeed, even the Cork Report had less than two and a half pages on international insolvency.[17] Accordingly, whilst the call for an international convention would doubtless be concurred in by all interested parties, a great deal remains to be done at the level of domestic legislation if a truly coherent set of rules applicable to cross-border insolvencies is ever to emerge as part of English law.[18]

In the meantime, it will regularly be the judge-made rules of English private international law to which practitioners and academics must make reference. The scope of operation of these rules is itself somewhat unusual. In many areas of English private international law (for instance, contracts, torts, negotiable instruments, transfers of property, trusts and so on) a key issue in both theoretical and practical terms will be *choice of law*. That is, in any particular case it may be crucial to determine which law governs the validity of a contract, of a transfer of property or the creation of a trust. Yet when it comes to the conduct of English insolvency proceedings, the judges have consistently obliterated choice of law issues: in an English bankruptcy, winding up or administration it is the Insolvency Act 1986, and not any foreign insolvency law, which must be applied.[19] Quite why the judges decided to adopt a restricted, even emasculated, approach to private international law in the insolvency field is not altogether certain, but this author would suggest that the purely statutory basis of bankruptcy law (and later companies winding up) has played a very large part: the judges had no inherent insolvency jurisdiction and simply could not point to any particular statutory provision that could reasonably be construed as permitting the application of a foreign insolvency law in an English

---

[15] Such as *Sill* v. *Worswick* (1791) 1 Hy BL 665 or *Re Blithman* (1866) L.R. 2 Eq. 23.

[16] For a recent judgment on the difficulties that this have given rise to, in relation to 'ancillary winding up', see *Re Bank of Credit and Commerce International S.A. (No. 10)* [1997] Ch. 213, p. 362, *infra*.

[17] *Report of the Review Committee on Insolvency Law and Practice* (Cmnd. 8558, 1982) pp. 429–431: cf. *Report on Bankruptcy and Related Aspects of Insolvency and Liquidation* (Scot. Law Com. No. 68, 1982) pp. 92–101.

[18] Even such a basic issue as the winding up of foreign companies is unnecessarily obscure: see p. 104, *infra*.

[19] *Re Suidair International Airways Ltd.* [1951] Ch. 165; cf. s. 426 of the Insolvency Act 1986, for details see chapter 15.

bankruptcy case.[20] In short, the problem is not just that many of the rules
of private international law are rather dated, but also that the removal of
choice of law issues has fundamentally handicapped any possibility of the
development through the cases of a theoretically coherent set of principles.

Turning away from English insolvency proceedings, the recognition in
England of foreign proceedings also presents major conceptual difficulties.
If one were today looking afresh at the recognition of foreign insolvency
proceedings, with a view to laying down the basis or bases of recognition,[1]
such concepts as the 'seat' of the debtor's business, the place of incorporation, the centre of the debtor's main interests, the habitual residence of the
individual debtor, and perhaps even domicile, might each be suggested with
varying degrees of enthusiasm. However, in the 1760s, when the general
principles of English private international law were at an embryonic stage,
and the judges were first dealing with the effect that might be given in
England to a foreign bankruptcy,[2] the issue was not approached as (what
would today be regarded as) a recognition issue.[3] For whilst it is true that
the judges looked to the domicile of the debtor, they did so not simply as a
basis of recognition but rather in order that they might apply the maxim
mobilia sequuntur personam,[4] the maxim being at that time the accepted
choice of law rule for the validity of a transfer of movable property.
Although the maxim has long since been discredited and replaced as the
relevant choice of law rule for the transfer of movables,[5] and although a
choice of law rule really has no necessary place when the question to be
decided is one of recognition,[6] the law on the recognition of foreign insolvencies is to this day influenced by the old maxim.[7] It is perhaps a testament
to the practical good sense of later judges (usually at first instance) that in
spite of such an inauspicious beginning, a workable set of rules on the
recognition of foreign insolvencies has emerged as part of English law.[8]

B. Opaque Legislation

If there have been difficulties and inadequacies in the judge-made rules, the
same can most definitely be said of the relevant English legislation. For
example, the winding up of foreign companies is heavily camouflaged in
Part V of the Insolvency Act 1986;[9] and even once the relevant provisions

---

[20] Insolvency, although unusual, is not unique in this regard. For example, when granting a
divorce the English courts only apply the English (and not any foreign) grounds for divorce,
see Dicey and Morris, *The Conflict of Laws* (12th ed., 1993) pp. 719–720. Divorce jurisdiction, it will be noted, is also exclusively statutory.

[1] The recognition of judgments and orders made in the course of foreign insolvency proceedings is discussed below, pp. 400–403.

[2] The landmark decision being *Solomons* v. *Ross* (1764) 1 Hy.Bl. 131n., and see p. 212 *infra*.

[3] Of course, the recognition of foreign judgments was at that time at a very early stage of
development, see *Dicey and Morris*, above n. 20, at pp. 455–456, *passim*.

[4] The transfer of movable property being governed by the personal law.

[5] The *lex situs* being applicable, *Dicey and Morris*, above n. 20, at p. 965.

[6] A foreign liquidation or re-organisation is recognised under English law without reliance
upon any notional transfer of the corporation's property.

[7] One particularly troublesome example being *Galbraith* v. *Grimshaw* [1910] A.C. 508, discussed below pp. 216–217 and 234.

[8] See, generally, chapters 5 and 6, *infra*.

[9] Discussed, pp. 93–94, *infra*.

have been uncovered, the sections give no guidance as to the factual nexus that must exist between a foreign company and England before there will be jurisdiction to make a winding up order.[10] Yet, even if these questions are answered, there remains the problem of whether any factual connection between the petitioning creditor (or other creditors) and England is also required.[11]

Similarly, where there has been a liquidation in a corporation's home State, one of the most basic practical questions the foreign representative may want answered is whether he or she can commence a winding up of the same corporation in England.[12] (The issue may just as easily arise where a foreign representative has been appointed in relation to an individual and wishes to know if he can commence bankruptcy proceedings in England.[13]) After careful analysis of Part IV and Part V of the 1986 Act it would appear[14] that, at least in some circumstances, a foreign representative may present a winding up petition – but there is no reasoned authority on the point and the legislation could scarcely be more unhelpful.

C. Unity, Territoriality and Universality

At the centre of the doctrine of 'unity of bankruptcy' lay the idea that there should be only one set of bankruptcy proceedings, recognised throughout the world, which should deal with all the debtor's assets and all the creditors' claims.[15] Apart from a conceptual neatness, a unity approach should in theory result in a considerable saving in costs and, accordingly, a larger estate available for distribution amongst the creditors.[16] In this regard the unity doctrine seems at first blush most attractive. This is particularly so if one thinks of bankruptcy in relatively simple terms (merely collecting assets, determining the creditors' claims and ultimately making distributions on a pari passu basis). Yet, increasing strains are put upon the credibility of the unity doctrine if one looks at insolvency in more modern terms. A modern insolvency involving, for example, a debtor who has carried on business in State A and State B, will very likely produce claims by the revenue authorities in both States. Unless the position has been modified by treaty,[17] however, it will be almost inevitable that tax debts owing to State A cannot be claimed in State B and vice versa.[18] No government is likely to be keen to embrace a theory that denies it the possibility of recovering its tax debts in these circumstances.[19] In fact,

---

[10] Discussed, p. 97, *infra*.

[11] Discussed, pp. 105–107, *infra*.

[12] The practical significance of this point is borne out by the fact that Art. 11 of the UNCITRAL Model Law specifically addresses the question. For a discussion of the English legislation, see pp. 228–230, *infra*.

[13] *Idem.*

[14] The point is that such an analysis should be unnecessary: the legislation should be clear.

[15] For a general analysis, see Fletcher, *Law of Insolvency* (2nd ed., 1995) pp. 684–689, Hanisch (1993) 2 I.I.R. 151 at 153–154, Johnson (1996) 5 I.I.R. 80 at 82–84 and Volken (1991) 230 Recueil des Cours. 347 at 387–400.

[16] Of course, this would not inevitably be the case, e.g. where the relevant jurisdiction had particularly inefficient insolvency laws.

[17] Which it would be if the EC Convention were to come into force (see Art. 39).

[18] See chapter 7, *infra*. The same is true in respect of social security claims.

[19] The right to commence a local insolvency is, of course, one means of enforcing tax debts.

governments have tended to try to ensure that their tax claims are met by according such debts preferential status in local insolvency proceedings. More generally, preferential debts (e.g. workers' salaries) in State A are (again in the absence of a treaty) unlikely to have the same status in State B and vice versa. Additionally, the priorities of preferential debts in State A and State B may be incompatible, each creating a preferential status unknown in the other jurisdiction. So too, different legal systems have very different types of secured interests (as well as other sorts of proprietary claims) and there is no universal approach as to whether – and if so, to what extent – the holders of security must follow along with any insolvency proceedings or, on the other hand, are permitted to take steps quite independently (even selfishly) to realise their security.[20]

Turning to corporate re-organisation and rescue – another more modern feature of international insolvencies – the unity doctrine is again put under great strain. One of the major objectives of corporate re-organisation is to preserve the company as a going concern, thereby saving jobs as well as helping the overall economy. Such considerations are almost bound to have strong territorial elements. Where a corporation has carried on business activities in both State X and State Y (although the major business has been operated in State Y) and a rescue is being proposed, officials and creditors in State X are not likely to be impressed by any plan that sacrifices jobs in their State so that a more complete re-organisation can occur in the corporation's home State.[1]

Despite the difficulties associated with the unity doctrine, particularly if it is proposed as an all-embracing theory,[2] a strictly territorial approach is especially unhelpful and unattractive. Whilst it could (superficially) be contended that a territorial approach has some advantages in terms of certainty,[3] it is totally out of step with modern commercial realities in the so-called global market place. Moreover, now that money and other intangible assets may be shifted around the world at the click of a mouse, the geographical location where assets are technically situated on a particular day may at best be a matter of chance – and, of course, territoriality plays into the hands of fraudsters, who do not leave the location of assets to chance.[4] Territoriality would tend to increase costs (thereby lessening the size of the overall estate available for distribution) as well as cause unfairness between creditors: particularly as a territorial approach is very often coupled with the ring-fencing of assets on a nationalistic basis.[5]

The English court has not adopted any doctrinaire position and, it can perhaps fairly be said, has taken a middle course. Thus, provided a foreign bankruptcy is entitled to recognition, it will vest the debtor's movable

---

[20] The floating charge (and the appointment of a receiver) is the classic example.

[1] Similar issues can arise where there are parent and subsidiary companies, incorporated in different jurisdictions, whose activities are interdependent. A notable example involved Lancer Boss/Steinbeck Boss, see Turing [1994] I.C.C.L.R. C-146.

[2] Rather than a guidepost.

[3] Although practitioners from jurisdictions that have adopted a strictly territorial approach are always on the look out for ways around the territoriality problem: see Miyake (1996) 24 Int. Bus. Law. 238, *passim*.

[4] Moreover, even without fraud, assets may happen to be located in a country the courts of which do not assert jurisdiction on the basis of assets alone.

[5] One of the objectives of the UNCITRAL Model Law, see Art. 13, is to eliminate discrimination.

property in England in the foreign trustee.[6] The English court, however, will not be deprived of its own bankruptcy jurisdiction simply because proceedings have been (or might be) commenced in the debtor's home State. The position is similar in relation to companies winding up. If a foreign liquidation is recognised, the liquidator can deal with the foreign corporation's property and rights in England; but foreign proceedings in no way prevent the making of a winding up order in England, whereupon the English liquidator will be solely entitled to represent the corporation in England.[7]

D. International Developments

Apart from the EC Convention on Insolvency Proceedings,[8] the two most significant recent developments at the international level, are the UNCI-TRAL Model Law on Cross-Border Insolvency (1997)[9] and the Cross-Border Insolvency Concordat,[10] the latter being approved by the Council of the Section on Business Law of the International Bar Association in September 1995. Both initiatives have taken flexibility and practicality as their watchwords.

The Concordat has been designed as something in the nature of a 'road map' to assist insolvency practitioners actually faced with concurrent proceedings in relation to the same debtor in two or more different jurisdictions. Rather than leaving the insolvency practitioners to start from scratch and try to forge a one-off agreement (acceptable to their respective courts) as to the proper co-ordination of the two sets of proceedings,[11] the Concordat sets out a small number of essential principles which can be adopted, with appropriate modification, to suit the particular facts involved. Experience has revealed the sorts of issues that are likely to be raised where there are concurrent re-organisations or liquidations; and the Concordat provides a clear and ready-made basis for negotiation at the earliest stages of the process. Once the insolvency practitioners (with court approval) have adapted the Concordat to come up with their own particular agreement or protocol, rapid progress with the actual administration of the insolvency process can be made.[12] Where one is dealing with two systems of insolvency law of roughly equal sophistication, it is unlikely (except in rare cases) in the context of the overall insolvency process to make

---

[6] The so-called 'universality' approach.

[7] Thus a foreign bankruptcy may have more consequences in England than a foreign liquidation – as once the English assets have vested in the foreign trustee, no English trustee will be able to get hold of those assets, see p. 343, *infra*.

[8] See p. 9, *infra*.

[9] Adopted by the United Nations Commission on International Trade Law at its thirtieth session (Vienna, 12–30 May 1997).

[10] For details, see Leonard (1996) 24 Int. Bus. Law. 203 and (1997) 6 I.I.R. 127, as well as Barratt (1996) 24 Int. Bus. Law. 208.

[11] As was done successfully in the Maxwell insolvency, see p. 335, *infra*.

[12] Leonard, above n. 10, at p. 132, sets out the following observation of Farley J in *Re Everfresh Beverages Inc.* (20 December 1995, unreported) Ontario Court of Justice: 'I would congratulate the parties for their initiative in taking their lead from the Concordat and in crafting the protocol which I believe will prove of significant value to all concerned, both in the aspect of eliminating certain procedural difficulties, reducing legal expenses and uncertainties and hopefully in maximizing everyone's recovery.' Note also *Re Hackett*. 184 Bankr. 656 (Bankr., S.D.N.Y. 1995).

a great deal of difference whether a particular matter is regulated by one law or the other:[13] for example, the collection and realisation of assets under Canadian law is probably just as efficient as under United States law. What matters more is that the relevant parties are aware from the outset who is responsible for what. Hence the principles under the Concordat concern such practical matters as the receipt of relevant notices, the right to appear in all proceedings, the division of responsibility between the various proceedings, the use of avoidance powers, as well as the mutual recognition of orders (including any ultimate compromise or discharge) made by the courts in either jurisdiction.[14] The Concordat has already been used as a template for constructing relevant agreements in cross-border cases;[15] and it would appear that the courts, particularly in North America, have seen it as a spring-board to yet more dynamic co-operative procedures and practices.[16]

The Concordat is likely to prove particularly useful where the two prima facie competing jurisdictions have a tradition of informal, non-treaty based co-operation and assistance in international insolvency matters.[17] The UNCITRAL Model Law, on the other hand, seeks to promote co-operation by facilitating the adoption by individual countries of model, but nevertheless flexible, legislation designed to achieve certain minimum recognition and assistance benchmarks. As the *Guide to Enactment of the UNCITRAL Model Law on Cross-Border Insolvency* puts it:[18]

> '1. The UNCITRAL Model Law on Cross-Border Insolvency, adopted in 1997, is designed to assist States to equip their insolvency laws with a modern, harmonized and fair framework to address more effectively instances of cross-border insolvency. Those instances include cases where the insolvent debtor has assets in more than one State or where some of the creditors of the debtor are not from the State where the insolvency proceeding is taking place.
> 2. The Model Law reflects practices in cross-border insolvency matters that are characteristic of modern, efficient insolvency systems. Thus, the States enacting the Model Law . . . would be introducing useful additions and improvements in national insolvency regimes designed to resolve problems arising in cross-border insolvency cases. Not only jurisdictions that currently have to deal with numerous cases of cross-border insolvency but also those that wish to be well prepared for the increasing likelihood of cases of cross-border insolvency will find the Model Law useful.'

As the *Guide* itself suggests,[19] for some countries the type of assistance and co-operation expected under the Model Law may be breaking new ground, whilst for other countries much of what is in the Model Law may in one way or another already be quite familiar.[20]

---

[13] See the comments of Lord Hoffmann in (1995) 4 I.I.R. 97 at 100–101.

[14] It is not altogether clear, however, that if the Concordat were used in a case involving English and US re-organisation proceedings, a US discharge of an English debt would inevitably be binding in England: see on discharge, generally, chapter 9, *infra*.

[15] Most notably in the *Everfresh* insolvency, see Leonard above n.12.

[16] There has recently been an historic joint hearing between the Alberta and US bankruptcy courts involving Forsyth J and Judge McFeeley, see *supra*, p. 2 at n.12.

[17] The US and Canada being the most obvious examples, but note also *Re Nakash* 190 B.R. 763 (Bankr., S.D.N.Y. 1996).

[18] Paras. 1 and 2.

[19] In para. 3 it is stressed that the Model Law 'respects the differences among national procedural laws and does not attempt a substantive unification of insolvency law'.

[20] Although it is doubtful whether any country would presently comply fully with the Model Law.

As far as English law is concerned, many of the essential principles under the Model Law have long been part of English law. For example, foreign creditors are already given the same rights as English creditors in relation to the commencement of and participation in English insolvency proceedings.[1] So too, foreign insolvency proceedings were first recognised in England more than two centuries ago[2] (although recognition does not prevent the commencement of proceedings against the same debtor under the English insolvency legislation);[3] and where foreign proceedings are recognised, no subsequent attachment of the debtor's property in England will confer any priority on an individual creditor.[4] Yet there are forms of assistance under the Model Law which are not always available under the present English law. For example, when acting under section 426 of the Insolvency Act 1986 the English court may (at the request of a foreign court from a relevant country or territory)[5] order the examination of witnesses in England – but the position is different under the common law.[6] This is also the case in relation to an order staying the commencement or continuation of an individual creditor's action against the debtor.[7] In addition, there are other issues in respect of which the common law and statutory provisions are particularly uncertain or obscure, where adoption of the straightforward rules laid down in the Model Law would be most welcome.[8] Unfortunately, whilst a number of countries[9] are already looking seriously at enacting the provisions (or at least the principles[10] embodied in the provisions) of the Model Law, the United Kingdom Government does not currently appear to be moving rapidly in that particular direction.[11]

2. THE EUROPEAN DIMENSION

A. EC Convention on Insolvency Proceedings

As long ago as 1960 the original Member States of the EEC recognised the need for a Bankruptcy Convention.[12] It was at that time envisaged that negotiations towards a Bankruptcy Convention would proceed in parallel with work on a convention on civil jurisdiction and judgments generally –

---

[1] See, for example, *Re BCCI S.A. (No. 10)* [1997] Ch. 213 at 242 *per* Scott V-C. The relevant provision in the Model Law is Art. 13.

[2] See *Solomons* v. *Ross* (1764) 1 H.Bl. 131n; recognition is dealt with in Chapter III of the Model Law, in particular Arts. 15–17.

[3] See, for an early example, *Re Cridland* (1814) 3 V. & B. 94, and note Art. 28 of the Model Law.

[4] See, for example, *Dulaney* v. *Merry and Sons* [1901]. 1 K.B. 536 (*infra*, p. 234) and Art. 20(1)(b) of the Model Law.

[5] See, generally, chapter 15, *infra*.

[6] See p. 404. Examinations fall within Art. 21(1)(d) of the Model Law.

[7] See Art. 21(1)(a).

[8] Such as the right of a foreign representative to commence insolvency proceedings in England, see p. 229, *infra*. Art. 11 of the Model Law is quite clear.

[9] Notably Canada, the United States, South Africa and Australia.

[10] The Model Law is designed to allow countries flexibility in terms of reform, see n. 19 above.

[11] The tendency has been to put off any general reform in England whilst awaiting a possible European Convention.

[12] For a summary of the history of negotiations, see *Seventh Report of the House of Lords Select Committee on the European Communities*, H.L. Paper 59 (1996) p. 5.

the latter being signed in 1968 at Brussels ('the Brussels Convention').[13] As bankruptcy and insolvency matters were deliberately excluded from the Brussels Convention,[14] attempts to reach agreement on a Bankruptcy Convention continued (somewhat sporadically) during the 1970s and 1980s between the Member States of the ever-enlarging EC. In the early 1990s new proposals (of a more limited nature than earlier versions) were put forward and, ultimately, on 23 November 1995 the Convention on Insolvency Proceedings was opened for signature. By Article 49(2) the Convention remained open for signature until 23 May 1996. Most of the Member States signed up rapidly,[15] although the United Kingdom took a more cautious approach. A consultative document was issued by the Insolvency Service of the DTI (containing, *inter alia*, the text of the Convention and an *Explanatory Report*)[16] and the Convention was considered by a Select Committee of the House of Lords, chaired by Lord Hoffmann.[17] In the end, however, the merits and demerits of the Convention were not decisive. By the middle of May 1996 all the other Member States had signed the Convention, but the United Kingdom Government was engaged in the 'beef war' with its European partners and the Commission.[18] The Government announced a blocking policy and the 23 May 1996 deadline passed with the Convention left unsigned. Although the Convention has lapsed, as it were, there is no inherent reason why it could not be revived at any time. The 'smart money',[19] however, is apparently that the Commission will push the matter forward by way of a Directive in late 1998 or 1999. This would appear to be what Mario Monti, European Financial Services Commissioner, was referring to when he stated recently:[20]

> 'In order to solve this situation, the Commission plans to examine all options to progress in this field and, in particular, whether a legislative proposal is necessary to enforce the measures contained in the 1995 Convention.'

It is inconceivable that the matter can be left in abeyance for very much longer.

A considerable amount of literature about the Convention on Insolvency Proceedings had already appeared;[1] and the approach adopted in this work is to highlight in each chapter the major changes that would be required in English law were the Convention to be adopted. Even if the Convention is

---

[13] For discussion of the background to the Brussels Convention (as implemented by the Civil Jurisdiction and Judgments Act. 1982) as well as the Lugano Convention, see Dicey and Morris, *The Conflict of Laws* (12th ed., 1993) pp. 270–274.

[14] See Art. 1(2), analysed, *infra*.

[15] See *EC Convention on Insolvency Proceedings: A Consultative Document*, The Insolvency Service, February. 1996 (Introduction) and the editorial comment at (1996) 5 I.I.R. 170. The text of the Convention is also at (1996) 35 I.L.M. 1123.

[16] *Idem*. The *Explanatory Report* at Annex B of the *Consultative Document* was prepared by M. Virgos and E. Schmidt and was at that time in draft form. The final version was published as EU Council Doc. 6500/96, DRS8 (CFC) (3 May. 1996).

[17] *Supra*, n. 12.

[18] The dispute followed the ban on British beef as a result of BSE or 'mad cow' disease: see (1996), Times, 23 May, p. 1.

[19] If this author may use the expression.

[20] See 'No Progress Yet on Insolvency Convention' *European Report*, 11 February 1998.

[1] See, in particular, Bogdan (1997) 6 I.I.R. 114, Fletcher (1997) 23 Brook. J. of Int. L. 25, Segal, *ibid.* at 57, Balz. 70 Am. Bankr. L.J. 485 (1996) and Johnson (1996) 5 I.I.R. 80.

never adopted, any Directive which may be promulgated by the Commission will in all probability track the key features of the Convention.[2]

The Convention by its terms only seeks to apply where a debtor has its centre of main interests in a Contracting State.[3] So if, for example, a Bahamian company carries on most of its business in New York, but also has an office in Paris, then nothing in the Convention will impact on current English law and practice.[4] Even where the debtor has its centre of main interests in a Contracting State, there are two further limitations: first, the Convention is expressed not to apply to credit institutions, insurance undertakings and (most forms of) investment undertakings;[5] secondly, and more importantly, by Article 1(1) the Convention applies to 'collective insolvency proceedings which entail the partial or total divestment of a debtor and the appointment of a liquidator'. (Happily, the term 'liquidator' is defined in Article 2, and Annex C, to cover not only a liquidator, in the English sense, but also a trustee, administrator and supervisor of a voluntary arrangement.)[6] But 'insolvency proceedings' does not encompass administrative receivership.[7] Where the Convention does indeed apply, the essential notion is that the courts of the country where the debtor has its centre of main interests should have the major responsibility for conducting any insolvency. Such main proceedings are entitled to recognition in all other Contracting States and the liquidator appointed in the main proceedings may exercise powers conferred on him in those proceedings in any other Contracting State[8] – although the liquidator must comply with the law of the Contracting State in which he intends to exercise any relevant powers.[9] Recognition of the main proceedings also extends not just to the proceedings themselves but also to any judgments or orders (such as setting aside a preference, or other transaction, or requiring a defaulting officer to contribute to the assets of an insolvent company) made in the course of the main proceedings.[10] The opening of main proceedings does not, however, prevent there being concurrent proceedings in another Contracting State.[11] Such proceedings, which are referred to as 'secondary proceedings',[12] are expressly limited in their territorial effect and may only be opened in a Contracting State

[2] Although if a Directive is used instead of a Convention, less consistency amongst the Member States will be achieved.

[3] See Art. 3(1) and para. 5 of the *Explanatory Report*. (References hereafter to the *Explanatory Report* are to the version contained in Annex B of the *Consultative Document*, see n. 15 above.)

[4] Thus the English court could make a winding up order on the basis of the presence of assets in England: see p. 99, *infra*.

[5] It is understood that work has been going on, for a number of years, on a Winding Up Directive which would govern (certain of) these types of undertakings.

[6] See Art. 2.

[7] Art. 2 states that: '"insolvency proceedings" should mean the collective proceedings referred to in Article. 1(1). These proceedings are listed in Annex A. . . .' In relation to the United Kingdom, Annex A lists: compulsory winding up, bankruptcy, administration of the insolvent estate of a deceased person, administration by a judicial factor, sequestration, creditors' voluntary winding up, administration and voluntary arrangements.

[8] See Art. 18(1), provided no insolvency proceedings have been opened in the other State.

[9] See Art. 18(3).

[10] See Art. 25; and p. 400, *infra* for discussion of insolvency judgments.

[11] Cf. the position under earlier versions of the Convention, Fletcher, *The Law of Insolvency* (2nd ed., 1995) pp. 771–773.

[12] Note Arts. 27–38.

where the debtor has an 'establishment'.[13] An 'establishment' is defined, perhaps not too helpfully, to mean 'any place of operations where the debtor carries out a non-transitory economic activity with human means and goods'.[14]

Although making important provision in relation to the jurisdiction to open[15] (and the subsequent recognition of) insolvency proceedings, the Convention has taken a conservative approach to the governing law of any such proceedings. Any proceedings, whether main or secondary, are to be governed by the law of the State in which the proceedings are being conducted.[16] In other words, English proceedings – whether based upon the centre of main interests or upon an establishment – would continue to be governed by the Insolvency Act 1986. Nevertheless, the Convention in Article 5 provides that the opening of proceedings in one Contracting State will not affect the rights *in rem* in respect of the property of the debtor which, at the time of the opening of the proceedings, is situate in another Contracting State.[17] Even though the Convention does not spell it out, the *Explanatory Report* makes it plain that *in rem* rights are considered to include rights under a floating charge.[18] Moreover, as one would expect, any creditor with an habitual residence, domicile or registered office in any Contracting State shall have the right to lodge claims in any insolvency proceeding.[19] The right to lodge claims extends to the tax authorities and social security authorities of any Contracting State,[20] thereby eliminating the traditional rule against the enforcement of foreign revenue debts.[1] The Convention also deals with the provision of information to creditors in any Contracting State and the need for co-operation between main and secondary proceedings.[2]

B. The Bankruptcy Exception under the Brussels Convention

(i) *General Principle*

Given the fact that it was envisaged that insolvency issues would be dealt with in a separate Bankruptcy Convention, it will be readily appreciated that insolvency was specifically excluded from the Brussels Convention on civil jurisdiction and judgments. Hence Article 1(2) states that the Convention does not apply in respect of:[3]

---

[13] See Art. 3(2).

[14] See Art. 2.

[15] The changes to the current position in English law in respect of jurisdiction are outlined *infra*, at pp. 58 and 136.

[16] See Art. 4.

[17] Specific provision is also made in the Convention in relation to, *inter alia*, set-off (Art. 6), reservation of title (Art. 7), immovable property (Art. 8), financial markets (Art. 9), contracts of employment (Art. 10) and pending actions (Art. 15).

[18] Above n. 3 at para. 85: '. . . there is a consensus in the group on the fact that forms such as the "floating charge" may qualify as a right in rem . . . .'

[19] See Art. 39. This is, of course, already the case in England.

[20] *Idem.*

[1] For the current position, see pp. 197–205, *infra*.

[2] See Arts. 31 and 40.

[3] For details of other, non-insolvency, exceptions see Dicey and Morris, *The Conflict of Laws* (12th ed., 1993) pp. 276–279.

'bankruptcy, proceedings relating to the winding up of insolvent companies or other legal persons, judicial arrangements, compositions and analogous proceedings . . . .'

The Jenard Report[4] explains further that 'analogous proceedings' refers to:[5]

'. . . those proceedings which, depending on the system of law involved, are based on the suspension of payments, the insolvency of the debtor or his inability to raise credit, and which involve the judicial authorities for the purpose either of compulsory and collective liquidation of assets or simply of supervision.'

Thus, for example, administration proceedings and individual voluntary arrangements would obviously come within the 'bankruptcy exception' and fall outside the Brussels Convention.[6] The same is, of course, the case in relation to compulsory winding up,[7] creditors' voluntary liquidation[8] and personal bankruptcy under the Insolvency Act 1986.

Moreover, the bankruptcy exception covers not only the insolvency process itself but also any proceedings directly derived from and closely connected to the bankruptcy or (insolvent) winding up.[9] The leading authority is the decision of the European Court in *Gourdain* v. *Nadler*.[10] It was held that an order obtained by a French *syndic* against the de facto manager of an insolvent company, imposing personal liability for the company's debts upon the manager on account of a failure to prove proper care in the management of the company's affairs,[11] could not be enforced in Germany under the Convention. The Court commented:[12]

'In this application, which derogates from the general rules of the law of liability, the . . . managers of the company are presumed to be liable and they can only discharge this burden by proving that they managed the affairs of the company with all the requisite energy and diligence. The period of limitation of three years for the application runs from the date when the final list of claims is drawn up . . . It is quite apparent that the legal foundation of [the relevant provision of French law], the object of which, in the event of the winding up of a commercial company, is to go beyond the legal person and proceed against its managers and their property is based solely on the provisions of the law of bankruptcy and winding up. . . .'

Similarly, it would inevitably follow that proceedings by a liquidator in England against directors for fraudulent or wrongful trading,[13] or against a creditor to set aside a preference,[14] would be excluded from the Brussels Convention.

---

[4] The Jenard Report is published at [1979] O.J. C59.
[5] *Ibid.*, at pp. 11–12.
[6] The same is true in relation to a company voluntary arrangement, note Annex A and Annex C to the EC Convention on Insolvency Proceedings.
[7] Where based upon the inability of the company to pay its debts.
[8] But not, of course, a members' voluntary winding up.
[9] *Gourdain* v. *Nadler* Case. 133/78 [1979] E.C.R. 733 at 744.
[10] *Idem.* Although *Gourdain* v. *Nadler* was cited in *Norsk Hydro and Aluminum AS* v. *Alumix Spa* [1998] I.L.Pr. 83, the decision of the majority of the Norwegian Supreme Court is very odd.
[11] Pursuant to Art. 99 of the French Law of 13 July. 1967.
[12] *Supra*, n. 9 at 744–745, approved in *Re Hayward* [1997] Ch. 45 at 51–52.
[13] *Dicey and Morris*, above n. 3, at pp. 277–278, approved in *Re Hayward*, at 53.
[14] In relation to transactions at an undervalue, see below.

Yet it would be quite wrong to suggest that merely because proceedings are brought by (or against)[15] a liquidator those proceedings must fall within the bankruptcy exception to the Brussels Convention. In *Grupo Torras S.A.* v. *Al-Sabah*[16] the first plaintiff had commenced proceedings in England in 1993 claiming, *inter alia*, damages against its directors for conspiracy and breach of duty. There were also claims by way of constructive trust. The first plaintiff was a Spanish company that had since December 1992 been in a state of suspension of payments pursuant to an order of the courts in Spain under the *Ley de Suspension de Pages de 26 Julio de 1922*. Mance J, applying *Gourdain* v. *Nadler*, rejected the argument that the proceedings in England came within the bankruptcy exception:[17] it was 'purely collateral' that the first plaintiff was in a state of suspension of payments.[18] The same is true where a trustee is proceeding against a defendant to recover debts owing to the bankrupt;[19] or where a liquidator has brought an action to avoid a transaction (entered into by the company prior to its going into liquidation) which is alleged to have constituted unlawful financial assistance[20] in relation to a purchase of the company's shares or an unauthorised return of capital to the shareholders.

In *Re Hayward*[1] Hayward and Hulse had in 1986 purchased a villa in Spain, the villa being held by them 'by indivisible halves'. In June 1987 Hayward was made bankrupt in England and his estate vested in the trustee. In December 1987 Hayward died intestate. In March 1992 Hayward's widow made a formal declaration in Spain whereby, after reciting that she was the person entitled under Hayward's intestacy, she purported to transfer her late husband's half-interest in the villa to Hulse. Thereafter Hulse was entered in the appropriate property register in Spain as the sole proprietor of the villa. Needless to say, the trustee was not happy about the purported transfer and brought an ordinary application[2] seeking a variety of relief, but in essence asserting the trustee's claim that he was entitled to the deceased's half-share in the villa as against Hulse and the deceased's widow. Rattee J accepted that had there been no bankruptcy the trustee would not have had any basis for his claim;[3] however, the nature of the claim was to recover from a third party (Hulse) 'assets said to belong to the bankrupt's estate and, therefore, to be vested in the trustee'.[4] Such a claim was analogous to a claim by a liquidator to recover from third parties debts owing to an insolvent company, and fell outside the bankruptcy exception.[5]

The basic point derived from the cases discussed above is that the nature of the claim will be decisive – rather than by whom the claim is brought. Thus, for example, where a trustee seeks an order (pursuant to section 291(2) of the Insolvency Act 1986) that the bankrupt convey foreign land

---

[15] See *Contant* v. *Somers* [1993] I.L.Pr. 379 (French Cour de Cassation), *passim*.

[16] [1995]. 1 Lloyd's Rep. 374. See also *Firswood* v. *Petra Bank* [1996] C.L.C. 608, p. 247, *infra*.

[17] *Ibid.*, at 400.

[18] *Idem.*

[19] See *Re Hayward*, above n. 12, at 54.

[20] There is a decision of Keane J in Ireland to this effect (*Credit Suisse* v. *CH (Ireland) Inc.*, (2 February. 1996, unreported), available on LEXIS).

[1] *Supra*, n. 12.

[2] In the bankruptcy proceedings in the Walsall County Court.

[3] *Supra*, n. 12, at 54.

[4] *Idem.*

[5] *Idem*, referring to an example given in *Dicey and Morris*, *supra*, n. 3, at pp. 277–278.

into the name of the trustee,[6] such proceedings would plainly come within the bankruptcy exception. In addition, whilst an ordinary civil action brought by a liquidator against one of the company's debtors to recover a debt will not come within the bankruptcy exception, the position will be otherwise were the court to make an order for the payment of a debt pursuant to section 237(2) consequent upon a section 236 examination of a person indebted to the company.[7]

(ii) *Section 423 of the Insolvency Act 1986*

Where a trustee wishes to set aside a transaction at an undervalue it will be usual for section 339 of the Insolvency Act 1986 to be invoked. Section 339, of course, provides that where an individual debtor has been adjudicated bankrupt and has (within a five year period) entered into a transaction at an undervalue, the trustee of the bankrupt's estate may apply to the court to have the transaction set aside. Section 238 deals with the situation where there has been a transaction at an undervalue entered into by a corporate debtor that has subsequently gone into liquidation (or administration).[8] Both these sections may only operate once there has been an insolvency; and only then in proceedings brought by a trustee or liquidator (or administrator) – proceedings cannot be brought by an individual creditor. Sections 238 and 339 clearly must be regarded as so closely and directly tied to the bankruptcy or winding up as to come within the bankruptcy exception and fall outside the Brussels Convention. An avoidance action under section 423, however, stands in a very different position.[9]

Section 423 applies to transactions at an undervalue and, after defining such a transaction, allows the court to make an order, *inter alia*, 'restoring the position to what it would have been if the transaction had not been entered into'.[10] Section 423(3) further states that, in relation to such a transaction entered into by a person, the court shall only set the transaction aside if it is satisfied that the transaction was entered into by him for the purpose:

'(a) of putting assets beyond the reach of a person who is making, or may at some time make, a claim against him, or
(b) of otherwise prejudicing the interests of such a person in relation to the claim which he is making or may make.'

Section 423 can be traced back in English law to the Fraudulent Conveyances Act 1571 and beyond that to the *actio Pauliana* of Roman law.[11] Prior to 1985 the relevant provision was found in section 172 of the Law of Property Act 1925, which was re-drafted and widened following the recommendations of the Cork Committee.[12] It is important to note that, in contrast to sections 238 and 339, an action under section 423 can be

---

[6] As in *Re Harris* (1896) 74 L.T. 221. See the criticism of *Ferguson's Trustee* v. *Ferguson.* 1990 S.L.T. (Sh. Ct.) 73, p. 308, *infra*.
[7] Although it would be highly unusual for such an order, i.e. pursuant to s. 237(2), to be made in the absence of very clear evidence.
[8] The time limit in relation to s. 238 is only two years: see s. 240(1).
[9] For a fuller discussion, see Smart (1998) 17 C.J.Q. 149 at 153–160.
[10] Section. 423(2)(a).
[11] For a summary, see Buckland, *A Textbook of Roman Law* (3rd ed., 1963) p. 596.
[12] *Report of the Review Committee on Insolvency Law and Practice* (Cmnd. 8558, 1982) para. 1238.

brought by a creditor.[13] There is no pre-condition that insolvency proceedings must have been commenced against the defendant. (Inevitably, no limitation period, unlike in relation to sections 238 and 339, is expressed in section 423.)[14]

Where an individual creditor brings a section 423 action against a defendant, there having been no bankruptcy or winding up, it is obvious that the bankruptcy exception does not apply. One may refer here to two decisions of the European Court arising out of the *action paulienne* provisions of the French Civil Code,[15] as well as a decision of Hirst J involving section 423 and the Lugano Convention.[16] Similarly, it must follow that a section 423 action brought by a creditor against a defendant who has been made bankrupt (or put into liquidation or administration) would also be outside the bankruptcy exception – the cause of action simply would not derive from the relevant bankruptcy (or winding up or administration). The more difficult question is whether an action brought by a trustee or liquidator would be excluded. In this regard a number of preliminary observations may be made. The first point is that such an action will not be excluded simply because it is brought by a trustee or liquidator.[17] Secondly, although section 423 is currently part of the Insolvency Act, it could quite reasonably be contained in non-insolvency legislation (as was the case for centuries under English law). Thirdly, it will be noted that all the exceptions[18] pursuant to Article 1, excluding as they do matters which would otherwise properly come within the Convention rules, must be strictly construed and such matters 'should only be excluded where they are the principal object of the proceedings'.[19] Fourthly, section 423 is not a provision which derogates from the general rules of the law of liability,[20] since section 423 is not reserved for trustees or liquidators.

A comparison between section 423 and section 339 shows, it is suggested, the nature of the former. A transaction may only be avoided under section 339 if there has been a bankruptcy order: without the trigger of an adjudication, section 339 is irrelevant. Further, and this emphasises the connection between section 339 and the bankruptcy itself, the provision has a time limit – five years prior to the date of the presentation of the bankruptcy petition. (It will be recalled that a limitation period was also found in *Gourdain* v. *Nadler* itself.)[1] There is no time limit under section 423; moreover, any relevant transaction is from the moment it is entered into liable to be impeached under section 423 – whether or not the debtor is ever made bankrupt. It is fair to say that the effect of a bankruptcy in respect of section 423 is not that it empowers the court to undo a transaction that

---

[13] See s. 424(1). Leave is required once the debtor has been made bankrupt, is being wound up or where an administration order has been made. For proceedings under s. 423 by a foreign representative, see p. 416, *infra*.

[14] There is also no presumption of impropriety in s. 423 in respect of associates.

[15] See *Reichert* v. *Dresdner Bank* Case 115/88 [1990] E.C.R. I-27 and *Reichert* v. *Dresdner Bank (No. 2)* Case. 261/90 [1992] I.L.Pr. 404 and, for details, Smart, *supra*, n. 9.

[16] *Aiglon* v. *Gau Shan Co. Ltd.* [1993]. 1 Lloyd's Rep. 164. Hirst J held, at 174, that a claim pursuant to s. 423 came within the Lugano Convention – there were, on the facts, no insolvency proceedings against the company.

[17] See, for example, *Grupo Torras S.A.* v. *Al-Sabah* [1995]. 1 Lloyd's Rep. 374, *supra*.

[18] Which will naturally be given an independent, Convention meaning.

[19] Cheshire and North, *Private International Law* (12th ed., 1992) p. 288.

[20] *Gourdain* v. *Nadler* Case. 133/78 [1979] E.C.R. 733 at 744, *supra*, p. 13.

[1] Discussed *supra*, p. 13.

would otherwise be unimpeachable, but rather that it adds the trustee to the list of parties who may bring an action. Moreover, section 424(2) states that whoever seeks to avoid a transaction under section 423 does so 'on behalf of every victim of the transaction'. In summary, whether a claim under section 423 is made by a creditor or by the trustee in bankruptcy, the nature of the cause of action is the same: it does not derive from any bankruptcy proceedings.

The conclusion that section 423 proceedings do not fall under the bankruptcy exception in Article 1(2) of the Brussels Convention is not without practical significance in a cross-border insolvency case. Firstly, the jurisdiction of the English court over a defendant will be governed by the rules under the Convention.[2] Second, and more significantly, any order made by the English court will be 'automatically' enforceable in other Convention States.[3] Thus, in practice, if a trustee or liquidator is minded to bring proceedings to set aside a transaction at an undervalue and anticipates that it may ultimately be necessary to have resort to a defendant's assets in a Brussels (or Lugano) State, section 423 will have advantages[4] over the more usual avoidance powers contained in section 339 and 238 of the Insolvency Act 1986 – at least until such time as provisions similar to those found in Article 25 of the EC Convention on Insolvency Proceedings[5] are brought into force in Member States.[6]

3. EXTRATERRITORIALITY

One issue that has been litigated in England on a number of occasions in recent years concerns the extraterritorial operation of the Insolvency Act 1986. Whether a particular provision applies extraterritorially is, of course, a question of construction. The following remarks of Lord Wilberforce in *Clark (Inspector of Taxes)* v. *Oceanic Contractors Inc.* are often taken as a starting point:[7]

> '. . . the general principle . . . is simply that, unless the contrary is expressly enacted or so plainly implied that the courts must give effect to it, United Kingdom legislation is applicable only to British subjects or to foreigners who by coming to the United Kingdom, whether for a short or long time, have made themselves subject to British jurisdiction.'

Although the two leading appellate authorities under the Insolvency Act 1986 have indeed concerned persons outside the jurisdiction,[8] it must not

---

[2] The difficulties as to service out are considered in Smart, *supra*, n. 9, at p. 156.
[3] The circumstances in which enforcement may be refused under the Brussels Convention are quite narrowly drawn (see Arts. 27–29).
[4] When a case comes within the Brussels Convention protective measures may well be available in the country where assets are located (see Art. 24).
[5] See also p. 401, *infra*.
[6] In addition, there may in the future be parties to the Lugano Convention (EFTA States) which are not part of the EU and do not come within any Convention on Insolvency Proceedings (or equivalent Directive).
[7] [1983]. 2 A.C. 130 at 145.
[8] See *Re Paramount Airways Ltd. (in administration)* [1993] Ch. 223 and *Re Seagull Manufacturing Co. Ltd.* [1993] Ch. 345 discussed below.

be overlooked that the question of extraterritoriality may just as easily arise in relation to property, acts or events abroad.

A. Property, Acts and Events Abroad

Happily, when it comes to property issues, the 1986 Act provides an all-embracing and extraterritorial definition.[9] Thus the duty of a liquidator to get in the company's property extends to assets worldwide; and, so too, all the bankrupt's assets will vest in the trustee. In contrast, if one turns to consider acts and events which may or may not come within a particular provision of the Act, it is very difficult to find any concrete guidance of general application – other than the obvious point that the wording and intent of the section in question must carefully be considered.[10] The case law tells us that the stay of proceedings upon the making of a winding up order (section 130(2)) is strictly territorial,[11] as indeed is section 183[12] – the latter deprives a creditor of the benefit of an attachment incomplete as of the date of commencement of the winding up. The same must inevitably be the case in relation to the avoidance of attachments actually put into effect after the date of commencement of the winding up (section 128). Similarly, if the avoidance of attachments is territorial, then one would expect the avoidance of property dispositions (section 127) to be treated likewise[13] – yet we know that the so-called statutory trust of the company's property applies to assets on a worldwide basis.[14] There is undoubtedly considerable (and undesirable) room for argument in relation to a number of these and similar provisions. Yet there is no inherent reason why modern legislation should not deal plainly with the matter.[15] In the meantime practitioners are probably best advised to reason by analogy from the current case law.

B. Persons Beyond the Jurisdiction

Returning to Lord Wilberforce's comments in *Oceanic*, made with reference to persons outside the jurisdiction, it will be noted that there are not just two ways of interpreting a particular statutory provision – territorially or extraterritorially – but rather three.[16] The presumption set out by his

---

[9] Insolvency Act. 1986, s. 436: '. . . every description of property wherever situated'.

[10] There is also a certain amount of case law. The power of a trustee (see s. 317) to disclaim leaseholds applies to foreign leaseholds (*Re Curzon Bros.* (1915) 84 L.J.K.B. 1000). In *Re RMCA Reinsurance Ltd.* [1994] B.C.C. 378 it was held that there was no territorial restriction in relation to the holding of meetings to sanction a scheme of arrangement (see also Bennett (1978) 52 A.L.J. 320). See also p. 386, *infra* (worker's preferences).

[11] *Re Vocalion (Foreign) Ltd.* [1932]. 2 Ch. 196, approved in *Hughes* v. *Hannover Rückversicherungs-Aktiengesellschaft* [1997]. 1 B.C.L.C. 497 at 520, and see pp. 279–280, *infra*.

[12] *Mitchell* v. *Carter; Re Buckingham International plc* [1997]. 1 B.C.L.C. 673 at 687.

[13] Although the wording of s. 127 might suggest an extraterritorial effect: '. . . any disposition of the company's property . . . is, unless the court otherwise orders, void'. Property, of course, embraces worldwide assets.

[14] See *Mitchell* v. *Carter, supra* n. 12, at 686 *per* Millett LJ.

[15] The problems that flow from some opaque drafting in the Insolvency Act have been touched upon above, see pp. 4–5.

[16] Or, more accurately, at least three.

Lordship, namely that a provision will apply to British subjects or to foreigners who are present in the United Kingdom, may to some extent be seen as occupying a middle ground: it is in a sense at once both territorial and extraterritorial. Territorial in that the presumption covers only foreigners actually present in the jurisdiction; extraterritorial in that it embraces British subjects wherever they happen to be.[17] The presumption can be displaced in favour of a wholly extraterritorial interpretation – whereupon a provision will apply to any (relevant) person anywhere in the world; or displaced in favour of a strictly territorial approach – so that a provision will only apply to persons actually present in the jurisdiction at the appropriate time.[18] It is of some significance, in this author's opinion, that the modern cases have taken either a wholly extraterritorial[19] or strictly territorial approach.[20] It is fair to say not merely that the presumption set out in *Oceanic* is quite easily displaced, but also that in the modern commercial environment it is largely inappropriate.

In *Re Paramount Airways Ltd. (in administration)*[1] the Court of Appeal held that the words 'any person' in section 238 of the 1986 Act (transactions at an undervalue) have their ordinary and natural meaning and, accordingly, applied extraterritorially – that is, to any person whether in the United Kingdom or not. It is quite clear from the judgments that the same result would be arrived at in relation to a preference (within section 239) given to 'any person'.[2] Having regard to the width of the ambit of the statutory avoidance powers, the Court of Appeal could not accept that Parliament would have intended a territorial or other restriction, particularly since any such restriction would be an open invitation for debtors to structure their transactions so as to fall outside the relevant provision. This point is particularly weighty as, it will be recalled,[3] there is generally no choice of law issues in insolvency proceedings under English law: the English court cannot apply a foreign avoidance power. Their Lordships, however, made it plain that whilst section 238 might operate extraterritorially, the court retained a discretion as to when the section could be successfully relied upon by an office holder against a party out of the jurisdiction.[4] Moreover, although not specifically addressed in *Paramount*, it must be that the 'transaction' referred to in section 238 may be a transaction anywhere in the world: the section is not limited to transactions occurring wholly or partly within the jurisdiction.[5]

An extraterritorial approach to the phrase 'any person' was shortly afterwards also adopted, by a differently constituted Court of Appeal, in

---

[17] See *Re Seagull Manufacturing Co. Ltd. (No. 2)* [1994] Ch. 91 at 105–106.

[18] A strictly territorial approach was taken in relation to private examination under the old legislation in *Re Tucker (R.C.) (a bankrupt), ex p Tucker* [1990] Ch. 148, *infra*.

[19] As in *Re Paramount Airways Ltd.* and *Re Seagull Manufacturing Co. Ltd., supra*, n. 8.

[20] As in *Re Tucker, supra*, n. 18.

[1] [1993] Ch. 223.

[2] A point confirmed in *Barclays Bank plc* v. *Homan* [1993] B.C.L.C. 680 at 690. It is also clear the s. 423 operates extraterritorially, see Smart (1998) 17 C.J.Q. 149 at 158.

[3] See *supra*, p. 3.

[4] Above n. 1, at 240. Discretion is discussed *infra*, p. 25. There is no discretion in relation to an order for public examination: *Re Seagull Manufacturing Co. Ltd. (No. 2)* [1994] Ch. 91 at 105.

[5] See also Smart (1996) 41 J.L.S. 141 in relation to Scottish authorities.

Re Seagull Manufacturing Co. Ltd.[6] – this time in the context of the public examination of a director under section 133 of the 1986 Act. The court, after looking at the Cork Report (paras. 654–656), stressed the particular role public examinations were intended to play in the investigation of company failures and concluded that the absence of a director from the jurisdiction could not be decisive.[7] Their Lordships also focused on a number of other points supporting an extraterritorial interpretation of section 133. Notably that, in comparison with private examination, the scope and number of persons falling within the public examination provision was relatively small;[8] and, second, that such persons would have voluntarily became involved in the management of the company (and accordingly had little valid reason to object if they were summoned for examination).[9]

C. Practical Considerations and Enforcement

The fact that relying upon *Re Seagull Manufacturing Co. Ltd.* the English court may be able to order a director or other officer beyond the jurisdiction to attend for public examination, does not mean that the director will attend – although it may be noted that a failure to attend is punishable as a contempt (section 134(1)). The options available to an English office holder in respect of a recalcitrant director, who has severed financial and other connections with the United Kingdom, may be somewhat limited.[10] The office holder may be able to commence some sort of ancillary case in the country where the director resides, or request that the foreign court grant an order in aid (under the applicable foreign insolvency legislation) directing an examination.[11] Where the foreign insolvency law does not have any procedure for assisting English insolvency proceedings, another route may yet be available. For, unlike as is (apparently) the case under English law,[12] some foreign courts[13] have allowed a foreign insolvency representative when conducting general investigatory and fact-finding activities to rely upon the Hague Convention on the Taking of Evidence Abroad in Civil and Commercial Matters 1970 (as brought into force under the local law). Moreover, in the future, it may well be that more and more countries adopt Article 21(1)(d) of the UNCITRAL Model Law, which specifically provides for the examination of witnesses and the collection of evidence.[14]

Where a person against whom an order for examination (public or private) has been made *is* within the jurisdiction, for however short a

---

[6] [1993] Ch. 345, a petition for leave to appeal to the House of Lords was dismissed, see [1994]. 2 All E.R. xx. See also *Re Seagull Manufacturing Co. Ltd. (No. 2)* [1994] Ch. 91.

[7] *Ibid.*, at 355–356.

[8] For private examination, see below.

[9] Peter Gibson J stated (at 356): '. . . I can see no reasons of comity which would prevent those who were voluntarily officers or otherwise participated in the formation or running of an English company to be capable of being summoned by the English court. . . .'

[10] Although it may be possible to examine relatives or advisers in England, as in *Re Murjani* [1996]. 1 All E.R. 65 (bankrupt's wife's solicitors).

[11] See *Re Seagull Manufacturing Co. Ltd.*, above n. 6, at 351.

[12] See *Re International Power Industries NV* [1985] B.C.L.C. 128, p. 403, *infra*.

[13] As discussed, p. 404, *infra*. See also *BCCI S.A.* v. *Haque* (1996) 42 C.B.R. (3d) 284.

[14] For a discussion of the Model Law, see pp. 7–9, *supra*.

period of time, the English court may make an order preventing that person's departure from England or allowing the departure upon the giving of security. Thus in *Re Bank of Credit and Commerce International S.A. (No. 7): Morris* v. *Al-Mirabi*[15] the applicant had come to England for a short visit, whereupon the liquidators of BCCI obtained an ex parte order for private examination (to take place the following week) and an injunction restraining the applicant from leaving the jurisdiction. The order was subsequently varied to permit the applicant to leave the country upon providing substantial security. Sir Donald Nicholls V-C upheld the order for substantial security. Although no authorities on this point were referred to by the Vice-Chancellor, the first reported case in which a similar order was made is *Re Oriental Credit Ltd.*[16] There Harman J granted an interim injunction against a director, in respect of whom an order for private examination had been made pursuant to the predecessor of section 236 of the Insolvency Act 1986, from leaving the jurisdiction. The order was subsequently varied to allow the director to leave, upon giving an undertaking to return, backed with security in the sum of £250,000.[17] Harman J rejected counsel's submission, based upon *The Siskina*,[18] that an interim injunction might only be granted for the enforcement or protection of some legal or equitable right, holding that an interim injunction could issue in aid of and ancillary to the order for examination – although his Lordship accepted that use of an interim injunction in this way was 'novel'.[19]

The difficulty in this regard is that in *Morris* v. *Murjani*[20] the Court of Appeal recently applied the basic principle in *The Siskina* (as confirmed in *Mercedes-Benz AG* v. *Leiduck*)[1] that an interim injunction would only issue where the infringement of some substantive right was threatened. In so doing, their Lordships cast some doubt upon the earlier approach of Harman J.[2] Nevertheless, it is submitted that the decision in *Re Oriental Credit Ltd.* remains good law. For in *Morris* v. *Murjani* the Court of Appeal only rejected the broad approach of Harman J – that substantive rights were not a general pre-condition for the granting of an interim injunction – and nowhere is it suggested that the actual ruling of Harman J was wrong on the facts. Moreover, in the course of giving the leading judgment, Peter Gibson LJ noted that counsel accepted 'that if an order under s. 366 [private examination] had been obtained, an injunction would lie'.[3] His Lordship clearly felt that the duty to comply with an order to attend for private examination would be sufficient to found an application for an interim injunction.[4] In addition, although it is not fully reported, there was

---

[15] [1994]. 1 B.C.L.C. 455. Note also *Re Skase* (1992) 114 A.L.R. 303 (warrant for arrest).
[16] [1988] Ch. 204.
[17] The Court of Appeal later reduced the amount of security: see [1988] 1 All E.R. at 896.
[18] See *Siskina* v. *Distos Compania Naviera S.A.* [1979] A.C. 210.
[19] Above, n. 16 at 208.
[20] [1996] 2 All E.R.384.
[1] [1996] A.C. 284, criticised by Collins (1996) 112 L.Q.R. 28.
[2] 'If and so far as any comments by Harman J are inconsistent with the approach which I would favour, they are not binding on this court.' ([1996] 2 All E.R. 384 at 389 *per* Peter Gibson LJ.)
[3] *Idem.*
[4] Peter Gibson LJ suggested (at 389) there was no substantial distinction between the duty to comply with an order for private examination under s. 366 and the duty imposed on a bankrupt by s. 333 to co-operate with the trustee – the latter being raised on the facts in *Morris* v. *Murjani*.

an appeal from the decision of Harman J in *Re Oriental Credit Ltd.*, wherein the Court of Appeal merely varied the judge's order by reducing the amount of security required.[5] In addition, *Re Oriental Credit Ltd.* has been cited with apparent approval on a number of occasions – including twice in the Court of Appeal.[6] The way to reconcile the judgment of Harman J with *Morris* v. *Murjani* would seem to this author to be as follows: an interim injunction must be founded upon the protection of a substantive right,[7] but the public duty to comply with an order for examination carries with it a sufficient (and corresponding) right in the office holder[8] – so that 'an ancillary order [may be] made with a view to reinforcing an obviously appropriate primary order'.[9]

In any event, where an order for examination (public or private) has been made and the defendant is required to produce documents, it is not necessary that such documents be within the jurisdiction.[10] Further, as to the extent to which an order requiring the production of documents held abroad involves an assertion of sovereignty, 'then that is an assertion which the legislature must be taken to have intended the courts to make in appropriate cases.'[11]

D. Private Examinations: *Re Tucker*

The provision for private examination[12] in relation to an insolvent company is found in section 236(2):

> 'The court may, on the application of the office holder, summon to appear before it –
> (a) any officer of the company,
> (b) any person known or suspected to have in his possession any property of the company or supposed to be indebted to the company, or
> (c) any person whom the court thinks capable of giving information concerning the promotion, formation, business, dealings, affairs or property of the company.'

Equivalent provision in respect of personal bankruptcy is to be found in section 366(1), although reference to any officer of the company is replaced by reference to 'the bankrupt or the bankrupt's spouse or former spouse'. Whilst there is some authority[13] that section 236(2) and 366(1) operate extraterritorially in relation to 'any officer' or 'the bankrupt' –

[5] See *supra*, n. 17.
[6] *Maclaine Watson & Co. Ltd.* v. *International Tin Council (No. 2)* [1989] Ch. 286 at 306 and *J.A. Mont (UK) Ltd.* v. *Mills* [1993] F.S.R. 577 at 588, see also *Mercantile Group (Europe) AG* v. *Aiyela* [1993] F.S.R. 745 at 758.
[7] *Morris* v. *Murjani* [1996] 2 All ER 384.
[8] *Re Oriental Credit Ltd* [1988] Ch 204.
[9] *J.A. Mont (UK) Ltd.* v. *Mills* [1993] F.S.R. 577 at 588 *per* Simon Brown LJ.
[10] See, for example, *Re Bank of Credit and Commerce International S.A.; Morris* v. *Bank of America National Trust & Savings Assoc.* [1997] B.C.C. 561; and note also *Re Maxwell Communications Corpn.; Homan* v. *Vogel* [1995]. 1 B.C.L.C. 521.
[11] *Per* Chadwick LJ in *Lehman Bros. Inc.* v. *Phillips; Re Mid East Trading Ltd.* [1998]. 1 All E.R. 577 at 592, distinguishing *MacKinnon* v. *Donaldson Lufkin & Jenrette Securities Corp.* [1986] Ch. 482.
[12] See Fletcher, *The Law of Insolvency* (2nd ed., 1995) pp. 152–155 and 561–563.
[13] *Re Seagull Manufacturing Co. Ltd.* [1993] Ch. 345: '. . . a debtor out of the jurisdiction could be examined privately . . . .' *per* Peter Gibson J at 357.

these individuals may be summoned to attend even though they are outside the United Kingdom – there is very considerable doubt whether 'any person' who may be indebted to or hold property of the debtor, or may be capable of giving any relevant information, is to be interpreted extraterritorially.[14]

It will be recalled that in *Re Seagull Manufacturing Co. Ltd.*, when dealing with the public examination of 'any person' who 'is or has been an officer of the company', the Court of Appeal took an extraterritorial approach. Their Lordships, however, placed considerable reliance upon the consideration that: (1) the range of persons falling within the scope of section 133 was inevitably narrow; and (2) such persons would have voluntarily involved themselves in the running of the company's business. The position is quite otherwise in respect of private examination[15] under, for example, section 236(2)(b) or (c) – any number of persons might be indebted to the company or capable of providing some information as to the company's business, and such persons would not generally have become involved in the company's management. In other words, it would be going a very long way to suggest that Parliament would have intended the private examination provisions to have such an extensive reach, amounting to a significant infringement of other countries' sovereignty.[16]

This sort of reasoning found favour in *Re Tucker (R.C.) (a bankrupt), ex p Tucker*,[17] where the Court of Appeal interpreted the private examination provision under section 25(1) of the Bankruptcy Act 1914 as strictly territorial. Section 25(1) stated:

> 'The court may . . . summon before it . . . any person known or suspected to have in his possession any of the estate or effects belonging to the debtor, or supposed to be indebted to the debtor, or any person whom the court may deem capable of giving information respecting the debtor, his dealings or property. . . .'

Dillon LJ rejected the argument that 'any person' in section 25(1) should be given its natural meaning – so as to cover[18] 'any person of any nationality in any part of the world' – and, after noting that the equivalent of section 25(1) appeared in the 1883 Act, commented:[19]

> '. . . in the light of the accepted practice of nations and comity . . . eyebrows might be raised at the notion that Parliament had in 1914 or 1883 given jurisdiction . . . to summon anyone in the world before it to be examined and produce documents.'

---

[14] The decision in *McIsaac, Petitioners* [1994] B.C.C. 410 might seem to favour extraterritoriality; however, the case involved an examination *in New York* and is, in any event, open to criticism: see Smart (1996) 41 J.L.S. 141 at 142–143.

[15] Note also the judgment of Mummery J at [1992] Ch. 128.

[16] The scope of provisions such as s. 234(2) of the 1986 Act is broader than public examination but narrower than private examination. It is likely that 'any person' who has possession of the company's property, books or records would be interpreted extraterritorially. There is some Scottish authority in relation to what was then s. 100 of the Companies Act 1862, see *British Canadian Lumbering & Timber Co. Ltd.* (1886) 14 R. 160 (subsequent enforcement proceedings in Ontario are reported at (1887) 2 O.P.R. 301, on appeal, (1890) 18 S.C.R. 708).

[17] [1990] Ch. 148 (the bankruptcy took place under the 1914 Act).

[18] *Ibid.*, at 156.

[19] *Ibid.*, at 156–157.

(Indeed, one may go back even further to the Act of 1849 where similar wording can be found;[20] and it can scarcely be in much doubt that in the middle of the nineteenth century a territorial approach to examinations would have been taken.[1]) Accordingly, although *Re Tucker* is not free from difficulty, having regard to the obvious similarity between the old Bankruptcy Act provisions and those currently found in the Insolvency Act 1986,[2] it seems the earlier decision of the Court of Appeal remains a major obstacle to an extraterritorial approach to the new sections.

Re Tucker also concerned the interpretation and application of section 25(6) of the 1914 Act, which provided:

> 'The court may, if it thinks fit, order that any person who if in England would be liable to be brought before it under this section shall be examined in Scotland or Ireland, or in any other place out of England.'

In *Re Drucker, ex p Basden (No. 2)*[3] Wright J had opined that the phrase 'any other place out of England' was to be given a restricted interpretation and only included places within British dominions – not, for example, France, Germany or Switzerland.[4] In *Re Tucker* the Court of Appeal rejected this interpretation: 'any other place out of England' meant precisely that. However, Dillon LJ did make it plain that an order would not be made under the subsection unless there were available machinery in the foreign country for compelling the examination of an unwilling person.[5] On the facts in *Re Tucker*,[6] as there was apparently no machinery to compel the appellant to attend an examination in Belgium (where the appellant resided), the court regarded it as a proper exercise of discretion not to make an order under section 25(6). Similarly, the power to order an examination 'in any place outside the United Kingdom' (under the current legislation)[7] gives the court jurisdiction to order an examination in, for example, France or Switzerland. But an order will not be made unless there is a real prospect of it being given effect in the foreign country. Again the practical relevance of the UNCITRAL Model Law provisions dealing with examinations may be noted.

---

[20] In s. 120 of the. 1849 Act it was stated: '. . . it shall be lawful for the court to summon before it any person known or suspected to have any of the estate of the bankrupt . . . or who is supposed to be indebted to the bankrupt, or any person the court may believe to be capable of giving information . . . '

[1] See *Park* v. *Robson* (1871) 10 M 10: the Scottish court having no power under the 1856 Act 'to compel the examination of a person who is out of the jurisdiction' (at 14).

[2] Although the Insolvency Act. 1986 is in many respects a totally new piece of legislation, and should be construed without restrictions derived from cases decided under different provisions, it does not appear from *Re Seagull Manufacturing Co. Ltd.* that *Re Tucker* can be simply dismissed as no longer relevant.

[3] [1902] 2 K.B. 210.

[4] The facts involved parties in Switzerland who would not submit for examination. The decision of Wright J was distinguished in *Re Fanta-Sea Swim Centre Inc.* (1973) 23 C.B.R. (NS) 12 – the company president was willing to be examined in New York, where he resided, but was not prepared to go to Ontario where he faced possible criminal charges.

[5] *Supra*, n. 17, at 161.

[6] The facts concerned the bankrupt's brother, resident in Belgium.

[7] Insolvency Act. 1986, s. 367(3); and note also s. 237(3) in relation to companies.

E. Exercise of Discretion

Whilst the Court of Appeal in *Re Paramount Airways Ltd.* took an extra-territorial approach to section 238, their Lordships were anxious to ensure that so wide a jurisdiction would not lead to unjustifiable consequences. There were, as Sir Donald Nicholls V-C put it,[8] 'two safeguards built into the statutory scheme'.

First, the power of the court pursuant to section 238(3) to make 'such order as it thinks fit' (in respect of a proven transaction at an undervalue) entitled the court not to make any order against a party to the transaction, unless that party 'was sufficiently connected with England for it to be just and proper to make the order against him'.[9] The presence of strong foreign elements would weigh heavily in this regard. When considering whether there was a sufficient connection with the jurisdiction the court would look at all the circumstances, to ensure that the court would not exercise 'oppressively or unreasonably' the very wide jurisdiction conferred under the Act.[10]

Secondly, where a defendant was abroad (and accordingly could not be served in England) no proceedings could be pursued unless the office holder first obtained leave to serve the proceedings on the defendant abroad. Leave to serve required an exercise of the court's discretion – although leave was specifically not governed by Order 11 of the Rules of the Supreme Court[11] – and the court would consider the strengths and weaknesses of the plaintiff's claim in this regard:[12]

> 'There must be a real issue, between the plaintiff and the defendant, which the plaintiff may reasonably ask the court to try . . . Where a foreign element is involved one of the factors which the court will consider is the apparent strength or weakness of the plaintiff's claim that the defendant has a sufficient connection with England, in respect of the relief sought.'

Speaking generally, therefore, when considering the granting of leave (the second 'safeguard') the court will need to be satisfied at the very least that – assuming the allegations of the office holder are made out at the trial – the facts display a sufficiently strong connection to England to justify the making of an order against the defendant. For it is obvious that leave will not be granted where, assuming the plaintiff makes out his case, the court would in any event not set aside the transaction because of a lack of connection with England (i.e. the first 'safeguard').

In this author's opinion, there must also be a third 'safeguard' against excessive jurisdiction – although the issue was not apparently addressed in *Re Paramount Airways Ltd.* The point may perhaps best be illustrated by way of an example. A Hong Kong listed company also has business interests in England and has been put into liquidation in both places. The company prior to its liquidation made certain payments to two of its directors (A and B) which, it is alleged, constitute preferences. The payments were made out of funds held in Hong Kong and were received by the two directors in Hong Kong, wherein both directors at that time resided.

---

[8] [1993] Ch. 223 at 239.
[9] *Idem.*
[10] *Ibid.*, at 240.
[11] See rule. 12.12 of the Insolvency Rules. 1986, SI 1986/1925 and *Re Busytoday Ltd.* [1992] 1 W.L.R. 683.
[12] *Supra*, n. 8, at 241.

Currently A is resident in Hong Kong – and cannot be served in England – whereas B is resident in England (although he travels frequently to Hong Kong). The English liquidator brings proceedings in England pursuant to section 239 of the Insolvency Act 1986 and effects service on B in England. Leave is required to serve A in Hong Kong; and having regard to the absence of any significant connection between the alleged preferences and England, coupled with an overwhelming connection to Hong Kong, leave would likely not be granted. But, of course, the refusal of leave in relation to A would have no direct consequences in relation to B – for B has already been served in England. In these circumstances it can only be that B might seek a stay of the proceedings against him in England, on the basis that there is another available forum (i.e. Hong Kong) which is the natural forum and where (equivalent) avoidance proceedings can more appropriately be pursued.[13] In other words, the proper forum is Hong Kong – England is *forum non conveniens*.[14] Nothing in *Re Paramount Airways Ltd.* suggests that the *forum conveniens* doctrine is not applicable to avoidance litigation, indeed on the facts the question simply did not arise. Moreover, once it is accepted that *forum conveniens* is relevant in the type of fact scenario given above, it follows that the location of the proper forum is bound to influence (if not determine) the exercise of the court's discretion to give leave serve proceedings abroad (i.e. the second safeguard). A relatively recent decision of Chadwick J has already moved in this direction.

In *Re Howard Holdings Inc.*[15] wrongful trading proceedings were being brought by the English liquidator of a Panamanian corporation, in respect of which a winding up order had previously been made in England, against its directors – all of whom were resident in Monaco. The corporation had been involved in the shipping business and its activities had a number of significant links to London. There was no evidence that the corporation was being wound up in Panama or elsewhere, or that England was not an appropriate jurisdiction in relation to the winding up. The liquidator sought leave to serve the wrongful trading proceedings in Monaco. Chadwick J noted the decision in *Re Paramount Airways Ltd.* and stated that in exercising its discretion 'the court must, it seems to me, be satisfied that the case is a proper case for service on a person who is abroad'. This meant that not only had there to be a 'real issue which the court may reasonably be asked to try', but also:[16]

> '. . . that the court must take account of the fact that the prospective respondent is abroad, and should not be required to answer claims in England unless there is good reason why England is the *proper place* for those claims to be litigated.'

On the facts, and having regard to the consideration that an alternative jurisdiction had not suggested by the directors, Chadwick J held that there was nothing unreasonable in the directors being required to answer the liquidator's claims in England.

---

[13] Hong Kong law is in substance the same as English law concerning preferences.
[14] In this example the *forum conveniens* doctrine will be suitably adapted to take into account that there are two liquidators and, accordingly, any avoidance action in Hong Kong would have to be conducted by the Hong Kong liquidator.
[15] (6 June 1997, unreported) (LEXIS transcript: Beverley F Nunnery).
[16] Emphasis added.

Looking at the issue of discretion in a more general way, it will come as no surprise to find English judges employing the proper or convenient forum doctrine in cross-border insolvency cases.[17] For, returning to some of the high-profile insolvencies mentioned at the very beginning of this chapter, similar developments have taken place in the United States and Canada.[18] Moreover, one might bear in mind the advice of Sir Peter Millett that the approach of the English judiciary to cross-border insolvency should be founded upon 'flexibility, co-operation and judicial restraint'.[19]

---

[17] See further, pp. 62–64 and 125–126, *infra*.

[18] See *Re Maxwell Communication Corpn plc*. 93 F. 3d. 1036 (1996) – discussed below p. 333 – and *Re Olympia & York Developments Ltd.* (1996). 29 O.R. (3d) 626 at 633 – set out below, p. 331.

[19] 'Cross-Border Insolvency: The Judicial Approach' (1997) 6 I.I.R. 99 at 103, and for more details see p. 392, *infra*.

Chapter 2

Jurisdiction in Bankruptcy

1. INTRODUCTION

When international elements arise in an insolvency, it will be relevant to determine those courts which may be likely to have jurisdiction over some, or all, of the matters in dispute. In particular, those advising as to the law of England must ascertain whether the English court has jurisdiction. With reference to personal insolvency, section 264(1) of the Insolvency Act 1986 specifies by whom a bankruptcy petition may be presented:[1]

> '(1) A petition for a bankruptcy order to be made against an individual may be presented to the court in accordance with the following provisions of this Part
> (a) by one of the individual's creditors or jointly by more than one of them,
> (b) by the individual himself,
> (c) by the supervisor of, or any person (other than the individual) who is for the time being bound by, a voluntary arrangement proposed by the individual and approved under Part VIII'.[2]

Jurisdictional requirements, in the form of forensic connections to England and Wales, are imposed under section 265 of the Insolvency Act 1986 where either the creditors or the debtor himself are seeking a bankruptcy order. Section 265(1) provides:

> 'A bankruptcy petition shall not be presented to the court under section 264(1)(a) or (b) unless the debtor
> (a) is domiciled in England and Wales,
> (b) is personally present in England and Wales on the day on which the petition is presented, or
> (c) at any time in the period of 3 years ending with that day
>   (i) has been ordinarily resident, or has had a place of residence in England and Wales, or
>   (ii) has carried on business in England and Wales.'

---

[1] Service of a petition is governed by Insolvency Rules, S.I. 1986/1925, r. 6.14. If personal service cannot be effected, because for instance the debtor is out of the jurisdiction, the Insolvency Rules provide for service outside the jurisdiction, r. 12.12. R.S.C. Order 11 has no application in insolvency proceedings: Insolvency Rules, r. 12.12.

[2] Section 264(1)(d) dealt with the presentation of a petition where a criminal bankruptcy order had been made. The power to make a criminal bankruptcy order was abolished by s. 101 of the Criminal Justice Act 1988 – with effect from 3 April 1989 (S.I. 1989/264). Section 264(1)(d) is prospectively repealed by s. 170(2) and Sch 16 of the 1988 Act from a date to be appointed.

Accordingly, five criteria are laid down: *domicile, presence, ordinary residence, place of residence* and the *carrying on of business*. If none of these criteria is satisfied, the English court will have no jurisdiction to hear a bankruptcy petition presented by either the creditors or the debtor. It will be noted that the presence of assets in England and Wales is not a basis of jurisdiction in bankruptcy. Having regard to the very broad range of jurisdictional criteria under section 265, the English court will be careful not to place a wider interpretation on the section than the context justifies; and, in any event, the burden will lie on the petitioner to establish that the debtor falls within the section.[3]

It should be noted that section 264 and section 265 by no means deal with all questions of jurisdiction. The sections relate only to the presentation of a bankruptcy petition and do not, for example, govern the jurisdiction of the English court to lend assistance to foreign insolvency proceedings or, where an English bankruptcy is already under way, to set aside a transaction entered into by a debtor abroad.[4] Similarly, the five jurisdictional bases in section 265 concern simply the existence of jurisdiction. Section 264(2) emphasises the discretionary nature of the court's power: a petition having validly been presented 'the court may make a bankruptcy order'. Thus the conditions in section 265 determine whether the English court is capable of making an order. Where section 265 is satisfied the court has a discretion not to make an order, or, even if an order has already been made, it is beyond doubt that the English court may stay its own proceedings. As was once stated by a judge quite familiar with international bankruptcies:[5]

> 'Theoretically at least, the idea of the bankruptcy law is that it should not be localised; but there are innumerable difficulties in the way of making a bankruptcy effective generally. It is obviously therefore of first importance that the court should exercise the jurisdiction . . . with extreme caution, in order not to precipitate the confusion which a conflict of jurisdiction and of law inevitably produces in commerce.'

When the court will exercise its discretion to stay proceedings is plainly dependent upon the facts of any given case.[6]

The jurisdictional criteria in section 265 (domicile, presence, ordinary residence, place of residence and the carrying on of business) are not laid down in any hierarchy. That domicile is first mentioned has no especial significance, indeed, it is evident that far more cases would fall under section 265(1)(c) than under section 265(1)(a). Domicile is exceptional, however, in that the concept is very much an idea of law, whereas the other criteria have no strictly defined legal meaning and (although borderline cases inevitably arise) are very much dependent on issues of fact.

Section 265(1)(b) is of particular (but not exclusive) use to a debtor, since it is likely that the debtor, when he himself petitions, may arrange to be present personally in England on the day on which the petition is presented.[7] The

---

[3] *Re Brauch* [1978] Ch. 316, *post.*

[4] See pp. 18–20 *supra.*

[5] *Re Chan Yue Shan* (1908) 4 H.K.L.R. 128 at 129 *per* Piggott CJ, the author of *Foreign Judgments* (2nd ed., 1908).

[6] The exercise of discretion is discussed in detail in chapter 3.

[7] This provision also means that any debtor who comes to England does so at his peril, for he may well be playing into the hands of his creditors: see *Re Thulin* [1995] 1 W.L.R. 165, discussed at p. 39, *infra.*

scope of section 265(1)(c) is undoubtedly the widest, for not only are three jurisdictional bases contained therein, but it is enough that the debtor has been ordinarily resident, or has had a place of residence or has carried on business in England *at any time in the period of three years* ending on the day the petition is presented.

Yet it is, perhaps, domicile which looks the furthest back in time. The nature of the rules of domicile in English law are such that as a forensic connection domicile has a most tenacious character; and many cases can be found in which a domicile once obtained has continued despite several years of absence from the country of domicile.[8]

In summary, if a debtor is actually in England on the day the petition is presented, section 265(1)(b) will be satisfied. Where the debtor, at any time during the period of three years ending with that day, has been ordinarily resident, has had a place of residence or has carried on business in England, the court will also have jurisdiction. Even if the debtor has not had any significant factual connection to England for greater than three years, it may yet be possible to establish jurisdiction under section 265(1)(a). This chapter now deals with each criterion in section 265 in the order there presented.

2. DOMICILE

Domicile is a notion of English law by which an individual is connected to a particular legal system. It may fairly be said that at one time domicile meant little more than, as Lord Cranworth once put it, 'home, the permanent home'.[9] In modern jurisprudence, however, the concept of domicile has been so keenly refined by technical legal rules that in many given instances an individual's domicile may bear no relationship to that person's home, permanent or otherwise. At the centre of modern domicile is the rule that at birth everyone is given a domicile and such domicile continues unless and until a subsequent domicile is acquired.[10] Accordingly, if the English court is called upon to determine whether a debtor is domiciled in England under section 265(1)(a) of the Insolvency Act 1986, it will generally be necessary to ascertain, first, the debtor's domicile at birth ('domicile of origin') and, secondly, whether the debtor has subsequently acquired a different domicile in particular by way of a 'domicile of choice', such being obtained by residing in a country with the intention of staying there permanently. This search for the initial domicile of origin, and any later domicile of choice, frequently necessitates extensive research into an

---

[8] The most celebrated examples being *Winans* v. *A-G* [1904] A.C. 287 and *Ramsay* v. *Liverpool Royal Infirmary* [1930] A.C. 588, *post*. It should be noted that domicile under the Insolvency Act 1986 is determined without reference to qualifications in the Civil Jurisdiction and Judgments Act 1982.

[9] *Whicker* v. *Hume* (1858) 7 HL Cas 124 at 160.

[10] Domicile is discussed in great detail in the standard works on private international law, Dicey and Morris, *The Conflict of Laws* (12th ed., 1993) chapter 7; Cheshire and North, *Private International Law* (12th ed., 1992) chapter 9. The special definition of domicile under the Civil Jurisdiction and Judgments Act 1982 is not relevant to s. 265(1) of the Insolvency Act 1986.

individual's past history[11] as well as present circumstances. The need for such research, not to mention the costs incurred, has regularly provoked criticism of the use of domicile as a connecting factor.

Authorities decided under the old bankruptcy legislation (Bankruptcy Act 1883, section 6(1)(d)) illustrate the nature of the inquiry the English court may be required to undertake with reference to section 265(1)(a) of the 1986 Act. In *Re Duleep Singh*[12] the debtor was the son of the Maharajah of the Punjab. The Maharajah had his domicile of origin in the Punjab but, in 1849 by the Treaty of Lahore, was obliged to renounce his sovereignty, leave the Punjab and live in England. The Maharajah resided in England until 1886, when he attempted unsuccessfully to return to the Punjab as ruler. Thereafter, the Maharajah resided in France and Russia. The debtor was born in England in 1866 and, even after his father's unsuccessful attempt to return to the Punjab, the debtor resided in England. In 1888 the debtor joined the British Army and went with his regiment to Canada. The question of the debtor's domicile arose for the purposes of bankruptcy jurisdiction in 1890 (a time when the debtor was no longer ordinarily resident in England). It was held that the debtor was not domiciled in England and that, therefore, the court had no jurisdiction; for the Maharajah, the debtor's father, never intended to settle permanently in England and had remained domiciled in the Punjab. When the debtor was born he took his father's domicile, that being in the Punjab. Although the debtor had thereafter lived in England and joined the British Army, such evidence was, as Lord Esher remarked, 'wholly insufficient' to establish the acquisition of an English domicile of choice.[13]

The somewhat artificial nature of domicile is well brought out by the decision in *Re Duleep Singh*. In order to determine the debtor's domicile, the Court of Appeal had to consider events that had taken place some 30 years previously. Moreover, it may be noted that although domiciled in the Punjab, the debtor had never set foot in the country[14] of his domicile.

A. Domicile of Origin

At birth a child acquires the domicile of its father or mother as a domicile of origin. If legitimate and born in the lifetime of the father, the child's domicile of origin will be the domicile of the father at the time the child was born. (Hence in *Re Duleep Singh*[15] the court sought to determine the Maharajah's domicile at the date of the debtor's birth.) If a child is posthumous, or is illegitimate, the domicile of origin will be that of the mother at the time of birth.[16] It must be stressed that once a domicile of origin is obtained (that is at birth) it is fixed; no new domicile of origin can be acquired. However, a domicile of origin can be superseded by the

---

[11] See *per* Kindersley V-C in *Drevon* v. *Drevon* (1864) 34 L.J. Ch. 129 at 133.

[12] (1890) 6 T.L.R. 385.

[13] *Ibid.* No question of a domicile of dependency arose.

[14] A debtor must, of course, be domiciled in a particular law district: a debtor cannot be domiciled in the United Kingdom nor in Canada; a debtor may be domiciled in England or Scotland, or Alberta or Ontario.

[15] *Supra.*

[16] *Dicey and Morris*, rule 9; *Udny* v. *Udny* (1869) L.R. 1 Sc. & Div. 441.

acquisition of a domicile of choice. A domicile of choice can be acquired, by a person of full age, through a combination of residence in a country and an intention to remain there permanently or indefinitely.

The residence element involved in a domicile of choice is in most cases easily satisfied and entails physical presence other than as a casual visitor. Even a single day's residence may suffice. On the other hand, the relevant intention, an intention to remain permanently or indefinitely, is difficult to establish and will not lightly be inferred by the courts. The cases of *Winans* v. *A-G*[17] and *Ramsay* v. *Liverpool Royal Infirmary*[18] are well-known. In the former, the deceased had resided principally in England for the last 37 years of his life; but it was held that, in the absence of the relevant intention, no domicile of choice in England had been established. In the latter the deceased, a native Scot, had spent the last 36 years of his life in England; but again the House of Lords held that, there being no clear evidence of an intention to stay permanently in England, the deceased had remained throughout domiciled in Scotland.[19]

The strength of the presumption in favour of the continuation of the domicile of origin is clearly shown in *Winans* v. *A-G* and *Ramsay* v. *Liverpool Royal Infirmary*.[20] Additionally, in each of the reported cases on domicile that arose under the Bankruptcy Act 1883 the English court concluded that the domicile of origin had not been displaced.[1] In *Re Barne*[2] the debtor, a domiciled Englishman, was a retired army officer who had taken his family to live in Belgium, but he had done so 'solely for educational and business purposes'.[3] The Court of Appeal held that the debtor remained domiciled in England. In *Re Langworthy*[4] the debtor, having an English domicile of origin, had deserted his wife and gone to reside in the Argentine Republic where he owned property. No evidence was led as to whether the debtor intended to settle permanently in the Argentine Republic. Cotton LJ stated:[5]

'His domicile of origin was English, and such it remained until a new domicile by choice was shown. No such domicile was established by the evidence.'

In *Re Duleep Singh*,[6] as we have seen, the debtor had a domicile of origin in the Punjab and, although he had lived only in England until joining his regiment in Canada, such residence was by itself 'wholly insufficient' to establish a domicile of choice in England,[7] whilst in *Re Mitchell*[8] the debtor, a Colonel in the British Army stationed in Guernsey, had his domicile of origin in (*semble*) Ireland. The only evidence as to a domicile of choice in England was that the headquarters of the debtor's regiment

---

[17] [1904] A.C. 287.
[18] [1930] A.C. 588.
[19] If such facts were to occur in the context of bankruptcy jurisdiction the debtor would in any event be ordinarily resident in England, *post*.
[20] [1904] A.C. 287 and [1930] A.C. 588 respectively.
[1] *Re Mitchell* (1884) 13 Q.B.D. 418, *Re Barne* (1886) 16 Q.B.D. 522, *Re Langworthy* (1887) 3 T.L.R. 544 and *Re Duleep Singh* (1890) 6 T.L.R. 385.
[2] (1886) 16 Q.B.D. 522.
[3] *Ibid.*, at 523.
[4] (1887) 3 T.L.R. 544.
[5] *Ibid.*, at 545.
[6] (1890) 6 T.L.R. 385, *ante*.
[7] *Ibid.*, n. 13, *ante*.
[8] (1884) 13 Q.B.D. 418.

were in England. Once again the Court of Appeal concluded that such circumstances did not give rise to a domicile of choice in England.

Thus the cases under the Bankruptcy Act 1883 give important practical guidance to a creditor seeking to petition relying on section 265(1)(a) of the Insolvency Act 1986. For whilst a domicile of choice may be acquired, if it can be established that the debtor's domicile of origin is English the creditor's case will be greatly advanced. Accordingly, one should not merely assume that the court will infer that the debtor's domicile of origin is English. Rather, specific evidence to establish the domicile of origin should be available.[9]

B. Domicile of Choice

(i) *Acquisition*

The acquisition of a domicile of choice[10] in the *Winans* v. *A-G* type of case (an individual residing in England for many years but without an intention to settle permanently) will not normally arise under section 265(1)(a) of the Insolvency Act 1986. For, quite simply, the debtor will be ordinarily resident in England whatever his subjective intentions may be. Thus, for the purposes of bankruptcy jurisdiction, the combination of residence and intention necessary to establish a domicile of choice will generally be relevant in two distinct fact situations.

The majority of cases, it is suggested, will involve a debtor who has an English domicile of origin but has lived in another country for some years, the question for the court being whether the debtor has replaced his English domicile of origin with a domicile of choice in that foreign country. For instance, the debtor (having an English domicile of origin) has spent several years living and working in New York. Here the debtor will be domiciled in England unless it is established that the debtor intends to remain permanently in New York. The debtor must, at one time, both be resident in New York and have the intention to remain there permanently.

The second, yet far rarer, situation in which the question of domicile may fall to be considered is where a debtor with a foreign domicile of origin is not currently residing in England, but has done so at some time in the past. In *Re Duleep Singh*,[11] it may be recalled, the debtor had a domicile of origin in the Punjab but had resided in England for many years. However, by the time the bankruptcy petition was presented, the debtor had already left England and his absence was such that he was no longer within the ordinarily resident provision of the Bankruptcy Act 1883.[12] Accordingly, the petitioner contended that the debtor had during the period of his residence in England acquired a domicile in England.

In either type of situation the legal test will be the same, as Scarman J once stated:[13]

---

[9] It is preferable to have evidence than to leave the court to infer that the domicile of origin be English: cf. *Re Barne* (1886) 16 Q.B.D. 522 at 524.

[10] The domicile of dependency is considered fully in *Dicey and Morris*, n. 10, *supra*.

[11] (1890) 6 T.L.R. 385, *ante*.

[12] The relevant period was then only one year before the presentation of the petition: Bankruptcy Act 1883, s. 6(1)(d).

[13] *Re Fuld's Estate (No. 3)* [1968] P. 675 at 684.

'A domicile of choice is acquired only if it be affirmatively shown that the *propositus* is resident within a territory subject to a distinct legal system with the intention, formed independently of external pressures, of residing there indefinitely.'

Or as Lord Westbury had put it a century earlier:[14]

'It must be a residence not for a limited period or particular purpose, but general and indefinite in its future contemplation.'

The court will not ask whether the debtor intended to acquire a domicile of choice, but rather whether the debtor was resident and intended to remain permanently.

(ii) *Conditional Intention*

In many instances an intention to reside permanently may be said to be conditional or contingent. Let us take the example of an individual with an English domicile of origin who has been residing in New York for several years, has established a business, a family and a home in New York and become a US citizen. Let us say further that this individual would, if asked, say he intended to stay permanently in New York. However, such intention (crucial to the acquisition of a domicile of choice) might easily be made to appear conditional in the light of the following questions. Would the individual be prepared to stay permanently in New York if (i) basic rate tax were increased to 60%, (ii) the US constitution were repealed, (iii) the passports of naturalised US citizens were revoked, and (iv) persons born outside the US were legally discriminated against? At some point it is likely that the intention to stay in New York might become qualified by reference to existing circumstances.[15]

However, it is not necessary to show an intention to remain whatever the circumstances or 'come what may'. The establishment of a permanent home in a new country does not have to be immutable. That the intention to remain permanently is to some extent conditional will not necessarily prevent the acquisition of a domicile of choice. If the condition can be clearly identified and is a 'reasonably anticipated contingency' then a domicile of choice will not be obtained.[16] Where, on the other hand, the condition (although clearly identified) is but a vague possibility, a domicile of choice may nevertheless be acquired.[17]

A modern example of a conditional intention amounting to no more than a vague possibility can be found in *Lawrence* v. *Lawrence*.[18] Robert Harley was a US citizen and (*semble*) had a domicile of origin in Pennsylvania,[19] but had resided most of his adult life in Brazil. Anthony Lincoln J said that:[20]

---

[14] *Udny* v. *Udny* (1869) L.R. 1 Sc. & Div. 441 at 458.
[15] More realistic scenarios might involve the individual getting divorced, losing his source of income or having to look after family members in England.
[16] *Re Fuld's Estate (No.3)* [1968] P. 675 at 684, *IRC* v. *Bullock* [1976] 1 W.L.R. 1178.
[17] *Re Furse* [1980] 3 All E.R. 838.
[18] [1985] Fam. 106.
[19] There can, of course, be no domicile in the United States.
[20] [1985] Fam. 106 at 110. The judgment of Anthony Lincoln J was affirmed by the Court of Appeal but without discussion of domicile.

'Mr Harley adopted Brazil as his permanent home, he loved Brazil. He was in all but nationality a Brazilian with a Brazilian lifestyle. He spoke Portuguese perfectly and adopted all the ways of Brazil. He lived not as an expatriate but as if he were indigenous. His matrimonial home was there.'

Yet Harley kept his US passport in case there was a revolution and he was compelled to leave Brazil. It was held that although the intention was subject to a contingency or condition, a domicile of choice was acquired:[1]

'Mr Harley. . . meant to live in Brazil permanently. He kept his passport just in case things got out of hand: if badly out of hand, he might or might not have to leave; if less than badly he would not. It was a matter of degree. The circumstances in which he might consider using the escape route were wholly indefinite, unpredictable and indefinable. The contingency was a vague one . . .

As the judge notes, whether a contingency may properly be described as 'vague' is a matter of degree and, naturally, the particular facts of each case will require careful consideration.

(iii) *Multiple Residence*

There is some authority which suggests that, in certain very limited circumstances, residence coupled with intention to remain permanently will *not* suffice to establish a domicile of choice.

In *Plummer* v. *IRC*,[2] a case involving residence in both England and Guernsey, Hoffmann J founded his decision upon the concept of 'chief residence'.[3] The taxpayer had an English domicile of origin but sought to establish that, during 1983 to 1985, a domicile of choice in Guernsey had been acquired. It was not in doubt that the taxpayer had the relevant intention. Further, it was accepted that the taxpayer was resident in Guernsey. However, during the period in question, the taxpayer was resident both in Guernsey and in England. Moreover, the taxpayer spent more time in England than in Guernsey. Hoffmann J concluded that no domicile of choice was acquired; and he did so on account solely of the quality of the residence in the alleged domicile of choice, when compared with the residence retained in the domicile of origin:[4]

'a person who retains a residence in his domicile of origin can acquire a domicile of choice in a new country only if the residence established in that country is his chief residence'.

In short, as the taxpayer's chief residence was in England (the domicile of origin) it was not possible whatever the taxpayer's intentions for a domicile of choice to be established in Guernsey.

Plummer v. *IRC* will not have a wide application in the context of bankruptcy jurisdiction. Cases on domicile and dual or multiple residence are certainly unusual. Moreover, the ratio of *Plummer* v. *IRC* is limited to circumstances in which a residence in the domicile of origin is retained. The reasoning of Hoffmann J would not apply in the following situation. A debtor with an English domicile of origin resides in Australia, spending

[1] [1985] Fam. 106.
[2] [1988] 1 W.L.R. 292 more fully reported at [1988] 1 All E.R. 97.
[3] [1988] 1 All E.R. 97 at 104.
[4] *Ibid.*, at 106.

seven months each year in New South Wales and the remaining months in Victoria, where the family home is situated. The debtor will acquire a domicile of choice in Victoria if it is shown that the necessary intention is present. It will not be relevant to inquire whether Victoria is the debtor's 'chief residence' in terms of the number of months and days spent residing there each year.

Nevertheless, it should be noted that the court in *Plummer* v. *IRC* did not refer to earlier (House of Lords) authorities upon domicile and multiple residence. In *Aikman* v. *Aikman*[5] the deceased had been born in 1761 with a Scottish domicile of origin but, it was argued, had acquired by 1820 an English domicile of choice. During the period 1812 to 1818 the deceased had houses in both England and Scotland and was accustomed to dividing his time more or less equally between the two places. In fact, from 1812 to 1815 the deceased spent more time in Scotland (the domicile of origin) than in England (the alleged domicile of choice). Their Lordships considered the matter as governed by the deceased's intention and did not mention the notion of chief residence. It is suggested that if the English court is called upon to determine a case of dual or multiple residence for the purposes of section 265(1)(a) of the Insolvency Act, the test of a combination of residence and intention as in *Aikman* v. *Aikman* is to be preferred: *Plummer* v. *IRC* should not be followed.[6]

C. Abandonment and Revival

A domicile of origin will continue, as we have seen, until replaced by a domicile of choice. A domicile of origin cannot simply be given up or abandoned.[7] Thus a debtor with an English domicile of origin may leave England intending never to return; however, that debtor will remain domiciled in England until a domicile of choice elsewhere is acquired.[8] A domicile of choice may be lost by mere abandonment.

A domicile of choice is acquired through a combination of residence and intention. Similarly, a domicile of choice will cease when both the residence and intention have been given up. When a domicile of choice is abandoned, it is the domicile of origin which automatically revives and continues unless and until replaced by a subsequent domicile of choice. The operation of the revival rule can be seen in the following example. The debtor was born in 1930 with an English domicile of origin. In 1955 the debtor moved to Denmark and, by 1960, intended to live there permanently. In 1995, having lived in Denmark for 40 years, the debtor was required by failing health to seek a warmer climate. The debtor, accordingly, leaves Denmark for good and goes to stay temporarily with members of his family in California. In 1995 the debtor's domicile of choice in Denmark is abandoned: the debtor

[5]   (1861) 4 L.T. 374.
[6]   The judgment of Hoffmann J makes no reference to the decision of the House of Lords in *Maxwell* v. *M'Clure* (1860) 2 L.T. 65 nor of the Court of Appeal in *Steiner* v. *IRC* [1973] S.T.C. 547, both cases suggesting a combination of residence and intention as the relevant test: see, *passim*, (1990) 10 O.J.L.S 572.
[7]   *Bell* v. *Kennedy* (1868) L.R. 1 Sc. & Div. 307.
[8]   Through a combination of residence and intention: note *Brown* v. *Brown* [1982] 3 F.L.R. 212, *passim*.

has given up residence and has no intention of returning. At this point the debtor's English domicile of origin automatically revives, quite irrespective of whether or not the debtor intends to spend even one day in England. But, continuing with our example, if in 1996 the debtor bought a home in California, deciding to stay there indefinitely, the English domicile of origin would be replaced by a domicile of choice in California.

It should be noted that a domicile of choice is only abandoned when both residence and intention are given up. For instance, a debtor with an Irish domicile of origin has acquired an English domicile of choice. In 1994 the debtor moves to Hong Kong to work in the financial sector on a five-year contract. In such circumstances the debtor's domicile of choice in England will continue if the debtor intends to return, albeit at a later date, to live in England.

D. Governing Law

A person's domicile is governed by the rules of English law.[9] It makes no difference whether an individual is domiciled in Scotland or Peru, it is English law alone to which reference must be made. In *Re Langworthy*[10] the Court of Appeal was called upon to consider, for the purpose of bankruptcy jurisdiction, whether a debtor with an English domicile of origin had acquired a domicile of choice in the Argentine Republic. It was held that no new domicile had been established by the evidence, yet Cotton LJ also commented:[11]

'[The debtor] had gone out to the Argentine Republic and had land there and was working a farm and dealing in cattle. But in the absence of evidence as to the law of the Republic, those facts were consistent with his retaining his domicile of origin, and that was enough to found the jurisdiction in bankruptcy . . .'

To the extent that his Lordship suggests that the acquisition of a domicile may depend upon the content of a foreign legal system, this comment cannot be supported.

E. Evidential Considerations

(i) *Burden and Standard of Proof*

The burden of proof rests upon the petitioner to show that a debtor falls under one of the heads of section 265(1) of the Insolvency Act 1986. The standard of proof required is the normal civil measure, a balance of probabilities. Although the court will not lightly infer a change of domicile, and there is a strong presumption in favour of the continuation of a domicile of origin, the acquisition of a domicile of choice need not be established beyond a reasonable doubt.[12]

[9] *Dicey and Morris*, rule 8.
[10] (1887) 3 T.L.R. 544, *ante.*
[11] *Ibid.*, at 545.
[12] *Re Fuld's Estate (No. 3)* [1968] P. 675 at 685–686.

The burden of proof remains throughout on the petitioner and that burden does not shift. In *Re Mitchell*[13] Baggallay LJ seems, at first glance, to have considered otherwise:[14]

> 'I am of the opinion that the onus is on the petitioning creditor to show that the debtor is domiciled in England. I can quite conceive that there may be cases in which there may be such an amount of *prima facie* evidence of an English domicile as to shift the burden on to the respondent.'

It is submitted that his Lordship meant no more than that if a petitioner produces seemingly clear evidence that the debtor has an English domicile then, as a matter of common sense, if the debtor does not challenge that evidence, the court will very likely find that the debtor has an English domicile. Yet at no time will the technical onus of proof be transferred from the petitioner to the debtor.

(ii) *Presumptions*

There is a presumption in favour of the continuation of an existing domicile. Such presumption is particularly strong in respect of the domicile of origin. Once a debtor is shown to have an English domicile of origin such domicile is, in the absence of evidence to establish a domicile of choice elsewhere, presumed to continue.[15] In some instances it may be that the debtor does not dispute his English domicile of origin; however, it will generally be prudent for some detailed evidence to be available in order to establish clearly the debtor's domicile of origin.

(iii) *Declarations of Intention*

When seeking to ascertain whether a domicile of choice has been acquired, the intentions of a debtor are of crucial importance. Naturally, therefore, expressions of intention made by a debtor may be taken into account. However, the court approaches declarations of intention with considerable caution.[16] In particular, the court would not be ignorant of the likelihood that a debtor might rather prefer to fall without the bankruptcy jurisdiction of the English court.

3. PERSONAL PRESENCE

By virtue of section 265(1)(b) a bankruptcy petition may be presented by a creditor or the debtor if the debtor is personally present in England on the day on which the petition is presented. Under the Bankruptcy Act 1914, and its predecessors, personal presence was not a sufficient forensic connection

[13] (1884) 13 Q.B.D. 418.
[14] *Ibid.*, at 421.
[15] *Bell* v. *Kennedy* (1868) L.R. 1 Sc. & Div. 307, *Winans* v. *A-G* [1904] A.C. 287 and *Ramsay* v. *Liverpool Royal Infirmary* [1930] A.C. 588.
[16] *Ross* v. *Ross* [1930] A.C. 1 at 6 *per* Lord Buckmaster.

to establish jurisdiction. The first example of the use of section 265(1)(b) to establish jurisdiction can be found in *Re Thulin*.[17] The debtor, a Swedish national who resided in Belgium, had in 1989 entered into a contract of loan with an English company. The contract was expressly governed by English law and subject to the non-exclusive jurisdiction of the English court. The debtor in 1991 defaulted on the loan and in July 1993 was served in England with a statutory demand, which was followed in due course by a bankruptcy petition. The debtor had come to England in July 1993 in order to try to prevent the sale of certain property, but had been arrested and charged with attempting to obtain property by deception. Although the debtor had been released on bail (and subsequently the charges had been dropped) he had been required to surrender his passport and was thus unable to leave the country when the petition was presented. A bankruptcy order was made in England even though the debtor had, in 1991, already been made bankrupt in Sweden.[18] Of course, in *Re Thulin* there was no suggestion that charges had been 'trumped up' against the debtor in order to detain him whilst a petition was being presented; such behaviour would inevitably cause the court to dismiss any petition.

Although personal presence is now a basis of jurisdiction under the Insolvency Act, the Act does not present a creditor with a means of requiring the debtor to come to England in the first place. However, it may be noted that in *Union Bank of Finland* v. *Lelakis*[19] it was held that, a default judgment having been obtained in England, the court in the exercise of its power under R.S.C. Ord. 48 could order a defendant abroad to attend in London for examination as to his assets. If a defendant were to comply with such an order and come to England, it would then be possible for any creditor to present a bankruptcy petition. Although it is suggested that if a plaintiff's real objective in invoking Ord. 48 were to facilitate the presentation of a bankruptcy petition, that would constitute an abuse of process of the court.

4. ORDINARY RESIDENCE

The English court will have jurisdiction if, at any time in the period of three years ending with the day on which the petition is presented, the debtor has been ordinarily resident in England.[20] The words 'ordinarily resident' are to be given in the context of section 265(1)(c)(i) their ordinary and natural meaning.[1] Moreover, whether a debtor is ordinarily resident in England is very much a question of fact and degree. Ordinary residence, unlike the notion of domicile, is largely free from complex and technical rules of law. Thus a debtor may at one time be ordinarily

[17] [1995] 1 W.L.R. 165. For the position under the Bankruptcy Acts, see *Re Hecquard* (1890) 24 Q.B.D. 71 at 74.
[18] See further pp. 71–72, *infra.*
[19] [1996] 4 All E.R. 305.
[20] Insolvency Act 1986, s. 265(1)(c)(i).
[1] The statutory framework does not require otherwise: see *Shah* v. *Barnet London Borough Council* [1983] 2 A.C. 309.

resident in two countries.[2] Additionally, a debtor may be ordinarily resident in England without any intention to remain in England permanently or indefinitely. In the broadest terms, ordinary residence means simply where a debtor normally lives albeit for a temporary period.

The leading authority upon ordinary residence is *Shah* v. *Barnet London Borough Council*,[3] wherein the House of Lords rejected the contention that ordinary residence was equivalent to 'real home'. As Lord Scarman observed:[4]

> '"ordinarily resident" refers to a man's abode in a particular place or country which he has adopted voluntarily and for settled purposes as part of the regular order of his life for the time being, whether of long or short duration'.

Hence ordinary residence in England may be acquired by a temporary stay in England, whether of long or short duration. The residence must be adopted voluntarily and for settled purposes. Such purposes are not in any way restricted and may include education, business or profession, employment, health, family or merely love of the place. Certainly, it is not required that a debtor be in England on commercial or business purposes.

Although the facts in *Shah* v. *Barnet London Borough Council* were far removed from insolvency, Lord Scarman's speech confirms the approach that had been adopted in bankruptcy cases. Indeed, the position was clearly stated in a Commonwealth decision, where it was held:[5]

> 'It is not necessary for a petitioner applying to be declared an insolvent to have resided for a long time at a place within the jurisdiction of the court. Even temporary residence for a time and for a particular purpose is enough to give the court jurisdiction to deal with an application for insolvency.'

There are several cases decided under the Bankruptcy Acts that give guidance as to when a temporary presence in England constitutes ordinary residence.[6]

A. Temporary Presence in England

It is apparent that if a debtor has moved to England intending to stay permanently or for a number of years, rather than months, that debtor will be ordinarily resident in England despite only a few weeks of physical presence. Yet such an intention is most definitely not a necessary element in ordinary residence.[7] In *Re Norris*[8] a foreign debtor staying in London hotels over a period of 18 months, returning periodically to his family in Brussels, was held to be ordinarily resident in England, Lord Halsbury LC

---

[2] *Re Norris* (1888) 4 T.L.R. 452, *post*. The doubts as to whether one can be 'habitually' resident in two countries, expressed in *Cameron* v. *Cameron* 1996 S.L.T. 306, are not relevant here.
[3] [1983] 2 A.C. 309.
[4] *Ibid.*, at 343.
[5] *Sheikh Abdul Rezak* v. *Basiruddin Ahmed* (1911) 27 C.W.N. 405.
[6] Particularly, *Re Norris* (1888) 4 T.L.R. 452, *Re Bright* (1901) 18 T.L.R. 37 and (1903) 19 T.L.R. 203, *Re A Debtor (1898)* (1898) 14 T.L.R. 569, *Re Erskine* (1893) 10 T.L.R. 32 and *Re Brauch* [1978] Ch. 316. Cf. *Nessa* v. *Chief Adjudication Officer*, [1998] 2 All ER 728.
[7] Thus ordinary residence is wholly different from domicile.
[8] (1888) 4 T.L.R. 452.

commenting that the debtor could at one time be ordinarily resident in both Belgium and England.[9] In *Re Bright*[10] an eight-month stay in England to conduct litigation amounted to ordinary residence. In *Re a Debtor (1898)*[11] residence in London, sometimes at an hotel and sometimes at a boarding house, for five months to conduct litigation was (*obiter*) considered sufficient to establish ordinary residence; although as Lindley MR observed such facts might be 'rather near the line'.[12] In comparison, the Court of Appeal in *Re Erskine*[13] held that a single five-month visit to England, but not motivated by any particular business or family reasons, did not confer jurisdiction in bankruptcy.[14] What distinguishes *Re Erskine* from *Re a Debtor (1898)* is that in *Re Erskine* the debtor had no particular reason for being in England: the debtor remained merely a visitor. To employ terminology taken from *Shah* v. *Barnet London Borough Council*,[15] in *Re Erskine* the debtor's presence in England was not for settled purposes.

The cases establish that, whilst the matter is one of fact, where a settled purpose can be found a stay in England even as brief as four or five months constitutes particularly strong evidence in favour of ordinary residence.[16]

Reference to cases decided under tax legislation reveals an approach wholly consistent with the bankruptcy authorities. In *Levene* v. *IRC*[17] the taxpayer was in England for four or five months each year over a five-year period for family, religious and medical reasons. The House of Lords upheld a finding of ordinary residence. In *IRC* v. *Lysaght*[18] the evidence was less clearly in favour of ordinary residence. In each of two years the taxpayer spent slightly over three months in England on frequent business trips. Viscount Cave LC was not satisfied that ordinary residence had been made out.[19] But a majority in their Lordships' House held that there was sufficient evidence to justify a finding of ordinary residence. *IRC* v. *Lysaght* is noteworthy since it must be considered very much a borderline decision. Although the taxpayer was only present for somewhat over three months each year it was the purpose behind the visits,

---

[9] (1888) 4 T.L.R. 452. Note also *Re Taylor* (1992) 37 F.C.R. 194.

[10] (1903) 19 T.L.R. 203, further facts are reported at (1903) 47 Sol. J. 253.

[11] (1898) 14 T.L.R. 569.

[12] *Ibid.*

[13] (1893) 10 T.L.R. 32.

[14] See also *Re Mackenzie* [1941] Ch. 69, *post.*

[15] [1983] 2 A.C. 309 at 343.

[16] This author has suggested, see (1989) 38 I.C.L.Q. 175 at 180, that ordinary residence may be reduced to something in the nature of a mathematical formula. Ordinary residence in England is established upon achieving a total of 6 points. 1 point is scored for each month of residence. A definite purpose (e.g. business) in coming to England will score 2. Repeated visits over a period of years adds 1. Hence in *Re Bright* (1903) 19 T.L.R. 203 the total is 10 (ordinary residence made out), eight months' residence to conduct litigation. In *Re a Debtor (1898)* 14 T.L.R. 569 the total is 7 (ordinary residence made out), five months' residence to conduct litigation. *Re Erskine* (1893) 10 T.L.R. 32 totals 5 (no ordinary residence), five months' residence but with no clear or settled purpose. This formula is, of course, no substitute for a proper consideration of all the facts.

[17] [1928] A.C. 217.

[18] [1928] A.C. 234.

[19] *Ibid.*, at 240.

taken with the regular and repeated nature of those visits, which amounted to ordinary residence.[20]

Accordingly, when called upon to determine if a debtor's presence 'has a sufficient degree of continuity to be properly described as settled',[1] the court will have regard to the length of and purpose for any visits; but also to be taken into account is whether those visits have been regular and repeated over a period of two or more years. In summary, where a debtor has been temporarily in England the following guidelines may be advanced. If a debtor spends the greater part of his time in England, ordinary residence can scarcely be in doubt. A stay of four or five months provided it is for purposes of business, family, employment, health, is strong evidence of ordinary residence.[2] Where a particular purpose is not apparent, residence for four or five months is unlikely to amount to ordinary residence,[3] unless visits to England have been regular and extended over a period of years. Finally, a stay of less than four months may constitute ordinary residence only where a settled purpose can be identified and, moreover, such visits have been regular and extended over a period of years.[4]

B. Prolonged Absence from England

The cases interpreting and applying ordinary residence as a jurisdictional test under the Bankruptcy Acts 1883 and 1914 concerned foreign debtors who were temporarily in England. Yet questions of ordinary residence may arise in very different circumstances, in particular, where a debtor who has been living in England (and has been ordinarily resident) leaves England to live abroad. It may be necessary in such a situation to determine when a period of ordinary residence in England has been brought to an end.[5]

(i) *Debtor Leaving England Permanently*

If a debtor after living for many years in England moves to Paris intending to stay there permanently, it is beyond doubt that the debtor will thereupon cease to be ordinarily resident in England.[6] For, quite simply, living in England no longer forms part of the regular order of the debtor's life. Nevertheless, the cessation of ordinary residence does not deprive the English court of jurisdiction under section 265(1)(c)(i) of the Insolvency Act 1986. A bankruptcy petition may be presented up to three years after

---

[20] On the formula suggested above, n. 16, *IRC* v. *Lysaght* totals slightly over 6 (ordinary residence barely made out), somewhat over three months' residence for business purposes and repeated over two years. *Levene* v. *IRC* totals 7–8 (ordinary residence made out), four to five months' residence for settled purposes repeated over a course of years.

[1] *Shah* v. *Barnet London Borough Council* [1983] 2 A.C. 309 at 344 *per* Lord Scarman.

[2] *Re a Debtor (1898)* (1898) 14 T.L.R. 569, *Levene* v. *IRC* [1928] A.C. 217 and *Miesegaes* v. *IRC* (1957) 37 T.C. 493 at 502.

[3] *Re Erskine* (1893) 10 T.L.R. 32.

[4] *IRC* v. *Lysaght* [1928] A.C. 234, see also *Kinloch* v. *IRC* (1929) 14 T.C. 736.

[5] However, the impact of the three-year time period under s. 265(1)(c)(i) should not be overlooked, *post*.

[6] See *Hopkins* v. *Hopkins* [1951] P. 116, *propositus* intending to settle permanently in Canada.

the end of a period of ordinary residence in England. Let us say a debtor who had been ordinarily resident in England left England for good on 30 November 1996; provided a petition be presented before December 1999 the English court will have jurisdiction.

(ii) *Intention to Return*

However in some instances it may not be immediately apparent when, or if, a debtor's ordinary residence has ended. For instance, although living abroad for several years, a debtor may intend at some later date to return to England. Obviously, temporary or occasional absences from England (such as on holiday) will not break a period of ordinary residence.[7] In *Stransky* v. *Stransky*[8] and *Lewis* v. *Lewis*[9] it was held (for the purpose of matrimonial jurisdiction) that periods of absence of eight months and nine months respectively did not end a wife's ordinary residence in England. But it must be noted that fact situations like those in *Stransky* v. *Stransky* and *Lewis* v. *Lewis* present no problem under section 265(1)(c)(i). If a debtor leaves England and returns one year or two years later, the English court will have bankruptcy jurisdiction throughout the period of absence by virtue of the three-year time period under section 265(1)(c)(i). Accordingly, where a debtor is out of England for less than three years it will simply not be relevant to determine if the debtor remained ordinarily resident in England throughout that absence.

Difficulties may arise, however, when a bankruptcy petition is presented after the debtor has already been living abroad for more than three years. For it may be necessary to decide if the debtor's intention to return to England at a future date will prevent the loss of ordinary residence. In *Lewis* v. *Lewis*[10] a wife was held to be ordinarily resident in England despite a nine-month absence in Australia, Willmer J commenting:[11]

> 'the stay in Australia was intended to be of only temporary duration, and at the date of departure, and indeed during the term of the wife's residence in Australia, there was always an intention at some time in the future to return to the matrimonial home in England'.

This *dictum* cannot be supported: its effect is to introduce the 'subjective test of domicile' which has been rejected by Lord Scarman in *Shah* v. *Barnet London Borough Council*.[12] Ordinary residence connotes where a person lives as part of the regular order of that person's life: an intention 'at some time in the future to return' does not prevent the loss of ordinary residence. Thus if a debtor were to leave England to take up employment abroad (and remain abroad for several years) it is clear that an intention to return to England would not prevent ordinary residence in England being lost. That the debtor owned a house in England, at which periods of annual

---

[7] *Shah* v. *Barnet London Borough Council* [1983] 2 A.C. 309 at 342 *per* Lord Scarman.
[8] [1954] P. 428. See also the judgment of Nolan J in *R.* v. *Immigration Appeal Tribunal, ex p Siggins* [1985] Imm. A.R. 14 – eight months' casual work in the USA, with an intention throughout to return to England, did not terminate ordinary residence in England.
[9] [1956] 1 W.L.R. 200.
[10] *Ibid.*
[11] *Ibid.*, at 204–205.
[12] [1983] 2 A.C. 309 at 343.

leave were spent, would not make the debtor ordinarily resident in England.[13] (Although the debtor would have a 'place of residence' in England.)

The following example presents the slightly different problem of precisely when ordinary residence is lost. In January 1995 a debtor, having been ordinarily resident in England, is sent by an employer to the Hong Kong office on a six-month secondment. The debtor's original intention is to return to England at the end of the six-month period. However, in June 1995, the debtor decides not to return to England and takes up a permanent position in Hong Kong. Would the English court have jurisdiction if a bankruptcy petition were presented in May 1998? That is, more than three years after the debtor left England, but within the three year period if the debtor remained ordinarily resident in England until June 1995. First, as has been shown, an intention to return to England does not of itself cause a debtor to remain ordinarily resident in England. Secondly, to the extent that an absence from England is 'temporary', ordinary residence will not be determined. If the debtor in our example had indeed returned to England at the end of the six-month secondment, there is clear authority that ordinary residence would not have been lost.[14] Accordingly, until June 1995 (when his absence ceased to be temporary) the debtor will have been ordinarily resident in England. Thus the three-year period under section 265(1)(c)(i) would start to run in June 1995, when the debtor's intention changed causing his absence no longer properly to be considered temporary. In such a manner, ordinary residence in England may in fact be continued for several months after a debtor has ceased to be physically present.

Quite when ordinary residence is terminated is a question of fact. It is suggested that there is strong evidence of a continuation of ordinary residence where the intended period of absence is eight months or less. It may even be that twelve months is not too long.[15] However, this author would not support the approach of the Federal Court of Australia in *Re Vassis*.[16] The debtor, a solicitor, fled Australia in January 1983 intending at some time to return there. The debtor did eventually return to Australia in February 1985. It was alleged that an act of bankruptcy was committed on 28 December 1983; and the Federal Court was required to rule as to whether the debtor was then ordinarily resident in Australia. Burchett J stated that the debtor:[17]

> 'was ordinarily resident in Australia, both at the time he departed, and throughout the period until his return two years later in February 1985, or at least until the crucial date, 28th December 1983, which was barely a year from his departure'.

Of course, if similar facts were to arise in England, the English court would in any event have jurisdiction on account of the three-year period in section

---

[13] *R.* v. *Lancashire County Council, ex p Huddleston* [1986] 2 All E.R. 941.

[14] *Lewis* v. *Lewis* [1956] 1 W.L.R. 200 and *Stransky* v. *Stransky* [1954] P. 428, the latter being approved on its facts by Lord Scarman in *Shah* v. *Barnet London Borough Council* [1983] 2 A.C. 309 at 342.

[15] Cf. *Reed* v. *Clark* [1986] Ch. 1 and *Rogers* v. *Inland Revenue* (1879) 1 T.C. 225: both decisions upon residence rather than ordinary residence.

[16] (1986) 64 A.L.R. 407.

[17] *Ibid.*, at 414.

265(1)(c)(i). Nevertheless, the effect of the reasoning of the Federal Court should be noted. In *Re Vassis* the debtor left Australia in January 1983 but (*per* Burchett J) was still ordinarily resident in Australia in January 1985, that is, before the debtor returned to Australia. If *Re Vassis* were followed in England it would mean that a debtor's intention to return to England could keep alive ordinary residence in England for at least some 24 months. Thus the three-year period in section 265(1)(c)(i) might only begin to run 24 months after a debtor had physically removed himself from England. It is submitted that an absence of 24 months must be considered as ending ordinary residence in England. A two-year period cannot properly be described as occasional or temporary; and the regular order of a debtor's life simply does not involve living in England.

In *Re Vassis* the alleged act of bankruptcy in fact was committed 11 months after the debtor fled Australia. Yet, it is submitted, the debtor was not then ordinarily resident in Australia. For *Re Vassis* did not involve an intended 11-month absence. The debtor left Australia with no clear or even vague intention as to when he would return. It may very well be as Burchett J suggested[18] that a university lecturer who goes on sabbatical leave for one year can be said to remain ordinarily resident in his home country. However, the university lecturer has a clear intention to return at the end of 12 months. In *Re Vassis* the debtor fled Australia with no clear intention as to the date of his return. An intention to return at some time in the future simply does not keep alive a period of ordinary residence.[19]

To sum up, in the normal type of case where a debtor leaves England intending to return in a couple of years, or at some indefinite time in the future, the three-year period under section 265(1)(c)(i) of the Insolvency Act 1986 will begin to run at once. However, if a debtor leaves England intending to be away for only a short period (let us say eight months) the debtor's ordinary residence in England may continue despite his physical absence: the three-year period under section 265(1)(c)(i) commencing only when the debtor's absence ceases to be temporary.

C. Involuntary Residence

In particular circumstances a debtor's presence in or absence from England may be said to be involuntary. Lord Scarman in *Shah* v. *Barnet London Borough Council* referred to residence 'adopted voluntarily and for settled purposes'.[20] The residence need not be voluntary but merely voluntarily adopted. In *Re MacKenzie*[1] an intestate (domiciled in Australia) had voluntarily come to England on a visit, but some four months later had become of unsound mind. The intestate died in England many years later, never having recovered. In the light of *Re Erskine*,[2] Morton J was in doubt whether a four-month visit to England (with no apparent settled purpose)

---

[18] (1986) 64 A.L.R. 407 at 415.

[19] Otherwise ordinary residence becomes too artificial a concept.

[20] [1983] 2 A.C. 309 at 343. See, however, the doubts expressed *obiter* in *Cameron* v. *Cameron* 1996 S.L.T. 306 at 311, as to whether Robinson Crusoe was habitually resident on his desert island.

[1] [1941] Ch. 69.

[2] (1893) 10 T.L.R. 32, *ante.*

amounted to ordinary residence. However, his Lordship took the intestate's involuntary residence into account, holding that prior to her death the intestate was ordinarily resident in England. Once residence has initially been taken up voluntarily, that it subsequently may become involuntary will not prevent the acquisition of ordinary residence.[3] Hence, if a debtor were to visit England and then be compelled to remain for many months (for instance, because of criminal proceedings) there would be compelling evidence to establish that the debtor had become ordinarily resident in England. Should a debtor be compelled to go to England, for example by being extradited, the presence of the debtor in England will establish jurisdiction pursuant to section 265(1)(b).

In the opposite situation, a debtor who has been ordinarily resident in England may be detained abroad perhaps for several years. Yet detention abroad does not continue a period of ordinary residence in England. Once it can no longer be said that the debtor usually lives in England, ordinary residence in England will come to an end.[4]

D. Illegal Residence

If a debtor has entered and remained illegally in the United Kingdom, it may well be that the English court would not allow the debtor to take advantage of that illegal residence and claim to be ordinarily resident under section 265(1)(c)(i) of the Insolvency Act. Yet it is not correct to maintain that illegal residence is no residence at all. That the debtor has been in England in breach of immigration laws will not prevent a creditor from relying on such illegal residence and petitioning under section 265(1)(c)(i).[5]

5. PLACE OF RESIDENCE

If a debtor has had a place of residence in England, at any time within the period of three years ending on the day on which the petition is presented, the English court will have jurisdiction under section 265(1)(c)(i) of the Insolvency Act 1986. Whether a debtor has a 'place of residence' is a question of fact, there being no absolute requirements either as to the nature of the 'place' or the period and quality of the 'residence' involved. Of course, a debtor may have a place of residence without being ordinarily resident in England. For instance, a debtor has been employed in Hong Kong for many years, returning to his house in England for periods of annual leave. Whilst the debtor will not be ordinarily resident in England, a place of residence undoubtedly exists.[6]

---

[3] For the unusual situation of presence which is from its very beginning involuntary see *Re Spek and Lawson* (1983) 2 D.L.R. (4th) 672 at 679.
[4] If a debtor were imprisoned abroad for several years ordinary residence in England would cease, whatever his intentions.
[5] Cf. *Puttick v. A-G* [1980] Fam. 1.
[6] Cf. *R. v. Lancashire County Council, ex p Huddleston* [1986] 2 All E.R. 941. Note also *Gairdner v. MacArthur* 1918 S.L.T. 123.

The Bankruptcy Act 1883 referred to a 'dwelling house'.[7] However, even under the old legislation, an actual house was not required. In *Re Hecquard*[8] a domiciled Frenchman took furnished rooms for three months in a house in London. The debtor occupied the rooms exclusively. The Court of Appeal held that the rooms were a dwelling house for the purposes of section 6(1)(d) of the 1883 Act. Merely staying occasionally at an hotel in England did not constitute a dwelling house.[9] But in *Re Hecquard* the debtor was plainly not staying at rooms in an hotel in the ordinary way.

The Insolvency Act does not expressly require that a debtor have any legal or equitable interest in a relevant 'place of residence';[10] and there is no reason why a mere licensee may not have a place of residence. Equally, that the debtor does indeed have legal title to a house in England does not inevitably mean that it is his place of residence. In *Re Brauch*[11] the debtor owned a house in London and, although he did not reside there, the debtor had there installed the mother of his son. The debtor made visits to the house and may have stayed nights. Nevertheless, the Court of Appeal upheld the registrar's determination that there was insufficient evidence to decide whether or not the debtor had a dwelling house; accordingly, as the burden of proof lay on the petitioning creditors, jurisdiction under this head was not made out.[12]

In *Re Brauch* the debtor, on the facts, was not shown to reside at the house in question. But the case certainly is no authority for the suggestion that putting a house into another person's name will enable the debtor to avoid the court's jurisdiction. *Loewenstein* v. *De Salis*[13] although concerned with residence under the Income Tax Act 1918 may serve as illustration. The appellant, a Belgian subject, was a director of, and controlling shareholder in, a company. The company owned property in England which the appellant used every year for the hunting season. For the appellant it was argued that the property was not his but rather belonged to the company. Rowlatt J, whilst not questioning the company's ownership of the property, held that it was nevertheless the appellant's residence:[14]

> 'Now I think that it is a case in which you do say you look at the substance of the matter. You do not look at the substance of the matter and say the man is the company, that is inaccurate, but you look at the substance of the matter and say: This is the house in which he could reside and did reside . . . He has got this house to come to when he likes; he does not own it; he has got no proprietary interest in it, but it is just as good as if he had it for the purpose of having it for a residence, and there it is.'

It is suggested that a similar approach is appropriate when considering whether, in substance, a debtor has a place of residence within section 265(1)(c)(i) of the Insolvency Act.

---

[7] Bankruptcy Act 1883, s. 6(1)(d); Bankruptcy Act 1914, s. 4(1)(d).
[8] (1890) 24 Q.B.D. 71.
[9] *Re Mitchell* (1884) 13 Q.B.D. 418 at 423 *per* Cotton LJ.
[10] See, generally, *Re Brauch* [1978] Ch. 316 at 334–335.
[11] [1978] Ch. 316.
[12] *Ibid.*, at 335.
[13] (1926) 10 T.C. 424.
[14] *Ibid.*, at 427–428.

Once a debtor has had a place of residence it may be given up, even though the debtor retains ownership and has not sold the property in question. In *Re Nordenfelt*[15] the debtor had a dwelling house in England but had taken his family to live in Paris and instructed an estate agent to let the house. The house not having been let, the furniture was offered for sale by auction, and that which was not sold was packed up ready for removal. It was held that the English court did not have jurisdiction, Lord Esher MR commenting:[16]

> 'If a man has a house belonging to him, but he has abandoned it as his dwelling house, that house is not his "dwelling house" within the meaning of this section.'

His Lordship expressly declined to offer any definition of the term 'dwelling house'. There is authority that *Re Nordenfelt* did not preclude the possibility that (under the old legislation) a debtor might have had a dwelling house without being actually resident in it. In *Re Brauch* Goff LJ stated:[17]

> 'I think it may be possible to find that the debtor had a dwelling house in England although he was not in fact in occupation of it any time during the year. But the more there is actual occupation, the easier it is to reach the conclusion that there was a dwelling house, and the shorter the actual occupation, the more difficult it becomes.'

The same approach will be taken in respect of 'a place of residence' under the Insolvency Act 1986; and it should be noted that where there is little or no evidence of occupation by a debtor the burden of proof will likely defeat the petitioner. In any event, as *Re Nordenfelt*[18] and *Re Brauch*[19] both suggest, merely because there is a place in England to which the debtor may resort and set himself down, does not of itself necessarily constitute a place of residence. The matter is one of fact and degree.

6. CARRYING ON BUSINESS

The English court will have jurisdiction under section 265(1)(c) of the Insolvency Act 1986 if the debtor has, at any time within the three-year period, carried on business in England and Wales. The ambit of this head of jurisdiction is widened by section 265(2) which provides:

> 'The reference in subsection (1)(c) to an individual carrying on business includes –
> (a) the carrying on of business by a firm or partnership of which the individual is a member, and
> (b) the carrying on of business by an agent or manager for the individual or for such firm or partnership.'

---

[15] [1895] 1 Q.B. 151.
[16] *Ibid.*, at 153.
[17] [1978] Ch. 316 at 335.
[18] [1895] 1 Q.B. 151.
[19] [1978] Ch. 316.

Leaving to one side for the moment at least the purely inclusive definition in subsection (2), the phrase 'carried on business' has no special legal meaning; although it must encompass[20] in general terms any trade, profession or other commercial or business enterprise. The carrying on of business is akin to the concept of 'ordinarily resident', in that the court will primarily be guided by the words of the statute itself, giving those words their ordinary and natural meaning. Whether a debtor has carried on business in England is to be determined as a matter of fact and degree.

It is plain that carrying on business has a broad meaning. The Insolvency Act does not in this context require any place, or established place, of business.[1] As a Scottish judge once commented:[2]

> 'The expression "carrying on business" is so wide that it would really touch all persons having business in the [jurisdiction] . . . '

The business must be carried on 'in' England not merely 'with' England.[3] Hence, if a foreign debtor were simply to order goods from an English manufacturer, there would be no evidence that the debtor had carried on business in England. Similarly, an Italian hotel proprietor would not be within section 265(1)(c)(ii) merely because a travel agent in England had received requests for bookings and transmitted them to Italy for confirmation.[4] Yet, it is important to stress that if a debtor has carried on business in England it is quite irrelevant that the chief place of business is elsewhere. Indeed, in some cases involving cross-border insolvency there is the likelihood that most of the debtor's activities will have been conducted abroad and the factual connection to England is somewhat marginal.[5]

As the carrying on of business is essentially a matter of fact, cases will arise wherein judicial opinions differ. In one case before the High Court of Australia[6] a tour company, registered in Victoria, operated bus tours that at times passed through Western Australia. Whilst the bus tours were passing through Western Australia debts were incurred for food, accommodation and camping facilities. Barwick CJ felt that such facts afforded no ground for concluding that the tour company had carried on business in Western Australia.[7] However, the majority held that there was evidence to support the finding in the lower courts that the company was carrying on business in Western Australia.[8] For a decision going the other way, reference may be made to another Commonwealth authority. In *Re R. S. Robinson & Sons Ltd.*[9] a company incorporated in Manitoba had on odd occasions purchased furs in Ontario, when the company's representatives happened to be in Ontario. The furs so purchased were exported under a non-resident

---

[20] See the Insolvency Act 1986, s. 436.
[1] Cf. the requirement of an established place of business for an oversea company under the Companies Act 1985, s. 744.
[2] *Lord Advocate* v. *Huron and Erie Loan and Savings Co.* 1911 S.C. 612 at 616 *per* the Lord President.
[3] For the situation where the debtor has an agent in England see p. 55, *post*.
[4] See *Luckins* v. *Highway Motel (Carnarvon) Pty. Ltd.* (1975) 133 C.L.R. 164 at 178–179.
[5] In such circumstances the English court's discretion to stay its proceedings in favour of a foreign forum comes very much into play: see chapter 3.
[6] *Luckins* v. *Highway Motel (Carnarvon) Pty. Ltd.* (1975) 133 C.L.R. 164.
[7] *Ibid.*, at 169.
[8] As the carrying on of business is essentially a question of fact, an appeal court will always be reluctant to interfere with the conclusions of a lower court.
[9] [1923] 1 D.L.R. 691. The Bankruptcy Act 1919 applied to incorporated companies.

licence. The Ontario court concluded that for the purposes of the Bankruptcy Act 1919 of Canada the company did not carry on business in Ontario. The reasoning of the court is, however, a little questionable, for reliance is placed upon the strength of the company's connection to Manitoba and the company's exclusive residence in that Province.[10] It should be noted that for the purposes of the Insolvency Act 1986 comparing the debtor's business activities in England to those in the debtor's home country is unlikely to advance the relevant inquiry under section 265(1)(c)(ii).[11]

A. Nature of the Business

(i) *Buying and Selling*

Trading in goods in the form of buying and selling is perhaps the most obvious example of carrying on business. Yet business may be carried on prior to the commencement of, or in the complete absence of, actual trading. In *Re Oriel Ltd.*[12] a foreign company owned various business premises but at the time in question was not trading therefrom. It was submitted that, absent evidence of trading activities, the company could not be carrying on business (or have an established place of business) in England. Such a contention was rejected, Oliver LJ commenting:[13]

> '[The company] did undoubtedly . . . acquire and hold properties, enter into an agreement which would render the equity in such properties more valuable as the loans were written off . . . and mortgage the properties to secure moneys lent. It was therefore engaged in carrying out objects for which it was incorporated in a way which, if persisted in, would produce a substantial profit. For the reasons given by the judge, I am for my part satisfied that he was right to conclude that the company was "carrying on business".'

Whilst *Re Oriel Ltd.* concerned provisions under the Companies Act 1948,[14] the decision supports the proposition that for the purposes of bankruptcy jurisdiction acts preliminary to trading may amount to evidence of carrying on business.

However, section 265(1)(c)(ii) of the Insolvency Act 1986 may be satisfied even where no trading (present or future) by the debtor is contemplated. Activities as diverse as speculating in land, promoting companies,[15] raising loan capital[16] and liaising with financial institutions[17] have been considered as carrying on business. Importantly, it has been held that merely because a person's main business is abroad, and those acts which have been done in England are incidental to such business, it does not follow that business is not carried on in England. In *South India*

---

[10] *Ibid.*, at 692–693.

[11] To say that a debtor does not carry on business in England because the debtor's business headquarters is abroad cannot be correct.

[12] [1986] 1 W.L.R. 180, a decision on company charges under what were then ss. 95 and 106 of the Companies Act 1948.

[13] [1986] 1 W.L.R. 180 at 187.

[14] N. 12, *ante.*

[15] *Re Brauch* [1978] Ch. 316.

[16] *Lord Advocate* v. *Huron and Erie Loan and Savings Co.* 1911 S.C. 612.

[17] *South India Shipping Corpn Ltd.* v. *Export-Import Bank of Korea* [1985] 1 W.L.R. 585.

Shipping Corpn Ltd. v. *Export-Import Bank of Korea*[18] the respondent bank incorporated in Korea had an office in England. The issue was whether the respondent had established a 'place of business' in Great Britain under the Companies Act 1948. There was no doubt that the respondent had a 'place' within the jurisdiction, but the Court of Appeal gave consideration to the extent to which the respondent carried on business in the jurisdiction. The respondent did not conclude any banking transactions at its English office, nor did it have any dealings with the general public. The role of the local office was limited to certain preliminary work in relation to loan transactions, encouraging trade between Korea and the United Kingdom and consulting with other banks and financial institutions. Ackner LJ concluded that such activities whilst merely incidental to the respondent's main business abroad constituted the carrying on of business.[19] Similarly, section 265(1)(c)(ii) of the Insolvency Act 1986 is in no way restricted to trading activities in England and Wales, nor is it necessary to show that contracts were actually concluded within the jurisdiction.

(ii) *A Series of Transactions*

In *Luckins* v. *Highway Motel (Carnarvon) Pty. Ltd.*[20] Gibbs J stated:[1]

> 'The expression "carrying on business" may have different meanings in different contexts. It would usually connote, at least, the doing of a succession of acts designed to advance some enterprise . . . pursued with a view to pecuniary gain.'

As his Honour noted, the carrying on of business will generally involve a series of acts or a number of transactions.[2] However, there is nothing in the words used in section 265 to suggest that one single transaction can never amount to carrying on business or, indeed, that a series of acts necessarily establishes the carrying on of business. Plainly, the matter is one of fact; and all that can be said is that the more business activities are conducted in England, the greater the evidence that the debtor has carried on business.

(iii) *The Individual's Business*

Under section 265(1)(c)(ii) it must be the debtor's business which has been carried on. Establishing that the debtor has carried on someone else's business is not enough.

Re Brauch[3] concerned a debtor, not domiciled in England, who was engaged in property speculation in England. The debtor divided his time

---

[18] [1985] 1 W.L.R. 585.
[19] *Ibid.*, at 591–592. In *Allinson* v. *Independent Press Cable Association of Australasia Ltd.* (1911) 28 T.L.R. 128 the Court of Appeal held that 'merely doing work ancillary to the business' of a foreign corporation did not give the English court jurisdiction over a foreign corporation. However, that decision concerned service under the old Rules of the Supreme Court with reference to the carrying on of business by an agent.
[20] (1975) 133 C.L.R. 164, *ante.*
[1] *Ibid.*, at 179.
[2] Note *Re Clark* [1914] 3 K.B. 1095 decided under s. 12 of the Bankruptcy and Deeds of Arrangement Act 1913.
[3] [1978] Ch. 316, *ante.*

between England and the Channel Islands, having an office in each. In essence, when the debtor found a suitable property in England he incorporated a company to acquire and develop the site. Each company was incorporated in Guernsey and, whilst the debtor was not always a director, each company was effectively under his control. In the Court of Appeal Goff LJ rejected the contention that 'carrying on business' included clerks, servants or others employed in a business, even where in complete control.[4] The business had to be the debtor's business. After referring to the doctrine of separate corporate personality as laid down in *Salomon* v. *A. Salomon and Co. Ltd.*,[5] his Lordship said:[6]

> 'in my judgment, it would be wrong to hold that section 4(1)(d) applies to a man who is running his company's business even though he be the sole beneficial shareholder and in complete control'.

Nevertheless, on the facts, it was held that the debtor did carry on business. For the debtor himself was finding suitable properties, obtaining valuations and negotiating the price, then promoting a company and causing the property to be vested in that company. Whilst the contractual liabilities incurred in respect of the development of a site were liabilities of the particular company concerned (and not liabilities of the debtor), those parts of the entire operation (namely, the preliminary stages) which were personally undertaken by the debtor constituted a business carried on by him and on his own behalf. The companies were 'part of the machinery by which the debtor implemented his business projects'.[7]

Whilst not doubting the decision in *Re Brauch* this author would suggest a bolder approach to the interpretation of section 265(1)(c)(ii). It is submitted that the principle in *Salomon* v. *A. Salomon and Co. Ltd.* has no relevance in the context of bankruptcy jurisdiction. The relevant inquiry is simply whether the debtor has carried on business. The question is not whether the business is the business of the company or the business of the debtor. For there is no inherent reason why one series of acts cannot be both the business of a company and of the debtor. *Salomon* v. *A. Salomon and Co. Ltd.* established that in English law a company has a separate legal personality from its corporators: the 'exceptions' to that doctrine involve the denial of such separate personality, or at least a temporary lifting of the corporate mask. The facts in *Re Brauch* did not require any denial of the companies' legal personalities, or any attempt to reveal the companies as mere shams – the relevant inquiry was whether, in the light of all the facts, the debtor in substance carried on business in England.[8]

Moreover, it is easily shown that the rule in *Salomon* v. *A. Salomon and Co. Ltd.* should have no relevance in the context of bankruptcy jurisdiction. For *Salomon* v. *A. Salomon and Co. Ltd.*, of course, embodies a rule of domestic English law, a rule applicable to companies incorporated under United Kingdom legislation. *Salomon* v. *A. Salomon and Co. Ltd.* does not of itself govern corporations brought into existence under German law, Turkish law or the law of the People's Republic of China. Such legal

---

[4] [1978] Ch. at 328.
[5] [1897] A.C. 22.
[6] [1978] Ch. 316 at 328. The relevant provision being then s. 4(1)(d) of the 1914 Act.
[7] *Ibid.*, at 336 *per* Buckley LJ.
[8] Accepting that the companies undoubtedly carried on business in England.

systems may well have very different rules as to whether a business carried on in the name of a corporation is to be regarded as the business of the corporators.[9]

It will also be noted that *Re Brauch* was decided upon a very narrow ground. The members of the Court of Appeal more than once observed that the basis of their decision was that the 'preliminary stages' of the overall property development schemes were the debtor's own separate business: the debtor had 'carried on a business which was distinct from the companies' activities, although associated with them'.[10] Accordingly, *Re Brauch* decided:

(i)   that a debtor will not be regarded as carrying on the business of a company merely because he is 'the sole beneficial shareholder and in complete control';[11] and

(ii) but that where the debtor has undertaken activities which, although associated with the companies' business, were carried out in his personal capacity, then the debtor may very well be carrying on his own business – even though it may be difficult precisely to define that business.[12]

There remains, however, the grey area that lies between these two propositions. What would have been the position if instead of acting personally the debtor in *Re Brauch* had incorporated a company in whose name all preliminary activities (finding properties, negotiating, arranging finance and so on) had been conducted?

In this author's view, the tentative approach adopted in *Re Brauch* is unsatisfactory. Fortunately, however, in a subsequent decision the Court of Appeal has tackled the issue in a far more robust manner. In *Ransome* v. *Chancery plc*[13] the debtor had left England in 1987 to live permanently in the Isle of Man. At that time the debtor acquired the entire share capital of an English company (in which he had previously held a minority interest) and those shares were then transferred to a Manx holding company in which the debtor held an 85% stake. Over the next few years a number of properties[14] in England were developed, either by the English company or by subsidiaries of the Manx company. The debtor entered into guarantees with Chancery plc in respect of the indebtedness of the various companies and, in due course, Chancery plc obtained judgment against the debtor and served a statutory demand followed by a bankruptcy petition. The debtor raised the question of jurisdiction, arguing that everything he had done in England was as a director of one or other of the companies involved.

---

[9]   'No doubt, for instance, a Jordanian company whose constitution provides for the personal liability of its general partners will, by its contracts in England, engage the liability of those persons if it chooses to trade here . . .' *per* Lord Oliver of Aylmerton in *Raynor (J.H.) (Mincing Lane) Ltd.* v. *Department of Trade and Industry* [1990] 2 A.C. at 509, citing *Johnson Matthey & Wallace Ltd.* v. *Alloush* (1984) 135 N.L.J. 1012.

[10] [1978] Ch. 316 at 336 *per* Buckley LJ.

[11] *Supra*, n. 6.

[12] In *Re Brauch* Goff LJ suggested (at 329) that the business could be described as promoting companies in land, or that of finding suitable sites for development, negotiating the price and financing the purchase.

[13] The case is only reported in *The Independent* 31 March 1994; the transcript from LEXIS is referred to hereafter.

[14] Some half a dozen or so.

The Court of Appeal upheld the determination of Chadwick J that the debtor was carrying on business in England. Dillon LJ (with whom Steyn and Peter Gibson LJJ concurred) referred to *Re Brauch* and concluded:[15]

'It seems to me that the present case is well within the approach in *Re Brauch* and the judge's conclusion was amply justified.'

This comment is more than a little enigmatic. For the 'approach' in *Re Brauch* was that the debtor had by his personal actions been conducting his own separate business, although closely associated with the business of the companies. In *Ransome* v. *Chancery plc* Dillon LJ did not attempt to identify any separate business of the debtor; rather his Lordship contented himself with the observation that:[16]

'The clear pattern that emerges is that Mr Ransome was the person who was organising the development of these properties and their acquisition for that purpose, whether they were offered to him or, as in some cases he found them himself or, in some cases, Mr Hart [a fellow director] raised the suggestion for him to consider, Mr Hart did not decide on whether a property should be acquired or not. It was Mr Ransome who did all that.'

The evidence relied upon by Dillon LJ – in addition to the fact that the debtor had entered into guarantees – seems to have involved little more than that the debtor himself and those with whom he dealt regarded the business as being carried on by the debtor personally.

In short, although the question must always remain one of fact, *Ransome* v. *Chancery plc* suggests that where a debtor is in control of a number of companies[17] then an appellate court will not likely interfere with the finding that the debtor has carried on business in England, even though the relevant business activities have been conducted in a perfectly genuine manner under a corporate umbrella.[18] Moreover, the cases suggest (although it would seem difficult to find any convincing logical justification) that the greater the number of companies involved and the more the debtor is potentially exposed to personal liability, the easier it will be satisfy section 265(1)(c)(ii).

B. The Time Element

The court has jurisdiction if the debtor has carried on business in England at any time in the period of three years ending on the day on which the petition is presented. Thus, if a petition is presented on 1 May 1998, it will be enough to show that the debtor had carried on business at any time since 1 May 1995.

It is important to note that a debtor does not cease to carry on business at the moment he, for instance, closes his shop door or otherwise stops

---

[15] See n. 13 *supra*.

[16] *Ibid.*

[17] Although everything that was done in *Ransome* v. *Chancery plc* could have been carried out by just a single company. For a decision the other way involving a single company, see *Turner* v. *Trevorrow* (1994) 126 A.L.R. 263 (Full Court).

[18] It will be necessary to establish that the debtor is beneficially interested in the companies, see *Turner* v. *Trevorrow*, *supra*, n. 18, rather than merely an employee.

trading. In *Theophile* v. *Solicitor-General*[19] the House of Lords held that, once a debtor has carried on business, such business does not cease until all debts arising out of the business have been discharged. *Theophile* was of course decided under the Bankruptcy Act 1914 and there was initially some doubt as to whether a different approach would be adopted under the new legislation: Hoffmann J has, however, ruled that the old authorities continue to apply.[20] Thus for the purposes of section 265(1)(c)(ii) the three-year period may be greatly extended. For, in effect, once having carried on business in England, a debtor will remain subject to the court's bankruptcy jurisdiction unless and until three years after the discharge of all trading debts and other liabilities arising out of that business.[1]

C. Section 265(2)

Section 265(2) provides that carrying on business includes:

'(a) the carrying on of business by a firm or partnership of which the individual is a member, and
(b) the carrying on of business by an agent or manager for the individual or for such firm or partnership.'

Hence, an individual, even if never personally in England, may be carrying on business by an agent or manager and accordingly fall within section 265(1)(c)(ii). So too all the partners in a foreign firm, or all the foreign members of an English partnership, will be within section 265(1)(c)(ii) where the firm has carried on business in England whether by resident partners or agents and managers.[2] Of course, the existence of an agency is a question of fact and may be established by way of an express or implied agreement.

(i) *Company as Agent*

As the Court of Appeal in *Re Brauch*[3] regarded the doctrine in *Salomon* v. *A. Salomon and Co. Ltd.*[4] as applicable to the carrying on of business in the context of bankruptcy jurisdiction, it is worthy of note that a company may indeed be the agent of an individual. If a company is shown to be the agent of the debtor and, as such, carrying on the debtor's business in England, jurisdiction under section 265(1)(c)(ii) will have been made out. However, an agency relationship cannot be implied simply because a debtor holds a 99% or even 100% beneficial interest in the company's shares[5] nor simply because the debtor is in effectual control.[6]

---

[19] [1950] A.C. 186, applied in *Re Bird* [1962] 1 W.L.R. 686 and *Re a Debtor (No. 784 of 1991)* [1992] Ch. 554.
[20] *Re a Debtor (No. 784 of 1991)* [1992] Ch. 554.
[1] This somewhat strained interpretation of carrying on business cannot be universally applied: see the discussion in respect of ss. 221 and 225 of the Insolvency Act 1986, p. 113, *post*.
[2] In relation to partnerships see the Insolvent Partnerships Order 1994 and *Re Vanilla Accumulation Ltd.*, (1998) Times, 24 February.
[3] [1978] Ch. 316.
[4] [1897] A.C. 22.
[5] *Woolfson* v. *Strathclyde Regional Council* (1978) 38 P. & C.R. 521.
[6] *Re Brauch* [1978] Ch. 316. See also *Adams* v. *Cape Industries plc* [1990] Ch. 433.

(ii) *The Carrying on of Business by an Agent*

Whether an agent is carrying on business for a debtor is a question of fact. Nevertheless, there is a certain body of authority which unless properly explained might seem to require a restrictive application of section 265(2). For a number of cases appear, at first blush, to lay down that a principal's business is carried on in England by an agent only if the agent is given authority to enter into contracts on the principal's behalf.

Okura & Co. Ltd. v. *Forsbacka Jernverks Aktiebolag*[7] concerned service of process on the defendant, a foreign corporation. The defendant had engaged an agent in England but the agent did not have general authority to enter into contracts for the defendant. Instead the agent's role was restricted to obtaining orders and submitting them for approval by the defendant abroad. The issue in the Court of Appeal was whether it had been established that the defendant was present or resident in England for the purposes of service which, as Phillimore LJ put it, 'in the case of a trading corporation residence means the carrying on of its business'.[8] It was held that absent evidence of the agent's contractual authority the foreign corporation was not carrying on its business in England.[9] Yet there are two reasons why *Okura & Co. Ltd.* v. *Forsbacka Jernverks Aktiebolag* is misleading in the particular context of bankruptcy jurisdiction.

Firstly, the question at issue in *Okura & Co. Ltd.* v. *Forsbacka Jernverks Aktiebolag* went beyond simply 'carrying on business'. Buckley LJ propounded a three-part formulation:[10]

> 'First, the acts relied on as showing that the corporation is carrying on business in this country must have continued for a sufficiently substantial period of time . . . Next, it is essential that these acts should have been done at some fixed place of business . . . The third essential, and one which it is always more difficult to satisfy, is that the corporation must be "here" by a person who carries on business for the corporation in this country.'

Indeed, in *Allinson* v. *Independent Press Cable Association of Australasia Ltd.*[11] the relevant approach to presence of a foreign corporation was succinctly stated by Buckley LJ in the following terms:[12]

> 'the test was whether the foreign corporation itself carried on its business at a fixed place within the jurisdiction, not whether its business was carried on at such a place'.

Thus in *Okura & Co. Ltd.* v. *Forsbacka Jernverks Aktiebolag* and in *Allinson* v. *Independent Press Cable Association of Australia Ltd.* it was not enough that the business of the corporation was carried on by someone (e.g. an agent) in England, it had additionally to be shown that the facts revealed that the corporation itself so carried on its business. The quite different requirement under section 265(2) of the Insolvency Act is simply that business is carried on by an agent for the debtor.

---

[7] [1914] 1 K.B 715.
[8] *Ibid.*, at 722.
[9] A like decision was reached in *Grant* v. *Anderson* [1892] 1 Q.B. 108 concerning a foreign partnership.
[10] [1914] 1 K.B. 715 at 718.
[11] (1911) 28 T.L.R. 128.
[12] *Ibid.*, at 129.

Moreover, recent English authority has revealed that even when dealing with a foreign corporation, it is not necessary as a rule of law that contracts be entered into in England. In *South India Shipping Corpn Ltd.* v. *Export-Import Bank of Korea*,[13] it will be recalled, the Court of Appeal held that the respondent bank had an established place of business in the United Kingdom (and hence carried on business) even though no banking trans-actions had been concluded in the United Kingdom. That pre-contractual negotiations may constitute carrying on business appears from the follow-ing passage in the judgment of Oliver LJ in *Re Oriel Ltd.*:[14]

> 'If, for instance, agents of an overseas company conduct business from time to time by meeting clients or potential customers in the public rooms of an hotel in London, they have, no doubt, "carried on business" in England, but I would for my part find it very difficult to persuade myself that the hotel lounge was "an established place of business".'

Moreover, reference to Scottish authority also supports the proposition that an agent's lack of contractual authority is not decisive. In *Lord Advocate* v. *Huron and Erie Loan and Savings Co.*[15] an Ontario corporation engaged agents in Scotland to tout for loans. The agents only forwarded applications to Ontario where debentures were in fact executed. The Lord President had no doubt that the corporation carried on business in the jurisdiction, even though 'everything in the way of making the contract itself by issuing the debenture, inscribing the debenture in the proper register, and so on is all done by the foreign company at its own domicile in Canada.'[16]

In summary, recent jurisprudence makes it quite plain that a foreign corporation may carry on business (and have an established place of business[17]) in England irrespective of an agent's contractual authority. The position can be no different for an individual debtor. More importantly, the words employed in section 265(2) contain no suggestion that an agent is required to have contractual authority before it can be said that the agent has carried on business in England for the debtor. There is accordingly no justification for a restrictive interpretation of section 265(2).

(iii) *By or Through an Agent*

Section 265(2) of the Insolvency Act 1986 uses a different wording from that found under the Bankruptcy Act 1914. The old provision made reference to carrying on business 'by means of' an agent;[18] whereas section 265(2) includes the carrying on of business 'by' an agent. It might, perhaps, be suggested that the current expression 'by' is narrower than the former 'by means of'.

---

[13] [1985] 1 W.L.R. 585, p. 51, *ante.* See also *Cleveland Museum of Art* v. *Capricorn Art International S.A.* [1990] 2 Lloyd's Rep. 166.
[14] [1986] 1 W.L.R. 180 at 184, *ante* p. 50.
[15] 1911 S.C. 612.
[16] *Ibid.,* at 616.
[17] See also the Companies Act 1985, s. 690.
[18] Bankruptcy Act 1914, s. 1(2).

In *Okura & Co. Ltd.* v. *Forsbacka Jernverks Aktiebolag* it was stated:[19]

> 'In my opinion the defendants are not "here" by an *alter ego* who does business for them here, or who is competent to bind them in any way. They are not doing business here *by a person but through a person*.'

It may also be noted that R.S.C. Order 11, rule 1(1)(d)(ii), refers to a contract made 'by or through' an agent trading in the jurisdiction;[20] and in *National Mortgage and Agency Co. of New Zealand Ltd.* v. *Gosselin*[1] it was held that where the English agent of a foreign firm forwarded orders to the foreign firm for acceptance abroad, the contracts were not made 'by' but rather 'through' the agent. In like circumstances it might be argued, in the context of section 265(2) of the Insolvency Act, that business is carried on in England not 'by' but merely 'through' an agent.

Of course, under the provisions of the Bankruptcy Act 1914 no such argument could succeed, for 'by means of' must include both 'by' and 'through'. It is difficult to accept an argument which contemplates that Parliament intended by the Insolvency Act to restrict the jurisdiction that the English court formerly exercised. Indeed, section 265 as a whole is far broader than its equivalent under the old legislation. Moreover, *dicta* from the old cases on the presence of a foreign corporation cannot (as has been shown) be taken as reliable guides to the interpretation of 'carrying on business' under section 265. So too, whilst not doubting the decision in *National Mortgage and Agency Co. of New Zealand Ltd.* v. *Gosselin*, section 265(2) unlike Order 11, rule 1(1)(d)(ii) draws no express distinction between 'by' and 'through'. In short, the word 'by' in section 265(2) should be taken as a shorthand form of 'by means of'. Accordingly, there is no substance in suggesting that if an agent lacks contractual authority then the debtor's business is not carried on by (but only through) that agent. It cannot be maintained that Parliament (other than by express words) would have intended a debtor to avoid the court's bankruptcy jurisdiction by such a device. Whether business has been carried on by an agent for a debtor is, quite simply, a matter of fact and degree. That an agent does not have contractual authority is a relevant matter but by no means decisive.

7. EUROPEAN CONVENTION ON INSOLVENCY PROCEEDINGS

The Convention, unlike English law, does not draw a distinction between jurisdiction over individual and corporate debtors. Article 3 envisages that the primary or 'main' insolvency proceeding should be opened in the Contracting State in which the centre of a debtor's main interests is located.[2] Additional insolvency proceedings (territorial in scope) may only be commenced in another Contracting State if the debtor has an establishment there. Thus Article 3(1) and (2) provides:

---

[19] [1914] 1 K.B. 715 at 721 *per* Buckley LJ (emphasis added).
[20] See, generally, *Dicey and Morris*, p. 329.
[1] (1922) 38 T.L.R. 832.
[2] See also p. 11, *supra*.

1. The courts of the Contracting State of the territory in which the centre of a debtor's main interests is situated shall have jurisdiction to open insolvency proceedings. In the case of a company or legal person, the place of the registered office shall be presumed to be the centre of its main interests in the absence of proof to the contrary.

2. Where the centre of a debtor's main interests is situated within the territory of a Contracting State, the courts of another Contracting State shall have jurisdiction to open insolvency proceedings against that debtor only if he possesses an establishment within the territory of that other Contracting State. The effects of those proceedings shall be restricted to the assets of the debtor situated in the territory of the latter Contracting State.

Article 3 would clearly require drastic amendment to the operation of section 265 of the Insolvency Act 1986.[3]

It will be noted, however, that the Convention only seeks to apply where the centre of a debtor's main interests does indeed lie in a Contracting State. If that centre is in fact in New York or Moscow then the Convention is not applicable; and this is the case even though the debtor's presence in let us say Germany is far more extensive than in England. On the other hand, if, for example, the centre of the debtor's main interests is in France, then bankruptcy proceedings could only be commenced under the Insolvency Act 1986 if there was an establishment in England; and such proceedings would be limited to assets in England.[4] An establishment is described in the Convention as 'any place of operations where the debtor carries out a non-transitory economic activity with human means and goods'.[5] The Convention also places restrictions upon when (and by whom) a petition relating to an establishment may be presented, if it is sought to do so prior to the opening of main insolvency proceedings.[6]

8. ILLUSTRATIONS

(1) Y was born in England with an English domicile of origin. After completing his education in England, Y went in 1970 to New York where he worked for several financial institutions. Having established a reputation as an astute financial adviser, in 1984 Y set up his own investment consultancy with offices in New York, California and Bermuda. Y was badly affected by the 1987 worldwide stockmarket crash and, in 1989, was forced to close down his business. In 1989 Y took up employment in Tokyo with a major Japanese bank. Y is domiciled in England.[7]

---

[3] But only in cases where the centre of the debtor's main interests is in another Contracting State.
[4] See Art. 3(2), set out above.
[5] This is by no means the sort of definition of a term one would expect to find in English legislation.
[6] See Art. 3(4).
[7] For as there is no evidence of the relevant intention, no domicile of choice has been acquired to replace the English domicile of origin.

(2) Born in 1956 with an English domicile of origin, A married a French-man in 1983 and went to live in France. Over the next 10 years A made France her home, intending to stay there indefinitely. In 1993, however, A's marriage broke up. Subsequently, A decided to make a new life for herself in Quebec. But A was unable to find suitable employment in Quebec and, after visiting Quebec one winter, A feels the climate in Quebec is a little too severe. A has been living since 1995 in British Columbia. A is domiciled in England.[8]

(3) P is a German businessman. Whilst P was on holiday in the Lake District a bankruptcy petition was presented by P's creditors. The English court has jurisdiction based on P's personal presence.[9]

(4) C was born in England but lived for many years in Spain. In 1996 C's father died in England. As a result, from August 1996 to October 1997, C spent a total of 9 months in England, dealing with his deceased father's estate and visiting relatives in England. During that period C made a number of trips back to Spain. In October 1997 C was ordinarily resident in England.[10]

(5) Z is a Parisian art dealer. In 1995 Z made three trips to England to attend various auctions in London. Z spent a total of 8 weeks in England. In 1996 Z was in England for some 15 weeks, over a period of several months, in connection with the art business. In 1995 Z was not ordinarily resident in England. However in 1996 Z was ordinarily resident.[11]

(6) R is an English physicist who after 10 years as an academic at the University of Oxford took up a more lucrative position in the United States. Although moving to America in 1994, R kept up his house in Oxford and has returned there for periods of leave in most, but not all, years. R has a place of residence in England.

(7) E is a Saudi businessman with a passion for horse racing. Every year E visits England for a week at the time of the Ascot races. E always stays in a suite of rooms at the same London hotel. E does not have a place of residence in England.[12]

(8) X is the proprietor of a New York fashion house. Each year X makes a number of visits to England to attend London fashion shows, negotiate with European suppliers of fashion wear and, in general, keep up the international reputation of X's New York fashion house. X carries on business in England.[13]

(9) S is a partner in a firm of estate agents based in Hong Kong. The firm has recently acquired representative offices in London, Vancouver and

---

[8] The domicile of origin has revived.
[9] *Re Thulin* [1995] 1 W.L.R. 165, *supra*.
[10] Cf. *Re Bright* (1903) 19 T.L.R. 203 and (1901) 18 T.L.R. 37.
[11] See *I.R.C.* v. *Lysaght* [1928] A.C. 234 and *Kinloch* v. *I.R.C.* (1929) 14 T.C. 736, *passim*.
[12] *Re Mitchell* (1884) 13 Q.B.D. 418 at 423 *per* Cotton LJ.
[13] See *South India Shipping Corpn Ltd.* v. *Export-Import Bank of Korea* [1985] 1 W.L.R. 585 and *Re Oriel Ltd.* [1986] 1 W.L.R. 180 at 184 *per* Oliver LJ.

Brisbane. The London office is run by a manager. The manager's duties include looking for suitable properties in England, showing such properties to clients visiting England, as well as advising clients generally on the property market and financing the purchase of property in England. However, agreements for the purchase of properties are invariably concluded at the head office in Hong Kong. The English court has jurisdiction over S. For S is a member of a firm carrying on business in England by a manager.

(10) B left England in the late 1980s to live permanently in the Isle of Man. B has a controlling interest in four English companies and one Manx company. Over the past few years several properties in England have been developed by one or other of the companies. Although all transactions relating to the properties have been entered into by the companies rather than B personally, B has made all relevant decisions. B (*semble*) carries on business in England.[14]

---

[14] The facts are based on *Ransome* v. *Chancery plc*, *supra* p. 53 except that there is here no mention of whether B has entered into any guarantees.

Chapter 3

The Exercise of Bankruptcy Jurisdiction: *Forum non Conveniens*

1. OUTLINE

Having regard to the breadth of the jurisdiction of the English court under section 265 of the Insolvency Act 1986,[1] it is hardly surprising to learn that such jurisdiction is not bound to be exercised automatically. Reference to the terms of the Insolvency Act itself, as well as the cases decided under the former Bankruptcy Acts,[2] reveals the matter as one of discretion. Section 266(3) of the Insolvency Act states:[3]

> 'The court has a general power, if it appears appropriate to do so on the grounds that there has been a contravention of the rules *or for any other reason*, to dismiss a bankruptcy petition or to stay proceedings on such a petition; and, where it stays proceedings on a bankruptcy petition, it may do so on such terms and conditions as it thinks fit.'

That the English court has a discretion to stay its own proceedings cannot be denied. Nevertheless, uncertainty prevails if one seeks to ascertain the precise principles upon which such discretion may be exercised when bankruptcy proceedings are under way not only in England but also in another country.[4]

The difficulties associated with concurrent bankruptcies in two or more jurisdictions may be briefly discussed. The extra cost of conducting an insolvency in more than one jurisdiction is an obvious disadvantage to the general body of creditors, for the fund ultimately available for distribution is likely to be diminished, to the particular prejudice of the unsecured creditors. Moreover, a conflict of jurisdiction between an English and a foreign court inevitably tends towards uncertainty and confusion which, it has often been said, should as far as possible be avoided in commercial matters.[5] Two competing courts may arrive at different conclusions,

---

[1] Chapter 2, *ante.*

[2] *Re Robinson* (1883) 22 Ch. D. 816 and *Re Behrends* (1865) 12 L.T. 149, *post.*

[3] Emphasis added. Note also s. 12 of the Bankruptcy Act 1914.

[4] Dicey and Morris, *The Conflicts of Laws* (12th ed., 1993) pp. 1159–1162.

[5] Two sets of proceedings may result in the 'creation of opposite and inconsistent systems' involving 'gross and palpable injustice' *per* Lord Meadowbank in *Stein's Case* (1813) 1 Rose 462 at 480–481. The *Cork Report* (*Insolvency Law and Practice: Report of the Review Committee*, 1982, Cmnd. 8558) paras. 1902–1906 draws attention to the dangers of 'conflict and confusion in cases of concurrent jurisdiction'. The general issue of costs has been highlighted by *Mirror Group Newspapers plc* v. *Maxwell* [1998] B.C.C. 324.

embarrassing both debtor and creditors alike.[6] Thus, in one example, a Canadian court held that certain creditors were entitled to a preference under the terms of a local enactment, and subsequently such preference was ordered to be given up by a court in Scotland.[7]

Despite the quite unsatisfactory consequences that may flow from having bankruptcy proceedings on foot both in England and abroad, the authorities decided under the Bankruptcy Acts 1861 to 1914 showed considerable reluctance on the part of the English court to stay its own proceedings. There are but few reported instances of a stay being granted, the last such case being decided over a century ago.[8] However, the exercise of discretion in questions of jurisdiction in English private international law has been affected by radical change. For the House of Lords in *Spiliada Maritime Corpn.* v. *Cansulex Ltd.*[9] has accepted a general doctrine of *forum non conveniens*, or the appropriate forum. As an essential starting point the English court will consider whether:[10]

'there is some other available forum, having competent jurisdiction, which is the appropriate forum for the trial of the action, i.e. in which the case may be tried more suitably for the interests of all the parties and the ends of justice'.

The general approach in *Spiliada* is of course taken directly from Scottish jurisprudence. Hence it is particularly important to have regard to the way prior foreign insolvency proceedings have been dealt with in Scottish bankruptcy law.

At one time it was held in Scotland[11] that the existence of a prior foreign bankruptcy (conducted in the country where the debtor was domiciled or carried on business[12]) rendered the Scottish court not merely *forum non conveniens* but rather *forum non competens*. A Scottish court could do nothing that purported to interfere with a process of universal distribution on foot abroad. However, the House of Lords (in a Scottish appeal) has observed that the matter should be one of 'judicial discretion' (an approach also favoured in more modern times by the Scottish Law Commission).[13] It is, in this author's view, difficult to think of any sound reason in principle why if English law has adopted the Scottish principles of *forum conveniens* in relation to civil litigation generally, English law should not also give due weight to the Scottish jurisprudence when it comes to the application of *forum non conveniens* to bankruptcy proceedings in particular. Moreover, since the first edition of this work was published, the English court has

---

[6] In *Re Baldwin* (1884) 77 L.T. Jo. 81, for instance, an English trustee was in contempt for failing to obey an order of the bankruptcy court in England, even though it was quite inconsistent with an order made by the Court of Session in Scotland.

[7] *Re Crawford and Co.* (1818) Nfld. LR 100 and *Bennet (Trustee for Crawford and Co.'s Creditors)* v. *Johnson* (1819) 2 Bell's Com. 686n.

[8] *Re Robinson* (1883) 22 Ch. D. 816, see [1989] J.B.L. 126 (Smart).

[9] [1987] A.C. 460: note also *De Dampierre* v. *De Dampierre* [1988] A.C. 92.

[10] *Per* Lord Kinnear in *Sim* v. *Robinow* (1892) 19 R. 665 at 668, applied by Lord Goff of Chieveley in *Spiliada Maritime Corpn.* v. *Cansulex Ltd.* [1987] A.C. 460 at 474.

[11] See *Stein's Case* (1813) 1 Rose 462, as well as *Goetze* v. *Aders* (1874) 2 R. 150.

[12] For, under Scots law, the carrying on of business establishes a so-called trading domicile, as in *Stein's Case, supra*; note also *Obers* v. *Paton's Trustee* (1897) 24 R. 719.

[13] See *Phosphate Sewage Co.* v. *Molleson* (1876) 1 App. Cas. 780 at 787; and note *Gibson* v. *Munro* (1894) 21 R. 840 at 847 and *Hutcheson & Co.'s Administrator* v. *Taylor's Executrix* 1931 S.C. 484 at 494. See also *Report on Bankruptcy and Related Aspects of Insolvency and Liquidation* (1982, Scottish Law Commission No. 68) pp. 100–101.

accepted (seemingly without controversy) that it may in the exercise of its discretion decline to wind up a foreign company, where a liquidation is underway in the clearly more appropriate foreign forum.[14] Also Lord Hoffmann, speaking in an extra-judicial capacity, has stated that:[15]

> 'As a general principle, the existence of insolvency proceedings in another country . . . has never precluded an English court from making a bankruptcy or winding up order if that appeared to be in the interests of English creditors . . . The making of an order is a matter of discretion and a judge will refuse if he thinks that the interests of creditors are adequately protected in the foreign proceedings.'

Sir Peter Millett has expressed similar views:[16]

> '. . . the existence of foreign insolvency proceedings does not bar the commencement of English insolvency proceedings, although their existence is a factor to be considered in deciding whether to make a winding up order in this country. The English court will renounce jurisdiction if it considers that the interests of justice and convenience require the liquidation to be conducted solely abroad.'

Although the doctrine of the appropriate forum has yet to be properly tested in a modern English bankruptcy case,[17] if it can be clearly shown that foreign insolvency proceedings are clearly more appropriate 'in the interests of all the parties and the ends of justice' a stay would surely be granted by the English court. The exercise of the discretion to stay an English bankruptcy must now be founded upon the appropriateness of the proceedings in the foreign court. But the existing bankruptcy authorities cannot simply be ignored. At the very least, the case law must be examined to reveal those factors which were in the past thought relevant to determine the exercise, by the English court, of the discretion to stay its own bankruptcy proceedings in favour of a foreign forum.

2. HISTORICAL INTRODUCTION: THE SCOTTISH INFLUENCE

In *Ex p Cridland*[18] the petitioner and another had been in partnership as merchants in England and Ireland. In January 1813 a separate commission of bankruptcy was issued in Ireland against the petitioner alone; shortly thereafter a joint commission (in respect of the partnership) issued in England. Lord Eldon LC treated the two sets of proceedings as raising 'a question certainly of great importance, and most distressing in every view of it'.[19] His Lordship considered that the English joint commission would not be superseded on account of the previous separate commission in Ireland. For a commission was the 'right of the subject' and the courts

---

[14] *Re Wallace Smith & Co. Ltd.* [1992] B.C.L.C. 970, discussed below.
[15] 'Cross-Border Insolvency' *The 1996 Lord Denning Lecture*, unpublished, 18 April 1996, p. 21.
[16] 'Cross-Border Insolvency: The Judicial Approach' (1997) 6 I.I.R. 99 at 103. For the use of *forum conveniens* in international insolvencies, see also *Re Olympia & York Developments Ltd.* (1996) 29 O.R. (3d) 626 at 633 *per* Blair J (set out at p. 331, *infra*).
[17] See the analysis of *Re Thulin* [1995] 1 W.L.R. 165, *infra*.
[18] (1814) 3 V. & B. 94.
[19] *Ibid.*, at 97.

in one country could not supervise a commission being conducted in another jurisdiction.[20] Similarly, in the year following the decision in *Ex p Cridland*, the Lord Chancellor refused to stay a prior English commission upon the mere ground of a subsequent sequestration in Scotland.[1]

However, there is nothing in *Re Cridland* to suggest that a stay of English proceedings would never be granted: too much reliance must not be placed on the Lord Chancellor's comment that a commission was the 'right of the subject'.[2] Upon the facts in *Re Cridland* the foreign proceedings were narrower than the English joint commission. To have stayed the English joint commission would have prejudiced the joint creditors, who obviously might have been unable to satisfy their joint claims in a separate commission in Ireland. Moreover, the Lord Chancellor approved the decision of the Court of Session in *Royal Bank of Scotland* v. *Cuthbert (Stein's Case)*.[3] *Stein's Case* involved a partnership trading in Scotland and England, in respect of which a joint commission had issued in England. The Court of Session, on the basis that the firm had trading domiciles in both England and Scotland, considered the case governed by the maxim *mobilia sequuntur personam*:[4] the English proceedings had vested the firm's movable property in the English commissioners, with the consequence that creditors in Scotland could not attach that property nor could a later sequestration of the joint estate issue.[5] In *Ex p Cridland* it was accepted as probable that an English court would reach a like conclusion when dealing with a prior Scottish sequestration.[6] Accordingly, the Lord Chancellor plainly envisaged circumstances in which an English commission might not issue on account of prior foreign proceedings.

To a certain extent, however, the reasoning in *Stein's Case* does not involve the actual exercise of discretion, the judges in the Court of Session being of the opinion that, once the joint estate had been subject to proceedings in England, the Scottish court lacked the power to permit a local sequestration in respect of property already subject to a foreign insolvency.[7] Thus, in *Goetze* v. *Aders* the Scottish court refused to award a sequestration of the estate of a German firm, already declared bankrupt in Germany, 'on the sole ground that the foreign sequestration renders sequestration in this country incompetent'.[8] Likewise in *Bank of Scotland* v. *Youde*[9] Lord Guthrie refused to grant sequestration of the estate of the debtor on the ground that bankruptcy proceedings had been commenced

---

[20] *Ibid.*, at 101.
[1] *Re Cockayne* (1815) 2 Rose 233. The Privy Council has held that a separate adjudication in England would not prevent a joint adjudication in Hong Kong: *Lyall* v. *Jardine, Matheson & Co.* (1870) L.R. 3 P.C. 318.
[2] See n. 20, *supra*.
[3] (1813) 1 Rose 462. *Stein's Case* was also approved in two House of Lords cases, *Selkrig* v. *Davies* (1814) 2 Rose 291 and *Geddes* v. *Mowat* (1824) 1 Glynn & J. 414, both Scottish appeals.
[4] Discussed generally in chapter 5, *post*.
[5] Although a sequestration of the individual estates might have been permitted, *per* Lord Bannatyne (1813) 1 Rose 462 at 483.
[6] (1814) 3 V. & B. 94 at 100. In the English court the matter has, however, always been one of discretion.
[7] As Lord Robertson put it (1813) 1 Rose 462 at 479: '. . . the only rule or principle that we can apply to the subject, is the priority, in point of time, of issuing the sequestration or commission'.
[8] (1874) 2 R. 150 at 155.
[9] (1908) 15 S.L.T. 847.

(many years previously) in England; and, as a result, all the debtor's estate wherever situated was already subject to English bankruptcy law and that 'left no room' for a sequestration in Scotland.[10]

A similar approach seems to have been taken in two English cases which perhaps unfortunately have been largely ignored. In *Re Wilson and Armstrong*[11] four partners carried on business in England and Scotland (although there was some question as to whether there was one partnership or two). On 12 July 1875 the joint estate and the separate estate of each of the partners (except Armstrong) was sequestrated in Scotland and, on the same day, Wilson and Armstrong filed their own joint petition in England. However, the creditors came to no resolution under the English petition (and eventually those proceedings terminated). In August 1875 Armstrong's personal estate was sequestrated in Scotland and a trustee was appointed there. In February 1876 Armstrong's separate creditors in England passed a resolution to liquidate by arrangement and a trustee was appointed. However, in the Court of Bankruptcy in England the registrar refused to register the resolutions of Armstrong's separate creditors in England:[12] 'on the ground that all the joint and separate assets were vested in the Scotch trustee'. Armstrong's English creditors appealed but the registrar's refusal was affirmed, the court commenting that 'to register these resolutions would cause an unseemly conflict between the English and Scotch courts'.[13] In *Re Wilson and Armstrong* the Court of Bankruptcy did not refer to domicile of the bankrupt, nor to the maxim *mobilia sequuntur personam*. But the result of the decision is plain enough: the foreign proceedings, as a result of which the property had been vested in the foreign assignee, were a ground for refusing the intervention of the English court to the potential embarrassment of the Scottish proceedings.[14] Armstrong's creditors then pursued a further appeal, apparently accepting the reasoning in the Court of Bankruptcy, but raising a new ground. For it was argued that although the Scottish trustee was appointed in August 1875 (and Armstrong's estate would then normally have vested in the Scottish trustee), the English proceedings should be regarded as being first in time. In that, it was contended, the English doctrine of relation back should apply, with the effect that the English proceedings against Armstrong should be treated as having commenced on 12 July 1875 when Wilson and Armstrong presented their joint petition – i.e. a month before any trustee was appointed in Scotland. The Court of Appeal accepted that Armstrong's estate had vested in the Scottish trustee and dismissed the appeal, on the basis that on the facts the doctrine of relation back could not apply.[15] It is perhaps not putting it too highly to say that

---

[10]   *Ibid.*, at 848.

[11]   (1876) 60 L.T. Jo. 434; affd *sub nom. Ex p Fenning; Re Wilson and Armstrong* (1876) 3 Ch.D. 455.

[12]   *Ibid.*, at 435.

[13]   *Ibid.*

[14]   The tenor of the report suggests the issue was one of discretion, rather than the very existence of jurisdiction.

[15]   The English creditors were asserting that the presentation of the joint petition in July 1875 was an act of bankruptcy by Armstrong, however, more than six months had elapsed between that act and the date when the creditors passed a resolution to liquidate by arrangement (February 1876).

the reasoning of the Court of Bankruptcy had the tacit approval of the Court of Appeal.[16]

In *Re Hughes*[17] the bankrupt carried on business in England and Ireland. An adjudication was made first in Ireland and three days later a petition was presented in England, under which an adjudication was subsequently made. A dispute arose concerning title to property in England as between the English and Irish assignees but the English court declined to interfere, it being stated:[18]

'The only question is as to the assets. By law all the property of the bankrupt, wherever situate, passes to the court which first acquires title to it. I do not think I ought to interfere in the matter. So far as I can understand it, the money must be paid over to the assignee in Ireland; and if the party complaining have any objection to make, he must oppose the bankrupt in the Court of Bankruptcy there.'

Thus *Re Hughes* shows the effect which a foreign insolvency may have directly upon property in England and, thereby indirectly, also upon the powers of the English court.[19]

Hence there is a line of authority, including *Stein's Case, Goetze* v. *Aders, Re Wilson and Armstrong*, and *Re Hughes* in addition to *Ex p Cridland*, which indicates that a local court may restrict the scope of its own bankruptcy proceedings on account of the consequences flowing from a foreign insolvency.[20] *Stein's Case* and *Goetze* v. *Aders* suggest that, at least at the time those cases were decided, the Scottish court considered itself incompetent to act in such circumstances. More recent Scottish authority, however, views the matter as one of discretion.[1]

Before leaving the Scottish judgments and their apparent influence upon the English jurisprudence, an observation of Lord Dunedin in *Galbraith* v. *Grimshaw* (an English appeal before the House of Lords) should be noted:[2]

'Now so far as general principle is concerned it is quite consistent with the comity of nations that it should be a rule of international law that if the court finds that there is already pending a process of universal distribution of a bankrupt's effects it should not allow steps to be taken in its territory which would interfere with that process of universal distribution; and that I take to be the doctrine at the bottom of the cases of which *Goetze* v. *Aders* is only one example.'

His Lordship's comment is interesting not least because it was put forward as a 'general principle'. If foreign insolvency proceedings are already under way and constitute a process of universal distribution, then Lord Dunedin suggests that the English court should be wary in

---

[16] Counsel for the Scottish trustee was not called upon by their Lordships.

[17] (1858) 31 L.T.O.S. 207.

[18] *Ibid.* Cf. *Re Rogers* (1859) 33 L.T.O.S. 30.

[19] As to the vesting of property in a foreign assignee see p. 222, *post*.

[20] In the English cases the matter was one of discretion.

[1] In *Phosphate Sewage Co.* v. *Molleson* (1876) 1 App. Cas. 780 at 787 the House of Lords put the sisting of Scottish bankruptcy proceedings on the basis of 'judicial discretion'. This is also made clear in *Gibson* v. *Munro* (1894) 21 R. 840 at 847.

[2] [1910] A.C. 508 at 513. For a recent example of comments upon similar lines, see the observations of Hoffmann J in *Banque Indosuez S.A.* v. *Ferromet Resources Inc.* [1993] B.C.L.C. 112 at 117 where his Lordship spoke of the English court doing its 'utmost' to co-operate with foreign insolvency proceedings and to avoid interference with the orderly administration of assets abroad.

the exercise of its bankruptcy jurisdiction, as the court 'should not allow steps to be taken . . . which would interfere with that process of universal distribution'. In other words, it is submitted, the English court should be quite willing in principle to stay its own proceedings. Of course, *Galbraith* v. *Grimshaw* concerned on its facts an English attachment and not bankruptcy proceedings in England. Nevertheless, Lord Dunedin's views were expressed as a general principle. Further, the reference to *Goetze* v. *Aders* (a decision upon *forum competens* not attachment) shows beyond question that Lord Dunedin had in mind concurrent bankruptcy proceedings.

3. THE BANKRUPTCY (SCOTLAND) ACT 1985

Prior to 1985, legislation provided that the Scottish court might recall a sequestration where (i) the majority of creditors in number and value resided in England or Northern Ireland; and (ii) the location of the debtor's property and other circumstances indicated that the debtor's estate should be distributed under the bankruptcy or insolvency laws of England or Northern Ireland.[3] As the Scottish Law Commission in its *Report on Bankruptcy and Related Aspects of Insolvency and Liquidation* in 1982 noted, this specific statutory provision operated alongside the more general principle that the Scottish court would not interfere where it found a process of universal distribution already underway in a foreign court.[4] The Commission, anxious as far as practicable to avoid 'the risk of concurrent proceedings'[5] in Scotland and elsewhere, made the following proposals. First, that as soon as a debtor or creditor became aware that there were concurrent proceedings in Scotland or any other country, there arose an obligation to bring that fact to the attention of the court. Secondly, where proceedings for a sequestration or an 'analogous remedy' had been commenced anywhere in the United Kingdom or abroad, the Scottish court might stay or dismiss a petition for sequestration. Those recommendations were given effect in section 10 of the Bankruptcy (Scotland) Act 1985, which specifically defines an 'analogous remedy' as meaning not only a bankruptcy order or administration order under English law, or the equivalent in Northern Ireland, but also the equivalent of bankruptcy, administration[6] or sequestration in 'any other country'.[7] In addition, the power of the Court of Session to recall an award of sequestration was expanded. The court has a general power to recall but (without prejudice to that general power) it may do so if it is satisfied that:[8]

> 'a majority in value of the creditors reside in a country other than Scotland and that it is *more appropriate* for the debtor's estate to be administered in that other country'.

---

[3] Bankruptcy (Scotland) Act 1913, s. 43, re-enacting earlier provisions.
[4] Scottish Law Commission No. 68, at pp. 100–101.
[5] *Ibid.*, at p. 99.
[6] That is, an administration order made in relation to an individual pursuant to County Courts Act 1984, s.112.
[7] See s. 10(5) of the 1985 Act.
[8] Section 17 (1)(b) (emphasis added); see also s. 17(1)(c).

It is, of course, not suggested that the provisions of the Scottish legislation apply directly in England. The English court does, however, have under the Insolvency Act 1986 a discretion to stay its own proceedings; moreover, the complications and confusion which may result from two or more sets of insolvency proceedings are no less in England than in Scotland. It can also forcefully be argued that the economic and social conditions either side of the border would suggest that the judicial response to concurrent bankruptcy proceedings should be similar.

4. THE DISCRETION OF THE ENGLISH COURT

As the Court of Bankruptcy in England was a court of equity, bankruptcy jurisdiction was, it seems, never bound to be exercised.[9] Even the wording of section 8 of the 1869 Act (a debtor 'shall be adjudicated bankrupt') did not render an adjudication so clearly *ex debito justitiae* as to take away the court's discretion. As James LJ once put it:[10]

'notwithstanding those words the court retains its old jurisdiction to refuse to make a man bankrupt for an improper purpose, and to annul an adjudication when the justice and convenience of the case require it'.

An early instance and indeed a most relevant example of the court staying its own bankruptcy proceedings is *Re Behrends*,[11] wherein the Court of Bankruptcy highlighted the more appropriate nature of the foreign forum. The debtor had traded as a general merchant in Hamburg and had, *in absentia*, been declared bankrupt there. The vast majority of his creditors were in Hamburg, although the debtor was present in England and there existed a few English creditors. The Court of Bankruptcy rejected a submission that the debtor's petition amounted to a fraud; nevertheless the English proceedings were stayed:[12]

'This man was, however, made bankrupt in Hamburg before he petitioned this court, and it may well be said that the place where his books of account and property were left, where his trading was carried on and the greater part of his debts were contracted, and where he was first made bankrupt, is the proper place for him to make such a disclosure of his affairs as his creditors may require.'

After facing his creditors in Hamburg, 'when he has there disclosed his affairs, and his conduct has been adjudicated upon',[13] the debtor would be permitted to apply for an order of discharge in England if he so wished.

The reasoning in *Re Behrends*, and in particular the reference to the 'proper place' for proceedings to be conducted, has never been the subject of judicial comment. However, that the English court has a discretion is confirmed by the decision of the Court of Appeal in *Re Robinson*.[14] In May

---

[9] The English court never permitted the bankruptcy legislation to be put to any inequitable use: *Ex p Gibson* (1865) 34 L.J. Bk. 31.
[10] *Re McCulloch* (1880) 14 Ch. D. 716 at 723; see also *Re Thulin* [1995] 1 W.L.R. 165, *infra*.
[11] (1865) 12 L.T. 149.
[12] *Ibid.*, at 150.
[13] *Ibid.*
[14] (1883) 22 Ch. D. 816, discussed in *Re Thulin*, *infra*.

1880 the debtor went to live in Scotland and, in August 1881, a sequestration was there awarded. In 1882 an English judgment creditor, who had made no claim in the Scottish proceedings, sought an adjudication in England. The registrar made an adjudication but that order was reversed on appeal, Jessel MR observing:[15]

'About the jurisdiction to make an adjudication I have no doubt . . . Of course there must be some reason for exercising it, and the mere existence of a bankruptcy in Scotland or in Ireland would, *prima facie*, be a reason for not exercising it. Here the Scotch sequestration is not closed; and it does not appear that there are any subsequent debts, or any assets in England, and there is no reason for exercising the jurisdiction. An adjudication would be altogether a vain thing. It might embarrass the proceedings in Scotland, and could be of no use to anyone.'

Baggallay LJ added that in his view had there been any assets in England the court *prima facie* would have made an adjudication.[16] Thus even a century ago there existed a discretion to decline to make an adjudication (as in *Re Robinson*) or, an adjudication having been made, to stay proceedings at some later stage (as in *Re Behrends*).

It must be stressed that if a stay is obtained it can only be on the basis of the exercise of discretion. The party seeking the stay must establish that the proceedings in the foreign court are clearly more appropriate in the interests of all parties and the ends of justice. An application founded merely upon the fact that the foreign proceedings were first in time is bound to fail. In *Re Artola Hermanos*[17] a partnership, with its head office in Paris, had a branch in England. Of the five partners, two resided in France, two in England and one in Spain. In 1889 the firm was declared bankrupt in France and a syndic appointed. Within a month a petition was filed in England and an interim receiver appointed. The Court of Appeal refused an application by the syndic to stay the English proceedings. Lord Coleridge CJ, citing *Stein's Case*, thought (*obiter*) that there was only one basis upon which a stay might be available, namely where the foreign bankruptcy was being conducted in the forum of the domicile of the bankrupt:[18]

'I can find no substantial ground no legal ground for interfering in a way which . . . has never been done in this country. The only cases in which the courts intimate that they would do this, if necessary . . . are where there were two bankruptcies going on, and one of them was going on in the country of the domicile of the bankrupt.'

---

[15] (1883) 22 Ch. D. at 818. Note *Bank of Scotland* v. *Youde* (1908) 15 S.L.T. 847, p. 65, *supra*. In *Re McCulloch* (1880) 14 Ch. D. 716 the Court of Appeal did not stay English proceedings despite a prior Irish bankruptcy; however, it is most relevant to observe that James LJ said (at 723): 'It is possible that after this debtor has been adjudged a bankrupt . . . one of the two courts may come to the conclusion that it is better that the proceedings on one of the petitions should be stayed, and possibly that one of the adjudications should be annulled.'

[16] (1883) 22 Ch. D. 816 at 818–819.

[17] (1890) 24 Q.B.D. 640.

[18] *Ibid.*, at 644–645. Fry LJ expressed himself with somewhat more caution, see (1890) 24 Q.B.D. 640 at 648–649.

There being no evidence that the bankrupts were domiciled in France, no stay was granted.[19] The reliance upon the law of the domicile is perhaps understandable, for at that time there was still very considerable doubt as to whether the English court could recognise any foreign bankruptcy except by reference to the debtor's domicile.[20] It would be illogical to argue that the English court should defer to foreign proceedings, if those proceedings would not be recognised in England.

However, in the modern context *Re Artola Hermanos* can have no influence upon the actual exercise of discretion by the English court. For the Court of Appeal did not in any way consider whether the interests of the general body of creditors would be best served by staying the English proceedings. But this is no criticism of their Lordships, as the case was put by counsel for the syndic on the basis of principle alone. Namely, that where a bankruptcy had been commenced abroad, 'and by the law of that country all the property of the bankrupt, wherever situated, is subject to be administered in that bankruptcy',[1] the English court will decline jurisdiction. It is scarcely surprising that such a contention, advanced quite without reference to the justice and convenience of the case, was rejected.

Nevertheless, whilst not questioning the decision in *Re Artola Hermanos*, the reasoning of the Lord Chief Justice (which is plainly *obiter*) cannot be supported. His Lordship felt justified in acting upon *Stein's Case* and in particular the fiction that movables follow the person, thus giving the courts of the domicile an exclusive position. However, the basis of *Stein's Case*, as has been shown, was that the foreign insolvency rendered the Scottish court incompetent. *Stein's Case* itself, unlike *Re Robinson* or *Re Behrends*, was not a decision upon the actual exercise of discretion. More importantly, it is clear beyond question that the courts of the domicile hold no exclusive position: a foreign bankruptcy may be recognised in England by virtue of a debtor's trading activities or submission to the jurisdiction of the foreign court.[2] Simply because there is a foreign insolvency entitled to recognition in England does not mean that English proceedings must be stayed. Whether the foreign court's jurisdiction be founded upon domicile, submission or carrying on business, the relevant inquiry for the English court remains unaltered: has it been shown that the foreign proceedings are clearly more appropriate?

This author's view that the doctrine of *forum conveniens* should be applicable to bankruptcy proceedings (just as it has been applied recently to winding up proceedings[3]) might appear at first sight to be in conflict with the decision in *Re Thulin*.[4] The debtor, a Swedish national who resided

---

[19] The exclusive reliance of Lord Coleridge CJ upon domicile is somewhat dubious: neither in *Re Robinson* (1883) 22 Ch. D. 816 nor *Re Behrends* (1865) 12 L.T. 149 (or indeed *Re Wilson and Armstrong* (1876) 60 L.T. Jo. 434) is any reference made to domicile. So too, in *Re O'Reardon* (1873) 9 Ch. App. 74 Mellish LJ referred merely to 'the simple ground of convenience' (at 78). The domicile of the bankrupt is wholly rejected in *Stabb, Preston & Prowse (Assignees)* v. *Stabb, Preston, Prowse & Co. (Trustees)* (1821) Nfld. L.R. 298 although it seems to have been a factor (though not an exclusive factor) in *Re Borovsky and Weinbaum* [1902] 2 K.B. 312 at 313, *passim*.

[20] For analysis see pp. 143–146, *infra*.

[1] (1890) 24 Q.B.D. 640 at 641. See the comments of Lord Hoffmann, set out at p. 64, *supra*.

[2] See pp. 146–153, *infra*.

[3] See *Re Wallace Smith & Co. Ltd.* [1992] B.C.L.C. 970, discussed p. 128, *infra*.

[4] [1995] 1 W.L.R. 165, p. 39, *supra*. The approval of the doctrine recently by Lord Hoffmann and Sir Peter Millett, see p. 64, *supra*, should now also be taken into consideration.

in Belgium and had apparently applied for US citizenship, had in 1989 entered into a contract of loan with an English company. The contract was expressly governed by English law and subject to the non-exclusive jurisdiction of the English court. The debtor in 1991 defaulted on the loan and in July 1993 was served in England with a statutory demand, which was followed in due course by a bankruptcy petition. The debtor had come to England in July 1993 in order to try to prevent the sale of certain property, but had been arrested and charged with attempting to obtain property by deception. Although the debtor had been released on bail (and subsequently the charges had been dropped) he had been required to surrender his passport and was thus unable to leave the country when the petition was presented. A bankruptcy order was made in England even though the debtor had in 1991 already been made bankrupt in Sweden. The debtor sought to have the order discharged on the ground that he had no assets in England:[5]

> 'The simple submission on the debtor's behalf as to why the court should exercise its discretion to dismiss or stay the petition is that, as the debtor has no assets in England, the bankruptcy order would be a vain thing: it would achieve nothing except additional wasted costs.'

Jules Sher Q.C.[6] held that the burden of proving 'no assets here' fell on the debtor; and on the facts the debtor had 'not even begun to discharge this onus and this is fatal to his appeal'.[7] The deputy judge added that even if the debtor had established that there were no assets in England, he would not have discharged the order.[8]

The first point to note is that in *Re Thulin* it was not doubted that the court has a discretion to stay bankruptcy proceedings. Secondly, as far as the basis of the exercise of that discretion, an argument of *forum non conveniens* simply was not advanced by counsel. Indeed, it could not realistically have been argued that the English court was *forum non conveniens* since, as the court noted, 'no evidence is put in concerning the Swedish bankruptcy';[9] and there was accordingly no reason to assume that 'an adjudication here might embarrass the proceedings in Sweden'.[10] Thirdly, although the court decided on the facts not to stay the English proceedings, that determination was not influenced by 'judicial chauvinism'[11] or made in disregard of the prior Swedish proceedings:[12]

> 'Even assuming that there are no assets in England, the English bankruptcy may yield benefits by way of reaching assets in a foreign country through recognition of the English bankruptcy, and assistance of, the courts of that foreign country. Such assets may not be capable of being recovered by the Swedish trustee in bankruptcy in the same way, or at all.'

---

[5] *Ibid.*, at 169.
[6] Sitting as a deputy judge of the High Court.
[7] *Supra* n. 4 at 171.
[8] The deputy judge expressed the view that he would have let the petitioning creditor 'have its order for what it was worth' (*ibid.*).
[9] *Ibid.*, at 170. Useful evidence could have included the stage which the Swedish proceedings had reached, whether the Swedish trustee was satisfied that the debtor had fully revealed his assets worldwide, and whether the petitioning creditor could yet prove in the Swedish proceedings without any prejudice: see the comments of Lord Hoffmann, p. 64, *supra*.
[10] *Ibid.*
[11] To employ Lord Diplock's well-known words in *The Abidan Daver* [1984] A. C. 398 at 411.
[12] *Supra* n. 4 at 170.

It would thus appear that the deputy judge, who had described the debtor as 'a businessman in a large way of business with a finger in many pies in many countries',[13] had in mind the possibility that the English proceedings could be used to recover assets abroad which the Swedish trustee might not be able to reach. In short, there is nothing in *Re Thulin* that prevents the English court in a suitable case (and where proper evidence is presented) from declining jurisdiction in favour of a clearly more appropriate foreign forum.

That there are so few illustrations of the English court declining jurisdiction or staying its proceedings in favour of a foreign forum would in any event more than justify reference to authorities in other common law jurisdictions. But the judgment of the Chief Justice of Newfoundland in *Stabb, Preston and Prowse (Assignees)* v. *Stabb, Preston, Prowse & Co. (Trustees)* must be considered as it is, quite simply, the clearest application of the relevant principles in a situation of cross-border insolvency. A firm carried on business in England and in Newfoundland. In 1821 the Supreme Court of Newfoundland declared the firm insolvent, a joint commission having been issued in England a few months previously. An application was made to supersede the Newfoundland insolvency and order the Newfoundland trustees to hand over assets to the English assignees. Forbes CJ considered the relevance of the maxim *mobilia sequuntur personam*, as applied in several English cases,[14] stating:[15]

'I must confess that my industry has hitherto been as unsuccessful in endeavouring to find such a principle of universal law, as my understanding has been to be convinced by the arguments upon which it rests; the proviso with which it is qualified, *viz.*, that it is operative only so far as it may not militate against the particular laws of the country in which the property may be placed, appears to me to destroy the only value it can have as a principle of universal law.'

Rejecting the view that the prior English proceedings prevented a subsequent local insolvency, the Chief Justice turned to consider the expediency of the case:[16]

'Abstract rules of justice should be framed with reference to the rights of parties: where the disposition of property depends upon the mere volition of the owner, such as the disposition of an estate by will, the personal domicile of the owner may afford a fair rule as to the distribution of his estate; but where the rights of other parties, as creditors, are concerned, the interests of such parties should be first consulted. *This resolves the question before the court into what it really is — a question of mere expediency, as to the best mode of distributing an insolvent's estate, with reference to the rights of those who are entitled to it.*'

Forbes CJ held that 'the interests of the body of creditors' would be best served by referring all parties to the proceedings in England:[17]

'In this case, nothing has been done but collecting the estate; and as the insolvents are all in England, and their concerns interwoven with a great number

---

[13] *Ibid.*, at 168.
[14] *Solomons* v. *Ross* (1764) 1 Hy. Bl. 131n., *Jollett* v. *Deponthieu* (1769) 1 Hy. Bl. 131n., *Sill* v. *Worswick* (1791) 1 Hy. Bl. 665, *Phillips* v. *Hunter* (1795) 2 Hy. Bl. 402 and *Hunter* v. *Potts* (1791) 4 Term Rep 182.
[15] (1821) Nfld. 298 at 303. The case is here discussed quite fully on account of the difficulty which practitioners may well have in obtaining a copy of the Newfoundland reports.
[16] *Ibid.*, at 304 (emphasis added).
[17] *Ibid.*, at 305. For the rights of preferred creditors, see p. 84, *post*.

of collateral partnerships, all of which centre in England, it does appear to me that justice will be most effectually done by directing the proceeds which have been realized in Newfoundland to be transferred to the assignees under the English commission, upon security given to the court to pay, in the first place, all preferable claims for servants' wages and current supplies, and referring all other creditors to England.'

Hence the Newfoundland court, having stated that it would be guided by the justice and convenience of the case, acted accordingly, not merely staying its own proceedings but specifically ordering local assets to be given over to foreign assignees, who would thereby be in a position to administer the claims of the ordinary creditors in both England and Newfoundland.

The conclusion in *Stabb, Preston and Prowse (Assignees)* v. *Stabb, Preston, Prowse & Co. (Trustees)* may be usefully compared with *Re O'Reardon*,[18] which also supports the proposition that the justice and convenience of a case will be borne in mind when deciding whether to hand local assets over to a foreign assignee. O'Reardon and Murphy carried on business in England and in Ireland. In December 1872 O'Reardon was made bankrupt in England. In February 1873 Murphy was adjudicated bankrupt in Ireland. Subsequently a joint commission issued in Ireland; and the Irish assignees applied to the English court for an order that certain joint estate be remitted to Ireland. Mellish LJ (Lord Selborne LC concurring) recognised that the English court had power to give assets to the Irish assignees.[19] However, the foreign assignees' claim was rejected on 'the simple ground of convenience':[20] the English adjudication had been first, the greater number of creditors lived in England and the English proceedings had already progressed to the stage that there were considerable assets ready for distribution in England.[1] Thus, in modern terminology, it certainly had not been shown that the Irish proceedings were clearly more appropriate.

5. THE EXERCISE OF DISCRETION IN CONTEMPORARY BANKRUPTCY PROCEEDINGS

There is little question that in the past the English court had at times felt obliged to exercise jurisdiction despite only slight connection to the forum. In *Ex p Pascal* the Court of Appeal upheld the validity of a debtor's summons[2] founded upon a foreign debt and taken out by a French creditor against a Peruvian debtor, even though the same creditor had already instituted bankruptcy proceedings in Peru where (*semble*) an adjudication had been made. However, it was recognised that at a later stage the debtor

---

[18] (1873) 9 Ch. App. 74. The case was not simply concerned with whether English proceedings should be stayed, but rather with the discretion to hand over English assets to a foreign assignee, see chapter 12, *post.*

[19] *Ibid.,* at 77.

[20] *Ibid.,* at 78.

[1] *Ibid.*

[2] Under the present law a statutory demand is regarded as an extra-judicial document (see *Practice Direction* [1988] 1 W.L.R. 461) so no question can arise as to staying such a demand on the basis that the creditor should be proceeding abroad.

might apply for a stay of any petition.[3] Clearly, in this type of situation the doctrine of the appropriate forum will be readily applicable. Yet the doctrine is not confined to such cases. That there exists a significant, even strong, factual link to the English forum does not preclude the granting of a stay. It will be recalled that in *Stabb, Preston and Prowse (Assignees)* v. *Stabb, Preston, Prowse & Co. (Trustees)*[4] the bankrupts carried on business within the jurisdiction, with both assets and creditors there situate; nevertheless the interests of the general body of creditors were in favour of a stay.

One thing is clear beyond peradventure: no single factor, or even combination of two or more factors, is necessarily decisive. Accordingly, some of the reasoning that has found favour in the English cases must now be discarded.[5]

In *Re a Debtor (No. 737 of 1928)*[6] Swiss creditors had presented a petition against a Swiss debtor who, although in the employ of a London firm, had carried on business on his own account purchasing goods from Switzerland. The larger debts were in Switzerland where the equivalent of a bankruptcy order had been made. The Court of Appeal rejected a submission that a receiving order ought not to have been made in England, Lord Hanworth MR commenting:[7]

> 'It appears to me that inasmuch as there are debts over here, the debtor is over here and the jurisdiction is not disputed, the registrar was acting well within his discretion in making the order. More than that, I think the order was rightly made.'

His Lordship's observation that jurisdiction was not disputed must at once be discounted. For the discretion to stay proceedings only arises once the jurisdiction of the court has been established. Accordingly, the decision of the Court of Appeal (far from analysing the justice and convenience of the case) was based upon two factors: that is, presence of the debtor and the existence of creditors in England. In respect of the former, a debtor may be present in England one day and gone the next; and as to the latter, that there was a minority of creditors in England cannot now be considered decisive. Indeed, it may be noted that in *Re Behrends*[8] the debtor was in England, together with certain creditors, but a stay was forthcoming.

It is trite that the appropriateness of competing courts can only be determined by reference to the facts of any given case. However, it is submitted that the following matters merit special attention.

---

[3] (1876) 1 Ch. D. 509 at 512: 'All that question will be open on the petition for adjudication, and if it be found that the distribution of the assets will take place abroad, the proceedings in this country may be stayed.'

[4] (1821) Nfld. 298.

[5] In particular, the judgment of Lord Coleridge CJ in *Re Artola Hermanos* (1890) 24 Q.B.D. 640 at 644–645, as well as much that is found in *Re McCulloch* (1880) 14 Ch. D. 716, *Re a Debtor* (No. 199 of 1922) [1922] 2 Ch. 470 and *Re a Debtor (No. 737 of 1928)* [1929] 1 Ch. 362, all *post*.

[6] [1929] 1 Ch. 362.

[7] *Ibid.*, at 370. If the facts of *Re a Debtor (No. 737 of 1928)* were to be repeated, the English court might still refuse a stay, for the debtor had carried on his business in England, thus relevant evidence would be available in England, just as such evidence was available in Hamburg in *Re Behrends* (1865) 12 L.T. 149, *ante*.

[8] (1865) 12 L.T. 149, *ante*.

A. Relevant Factors

(i) *Proof*

As jurisdiction under section 265(1) of the Insolvency Act 1986 is founded as of right, it is not for the petitioner to contend that England is the proper place for insolvency proceedings. Rather it is up to the party seeking the stay to show that the foreign court is clearly more appropriate. Only once it has been shown that the foreign proceedings are clearly more appropriate, in the interests of all the parties and for the ends of justice, will the burden of proof then shift to the other party to put forward special circumstances by reason of which justice requires that proceedings continue in England.[9] The need for evidence concerning the effect of a foreign insolvency must be noted. Accordingly in practice the party seeking the stay should be armed with appropriate expert evidence. Such matters as the jurisdiction of the foreign court; the effect of the foreign proceedings upon the debtor's property and obligations; the territorial application of the foreign law; the rights of English creditors in the foreign proceedings; and the authority of the foreign assignee, suggest themselves as likely to be relevant.[10]

(ii) *Foreign and Local Proceedings*

It may be important to contrast the amount of progress that has been made in the foreign and local proceedings at the time a stay is sought.[11] In *Re O'Reardon*[12] one factor relevant to the question of convenience was that assets were already available for distribution in the English proceedings. In *Re Crawford and Co.*[13] the Chief Justice of the Supreme Court of Newfoundland refused a stay where part of the local assets had already been distributed. In *Stabb, Preston and Prowse (Assignees)* v. *Stabb, Preston, Prowse & Co. (Trustees)* the Chief Justice distinguished his earlier decision in *Re Crawford and Co.* and granted a stay, noting that 'nothing has been done but collecting the estate'.[14] Similarly, that the foreign proceedings are already well advanced will be a matter properly to be taken into account, for it may tend to indicate the efficiency, expedition and

---

[9] *Spiliada Maritime Corpn.* v. *Cansulex Ltd.* [1987] A.C. 460 at 474. See also *Re Harrods (Buenos Aires) Ltd (No. 2)* [1991] 4 All E.R. 348 at 356, where the application of the doctrine of *forum non conveniens* in relation to (solvent) winding up is considered. The existence of a foreign insolvency is not *prima facie* a reason for a stay: the observation of Jessel MR in *Re Robinson* (1883) 22 Ch. D. 816 at 818, p. 70, *ante*, cannot be supported.

[10] *Cf Re Thulin* [1995] 1 W.L.R. 165, p. 71, *supra*.

[11] In *Livingstone's Creditors* v. *Livingstone's Trustees* 1937 S.L.T. 391 the Scottish court refused to recall a sequestration in favour of English bankruptcy proceedings, even though a substantial majority of creditors resided in England (where business had been carried on) because *inter alia* those creditors had failed to make the application timeously but had allowed the Scottish proceedings to reach an advanced stage before applying. An application for a stay on the basis of *forum conveniens* should be made at the earliest appropriate time: see *Mansour* v. *Mansour* [1989] 1 F.L.R. 418. In particular, it would be wrong to advise a party (as was done in *Re Cockayne* (1815) 2 Rose 233) to ignore the English proceedings until almost completed and then apply for a stay.

[12] (1873) 9 Ch. App. 74, *ante*.

[13] (1818) Nfld. L.R. 100. The decision was subsequently reversed by the Privy Council, though merely because of an irregularity in the proceedings, (1818) Nfld. L.R. 242.

[14] (1821) Nfld. L.R. 298 at 305.

economy of those proceedings.[15] The state of the relevant proceedings is but one consideration. Plainly the English court would never feel precluded from exercising jurisdiction merely on account of the speed of a party's recourse to a foreign tribunal.

(iii) *Locality of Creditors*

That there exists a majority of creditors in the English or in the foreign court is obviously relevant to the identification of the clearly more appropriate forum.[16] Yet the location of the majority is not of itself decisive.[17] It is not difficult to imagine a situation wherein England has a bare majority of creditors, but the weight of other factors favours the foreign forum: the debtor's business (and the evidence relevant thereto) is centred in the foreign jurisdiction; the foreign proceedings are already well advanced; nearly all the assets are there located; the debtor and a substantial body of creditors (albeit a minority) reside in the foreign jurisdiction.

As a general rule English private international law looks to the legal rather than political unit (e.g. the Provinces of Canada not the country as a whole). Let us say, however, that insolvency proceedings are on foot in British Columbia and in England, with creditors equally distributed between England, British Columbia and Alberta. In such a situation the creditors in British Columbia and Alberta may be considered as a single group, particularly if they are subject to a common bankruptcy law.

(iv) *Foreign Injunctions*

Upon entering a proof in foreign proceedings a creditor does not thereby automatically preclude himself from claiming in any English insolvency.[18] Even if the foreign court grants an injunction prohibiting a creditor from lodging a claim in England, the English court is not obliged to enforce that injunction by staying its own proceedings.[19] When determining where the interests of justice lie, the English court will bear in mind the conduct of creditors and any orders of the foreign court. In *Banque Indosuez S.A.* v. *Ferromet Resources Inc.* Hoffmann J discharged interlocutory injunctions (granted in the course of litigation in England) which the plaintiff had

---

[15] *Spiliada Maritime Corpn.* v. *Cansulex Ltd.* [1987] A.C. 460 at 485. See also *Phosphate Sewage Co.* v. *Molleson* (1876) 1 App. Cas. 780 at 788–789 *per* Lord Selborne.

[16] Note Bankruptcy (Scotland) Act 1985, s. 17(1)(b), and the former s. 12 of the Bankruptcy Act 1914, in respect of the recall of a sequestration.

[17] It may also be noted that the power of the court in Scotland to stay a petition for sequestration, see Bankruptcy (Scotland) Act 1985, s. 10(4), does not require that a majority of creditors reside within the jurisdiction of the foreign court.

[18] Although a creditor may have to account for any dividend received abroad, chapter 10, *post.*

[19] See the discussion in *Banque Indosuez S.A.* v. *Ferromet Resources Inc.* [1993] B.C.L.C. 112, *Felixstowe Dock and Rly Co.* v. *United States Lines Inc.* [1989] Q.B. 360, *Brand* v. *Green* (1900) 13 Man. R. 101, *Bank of Nova Scotia* v. *Booth* (1910) 19 Man. R. 471, *Nemaha Energy Inc.* v. *Wood & Locker Inc.* (1985) 68 B.C.L.R. 187 and *Pitts* v. *Hill* (1987) 66 C.B.R. (N.S.) 273, chapter 8, *post.*

obtained in breach of an automatic worldwide stay of proceedings under the US Bankruptcy Code, commenting:[20]

> 'The court is not of course bound by the stay under United States law but will do its utmost to co-operate with the United States Bankruptcy Court and avoid any action which might disturb the orderly administration of [the debtor] under Chapter 11 [of the US Bankruptcy Code].'

In particular the English court will be most anxious to ensure that no attempt is being made to use English proceedings to gain an unfair advantage over the general body of creditors. However, the desire of a foreign court to exercise exclusive jurisdiction will not render proceedings in that foreign court clearly more appropriate.

(v) *The Presence of Assets in England*

From the decided cases it is easy to assume that the presence of assets in England is in itself a sufficient reason for exercising jurisdiction. In *Re Robinson*[1] and *Re Behrends*[2] there were no assets in England and a stay was in each case granted. Where there have been assets in England, no stay has been forthcoming.[3] Moreover, in *Re Hecquard*[4] the Court of Appeal was minded to exercise jurisdiction in light of the possibility that an English trustee in bankruptcy might be able to set aside transactions and thereby gather in assets. A similar approach seems to have been taken in *Re Thulin*.[5] It must be stressed, however, that in contemporary bankruptcy proceedings the presence of assets in England is merely one factor to be taken into account. Moreover, as has often been remarked, the nature of international business and communications is such that assets can be moved into and out of England at the 'press of a button' (or the click of a mouse).[6] Hence whether or not there are any assets in England at a particular date may be a matter of chance. But, more importantly, it will be noted that if there has already been a prior foreign bankruptcy (entitled to recognition in England) then all movable property may well have vested in the foreign trustee – leaving nothing in England which an English trustee can recover.[7]

(vi) *Immovable Property in England*

Leaving to one side adjudications in Scotland and Northern Ireland, a foreign bankruptcy decree will not vest English land in the foreign assignee.[8]

---

[20] [1993] B.C.L.C. 112 at 117, see further p. 232, *infra.*
[1] (1883) 22 Ch. D. 816.
[2] (1865) 12 L.T. 149.
[3] *Re McCulloch* (1880) 14 Ch. D. 716 and *Re a Debtor (No. 199 of 1922)* [1922] 2 Ch. 470. These two cases can no longer be safely relied upon.
[4] (1889) 24 Q.B.D. 71 at 76.
[5] [1995] 1 W.L.R. 165 at 170, although the deputy judge appears to have thought that assets *outside* England would also be recovered (assets which the Swedish trustee might not have been able to recover), p. 72, *supra.*
[6] *Re Thulin*, at 171.
[7] See the cases discussed at p. 342, *infra.*
[8] *Waite* v. *Bingley* (1882) 21 Ch. D. 674 at 681–682: see also p. 220, *infra.*

However, the English court may make an order to allow a foreign assignee to dispose of immovables in England. Such an order may be made under the inherent jurisdiction[9] of the court or section 426 of the Insolvency Act 1986.[10] Accordingly, that the debtor has land in England is no obstacle to a stay of English proceedings.

(vii) *Statutory Provisions for Co-operation*

An application to stay English bankruptcy proceedings should be made at the earliest reasonable opportunity.[11] At that early stage, however, it may well be that the petitioning creditor argues, for example, that English proceedings should be allowed to continue because the English court may in the future be required to examine witnesses in England or recover assets which cannot be recovered by the foreign trustee.[12] Obviously such arguments cannot simply be ignored and their weight will very much depend upon the facts of any particular case. Yet, it should be noted that section 426 of the Insolvency Act 1986 establishes a framework whereunder the English court may grant assistance to an insolvency court in Scotland or Northern Ireland or in any other 'relevant country or territory'.[13] (At the time of writing some 19 foreign countries or territories, in addition to the Isle of Man and the Channel Islands, have been designated for the purposes of section 426.[14]) It has been held that, where a request has been received from a relevant foreign court, section 426 allows the English court to exercise any and all powers that arise:

(i)   under its inherent jurisdiction;
(ii)   under English insolvency law; and
(iii) under the foreign insolvency law.[15]

Hence, if a bankruptcy has been commenced in a relevant country or territory, the foreign court may ask the English court to examine witnesses or exercise English avoidance powers under the Insolvency Act 1986.[16] In such a way the strength of any argument by a petitioning creditor that a full-scale English bankruptcy is necessary will be reduced. If there are any powers which the English court has that the foreign court does not, or if persons are subject to the jurisdiction of the English court but not subject to the foreign court's jurisdiction, a section 426 request can always be submitted to the English court. (Indeed, a section 426 request could be framed so as specifically to request that the English court lends assistance to the foreign proceedings by staying the English bankruptcy. Under the

---

[9]   *Re Kooperman* [1928] W.N. 101, *Re Osborn* [1931–1932] B. & C.R. 189 and *Re Bolton* [1920] 2 I.R. 324. *Ex p Stegmann* 1902 T.S. 40 contains a relevant discussion of the appropriate principles.

[10] Which makes provision for international co-operation, see below.

[11] See p. 76, *supra*.

[12] *Re Thulin*, *supra* n. 6 at 170 suggests similar contentions.

[13] For a full analysis of s. 426, see p. 405, *infra*.

[14] Neither the United States nor any European country, other than Ireland, has been so designated.

[15] *Hughes* v. *Hannover Rückversicherungs-Aktiengesellschaft* [1997] 1 B.C.L.C. 497.

[16] The absence of any treaty between the United Kingdom and Sweden for international co-operation in insolvency matters was noted in *Re Thulin*, *supra* n. 12, and contrasted with mutual co-operation between England and Scotland in *Re Robinson* (1883) 22 Ch.D. 816.

old Bankruptcy Act provision an English court made such a request to a court in the Cape, which stayed its proceedings.[17]) It may also be noted that Australian courts have relied upon a similar statutory provision when staying a case in favour of bankruptcy proceedings in New Zealand.[18]

(Even in respect of countries that are not within section 426, a more limited range of assistance has since April 1997 been available.[19])

(viii) *Notice and Claims*

The facts of *Re Robinson*,[20] in which the English creditor did not prove his debt in the Scottish sequestration, show that an English creditor cannot simply by ignoring the foreign insolvency proceedings ensure that the English court will exercise jurisdiction. The test is where the interests of all the parties lie.

Whether or not the English creditors have also made a claim (or are minded to participate) in the foreign proceedings may in some instances be a relevant consideration. However, the facts of each particular case must be taken into account. Certainly there is no basis for contending that an English creditor, upon entering a proof abroad, makes some kind of election in favour of the exclusive jurisdiction of the foreign forum. Equally, that a local creditor had no notice of the foreign proceedings at the time they were commenced has little relevance in ascertaining whether the foreign court is clearly more appropriate.[1]

(ix) *Domicile*

At one stage it was held in the Scottish courts,[2] and suggested in the English Court of Appeal,[3] that the courts of the domicile were in a special position when it came to making an adjudication in bankruptcy. Now, however, it is quite plain that an English judge is not in any way restricted by the domicile of a debtor.[4] Whether the debtor be domiciled in England or elsewhere, the matter is one of discretion: English proceedings should be stayed in favour of a clearly more appropriate forum.

---

[17] *Howse, Sons & Co. (Trustee)* v. *Howse, Sons & Co. (Trustees)* (1884) 3 J. 14, discussed below.

[18] *Radich* v. *Bank of New Zealand* (1993) 116 A.L.R. 676. For an earlier illustration, see *Re Becker*, 29 May 1992, No. Q P755 of 1992 FED No. 342; this case is on LEXIS or can be found through the Aust LII web-site.

[19] Discussed fully below, at p. 397.

[20] (1883) 22 Ch. D. 816.

[1] In *Howse, Sons & Co. (Trustee)* v. *Howse, Sons, & Co. (Trustees)* (1884) 3 J. 14 the court in England had sought the aid of the courts of the Cape Colony. Some of the Cape creditors had participated in the English proceedings, others had not (*ibid.*, at 19). The Cape court lent its assistance, setting aside its own sequestration.

[2] *Stein's Case* (1813) 1 Rose 462 and *Goetze* v. *Aders* (1874) 2 R. 150, *ante*.

[3] *Re Artola Hermanos* (1890) 24 Q.B.D. 640 at 644–645 *per* Lord Coleridge CJ.

[4] It may be noted that in *Re Cockayne* (1815) 2 Rose 233 the bankrupt was domiciled in Scotland yet no stay was granted. For detailed consideration of the recognition of foreign bankruptcies, see chapter 5, *post*.

(x) *Debtor's Petition in Foreign Proceedings*

The mere fact that it is the debtor who presents a petition in England or abroad obviously raises no inference of fraud. A vague suspicion of impropriety will not be considered as an established fraud. Thus if the debtor has petitioned abroad in a situation which has 'more or less of suspicion attaching to it', the question of whether the debtor has been fraudulent may be left to the foreign court.[5] But where it is shown that the debtor has acted fraudulently in commencing proceedings in a foreign court, plainly the English court will not accede to an application to stay its own proceedings.

Yet in the absence of fraud the English court will grant a stay in favour of a more appropriate forum regardless of by whom the foreign proceedings were commenced. It is surely irrelevant that the foreign proceedings were set in motion by the debtor: either it is shown that the foreign court is clearly more appropriate, in the interests of justice, or it is not.

In *Re a Debtor (No. 199 of 1922)*[6] a bankruptcy notice had been served on the debtor who, three days before the expiration of the time fixed for compliance, petitioned the Scottish court and obtained an order of sequestration. The registrar in the exercise of his discretion made a receiving order despite the sequestration. That order was upheld, Warrington LJ observing:[7]

> 'I only desire to say on the first point that the fact that the petition for sequestration in Scotland was presented by the debtor himself seems to me to be fatal; but I must not be taken to intimate that my view would have been different if the petition had been presented by a creditor. That point may one day have to be decided.'

This observation has been taken as suggesting that the English court is less likely to stay its own proceedings where the debtor has himself petitioned the foreign court.[8] However, the 'first point' to which the learned Lord Justice addressed his comments was whether the debtor had indeed committed any act of bankruptcy.[9] The 'first point' did not concern the exercise of discretion at all.[10] Indeed, it may be noted that in *Re a Debtor (No. 199 of 1922)*[11] Lord Sterndale MR (who gave the leading judgment) when dealing with the court's discretion did not refer to the circumstance that the debtor had petitioned the foreign court.

In short, absent fraud, the appropriateness of the competing courts should not be influenced by whether or not the debtor initiated directly or indirectly the foreign proceedings.

---

[5] *Re McCulloch* (1880) 14 Ch. D. 716 at 720.
[6] [1922] 2 Ch. 470.
[7] *Ibid.*, at 474.
[8] *Dicey and Morris*, p. 1162.
[9] It had been argued by counsel for the debtor that, once the sequestration took place in Scotland, the debtor had been prevented from complying with the English bankruptcy notice: see [1922] 2 Ch. 470 at 471 and 473.
[10] The exercise of discretion was the third point at issue.
[11] [1922] 2 Ch. 470 at 473–474.

(xi) *The Availability of Evidence*

The location and availability of evidence and of witnesses must, of course, be an important factor in deciding whether foreign proceedings are clearly more appropriate. It will be recalled that a stay was granted in *Re Behrends*,[12] the facts revealing that the debtor's business was carried on in Hamburg 'where his books of account and property were left'.[13] In *Stabb, Preston and Prowse (Assignees)* v. *Stabb, Preston, Prowse & Co (Trustees)*[14] the Newfoundland court stayed its own proceedings in favour of the English court. The insolvents were all in England and 'their concerns interwoven with a great number of collateral partnerships, all of which centre in England'.[15] Accordingly, the insolvents were available as witnesses in England where additionally the most part of the evidence relating to the insolvents' diverse business interests was located.

(xii) *Foreign Revenue Claims*

Revenue debts are by no means unfamiliar in contemporary insolvency. Let us say that proceedings have been commenced in England and in France and, further, that each taxing authority has lodged claims in its own country. The presence of French revenue claims in the French proceedings is no reason for the English court to refuse a stay, if the French court is the clearly more appropriate forum. It is only where the foreign proceedings amount, in substance, to nothing more than an attempt to enforce a foreign revenue debt in England that the rule against foreign revenue laws can claim any application.[16]

B. Special Circumstances Requiring Proceedings in England

If the party applying for a stay fails to show that the foreign court is clearly more appropriate, that is the end of the matter; the application must be dismissed. Where the appropriateness of the foreign proceedings is made out (the burden of proof having been upon the applicant) a stay will generally be forthcoming. Nevertheless the English court will not grant a stay, even though the foreign proceedings are indeed more appropriate, if there exist special circumstances by reason of which justice requires the continuation of the English bankruptcy. A stay must be refused if substantial justice would not be done in the otherwise appropriate forum.[17] Plainly there will be few instances in which such circumstances may likely be established. The burden is here upon the party resisting the application for a stay.[18]

---

[12] (1865) 12 L.T. 149.

[13] *Ibid.*, at 150.

[14] (1821) Nfld. L.R. 298, p. 73, *supra.*

[15] *Ibid.*, at 305; pp. 73–74, *ante.*

[16] For UK revenue claims and the staying of English proceedings, see p. 205, *post.* The rule against foreign revenue claims is considered further in chapter 7.

[17] *Spiliada Maritime Corpn.* v. *Cansulex Ltd.* [1987] A.C. 460 at 476: see also the remarks of Lord Hoffmann, p. 64, *supra.*

[18] *Ibid.*

(i) *Prejudice to English Creditors*

Merely because the English creditors will lose some advantage by not being allowed to bring their claims in England does not, of course, mean that substantial justice would not be done in the foreign court.[19] The matter is one of degree. If the proceedings in the foreign forum are not, to borrow Lord Dunedin's expression in *Galbraith* v. *Grimshaw*,[20] a process of universal distribution but instead discriminate against the English creditors, it may well be said that substantial justice would not be done in the foreign court.

Brief reference may here be made to *Felixstowe Dock and Rly Co.* v. *United States Lines Inc.*[1] The defendant corporation ('U.S.L.') was under reorganisation in the United States in accordance with Chapter 11 of the US Federal Bankruptcy Code. Although no insolvency proceedings had been initiated in England, the plaintiff creditors had obtained Mareva injunctions. For the defendant it was argued, broadly speaking, that the English court should not interfere in the Chapter 11 process under way in the United States. Hirst J dismissed the defendant's application to discharge the Mareva injunctions, noting that the Chapter 11 process was limited to a reorganisation in North America and could confer no benefit upon those creditors such as the plaintiffs in Europe:[2]

> 'If these were ordinary winding up proceedings under which U.S.L.'s assets would be collected and distributed totally and rateably amongst all its creditors, U.S.L.'s arguments under this head would have substantial force. But it is nothing of the kind. This is a scheme to reorganise the company as a going concern, but on a much narrower commercial base limited to North America.'

Whilst serious doubts have been expressed as to the correctness of the judge's finding on the facts[3] (which was of course based solely upon the evidence as presented before him), namely that the US proceedings in effect discriminated against European creditors, *Felixstowe Dock and Rly Co.* v. *United States Lines Inc.* illustrates a basic principle: the English court will set its face against lending assistance to a foreign court where the English creditors would be unfairly discriminated against in the foreign proceedings. In contrast, one may refer to *Banque Indosuez S.A.* v. *Ferromet Resources Inc.*[4] where Hoffmann J was happy to discharge Mareva injunctions in order to assist a Chapter 11 administration underway in the US Bankruptcy Court, there being no suggestion of discrimination against English creditors.

---

[19] See, generally, the discussion in *Re Harrods (Buenos Aires) Ltd.* [1991] 4 All E.R. 348. Such an advantage was not permitted to the English creditor in *Re Robinson* (1883) 22 Ch. D. 816, p. 87, n. 10, *post*. An advantage to the creditors in England may very well work a disadvantage to creditors in the foreign proceedings (if only because those creditors then have to seek legal advice as whether or not to enter proofs in both sets of proceedings); so too, where for example a prior transaction is set aside, the advantage to English creditors may be a disadvantage to the debtor's family members and indirectly the debtor himself.

[20] [1910] A.C. 508 at 513.

[1] [1989] Q.B. 360.

[2] *Ibid.*, at 386.

[3] See, for example, Fletcher (1993) 6 Insol. Int. 10.

[4] [1993] B.C.L.C. 112, see also p. 77, *supra*: note also Lord Hoffmann's remarks set out at p. 64, *supra* in relation to the exercise of discretion.

(ii) *Preferential Creditors*

A stay of English proceedings might easily result in preferential creditors[5] (according to English law) being left to claim before the foreign court, wherein no like preferences are available. Such circumstances might go some way to justifying the continuation of English proceedings. In *Howse, Sons & Co. (Trustee)* v. *Howse, Sons & Co. (Trustees)*[6] there were concurrent bankruptcy proceedings in England and the Cape; and the English court had, acting under section 74 of the Bankruptcy Act 1869,[7] requested that the Cape court stay its own proceedings. Upon the facts a stay was granted; however, De Villiers CJ observed:[8]

'If the decision in favour of one country were to involve the loss of right of preference acquired before insolvency by creditors in the other country, I should certainly answer that the assets in each country ought to be administered under the supervision of the courts of that country. . . .'

It should be noted that the Chief Justice of the Cape Colony was only speaking generally. It may well be, in a particular case, that the value of assets in England is so small that the rights of a class of preferential creditors would be virtually worthless; thus there could be no compelling reason to refuse a stay.[9]

In any event, where the foreign court is clearly more appropriate the claims of preferential creditors may easily be preserved upon the basis suggested in *Stabb, Preston and Prowse (Assignees)* v. *Stabb, Preston, Prowse & Co. (Trustees)*.[10] It will be recalled that insolvency proceedings had been commenced in England and in Newfoundland. The Chief Justice of the Supreme Court of Newfoundland considered:[11]

'that justice will be most effectually done by directing the proceeds which have been realised in Newfoundland, to be transferred to the assignees under the English commission . . .'

Forbes CJ then continued:[12]

'upon security given to the court to pay, in the first place, all preferable claims for servants' wages and current supplies, and referring all other creditors to England.'

A similar solution commended itself to the Manitoba court in *Re National Benefit Assurance Co.*,[13] a decision upon the ancillary winding up of foreign corporations. The company was incorporated and carried on business in England. Business was also conducted in Canada. The company had been put into liquidation in England and a liquidator had also been appointed in an ancillary winding up in Manitoba. The Manitoba Court of Appeal determined that the claims of all the ordinary creditors would best be dealt with in England. Hence the assets gathered

---

[5] For instance, employees entitled to preference in respect of remuneration in accordance with the Insolvency Act 1986, Sch. 6.
[6] (1884) 3 J. 14.
[7] See now Insolvency Act 1986, s. 426, chapter 15, *post.*
[8] (1884) 3 J. 14 at 22.
[9] Or the only asset may be land and exhausted upon satisfaction of the mortgagees.
[10] (1821) Nfld. L.R. 298.
[11] *Ibid.*, at 305.
[12] *Ibid.*, like views were expressed in *Re Slade* (1862) 4 Nfld. L.R. 710.
[13] [1927] 3 D.L.R. 289.

in by the Canadian liquidator were ordered to be paid over to the English liquidator, but only after payment of preferred creditors in the Canadian proceedings:[14]

> 'As there can be no apprehension that the Canadian creditors will not have equal treatment with all other creditors, there is no reason why the assets in the hands of the Canadian liquidator should not now be remitted to the English liquidator, less amounts required to pay Canadian preferred creditors . . .'

Similar reasoning would clearly apply where the set-off rules in England were more favourable to a creditor than the equivalent rules in the foreign proceedings.[15]

(iii) *The Priority of Secured Creditors*

The priority of creditors, which includes preferred as well as secured creditors, is of course a matter governed in general by the *lex fori*. If English proceedings are stayed in favour of a foreign forum, that foreign court will in all probability apply its own rules regarding priorities. Thus a stay may, *prima facie*, work an injustice to a creditor who, possessed of a secured interest under English law, is regarded as unsecured according to the procedural rules of the foreign court.

At this stage two points must be made clear. Firstly, priority depends not merely upon the nature of a creditor's right but is a privilege conferred by the *lex fori*. Although it may be that where a stay is granted a creditor may have no opportunity to take advantage of the privilege available under English law as the *lex fori*, yet it does not inevitably follow that an injustice will be occasioned. Let us say that a creditor, who has carried on business in Finland, has a lien that arose under the law of Finland. Such a creditor is not prejudiced if prevented by an application of the doctrine of the appropriate forum from pursuing his claim in an English bankruptcy. For the creditor could not reasonably have anticipated the privilege conferred by the procedural rules of the English court. Second, in any event, even if a secured creditor would indeed suffer an injustice,[16] the English court may rely upon the solution adopted with reference to preferred creditors in *Stabb, Preston and Prowse (Assignees)* v. *Stabb, Preston, Prowse & Co. (Trustees)*[17] and *Re National Benefit Assurance Co.*[18] That is, rather than conducting a

---

[14] *Ibid.*, at 302 *per* Trueman JA. In *Re African Farm Ltd.* 1906 T.S. 373, cited with approval in the decision in *The Cornelis Verolme* [1997] 2 N.Z.L.R. 110, the Full Court in the Transvaal, without ordering an ancillary winding up, recognised the appointment of an English liquidator and his authority to deal with local assets, subject to conditions to protect preferred creditors: 'But clearly our recognition must be coupled with conditions calculated, as far as possible, to protect local creditors, to recognise preferences over Transvaal assets duly constituted here, and to enable the free balance to be distributed as part of a scheme of administration which will have regard to the whole of the company's debts wherever found, and to its total assets wherever situated.' (*Per* Innes CJ at 382.)

[15] See *Re Bank of Credit and Commerce International S.A. (No. 10)* [1996] 4 All E.R. 796, discussed below p. 318.

[16] Such injustice is only possible where the creditor (and his rights) are particularly closely linked to the English forum.

[17] (1821) Nfld. L.R. 298, *ante.*

[18] [1927] 3 D.L.R. 289, *ante.*

full-scale bankruptcy,[19] the English court may grant a stay on condition that the relevant assets are applied in satisfaction of the secured creditors' claims. The secured creditors having been satisfied to the extent of their security, the remaining English assets may then be given over to the foreign assignee, who will be in a position to deal with the whole of the debtor's assets and the claims of all the ordinary creditors in a single set of proceedings – moreover, a set of proceedings being conducted in the clearly more appropriate forum.

Reference may here be made to the recent decision of the New Zealand courts in *The Cornelis Verolme*.[20] The ship was arrested in New Zealand and two days later the owner was declared bankrupt[1] by a court in Belgium. Belgian insolvency law (like English law) sought to apply to assets anywhere in the world and the Belgian court ordered that the ship be released to the control of the Belgian trustee in bankruptcy. The master and crew, however, objected to the release of the ship, arguing that in accordance with New Zealand law they had a maritime lien. The New Zealand court accepted that the Belgian insolvency proceedings were entitled to recognition and that such recognition carried with it the active assistance of the New Zealand courts.[2] Williams J. ordered the release of the vessel against adequate security in New Zealand to satisfy any *in rem* claims of the master and crew (together with costs).[3]

(iv) *Property Recoverable only in English Proceedings*

The case law reveals examples in which it has been of significance that the English court might set aside transactions unimpeachable in the foreign proceedings. In *Re a Debtor (No. 199 of 1922)*[4] a Scottish sequestration had already issued, but the Court of Appeal declined to stay English proceedings against a debtor who had made a voluntary settlement which could not be set aside under the law of Scotland.[5] (Of course, it should now be argued that, even if the court in Scotland could not set aside the settlement, the Scottish court could make a section 426 request to the English court.[6]) In *Re McCulloch*,[7] proceedings having been commenced in England and in Ireland, Thesiger LJ commented upon the availability in the English court of the doctrine of relation back:[8]

---

[19] Which will lead to an increase in costs, itself a disadvantage to the general body of creditors, as well as putting creditors in the difficult position of having to decide whether or not to enter proofs in both sets of proceedings.

[20] [1997] 2 N.Z.L.R. 110; for recognition generally see chapters 5 and 6.

[1] The shipowner was a company, but the judge refers throughout to bankruptcy under the foreign (Belgian) law, rather than winding up.

[2] Reference was made to the First Edition of this work and to *Re African Farms Ltd.* 1906 T.S. 373.

[3] *Supra* n. 20 at 127.

[4] [1922] 2 Ch. 470.

[5] The decision seems to rest largely upon the presence of assets in England: 'It is true that in *In re Robinson* the discretion was exercised in the other way, but in that case there were no assets in England, and here there are.' (*Per* Lord Sterndale MR [1922] 2 Ch. 470 at 473–474.)

[6] See p. 79, *supra*.

[7] (1880) 14 Ch. D. 716.

[8] *Ibid.*, at 724–725.

'Then, as regards the creditors generally, I think it is reasonable, at all events at present, that the English bankruptcy should stand, as it is obvious that there may be transactions which may possibly be overreached . . . in the English bankruptcy which could not be overreached in the Irish bankruptcy, owing to there being no such relation back under the Irish bankruptcy law as there is under the English.'

Nevertheless, even under the old authorities it was plain that the court retained a discretion. It will be recalled that in *Re Robinson*[9] the English Court of Appeal declined to exercise jurisdiction. Yet counsel for the petitioning creditor, referring to *Re McCulloch*, had sought to be permitted 'to examine the debtor and to set aside any transaction which he may have entered into here'.[10] Thus it is not correct on the authorities to argue that because property may be recovered only in the English proceedings (and not by the foreign court) justice requires that the English bankruptcy continues.

In addition, the above observation of Thesiger LJ in *Re McCulloch* must be reconsidered. If the foreign court is clearly more appropriate then the burden of establishing circumstances by reason of which justice requires that the English proceedings are not stayed, falls upon the party resisting the application for a stay. Accordingly, it cannot be enough that there 'may be' transactions which 'may possibly' be overreached. Positive proof of a lack of substantial justice in the foreign court is required.

Certainly, it will not be sufficient merely to argue that no thorough investigation of the facts will occur unless the English court acts. A recent example drawn from corporate insolvency is relevant in this regard. In *New Hampshire Insurance Co.* v. *Rush & Tomkins Group plc*[11] the appellant as a contingent creditor had petitioned in England for the winding up of two Dutch companies (referred to as 'NV' and 'International NV') which were part of a much larger group of companies, the Rush & Tomkins Group. (The English companies in the Group were in compulsory liquidation in England.) The Dutch companies were subject to insolvency proceedings in Holland and a Mr De Ruuk had been appointed as trustee in bankruptcy there. The evidence of Mr De Ruuk was to the effect that the making of English winding up orders 'would lead to confusion and duplication of time and costs which will, in turn, reduce the assets of the company available for distribution to all creditors.' At first instance Jonathan Parker J had ruled that:

(1) although the Dutch companies were factually connected to England,[12] there was no reasonable possibility that any benefit would accrue to the creditors from an English winding up, so that the court lacked jurisdiction to make a winding up order; and in the alternative
(2) even if the court did have jurisdiction, it was a jurisdiction which in its discretion the court would not exercise.

The appeal centred around the ownership of a substantial sum of money said to be in England, which after investigation Mr De Ruuk had concluded did not belong to either of the Dutch companies. The appellant

---

[9] (1883) 22 Ch. D. 816.
[10] *Ibid.*, at 818.
[11] (3 October 1996, unreported), CA (LEXIS transcript: Smith Bernal).
[12] The precise connections required in order to found winding up jurisdiction in relation to a foreign company are analysed in the following chapter.

maintained that Mr De Ruuk had not adequately investigated the question of ownership of the money and that no proper investigation would occur unless an English liquidator were appointed. The Court of Appeal emphatically rejected the appellant's attack on the integrity or competence of the Dutch trustee and suggested that the appellant should lodge a formal proof in the Dutch insolvency proceedings and then apply to the Dutch court for any appropriate remedy. Millett LJ observed:

> 'It would be something of an impertinence for the English court to take the view that if a trustee in bankruptcy appointed by the Dutch court is not performing his task properly, the proper remedy is for the English court to appoint its own officer to see that he does. If Mr De Ruuk's conduct gives rise to any cause for concern then it is to the Dutch court that those concerns ought, in my opinion, to be addressed.'

Having regard to all the circumstances, it was not appropriate for an English liquidator to be appointed.

The facts of each particular case must be borne in mind. If a debtor has made a voluntary settlement of property in Spain (governed by the law of Spain) as a matter of principle there can be no inherent reason why the English court, not being the appropriate forum, should wish to intervene, particularly not at the instance of Spanish creditors. On the other hand, the justice of the case may be quite different if the property is in England and there are English creditors who might reasonably have anticipated the protection of English curial law. In short, there will be no lack of substantial justice unless it is shown that the transaction sought to be avoided is very closely linked to the English forum.

It is necessary to examine more closely the type of case where the English court is not the appropriate forum, yet substantial justice does require that the English proceedings be used to set aside a transaction, thereby gathering in assets which would not be available for distribution under the laws of the more appropriate foreign forum. Let us say that, in a given instance, proceedings have begun not only in France but also in England. (France is not a 'relevant country or territory' for the purposes of section 426 of the Insolvency Act 1986.) Further, the French court is clearly the more appropriate forum. However, the debtor had made a settlement of property in England which, although it would be set aside in England, is unimpeachable in the foreign court. Additionally, the English creditors would be so prejudiced should the voluntary settlement not be set aside that, it is suggested, justice requires that the English proceedings continue. If the English court conducts a full-scale bankruptcy the settlement will be set aside and those assets recovered can be applied for the benefit of the creditors. Yet the creditors would include the English creditors as well as any French creditors who might prove in England. In other words, both English and French creditors may seek to share in the proceeds recovered under English law: assets in England are not in any way exclusively reserved for English creditors.[13] At the same time, of course, the foreign court would be conducting its own insolvency proceedings. Hence, with concurrent sets of proceedings, the courts of each country would seek to regulate their own proceedings, as far as practicable, to bring about an equalisation of dividends between the

---

[13] *Re Azoff-Don Commercial Bank* [1954] Ch. 315.

different groups of creditors.[14] This, quite obviously, may involve a number of applications to both the English and French courts.[15] A more straightforward solution is available. First, if justice does indeed require that the creditors have the benefit of setting aside a transaction then proceedings must be commenced in England, as well as in the more appropriate foreign court. Secondly, English proceedings need not develop into a full-scale bankruptcy but must be restricted to gathering in all assets in England liable to English bankruptcy law. Thirdly, once all the assets in England have been collected, they shall be given over to the foreign assignee; and all the creditors may then claim in the foreign, more appropriate forum. In such a manner the English creditors suffer no injustice, two sets of full proceedings are not required and, just as importantly, issues are determined in the proper forum.

Whilst there is no English bankruptcy case wherein the court has restricted its own proceedings to gathering assets in England, to be given over at a later stage to a foreign assignee, such a procedure is very familiar with reference to winding up.[16] The decisions upon the ancillary winding up of a foreign corporation support a broad proposition applicable to cross-border insolvency generally: English proceedings may be limited in their scope, being merely auxiliary to or in aid of a more appropriate foreign court.[17] In particular, English proceedings (which are governed by English law) may be usefully employed to gather in assets in England; those assets will subsequently be remitted to the foreign court, in which all the creditors' claims and all the insolvent's assets may be administered.

Moreover, where all that is required in England is to set aside a settlement (or other transaction unfairly prejudicial to creditors[18]) there is no reason why in appropriate circumstances a foreign trustee cannot be left to pursue a claim under section 423 of the Insolvency Act 1986, without the intervention of any bankruptcy proceedings in England.[19]

(v) *Discharge*

Leaving to one side United Kingdom bankruptcies, it is often maintained that the effect of a foreign discharge is an issue exclusively governed by the proper or applicable law.[20] Hence if a discharge is obtained in a French court, the debtor will not subsequently be protected from an action in England if the contract between the plaintiff and the debtor was governed by English law. For under English law the discharge will not be effective in respect of English contracts even though the foreign decree may vest the debtor's property in England in the foreign assignee. Thus in *Smith* v. *Buchanan*[1] the defendants had obtained a discharge in insolvency proceedings in the State of Maryland. Nevertheless, the defendants were not

---

[14] Discussed, generally, chapter 12, *post.*
[15] Once again increasing costs.
[16] Chapter 14, *post.*
[17] This proposition is reinforced by the power given to the English court by s. 426 of the Insolvency Act 1986 to act in aid of a foreign court, *supra.*
[18] An unfair preference, on the other hand, cannot be brought within s. 423 of the 1986 Act.
[19] See, for details, p. 416, *infra* and *McNeil* v. *Sharp* (1915) 70 D.L.R. 740.
[20] See chapter 9, below for a full analysis.
[1] (1800) 1 East 6.

thereby protected from *assumpsit* in England for goods sold and delivered under a contract governed by English law.

In the context of *forum conveniens*, it might be contended by English creditors that English proceedings should not be stayed in favour of a foreign forum because no foreign discharge can extinguish obligations arising under a contract governed by English law. Such a contention is simply irrelevant. If the foreign court is clearly more appropriate then English proceedings should be stayed. As a result English creditors will, in all probability, bring their claims in the foreign forum.[2]

If an English creditor fails before the English court on the question of the exercise of jurisdiction, that creditor is not required and cannot be compelled to claim in the clearly more appropriate foreign forum. However, if an English creditor chooses not to prove in the foreign court, even though English bankruptcy proceedings have been stayed, it would be vexatious and an abuse of process should that creditor bring an action in England.[3] In any event, it is inconceivable that the mere refusal by an English creditor to claim in the foreign forum can have any influence on whether English proceedings should be stayed in favour of the foreign forum. If it were otherwise, the interests of all the parties and the ends of justice would take second place to the whims of English creditors.

6. SUMMARY

Whilst insolvency proceedings are by their very nature different from normal civil litigation (in the form of a *lis inter partes*), the existence of a discretion to stay English bankruptcy proceedings[4] in favour of a clearly more appropriate foreign forum should be beyond question. The general principle governing the exercise of that discretion is clear: it is the interests of all the parties, not just the English creditors, and the ends of justice which must be determinative. But there is no shorthand method of forecasting the outcome of the application of that general principle. The facts of each particular case must be most carefully considered. In a given instance it may be plain that the English proceedings can simply be stayed.[5] In other circumstances, a more flexible approach will be required – the English court using its proceedings in a limited way to satisfy the particular claims of certain creditors (e.g. preferred or secured creditors) who would otherwise be unfairly disadvantaged by the granting of a stay.[6]

---

[2] The consequences of a creditor (under an English contract) *participating* in the foreign insolvency proceedings, is analysed below at pp. 263—266.

[3] An action in England might also be stayed under s. 285 of the Insolvency Act 1986. Certainly, where the English court is conducting an ancillary winding up (and the principal liquidation is abroad) it has used its powers to restrain actions brought by creditors in England or elsewhere: see *Re Queensland Mercantile Agency Co. Ltd.* (1888) 58 L.T. 878.

[4] The matter appears more settled in respect of winding up proceedings: see *Re Wallace Smith & Co. Ltd.* [1992] B.C.L.C. 970, p. 127, *infra*. See also the comments of Lord Hoffmann and Sir Peter Millett, p. 64, *supra*.

[5] Or the English court may decline to make an adjudication as in *Re Robinson* (1883) 22 Ch. D. 816.

[6] *Stabb, Preston and Prowse (Assignees)* v. *Stabb, Preston, Prowse & Co. (Trustees)* (1821) Nfld. L.R. 298, *ante*, being the best illustration.

7. EUROPEAN CONVENTION ON INSOLVENCY PROCEEDINGS

One of the main principles of the Convention is to identify which court is the natural forum for any insolvency, conferring international jurisdiction thereon.[7] Thus if the debtor has its centre of main interests in England, the English court would conduct the primary proceeding. Whereas if the centre of the debtor's main interests was in another Convention country, the English court would only have (a limited) jurisdiction in relation to an establishment in England.[8] A liquidator appointed in any such territorial proceedings is required to render co-operation to the liquidator in the main proceedings abroad.[9] Thus the way the Convention is framed would do away with the need for any application to stay proceedings in favour of a more appropriate foreign forum in another Convention country.

8. ILLUSTRATIONS

(1) Y, a French citizen domiciled in France, has for several years been living and carrying on business in England. Y's business involves the manufacture and sale, both retail and wholesale, of French-style food-stuffs in England. The majority of creditors and most of Y's assets are in England, although a number of creditors are in France. The French creditors commenced insolvency proceedings in France and, subsequent thereto, Y presented a petition in England. The French creditors have applied for a stay of the English proceedings. No stay will be granted.[10]

(2) K is a property developer with extensive interests in Panonian holiday resort developments. K lives with his family in Panonia but also, at times, arranges to stay in London. K regularly visits England as well as other European and Scandinavian cities in order to sell holiday homes in Panonia. Insolvency proceedings are under way in Panonia; a petition has also been presented by creditors in England. Although K's business activities were centred in Panonia, creditors are distributed throughout Europe and Scandinavia, there being no absolute majority in any one country. Nevertheless, the English creditors amount to less than 10% of the whole body of creditors. The creditors in Panonia constitute some 40%. Many of the English creditors are purchasers from K of property in Panonia, it being alleged that K has sold inferior and sub-standard property in breach of the terms of the parties' agreement. Such agreements are governed by the laws of Panonia. The relevant application having been made, a stay of English proceedings would be granted.

---

[7] Article 3(1).
[8] Article 3(2).
[9] Article 31.
[10] The French court is not clearly more appropriate.

(3) As in Illustration 2, above, however, the English creditors[11] establish that they would be discriminated against under the laws of Panonia, the Panonian creditors having first claim to K's assets. The English proceedings would not be stayed.

(4) The debtor was engaged in a large number of business ventures in New York and throughout the United States. The debtor also had an office in England. Insolvency proceedings have been commenced in New York. A petition has also been presented by a creditor in England. The majority of creditors is in the United States where, in addition, the debtor's assets are largely located. The English claims constitute less than 3% of the overall amount. Important documentary evidence and relevant witnesses are in the United States. There is no suggestion that the English creditors would not receive fair treatment in the United States; and most English creditors have no objection to a stay of the English proceedings. However, there are preferred creditors in England, according to English law, who would not enjoy such preference in the New York court. The English court will order a stay on condition that the English assets, once collected in, are used first to satisfy the preferred creditors, the remaining assets to be given over to the foreign court.[12]

(5) As in Illustration 4, above, however in the New York proceedings the revenue authorities of the United States have entered claims amounting to some 20% of the total debts. As the New York proceedings are not simply, as a matter of substance, an attempt to enforce a revenue debt,[13] the English court may stay its own proceedings upon condition that the preferred creditors are satisfied as in Illustration 4.

---

[11] The burden of proof being upon the creditors resisting the stay.

[12] *Stabb, Preston and Prowse (Assignees)* v. *Stabb, Preston, Prowse & Co. (Trustees)* (1821) Nfld. LR 298 and *Re National Benefit Assurance Co.* [1927] 3 D.L.R. 289. See also chapter 14.

[13] Chapter 7, *post.*

Chapter 4

Companies: Winding Up and Administration

1. INTRODUCTION

When dealing with a corporation, be it English or otherwise, the law of the place of incorporation has always been considered as playing an important though by no means exclusive role. Thus it can come as no surprise to learn that the English court may wind up an English company: just as such a company is created under United Kingdom legislation so too may it be dissolved.[1] Yet it is equally plain on the authorities that the English court has a broad statutory jurisdiction to make a winding up order in respect of a foreign company,[2] although, of course, a foreign company can only actually be dissolved under the law of the country in which it was incorporated.[3] By virtue of provisions derived from the Companies Acts[4] but now found in Part V of the Insolvency Act 1986, foreign companies come within the category of 'unregistered companies' and fall to be wound up accordingly. In particular, the predecessors of what are now sections 220 and 221 of the Insolvency Act 1986 have often been relied upon as founding jurisdiction. However, it must be stated at the outset that Part V of the Insolvency Act 1986 is not altogether satisfactory. Whereas jurisdiction in matters of personal insolvency is clearly and directly spelt out under the Act,[5] the jurisdiction to wind up foreign companies is somewhat disguised. For, perhaps surprisingly, sections 220 and 221 do not expressly mention foreign companies; and the one section in Part V which refers in terms to 'companies incorporated outside Great Britain' (section 225) is largely otiose. Moreover, albeit only in a limited range of situations, Part V of the Act is not comprehensive and reference must also at times[6] be made to the Civil Jurisdiction and Judgments Act 1982. Accordingly, practitioners

---

[1] See the Insolvency Act 1986, s. 117.
[2] See *Banque des Marchands de Moscou (Koupetschesky)* v. *Kindersley* [1951] Ch. 112, *Re Compania Merabello San Nicholas S.A.* [1973] Ch. 75, *Re a Company (No. 00359 of 1987)* [1988] Ch. 210 and *Re Mid East Trading Ltd.* [1997] 3 All E.R. 481; *discussed post.*
[3] *Re Matheson Bros Ltd.* (1984) 27 Ch. D. 225 at 229 *per* Kay J; *Mercantile Credits Ltd.* v. *Foster Clark (Australia) Ltd.* (1964) 112 C.L.R. 169 at 176.
[4] Companies Act 1862, s. 199; Companies Act 1929, s. 338; Companies Act 1948, s. 399; Companies Act 1985, s. 666.
[5] Insolvency Act 1986, s. 265; chapter 2, *ante.*
[6] In particular where a company is solvent and has its 'seat' in a Contracting State other than the United Kingdom: Civil Jurisdiction and Judgments Act 1982, s. 43; Sch. 1, Arts. 1(2) and 16(2); discussed *post.*

must approach the jurisdiction to wind up foreign companies with some care. Nor should it be overlooked that once jurisdiction is established there exists a discretion to stay an English winding up in favour of proceedings in a foreign forum.

Yet if the statutory framework in relation to the winding up in England of foreign companies is to a certain extent unsatisfactory, it is somewhat worse when it comes to the making of administration orders. Of course, under Part II of the Insolvency Act 1986 the court may make an administration order in relation to an English company, but whether an order can generally be made with reference to a foreign company has provoked considerable debate.[7] It is by no means clear why Parliament did not expressly deal with the matter in the 1986 legislation.

2. UNITED KINGDOM COMPANIES AND WINDING UP

Under section 117 of the Insolvency Act 1986 the High Court has jurisdiction to wind up any company registered in England. Like jurisdiction is pursuant to section 120 exercised by the Court of Session with regard to companies registered in Scotland. The English court cannot wind up Scottish companies.[8] Northern Ireland companies will normally be wound up in Northern Ireland, pursuant to the Insolvency (Northern Ireland) Order.[9]

In the first edition this author expressed the view that the English court had no power (except in one particular circumstance) to wind up a company incorporated in Northern Ireland. The opposite conclusion was reached in *Re a Company (No. 007946 of 1993)* by Morritt J.[10] Nevertheless, it is respectfully submitted that his Lordship's decision is wrong; and (even if correct) in practice it may be inadvisable to rely upon the judgment of Morritt J rather than following the obvious route of having the company liquidated in Northern Ireland.

The existence of the jurisdiction of the English court in respect of English companies is without qualification. Nothing in the Civil Jurisdiction and Judgments Act 1982 has any bearing upon the matter.[11] Moreover, an English company may be wound up in England quite irrespective of the nationality of its shareholders, the country in which its business has been conducted or, indeed, that a foreign court has already sought to put the company into liquidation. In *Re Suresnes Racecourse Co. Ltd.*[12] an English registered company had its business offices and the bulk of its assets in France, where the local courts had appointed a liquidator: nevertheless, Kekewich J made an order upon the petition of an English creditor. *North Australian Territory Co. Ltd.* v. *Goldsbrough, Mort and Co. Ltd.*[13]

---

[7] See, p. 130, *infra*.

[8] *Re Scottish Joint Stock Trust Bank* [1900] W.N.114; but if a company registered in England has by mistake its registered office in Scotland it may still only be wound up in England: see *Re Baby Moon (U.K.) Ltd* [1985] P.C.C. 103.

[9] S.I. 1989, No. 2405 N.I. 19.

[10] The issue is discussed fully, at p. 113 *infra*.

[11] The effect of s. 43 of the 1982 Act is that an English company cannot have its seat outside the United Kingdom for the purpose of Article 16(2); discussed *post*.

[12] (1890) 90 L.T. Jo. 55.

[13] (1889) 61 L.T. 716 applied in *Re B.C.C.I. (No. 10)* [1997] Ch. 213 at 241.

concerned an English company with a branch and the most part of its business in Australia. On 9th August 1889 the shareholders in England resolved that the company should be wound up voluntarily. But on 1st August 1889 a winding up petition had already been presented to the Supreme Court of South Australia and an order made by that court. Kay J held that the foreign compulsory order would not in the least degree affect the validity of a voluntary winding up in England. In short, that one is dealing with an English company is itself the only fact necessary to found jurisdiction.[14]

3. WINDING UP FOREIGN COMPANIES

A. General

There is no shortage of reported instances wherein the English court has wound up a foreign company. In each case[15] the English court has acted under provisions corresponding to sections 220 and 221 of the Insolvency Act 1986. Foreign companies are within the definition of unregistered companies in section 220 and fall to be wound up accordingly. Section 221(5), by no means a narrowly drawn provision, specifies the circumstances in which an unregistered company may be wound up:

'(a) if the company is dissolved, or has ceased to carry on business, or is carrying on business only for the purpose of winding up its affairs;

(b) if the company is unable to pay its debts;

(c) if the court is of the opinion that it is just and equitable that the company should be wound up.'

Brief reference to the facts of a selection of cases gives some general indication of the range of situations in which a foreign company may be wound up.

In one instance a New Zealand company had conducted a certain amount of trade through a branch office in London. The company's shareholders and creditors were mostly in New Zealand where winding up proceedings were already under way. The company had assets and liabilities in London. Kay J determined that the English court had jurisdiction to make a winding up order.[16]

In *Banque des Marchands de Moscou (Koupetschesky)* v. *Kindersley*[17] the plaintiff bank was a Russian corporation which had been dissolved by decrees of the Soviet Government in 1918. In 1932 a winding up order had been made in England. The validity of that winding up order was challenged when, in 1949, an action was brought by the liquidator against

---

[14] Although in the case of a solvent English company the English court might decline jurisdiction in favour of a more appropriate foreign forum, see *Re Harrods (Buenos Aires) Ltd.* [1992] Ch, 72, it would be unlikely to do so where the company was insolvent: England being the place where the primary liquidation would in principle occur.

[15] In *Re Tea Trading Co.; K. & C. Popoff Bros.* [1933] Ch. 647 the equivalent of s. 225 may have been used.

[16] *Re Matheson Bros Ltd.* (1884) 27 Ch. D. 225, although Kay J on the facts exercised his discretion not to make an order: note also *Re Syria Ottoman Rly Co.* (1904) 20 T.L.R. 217.

[17] [1951] Ch. 112 affirming [1950] 2 All E.R. 105: see Lipstein (1952) 11 C.L.J. 198, *passim*.

the defendants. The bank had not established any branch office in England. However, an agent of the bank had visited England to transact business. Moreover, there were considerable assets in England. The Court of Appeal held that there was jurisdiction to make the winding up order and such order had rightly been made.

In *Compania Merabello San Nicholas S.A.*[18] the petitioners had obtained judgment in England (for breach of a contract of carriage) against the company. The company was a so-called 'one-ship company' incorporated in Panama. At all material times the company's ship had been insured with a mutual insurance club ('Oceanus'). Neither the company nor Oceanus had satisfied the petitioners' judgment and the only known asset of the company was its right against Oceanus (a right which must have been situated in England). The English court made a winding up order, the consequence being that the right of the company against Oceanus automatically vested in the petitioners pursuant to the Third Parties (Rights Against Insurers) Act 1930.

In a more recent example[19] a Guernsey company, which had substantial interests in Portuguese real estate and Portuguese companies, was controlled and run by an individual resident in England – although the company itself did not have any place of business in England. A number of loans had been made by the petitioner to the company, those loans having been negotiated, dealt with and drawn down in London. Despite the fact that the company did not have any assets in England, Harman J made a winding up order.[20]

Before turning to consider in detail Part V of the 1986 Act, brief reference may be made to issues of State immunity. *Re Rafidain Bank*[1] concerned an insolvent Iraqi bank (owned by the State of Iraq) in respect of which provisional liquidators had been appointed following the presentation of a winding up petition by the Bank of England. The Iraqi embassy's accounts with Rafidain Bank were in credit and the embassy had requested that the provisional liquidators pay over certain sums to enable the embassy to meet various commitments. One of the arguments raised by the embassy was that the winding up impleaded a foreign State, in that the appointment of the provisional liquidators prevented the embassy having access to its funds. That contention was rejected by Browne-Wilkinson V-C on the basis that the winding up did not call into question the title of the State of Iraq to the debt owed by Rafidain Bank, rather the proceedings merely suspended the right immediately to enforce payment thereof.[2] Moreover, the fact that it might be said that the State of Iraq as a creditor had an interest in the assets of Rafidain Bank in no way prevented the exercise of the court's winding up jurisdiction.[3] The Vice-Chancellor left open the question as to whether the winding up petition itself impleaded a foreign State, for Rafidain Bank was actually owned by the State of Iraq. However, the older authorities make it fairly plain that simply because a foreign government owns some or all of the shares in a

---

[18] [1973] Ch. 75.
[19] *Re a Company (No. 003102 of 1991), ex p Nyckeln Finance Co Ltd.* [1991] B.C.L.C. 539.
[20] Applying *Re a Company (No. 00359 of 1987)* [1988] Ch. 210, discussed below.
[1] [1992] B.C.L.C. 301.
[2] *Ibid.*, at 304.
[3] *Ibid.*, referring to s. 6(3) of the State Immunity Act 1978.

company does not mean that a claim for immunity from winding up proceedings can be maintained.[4]

B. Definition of Unregistered Companies

Section 220 of the Insolvency Act defines the expression 'unregistered company' as including 'any association and any company' with the following exceptions:

'(a) [repealed]
(b) a company registered in any part of the United Kingdom under the Joint Stock Companies Acts or under legislation (past or present) relating to companies in Great Britain.'

Thus a wide range of business associations fall within section 220. It is not necessary to ascertain the precise scope of section 220 as foreign companies are undoubtedly included.[5] A foreign company is considered to be an 'unregistered company' whether or not it has submitted particular for registration under sections 690 or 690A of the Companies Act 1985.[6]

C. Jurisdictional Criteria under Section 221

Section 221(1) permits the winding up under the Insolvency Act 1986 of any unregistered company, whilst section 221(5) lays down five situations in which the court may act: (i) if the company has been dissolved; (ii) if the company has ceased to carry on business; (iii) if the company is carrying on business only for the purposes of winding up its affairs; (iv) if the company is unable to pay its debts; or (v) if it is just and equitable that the company should be wound up. The circumstances laid down in section 221(5) are independent and not cumulative.[7]

It must be noted that section 221(5) identifies no specific jurisdictional requirement. That is, no particular factual nexus or link to England is expressed. On the face of it therefore it may seem that the English court is given jurisdiction to wind up any foreign company which is, for example, unable to pay its debts. Such a company might have neither English creditors nor debtors, no assets in England nor shareholders; so too it might never have carried on business in England either by opening a

---

[4] *Per* Lord Maugham in *The Cristina* [1938] A.C. 485 at 520, citing *Re Russian Bank for Foreign Trade* [1933] Ch. 745 at 769.

[5] Section 220 does not, however, include international organisations established by treaties. 'English judges cannot meddle with unincorporated treaties' *per* Lord Templeman in *J. H. Rayner (Mincing Lane) Ltd.* v. *Department of Trade and Industry* [1990] 2 A.C. 418 at 482. See also *per* the Court of Appeal [1989] Ch. 309 at 330–331. Note also *Arab Monetary Fund* v. *Hashim (No. 3)* [1991] 2 A.C.114 and *Westland Helicopters Ltd.* v. *Arab Organisation for Industrialisation* [1995] Q.B. 282.

[6] The comment of Harman J in *Re a Company (No. 003102 of 1991) ex p Nyckeln Finance Co. Ltd.* [1991] B.C.L.C. 539 at 540: 'The company has never filed any particulars pursuant to . . . the Companies Act 1985. It is thus an unregistered company within the meaning of s. 220 of the Insolvency Act 1986', should not be taken literally. See also *SFC* v. *MKI Corpn. Ltd.* [1995] 2 H.K.C. 79.

[7] *Banque des Marchands de Moscou (Koupetschesky)* v. *Kindersley* [1951] Ch. 112 at 125 *per* Evershed MR.

branch (or representative office) or by means of an agent. This would indeed be an exorbitant jurisdiction. However, the English court has been unwilling to claim jurisdiction to wind up any company anywhere in the world regardless of connection to the forum.[8] Hence it is to the cases that one must turn to ascertain those facts which have, in the past, been considered as constituting a sufficient connection to justify intervention by means of an English winding up order. In effect, the judges have suggested three major jurisdictional bases.

(i) *Branch Office in England*

In *Re Matheson Bros Ltd.*[9] it was decided that the Companies Act 1862 conferred jurisdiction to wind up a New Zealand company; the company had a branch office and assets in England. That decision was distinguished in *Re Lloyd Generale Italiano*,[10] Pearson J holding that there was no jurisdiction to wind up an Italian company that had merely carried on business through an agent in England and which did not have a branch office or any assets in England. His Lordship's determination was more than likely founded upon the absence of a branch office. The judgment contains no reference, not even in passing, to the lack of English assets.

It may well be that in practice a foreign company will indeed have an office and carry on business in England. In such a situation there is no question that the English court will have jurisdiction. The collapse of BCCI, perhaps the most celebrated cross-border insolvency of all time, of course involved branch offices in England[11] (and elsewhere[12]). Yet matters have not stood still since the decision in *Re Lloyd Generale Italiano*. Subsequent cases have significantly lowered the jurisdictional hurdle.

(ii) *Place of Business in England*

In *Tovarishestvo Manufactur Liudvig–Rabenek*[13] Cohen J held that it was not necessary that a foreign company have a branch office in England, provided there was a 'place of business' albeit a temporary office or merely an hotel room where the directors transacted business. However, the Court

---

[8] 'As a matter of general principle, our courts would not assume, and Parliament should not be taken to have intended to confer, jurisdiction over matters which naturally and properly lie within the competence of the courts of other countries': *per* Evershed MR in *Banque des Marchands de Moscou (Koupetschesky)* v. *Kindersley* [1951] Ch. 112 at 125–126. See also *Re Titan International Inc* [1998] 1 B.C.L.C. 102 at 106 *per* Peter Gibson LJ.

[9] See p. 95, n. 16, *supra*.

[10] (1885) 29 Ch. D. 219, reconsidered below.

[11] A good summary of the facts and international insolvency law issues can be found in *Re Bank of Credit and Commerce International S.A. (No. 10)* [1997] Ch. 213.

[12] For an example of the insolvency of a branch in France, see *Bank of Credit and Commerce International* v. *Forde* [1993] I.L.Pr. 377.

[13] [1944] Ch. 404. Cf. *Re a Company (No. 003102 of 1991), ex p Nyckeln Finance Co. Ltd.* [1991] B.C.L.C. 539, foreign company's affairs conducted from a hotel in Watford: and note *Re Dendre Valley Rly and Canal Co.* (1850) 19 LJ Ch. 474 (Belgian company with board of directors in London).

of Appeal in *Banque des Marchands de Moscou (Koupetschesky)* v. *Kindersley* took a different view.[14] Sir Raymond Evershed MR rejected the proposition that a place of business in England, still less a branch office, was a condition to the existence of jurisdiction in the English court to wind up a foreign company. Evershed MR considered that jurisdiction was made out provided there were assets in England together with persons concerned or interested in the proper distribution of those assets.[15] The Master of the Rolls explained *Re Lloyd Generale Italiano* on the basis that the Italian company did not have any assets in England. In summary, as a general rule the English court may wind up a foreign company with assets in England whether or not that company has, or ever had, any branch or place of business in England.

(iii) *Presence of Assets*

Banque des Marchands de Moscou (Koupetschesky) v. *Kindersley*[16] has been approved both in England[17] and elsewhere.[18] Later cases have, in particular, given guidance upon the need for assets in England. First, the assets in question need not be 'commercial' assets or in any way derived from the carrying on of business in England; assets of whatever nature will suffice.[19] A right of action belonging to the company which has a reasonable (but not guaranteed) possibility of success is considered to be an asset for these purposes.[20] Secondly, there is no requirement that the assets in England be of substantial value; some asset, though negligible in worth, will be enough. Hence in *Re Wallace Smith & Co. Ltd.*[1] a modest amount in a London bank account, though trivial in comparison to the company's assets abroad, was sufficient to found jurisdiction: although the court declined to exercise its jurisdiction as there was a clearly more appropriate forum abroad.[2] Thirdly, a petitioner does not have to show that the asset or assets in question will come into the hands of the liquidator and later be distributed in the course of a winding up. For, it may be recalled, in *Re Compania Merabello San Nicholas S.A.* the court made a winding up order even though its immediate effect was to take the relevant asset (situated in

---

[14] [1951] Ch. 112 at 127. Evershed MR thought that the facts would, in any event, have satisfied a requirement of 'place of business'.

[15] *Ibid.*, at 126. The requirement that there are one or more persons interested in the proper distribution of the assets over whom jurisdiction can be exercised, is examined below at p. 105.

[16] [1951] Ch. 112. Note, *passim, Rose* v. *Laskington Ltd.* [1990] 1 Q.B. 562 at 572.

[17] See *Re Azoff-Don Commercial Bank* [1954] Ch. 315, *Re Compania Merabello San Nicholas S.A.* [1973] Ch. 75, *Re Allobrogia SS Corpn* [1978] 3 All E.R. 423 and *Re Real Estate Development Co.* [1991] B.C.L.C. 210 at 213.

[18] *Tong Aik (Far East) Ltd.* v. *Eastern Minerals and Trading (1959) Ltd.* [1965] 2 M.L.J. 149 (Singapore), *Re Kailis Groote Eylandt Fisheries Pty. Ltd.* (1977) 2 A.C.L.R. 574 (South Australia), *I.R.C.* v. *Highland Engineering Ltd.* 1975 S.L.T. 203 (Scotland) and *Re Irish Shipping Ltd.* [1985] H.K.L.R. 437 (Hong Kong).

[19] *Re Compania Merabello San Nicholas S.A.* [1973] Ch. 75 at 88 *per* Megarry J. However, claims which only arise by virtue of a winding up order, such as for wrongful or fraudulent trading, are not assets for this purpose, *per* Peter Gibson J in *Re a Company (No. 00359 of 1987)* [1988] Ch. 210 at 221: see also *Re Real Estate Development Co., supra,* at 222.

[20] *Re Allobrogia SS Corpn.* [1978] 3 All E.R. 423.

[1] [1992] B.C.L.C. 970.

[2] Discussed further, p. 127, *infra.*

England) out of any winding up and vest it directly in the petitioners. In that case Megarry J summarised the essentials of this area of the law in the following oft-cited passage:[3]

> '(1) There is no need to establish that the company ever had a place of business here. (2) There is no need to establish that the company ever carried on business here, unless perhaps the petition is based upon the company carrying on or having carried on business. (3) A proper connection with the jurisdiction must be established by sufficient evidence to show (a) that the company has some asset or assets within the jurisdiction, and (b) that there are one or more persons concerned in the proper distribution of the assets over whom the jurisdiction is exercisable. (4) It suffices if the assets of the company within the jurisdiction are of any nature; they need not be "commercial" assets, or assets which indicate that the company formerly carried on business here. (5) The assets need not be assets which will be distributable to creditors by the liquidator in the winding up: it suffices if by the making of the winding up order they will be of benefit to a creditor or creditors in some other way. (6) If it is shown that there is no reasonable possibility of benefit accruing to creditors from making the winding up order, the jurisdiction is excluded.'

Whether there are assets within the jurisdiction is to be determined as at the moment the petition is presented.[4]

(iv) *A More Flexible Approach*

As section 221 does not specify any jurisdictional criteria the matter has inevitably been left to the courts. Judges in the past sought to identify one single factor as the fundamental basis of jurisdiction – such as the presence of assets test. Yet reliance upon one single factor is not only rigid but may also lead to arbitrary results. For example, a foreign company fearing that a winding up petition is likely may deliberately remove all its assets from England the very day before the petition is presented. Certainly, it is relevant to observe that in *Derby & Co. Ltd.* v. *Weldon (Nos. 3 and 4)*[5] the Court of Appeal held that the absence of English assets does not prevent the granting (either pre-judgment or post-judgment) of a Mareva injunction against a foreign company, coupled with the appointment of a receiver. As Lord Donaldson of Lymington MR commented:[6]

> 'We live in a time of rapidly growing commercial and financial sophistication and it behoves the courts to adapt their practices to meet the current wiles of those defendants who are prepared to devote as much energy to making themselves immune to the courts' orders as to resisting the making of such orders on the merits of their case.'

---

[3] [1973] Ch. 75 at 91–92.
[4] See *Re Real Estate Development Co.* [1991] B.C.L.C. 210 at 217 and *Re Kailis Groote Eylandt Fisheries Pty. Ltd.* (1977) 2 A.C.L.R. 574. The view (*obiter*) of Jones J in *Re Irish Shipping Ltd.* [1985] H.K.L.R. 437 at 444, that it was sufficient if there were assets within the jurisdiction when the petition is heard, cannot be supported. Either the court has jurisdiction when the petition is presented or it does not.
[5] [1990] Ch. 65.
[6] *Ibid.*, at 77.

Similar observations have been made not infrequently in the context of cross-border insolvency.[7] It is remarkable that Parliament in the Insolvency Act 1986 increased the number of bases of jurisdiction in bankruptcy to five,[8] but left the winding up of foreign companies unaltered and very much at large.

The English court has not found the presence of assets test wholly satisfactory, and in the two leading first instance cases, *Re Eloc Electro-Optieck and Communicatie B.V.* and *Re a Company (No. 00359 of 1987)*,[9] significant qualifications were advanced. Such qualifications have been approved and applied by trial judges several times and have recently been considered by the Court of Appeal.[10]

In the former, a Dutch company had engaged the petitioners to carry on its business in England. The petitioners were owed sums in respect of outstanding salaries and other remuneration. The company had no assets in England. However if a winding up order were made the petitioners could apply for payments from the Secretary of State out of the Redundancy Fund in accordance with the Employment Protection (Consolidation) Act 1978. Whilst there were indeed no assets of the company in England, Nourse J emphasised that Megarry J's summary in *Re Compania Merabello San Nicholas S.A.* was relevant 'so far as *normal* cases are concerned'[11] but was not universally applicable. In particular, his Lordship thought that 'the ownership of assets by the company is not a matter of crucial importance'.[12] Hence, a winding up order was made, even though the assets which the petitioners sought belonged not to the company but to an outside source.

In the latter case, the business of a Liberian company ('Okeanos') was managed in England by an associated company. The petitioning bank had in 1984 agreed to lend Okeanos around 13.5 million for the construction of a bulk carrier, Okeanos granting the bank a first preferred mortgage on the ship. In January 1987, Okeanos having defaulted, the bank recovered judgment in England and within a month a winding up petition was presented. Yet Okeanos had no assets in England: its only known asset (the ship) being 'semi laid-up' somewhere off Indonesia. Peter Gibson J, after reviewing the authorities, arrived at a noteworthy conclusion:[13]

> 'In the circumstances, I am prepared consistently with the *Eloc* case [1982] Ch. 43 to hold that the presence of assets in this country is not an essential condition for the court to have jurisdiction in relation to the winding up of a foreign company. In my judgment, provided a sufficient connection with the jurisdiction is shown, and there is a reasonable possibility of benefit for the creditors from the winding up, the court has jurisdiction to wind up the foreign company.'

With particular reference to the circumstances that the loan agreement was governed by English law, that the company by its agents had carried on

---

[7] See, for example, *per* Williams J in *The Cornelis Verolme* [1997] 2 N.Z.L.R. 110 at 126 and *per* Millett LJ in *Credit Suisse Fides Trust S.A.* v. *Cuoghi* [1997] 3 All E.R. 724 at 730.

[8] Namely, presence, domicile, ordinary residence, place of residence and the carrying on of business; Insolvency Act 1986, s. 265; chapter 2, *ante*.

[9] [1982] Ch. 43 and [1988] Ch. 210 (*sub nom. International Westminster Bank p.l.c.* v. *Okeanos Maritime Corpn.* [1987] B.C.L.C. 450, noted [1989] Lloyd's M.C.L.Q. 20).

[10] *Re Titan International Inc.* [1998] 1 B.C.L.C. 102, *infra*.

[11] [1982] Ch. 43 at 46 (original emphasis).

[12] *Ibid.*, at 48.

[13] [1988] Ch. 210 at 225–226.

business in England, and that there was no other more appropriate foreign jurisdiction[14] in which a winding up might be conducted, it was held that Okeanos had a sufficiently close connection with the forum to confer jurisdiction.[15]

(v) *Sufficient Connection Between the Company and England*

The sufficient connection test put forward by Peter Gibson J has been adopted and applied a number of times in the Chancery Division[16] and recently the matter came for the first time before the Court of Appeal.[17] Their Lordships rejected the submission that 'it is an essential condition . . . in all cases that there must be assets in the jurisdiction'.[18] The position may be summarised as follows:[19]

> '(1) that there must be a sufficient connection with England and Wales which may, but does not necessarily have to, consist of assets within the jurisdiction; (2) that there must be a reasonable possibility if a winding up order is made, of benefit for those applying for the winding up order; (3) one or more persons interested in the distribution of assets of the company must be persons over whom the court can exercise jurisdiction.'

Whether the connection between a foreign company and England (in the absence of assets in England) is sufficient to justify the court setting in motion its winding up procedures must always be a question of fact. In *Re a Company (No. 003102 of 1991), ex p Nyckeln Finance Co. Ltd.* that the company's business was in effect run out of an hotel room near Watford was considered a sufficient connection.[20] In *Re Mid East Trading Ltd.*,[1] where a Lebanese company which had acted as an investment adviser and had placed a substantial amount of business through the London office of Lehman Brothers Inc., the same conclusion was reached; and this was so even though there was no evidence that any of the company's clients were resident in England.[2]

On the other hand, Knox J ruled there was no jurisdiction in *Re Real Estate Development Co.*[3] A French bank had in mid-May 1986 obtained judgment in France against a Kuwaiti company ('the company'). That judgment was in August 1986 registered in England.[4] In early May 1986, shortly before the French court delivered its judgment, the company transferred its shareholding in an English company to another Kuwaiti

---

[14] The issue of a more appropriate foreign forum is dealt with below, p. 125.

[15] *Ibid.*, at 227.

[16] See *Re Real Estate Development Co.* [1991] B.C.L.C. 210, *Re a Company (No. 003102 of 1991), ex p Nyckeln Finance Co. Ltd.* [1991] B.C.L.C. 539, *Re Wallace Smith & Co. Ltd.* [1992] B.C.L.C. 970 and *Re Mid East Trading Ltd.* [1997] 3 All E.R. 481.

[17] *Re Titan International Inc.* [1998] 1 B.C.L.C. 102.

[18] *Ibid.*, at 107.

[19] Per Knox J in *Re Real Estate Development Co.*, *supra*, 217, approved in *Re Mid East Trading Ltd.*

[20] In fact, even under the test applied 50 years ago – a place of business – there would have been jurisdiction: see *Re Tovarishestvo Manufactur Liudvig-Rabenek* [1944] Ch. 404.

[1] *Supra.* The case went on appeal, see [1998] 1 All E.R. 577, but not on the jurisdiction issue.

[2] The judge said that 'the business was conducted with the assistance of and using the facilities of [Lehman Brothers] in England', *supra*, at 491.

[3] *Supra*, n. 16.

[4] This was prior to the Civil Jurisdiction and Judgments Act 1982 coming into effect.

company for a nil consideration. The shares in the English company were the only asset that the company had ever owned in England and there was no evidence led as to any business activity on the part of the company in England. Knox J concluded that there was no sufficient connection. His Lordship noted that whilst it had been suggested that, were the company to be wound up, a liquidator might have a good case to set aside the transfer of shares as a transaction defrauding creditors, the possibility of such an action depended upon the making of a winding up order; and, therefore, that prospective cause of action could not be regarded as an asset locally situated in England at the date of the presentation of the winding up petition.[5] Whilst not doubting the correctness of the ruling of Knox J, it is important to note that a quite different approach to the type of fact situation in *Re Real Estate Development Co.* should now be taken. The French bank, even before obtaining judgment in France, would invoke section 25 of the Civil Jurisdiction and Judgments Act 1982 to obtain a Mareva injunction in aid of the French proceedings.[6] (Thereby preventing the company from disposing of the English shares.) Moreover, as from April 1997 the restrictions formerly imposed by section 25 upon the granting of interim relief have been removed – so that in particular the English court can now grant interim relief in aid of any foreign proceedings, whether or not commenced in State party to the Brussels or Lugano Conventions.[7]

Re Titan International Inc.[8] involved a multi-level snowball or money circulation scheme which the authorities in the United Kingdom were anxious to close down in the public interest. The scheme, itself a variation on an earlier 'Titan' scheme,[9] was run by 'LLC', a limited liability company incorporated in Wyoming and in respect of which provisional liquidators had (by the time the case came before the Court of Appeal) been appointed. LLC carried out all relevant activities in England, but then sent a certain proportion of the funds collected from 'members' to Titan International Inc. ('the company') which was an offshore investment vehicle for the scheme. Both LLC and the company were under the control of a certain individual. Although the winding up petition was a public interest petition, pursuant to section 124A of the Insolvency Act 1986, the Court of Appeal approved the approach in *Re Real Estate Development Co.*, rejected the contention that the presence of assets was an essential prerequisite for the existence of jurisdiction and applied the sufficient connection test.[10] (Peter Gibson LJ delivered the leading judgment and modestly did not mention his earlier decision.) On the facts, however, their Lordships ruled that the company had no assets in England and had not at any time carried out any activities in England. Peter Gibson LJ observed:[11]

'To arrogate to the English court jurisdiction to wind up a foreign company merely because of its association as an investment vehicle outside the jurisdiction with another foreign company that has been active within the jurisdiction

[5] At 222, applying *Re a Company (No. 000359 of 1987)* [1988] Ch. 210.
[6] Assuming that the assets were at risk of dissipation, of course.
[7] See the discussion of the amendment in 1997 at p. 397, *infra*.
[8] [1998] 1 B.C.L.C. 102. See also *Re Vanilla Accumulation Ltd.*, (1998) Times, 24 February (Dutch 'partnership').
[9] See *Re Senator Hanseatische Verwaltungsgesellschaft mbH* [1996] 2 B.C.L.C. 562.
[10] *Supra* n. 8 at 107.
[11] *Ibid.*, at 108–109.

would be in my view to make a giant, impermissible and unjustified extension of the jurisdiction of the English court.'

(vi)   *Criticism of the Sufficient Connection Test*

Although the appropriateness of the sufficient connection test has not been called into question by any English court, the test is not without its difficulties. Of course, as has been noted, there is no logical reason why the jurisdiction of the court should depend solely upon the presence of assets (or indeed any other single factor). Equally plain is that a presence of assets test may produce lamentable results.[12] Nevertheless, reference to whether a foreign company has a sufficient connection to England is, in this author's opinion, open to serious criticism.

As a basis of jurisdiction, close or sufficient connection is too vague. A number of different factors taken singly or in combination might be indicative of some connection. Hence the whole history of a company might have to be examined and debated. It may be noted that *Re a Company (No. 000359 of 1987)* was heard over six days; a more complex case might involve a longer hearing just to determine that the English court lacked jurisdiction.[13] These difficulties are enhanced if as Peter Gibson J thought the very existence of jurisdiction depends upon 'whether any other jurisdiction is more appropriate for the winding up.'[14] This approach was also taken by Harman J in *Re a Company (No. 003102 of 1991)*, ex p Nyckeln Finance Co. Ltd. when determining that neither the place of incorporation of the company or the courts of Portugal, where the assets were located, was more appropriate than England (where the business had been managed).[15] With respect to Peter Gibson and Harman JJ, the better view must surely be that the appropriateness of a foreign forum goes to the *exercise* of jurisdiction rather than its very existence. It is significant to note that the most recent decision upon this particular issue has taken the view that the matter is one of discretion.[16] In any event, even if one accepts that the appropriateness of a foreign forum is a discretion issue, a jurisdictional test based upon sufficient connection remains inherently uncertain.[17]

Moreover, from a theoretical standpoint, a sufficient connection test raises something of an inconsistency. The test has been described as a means 'to establish a link of genuine substance between the company and this country'.[18] Yet it is fair to ask whether the presence of assets of a trifling amount constitutes a link of any substance, genuine or otherwise. The inconsistency between 'any asset' and 'substantial connection' is perhaps one reason why a court in Hong Kong, attempting to apply the

---

[12] See, for example *Re Eloc Electro-Optieck and Communicatie B.V.* [1982] Ch. 43 at 48 *per* Nourse J.

[13] The hearing in *Re Real Estate Development Co.*, *supra*, took place over three days to decide there was no jurisdiction.

[14] [1988] Ch. 210 at 226.

[15] [1991] B.C.L.C. 539 at 541.

[16] See *Re Wallace Smith & Co. Ltd.* [1992] B.C.L.C. 970, discussed below, p. 127.

[17] For a defence of sufficient connection, see Morse, 'Principles and Pragmatism in English Cross-Border Insolvency' in *Insolvency Law: Theory and Practice* (ed. Rajak) (1993) pp. 206–209.

[18] *Re Real Estate Development Co.* [1991] B.C.L.C. 210 at 217, *per* Knox J.

English cases and having found that there were assets in the jurisdiction, then went on to look at all the circumstances to see if there was a sufficient connection to Hong Kong.[19] It would appear on the authorities, however, that the view of English judges is that provided there are some assets (even if trivial) no genuine link is required.[20]

In the first edition of this work it was suggested that a sufficient connection approach was too uncertain and that jurisdiction should rather be founded upon specific forensic connections to the forum.[1] It was also pointed out that the facts in *Re Eloc Electro-Optieck* and *Re a Company (No. 000359 of 1987)*[2] permitted of a simple explanation: in both cases the foreign company carried on business in England through its agents. It would be inconceivable that the English court would have held in favour of jurisdiction in *Re A Company* if the company's ship agents had been based in Paris or Athens instead of London. Fortunately, the more recent cases are quite consistent with the suggested approach. In neither *Re Real Estate Development Co.* or *Re Titan International Inc.*[3] (no jurisdiction) were any business activities by the company in question carried on in England. Whereas in the two cases where jurisdiction was made out,[4] the judges ruled on the facts that business had been carried on to a greater or lesser degree in England.[5] Thus, whilst it is now perhaps too late even for the Court of Appeal to side-step the sufficient connection test,[6] it is still maintained that (in the absence of assets) it is only where business has in one way or another been carried on in England that the court should have jurisdiction to wind up a foreign company. Further, as a matter of common sense, if a foreign company has no assets and has never carried on business directly or indirectly in England, there can be little justification for intervention by the English court whatever other connections to England may exist.

(vii) *Petitioner's Connection to the Forum*

It will be recalled that the third requirement in the summary of Knox J in *Re Real Estate Development Co.* was that 'one or more persons interested in the distribution of assets of the company must be persons over whom the court can exercise jurisdiction'.[7] It is important to stress at the outset that this 'third requirement' applies even where there are assets in England: this

---

[19] *Re China Tianjin International Economic and Technical Co-operative Corpn.* [1994] 2 H.K.L.R. 327, see Booth and Smart [1996] J.I.B.L. 216.

[20] It is stated in *7(3) Halsbury's Laws* (4th ed) (1996 reissue) para. 2909: 'A foreign company . . . may be wound up as an unregistered company if it has assets in England, or if a sufficient connection with England and Wales can be shown. . . .' This was approved in *Re Mid East Trading Ltd.* [1997] 3 All E.R. 481 at 490.

[1] At p. 64, see also n. 17, *supra*.

[2] Both *supra*.

[3] Both *supra*.

[4] *Re a Company (No. 0003102 of 1991), ex p Nyckeln Finance Co. Ltd.* [1991] B.C.L.C. 539 and *Re Mid East Trading Ltd.* [1997] 3 All E.R. 481.

[5] Although this commentator would suggest that *Re Mid East Trading Ltd.* was perhaps somewhat near the line.

[6] For the test was applied by their Lordships in *Re Titan International Inc.*, above, as well as being approved *obiter* in *Re Paramount Airways Ltd.* [1993] Ch. 223 at 240.

[7] *Supra*, p. 102.

third requirement is not just part of a 'sufficient connection' test.[8] Indeed, it was Evershed MR who as long ago as 1950 stated:[9]

'There must be assets here . . . and persons subject, or at least submitting, to the jurisdiction . . . .'

The practical difficulty, however, is to ascertain the scope of this third requirement. There appears to be sufficiently clear authority to establish the following:

(1)   if the petitioning creditor is English[10] (or has been resident or employed in England[11]) this requirement will be satisfied;
(2)   but it cannot be stated that the petitioning creditor must be resident in England;[12] and
(3)   it is not necessary that any potential creditor is English – that all the creditors are foreign does not of itself preclude the court from making a winding up order.[13]

Beyond, however, these general principles the waters become somewhat muddied. In *Re Real Estate Development Co.* Knox J pointed out that the reason for this requirement was not so that the court can control the winding up process, for the liquidator will throughout be subject to the directions of the court.[14] Similarly, it would be meaningless if all this requirement was concerned with were that someone had submitted to the jurisdiction of the English court: for whenever a petition for winding up is presented someone will be submitting to the court's control. Rather Knox J's view was that this requirement was designed to ensure that those persons who were likely to benefit from the winding up:[15]

'. . . qualify for one reason or another as persons on whose behalf it would be right to set in motion the winding up petition over a foreign company.'

In other words, Knox J was concerned on the facts to see that there was a sufficient connection with England not only in relation to the company but also in respect of the potential beneficiaries under the winding up process.[16] In a cross-border insolvency context this means a sufficient connection between the *creditors* and the forum.

---

[8]   The requirements are (1) that there is a sufficient connection, which may or may not consist of assets; (2) that there is a reasonable possibility of benefit; and (3) that the court must be able to exercise jurisdiction over one or more persons interested in the distribution of the company's assets: see *Re Titan International Inc.* [1998] 1 B.C.L.C. 102 at 107.

[9]   *Banque des Marchands de Moscou (Koupetschesky)* v. *Kindersley* [1951] Ch. 112 at 125, [1950] 2 All E.R. 549 at 556.

[10] As in *Re a Company (No. 003102 of 1991), ex p Nyckeln Finance Co. Ltd., supra.*

[11] In *Re Real Estate Development Co.* [1991] B.C.L.C. 210 at 218 Knox J observed: 'In the *Eloc* case the petitioners were citizens of the United States, but the jurisdiction was exercised, so there is no question of a rule that foreign petitioners do not qualify. In their case, I venture to suggest, it was exercised and arose because they had been employees in this country. . . .'

[12] In *Re Azoff-Don Commercial Bank* [1954] Ch. 315 the joint petitioners were all foreign banks.

[13] See *Re Kailis Groote Eylandt Fisheries Pty. Ltd.* (1977) 2 A.C.L.R. 574 at 579.

[14] *Supra,* n. 11, at 217.

[15] *Ibid.*

[16] As his Lordship stated (at 217): 'Throughout the investigation into whether the court has jurisdiction, the aim is to discover a sufficient connection with this jurisdiction *and that is as true in relation to the potential beneficiaries* as it is in relation to the company which it is sought to wind up.' (Emphasis added.)

It will be recalled that in *Re Real Estate Development Co.* the petitioners were French and had no connection with England, except that their French judgment had been registered in England. Knox J expressly held that there had not been shown 'a sufficient nexus between this country and those who might benefit from the making of a winding up order'.[17] Thus there was no jurisdiction to make an order. In *Re Mid East Trading Ltd.*[18] Evans-Lombe J quoted with approval the approach of Knox J and rejected counsel's submission that it followed from Knox J's judgment that 'some at least of the potential proving creditors must be resident' in England.[19] Evans-Lombe J made a winding up order[20] but, oddly, gave no indication of what facts established the genuine link between the petitioner and England.[1]

A variation upon the facts in *Re Real Estate Development Co.* illustrates the type of case in which this third requirement presents serious problems. Let us say that the facts are exactly as before Knox J except that the Kuwaiti company does indeed have assets in England. According to the judgment of Knox J the court could have no jurisdiction to make a winding up order because of the absence of 'a sufficient connection with this jurisdiction . . . in relation to the potential beneficiaries' of the winding up.[2] Yet as the presentation of a winding up petition by a creditor in respect of an undisputed debt is perfectly legitimate (and the company has assets in England), it strikes this author as surprising that the question of jurisdiction comes down to whether the petitioner is English or French: the court has jurisdiction if the creditor is English, but not if the petitioner is French.[3]

This author would suggest that the connections of the petitioner to England should no longer form part of any relevant inquiry when it comes to establishing the existence of jurisdiction to wind up a foreign company.[4] Rather such considerations should be taken into account if and when the English court is asked not to *exercise* a jurisdiction it undoubtedly possesses.[5]

(viii) Re Lloyd Generale Italiano *Reconsidered*

The readiness to claim jurisdiction over foreign companies is highlighted by the fact that *Re Lloyd Generale Italiano*[6] is only one of a handful of

---

[17] *Ibid.*, at 222.
[18] [1997] 3 All E.R. 481; *supra*, p. 102.
[19] *Ibid.*, at 491.
[20] This part of the judgment was not appealed: see [1998] 1 All E.R. 577 at 580.
[1] It may have been that the investors' money had initially been transferred to England.
[2] *Supra*, n. 16.
[3] It may be noted that in *Re China Tianjin International Economic and Technical Co-operative Corpn.*, *supra*, p. 105 n. 19, the Hong Kong court wound up a foreign company (as an unregistered company) which had assets in Hong Kong, on a petition presented by an English judgment creditor who had no connection to Hong Kong other than that the English judgment had been registered in Hong Kong prior to the presentation of the winding up petition.
[4] This conclusion is not intended as any criticism of Knox J who was merely applying the established authorities.
[5] Discussed p. 125, *infra*.
[6] (1885) 29 Ch. D. 219.

reported examples in which the English court has held it lacked jurisdiction.[7] Thus it may be of interest to analyse the facts of that case in the modern context. An Italian company had extensive insurance business in Italy, England and elsewhere, the business in England being conducted by agents. The company had been put into liquidation in Italy and the liquidators wished to send money to England for payment of a dividend to the English creditors. The Italian liquidators, however, feared that if funds were sent to England, other than to a liquidator appointed in an English winding up, such money might be attached by certain of the English creditors. Thus it was the Italian liquidators who sought the English winding up in the name of the company. The company had no branch office or assets in England. Pearson J held that as the company had no office in England no winding up order could be made.

If the facts in *Re Lloyd Generale Italiano* were to reoccur, the English court would undoubtedly now have jurisdiction. For the company carried on business in England through agents.[8] The judgment of Pearson J would not now be followed. For, apart from being at first instance, the case has been so much explained that, as Megarry J once said, one 'cannot see what was left of the decision'.[9] If today one were advising the Italian liquidators, they should also be told to transfer some assets to the company's agent in England and then present a petition. The English court would accordingly have jurisdiction under two heads: carrying on business, as well as assets in England.

It should also be noted that a quite different course of action would currently be available to the foreign liquidators in *Re Lloyd Generale Italiano*. The liquidators had sought a winding up because they feared that one or more English creditors might attach any dividends or other property sent to England. However, in bankruptcy there is the authority of the House of Lords that the title of a foreign assignee will prevail over a creditor who attempts to attach property *after* the making of a foreign adjudication.[10] A like rule applies in corporate matters, although of course the company's property may not actually vest in a foreign liquidator. The case of *Felixstowe Dock and Rly Co.* v. *United States Lines Inc.*[11] illustrates the relevant principle. A United States company was undergoing reorganisation pursuant to the US Bankruptcy Code. The plaintiffs obtained Mareva injunctions restraining the company from removing certain assets out of England (and into the US proceedings). Hirst J determined upon the very particular facts that the Mareva injunctions would

---

[7] See also *Re Real Estate Development Co.* and *Re Titan International Inc.*, both *supra*. The Supreme Court of South Australia held it had no jurisdiction in *Re Kailis Groote Eylandt Fisheries Pty. Ltd.* (1977) 2 A.C.L.R. 574, the company had no assets and had never carried on business in South Australia. Assets were subsequently sent to South Australia and new proceedings commenced: see (1977) 3 A.C.L.R. 288, *passim*.

[8] The benefit to the creditors would be an undertaking by the foreign liquidators to remit assets to England upon the making of a winding up order. There were also creditors in England, thereby satisfying the 'third' requirement, above.

[9] *Re Compania Merabello San Nicholas S.A.* [1973] Ch. 75 at 85. That *Re Lloyd Generale Italiano* (1885) 29 Ch. D. 219 has been effectively overruled is evidenced by the fact that the case was not even cited in any case since 1973.

[10] *Galbraith* v. *Grimshaw* [1910] A.C. 508.

[11] [1989] Q.B. 360; p. 394, *post*.

not be discharged.[12] Nevertheless, his Lordship made it plain that where a corporation was in liquidation abroad the English court would not allow a judgment creditor to obtain a priority by attaching assets in England, such a judgment creditor would have to seek a winding up order.[13] Thus in *Re Lloyd Generale Italiano* any English creditor who sought to attach the company's property in England would now not be permitted to obtain a priority over other creditors. Rather that creditor would be allowed to proceed to judgment but would then have to petition for a winding up. As a general rule, once appointed, a foreign trustee or liquidator need not fear subsequent attachment by an English creditor attempting to obtain some advantage over the general body of creditors.

(ix) *Allocating Jurisdiction within the United Kingdom*

Section 221 of the Insolvency Act 1986 also deals with the distribution of jurisdiction within the United Kingdom according to where a foreign company has a principal place of business. Section 221(2) and (3) provides:

> '(2) If an unregistered company has a principal place of business situated in Northern Ireland, it shall not be wound up under this Part unless it has a principal place of business situated in England and Wales or Scotland, or in both England and Wales and Scotland.
> (3) For the purpose of determining a court's winding up jurisdiction, an unregistered company is deemed
> (a) to be registered in England and Wales or Scotland, according as its principal place of business is situated in England and Wales or Scotland, or
> (b) if it has a principal place of business situate in both countries, to be registered in both countries;
> and the principal place of business situated in that part of Great Britain in which proceedings are being instituted is, for all purposes of the winding up, deemed to be the registered office of the company.'

With reference to foreign companies these subsections do not require that there must be a principal place of business in England before the English court can order a winding up.[14] The subsections are relevant where the English court does, *prima facie*, have jurisdiction but the foreign company has a principal place of business in Northern Ireland or in Scotland. According to section 221(2) if a foreign company has a principal place of business in Northern Ireland, and no such place of business in England, the English court cannot make a winding up order. The effect of section 221(3) is that if a foreign company has a principal place of business in Scotland but no principal place of business in England, the company is deemed to be registered in Scotland and therefore any winding up must be in Scotland rather than in England.

---

[12] *Ibid.*, at 389. See now, in the normal type of case where there is no discrimination against English creditors, *Banque Indosuez S.A.* v. *Ferromet Resources Inc.* [1993] B.C.L.C. 112.

[13] As Hirst J observed (at 389): 'so far as prejudice is concerned, I am satisfied that U.S.L. will suffer no material prejudice if the Mareva injunctions continue, since the assets will remain safely here, and there is no prospect of their being distributed without the intervention of ancillary winding up proceedings'.

[14] *Re Compania Merabello San Nicholas S.A.* [1973] Ch. 75 at 84, cf. Lipstein (1952) 11 C.L.J. 198.

In summary (even where there are, for example, assets in England) the English court has no jurisdiction to wind up a foreign company which has a principal place of business in Northern Ireland or in Scotland and which does not have a principal place of business in England.

The existence of a principal place of business in any part of the United Kingdom is a question of fact. A foreign company may well have more than one principal place of business, as section 221(3)(b) clearly indicates.[15] Principal place of business does not mean the place of business to which major importance ought to be attached. Thus if a foreign company has offices in New York, Paris and Glasgow, the English court is not required to identify one single office as the company's major place of business worldwide. The relevant inquiry for the purposes of section 221(3) is whether there is a principal place of business in Scotland.[16] If there is only one office in Scotland (for example, in Glasgow) that will be a principal place of business in Scotland.

D. The Operation and Effect of Part V

Sections 220 and 221 fall within Part V of the Act ('Winding Up of Unregistered Companies'). Part V does not purport to contain any sort of comprehensive approach to the winding up of unregistered companies – indeed Part V has only ten sections – rather it is specified in section 221(1) that, subject to any exceptions or additions in the section, 'all the provisions of this Act and the Companies Act about winding up apply to an unregistered company'.[17] This is re-enforced by section 229(1) which states that the 'provisions of this Part . . . are in addition to and not in restriction of any provisions in Part IV with respect to winding up companies by the court.' Thus, for instance, although section 221(5) details the circumstances in which an unregistered company may be wound up – in particular that it is unable to pay its debts – and it would appear that the section is exhaustive (so that a foreign company may not resolve that it be *compulsorily* wound up pursuant to what is now section 122(1)(a)),[18] one must look to section 124 (in Part IV) to ascertain by whom a petition may be presented.[19] Similarly, if it is sought to appoint a provisional liquidator in relation to a foreign company, then section 135 must be applied.[20] There are, however, two particular issues which require some comment.

First, it is plain that once a winding up order has been made or a provisional liquidator has been appointed 'no action or proceeding shall be proceeded with or commenced against the company or its property,

---

[15] A recent example of a foreign company having principal places of business in both England and Scotland can be found in relation to BCCI; see *Re BCCI S.A. (No. 10)* [1997] Ch. 213 at 254.

[16] See *Re Naamlooze Vennootechap Handelmaatschappij Wokar* [1946] Ch. 98 in which principal place of business is discussed in the context of the Companies (Winding Up) Rules 1929, SR & O 1929/612 see now Insolvency Rules, S.I. 1986/1925, r. 4.8.

[17] One of those exceptions being that no unregistered company may be wound up voluntarily under the Act (s.221(4)).

[18] *Per* Mustill J in *Orri* v. *Moundreas*, 4 March 1981, QBD; the abbreviated report of the decision at [1981] Com L.R. 168 does not address this particular issue.

[19] See also p. 229, *infra*, for presentation of a petition by a foreign liquidator.

[20] See further p. 399, *infra*.

except by leave of the court' (section 130(2)): the word 'company' is deemed to include a foreign company which is being wound up.[1] Yet the wording employed in section 128(1) (avoidance of attachments) is significantly different:

> 'Where a company registered in England and Wales is being wound up by the court, any attachment, sequestration, distress or execution put in force against the estate or effects of the company after the commencement of the winding up is void.'

Where the English court takes jurisdiction over a foreign company on the basis of the presence of assets,[2] it may fairly be asked whether that company can be considered a 'company registered in England and Wales'. Arden J in *Re Lineas Navieras Bolivianas S.A.M. (The Bolivia)*[3] has answered that question in the affirmative, concluding that 'the effect of Part V of the Act is to make the whole of Part IV applicable in the case of an unregistered company'.[4] In substance, therefore, section 128(1) has been interpreted as if it stated: 'Where a *company* is being wound up by the court in England. . . . '[5] Although the legislative history of section 128 is more than a little ambiguous, it is respectfully submitted that Arden J's conclusion is correct.[6] Thus, in addition, where a court in Scotland is winding up a foreign company, it may be taken that any provisions expressed to apply in the winding up 'of a company registered in Scotland' will be likewise applicable.[7]

Second, section 227 (which comes towards the end of Part V) appears to contain an error. The section states:

> 'The provisions of this Part with respect to staying, sisting or restraining actions and proceedings against a company . . . extend, in the case of an unregistered company, . . . to actions and proceedings against any contributory of the company.'

The difficulty is that 'this Part' (i.e. Part V) does not in fact contain any provisions with respect to the staying, sisting or restraining of actions against a company. It seems fairly obvious, at least to this author, that section 227 should refer to the provisions of *this Act*, which was the wording that had been used at one time in the past.[8]

It is perhaps unnecessary to mention again that the time has surely come when the notion of winding up foreign companies as unregistered companies should be abandoned and replaced with specific, modern legislation.

---

[1] This was made expressly apparent under the former legislation. Companies Act 1985, s. 674(2): 'an unregistered company is not, except in the event of it being wound up, deemed to be a company under this Act, and then only to the extent provided by this Part'. See now the Insolvency Act 1986, s. 229(2).

[2] Where there is a place of business in England s. 221(3) deems the company to be registered in England.

[3] [1995] B.C.C. 666, noted Smart [1996] L.M.C.L.Q. 168.

[4] *Ibid.*, at 669.

[5] Such wording is, for example, used in ss. 168 and 178 of the Insolvency Act 1986.

[6] For details see the comment above, n. 3.

[7] For example, the Insolvency Act 1986, s. 185.

[8] See, for instance, the Companies Act 1948, s. 402.

4. OVERSEA COMPANIES: INSOLVENCY ACT 1986, SECTION 225

Foreign companies have been wound up by the English court under section 221 of the Insolvency Act 1986 and its predecessors. It must be noted, however, that the Insolvency Act offers an alternative in the form of section 225 which provides:[9]

> 'Where a company incorporated outside Great Britain which has been carrying on business in Great Britain ceases to carry on business in Great Britain, it may be wound up as an unregistered company under this Act, notwithstanding that it has been dissolved or otherwise ceased to exist as a company under or by virtue of the laws of the country under which it was incorporated.'

This provision does not seem ever to have been expressly relied upon by an English court, no doubt because in practice any case falling under section 225 will also be within the more widely drawn section 221. Thus, for example, in *IRC* v. *Highland Engineering Ltd.*[10] a dissolved New Zealand company was wound up in Scotland, relying upon the predecessors of sections 220 and 221.

Those familiar with United Kingdom companies legislation, past or present, may observe that section 225 of the Insolvency Act is somewhat oddly entitled: 'Oversea company may be wound up though dissolved'. The heading is inappropriate. Section 225 deals with foreign companies that have been carrying on business in Great Britain, whereas the term 'oversea company' is normally used to refer to a foreign company which has an 'established place of business in Great Britain'.[11] A foreign company may carry on business (within section 225) without being an oversea company (which must have an established place of business).

A. Ceases to Carry on Business

Section 225 is narrower than section 221 as the former can only be of relevance when a foreign company which has carried on business in Great Britain ceases to do so. The operation of a provision in substance identical to section 225 was considered by the Privy Council in *Dairen Kisen Kabushiki Kaisha* v. *Shiang Kee.*[12] A company incorporated in China but with a branch office in Hong Kong had been dissolved in China. The power of the Hong Kong court to make a winding up order was confirmed by the Privy Council, Lord Romer commenting:[13]

---

[9] First introduced as s. 91 of the Companies Act 1928 in, seemingly, an attempt to deal with Russian companies dissolved by decrees of the Soviet Government: see, generally, *Russian and English Bank* v. *Baring Bros.* [1936] A.C. 405; M. Mann (1952) 15 M.L.R. 479 and (1955) 4 I.C.L.Q. 226.

[10] 1975 S.L.T. 203. 'What is now [section 225] was enacted merely for the removal of doubt' *per* Megarry J in *Re Compania Merabello San Nicholas S.A.* [1973] Ch. 75 at 86.

[11] Companies Act 1985, s. 744: see also s. 690A.

[12] [1941] A.C. 373; s. 313(2) of the Companies Ordinance 1932 now re-enacted as s. 327A of the Companies Ordinance (*Cap.* 32).

[13] *Ibid.*, at 376.

'As the company had ceased to exist, it had necessarily ceased to carry on business in the Colony, and in such circumstances the sub-section in terms empowers the court to wind it up notwithstanding that it has been dissolved and ceased to exist by virtue of the law of the Republic of China.'

Thus we have the authority of Lord Romer for the proposition that when a foreign company is dissolved abroad, it must thereby cease to carry on business in Great Britain.

However, where a foreign company has not been dissolved abroad the question remains as to when the company ceases to carry on business in Great Britain under section 225. The most attractive approach, on first impression, is to say that whether a foreign company has ceased to carry on business in Great Britain is simply a matter of fact. But it may be recalled that carrying on business was given a particular meaning by the House of Lords in *Theophile* v. *Solicitor-General*.[14] There it was decided, for the purposes of bankruptcy jurisdiction, that a debtor continues to carry on business until all debts arising out of the business are satisfied:[15]

'In a sense it is true that the appellant was not actively carrying on business . . . but . . . trading does not cease when, as the expression is, "the shutters are put up", but continues until the sums due are collected and all debts are paid.'

Theophile v. *Solicitor-General*, although a bankruptcy case, has been applied to carrying on business by a company in the course of a winding up.[16] Moreover, Hoffmann J has confirmed that, under the Insolvency Act 1986, *Theophile* v. *Solicitor–General* remains good law for the purpose of bankruptcy jurisdiction.[17] Nevertheless, it would be nonsense to rely upon the decision of the House of Lords when interpreting section 225. Otherwise, so long as there were creditors in Great Britain the company would still be carrying on business and section 225 would not apply. For the purposes of section 225 a foreign company ceases to carry on business when 'the shutters are put up' or the company otherwise ceases actively to carry on business.

B. Companies Registered in Northern Ireland

Section 225 expressly applies to companies incorporated outside Great Britain and that, it has always been accepted, covers a company incorporated in Northern Ireland. In contrast, the definition of unregistered company in section 220 does not expressly refer to companies incorporated outside Great Britain. For 'unregistered company' includes 'any company' excepting a company registered 'under the legislation (past or present) relating to companies in Great Britain'. It may very well be that by implication a company registered in Northern Ireland is an unregistered company, for only companies registered in Great Britain are excluded. However, section 441(2) of the Insolvency Act must be taken into account:

[14] [1950] A.C. 186; considering s. 1(1)(d) of the Bankruptcy Act 1914, see now s. 265(1)(c)(ii) of the Insolvency Act 1986, p. 55, *infra*.

[15] *Ibid.*, at 201, *per* Lord Porter.

[16] *Re Sarflax Ltd.* [1979] Ch. 592, with reference to s. 332 of the Companies Act 1948, now s. 213 of the Insolvency Act 1986.

[17] *Re a Debtor (No. 784 of 1991)* [1992] Ch. 554.

'(2) Subject . . . to any provision expressly relating to companies incorporated elsewhere than in Great Britain, nothing in this Act extends to Northern Ireland or applies to or in relation to companies registered or incorporated in Northern Ireland.'

The traditional view was that as section 220 did not 'expressly' relate to companies incorporated elsewhere than in Great Britain, section 441(2) took effect to exclude section 220 in relation to companies registered in Northern Ireland: companies registered in Northern Ireland were not unregistered companies within section 220. On the other hand, section 225 did 'expressly' relate to companies incorporated elsewhere than in Great Britain and its operation with reference to companies registered in Northern Ireland was therefore preserved by section 441(2). In short, it was argued that whilst a company registered in Northern Ireland was not an 'unregistered company' within section 220, it could be wound up 'as an unregistered company' pursuant to section 225.[18]

In *Re a Company (No. 007946 of 1993)*[19] this approach was rejected by Morritt J, who held that any company incorporated in Northern Ireland could be wound up pursuant to section 220. The facts concerned a company ('the company') incorporated in Northern Ireland which had carried on business in England. In February 1993 the Secretary of State for Trade and Industry authorised two of his officers to require the company to produce certain documents. As a consequence of such information, the Secretary of State considered it in the public interest that the company be wound up and presented a petition under section 124A of the 1986 Act.[20] Section 124A allows the presentation of a petition 'if it is expedient in the public interest that a company should be wound up'. The expression 'company' is given, by section 251 of the 1986 Act, the same meaning it has under the Companies Acts 1985; namely, unless the contrary intention appears, a company registered (in England or Scotland) under the Companies Act 1985 or its predecessors.[1] Faced with the difficulty that a company incorporated in Northern Ireland under the Companies Acts (Northern Ireland) 1960–1982 did not *prima facie* appear to be a 'company' within the 1986 Act, the Secretary of State argued, in substance:

---

[18] This view was expressed in Rule 158(2) of *Dicey and Morris* (12th ed., 1993).

[19] [1994] Ch. 198, *sub nom. Re Normandy Marketing Ltd.* [1993] B.C.C. 879. For more detailed comment see Smart (1996) 45 I.C.L.Q. 177, in particular at pp. 178–179 for discussion of *DSQ Properties Ltd.* v. *Lotus Cars Ltd.* [1987] 1 W.L.R. 127 at 132 which suggested (albeit *obiter*) that a company incorporated in Northern Ireland could generally only be wound up in Northern Ireland.

[20] Section 124A, introduced by s. 60 of the Companies Act 1989, states: '(1) where it appears to the Secretary of State from – a) any report made or information obtained under Part XIV of the Companies Act 1985 (company investigations, &c) . . . that it is expedient in the public interest that a company should be wound up, he may present a petition for it to be wound up if the court thinks it just and equitable for it to be so.' For a discussion on the history of s. 124A see Smart, *supra* n. 19, at pp. 187–189.

[1] Companies Act 1985, s. 735(1) and (4). Section 124A (introduced by the Companies Act 1989, s. 60) makes no attempt to define the word 'company'. This must presumably have been deliberate on the part of the draftsman who elsewhere in the 1989 Act gave an extended definition to 'company'; e.g. Sch 22, para. 14(3): '"Company" means a company within the meaning of s. 735(1) of the Companies Act 1985 *or a company which may be wound up under Part V of the Insolvency Act 1986 (unregistered companies)*' (emphasis added).

(1)   that if an entity could be wound up as an unregistered company within section 220 then Part IV of the 1986 Act (which included section 124A) became applicable; and

(2)   a Northern Irish company could be wound up as an unregistered company.

The arguments in *Re a Company* were very largely confined to this latter proposition and, in particular, whether or not section 220 was a provision 'expressly relating to' companies incorporated outside Great Britain within section 441(2) of the Insolvency Act.[2]

His Lordship noted that the wording of section 441(2) was expressly relating to and not referring to: 'The former includes but is not confined to the latter'.[3] Moreover, whilst any provision (e.g. section 225) which expressly referred to companies incorporated outside Great Britain would necessarily also expressly relate to such companies, it was possible as a matter of ordinary English usage to have an express relation without an express reference: 'for example, a provision which referred expressly to citrus fruit would be a provision expressly relating to oranges and lemons, even though they were not expressly mentioned in the provision'.[4] In this manner his Lordship concluded that, as the words 'any company' in section 220 were unlimited and without restriction, section 220 was 'a provision expressly relating to companies incorporated elsewhere than in Great Britain notwithstanding that there is no express reference to such a company'.[5]

Morritt J opined that there were other provisions in Part V of the 1986 Act which 'clearly' pointed to the conclusion that Northern Irish companies were not excluded from section 220.[6] His Lordship referred to section 221(2) as relevant in two regards. It will be recalled that section 221(2) states:

'If an unregistered company has a principal place of business situated in Northern Ireland, it shall not be wound up under this Part unless it has a principal place of business situated in England and Wales or Scotland, or in both England and Wales and Scotland.'

First, Morritt J believed that section 221(2) suggested 'that the draftsman considered that a company incorporated in Northern Ireland could be wound up in England as an unregistered company because a company with a principal place of business in Northern Ireland would most commonly be a company incorporated there'.[7] Second, section 221(2) disposed of the company's contention that including Northern Irish companies in section 220 would have the dramatic (and surely unintended) effect of subjecting all Northern Irish companies to substantially all of the provisions of the 1986 Act: 'Section 221(2) shows that only those companies incorporated in Northern Ireland which also have a

---

[2]   It does not seem to have been doubted that the Secretary of State could have arranged for a petition to have been presented in Northern Ireland.

[3]   [1994] Ch. 198, 203.

[4]   *Ibid.*

[5]   *Ibid.*

[6]   *Ibid.*

[7]   *Ibid.*, see however the discussion below.

principal place of business in England and Wales are liable to be wound up in England'.[8]

In addition, Morritt J referred to section 225, which as his Lordship noted had been enacted apparently to remove any doubt as to the winding up of Russian banks that had already been dissolved by Soviet decrees.[9] 'It would be most surprising', said Morritt J,[10] 'if a company incorporated in Northern Ireland might be wound up in England if it had ceased to carry on business in England and had been dissolved in Northern Ireland, but not otherwise. This would be the consequence of the company's argument and of the view expressed in *Dicey and Morris*.'

This author would not disagree with the view of Morritt J that a provision may expressly relate to a particular matter even though that particular matter is not expressly mentioned or spelt out.[11] Clearly there is at first blush a good argument that Northern Irish companies fall within the wording of section 220 of the 1986 Act. However, the issue although arguable is by no means clear cut one way or the other; and one is required to look at other statutory provisions to try to fix the intention of the legislature.

(i) *Section 221(2)*

Morritt J, as mentioned above, considered section 221(2) of the 1986 Act and formed the impression that the draftsman would have intended that Northern Irish companies fall under section 220 because companies having a principal place of business in Northern Ireland would most commonly be incorporated there. In this regard there is no doubt that Morritt J arrived at a wholly misconceived interpretation of section 221(2).

Prior to the division of Ireland in the early 1920s it was quite clear that the courts of one part of the United Kingdom had no jurisdiction whatsoever to wind up companies incorporated under the Companies Acts in any other part.[12] But the predecessor of section 221(2) was found in the Companies (Consolidation) Act 1908 (section 268(1)) and indeed the Companies Act 1862 (section 199(1)). The draftsman of section 199(1) of

---

[8]   *Idem*, at 204. Whilst this comment is strictly correct, care must be taken with reference to a 'principal place of business'. That expression does not of course mean that a company must have its major commercial or business dealings in England. If a foreign company has some place of business in England that will be its principal place of business for the purposes of s. 221(2): 'It is irrelevant that it had also a principal place of business abroad and that – if, indeed it be the fact – that foreign place of business was, on comparison, the one to which major importance ought to be attached' (*per* Uthwatt J in *Re Naamlooze Vennoorschap Handelmaatschappij Wokar* [1946] Ch. 98, 100).

[9]   See *supra* p. 112, n. 9.

[10] *Supra*, n. 3 at 204.

[11] No authority on the construction of the words 'expressly relate to' was cited before Morritt J; however, *Shanmugan* v. *Comr for Registration* [1962] A.C. 515 might be mentioned. The facts had nothing to do with Northern Ireland or companies at all – rather the Privy Council had to decide whether certain legislation amounted to an 'express provision' within the Interpretation Ordinance of Ceylon. Lord Radcliffe stated: 'To be "express provision" with regard to something it is not necessary that that thing should be specifically mentioned; it is sufficient that it is directly covered by the language however broad the language may be.'

[12] *Per* Jessel MR in *Re International Pulp and Paper Co.* (1876) 3 Ch.D. 594, 598–599 ('though the company may carry on business in any part of the United Kingdom, yet the place of its registered office shews the court which is to wind it up'). See also *Re Scottish Joint Stock Trust Bank* [1900] W.N. 114.

the Companies Act 1862 could not possibly have had in mind the English court winding up companies incorporated in Ireland, because such was against the very scheme and letter of the Act itself.[13] The fact that the equivalent of section 221(2) of the 1986 Act is to be found in the companies legislation in force prior to the division of Ireland (when Irish companies certainly could be wound up only in Ireland) shows that section 221(2) cannot possibly suggest that the English court today has jurisdiction to wind up a Northern Irish company.

(ii) *Section 225*

In *Re a Company* Morritt J thought it would be 'most surprising' if, as his Lordship believed *Dicey and Morris* stated, a company incorporated in Northern Ireland might be wound up in England 'if it had ceased to carry on business in England and had been dissolved in Northern Ireland, but not otherwise'.[14] However, this misinterprets the effect of section 225 (and misstates the view actually expressed in *Dicey and Morris*). Section 225 requires that the company in question carried on business in Great Britain and has ceased to do so; it in no way requires that the company has ceased to carry on business and has been dissolved. The wording of section 225 is clear: a company that has ceased to carry on business may be wound up 'notwithstanding that it has been dissolved' in the country of incorporation. In any event, it could not possibly be that section 225 requires that a company has ceased to carry on business and that it has been dissolved, because if a company has been dissolved it will necessarily have ceased to carry on business in Great Britain.[15]

Section 225 is certainly a somewhat anomalous provision: not least because authority tells us that dissolved companies can in any event be wound up with reference to section 220.[16] But it is quite plain why section 225 refers in terms to companies incorporated 'outside Great Britain' (thereby including Northern Irish companies). Section 225 was originally enacted (as section 91 of the Companies Act 1928, later re-enacted as section 338(2) of the Companies Act 1929) well after the division of Ireland. The section, as its heading indicates, was drafted with oversea companies in mind. In section 274 of the Companies (Consolidation) Act 1908 (prior to the division of Ireland) oversea companies were defined as those incorporated outside the United Kingdom which established a place of business in the United Kingdom. After the division of Ireland and the establishment of a separate legislature for Northern Ireland, the Companies Acts passed at Westminster in general applied only to Great Britain: thus in the Companies Act 1929 the regulation of oversea companies dealt with companies incorporated outside *Great Britain* which

---

[13] The Companies Act 1862 gave jurisdiction (by s. 81) to the Irish court to wind up Irish companies.

[14] See n. 10, *supra*.

[15] *Per* Lord Romer in *Dairen Kisen Kabushiki Kaisha* v. *Shiang Kee* [1941] A.C. 373, 376, above p. 113.

[16] Under s. 221(5)(a), see *Russian and English Bank* v. *Baring Bros.* [1936] A.C. 405, 424–425 and, more recently, *IRC* v. *Highland Engineering Ltd* 1975 S.L.T. 203 (a dissolved New Zealand company).

established a place of business in Great Britain.[17] When drafting the predecessor of section 225 of the 1986 Act it was perhaps inevitable that the section would be in line with the rest of the legislation regulating oversea companies and refer to companies incorporated outside Great Britain (thereby including Northern Irish companies).

It has always been thought that section 225 does not qualify the interpretation of section 220 or 221. It is difficult to argue, therefore,[18] that the existence of a most narrowly confined jurisdiction under section 225 is any evidence of an intention on the part of the legislature in favour of a less narrowly confined jurisdiction under sections 220 and 221.

(iii) *Section 570 of the Companies Act 1985*

Section 220 and Part V of the 1986 Act are derived from section 665 and Part XXI of the Companies Act 1985. In *Re a Company* Morritt J did not contend that the 1986 Act created a jurisdiction which had not existed under the Companies Act 1985. Yet reference to section 570 of the Companies Act 1985 suggests very strongly, to this author at least, that Parliament would not have intended that a Northern Irish company be wound up in England.

Section 570, which was by sub-section (5) extended to Northern Ireland, dealt with the enforcement throughout the United Kingdom of winding up orders and connected matters:[19]

> '(1) An order made by the court in England and Wales for or in the course of winding up a company shall be enforced in Scotland and Northern Ireland in the courts that would respectively have jurisdiction in respect of that company if registered in Scotland or Northern Ireland and in the same manner in all respects as if the order had been made by those courts.'

This meant that when the English court made a winding up order, or any other order in the course of winding up a company, such order would be entitled to immediate effect in Scotland and Northern Ireland. In *Boyd* v. *Lee Guinness Ltd.*[20] an English company which had carried on business in Northern Ireland had gone into liquidation in England. The Court of Appeal in Northern Ireland held that it was bound to give automatic effect to the English winding up order and stay any action or proceeding against the company in Northern Ireland. It is one thing for the court in Northern Ireland to follow the lead of the English court when the latter is winding up an English company (even one which has carried on business in Northern Ireland). But it is quite another matter to suggest that Parliament intended that the English court could wind up Northern Irish companies and the courts of Northern Ireland would be bound by section 570 of the Companies Act 1985 to defer to the English court and enforce orders of

---

[17] See s. 343, *passim*.

[18] As Morritt J appeared to do in *Re a Company*.

[19] Section 570(1) of the Companies Act 1985 re-enacted s. 276(1) of the Companies Act 1948. Section 570 was repealed by s. 438 of and Sch 12 to the Insolvency Act 1986 and replaced by the more broadly drafted s. 426 of the 1986 Act, which makes provision for co-operation between courts exercising jurisdiction in relation to insolvency (both corporate and personal): see chapter 15, *infra*.

[20] [1963] N.I. 49.

the English court 'in the same manner in all respects' as if such orders had been made in Northern Ireland.

One might at this stage recall the advice of Evershed MR:[1]

> 'As a matter of general principle, our courts would not assume, and Parliament should not be taken to have intended to confer, jurisdiction over matters which naturally and properly lie within the competence of the courts of other countries.'

The winding up of Northern Irish companies surely falls naturally within the province of the courts of Northern Ireland.

In addition, the wording of section 570 of the Companies Act 1985 did not hint at any difference between Scotland and Northern Ireland; and most certainly a Scottish company cannot be wound up in England. Moreover, section 570 identified the relevant courts in Scotland and Northern Ireland as those courts which 'would respectively have jurisdiction in respect of that company *if* registered in Scotland or Northern Ireland': which suggests that the company in question would not be one which actually was registered in the requested country.

(iv) *Section 72 of the Financial Services Act 1986*

There is of course a deal of legislation, quite apart from the Companies Act 1985 and the Insolvency Act 1986, which touches upon company and insolvency law. Certain provisions in such legislation refer back to the winding up jurisdiction of the English court, but there is one particular provision which must be noted. Section 72(1) of the Financial Services Act 1986 explains the circumstances in which the Secretary of State can petition for the winding up of an 'authorised person' or 'authorised representative' (in relation to investment business). Section 72(2) states:

> 'Sub-section (1) above applies to any authorised person . . . or any authorised representative who is:
> (a) a company within the meaning of s.735 of the Companies Act 1985;
> (b) an unregistered company within the meaning of s.220 of the Insolvency Act 1986;
> (c) an oversea company within the meaning of s.744 of the Companies Act 1985; or
> (d) a partnership.'

The relationship between section 72(2)(b) and (c) is crucial. Parliament must have intended that section 72(2)(c) add something to what is already found in section 72(2)(b). Or, to put it the other way, Parliament would not have intended every company within section 72(2)(c) to have been already provided for in section 72(2)(b). Yet if *Re a Company* is correctly decided, section 72(2)(c) is mere surplusage.[2]

---

[1] See p. 98, n. 8 *supra*.

[2] It is to be noted that s. 72(2) refers specifically to s. 220 rather than to Part V of the Insolvency Act 1986 as a whole. A reference to Part V, obviously, would include not only s. 220 but also s. 225 (which may apply to a Northern Irish company which has carried on business in England).

An oversea company under section 744 of the Companies Act 1985 is a company incorporated outside Great Britain which establishes a place of business in Great Britain. (It will be recalled that this includes a Northern Irish company with a place of business in Great Britain.) An unregistered company under section 220 of the Insolvency Act 1986 includes any foreign company regardless of whether or not it has a place of business in England or Scotland. If, as Morritt J held, Northern Irish companies fall within section 220 as unregistered companies, there is no company which comes within section 72(2)(c) that is not already covered by section 72(2)(b). However, if *Dicey and Morris* is correct, companies incorporated in Northern Ireland may fall within section 72(2)(c) even though they are outside section 72(2)(b). Only if *Dicey and Morris* is correct can any scope of operation be given to section 72(2)(c). Section 72(2) is most strongly against the determination in *Re a Company* because the draftsman must have had Northern Ireland and Northern Irish companies in mind. For the very next section deals with winding up orders in Northern Ireland and subsection (2) of section 73 repeats the provisions of section 72(2), merely changing references to the Companies Act 1985 and Insolvency Act 1986 to the Companies (Northern Ireland) Order 1986 and the Insolvency (Northern Ireland) Order 1989.[3]

(v) *Summary*

In conclusion, the ruling that a company incorporated in Northern Ireland can be wound up in England as an unregistered company, under section 220 of the Insolvency Act 1986, cannot be supported. For Morritt J arrived at a wholly erroneous interpretation of the intent underlying section 221(2). In addition, a consideration of provisions such as section 570 of the Companies Act 1985 and, in particular, section 72(2) of the Financial Services Act 1986 compels one to conclude that Parliament would not have intended that Northern Irish companies fall within section 220 of the Insolvency Act 1986. The general rule that found expression prior to the decision of Morritt J should still be applied: a company incorporated in one part of the United Kingdom can be wound up only in the place of incorporation.

Finally, from an insolvency point of view it might be most unwise to advise a creditor to rely upon the decision of Morritt J and seek to have a Northern Irish company which has a place of business in England wound up by the English court. (Of course, even on the reasoning of Morritt J there could be no jurisdiction to wind up a Northern Irish company that does not have a place of business in England.) For, even if a judge were minded to follow the decision in *Re a Company*,[4] it must always be remembered that the English court has a discretion and may, in particular, decline to make a winding up order where the courts in the country of incorporation are a more appropriate forum.[5]

---

[3] S.I. 1986/2404, N.I. 18 and S.I. 1989/2405, N.I. 19 respectively.
[4] There would be a costs issue, in any event.
[5] Discussed *infra*, p. 125.

5. CIVIL JURISDICTION AND JUDGMENTS ACT 1982

The Brussels and Lugano Conventions on jurisdiction and enforcement of judgments in civil and commercial matters are given effect by the Civil Jurisdiction and Judgments Act 1982 (as amended[6]). The relevant provision of the Conventions is Article 16(2). Article 16(2) lays down that the courts of the State in which a company has its 'seat' shall have exclusive jurisdiction in proceedings for the dissolution of that company. If Article 16(2) stood unqualified it would plainly very much alter the jurisdiction of the English court to wind up foreign companies. However, the operation in practice of Article 16(2) has been heavily qualified both in the Conventions and by the terms of the Civil Jurisdiction and Judgments Act.

Nothing in the Conventions affects 'bankruptcy, proceedings relating to the winding up of insolvent companies or other legal persons, judicial arrangements, compositions and analogous proceedings'.[7] Thus the Conventions can only operate in respect of the winding up of solvent companies. If a company is plainly insolvent the practitioner need not be concerned about the Conventions and the 1982 Act. Moreover, even when dealing with a solvent company the Act effectively excludes the operation of the Conventions to United Kingdom registered companies.[8]

A. United Kingdom Companies

If a company, United Kingdom registered or otherwise, is insolvent the Conventions cannot apply. Where a United Kingdom company is solvent its seat for the purposes of Article 16(2) (exclusive jurisdiction) is laid down in section 43 of the Civil Jurisdiction and Judgments Act 1982. The substance of section 43 is that if a company has been registered in any part of the United Kingdom it cannot be regarded as having its seat in a Contracting State other than the United Kingdom.[9] Thus an English registered company simply cannot have its seat in France or Germany for the purposes of Article 16(2). Additionally, nothing in Article 16(2) affects the jurisdiction of a court in one part of the United Kingdom to wind up a company incorporated in another part of the United Kingdom.[10]

In short, as respects a United Kingdom registered company, nothing in the Conventions affects that jurisdiction of the English court which exists under the Insolvency Act 1986.

B. Foreign Companies

As the Conventions do not apply in an insolvency they are unlikely to have any dramatic impact upon the winding up of foreign companies: in

---

[6] By, in particular, the Civil Jurisdiction and Judgments Act 1991.
[7] Civil Jurisdiction and Judgments Act 1982, Sch. 1, Art. 1(2); see Case 133/78 *Gourdain* v. *Nadler* [1979] E.C.R. 733 and p. 13, *supra*.
[8] Section 43(2), (3) and (7)(a), *post*.
[9] Section 43(2) and (7)(a).
[10] Civil Jurisdiction and Judgments Act 1982, s. 17(1) and Sch. 5.

practice, creditors will generally only seek an English winding up order where a foreign company is insolvent. But in those instances where a foreign company is solvent the provisions of the Conventions must be carefully considered.

As Article 16(2) confers exclusive jurisdiction according to the seat of a solvent company, two consequences follow: first, the English court may be denied a jurisdiction that would have existed in respect of an insolvent company; and, secondly, a basis of jurisdiction is established – when a solvent foreign company has its seat in England.

(i) *Seat Abroad*

Under the Insolvency Act 1986 the English court has a wide jurisdiction to wind up foreign companies as unregistered companies.[11] Article 16(2) restricts that jurisdiction where a foreign company has its seat in a Contracting State abroad. The framework for determining where, for the purposes of Article 16(2), a company has its seat is laid down in section 43 of the Civil Jurisdiction and Judgments Act 1982. Section 43(6) and (7) provides:

> '(6) Subject to sub-section (7), a corporation or association has its seat in a Contracting State other than the United Kingdom if and only if –
> (a) it was incorporated or formed under the law of that State; or
> (b) its central management and control is exercised in that State.
> (7) A corporation or association shall not be regarded as having its seat in a Contracting State other than the United Kingdom if –
> (a) . . .
> (b) it is shown that the courts of that other State would not regard it for the purposes of Article 16(2) as having its seat there.'

Thus, a foreign company will have its seat in a Contracting State if it is: (i) either incorporated there or has its central management and control there; and (ii) the courts of that State would also treat the company as having its seat there.

An example best illustrates the type of situation in which Article 16(2) will apply to deny the English court jurisdiction. Let us say a French trading company is based in Paris, where its central management and control is exercised, but has a branch in England. The company is solvent. Assuming that under French law the company has its seat in France, the English court will have no jurisdiction on account of Article 16(2). It may be noted, however, that should the company be wound up in France, relevant particulars of that winding up must be registered in England pursuant to section 703P of the Companies Act 1985.[12]

(ii) *Seat in England*

If a foreign solvent company's central management and control is exercised in England that company will have its seat in England and the English

---

[11] In particular, where the company has carried on business in England or has assets in England, *ante*.

[12] Companies Act, s. 703P applies, in fact, to both solvent and insolvent companies.

court will have jurisdiction under Article 16(2).[13] As Article 16(2) does not lay down a code for winding up solvent companies, the provisions of the Insolvency Act 1986 will apply.[14]

However, jurisdiction under this head may not in fact be truly exclusive. Section 43 of the Act determines seat by reference to incorporation *or* central management and control: two 'seats' may therefore exist. For example, if a company is incorporated in Ireland but has its central management and control in England, it will have its seat in England. But, in addition, if Irish law defines seat by reference to the place of incorporation the company will also have its seat in Ireland.[15] Such cases will be rare indeed. Nevertheless, where two courts claim exclusive jurisdiction under the Conventions, it appears that 'any court other than the court first seized shall decline jurisdiction in favour of that court'.[16]

6. SUMMARY

United Kingdom Companies

(i)   The English court may wind up any company registered in England.[17]

(ii) The English court has no jurisdiction to wind up a company registered in Scotland.[18]

(iii) The English court (*semble*[19]) has no jurisdiction to wind up a company registered in Northern Ireland, except a company which carried on business in Great Britain but has ceased to carry on that business;[20] such a company may be wound up as an unregistered company in accordance with (iv) and (v), *infra*.

Foreign Companies – Insolvent

(iv) The English court has jurisdiction to wind up an insolvent foreign company if:

(a) there are assets in England[1] or the company has carried on business in England either through a branch office or by means of agents;[2] and

(b) there is a reasonable possibility of benefit accruing to creditors from the making of a winding up order.[3]

---

[13] Civil Jurisdiction and Judgments Act 1982, s. 43(2)(b) and (3)(b).

[14] In particular, s. 221 as interpreted through the cases, *ante*.

[15] *Dicey and Morris*, pp. 1118–1119.

[16] Art. 23: such instances are not likely to arise in practice on a frequent basis.

[17] Insolvency Act 1986, s. 117.

[18] Insolvency Act 1986, s. 120. *Re Scottish Joint Stock Trust Bank* [1900] W.N. 114.

[19] This is on the basis that *Re a Company (No. 007946 of 1993)*, above, is wrongly decided.

[20] Insolvency Act 1986, s. 225.

[1] *Banque des Marchands de Moscou (Koupetschesky)* v. *Kindersley* [1951] Ch. 112.

[2] Interpreting the cases discussed above, pp. 104–105.

[3] *Re Compania Merabello San Nicholas S.A.* [1973] Ch. 75. Such creditors need not be English; *Re Azoff-Don Commercial Bank* [1954] Ch. 315 and *Re Kailis Groote Eylandt Fisheries Pty. Ltd.* (1977) 2 A.C.L.R. 574. This author would suggest that any 'third requirement' (*supra*, p. 107) is better regarded as going to discretion, discussed below.

(v) There is no jurisdiction under (iv), *supra*, if the company has a principal place of business in Scotland or in Northern Ireland and does not have a principal place of business in England.[4]

Foreign Companies – Solvent

(vi) The English court has jurisdiction to wind up a solvent foreign company as an unregistered company in accordance with (iv) and (v), *supra*, except where the company has its seat in a State party to the Brussels or Lugano Conventions.[5] However, this exception will not apply if the company's central management and control is exercised in England and the English court is first seized of the matter.[6]

(vii) The English court has jurisdiction to wind up as an unregistered company a solvent foreign company whose central management and control is exercised in England. But if such a company also has its seat in a State party to the Brussels or Lugano Conventions, and the courts of that State are already seized, the English court must decline jurisdiction.[7]

7. SERVICE OF PETITION

The Insolvency Rules lay down detailed provisions in relation to service of a petition.[8] The following propositions emerge. A petition in respect of an English company shall be served at the company's registered office, unless service there is not practicable. Rule 4.8(5) states that in respect of an oversea company service may be effected in any manner provided for by section 695 of the Companies Act 1985; which means service upon any person who has been authorised to accept service[9] or (in case of default) at any place of business established in Great Britain. As 'oversea company' means[10] any company incorporated outside Great Britain which establishes a place of business in Great Britain, Rule 4.8(5) will presumably apply to both: (1) companies that are required to register under section 691 of the 1985 Act;[11] and (2) companies that have established a branch in Great Britain and (since 1992) have been registered pursuant to section 690A and Schedule 21A of the 1985 Act.[12] A petition may also be served at any unregistered (thereby including foreign) company's last known principal place of business in Great Britain.[13]

---

[4] Insolvency Act 1986, s. 221(2) and (3).
[5] Civil Jurisdiction and Judgments Act 1982, s. 43 and Sch. 1, Art. 1(2) and 16(2).
[6] *Ibid.* s. 43 and Sch. 1, Art. 23.
[7] *Ibid.* s. 43 and Sch. 1, Art. 1(2), 16(2) and 23.
[8] See S.I. 1986/1925, r. 4.8 and r. 12.12. For service generally see *Re Busytoday Ltd.* [1992] 1 W.L.R. 683.
[9] See *Rome* v. *Punjab National Bank (No. 2)* [1989] 1 W.L.R. 1211.
[10] Companies Act 1985, s. 744.
[11] Such will these days be few in number, as most foreign companies that carry on business in England will now fall under s. 690A of the Companies Act 1985 (as amended).
[12] Section 690A was introduced by S.I. 1992/3179 (Branch Registration under the EC Eleventh Company Law Directive).
[13] Rule 4.8(4), see also *Re Naamlooze Vennootschap Handelmaatschappij Wokar* [1946] Ch. 98.

Plainly, if a foreign company has never had any place from which it carried on business within the jurisdiction, an order for substituted service will be required. The Insolvency Rules make such provision.[14]

8. DISCRETION OF THE ENGLISH COURT

Although the English court may have jurisdiction to wind up a company, it does not follow that such jurisdiction must inevitably be exercised. There is a discretion to decline jurisdiction and refuse to make a winding up order or, an order having already been made, to stay those proceedings. This discretion, which was expressly recognised recently in *Re Wallace Smith & Co. Ltd.*,[15] is in many ways similar to that which exists in respect of bankruptcy (discussed in the previous chapter). When an English insolvency case, personal or corporate, contains foreign elements it will be relevant to bear in mind the doctrine of the convenient or appropriate forum. However, the doctrine of the appropriate forum must be modified to take into account the fundamental nature of corporate personality. For there is a great deal of authority to establish the general rule that a winding up may be either principal or ancillary. English judges have often maintained that the courts of the country in which a company was incorporated shall conduct the principal liquidation; and all other liquidations should be ancillary or auxiliary to that principal liquidation.[16] Thus the exercise of jurisdiction to make a winding up order will, to a certain extent, depend upon whether the company in question is English or foreign.

A. English Companies

The English court has jurisdiction to wind up an English company regardless of the location of the company's business or the nationality of its shareholders. But the Insolvency Act 1986 does not require that a winding up order be made.[17] The matter is one of discretion and, doubtless, the English court would not allow its proceedings to be put to an inequitable use, nor would an order be made if to do so would defeat the ends of justice.[18] Further, section 147 of the Insolvency Act states:

> '(1) The court may at any time after an order for winding up, on the application either of the liquidator or the official receiver or any creditor or contributory, and on proof to the satisfaction of the court that all proceedings in the winding

---

[14] S.I. 1986/1925, r. 12.12 and r. 12.11. Substituted service was, for example, ordered in *Re Compania Merabello San Nicholas S.A.* [1973] Ch. 75.

[15] [1992] B.C.L.C. 970, discussed below. Lord Hoffmann and Sir Peter Millett have also expressed similar views, see p. 64, *supra*.

[16] *Re English, Scottish and Australian Chartered Bank* [1893] 3 Ch. 385 and the comments of Scott V-C in *Re Bank of Credit and Commerce International S.A. (No. 10)* [1997] Ch. 213, below chapter 14.

[17] Insolvency Act 1986, s. 122: 'A company may be wound up if. . . .' The discretion to stay proceedings is contained in s. 147, see *post*.

[18] For the court will never exercise its jurisdiction so as to defeat the ends of justice: *per* Mustill LJ in *A-G v. Arthur Andersen & Co.* [1989] E.C.C. 224 at 229.

up ought to be stayed or sisted, make an order staying or sisting the proceedings, either altogether or for a limited time, on such terms and conditions as the court thinks fit.'

When winding up an English company it has often been said that the court is conducting the principal liquidation, a liquidation in any other country being merely ancillary.[19] Hence English proceedings should not normally be stayed simply because the company's business has been largely conducted in a foreign country, wherein is located the most part of the company's assets and creditors. Rather, the English court and the English liquidator should seek to co-operate with the foreign court, attempting as far as possible to reduce costs and promote substantial equality between creditors in different countries.[20] However, it may well be that an English winding up would be stayed if the proceedings would in substance serve no useful purpose. To take an example, let us say that a company although incorporated in England has carried on all its business in a foreign country, where all its creditors and assets are situated; and that any English winding up order would simply be ignored in that foreign country. A stay might well be forthcoming in such circumstances. In *Re Harrods (Buenos Aires) Ltd.*[1] an English company carried on all its business and was managed and controlled in Argentina. The company no longer had any substantial connection with England. After a dispute between the shareholders had arisen, an unfair prejudice petition was presented in England coupled with a just and equitable winding up petition (in the alternative). The English proceedings, including the winding up petition, were stayed by the Court of Appeal in favour of the natural forum, namely Argentina. Dillon LJ observed:[2]

'. . . the evidence raises a doubt whether a winding up order made against the company by the English court would be recognised by the Argentine courts; as the assets are in Argentina a winding up order made by the English court would be of very limited use if it was not recognised in Argentina.'

Although *Re Harrods (Buenos Aires) Ltd.* was not an insolvency case, had the company been insolvent any English winding up order would have been equally in vain.

Some guidance may also be found in *Re Stewart & Matthews Ltd.*[3] A company incorporated in Manitoba carried on its business in America in the State of Minnesota. Its business consisted of selling farm land, much of which was in the Province of Saskatchewan (in Canada, of course). No business was carried on in Manitoba. In July 1914 the company petitioned the bankruptcy court in Minnesota and a trustee in bankruptcy was in due course appointed. The majority of shareholders resided in the United States and all of the (small number of) Canadian creditors had proved their claims in the American proceedings. More than a year after the commencement of the insolvency in Minnesota, a winding up order was made in Manitoba. An application was subsequently made in Manitoba,

---

[19] *North Australian Territory Co. Ltd.* v. *Goldsbrough, Mort & Co. Ltd.* (1890) 61 L.T. 716 at 717.

[20] See also *Smith & Co.* v. *Salem Flour Mills Co. Ltd.* (1887) 14 R. 441, *passim.*

[1] [1991] 4 All E.R. 348. The impact of this decision upon the recognition of foreign liquidations is considered below, p. 173.

[2] *Ibid.*, at 356. (Dillon LJ was dissenting, but not in this regard.)

[3] (1916) 10 W.W.R. 154 (Manitoba).

supported by a majority of all the company's creditors, for a stay of the proceedings in Manitoba. The court pointed out the value of the winding up order, in that it had secured the assets in Canada, but was satisfied that (in the exercise of its discretion) it was in the best interests of all the creditors that the proceedings should be stayed. The US proceedings were just as efficient as those under the Canadian legislation, the US court had ample investigatory powers, and the proceedings did not discriminate against the Canadian creditors. The liquidator in Manitoba was instructed to take whatever steps were necessary to make any Canadian assets that had not yet vested in the US trustee in bankruptcy available for distribution in the US proceedings: but otherwise to take no further action until such became necessary in aid of the US proceedings.[4]

B. Foreign Companies

The exercise of discretion is of particular relevance in respect of foreign companies. In *Banque des Marchands de Moscou (Koupetschesky)* v. *Kindersley*[5] it will be recalled the Court of Appeal greatly enlarged the then jurisdiction over foreign companies, holding that the English court may wind up a company with assets in England. Yet Sir Raymond Evershed MR emphasised the discretionary nature of the jurisdiction and the role of the law of the place of incorporation:[6]

'*Prima facie* if the local law of the dissolved foreign corporation provided for the due administration of all the property and assets of the corporation wherever situate among the persons properly entitled to participate therein, the case would not be one for interference by the machinery of the English courts.'

In *Re a Company (No. 00359 of 1987)*[7] Peter Gibson J was willing to wind up a Liberian company which did not even have any assets in England. However, his Lordship made it abundantly clear that no order would have been forthcoming if some foreign court had been a more appropriate jurisdiction for the liquidation.[8]

Re Wallace Smith & Co. Ltd.[9] concerned a winding up petition presented against an Ontario company ('the company') by an English company which was itself in liquidation in England. Both companies had been part of the same group and there was no question that the company did have assets[10]

---

[4] *Ibid.*, at 159.

[5] [1951] Ch. 112.

[6] *Ibid.*, at 126 cited in *Re Real Estate Development Co.* [1991] B.C.L.C. 210 at 213. Costs must also be considered, see generally *Mirror Group Newspapers plc* v. *Maxwell* [1998] B.C.C. 324.

[7] [1988] Ch. 210: see the discussion at pp. 101–102, *supra*. The discretion to stay winding up proceedings in respect of a foreign company on the basis of *forum non conveniens* was also recognised in *Re Buildmat (Australia) Pty. Ltd.* (1981) 5 A.C.L.R. 689 at 692.

[8] *Ibid.*, at 227. In *Tong Aik (Far East) Ltd.* v. *Eastern Minerals and Trading (1959) Ltd.* [1965] 2 M.L.J. 149 the Singapore court declined to wind up a Malayan company where appropriate proceedings could be taken under the companies legislation of the Federation of Malaya.

[9] [1992] B.C.L.C. 970, Edward Nugee Q.C. sitting as a deputy judge of the High Court. Strong support for the application of the *forum conveniens* approach to insolvency cases has also recently been given (extra-judicially) by Lord Hoffmann and Sir Peter Millett, see p. 64 above.

[10] An account in credit to the sum of £25,000 in London.

(and at least one creditor, namely the petitioner) in England. The petition was based upon an alleged unpaid debt. On the facts it was ruled that the debt was bona fide disputed and the petition was dismissed accordingly. But the court also held that, in any event, the petition would have been dismissed on the basis that Ontario was a clearly more appropriate forum for the winding up. It could not be said that the existence of a more appropriate foreign forum was an 'essential factor'[11] in determining whether a foreign company was to be wound up in England:[12]

'. . . because there are cases, such as *Re Commercial Bank of South Australia* (1886) 33 Ch. D. 174, in which the court will make a winding up order in England which is ancillary to a winding up order made in the jurisdiction in which the company is incorporated; and clearly in such a case it could not be said that England was the more appropriate jurisdiction in which to make a winding up order; but the question is nevertheless an important one for the court to consider in deciding how to exercise its discretion.'

The company had a relatively modest connection to England (compared with Ontario); and it appeared that the liquidators of the petitioner were hoping also to be appointed as liquidators of the company with a view to gaining control over certain constructive trust litigation that the petitioner had already commenced against the company in Ontario. Although the existence of the constructive trust litigation was important upon the facts in *Re Wallace Smith & Co. Ltd.*, the court subsequently confirmed[13] that, as a general proposition, even though the court might have undoubted jurisdiction and there was a reasonable possibility of benefit to creditors, the existence of a more appropriate forum was a factor to be considered when it came to the exercise of the court's discretion. This author would suggest that not only the forensic links between the company and England, but also the connections of the petitioner (and other potential creditors) to England will be taken into account.

A relevant example of the exercise of discretion can be found in the Canadian case *Re Halifax Sugar Refinery Co.*[14] An English company (managed in England) had carried on a manufacturing business in Nova Scotia, where it had considerable assets and a small number of shareholders and creditors. The company was put into liquidation in England and many months later a petition was presented by a creditor in Nova Scotia. (The petition was not supported by other creditors in the Province.) The petitioner had also entered a claim in the English liquidation, part of which had been admitted although most had been rejected by the liquidator.[15] The court in Canada considered[16] whether the case called 'for the exercise of this jurisdiction even as ancillary to the liquidation in England' and ruled that it did not. It was held that ancillary proceedings

[11] In the sense of being a 'prerequisite for the making of a winding up order in England': *Re Wallace Smith Group Ltd.* [1992] B.C.L.C. 970 at 1007.
[12] *Re Wallace Smith & Co. Ltd.* [1992] B.C.L.C. 970 at 985. For ancillary winding up, see generally chapter 14.
[13] *Re Wallace Smith Group Ltd., supra,* n.11.
[14] (1889) 22 N.S.R. 71. See also *Re New England Brewing Co. Ltd., infra,* p. 366.
[15] The liquidator's decision had been affirmed by the English court: (1889) 22 N.S.R. 71 at 77. In addition, the petitioner had alleged that there had been a fraudulent conveyance of the company's real estate in the Province, but the court ruled (at 80) that the English court was equally well equipped to investigate the alleged impropriety.
[16] *Supra,* n. 14 at 79. See also *Gavigan v. AMPL* (1997) 8 N.Z.C.L.C. 261, 449.

would serve no useful purpose, since any relevant action that might be taken by a local liquidator could equally well be taken by the English liquidator.

Whether any useful or appropriate purpose would be served by having a local liquidation in respect of a foreign company recently arose before the Court of Appeal in England. Although the decision contains no reference to previous authority, or any attempt to analyse the guiding principles, it is nevertheless a useful illustration. In *New Hampshire Insurance Co.* v. *Rush & Tomkins Group plc*[17] the appellant had petitioned for the winding up of two Dutch companies which were part of a much larger group of companies, the Rush & Tomkins Group. The English companies in the Group were in compulsory liquidation in England. The Dutch companies were subject to insolvency proceedings in Holland and a Mr De Ruuk had been appointed as trustee in bankruptcy. The appellant had not yet entered a proof in the Dutch proceedings. The evidence of Mr De Ruuk was that the making of English winding up orders 'would lead to confusion and duplication of time and costs which will, in turn, reduce the assets of the company available for distribution to all creditors.' At first instance Jonathan Parker J had ruled that:

(1)   although the Dutch companies had a sufficient connection to England (this issue was agreed on appeal), there was no reasonable possibility that any benefit would accrue to the creditors from an English winding up – accordingly there was no jurisdiction; and, in the alternative,
(2)   even if the court did have jurisdiction, it would not be exercised.

The argument before their Lordships mainly concerned the ownership of a substantial sum of money in England which, in the relevant accounts, was shown as belonging to one of the Dutch companies. After investigating the matter, however, Mr De Ruuk had concluded that the money was not in fact owing to either of the Dutch companies. The appellant maintained that Mr De Ruuk had not adequately investigated the issue and that no proper investigation would occur unless an English liquidator were appointed. The Court of Appeal emphatically rejected the appellant's attack on the integrity or competence of the Dutch trustee and upheld the decision of the judge, suggesting that the appellant should lodge a formal proof in the Dutch insolvency proceedings so as to be able to apply before the Dutch court for any appropriate remedy. Millett LJ observed:

'It would be something of an impertinence for the English court to take the view that if a trustee in bankruptcy appointed by the Dutch court is not performing his task properly, the proper remedy is for the English court to appoint its own officer to see that he does. If Mr De Ruuk's conduct gives rise to any cause for concern then it is to the Dutch court that those concerns ought, in my opinion, to be addressed.'

In short, it was not appropriate for an English liquidator to be appointed.

The authorities establish that the English court may decline to exercise its jurisdiction to wind up a foreign company where proceedings are already under way, or may be commenced, in some other more appropriate foreign

---

[17] (3 October 1996, unreported, CA) (LEXIS transcript: Smith Bernal).

court.[18] In the alternative, the English court may make a winding up order but with the objective of conducting an ancillary winding up – that is, limiting the scope of the English proceedings so as to assist the principal liquidator abroad.[19] The ancillary winding up of foreign companies is developed further below.[20]

9. ADMINISTRATION ORDERS

A. Introduction

It obviously goes without saying that the court in England has jurisdiction to make an administration order pursuant to Part II of the Insolvency Act 1986 in respect of a company formed and registered in England under the Companies Act 1985. But, unfortunately, no thought appears to have been given when drawing up Part II as to whether or not the court should also have jurisdiction over a foreign company and, if so, in what circumstances. Accordingly, one's starting point must be that when the word 'company' appears in Part II it refers to a company formed and registered under the Companies Acts and does not encompass foreign companies.[1] Indeed, it will be noted that, in a case[2] shortly after the coming into force of the 1986 legislation, it was accepted that an administration order could not generally be made in relation to a foreign company.[3] Similarly, although in *Re Dallhold Estates (UK) Pty. Ltd.*[4] an administration order was made in relation to an Australian company, that order was only made acting under section 426 of the Insolvency Act 1986 – again it being assumed that Part II did not generally extend to foreign companies.[5] More recently, however, the question has generated a certain amount of controversy as distinguished commentators have argued that foreign companies may generally fall within Part II.[6] Such arguments have particularly drawn support from *Re International Bulk Commodities Ltd.* in which it was held that an administrative receiver (under Part III of the Insolvency Act 1986) could be appointed in relation to a foreign company.[7] It is argued that 'company'

[18] See also *Re Matheson Bros.* (1884) 27 Ch.D. 225, p. 95, *supra*.
[19] See, for example, *Re Federal Bank of Australia* (1893) 62 L.J. Ch. 561.
[20] See chapter 14, *infra*.
[1] The meaning of 'company' is dealt with in detail below.
[2] *Felixstowe Dock and Rly Co. v. US Lines Inc.* [1989] QB 360 at 367.
[3] See also Picarda, *The Law Relating to Receivers, Managers and Administrators* (2nd ed., 1990) pp. 501–502 and the discussion in Lightman and Moss, *The Law of Receivers of Companies* (2nd ed., 1994) pp. 418–421 and in Fletcher, Higham and Trower, *The Law and Practice of Corporate Administrations* (1994) pp. 251–254.
[4] [1992] B.C.L.C. 621.
[5] *Ibid.*, at 623. *Dallhold* was approved by the Court of Appeal in *Hughes* v. *Hannover Rückversicherungs-Aktiengesellschaft* [1997] 1 B.C.L.C. 497, where Morritt LJ made the following observation, at 511: 'The problem as explained by Chadwick J (at 623 [in *Dallhold*]) was that s. 8 of the Insolvency Act 1986 only applied to a company registered in England'. For discussion of s. 426 see chapter 15.
[6] A survey of arguments and case law can be found in Moss 'Insolvency Administration for Foreign Companies in England' (1993) 15 *Comparative Yearbook of International Business* 3–19; Moss and Segal 'Cross-Border Issues' in *Insolvency of Banks: Managing the Risks* (1996) Oditah (ed.) pp. 71–76.
[7] [1993] Ch. 77: the decision was not followed in *Re Devon and Somerset Farmers Ltd.* [1994] Ch. 57 (in relation to an English unregistered company).

under Part II should be interpreted to include any company which may be wound up as an unregistered company pursuant to Part V.

There is no doubt that the meaning to be given to 'company' must be determined by the (presumed) intention of Parliament – although it is equally apparent that Parliament did not actually consider the matter one way or the other. Although 'company' is defined in the legislation as meaning a company incorporated under the Companies Acts, that prima facie definition can be displaced. Yet, it is worth making the point that had the administration procedure been introduced into English law in 1985 under the Companies Act[8] there would, in this author's view, have been virtually no possible room for arguing that, for the purposes of administration, 'company' included any foreign company that might be wound up as an unregistered company. For section 674(2) of the Companies Act 1985 made it very plain that, except for the purposes of winding up, an unregistered company was not a 'company' under the Companies Act:

'. . . an unregistered company is not, except in the event of its being wound up, deemed to be a company under this Act, and only then to the extent provided by this Part.'

The current equivalent of this provision is to be found in section 229(2) of the Insolvency Act 1986 and states:

'. . . an unregistered company is not, except in the event of its being wound up, deemed to be a company under the Companies Act, and then only then to the extent provided by this Part of this Act.'

It is only because section 229(2) states that an unregistered company is not 'a company under the Companies Act', rather than 'a company under *this* Act', that it is even possible to argue that the word company in Part II includes any unregistered company. But certainly the legislative history of section 229(2) weighs heavily against any extended definition of 'company'.

Two theoretical issues, which have hitherto attracted little (if any) attention, also must be mentioned at the outset. First, it is clear that 'company' generally means a company incorporated (in Britain) under the Companies Acts. If that prima facie meaning is displaced, by circumstances indicating a contrary intention on the part of Parliament, then 'company' might be expected to mean 'a company wherever incorporated'. But this (second) meaning cannot realistically be given to the word 'company' for the purposes of Part II, because to do so would result in the court having jurisdiction to put into administration *any* foreign company, irrespective of whether that foreign company carried on business or had assets in England. The only realistic way of seeking to establish a factual link (or forensic connection) between the English court and a foreign company is by making reference to the concept of 'unregistered companies' under Part V of the 1986 Act: for case law as we have seen has established that (*inter alia*) any foreign company that has assets in England comes within Part V. Hence those commentators who maintain that foreign companies fall within Part II are arguing not only that the prima facie meaning of 'company' is displaced, but also that the expected expanded meaning – a company wherever incorporated – is similarly not accepted. Instead, a third meaning is being advanced. There is in effect a double hurdle to be

---

[8] It was, of course, introduced in the Insolvency Act 1985.

overcome by those who reject the 'traditional' approach. It will in addition be noted that if reference is to be made to unregistered companies then Parliament must have intended Part II to apply not only to foreign companies but also to corporations incorporated in Britain other than under the Companies Acts[9] – but in each case Parliament failed expressly so to provide.

Secondly, the difficulty of establishing a connection between Part II and Part V is, in this author's opinion, further increased upon consideration of the scope of Part V itself. It has been held that a foreign company which has already been dissolved in its country of incorporation is nevertheless an unregistered company for the purposes of sections 220 and 221 and can be wound up in England under Part V.[10] Yet if the word 'company' in Part II is construed as including Part V unregistered companies, it follows that the English court has jurisdiction to make an administration order in relation to a foreign company that no longer exists in its country of incorporation. This is bordering on the preposterous. It is one thing to maintain that Parliament intended the court to be able to wind up an English branch of a dissolved foreign corporation, it is quite another matter to suggest that the operations of such a branch can be reorganised under Part II. For once a corporation has been dissolved in its country of incorporation, it necessarily has ceased to exist as a legal person and can no longer sue, be sued or enter into contracts, still less can it have its business operations restructured. Quite simply, from a theoretical standpoint Part V does not fit with Part II.

B. The Interpretation of 'Company'

Section 8 of the 1986 Act lays down the power of the court to make an administration order. The first requirement (see s 8(1)(a)) is that the court must be satisfied that a 'company' is or is likely to become 'unable to pay its debts' within section 123 of the Act.[11] The 1986 Act does not contain a specific definition of the term 'company'; however, the effect of section 251 is that 'company' must be given the same meaning it has under the Companies Act 1985: section 735 of which defines a 'company' as meaning (unless a contrary intention appears) 'a company formed and registered under this Act'. Hence the starting point is that a foreign company is not a 'company' and therefore falls outside the scope of Part II of the 1986 Act.

From the point of view of the practitioner it clearly would be more convenient if the English court could put a foreign company into administration. One has only to take the example of a proposed rescue of a group of companies, where all but one of the companies in the group are English companies. The potential inability adequately to regulate the affairs of the one foreign company in the group could not only make any rescue more complex, but might even prejudice the chances of success in relation to the

---

9   See *Re Devon and Somerset Farmers Ltd.*, *supra* n. 7, *passim.*
10   See p. 112, *supra.*
11   The reference to s. 123 is of significance, see text below.

group as a whole.[12] Moreover, administration was designed to be an alternative to liquidation and if (as is the case) the English court can wind up a foreign company, then there can be no inherent reason why as a matter of policy the court cannot put a foreign company into administration. Indeed, it has been noted that one of the purposes of an administration order (as listed in section 8(3) of the 1986 Act) is to facilitate the approval of a scheme of arrangement pursuant to section 425 of the Companies Act 1985; and that as a scheme of arrangement can be entered into with respect to a foreign company, so too the court should be able to make an administration order in relation to a foreign company,[13] just as in *Re International Bulk Commodities Ltd.* it was ruled that a foreign company could be put into administrative receivership.

In response to such arguments it might be pointed out that the question whether a foreign company might come within Part II was expressly left open in *Re International Bulk Commodities Ltd.*, Mummery J stating that he was 'unable to derive any assistance from the provisions relating to administrators on the question of administrative receiverships'.[14] Moreover, the primary argument that found favour before Mummery J derived from the fact that the concept of administrative receivership rests upon a contractual base: where a debenture was governed by English law it had always been the case (prior to 1986) that 'the existing regime of contractual receivers appointed by debenture holders' was applicable to both registered and unregistered companies.[15] Administrative receivership simply gave 'statutory recognition' to the existing regime of contractual receivers; and there was no reason to suppose that Parliament intended to create a two-tier system.[16] On the other hand, of course, administration does not rest upon a contractual base; and was introduced in 1985 as an entirely new procedure.

Moreover, in relation to a scheme of arrangement it may be pointed out that a scheme can only be entered into with respect to a foreign company because the Companies Act makes express provision to that effect: section 425(6) defines a 'company' for the purpose of the section as meaning 'any company liable to be wound up'. If Parliament had intended the courts to exercise a like jurisdiction in the case of administration orders, it could simply have said so. Further, there are provisions in Part II itself which could be interpreted as favouring the traditional view.[17] Section 10 deals with the effect of an application for an administration order and states that, during the relevant period, 'no resolution may be passed or order made for the winding up of the company' (see s 10(1)(a)). Yet a foreign company can never be put into voluntary or compulsory liquidation[18] by

---

[12] A scheme of arrangement pursuant to s. 425 of the Companies Act 1985 can be entered into with reference to a foreign companies: see text below. Moreover, in practice, a winding up petition can be presented and provisional liquidators appointed in respect of a foreign company, thereby staying any actions against the company and hopefully giving time for negotiations to reach a satisfactory rescue plan: see Moss and Segal, *supra* n. 6 at pp. 72–73.

[13] Moss, *supra* n. 6 at p. 11.

[14] [1993] Ch. 77 at 88. Indeed, Mummery J did not make any reference to the view of Chadwick J in *Dallhold*, above n. 4.

[15] *Ibid.*, at 84.

[16] *Ibid.*

[17] Other arguments are put forward in Fletcher, Higham and Trower, *supra*, n. 3.

[18] As to a resolution for voluntary liquidation see s. 221(4); in relation to a resolution for compulsory liquidation, see p. 110, *supra*.

resolution under the 1986 Act and, accordingly, it might appear that the reference to the passing of a winding up resolution would tend to show an intention that foreign companies were not within the ambit of Part II. One might also look at section 8(1)(a) which states that the court may make an administration order (*inter alia*) if a company is or is likely to become unable to pay its debts 'within the meaning given to that expression by section 123 of this Act'. The point here is that section 123 is not applicable in relation to unregistered companies: the inability of an unregistered company to pay its debts is determined by reference to sections 222–224.

This author would suggest that the more one looks into the provisions of Part II, the more apparent it becomes that Parliament did not give any thought one way or the other as to whether or not foreign companies should be subject to the administration regime. The same is true, it is submitted, when one turns to the Insolvency Rules. For example, service of a winding up petition (rule 4.8) is drafted so as to cover not merely companies registered under the Companies Act but also unregistered and oversea companies. Service of a petition for administration is similarly drafted, except that the relevant rule (rule 2.7) contains no mention of unregistered or oversea companies: it was obviously drafted with only English companies in mind.[19] The point, quite simply, is that it is very difficult convincingly to maintain that Parliament intended to displace the meaning normally given to the word 'company', if in reality that issue never entered the draftsman's mind at the time.

C. The 1989 Order

By 1989, however, the question of whether foreign companies could be put into administration must have been in the forefront of the draftsman's mind. Prior to 1989, Part II of the 1986 Act did not apply to banks – or more precisely authorised institutions or former authorised institutions within the meaning of the Banking Act 1987.[20] The Banks (Administration Proceedings) Order 1989 ('the 1989 Order')[1] applies Part II (with modification) to those authorised institutions or former authorised institutions 'which are companies within the meaning of section 735 of the Companies Act 1985'.[2] The exclusion of foreign authorised institutions is quite consistent with the view that foreign companies generally are outside the scope of Part II. Indeed, any other approach would lead to bizarre conclusions. It is clear that an English bank (being an authorised institution) can now be put into administration, whereas a foreign authorised institution cannot. However, not every foreign bank is an authorised institution; for example, a foreign bank may have assets in England but if it does not carry on any type of banking business in

---

[19] If anything, it could be argued that this points against including foreign companies within Part II.

[20] See s. 8(4)(b) of the 1986 Act (as amended by the Banking Act 1987).

[1] S.I. 1989/1276.

[2] See Art. 2 of the 1989 Order.

England it will not be an authorised institution.[3] Such a foreign bank is neither included or excluded from the scope of Part II by the 1989 Order and must stand in the same position as any other foreign company with assets in England: either it is a 'company' for the purposes of Part II, or it is not. To argue that a foreign bank which only has assets in England can be put into administration but a foreign bank that actually carries on business in England cannot, is an argument that only has to be stated to be rejected.[4]

D. The 1992 Regulations

The Oversea Companies and Credit and Financial Institutions (Branch Disclosure) Regulations 1992 ('the 1992 Regulations')[5] inserted various provisions into Part XXIII of the Companies Act 1985. The 1992 Regulations deal with branch registration pursuant to the Eleventh Company Law Directive (89/666/EEC) and apply to any limited company incorporated outside the United Kingdom and Gibraltar which has a branch in Great Britain.[6] A new Chapter IV was added to Part XXIII and concerns the registration of specified particulars where a foreign company with a branch in Great Britain goes into liquidation or becomes subject to other insolvency proceedings. Section 703P details the particulars to be delivered to the registrar when a foreign company goes into liquidation. Section 703Q concerns particulars where a foreign company becomes subject to insolvency proceedings other than liquidation. The particulars required under the two sections are broadly similar. However, section 703P(8) provides that no return is required under section 703P in respect of a winding up under Part V of the Insolvency Act 1986; this is obviously because if a foreign company is being wound up under Part V all appropriate information will already be available in England. But section 703Q contains no similar exemption in relation to other insolvency proceedings.[7]

In short, the draftsman of the 1992 Regulations must have had in mind both the winding up and reorganisation of foreign companies. The reference to Part V when dealing with winding up clearly contrasts with the absence of any mention of Part II in relation to insolvency proceedings other than winding up. It is difficult to resist the conclusion that the draftsman of the 1992 Regulations took the same view as the draftsman of the 1989 Order: foreign companies were not considered to come within Part II.

---

[3] The need to obtain authorisation (from the Bank of England) is triggered by the carrying on of deposit-taking activities within the United Kingdom: Banking Act 1987, ss. 8 and 106.

[4] Clearly, the more the connection to England, the greater the justification for subjecting a foreign company to the administration regime.

[5] S.I. 1992/3179.

[6] See now s. 690A of the Companies Act 1985 as inserted by the 1992 Regulations, s. 690 thus currently only covers those companies falling outside s. 690A.

[7] It can be strongly argued that if it had been the case that foreign companies fell within Part II then the draftsman would have included appropriate provision (corresponding to s. 703P(8)) in s. 703Q. The 1992 Regulations have until now seemingly been overlooked by commentators.

E. Conclusion

Whilst it would undoubtedly be convenient if foreign companies came within Part II of the 1986 Act, there are weighty arguments against such an interpretation of the current legislation. In particular, the 1989 Order and the 1992 Regulations indicate that Parliament did not intend the prima facie meaning of the word 'company' to be displaced for the purposes of Part II.[8] This lack of jurisdiction in the English court may in some instances be remedied by reliance upon section 426 of the 1986 Act. A section 426 request is, however, a complex procedure and, more significantly, is only available in respect of a restricted group of countries: the United States, Japan, Germany and France are noticeably not included. In other cases, it may well be that a winding up petition can be presented in relation to a foreign company and then a provisional liquidator appointed: thereby staving off individual creditors and hopefully gaining enough time in which to reach a negotiated restructuring. Of course, it goes without saying that amendment to Part II – setting out the particular circumstances in which foreign companies can be put into administration – is very much desired.

10. EUROPEAN CONVENTION ON INSOLVENCY PROCEEDINGS

The Convention applies to 'insolvency proceedings' which are defined in Article 2 and listed in Annex A:[9] both winding up and administration proceedings are there included. Article 3 envisages that the primary or 'main' proceedings should be opened in the Contracting State in which the centre of the debtor's main interests is located. Additional proceedings (territorial in scope) may only be commenced in another Contracting State in which the debtor has an establishment. Thus Article 3(1) and (2) states:

> '1. The courts of the Contracting State of the territory in which the centre of a debtor's main interests is situated shall have jurisdiction to open insolvency proceedings. In the case of a company or legal person, the place of the registered office shall be presumed to be the centre of its main interests in the absence of proof to the contrary.
>
> 2. Where the centre of a debtor's main interests is situated within the territory of a Contracting State, the courts of another Contracting State shall have jurisdiction to open insolvency proceedings against that debtor only if he possesses an establishment within the territory of that other Contracting State. The effects of those proceedings shall be restricted to the assets of the debtor situated in the territory of the latter Contracting State.'

It will be noted, however, that the Convention only seeks to apply where the centre of a debtor's main interests does indeed lie in a Contracting

---

[8] As far as the case law is concerned, it is submitted that the weightier view is that Part II does not apply to foreign companies; see *infra*, p. 130, n. 5 in relation to *Hughes* v. *Hannover*. See also *Arab Bank plc* v. *Mercantile Holdings Ltd.* [1994] Ch. 71 at 82–83, where a restricted approach to the meaning of 'company' was adopted in relation to s. 151 of the Companies Act 1985 (unlawful financial assistance).

[9] See p. 11, n. 7, *supra*.

State. If that centre is actually in Singapore or Mexico then the Convention simply does not apply and this is so even though the debtor's commercial operations in (for example) Spain are far more extensive than in England.[10]

In comparison, if the debtor's main interests are centered in Spain then winding up proceedings could only be commenced in England (even in relation to an English registered company[11]) if there were an establishment in England;[12] and such proceedings would be limited to assets located in England.

With regard to administration proceedings,[13] Article 3(2) must also be taken into consideration:

> 'Where insolvency proceedings have been opened under paragraph 1, any proceedings opened subsequently under paragraph 2 shall be secondary proceedings. These latter proceedings must be winding-up proceedings.'

'Winding up proceedings' does not include Part II administration.[14] Thus if the centre of main interest is, for example, in Ireland and company examinership proceedings have already been commenced there, the only order that could be made in England (even when dealing with an English company) would be a winding up order.[15]

Although Article 3 provides that where the centre of main interests is located (or where an establishment is located) the courts 'shall have jurisdiction to open insolvency proceedings', it must be doubtful whether Article 3 by itself overcomes the difficulty currently under Part II of the Insolvency Act 1986, namely that here is no jurisdiction to make an administration order in respect of a foreign company.[16] The point is perhaps not worth extensive discussion since, no doubt, any legislation introducing the Convention into English law would expand the meaning to be given to 'company' in Part II accordingly.

In summary, the most significant change that would result (in terms of jurisdiction over companies) should the Convention become law is that the presence of assets would no longer be sufficient to found winding up jurisdiction in cases where a company has it centre of main interests in a Contracting State other than the United Kingdom.

11. ILLUSTRATIONS

(1) Q Co. Ltd., registered in England, carries on business as an insurance consultant in England and to a greater extent in Australia and the Far

---

[10] See p. 11, *supra*.

[11] The presumption in Art. 3(1) that a company has its centre of main interests where it is registered is rebuttable.

[12] Assets would not be a sufficient basis for jurisdiction.

[13] See generally pp. 130–136, *supra*.

[14] Article 2 tells us that 'winding up proceedings' are such proceedings (listed in Annex B) as involve 'realising the assets of the debtor'.

[15] Although by Arts. 17 and 18 the representative appointed in Ireland would prima facie be entitled to exercise in England the powers conferred under the Irish legislation.

[16] *Supra*, p. 136.

East. Q Co. Ltd. is insolvent and winding up proceedings have been commenced in South Australia. The English court has jurisdiction to wind up Q Co. Ltd.[17]

(2) X is a corporation created under the laws of Liberia. X appointed agents to carry on its business in England and elsewhere. X is known to be in dire financial straits, it has recently terminated the appointment of its English agents and removed any and all its assets from the jurisdiction. There is a substantial body of English creditors. The English court has jurisdiction to make a winding up order.[18]

(3) N, a Delaware corporation, trades as a general merchant in New York State and throughout North America. N has not carried on business in England but, on occasion, has ordered goods from and sold goods to English firms. N has, accordingly, a small number of both debtors and creditors in England. N is insolvent. The English court has jurisdiction to order a winding up.[19]

(4) As in Illustration 3, above, however, N is already in liquidation in New York. It has been established that the English creditors will in no way be prejudiced in the New York proceedings. Moreover, no difficulty is envisaged with reference to the US trustee recovering the assets in England. The English court will decline to make a winding up order.[20]

(5) G is a French *société anonyme*. G's business is substantially conducted and controlled in France. G has a small office in England. G is solvent. Assuming that under the law of France G has its seat in France, the English court lacks jurisdiction.[1]

(6) L is an Italian corporation but with offices in several European cities. L's United Kingdom and Ireland operations are controlled from a branch office in Scotland. L is insolvent but has assets in England. The English court has no jurisdiction to make a winding up order.[2]

(7) K is a New Zealand registered company. K has for many years operated a branch office in England. A winding up petition has recently been presented by creditors in the New Zealand court. The majority of K's assets and creditors are in New Zealand, but there are valuable assets and a substantial body of creditors in England. The court has jurisdiction to make an order. However, the English winding up will be ancillary to the principal liquidation in New Zealand.[3]

---

[17] *North Australian Territory Co. Ltd.* v. *Goldsbrough, Mort and Co. Ltd.* (1889) 61 L.T. 716, *Re Suresnes Racecourse Co. Ltd.* (1890) 90 L.T. Jo. 55.

[18] Insolvency Act 1986, s. 221. For business has been carried on in England by means of agents thereby satisfying the 'sufficient connection' test, *ante*.

[19] Insolvency Act 1986, s. 221. There are assets within the jurisdiction, namely the company's debtors: see, *passim, Re Irish Shipping Ltd.* [1985] H.K.L.R. 437.

[20] *See Re Wallace Smith & Co. Ltd., supra.*

[1] Civil Jurisdiction and Judgments Act 1982, s. 43 and Sch. 1, Art. 1(2) and 16(2).

[2] Insolvency Act 1986, s. 221(3).

[3] *Re Matheson Bros Ltd.* (1884) 27 Ch. D. 225, and chapter 14.

(8) WA Pty. Ltd. is an Australian company that has carried on business in England. The company has substantial assets in England that could be realised more advantageously if the company were put into administration than if it were wound up. The English court may put the company into administration, but only upon the receipt of a request to that effect from a court in Australia.[4]

(9) RF Inc. is a corporation incorporated in Delaware, all of its directors reside in the United States or elsewhere outside England. RF Inc. has never carried on business in England, but at one time owned a significant shareholding in Subco Ltd. (an English company). RF Inc. sold that shareholding some months ago. Creditor SA is a French company that recently obtained judgment in France against RF Inc. and subsequently registered that judgment in England. Creditor SA wishes to put RF Inc. into liquidation in England. RF Inc. has no assets in England. The court has no jurisdiction to make a winding up order.[5]

(10) The facts are as in example (9) above, except that RF Inc. has a bank account in England in credit. There is jurisdiction to make a winding up order (even though the petitioner has no connection to England and there is no evidence that there are any English creditors of RF Inc.)[6]

---

[4] See Insolvency Act 1986, s. 426 and *Re Dallhold Estates (UK) Pty. Ltd.* [1992] B.C.L.C. 621, above.
[5] See the discussion of *Re Real Estate Development Co.* [1991] B.C.L.C. 210, p. 102, *supra.*
[6] *Ibid.*

Chapter 5

Foreign Bankruptcies: Bases of Recognition

1. INTRODUCTION

At the outset it must be stressed that there are two issues which should so far as possible be kept separate and distinct. It is one thing to decide whether a foreign insolvency may be recognised in England, but it is quite a different matter to determine the consequences of such recognition. In the past, a deal of confusion[1] has been occasioned by the failure to distinguish between the bases of recognition and the consequences of recognition. This chapter deals with when a foreign bankruptcy decree may be recognised. The consequences of such recognition are described in detail in chapter 8.

A. Domicile, Submission and the Carrying on of Business

It was settled more than two centuries ago in *Solomons* v. *Ross*[2] that the English court might recognise and give effect to foreign insolvency proceedings. What has been unclear, however, is the foundation upon which recognition may be afforded. In short, a number of possible bases of recognition can find more or less support in the decided cases: domicile, submission, the carrying on of business, residence and comity have all been judicially suggested. Unfortunately, no English court has ever embarked upon a proper review of this 'vexed and controversial'[3] topic. Nevertheless, it is here maintained that there are in fact three clearly established criteria: domicile,[4] submission[5] and the carrying on of business.[6]

---

[1] Stemming from, in particular, *Re Blithman* (1866) L.R. 2 Eq. 23, *post*.
[2] (1764) 1 Hy. Bl. 131n. See Raeburn (1949) 26 B.Y.I.L. 177 at 186–187 and Nadelmann (1946) 9 M.L.R. 154. As to what was decided in the case, see p. 250, *infra*.
[3] Dicey and Morris, *The Conflict of Laws* (12th ed., 1993) p. 1172.
[4] *Re Blithman* (1866) L.R. 2 Eq. 23.
[5] *Re Davidson's Settlement Trusts* (1873) L.R. 15 Eq. 383 and *Re Anderson* [1911] 1 K.B. 896, discussed in Raeburn (1949) 26 B.Y.I.L. 177 at 190–202 and in Blom-Cooper *Bankruptcy in Private International Law* (1954), pp. 93–100.
[6] *Re Vanzeller* (1832) 2 L.J.Bcy. 18; affd (1834) 1 Mont. & A 345, *Ex p Wucherer* (1832) 2 Deac. & Ch. 27, *Clark* v. *Mullick* (1840) 3 Moo. P.C. 252, *Goldsmid* v. *Cazenove* (1859) 7 HL Cas 785 and *Re Behrends* (1865) 12 L.T. 149, discussed *post*. In Scotland there is no doubt that carrying on a business is a sufficient basis of recognition: *Stein's Case* (1813) 1

B. The Nature of a Foreign Insolvency

The very nature of insolvency must influence the approach of an English court to the question of recognition. It might be tempting to say, as judges have on occasion,[7] that a foreign insolvency decree is a type of foreign judgment and therefore the rules on the recognition of foreign judgments should be applied. However, such a contention cannot be supported. A judgment, be it foreign or English, generally concerns only the parties thereto; yet an insolvency has a broader impact.[8] The status of an insolvent is likely to be affected; indeed, a corporation may even cease to exist. More importantly, the rights of third parties against the insolvent are affected, the insolvent's assets being distributed in a manner which may well purport to bind all the creditors. In this regard perhaps the clearest statement as to the nature of a foreign insolvency is found in the judgment of Innes JP in *Ex parte Stegmann*:[9]

> 'It is not the mere settlement by a foreign tribunal of a dispute between two litigants; it affects the rights of third parties who were never before the foreign court; and not only does it affect such rights, but it regulates in the future the dealings between the insolvent and all other persons. It is, in fact, a species of arrest or execution upon the property of the insolvent, followed by a distribution of it among his various creditors; it restricts the ordinary legal remedies of those creditors, and it imposes upon the insolvent disabilities which tend in the direction of an impairment of his status. To enforce such a decree absolutely and entirely in this country, as if it were a foreign judgment, is, therefore, out of the question.'

There are indeed a number of incidents of foreign insolvency proceedings to which the English court will not, at least automatically or unconditionally, give effect.[10] On the other hand, it must be stressed that the general attitude of English law to foreign insolvencies is characterised by marked generosity. No foreign judgment has a positive effect in England unless and until it is duly enforced, but a foreign insolvency does not require any formal process of registration: thus it has been settled for more than two centuries that, in appropriate circumstances, a foreign bankruptcy will at once vest the debtor's movable property in England in the foreign assignee. Moreover, an English judge has suggested that, where a debtor's movables vest in the foreign assignee, persons in England with custody of such property must give it up to the foreign assignee and will be penalized in costs should they insist upon the assignee first bringing an action in the English courts.[11]

Rose 462, *Obers* v. *Paton's Trustees* (1897) 24 R. 719 and *Hutcheson & Co.'s Administrator* v. *Taylor's Executrix* 1931 S.C. 484, but these cases rely to a certain degree upon a forensic domicile under Scottish law.

[7] *Per* Lord Romilly MR in *Re Blithman* (1866) L.R. 2 Eq. 23 at 26 and *per* Faucett J in *Proudfoot* v. *Stubbins* (1886) 7 L.R. 131 at 133 (N.S.W.).

[8] Although part of a foreign bankruptcy proceeding may constitute the equivalent of a judgment enforceable in England; see *Berliner Industriebank A.G.* v. *Jost* [1971] 2 Q.B. 463.

[9] 1902 T.S. 40 at 47.

[10] A foreign stay order has no automatic effect: see, e.g., *Banque Indosuez S.A.* v. *Ferromet Resources Inc.* [1993] B.C.L.C. 112, discussed below, p. 237; so too a foreign decree will never vest immovables in England in the foreign representative, although the court has a discretion to appoint the foreign representative as receiver of such property, *Re Kooperman* [1928] W.N. 101, discussed p. 222, *infra*.

[11] *Pélégrin* v. *Coutts & Co.* [1915] 1 Ch. 696 at 701–702, *per* Sargant J.

As a foreign decree of insolvency cannot be equated with an ordinary foreign judgment, the rules on the recognition of foreign insolvencies have quite separately to be determined.

Before turning to consider the detailed content and operation of the rules on recognition with reference to bankruptcy, two further points must be made plain. First, an insolvency may occur without the intervention of a foreign court,[12] and it is incorrect to maintain that only an insolvency pronounced by a foreign court may be recognised in England. Secondly, the familiar distinction in English law between bankruptcy and the winding up of a company may be without parallel in a foreign legal system.[13] The foreign law may draw no distinction between individual and corporate insolvency. Moreover, the foreign proceedings might be radically different from anything that can be done in a United Kingdom court. This may very well be the reason cases can be found in which foreign corporate insolvencies have been recognised with reference to the rules on bankruptcy,[14] or even some kind of combination of bankruptcy, winding up and administration.[15] That foreign insolvency proceedings are of a nature unknown to English law is certainly no reason to deny recognition.[16] So too, as a matter of common sense, because a foreign legal system may not draw any clear distinction between individual and corporate insolvency, the English law rules on recognition of on the one hand foreign bankruptcies and on the other foreign liquidations should be broadly similar in their operation. (The recognition of foreign liquidations is considered further in chapter 6.)

2. UNITED KINGDOM BANKRUPTCIES

A bankruptcy pronounced in the courts of Scotland or Northern Ireland is without more entitled to recognition in England.[17] It has been long established that the English court will not question the jurisdiction of a bankruptcy court in another part of the United Kingdom. As a Scottish judge once put it with reference to the Bankruptcy Act 1861:[18]

> 'This is not a question of international law . . . for we are here dealing with . . . the operation of an Act of the Imperial Parliament, to which we are bound to give effect.'

---

[12] There may be some type of voluntary liquidation with, or without, the assistance of a tribunal, Senate, Chamber or whatever other institution that may be specified in the local law. See also Wolff *Private International Law* (2nd ed., 1950), p. 564, n. 2.

[13] The term 'bankruptcy' may include both individual and corporate insolvency, as under the US Federal Bankruptcy Code, e.g. *Felixstowe Dock and Rly Co. v. United States Lines Inc.* [1989] Q.B. 360.

[14] As in, for instance, *Pitts v. Hill* (1987) 66 C.B.R. (N.S.) 273 or *Modern Terminals (Berth 5) Ltd. v. States SS Co.* [1979] H.K.L.R. 512. See also *New Hampshire Insurance Co. v. Rush & Tomkins Group plc, supra,* p. 129 (Dutch 'trustee in bankruptcy' appointed in relation to Dutch companies).

[15] As (*semble*) in *Macaulay v. Guaranty Trust Co of New York* (1927) 44 T.L.R. 99.

[16] See pp. 187–188, *infra.*

[17] *Galbraith v. Grimshaw* [1910] A.C. 508 at 511–512.

[18] *Per* the Lord Justice-Clerk in *Young v. Buckel* (1864) 2 M. 1077 at 1080. Note also *Wilkie v. Cathcart* (1870) 9 M. 168 and *Salaman v. Tod* 1911 S.C. 1214.

Under the current legislation the relevant provision is section 426(1) of the Insolvency Act 1986:[19]

> 'An order made by a court in any part of the United Kingdom in the exercise of jurisdiction in relation to insolvency shall be enforced in any other part of the United Kingdom as if it were made by a court exercising corresponding jurisdiction in that other part.'

Section 426(1) speaks only of enforcement, but that must inevitably carry with it recognition of the proceedings in Scotland or Northern Ireland. Whilst it is beyond doubt that a decree pronounced in another part of the United Kingdom must be recognised in England, the consequences thereof fall to be considered in chapter 8.

3. FOREIGN BANKRUPTCIES

A. Outline

The maxim *mobilia sequuntur personam* has played some considerable part in the formation of the English rules on the recognition of foreign bankruptcies. The use to which the maxim has at times been put has been twofold: firstly, as a basis of recognition of a bankruptcy or equivalent decree pronounced by a foreign court and, second, to justify restricting recognition to one single basis, namely domicile.[20] In the modern context it is fair to say the maxim is very much outworn,[1] not least because it has been established that as a general principle the transfer of movable property is governed by the *lex situs* irrespective of the domiciliary laws of transferor or transferee. With reference to foreign bankruptcies there is no doubt that, whilst domicile remains a basis of recognition, it occupies no exclusive position.

As long ago as 1754 the doctrine *mobilia sequuntur personam* was judicially condemned as 'an abstract notion not founded in nature nor agreeable to reason'.[2] The inherent weakness of the doctrine has, moreover, been revealed in a number of cases;[3] and, in any event, it is probable that the maxim originated from little more than a simple desire to justify that which comity, convenience and common sense required.[4] But one thing is certain: a rigid approach to recognition, an approach founded solely upon domicile, cannot be reconciled with authority. There are at least seven cases, albeit only at first instance, where the English court has expressly recognised a foreign bankruptcy where the debtor has been a party to the proceedings in the foreign court.[5]

---

[19] For the detailed operation of s. 426 of the Insolvency Act 1986 see chapter 15 *post*.
[20] See the discussion in the Court of Appeal in *Re Artola Hermanos* (1890) 24 Q.B.D. 640, p. 71, *ante*.
[1] Its application to bankruptcy has been critically reviewed by Raeburn (1949) 26 B.Y.I.L. 177.
[2] *Bradshaw and Ross* v. *Fairholm* (1754) Kilk 280.
[3] See pp. 73–74, *ante* and n. 5, *infra*.
[4] See, *passim*, the comments of Innes JP in *Ex p Stegmann* 1902 T.S. 40 at 47.
[5] *Re Davidson's Settlement Trusts* (1873) L.R. 15 Eq. 383, *Re Lawson's Trusts* [1896] 1 Ch. 175, *Re Anderson* [1911] 1 K.B. 896, *Re Craig* (1916) 86 L.J. Ch. 62, *Re Burke* (1919) 54 L.Jo. 430, *Bergerem v Marsh* (1921) 91 L.J.K.B. 80 and *Re Kooperman* [1928] W.N. 101. See also the decision of the Court of Appeal in *Ex p Dever* (1885) 14 Q.B.D. 611. Cf. *Harris* v. *Russell* (1868) 2 Q.S.C.R. 17, *passim*.

However, even two bases of recognition (domicile and submission) would not be sufficient. From a practical point of view, an example may best illustrate that reference merely to either the domicile of the bankrupt or participation by the bankrupt in the foreign proceedings is too restrictive. Let us say that a debtor has a domicile in New Zealand yet carries out extensive trade in France, where the debtor also resides. The debtor, finding himself in dire financial circumstances, quits France and takes up residence in Panama. Insolvency proceedings are commenced in France (the debtor taking no part therein) and a syndic is appointed by the French court. Subsequently, the syndic comes to England and attempts to recover the debtor's assets in England. If it be correct that recognition is limited to domicile or submission, then the French proceedings could not be recognised in England. (Nor, incidentally, would the English court[6] have jurisdiction under section 265 of the Insolvency Act 1986.) Obviously, the most practically relevant basis of recognition would be the carrying on of business within the jurisdiction of the foreign court. Yet the English rules, if they were limited to domicile and submission, would favour the fraudulent bankrupt (who runs up debts then flees) over those bankrupts who make every effort to participate in the foreign proceedings and co-operate with the foreign assignee.

Relevant authorities have in the past been overlooked. But fortunately, there are indeed several cases which establish that a foreign bankruptcy might be recognised by the English court if the bankrupt has carried on business within the jurisdiction of the foreign court.[7]

B. Domicile

Re Blithman[8] is an important decision in the history of the recognition of foreign bankruptcies. The facts concerned a fund of personal property in England. The deceased, Henwood, who was entitled to a reversionary interest in a trust, became insolvent in South Australia. Subsequently, the property fell into possession but, before the money was paid out, Henwood died. The trustees of the fund paid the money into court, and the question for Lord Romilly MR was entitlement to the fund as between Henwood's assignees under the South Australian insolvency and Henwood's executrix. His Lordship ordered an inquiry into Henwood's domicile, stating:[9]

> 'this is a question of domicile, and depends upon domicile alone; and that if Henwood was a domiciled Australian at the time, then that this property passed to the assignees, but that if he was not, then it passes to his legal personal representative, and she is the person entitled to receive it.'

Lord Romilly's judgment, accordingly, is very much based upon the domicile of the bankrupt.[10]

---

[6] Chapter 2, *ante*. Cf. the position under the European Convention, p. 162, *infra*.
[7] See p. 153, *post*; also Smart (1989) 9 O.J.L.S. 557.
[8] (1866) L.R. 2 Eq. 23.
[9] *Ibid.*, at 26.
[10] Although it by no means follows that recognition was denied to the South Australian proceedings; see p. 153, *post*.

In *Re Blithman* the Master of the Rolls considered whether the insolvent was a 'domiciled Australian'. It is of course not strictly correct to speak of a domicile in Australia: there must be a domicile in a particular State, i.e. South Australia.[11]

Although it cannot be denied that the English court may recognise a bankruptcy pronounced by the courts of the place in which the debtor was domiciled at the commencement of those proceedings, the question arises as to whether this basis of recognition should be given an extended operation. Thus a bankruptcy may not actually be pronounced in the courts of the domicile, but it may be recognised as effective under the domiciliary law. For instance, a debtor is domiciled in Malaysia but is declared bankrupt in Singapore, that Singapore decree being recognised as effective in Malaysia. Whilst there is no English authority directly upon this point, in such circumstances the Singaporean decree should be recognised in England. Certainly, at common law foreign decrees of divorce were recognised in like situations.[12] Moreover, an extended operation of domicile as a basis of recognition would be wholly consistent with the especial significance which English judges have generally given domicile in matters of cross-border insolvency.[13]

One bankruptcy case that tends to support an extended operation of domicile is *Re Tuticorin Cotton Press Co. Ltd.*[14] Alston was a domiciled Scot who had held shares in the Tuticorin Cotton Press Co. Ltd., an English registered company. There had in England been a winding up of the company, which resulted in a surplus. However, prior to the winding up, Alston had died. Subsequent to Alston's death (but prior to the winding up) Alston's estate had been sequestrated in Scotland. At the time of his death Alston had been a partner in a Scottish firm, C.R. & Co. Moreover, C. R. & Co. had itself been in partnership in Ceylon with two persons, Buchanan and Bois, under the style of A.S. & Co. In Scotland C.R. & Co. was also insolvent, and Muir was appointed trustee of both the estates of Alston and of C.R. & Co. To further complicate matters, Buchanan and Bois had been made bankrupt according to the laws of Ceylon and one Brown had been appointed assignee of their estates. In the course of the sequestration in Scotland it was alleged that Alston had held the shares in the Tuticorin Cotton Press Co. Ltd. in trust for the Ceylon firm, A.S. & Co. The Lord Ordinary in Scotland declared that Muir (as trustee of the sequestrated estate of C.R. & Co.) and Brown (as assignee under the law of Ceylon of Buchanan and Bois) were beneficially jointly entitled to the shares, with the legal title thereto being vested in Muir alone. In the English court the liquidator of the Tuticorin Cotton Press Co. Ltd. took out a summons for directions in respect of entitlement to the surplus payable on the shares held by Alston prior to his death. Vaughan Williams J,

---

[11] A like inaccuracy appears in *Semphill* v. *Queensland Sheep Investment Co. Ltd.* (1873) 29 L.T. 737 at 742.

[12] Under the so-called rule in *Armitage* v. *A-G* [1906] P. 135. See also the observation of Goulding J in relation to a foreign receiver in *Schemmer* v. *Property Resources Ltd.* [1975] Ch. 273 at 287.

[13] This is, of course, particularly so in respect of foreign corporations. However, even in respect of a foreign corporation, it is submitted that the corporate domicile occupies no *exclusive* position; see chapter 6, *post*.

[14] (1894) 64 L.J. Ch. 198, more fully reported at 71 L.T. 723. Cf. *Felixstowe Dock and Rly Co.* v. *United States Lines Inc.* [1989] Q.B. 360, p. 167, *post* (recognition of proceedings in United States District Court with reference to Delaware corporation).

expressly applying Scots law, held that legal title was vested in the Scottish sequestrator (Muir) to whom the liquidator should pay the surplus upon being given a joint receipt by Muir and Brown. For, it will be recalled, the Scottish court had determined that Muir and Brown were jointly beneficially entitled to the shares.

An analysis of *Re Tuticorin Cotton Press Co. Ltd.* in terms of the recognition of foreign bankruptcies reveals a number of propositions. First, the shares were registered in the name of Alston, who had died domiciled in Scotland. Secondly, under Scottish law title had vested in the Scottish sequestrator. Thirdly, the rights of the assignee appointed under the law of Ceylon were recognised in Scotland, the foreign assignee being jointly entitled with the Scottish sequestrator to the beneficial interest in the shares. Fourthly, Alston was not domiciled in Ceylon, nor was there any suggestion that Buchanan or Bois were domiciled in Ceylon. The rights of the Ceylonese assignee were given effect in England because they had been recognised under Scots law, the law of the domicile.

Hence, a foreign bankruptcy may be recognised in England if pronounced, or recognised as effective, under the law of the debtor's domicile.

C. Submission

Subsequent to *Re Blithman*[15] came several cases establishing that the bankruptcy jurisdiction of a foreign court may also be recognised in England if the bankrupt himself petitioned the foreign court, or otherwise submitted to its jurisdiction by appearing in the foreign court or presenting an appeal against an adjudication.[16] Reference may here be made to *Re Davidson's Settlement Trusts*[17] which concerned a fund of property in England. Prior to his death in 1868, the deceased had been adjudicated insolvent upon his own petition in Queensland. The question for the English court was entitlement to the fund as between the deceased's estate and the foreign assignee. James LJ (sitting as a judge of first instance) held that the domicile of the deceased was irrelevant. As the deceased had voluntarily submitted to the bankruptcy jurisdiction of the foreign court, the representative of the deceased's estate could not dispute the title of the foreign assignee.

Re Davidson's Settlement Trusts has been applied not merely where the debtor himself petitioned the foreign court,[18] but also where the debtor appeared personally or by a legal representative in the foreign proceedings[19] or appealed against an adjudication.[20] Thus in *Bergerem* v. *Marsh*[1] the defendant had been a partner in a Belgian *société en nom collectif*. That partnership was declared bankrupt, along with the defendant personally,

---

[15] (1866) L.R. 2 Eq. 23.

[16] See p. 143, n. 5, *ante*.

[17] (1873) L.R. 15 Eq. 383.

[18] *Re Lawson's Trusts* [1896] 1 Ch. 175, *Hunt* v. *Fripp* [1898] 1 Ch. 675 and *Re Burke* (1919) 54 L. Jo. 430. Cf. *Re Aylwin's Trusts* (1873) L.R. 16 Eq. 585.

[19] *Re Anderson* [1911] 1 K.B. 896 and *Re Craig* (1916) 86 L.J. Ch. 62.

[20] *Bergerem* v. *Marsh* (1921) 91 L.J.K.B. 80.

[1] *Ibid.* The decision was cited with approval by Parker LJ in *Metliss* v. *National Bank of Greece and Athens S.A.* [1957] 2 Q.B. 33 at 54.

by the Belgian court acting of its own motion. The defendant received notice of the decision of the Belgian court and lodged an unsuccessful appeal. Bailhache J recognised the Belgian bankruptcy by reference to the defendant's submission to the jurisdiction of the foreign tribunal. However, it was not brought to the attention of James LJ in *Re Davidson's Settlement Trusts* (nor has it seemingly been noticed in subsequent cases or commentaries) that two reports of *Re Blithman* assert that the bankrupt had indeed himself petitioned the South Australian court.[2] There is, nevertheless, no insuperable difficulty in reconciling the two cases.[3]

There is no clear appellate authority upon the apparent conflict between *Re Blithman* and *Re Davidson's Settlement Trusts*. But the decision in *Ex p Dever*[4] should briefly be noted. The facts concerned the proceeds of certain bills of exchange drawn by a firm in Colombo upon the liquidating debtors in England. The Colombo firm consisted of two partners, one of whom had gone insane and was resident in Germany. On the petition of the active partner, the firm was adjudicated insolvent in Ceylon and a trustee appointed. One question for the English Court of Appeal was whether the drawer's estate was in forced administration for the purposes of the rule in *Ex p Waring*.[5] Although authorities were not cited, the foreign insolvency was recognised by the members of the Court of Appeal:[6]

> 'It is clear that the estate of the acceptors is being administered under a forced administration. It has been disputed whether the drawers' estate is also under a forced administration, but the evidence which has been given as to the facts and the law of Colombo, seems to me to show that the partnership estate of the drawers is under a forced administration at Colombo.'

The drawer's insolvency was recognised in England and, moreover, the foreign trustee was represented by counsel before the English court.

Precisely what constitutes the necessary submission to the jurisdiction of a foreign court will vary according to the facts of any given case. Plainly, as in *Re Davidson's Settlement Trusts*,[7] participating in the foreign proceedings will amount to a submission. Appearing in the foreign court merely to contest jurisdiction alone (not arguing on the merits or requesting the exercise of the court's discretion against making an order) should not be seen as a submission. So too, it is suggested, the relevant submission must be a submission to the *bankruptcy* jurisdiction of the foreign court. In *Young* v. *Buckel*,[8] a decision of the Court of Session, Young had unsuccessfully defended an action in the Court of Common Pleas in England. The judgment creditor subsequently served a debtor's summons which resulted in an adjudication being made against Young in England. Young was domiciled and resident in Scotland and took no part in the English bankruptcy proceedings. The Court of Session recognised the English

---

[2] See 14 L.T. 6 at 7 (and 12 Jur. N.S. 84): 'and in 1863 took the benefit of the Act in force in that colony for the benefit of insolvent debtors. . . .'
[3] See p. 156, *post*.
[4] (1885) 14 Q.B.D. 611. See also the approval of *Bergerem* v. *Marsh* by Parker LJ in *Metliss* v. *National Bank of Greece and Athens S.A*, n. 1 *supra*.
[5] (1815) 19 Ves. 345.
[6] (1885) 14 Q.B.D. 611 at 621 *per* Brett MR.
[7] (1873) L.R. 15 Eq. 383.
[8] (1864) 2 M. 1077.

bankruptcy as 'a good and effectual deliverance of a court of competent jurisdiction'.[9] At first blush *Young* v. *Buckel* might suggest a most broad interpretation of submission: if a debtor has submitted to the jurisdiction of a foreign court by appearing in an action, then a subsequent bankruptcy founded upon a judgment debt may be recognised. But, in fact, *Young* v. *Buckel* involved a United Kingdom bankruptcy, the Scottish court being obliged to recognise the English bankruptcy as it had been obtained pursuant to an Act of the Imperial Parliament. *Young* v. *Buckel* is not an authority upon submission. In this context, submission refers to some participation by the bankrupt in the foreign bankruptcy proceedings.

D. Carrying on Business

The development of the English law rules on the recognition of foreign bankruptcies has been considerably confused by the generally held belief that, at the time *Re Blithman*[10] was decided, the domicile of the bankrupt constituted the sole available basis of recognition.[11] However, even by the mid-nineteenth century there existed a sufficient body of authority to establish that a foreign bankruptcy might be recognised by the English court if the bankrupt carried on business within the jurisdiction of the foreign court.

These older English cases may best be explained by being divided into three categories: Double Proof; Foreign Dividends; and Foreign Assignees in the English Court.

(i) *Double Proof*

Before the passing of the Bankruptcy Act 1861 if there were two commissions of bankruptcy taking place in England (for instance, joint and separate commissions) a bill holder would not be permitted to prove in both proceedings, but was put to an election.[12] The rules on double proof were similarly applied where there was a commission in England and an insolvency abroad. In *Re Vanzeller*[13] the bankrupt carried on business on his own account in England and as a member of a firm in Brazil. In 1830 the property of the firm was sequestrated in Brazil, and subsequently a commission issued in England against the bankrupt. A bill holder, having already participated in the Brazilian insolvency, sought to receive a dividend in England. The Court of Review treated the foreign insolvency in a like manner to a joint commission in England and would not permit a double proof, Sir George Rose stating:[14] 'I entertain no doubt, that the effect of a sequestration abroad is precisely the same as a commission here

---

[9] *Ibid.*, at 1081. English proceedings are reported as *Ex p Young* (1862) 7 L.T. 534.
[10] (1866) L.R. 2 Eq. 23.
[11] See, generally, Smart (1989) 9 O.J.L.S. 557.
[12] The doctrine was laid down in *Ex p Moult* (1832) 1 Deac. & Ch. 44.
[13] (1832) 2 L.J. Bcy. 18, affirmed by the Lord Chancellor in a two line judgment (1834) 1 Mont. & A. 345 at 357.
[14] (1832) 2 L.J. Bcy. 18 at 20. Sir George Rose was, perhaps, a little over-enthusiastic in his observation that the effect of a foreign insolvency is precisely the same as an English bankruptcy. The consequences of recognition are discussed in chapter 8.

. . .'. *Re Vanzeller* does not, however, reveal the basis upon which the Brazilian sequestration was recognised. Undoubtedly, business was carried on in Brazil. Yet, equally, it might be argued that the sequestration in Brazil was treated as effective in the Court of Review because of an estoppel: the bill holder having taken part in the foreign proceedings could not, when later in England, deny the validity of those proceedings. However, *Re Vanzeller* certainly contains no suggestion that the bankrupt's domicile was determinative of recognition.

Goldsmid v. Cazenove[15] also raised the question of double proof, following insolvencies in England and Brazil. Deane and Youle carried on business at Liverpool as well as, with a third person, at Pernambuco. In 1854 Deane and Youle were declared bankrupt in England and, in the following year, the Pernambuco firm entered into a *concordata*, ratified according to Brazilian law. The House of Lords held that a bill holder, having received a dividend in Brazil, could not also prove under the English commission. As in *Re Vanzeller*, the basis of recognition of the Brazilian insolvency was not discussed in their Lordships' House, although it may be noted that, in the court below, Knight Bruce LJ had mentioned, but without attaching any particular importance to it, the 'foreign domicile of the Pernambuco firm'[16] – a reference which points to the carrying on of business in Brazil as a foundation of the foreign court's jurisdiction.[17]

(ii) *Foreign Dividends*

It is well settled that, in a situation involving a multiplicity of bankruptcies, a creditor who has received a dividend in a foreign insolvency will not generally be permitted to prove in England without 'bringing into the common fund what he has received abroad'.[18] In *Banco de Portugal* v. *Waddell*[19] the members of a firm which carried on business in London and Oporto were made bankrupt, first in England and then in Portugal. A creditor who received a dividend in the Portuguese proceedings was permitted by the House of Lords to prove in England, but only upon accounting for what had been received in Portugal. Lord Blackburn stated:[20]

> 'It seems to me . . . that the Court of Bankruptcy in England had the right to administer all the personal property of these bankrupts, wherever that property was, whether in Portugal or in England; that when a Portuguese subject in any way got hold of part of that property under the Portuguese law, he was entitled to hold it, but when he had so got hold of part of the property, and he came to England to take advantage of the proceedings under the Bankruptcy Act, he could only do so upon appropriating that which he had received under the Portuguese law in payment of dividends, and taking no dividends until that sum was exhausted.'

[15] (1859) 7 HL Cas. 785.
[16] (1857) 1 De G. & J. 257 at 282.
[17] The doctrine of commercial domicile, or trading domicile, has no part in English private international law. Hence it seems likely that Knight Bruce LJ meant little more than that the firm had a place of business in Pernambuco.
[18] *Selkrig* v. *Davies* (1814) 2 Rose 291 at 318 *per* Lord Eldon LC.
[19] (1880) 5 App. Cas. 161.
[20] *Ibid.*, at 175.

Lord Blackburn's observation carries with it recognition of the Portuguese bankruptcy. Had the foreign creditor chosen to ignore the English proceedings, that would have been an end of the matter. Yet even when the foreign creditor entered a proof in the English bankruptcy, his rights (derived from the foreign proceedings) were not set aside, but rather the benefit received abroad had to be taken into consideration when distributing dividends in England.[1] Thus, in *Banco de Portugal* v. *Waddell* the Portuguese insolvency was recognised in England. The foreign creditor could retain the dividend derived from the foreign insolvency, but was prevented from taking advantage of the English proceedings until the dividend paid in England matched the sum the foreign creditor had already received in Portugal.[2]

This analysis of *Banco de Portugal* v. *Waddell* reveals that their Lordships were willing to recognise a foreign bankruptcy, at least to the extent of allowing a foreign creditor, who did not prove in England, to retain property obtained in a foreign insolvency. Their Lordships do not, however, identify the basis of recognition. Where a foreign creditor, having received property abroad, does not take part in the English bankruptcy, recognition cannot be explained by way of an estoppel on the part of the foreign creditor. For recognition, permitting the retention of property received abroad, affects not only the foreign creditor but more particularly the trustee in England and all the English creditors. In *Banco de Portugal* v. *Waddell* no mention is made of the domicile of the bankrupts, and it may be noted that, as in *Re Vanzeller and Goldsmid* v. *Cazenove*, business was carried on in the foreign jurisdiction. Of course, *Banco de Portugal* v. *Waddell* was decided after *Re Blithman*, yet their Lordships were undoubtedly applying the law as it had been laid down in *Selkrig* v. *Davies*[3] some 50 years before *Re Blithman*.

(iii) *Foreign Assignees in the English Court*

The right of a foreign assignee to sue in England, in respect of the obligations of the bankrupt, was demonstrated in a number of cases decided in the 1830s. These cases highlight a liberal approach by the English court to the recognition of foreign bankruptcies and, in particular, an approach not restricted to domicile but favouring the carrying on of business in the foreign jurisdiction.

In *Ex p Wucherer*[4] the bankrupt carried on business on his own account in England and as a member of a firm trading in Brazil. In September 1830 the Brazilian house shipped, from Brazil, certain goods which were to be sold by the bankrupt on account of the Brazilian house. In December 1830 a 'cession' of the property of the firm took place in Brazil, as a result of which the petitioners were appointed assignees according to Brazilian law. In July 1831 a separate commission issued against the bankrupt in England. The proceeds of sale of the goods having been

---

[1] See also at 167 *per* Cairns LC.
[2] See also *Ex p Wilson* (1872) 7 Ch. App. 490 and chapter 12, *post*.
[3] (1814) 2 Rose 291.
[4] (1832) 2 Deac. & Ch. 27. The case arose out of the insolvency of the same firm as in *Re Vanzeller* (1833) 2 L.J. Bcy. 18, *ante*.

received by the English assignees, an order was sought directing the English assignees to hand over the proceeds of sale to the petitioners (that is, the Brazilian assignees) for the benefit of the creditors of the Brazilian firm. The Court of Review was satisfied that the goods had throughout belonged to the Brazilian firm and, accordingly, ordered the English assignees to pay the proceeds of sale to the Brazilian assignees.

Ex p Wucherer is an interesting decision, for its facts reveal that not only were foreign assignees permitted to maintain an action in England but, in addition, the foreign assignees recovered property in England in the hands of assignees under an English commission. However, the judges in the Court of Review did not seek to explain the basis upon which the Brazilian insolvency was recognised. Nevertheless, the lack of any reference to domicile supports the submission that, prior to *Re Blithman*, recognition was not restricted to the domicile of the bankrupt. It may also be noted that in *Ex p Brown*[5] foreign assignees were represented before the Court of Review, again there being no inquiry into the domicile of the bankrupts.

Moreover, a positive pronouncement upon the recognition of foreign insolvencies can be found in *Alivon* v. *Furnival*.[6] An action was brought in England upon a French judgment by syndics of a merchant who had become bankrupt according to the laws of France. The defendant questioned the right of the syndics to maintain the action; for, in particular, although three syndics had been appointed in France, only two of them were plaintiffs in the English suit. The Court of Exchequer, making reference not to domicile but to the comity of nations, recognised the right of the syndics to sue in England:[7]

> 'The property in the effects of the bankrupt does not appear to be absolutely transferred to these syndics in the way that those of a bankrupt are in this country; but it should seem that the syndics act as mandatories or agents for the creditors; the whole three or any two or one of them having the power to sue for and recover the debts in their own names. This is a peculiar right of action, created by the law of that country; and we think it may by the comity of nations be enforced in this, as much as the right of foreign assignees or curators, or foreign corporations, appointed or created in a different way from that which the law of this country requires.'

Whilst *Alivon* v. *Furnival* involved a foreign receiver and not actually a foreign assignee, there is nothing in the judgment to suggest that any distinction should be drawn between the two. Indeed, in 1927, Clauson J is reported to have considered *Alivon* v. *Furnival* as:[8]

> 'an authority for the proposition that, if receivers *or assignees in bankruptcy* had, according to the law of the country in which they had been appointed, a right to sue in their own names for a chose in action . . . that gave them a right which this country, by the comity of nations, would treat as though it were a right of action at common law . . . .'

This observation is *obiter* since his Lordship was in fact dealing with interim receivers of a Delaware corporation. Nevertheless, Clauson J appears to have favoured a liberal approach to recognition in general.

---

[5] (1838) 7 L.J. Bcy. 29 at 31.
[6] (1834) 1 Cr. M. & R. 277.
[7] *Ibid.*, at 296.
[8] *Macaulay* v. *Guaranty Trust Co of New York* (1927) 44 T.L.R. 99 at 100 (emphasis added). The case involved *interim* receivers, see p. 194, *infra*.

The right of a foreign assignee to enforce the obligations of the bankrupt also received the attention of the Privy Council in *Clark* v. *Mullick*.[9] Their Lordships were hearing an appeal from the Supreme Court in Calcutta in respect of the effect to be given in India to an English bankruptcy. The assignee of an English bankrupt had brought an action of assumpsit in Calcutta but the Supreme Court had entered a non-suit. The Privy Council, affirming the court below, held that the relevant English legislation[10] *did not* extend to India and that the assignee had failed to prove the bankruptcy and assignment in England. However, had the English bankruptcy been proved, the assignee's rights would have been recognised, for Lord Brougham stated:[11]

'It is not denied, that an assignment validly made under a commission here, has the effect of carrying to the assignee a right to sue in India for debts due to the bankrupt. This follows from all the rights of the bankrupt being duly vested in the assignee vested in him by operation of the bankrupt laws as effectually as if he had himself made a voluntary transfer of them good by the law of the country where it was executed. But the question is whether or not this assignment had been duly proved?'

A more liberal attitude to the recognition of foreign bankruptcies is difficult to envisage – Lord Brougham's only express requirement being that the title of the assignee be 'good by the law of the country where it was executed'.

One further example in which the English court displayed a willingness to recognise a foreign bankruptcy, pronounced by the courts in whose jurisdiction the bankrupt carried on business, is *Re Behrends*.[12] The bankrupt had carried on business in Hamburg since 1852. In 1863 the bankrupt left Hamburg and was subsequently made bankrupt there. Assignees or *curatores bonorum* were appointed in the Hamburg proceedings. In 1864 the bankrupt came to England and thereafter presented a petition. The vast majority of the creditors resided in Hamburg. The Court of Bankruptcy determined that the English proceedings would be adjourned *sine die* with liberty to the bankrupt to apply for his discharge in England after the termination of proceedings in Hamburg:[13]

'This man was, however, made bankrupt in Hamburg before he petitioned this court, and it may well be said that the place where his books of account and property were left, where his trading was carried on and the greater part of his debts were contracted, and where he was first made bankrupt, is the proper place for him to make such a disclosure of his affairs as his creditors may require.'

Although the Hamburg *curatores bonorum* did not seek to appear before the English court, there can be no question that the court was willing to recognise the foreign proceedings, conducted in the jurisdiction in which the bankrupt had carried on business.

---

[9] (1840) 3 Moo. P.C.C. 252.
[10] 2nd and 3rd Will IV c.114 and 6 Geo IV c.16.
[11] (1839) 3 Moo. P.C.C. 252 at 279.
[12] (1865) 12 L.T. 149. This is also an interesting case on *forum non conveniens* and is discussed in chapter 3.
[13] *Ibid.*, at 150.

(iv) *Summary*

Prior to the decision in *Re Blithman* the domicile of the bankrupt did not constitute the sole basis of recognition by the English court of a foreign bankruptcy. The facts of two cases in the Court of Review (*Re Vanzeller* and *Ex parte Wucherer*) both involved the carrying on of business within the jurisdiction of the foreign court. Likewise, business was carried on in Brazil in *Goldsmid* v. *Cazenove*, in France in *Alivon* v. *Furnival*, in Hamburg in *Re Behrends* and in England in the Privy Council case of *Clark* v. *Mullick*. In these cases the court was prepared to recognise a foreign insolvency without any reference to the question of the domicile of the bankrupt. It is, of course, correct that the judgments in these cases (with the exception of *Alivon* v. *Furnival*) contain no analysis of the basis of recognition of the foreign insolvency concerned, whilst in *Alivon* v. *Furnival* the Court of Exchequer made no more specific reference than to the comity of nations. Nevertheless, it cannot be supposed that in every instance the judges were unaware of, or failed to take into consideration, the fact that the insolvency before them was pronounced in a foreign court. Indeed, authorities on the private international law of bankruptcy were cited (either by counsel or the court) in *Re Vanzeller*,[14] *Alivon* v. *Furnival*[15] and, at some length, in *Clark* v. *Mullick*.[16]

Accordingly, several cases can be found, each decided prior to *Re Blithman*, which reveal that recognition of a foreign insolvency was not dependent solely upon domicile. It is submitted that the common feature of all these cases is the carrying on of business; and, when taken together, these cases can lead to no conclusion other than that a foreign bankruptcy might be recognised in England if the bankrupt carried on business within the jurisdiction of the foreign court.[17]

E. *Re Blithman* Explained

A proper understanding of *Re Blithman* supports the proposition that an English court could recognise a foreign bankruptcy regardless of the domicile of the bankrupt.

The facts of *Re Blithman*, it will be recalled, involved a trust fund of property in England. Lord Romilly MR resolved that, as between assignees under the South Australian insolvency and an English personal representative, the domicile of the deceased was the determining factor:[18]

---

[14] In which counsel discussed *Phillips* v. *Hunter* (1795) 2 Hy. Bl. 402, see (1834) 1 Mont. & A. 345 at 356 before the Lord Chancellor.

[15] Parke B cited *Solomons* v. *Ross* (1764) 1 Hy. Bl. 131n. at (1834) 1 Cr. M. & R. 277 at 296.

[16] In which counsel cited *Alivon* v. *Furnival* (1834) 1 Cr. M. & R. 277, *Phillips* v. *Hunter* (1795) 2 Hy. Bl. 402, *Selkrig* v. *Davies* (1814) 2 Rose 291, *Sill* v. *Worswick* (1791) 1 Hy. Bl. 665, *Solomons* v. *Ross* (1764) 1 Hy. Bl. 131n., *Neal* v. *Cottingham* (1770) 1 Hy. Bl. 134n., *Jollett* v. *Deponthieu* (1769) 1 Hy. Bl. 131n. and *Stein's Case: Royal Bank of Scotland* v. *Cuthber* (1813) 1 Rose 462. The cases are analysed in chapter 10 in the context of foreign attachments.

[17] In *Re Borovsky and Weinbaum* [1902] 2 K.B. 312 a Belgian curator was heard in the English court, the bankrupts having carried on business in Antwerp and London.

[18] (1866) L.R. 2 Eq. 23 at 26.

'if Henwood was a domiciled Australian at the time, then that this property passed to the assignees, but that if he was not, then it passes to his legal personal representative, and she is the person entitled to receive it.'

Yet his Lordship's determination, whilst unquestionably in favour of the domicile, cannot be taken as amounting to a denial of recognition of the South Australian insolvency. For the judgment immediately continues:[19]

'That does not dispose of everything, but it was argued with great force, although I do not think it affects this particular question, that if the domicile was not Australian, nevertheless, by reason of the comity of nations, this would follow that the insolvency being in the nature of a foreign judgment, the court would give effect to it, and give the parties the benefit of it against the property of the insolvent in this country; and Mr. Martelli cited several cases to establish that point.[20] I am disposed to assent to that, but I do not think it would entitle the assignees to receive this sum of money.'

Thus the judgment of the Master of the Rolls reveals two propositions. Firstly, his Lordship was disposed to assent to the contention that 'by reason of the comity of nations' effect could be given in England to the South Australian insolvency. Secondly, if the deceased were domiciled in England, the assignees would not receive the fund in preference to the English personal representative. Only the first proposition is a matter of recognition. The second proposition (upon which is founded the actual decision in *Re Blithman*) expresses the *effect or consequence* of such recognition: that is, even though the foreign bankruptcy might be recognised, the claim of the assignees to property in England could not prevail over that of the personal representative of a domiciled Englishman.

The distinction between recognition and the *consequences* of recognition is quite familiar, at least in modern English private international law. Thus a foreign bankruptcy may be recognised but it will not have the effect of transferring immovables in England to the foreign assignee.[1] So too, in respect of movable property in England, a foreign bankruptcy if recognised will not override any prior attachments by creditors in England.[2] *Re Blithman* is a decision upon the consequence of recognition: although the South Australian insolvency might be recognised nevertheless the money in court would, assuming the bankrupt's domicile to be English, be paid to the personal representative. Indeed, *Re Blithman* cannot properly be explained as decided upon the issue of recognition, rather than the consequence of recognition. If the South Australian insolvency were simply not recognised, Lord Romilly could not have been 'disposed to assent' to counsel's submission that by reason of the comity of nations the court could give effect to the foreign insolvency. Similarly, if his Lordship had denied recognition, *cadit quaestio*, the assignees' claim would have been at an end: yet Lord Romilly clearly considered that the assignees might take further proceedings, even if the bankrupt had been domiciled in England:[3]

---

[19] *Ibid.*

[20] Mr. Martelli being counsel for the foreign assignees. The cases cited were the well-known decisions in *Solomons* v. *Ross* (1764) 1 Hy. Bl. 131n., *Sill* v. *Worswick* (1791) 1 Hy. Bl. 665 and *Selkrig* v. *Davies* (1814) 2 Rose 291.

[1] *Waite* v. *Bingley* (1882) 21 Ch. D. 674, chapter 8, *post*.

[2] *Galbraith* v. *Grimshaw* [1910] A.C. 508.

[3] (1866) L.R. 2 Eq. 23 at 26 (emphasis added).

'I am therefore of the opinion that, upon this occasion, assuming the domicile to be English, the money ought to be paid to the petitioner, who is the legal personal representative, *and that it is for the assignees to take such steps as they may think fit for the purpose of asserting their claim.*'

Quite simply, if recognition had been denied, the assignees could not have had any claim of which the English court might have had cognisance.

That *Re Blithman* turns upon the consequence of recognition becomes readily apparent when other reports of the case are considered.[4] It will be recalled that counsel for the assignees contended that, by reason of the comity of nations, effect could be given to the South Australian insolvency even if the bankrupt were not domiciled there. The *Law Report* states that Lord Romilly was 'disposed to assent to that'.[5] However, in the *Law Journal* Lord Romilly is reported as commenting:[6]

'I am disposed to assent to that view, but not so as to give effect to it in the way I am asked to do. I think that the personal representatives must receive the fund in the first instance, and then the assignees may take proceedings against her to get at the fund.'

Thus, as indeed the *Law Report* itself suggests, although the personal representatives would receive the fund, the foreign assignees could subsequently take proceedings against the personal representative 'for the purpose of asserting their claim'.[7] If recognition had been denied to the South Australian insolvency, the assignees would have lacked *locus standi* to take subsequent proceedings against the personal representative.[8]

Accordingly, the judgment in *Re Blithman* supports an approach to recognition not limited to domicile but, at the same time, purports to restrict the effect or consequence of that recognition.

The restrictive effect or consequence of recognition contemplated by Lord Romilly may briefly be considered. As a decision restricting the effect of recognition of a foreign bankruptcy, *Re Blithman* can claim only a very limited scope of application. For the case depends upon a combination of three particular factors: (i) that the bankrupt was domiciled in England; (ii) that there is property in England; and (iii) that such property is claimed by the English personal representative of the bankrupt. Accordingly if, for instance, the property in question is not in England, *Re Blithman* does not require any restriction upon the effect of a foreign bankruptcy recognised by the English court.[9] So too, if property in England is claimed not by the personal representatives in England but by the bankrupt's creditors or an English trustee, *Re Blithman* will not apply. In this context it may be recalled that *Ex p Wucherer*, decided in 1832, involved a dispute between English

---

[4] See 35 L.J. Ch. 255, 35 Beav. 219, 14 L.T. 6 and 12 Jur. N.S. 84.
[5] See p. 154, text to n. 19, *ante*.
[6] 35 L.J. Ch. 255 at 257, see also 35 Beav. 219 at 222.
[7] Note 3, *ante*.
[8] See, *passim*, *Re Artola Hermanos* (1890) 24 Q.B.D. 640 at 644 *et seq.* Lord Romilly also seems to have recognised the foreign proceedings as vesting the property *in Australia* in the assignees: 'the property of the insolvent in Australia vested in his assignees there, in the same way that the property of an insolvent here would vest in assignees here' (35 L.J. Ch. 255 at 257, see also 14 L.T. 6 at 7).
[9] Lord Romilly himself is reported as stating that 'the property of the insolvent in Australia vested in his assignees there', n. 8, *ante*.

and foreign assignees, and the Court of Review gave full effect to the foreign assignees' title to property in England.[10] Lastly, *Re Blithman* will only be relevant where the deceased had been domiciled in England. To take an example: if the deceased were pronounced bankrupt in Queensland (where business had been carried on) but had been domiciled in New Zealand, *Re Blithman* would at once be distinguishable, and there would be no reason to restrict the effect in England of the Queensland bankruptcy.

Thus, in the absence of evidence that the deceased's domicile was English, a foreign assignee's right to property in England, even as against a personal representative appointed in England, will not be restricted by reference to *Re Blithman*. However, it remains necessary to reconcile *Re Blithman* and *Re Davidson's Settlement Trusts* as both cases did involve a dispute over property in England between a foreign assignee and the English personal representative of a deceased who (*semble*) had been domiciled in England. The two cases cannot be reconciled by reference to the bases of recognition. It is simplistic, indeed incorrect, to state that in *Re Blithman* the South Australian insolvency was not recognised, whereas in *Re Davidson's Settlement Trusts* the Queensland insolvency was recognised, as the deceased had himself presented the petition in the foreign court. For *Re Blithman* is a decision upon the consequence of recognition and Lord Romilly did not deny recognition to the South Australian decree. Nevertheless, *Re Blithman* and *Re Davidson's Settlement Trusts* may be reconciled by way of the 'estoppel' that arose in the latter decision.[11] In *Re Blithman* the foreign insolvency was given a restricted effect and the deceased's personal representative received the property in England: in *Re Davidson's Settlement Trusts*, as the deceased had himself presented the petition in the foreign court, it did not lie in the mouth of his personal representative to dispute the effect of the foreign insolvency; accordingly, the property in England was received by the foreign assignee. This explanation, it is submitted, will hold good even if the deceased in *Re Blithman* had petitioned the South Australian court (as is suggested in two reports of the case[12]). Since neither Lord Romilly nor counsel referred to the manner in which the foreign proceedings were commenced, there is nothing to prevent *Re Davidson's Settlement Trusts* operating as a gloss upon the earlier decision. Lord Romilly's restrictive approach to the effect of recognition may not be raised by persons claiming through the bankrupt, where the bankrupt has himself invoked the jurisdiction of the foreign court.

To summarise, *Re Blithman* is undoubtedly an important case in historical terms; however, the decision can now claim only a most limited application. *Re Blithman* rests upon the effect or consequence of recognition, and its application depends not upon any general principle but rather upon its particular facts: property in England claimed by the personal representative of a person domiciled in England. Moreover, *Re Blithman* cannot be prayed in aid by the personal representative if the bankrupt presented the petition abroad, or consented to the jurisdiction of the

---

[10] This explanation is applicable to *Re Anderson* [1911] 1 K.B. 896, *Re Craig* (1916) 86 L.J. Ch. 62 and *Bergerem* v. *Marsh* (1921) 91 L.J.K.B. 80.

[11] This explanation would similarly apply to *Re Lawson's Trust* [1896] 1 Ch. 175 and *Re Burke* (1919) 54 L.Jo. 430.

[12] 14 L.T. 6 at 7 and 12 Jur. N.S. 84, p. 147 n. 2, *ante*.

foreign court. In addition, Lord Romilly himself envisaged that foreign assignees (although not entitled to property in preference to the personal representative) might in any event bring proceedings against the personal representative 'for the purpose of asserting their claim'.

F. Recognition on Other Grounds

The vast majority of foreign bankruptcies are likely to fall within one of the three heads of jurisdiction discussed above: domicile, submission and carrying on business. Yet it is relevant to inquire whether any other grounds of recognition can be made out as a matter of either authority or principle.

(i) *Residence*

There appears to be no English decision recognising a foreign bankruptcy on the basis of the residence of the bankrupt.[13] In *Watson* v. *Renton*[14] Lord Eskgrove stated:[15]

'Every act and every deed relating to a movable estate, executed conformably to the custom of the place *where the person is resident* will be good and effectual in law.'

But his Lordship's reference to residence is merely *obiter*, for *Watson* v. *Renton* concerned the discharge of a (*semble*) Scottish contract by an English commission.

Perhaps the strongest argument in favour of residence is by way of analogy to carrying on business. Where a trader has carried on business within the jurisdiction of the foreign court, a foreign bankruptcy may be recognised in England. Carrying on business may be seen as constituting business presence within the jurisdiction of the foreign court. But carrying on business is, of course, of no relevance to an individual who has not in any way traded. There is, moreover, no inherent reason for the English rules on recognition to be more favourable in respect of a trader than an ordinary individual. In terms of the individual, residence is the equivalent of the business presence of a trader arising from the carrying on of business. Hence it is suggested that residence within the jurisdiction of the foreign court should be regarded as a sufficient foundation for recognition of a foreign bankruptcy.

(ii) *Comity and Reciprocity*

As we have seen, in *Alivon* v. *Furnival*, *Macaulay* v. *Guaranty Trust Company of New York* and *Re Blithman*[16] the judges made reference to the comity of nations. So too, in the Court of Session in *Obers* v. *Paton's Trustee*[17] the Lord President opined:[18]

---

[13] The courts in South Africa have rejected residence, but in so doing made it clear that they were applying Roman-Dutch law rather than English common law: see *Ex p Palmer* 1993 (3) S.A. 359 at 365.
[14] (1792) Bell S.C. 92.
[15] *Ibid.*, at 100.
[16] (1834) 1 Cr. M & R. 277, (1927) 44 T.L.R. 99 and (1866) L.R. 2 Eq. 23 respectively, *ante*.
[17] (1897) 24 R. 719.
[18] *Ibid.*, at 732.

'It seems difficult to the degree of impossibility for this court to decline on principle to recognise if done abroad what it is itself bound to do and daily does at home.'

Thus, it might be argued that the English court should recognise the jurisdiction of a foreign court over a bankrupt where, *mutatis mutandis*, the English court would itself claim jurisdiction under section 265 of the Insolvency Act 1986 (section 265 referring to domicile, presence, ordinary residence, place of residence and the carrying on of business in England and Wales). A like contention was accepted by the English Court of Appeal in respect of the recognition of foreign divorces in *Travers* v. *Holley*.[19]

However, there have always been compelling theoretical objections to a doctrine of comity. As was stated even two centuries ago:[20]

'Though much has been said about *comitas*, it is an improper term; there is no such thing as a decision from complaisance. Where judges determine by the law of another country, they do it *ex justicia*; they are bound to do it.'

As the English court is not bound to exercise jurisdiction under section 265 of the Insolvency Act 1986, the court would on the basis of comity not be bound to recognise any foreign insolvency. Recognition would become an exercise of judicial discretion. Moreover, the criteria relevant to the exercise by the English court of its bankruptcy jurisdiction[1] cannot be applied in the context of recognition of foreign insolvencies.

More significantly, an argument based upon *Travers* v. *Holley* was not accepted by the Court of Appeal in the context of a company insolvency in *Re Trepca Mines Ltd*.[2] Comity was also rejected in *Felixstowe Dock and Rly Co.* v. *United States Lines Inc*.[3] The latter case concerned a US corporation (the defendant) which had carried on business throughout the world and was registered in England as an oversea company under section 691 of the Companies Act 1985. The defendant corporation was under reorganisation in the United States in accordance with Chapter 11 of the US Federal Bankruptcy Code. The reorganisation envisaged the continuation of the defendant's business in North America, but the cessation of operations in Europe. The plaintiffs commenced proceedings in England against the defendant and obtained Mareva injunctions, restraining the defendant from removing certain assets out of the jurisdiction. But a United States court had, prior to the issue of the Mareva injunctions in England, granted a restraining order which purported to stay all actions against the defendant worldwide. The defendant sought to have the Mareva injunctions discharged on the basis that, by reference to international comity, the English court should give effect to the order of the United States bankruptcy court. Hirst J dismissed the defendant's application upon the very peculiar facts (as found) in that case, rejecting the defendant's appeal to comity.[4]

---

[19] [1953] P. 246.

[20] *Watson* v. *Renton* (1792) Bell S.C. 92 at 106 *per* the Lord Justice-Clerk.

[1] Chapter 3, *ante*.

[2] [1960] 1 W.L.R. 1273; see also the comments of Goulding J in *Schemmer* v. *Property Resources Ltd.* [1975] Ch. 273 at 285.

[3] [1989] Q.B. 360. See, generally, p. 231, *infra*.

[4] *Ibid.*, at 375. Cf. the approach of Hoffmann J in *Banque Indosuez S.A.* v. *Ferromet Resources Inc.* [1993] B.C.L.C. 112, p. 232, *infra*.

Of course, *Felixstowe Dock and Rly Co.* v. *United States Lines Inc.* may be distinguished as the US proceeding was undoubtedly recognised in England, the question before Hirst J being whether effect would be given to a foreign restraining order in the particular circumstances of that case. Similarly, *Re Trepca Mines Ltd.* concerned the recognition of a foreign judgment in an English winding up and did not deal with the recognition of foreign insolvency proceedings. Nevertheless, it is maintained that the judicial tide, as it were, has very much turned against comity. Comity should not be regarded as a separate basis for the recognition of foreign bankruptcies.

(iii) *Presence of Assets*

It is thought that the English court will not accord recognition to a foreign bankruptcy founded upon nothing more than the presence of assets within the jurisdiction of the foreign court.[5] Thus, for example, a foreign assignee so appointed would not be entitled to claim the bankrupt's movable property in England.

Although a foreign bankruptcy based solely upon the presence of assets will not be recognised in England, it does not follow that the foreign bankruptcy law will be wholly ineffectual. Let us say that bankruptcy proceedings are commenced in Panama. The debtor is not domiciled or resident in Panama, nor has the debtor carried on business there or participated in those proceedings. There are, however, assets in Panama. The assets are gathered in by the Panamanian trustee, who sells them in accordance with the law of Panama to X. The funds so realised are distributed to creditors in the Panamanian proceedings. X subsequently brings those assets, formerly belonging to the debtor, to England. The debtor will not be able successfully to challenge X's title. It is not that the Panamanian bankruptcy is recognised in England, but rather X has validly acquired title to movable property according to the *lex situs*. Such title remains valid even when the property is removed from Panama (the original *situs*) and taken to England.[6]

Accordingly, even though a foreign bankruptcy be not recognised in the English court, the foreign law may still have some effect as the *lex situs* governing the transfer of title to movable property in that foreign country.

G. Statutory Bases of Recognition

(i) *Insolvency Act 1986, section 426*

Section 426(4) of the Insolvency Act 1986 provides:[7]

> 'The courts having jurisdiction in relation to insolvency law in any part of the United Kingdom shall assist the courts having corresponding jurisdiction in any other part of the United Kingdom or any other relevant country or territory.'

---

[5] *Dicey and Morris*, p. 1174.
[6] *Cammell* v. *Sewell* (1860) 5 H. & N. 728, *Winkworth* v. *Christie, Manson and Woods Ltd.* [1980] Ch. 496.
[7] Considered in detail in chapter 15.

In practice, it is very likely that bankruptcy proceedings in a foreign court which has requested the assistance of the English court under section 426(4) would be entitled to recognition in England under the existing common law rules. For, taken together, domicile, submission, carrying on business and residence constitute a liberal approach to the question of recognition. But if the requesting court's jurisdiction fell outside the common law rules, there is nothing in section 426 which necessarily prevents the English court from lending its assistance. In *Re Kooperman*[8] the English court, acting under its inherent jurisdiction, lent its assistance to a foreign trustee, the facts revealing that the bankrupt had submitted to the jurisdiction of the foreign court. However, *Re Kooperman* obviously should not be relied upon to restrict the application of section 426, the section not being restricted to cases where recognition is in any event available at common law.[9]

(ii) *Recognition of Trusts Act 1987*

It may well be, at least in theory, that the provisions of the Recognition of Trusts Act 1987 are relevant to the recognition of foreign bankruptcies.[10] At the outset, however, it must be noted that such relevance is very much marginal. The 1987 Act gives effect in the United Kingdom to the Hague Convention of 1984 on the recognition of trusts. The Act does not specifically address the recognition of foreign bankruptcies. Nevertheless, Article 2 of the Convention identifies a 'trust' as:

> 'the legal relationship created inter vivos or on death by a person, the settlor, when assets have been placed under the control of a trustee for the benefit of a beneficiary or for a specified purpose.'

Article 3 further provides:

> 'The Convention applies only to trusts created voluntarily and evidenced in writing.'

Obviously, most foreign bankruptcies would not fall within Articles 2 and 3. However, at least on the face of it, certain foreign bankruptcies appear to satisfy those Articles: specifically, where a debtor voluntarily conveys property to a trustee for a 'specified purpose', namely the distribution of such assets amongst the creditors.

Recognition under the Hague Convention is dealt with in Chapter III thereof and:

> 'shall imply, as a minimum, that the trust property constitutes a separate fund, that the trustee may sue and be sued in his capacity as trustee, and that he may appear or act in this capacity before a notary or any person acting in an official capacity'.

However, it is unnecessary to inquire further into the operation of the Recognition of Trusts Act 1987 in respect of foreign bankruptcies, for any bankruptcy which may fall within Articles 2 and 3 will inevitably be

---

[8] [1928] W.N. 101.
[9] See p. 417, *post*.
[10] The Act is considered generally, but without reference to bankruptcy, by Hayton (1987) 36 I.C.L.Q. 260.

recognised under the common law rules, the bankrupt having instituted the foreign insolvency proceedings. As a practical matter, it is plainly wiser to rely upon cases such as *Re Davidson's Settlement Trusts*[11] and *Bergerem* v. *Marsh*[12] than to speculate as to the operation of the Recognition of Trusts Act 1987.

H. Bankruptcy and Death

Under a particular foreign legal system it may be permitted to a foreign court to pronounce a bankruptcy decree in respect of the estate of a deceased debtor. Such authority as exists suggests that the jurisdiction of a foreign court is not confined to bankruptcy proceedings in respect of living debtors.

In *Re Burke*[13] the debtor had himself petitioned the foreign court, but died prior to the adjudication. Nevertheless, the English court did recognise the foreign proceedings in respect of the deceased. It is submitted that, with reference to recognition, no distinction is to be drawn between foreign bankruptcy proceedings commenced before or after the demise of a debtor.

In the Scottish case of *Hutcheson & Co.'s Administrator* v. *Taylor's Executrix* Taylor, a domiciled Scot who had up until his death been a member of a trading partnership in Portugal, had died in 1925. In 1927 an order was made by a court in Portugal declaring both the firm and the individual partners thereof (including Taylor) insolvent. The Court of Session recognised the Portuguese bankruptcy, even though it had been commenced more than two years after Taylor's demise.[14]

4. SUMMARY

Bankruptcies pronounced in Scotland or in Northern Ireland are, without more, to be recognised in England. Other foreign bankruptcies will be recognised in England as follows:

(i)   where the bankruptcy has been pronounced under, or is recognised by, the law of the debtor's domicile;[15]

(ii) where the debtor participated in the foreign proceedings;

(iii) where the debtor carried on business, or (*semble*) was resident, in the foreign jurisdiction.[16]

---

[11] (1873) L.R. 15 Eq. 383, *ante*.

[12] (1921) 91 L.J.K.B. 80, *ante*.

[13] (1919) 54 L. Jo. 430. See also the comments of Vaughan Williams J in the course of argument in *Re Tuticorin Cotton Press Co. Ltd.* (1894) 71 L.T. 723. Cf. *Araya* v. *Coghill* 1921 S.C. 462.

[14] 1931 S.C. 484, 493–494. For details of this decision see p. 230, *infra*.

[15] The debtor's domicile at the time the foreign proceedings are commenced (or the debtor's domicile immediately prior to death) being the relevant consideration.

[16] That is, carrying on business or (*semble*) residence prior to the commencement of the foreign proceedings or prior to the debtor's death.

5. EUROPEAN CONVENTION ON INSOLVENCY PROCEEDINGS

If the European Convention on Insolvency Proceedings were to be introduced into English law it would add one significant ground to the bases of recognition currently existing under the common law rules. In Article 3 the Convention envisages that any primary or main proceedings should be opened in the Contracting State in which a debtor has its 'centre of main interests'. Such proceedings, obviously, are entitled to recognition in every other Contracting State.[17] The precise place where a debtor has its centre of main interests will always be a question of fact, and may or may not be where the debtor is domiciled.[18] Where the debtor also has an establishment in another Contracting State, secondary proceedings may be opened in that country. By virtue of Article 16, any secondary proceedings would also be entitled to recognition in England (although generally the effect of any secondary proceedings would be purely territorial).[19]

6. ILLUSTRATIONS

(1) For many years A carried on business in Germany. In early 1996 A, in dire financial straits, left Germany and has not since returned. Insolvency proceedings were commenced in Germany by A's creditors and shortly thereafter an assignee was appointed. The German insolvency is entitled to recognition in England.[20]

(2) X recently died domiciled and resident in Mondavia. X's estate is insolvent and has been sequestrated under Mondavian law. The Mondavian sequestration will be recognised in England.[1]

(3) The courts in Northern Ireland have made a bankruptcy order in respect of P, a Spanish national, domiciled and resident in Spain. The Northern Ireland proceedings are entitled to recognition in England.[2]

(4) Q, domiciled and resident in England, is a member of a firm that has carried on business in Belgium. The firm, and the partners thereof, have been declared insolvent by a Belgian court and a trustee appointed. Q participated in the Belgian proceedings. The Belgian insolvency will be recognised in England.[3]

---

[17] See Art. 16.
[18] In relation to a company, that centre is rebuttably presumed (see Art. 3(1)) to be where the company is registered (i.e. domiciled).
[19] See Art. 3(2) and p. 11, *supra*.
[20] Cf. *Re Behrends* (1865) 12 L.T. 149, *ante*.
[1] Cf. *Re Tuticorin Cotton Press Co. Ltd.* (1894) 71 L.T. 723, *Hutcheson & Co.'s Administrator* v. *Taylor's Executrix* 1931 S.C. 484 and *Araya* v. *Coghill* 1921 S.C. 462.
[2] *Supra*, p. 142.
[3] Cf. *Bergerem* v. *Marsh* (1921) 91 L.J.K.B. 80.

(5) T, a resident of Ireland, is hopelessly insolvent. T's only known assets of any substantial value are a holiday home in South Africa and certain shares in an English registered company. T's only connection to South Africa is the holiday home in which T stays for one or two weeks each winter. On a creditor's petition, a court in South Africa has declared T bankrupt and appointed a trustee. T was present in South Africa on the day the creditor's petition was presented, but T has taken no part in the South African proceedings. The South African bankruptcy will not be recognised in England as affecting assets in England.[4]

---

[4] Neither the presence of assets nor comity (the English court has jurisdiction if a debtor is personally present) being a sufficient foundation for recognition.

Chapter 6

Foreign Liquidations: Bases of Recognition

1. INTRODUCTION

A foreign corporation, having been brought into existence under a foreign legal system, may obviously be dissolved pursuant to the law of the place of incorporation. As Lord Romer once put it with reference to a dissolved Chinese company:[1]

> 'The company has ceased to exist by an act of the country by whose acts and under whose laws it was made a juristic entity, and must, accordingly, be treated as non-existent by all courts administering English law . . . .'

So too a liquidation (whether or not intended to result in dissolution) conducted in accordance with the law of the place of incorporation will be recognised in England.

Of course, in contrast to bankruptcy, it may very well be that the property of a foreign corporation is not actually vested in the foreign liquidator. Nevertheless, the authority of a liquidator to administer assets of a corporation will be recognised in England. It will also be noted that, as is the case with regard to a foreign trustee in bankruptcy, there is no requirement that a foreign liquidator must apply to the English court for an order granting recognition before being able to represent the corporation and deal with its assets in England. The recognition by the English court of a liquidator appointed under the law of the place of incorporation is sufficiently well established that the matter may at times scarcely merit the detailed attention of the court. A good example may be found in *Baden, Delvaux and Lecuit* v. *Société Générale pour Favoriser le Développement du Commerce et de l'Industrie en France S.A.*,[2] where not one but four foreign liquidations were recognised. Indeed, the strength of the law of the place of incorporation is such that English judges have often maintained that, upon a liquidation being conducted under the law of the place of incorporation, any winding up in the English court should *prima facie* be ancillary to the principal liquidation abroad.[3]

---

[1] *Dairen Kisen Kabushiki Kaisha* v. *Shiang Kee* [1941] A.C. 373 at 376.

[2] [1983] B.C.L.C. 325 ([1993] 1 W.L.R. 509 note). For the recognition of foreign receivers see, *passim*, *Schemmer* v. *Property Resources Ltd.* [1975] Ch. 273 and *White* v. *Verkouille* [1990] 2 Qd. R. 191.

[3] *Re Bank of Credit and Commerce International S.A. (No. 10)* [1997] Ch. 213 and generally chapter 14, *infra*.

Leaving to one side the law of the place of incorporation, there is little English authority to establish that any other foreign liquidation may be recognised. It is not difficult to find examples[4] in which a company incorporated in Panama or Liberia (often with a small number of bearer shares) has long since ceased to have any real connection with its place of incorporation. There is no doubt, a sufficient jurisdictional nexus having been made out, that the English court may wind up such a company under the provisions of the Insolvency Act 1986. But whether the English court would accord recognition to the liquidation of a Panamanian company taking place in like circumstances in France or New York requires some consideration. That consideration must now be taken in the light of the insolvency in Maxwell Communications Corporation plc. For there it was expressly acknowledged in the Court of Appeal that Hoffmann J had recognised the Chapter 11 proceedings being conducted in New York in respect of an English company.[5]

As a practical point it should be noted that if there is no liquidation taking place under the law of the place of incorporation, it may be more convenient to obtain an English winding up order than to seek recognition of liquidation proceedings being conducted in a third country. (This is, perhaps, one reason why there is a shortage of relevant English authority on this issue.) The same is also true even where there is a liquidation in the place of incorporation. The foreign liquidator may often favour an English winding up,[6] not least so that advantage may be taken of the avoidance powers available under the English legislation.[7]

The recognition of foreign re-organisations is examined below.

2. UNITED KINGDOM LIQUIDATIONS

When the Companies Act 1862 was enacted it applied throughout the whole of the United Kingdom.[8] It followed that a court in England would not question the jurisdiction of a court in Scotland or Ireland to make a winding up order[9] (whether the order were made in relation to a Scottish or Irish company, or a foreign company). Although the Insolvency Act 1986 does not generally apply to the whole of the United Kingdom,[10] the English court must still be bound to recognise any winding up in Scotland or Northern Ireland – just as a sequestration or bankruptcy conducted in either country will be recognised in England.[11] This proposition, if it

[4] See *Re Compania Merabello San Nicholas S.A.* [1973] Ch. 75, *passim.*
[5] *Barclays Bank plc* v. *Homann* [1993] B.C.L.C. 680 at 706 *per* Leggatt LJ.
[6] As to the presentation of a petition by a foreign liquidator, see p. 229, *infra.*
[7] See the observations of the Lord President in *Queensland Mercantile and Agency Co. Ltd.* v. *Australasian Investment Co. Ltd.* (1888) 15 R. 935 at 939 (set out below) or of Lord Morison in *Hutcheson & Co.'s Administrator* v. *Taylor's Executrix* 1931 S.C. 484 at 494.
[8] Cf. the position under the Winding Up Acts 1848 and 1849: *Edinburgh & Glasgow Bank* v. *Ewan* (1852) 14 D. 547.
[9] This author would prefer the opinion expressed by Lord Shand in *Queensland Mercantile and Agency Co. Ltd.* v. *Australasian Investment Co. Ltd.* (1888) 15 R. 935 at 943, to the view of the other judges in the Court of Session in that case.
[10] See s. 441 and p. 113, *supra.*
[11] See p. 142, *supra.*

could be in any doubt, finds support in the fact that a winding up in Scotland or Northern Ireland in relation to a foreign corporation may in appropriate circumstances deprive the English court of the winding up jurisdiction it would otherwise possess.[12]

In addition to recognition pursuant to general principles, section 426(I) of the Insolvency Act 1986 will also be noted:[13]

> 'An order made by a court in any part of the United Kingdom in the exercise of jurisdiction in relation to insolvency law shall be enforced in any other part of the United Kingdom as if it were made by a court exercising the corresponding jurisdiction in that other part.'

But even without reference to section 426 a liquidator appointed in Scotland or Northern Ireland, in respect of a local or foreign company, will be recognised in England.

3. FOREIGN LIQUIDATIONS: THE LAW OF THE PLACE OF INCORPORATION

A. Place of Incorporation

A corporation is regarded as domiciled in the country in which it has been incorporated. The law of the place of incorporation is treated as the personal law of the corporation and governs such issues as formation, dissolution, amalgamation, corporate capacity, the rights and liabilities of members as well as matters of internal management in general.[14] Just as the domicile of a debtor is a basis of recognition of foreign bankruptcies, so too a liquidation in the corporate domicile (that is in accordance with the law of the place of incorporation) will be recognised in England. A relatively recent illustration is *Baden, Delvaux and Lecuit* v. *Société Générale pour Favoriser le Développement du Commerce et de l'Industrie en France S.A.*[15] A group of companies and other legal entities provided financial services throughout the world as part of the Investment Overseas Services ('IOS') complex. The plaintiffs were liquidators of four 'dollar funds' under the IOS umbrella. The four dollar funds were constituted through two Ontario companies, a corporation established under the laws of the Netherlands Antilles and an 'indivision' (referred to as 'ITT'), a legal entity under the law of Luxembourg. Peter Gibson J recognised the liquidations that had taken place in Ontario, Curacao and Luxembourg respectively. It may be noted that ITT, a legal entity under the law of Luxembourg, did not have any exact parallel in English law. Further, ITT was not a corporate entity but it was 'a body that under Luxembourg law could be dissolved'.[16] Such dissolution, resulting in the appointment of the plaintiffs as liquidators, was recognised in England. (Although not cited in the English court, in *Re ITT*[17] the same

---

[12] See Insolvency Act 1986, s. 221(2) and (3), p. 109, *supra*.
[13] An analysis of s. 426 in relation to intra-United Kingdom insolvencies is found at p. 213, *infra*.
[14] Chapter 13, *post*.
[15] [1983] B.C.L.C. 325.
[16] *Ibid.*, at 333.
[17] (1975) 58 D.L.R. (3d) 55.

Luxembourg liquidators had also been recognised by the High Court of Ontario.)

In those rare instances where multiple incorporation has validly occurred, that is a corporation has been incorporated under not one but two legal systems, a corporation must be regarded as having two domiciles (at least until one of the incorporations is cancelled). Accordingly, a liquidation taking place under either domiciliary law may be recognised by the English court.[18]

B. Recognised in the Place of Incorporation

In *Macaulay* v. *Guaranty Trust Co of New York*[19] a Delaware corporation had been declared insolvent by the Court of Chancery in the State of Delaware and interim receivers appointed. The interim receivers were recognised in England as entitled to enforce the obligations of the Delaware corporation. *Macaulay* v. *Guaranty Trust Co of New York* may usefully be compared with more recent authority involving US corporations. For bankruptcy in the United States is a Federal matter governed by the Federal Bankruptcy Code (which, incidentally, draws no distinction between bankruptcy and winding up). Thus in *Felixstowe Dock and Rly Co.* v. *United States Lines Inc.*[20] a Delaware corporation was undergoing reorganisation in accordance with Chapter 11 of the Federal Bankruptcy Code in the United States District Court for the Southern District of New York (in Bankruptcy). Hirst J recognised the US proceedings.[1] Accordingly, a foreign liquidation may be recognised in England when it is effective as part of the law of the place of incorporation, regardless of the particular court (State or Federal) in which the proceedings are being conducted.

Whilst *Felixstowe Dock and Rly Co.* v. *United States Lines Inc.* concerned Federal legislation, recognition must also be available in England where a liquidation is *recognised* under the law of the place of incorporation. Let us say that a country consists of State X and State Y. Each State has its own companies and winding up legislation, but any liquidation in State Y is recognised in State X. A company, incorporated in State X, has been put into liquidation in State Y and liquidators there appointed. The liquidators being recognised under the law of the State X (the place of incorporation) are entitled to recognition in England. The same principle would apply where a company has been incorporated in one country and liquidated elsewhere, the foreign liquidation being recognised under the law of the place of incorporation.

Hence, as a general rule, a liquidation which is either granted or recognised under the law of the place of incorporation is entitled to recognition in England.[2]

---

[18] Multiple incorporation is considered in detail in chapter 13.
[19] (1927) 44 T.L.R. 99: see further, *infra* p. 194.
[20] [1989] Q.B. 360.
[1] Hirst J did not, however, give effect in England to a restraining order of the US District Court which apparently on the facts would have prejudiced creditors in England: [1989] Q.B. 360 at 389. See further p. 394, *post*.
[2] For the equivalent proposition with reference to foreign bankruptcies see p. 146, *ante*.

4. FOREIGN LIQUIDATIONS: OTHER BASES OF RECOGNITION

A. Place of Incorporation not Exclusive

(i) *A Pragmatic Approach*

The importance of the law of the place of incorporation cannot be denied, a circumstance well illustrated by the proposition that the winding up in England of a foreign company will, in general, be carefully limited in scope and ancillary to the principal liquidation in the place of incorporation. However, it does not inevitably follow that no other foreign liquidation is capable of being recognised in England. The recognition of foreign liquidations other than by virtue of the law of the place of incorporation is far from settled in English law. But the balance of principle, authority and simple convenience is against granting an exclusive role to the law of the place of incorporation.[3]

North Australian Territory Co. Ltd. v. *Goldsbrough, Mort and Co. Ltd.*[4] concerned an English company which had a branch office, together with the bulk of its business, in Australia. The shareholders in England resolved that the company should be wound up voluntarily. However, a compulsory order had already been made in the Supreme Court of South Australia. Kay J held that the foreign compulsory order did not 'in the least degree interfere with a voluntary winding up in this country'.[5] But recognition of the foreign proceedings was not absolutely denied:[6]

> 'any order made by the Australian courts for winding up in Australia would merely be ancillary, just as in the converse case an order made in this country for winding up an Australian company could only be ancillary to a winding up taking place in Australia.'

Kay J accordingly envisaged recognition of the foreign proceedings as an ancillary winding up, effective within the jurisdiction of the foreign court.[7] But it was definitely not a consequence of such recognition that the English winding up would be superseded.

That recognition may be accorded to a liquidation other than in the place of incorporation is further supported by reference to the decision of the Court of Session in *Queensland Mercantile and Agency Co. Ltd.* v. *Australasian Investment Co. Ltd.*[8] A Queensland company was ordered to be wound up by the courts in Queensland. Subsequently the foreign

---

[3] See the discussion of *Barclays Bank plc* v. *Homan* [1993] B.C.L.C. 680, at p. 170 below. In *Re ITT* (1975) 58 D.L.R. (3d) 55 at 58 Houlden JA, having recognised the Luxembourg liquidation, stated: 'Indeed, I do not think that any other jurisdiction would have had authority to appoint liquidators for ITT.' This comment is plainly *obiter* and made without reference to relevant English authority. Moreover, the evidence before the Ontario court did not suggest that ITT had carried on business within, or submitted to, the jurisdiction of any other foreign court. Note also the discussion of *National Trust Co. Ltd.* v. *Ebro Irrigation & Power Co. Ltd.* [1954] 3 D.L.R. 326, *infra*.

[4] (1889) 61 L.T. 716, applied in *Re Bank of Credit and Commerce International S.A. (No. 10)* [1997] Ch. 213 at 242.

[5] *Ibid.*, at 717.

[6] *Ibid.*

[7] This seems also to have been the view of Lord Blanesburgh in *Employers' Liability Assurance Corpn.* v. *Sedgwick, Collins & Co.* [1927] A.C. 95 at 125 and of Griffith CJ in *Re Alfred Shaw and Co. Ltd.* (1897) 8 Q.L.J. 93 at 96.

[8] (1888) 15 R. 935.

liquidator sought assistance from the English court and a winding up order was made in England 'and the winding up here was directed to be ancillary to the proceedings in Australia'.[9] In the course of the ancillary winding up in England North J ordered a stay of certain proceedings already under way in Scotland.[10] The effect of his Lordship's restraining order was thereafter considered in the Court of Session, which specifically noted that England was not the place of incorporation.[11] The Scottish court gave effect to the order of North J and, in so doing, recognised a liquidation other than under the law of the place of incorporation. The Lord President made it plain that recognition was not restricted to the sole basis of place of incorporation:[12]

> 'although there is a winding up in the colony which would enable the liquidator there to ingather the whole assets of the company, if he can reach them, it may aid him very much in the performance of that duty that there should be another liquidation in England or elsewhere where also the company has been carrying on business. There seems to me to be nothing incompatible in the coexistence of the two.'

It may be noted that the Lord President linked recognition to a jurisdictional basis: the carrying on of business.

There is, it is respectfully submitted, a deal of sense in according recognition in circumstances like those arising in *Queensland Mercantile and Agency Co. Ltd.* v. *Australasian Investment Co. Ltd.* A liquidator appointed in the place of incorporation may well require the assistance of a foreign court. Such assistance may be desirable, indeed it may even be a necessity, either because only limited powers are available to the liquidator under the law of the place of incorporation or, more likely, on account of the laws of the foreign court concerned.

(ii) *Maxwell Communications Corporation plc*

The most telling sign that the English court is prepared to adopt a flexible approach to the recognition of foreign insolvencies, and in particular one not restricted to the place of incorporation, comes by way of the Maxwell saga. It is, of course, well-known that the English administrators and the US examiner reached unprecedented heights of mutual respect and co-operation in their conduct of the proceedings.[13] But the very fact that MCC was an English company should not be overlooked. MCC had filed a Chapter 11 petition in the Southern District of New York the day before it presented a petition for administration in England. In terms of recognition, the company had submitted to the jurisdiction of the US courts. The very foundation of the co-operation in the Maxwell case with the US court and the examiner goes against any suggestion that recognition is restricted

---

[9] (1888) 58 L.T. 878 at 879.
[10] (1888) 58 L.T. 878; for discussion of the judgment of North J see p. 377, *post.*
[11] (1888) 15 R. 935. Recognition by the Scottish court was apparently not simply dependent upon United Kingdom legislation. Only Lord Shand expressed the view (at 943) that the Scottish court was incompetent to entertain objections to an order of the English court made under the Companies Act 1862. (This commentator favours the opinion of Lord Shand, see *supra*, p. 165, n. 9.)
[12] (1888) 15 R. 935 at 939. See also *BCCI S.A.* v. *Haque* (1996) 42 C.B.R. (3d) 95, English ancillary liquidation lent assistance in Ontario in respect of witness examination.
[13] See p. 332, *infra.*

to the corporate domicile. Nor did the matter pass without comment from the English judges. In *Barclays Bank plc* v. *Homan* Leggatt LJ, referring to the approval by Hoffmann J of the Protocol between the administrators and the examiner, stated:[14]

> 'Hoffmann J recognised the jurisdiction of the United States Bankruptcy Court when he made his order of 31 December 1991. This court having recognised the jurisdiction of the United States court in relation to this insolvency, it would, in my judgment, offend against comity for this court now to decree which claims the administrators can, and which they cannot, allege in the United States court are preferences.'

The case is a particularly strong one since MCC was an English company and was already subject, at the time of the order of Hoffmann J, to insolvency proceedings in England.

(iii) *Additional Authorities*

The decision of the Ontario court in *National Trust Co. Ltd.* v. *Ebro Irrigation & Power Co. Ltd.* has at times been taken as authority for the proposition that only a winding up in the place of incorporation can be recognised at common law.[15] The case, however, is not even remotely decided upon this supposed basis. Ebro and Catalonian were subsidiaries of Barcelona Traction, Light & Power Co. Ltd. All three companies were incorporated in Canada. Ebro and Catalonian carried on business in Spain, Barcelona did not. In 1948 a court in Spain declared Barcelona bankrupt and, as part of related so-called 'ancillary relief',[16] appointed functionaries to seize all the assets of Ebro and Catalonian. It must be stressed that neither Ebro or Catalonian were ever the subject of insolvency proceedings in Spain. The functionaries purported to dismiss the duly appointed directors of Ebro and Catalonian, cancel all the shares and bonds issued by the companies and then issue new shares and bonds to a Spanish company that had been formed to take over the business previously operated by Ebro and Catalonian in Spain. Schroeder J decided, not surprisingly, that the purported cancellation and issue of new shares and bonds by (and all other acts of) the functionaries were 'completely invalid and ineffective'.[17] For the power to regulate the internal affairs of a company (including the appointment and removal of directors, the holding of meetings and the right to issue and transfer shares and bonds) was a matter exclusively falling within the law of the place of incorporation. The judge's conclusion could scarcely be doubted; and no question of the recognition of insolvency proceedings in respect of Ebro or Catalonian (which had carried on business in Spain) could have arisen at any time – since no such proceedings had ever been instituted there. Moreover, the only bankruptcy was in relation to Barcelona and it could hardly be argued

---

[14] [1993] B.C.L.C. 680 at 706 (Mann LJ agreed with Leggatt LJ).

[15] [1954] 3 D.L.R. 326. See the remarks of Houlden JA in *Re ITT* (1975) 58 D.L.R. (3d) 55 at 58, set out *supra* p. 168, n. 3.

[16] [1954] 3 D.L.R. 326 at 333. The expert evidence of Spanish lawyers was that there was no basis under the law of Spain for the action that had been taken in the case. Barcelona was also prevented by procedural machinations from presenting any objections to the bankruptcy proceedings (see *ibid.* at 328).

[17] *Ibid.*, at 345.

that such proceedings were entitled to recognition, as Barcelona on the facts had not carried on business or even owned assets in Spain.[18] Indeed, from a cross-border insolvency perspective, it might fairly be argued that Schroeder J could have summarily disposed of all arguments based on the law of Spain and the acts of the Spanish functionaries: quite simply, all relevant (purported) acts flowed from the bankruptcy proceedings in the Spanish court and those proceedings, conducted in relation to a foreign company that had not carried on business in Spain nor submitted to the jurisdiction, could not be recognised in Ontario; and, in particular, were not to be recognised as affecting the company's assets[19] in Ontario.

That corporate domicile is not the only basis upon which a liquidation may be recognised at common law is borne out by reference to a recent decision in the Hong Kong Court of Appeal.[20] BCCI (Overseas) Ltd. ('Overseas') was incorporated in the Cayman Islands and in 1983 had opened a branch in Macau. In 1991 the officers in charge of the Macau branch placed funds from the branch on deposit with a bank in Hong Kong. In January 1992 Overseas was put into compulsory liquidation by order of the Grand Court of the Cayman Islands and, later that year, the Macau branch was ordered to be liquidated out of court by an executive order of the Governor of Macau. Under the law of Macau any assets recovered by the Macau liquidator would be ring-fenced.[1] Subsequently both the Cayman liquidators and the Macau liquidator claimed the funds on deposit in Hong Kong. (The proceedings were originally brought against the Macau branch of Overseas however, as no such separate legal entity existed, the court ordered the substitution of the Macau liquidator as the named defendant.) It was held that the Macau liquidator, as the representative of the creditors entitled to prove in the Macau liquidation, could be a party to proceedings in Hong Kong – and therefore, of course, the liquidation in Macau was recognised – but that the fate of the funds on deposit in Hong Kong was governed by Hong Kong law as the *lex situs*. The funds were ordered to be paid to the Cayman liquidator, primarily because the liquidation there provided for *pari passu* distribution.[2] It may be noted that a similar situation had once arisen in Singapore. In *Re Lee Wah Bank Ltd.*[3] a Hong Kong bank had a branch in Saigon. The Saigon branch had a separate current account in credit in Singapore at a time when winding up proceedings were commenced in Hong Kong and Saigon. The Hong Kong liquidator and the Saigon liquidator both claimed the money.[4] It was held that either liquidator could give a good receipt for the money and that the court had a discretion to direct payment to either

---

[18] *Ibid.*

[19] In particular, Barcelona's shareholding in the two Canadian subsidiaries. Those shares, of course, being situated in Canada.

[20] *Bank of Credit and Commerce International (Overseas) Ltd.* v. *Bank of Credit and Commerce International (Overseas) Ltd. (Macau Branch)* [1997] H.K.L.R.D. 304.

[1] That is, the assets were to be applied first to satisfy the debts of creditors in Macau before any other creditors could claim.

[2] *Supra*, n. 20 at 309.

[3] (1926) 2 Malayan Cases 81.

[4] The Hong Kong liquidator argued that he had the power to revoke the authority of the Saigon liquidator, but this contention was rejected by Murison CJ who stated (at 84): 'To say that the Hong Kong liquidator can revoke any authority of the liquidator, appointed by a court in another country, is to say that the courts of one country can dictate to the courts of another, which is an untenable proposition.'

liquidator; however, following the normal rule the money would be given to the Hong Kong liquidator as he was conducting the principal liquidation in accordance with the law of the domicile of the company. Although the results in both these cases are by no means surprising, the important point to note is that the liquidator of the relevant branch was recognised: the courts did not take the approach that because there was a liquidation in the place of incorporation that in itself automatically put an end to any dispute.

There is a further instance where a liquidation other than in the place of incorporation may be recognised in England, namely where there is no likelihood of a liquidation under the law of the place of incorporation. If the English rules on recognition were restricted to the place of incorporation and a liquidation has not or even cannot there occur, then no foreign liquidation whatsoever could be recognised. Plainly this would be most unsatisfactory. Accordingly, the editors of *Dicey and Morris* suggest that recognition is possible 'where there is no likelihood of a liquidation in the country of incorporation'.[5]

Yet perhaps the most illuminating discussion is to be found in *Re Russo-Asiatic Bank*,[6] decided in Hong Kong. A banking corporation established in Russia had branches, *inter alia*, in London, Shanghai and Hong Kong. The Hong Kong court, applying the then English authorities,[7] denied effect to certain Soviet decrees dissolving the Russo-Asiatic Bank. Liquidations of the branch offices took place in London, Shanghai and Hong Kong, the Hong Kong winding up resulting in a surplus. There was no liquidation in the place of incorporation. The Shanghai liquidators applied for an order that they be given the surplus assets from the Hong Kong winding up. The London liquidator merely sought to represent the creditors in the English proceedings and to enter claims in the Hong Kong winding up on behalf of those creditors. The Hong Kong court did not simply rule that as the Russo-Asiatic Bank was neither incorporated in London nor in Shanghai recognition could not be accorded to those proceedings. Rather Sir Henry Gollan CJ chose a more careful route:[8]

'But the rule that the liquidation in Hong Kong of a branch of a foreign company should be ancillary to a liquidation in the country of its domicile can have no application in the circumstances of this case . . . As the liquidation proceedings in Hong Kong cannot be taken as ancillary to those in Russia, it follows that there is no court elsewhere which can . . . be regarded as the principal court to govern the liquidation.

There is no precedent to guide me in the exceptional circumstances of this case. But, it appears to me that, on principle, there is no reason why the London liquidator should not put in proofs on behalf of the creditors whom he represents, and I give him leave to do so. So far as the claim of the Shanghai liquidators for payment to them of the surplus is concerned, I dismiss it.'

Upon the facts of *Re Russo-Asiatic Bank* it would have been peculiar had the Hong Kong court regarded the Shanghai liquidators as possessing a status equivalent to that of a liquidator appointed by the courts of the

---

[5] At p. 1138. (12th ed., 1993) The relevant passage in *Dicey and Morris* was cited with apparent approval in *Felixstowe Dock and Rly Co. v. United States Lines Inc.* [1989] Q.B. 360 at 374–375.

[6] (1930) 24 H.K.L.R. 16: affirmed without discussion, *ibid.* at 100.

[7] *Russian Commercial and Industrial Bank* v. *Comptoire d'Escompte de Mulhouse* [1925] A.C. 112; see now *Lazard Bros* v. *Midland Bank* [1933] A.C. 289.

[8] (1930) 24 H.K.L.R. 16 at 20–21.

place of incorporation. The claim of the Shanghai liquidators to represent the Bank could be no stronger than that of the London or indeed Hong Kong liquidators: branch offices existed at all three places. Yet *Re Russo-Asiatic Bank* certainly does not suggest that any liquidation other than in the place of incorporation must necessarily be disregarded. The London and Shanghai liquidators, appointed in foreign proceedings, were represented in the Hong Kong court. More particularly, Sir Henry Gollan CJ recognised the English liquidation, at least to the extent of permitting the London liquidator to enter claims on behalf of the creditors that liquidator had been appointed to represent by the English court.

(iv) *Jurisdiction and Recognition*

The impact of the decision in *Re Harrods (Buenos Aires) Ltd. (No. 2)*[9] – a case on *forum conveniens* – must be considered in the context of the recognition of foreign liquidations. It will be recalled that the company, incorporated in England, had carried on its business in Argentina and was overwhelmingly more closely connected to Argentina than to England. A 49% minority shareholder petitioned in England invoking the unfair prejudice remedy and, in the alternative, seeking a just and equitable winding up order. The Court of Appeal stayed the English proceedings on the basis that Argentina was clearly the more appropriate forum, even though any remedy in Argentina would have to be by way of winding up.[10] At this point one may ask the question, assuming that a winding up order were made in Argentina, whether the English court would then recognise the winding up in Argentina. There can, it is suggested, be only one realistic answer to this question. To stay your own proceedings in favour of those in a foreign forum, but subsequently refuse to recognise the relevant foreign proceedings, would be both illogical and contrary to all commonsense. If, for example, the liquidator appointed in Argentina had sought to recover certain books of account (or other property belonging to the company) in England, recognition would be bound to be forthcoming.

Of course, the company in *Re Harrods (Buenos Aires) Ltd. (No. 2)* was not insolvent, but as far as this author is aware it has never been suggested that there are two sets of rules on the recognition of foreign liquidations – one where the company is solvent and another (more restricted) where the company is insolvent. (In addition, there are a variety of different approaches to the test of insolvency and, without any statutory guidance, which approach would the court adopt when trying to ascertain whether the company in question was insolvent at the date of the order in the foreign proceedings.) In any event, the decision in the Court of Appeal is very much against the contention that as a matter of general principle only a liquidation in the place of incorporation can be recognised in England – this is particularly so because the company that was to be wound up in the foreign proceedings was an English company.

It is also instructive to make reference to the Canadian case of *Re Stewart & Matthews Ltd.*[11] A company incorporated in Manitoba carried

---

[9] [1991] 4 All E.R. 348, *supra*, p. 126.
[10] There was no alternative remedy in Argentina, *ibid.*, at 356.
[11] (1916) 10 W.W.R. 154, *supra* p. 126.

on its business in America in the State of Minnesota. No business was carried on in Manitoba. In July 1914 the company petitioned the bankruptcy court in Minnesota and a trustee in bankruptcy was in due course appointed. The majority of shareholders resided in the United States and all of the (small number of) Canadian creditors had proved their claims in the American proceedings. More than a year after the commencement of the insolvency in Minnesota, a winding up order was also made in Manitoba. An application was subsequently presented in Manitoba, supported by a majority of all the company's creditors, for a stay of the proceedings in Manitoba. The court pointed out the value of the winding up order, in that it had secured the assets in Canada, but was satisfied that (in the exercise of its discretion) it was in the best interests of all the creditors that the proceedings should be stayed. The US proceedings were just as efficient as those under the Canadian legislation, the US court had ample investigatory powers, and the proceedings did not discriminate against the Canadian creditors. The liquidator in Manitoba was instructed to take whatever steps were necessary to make any Canadian assets that had not yet vested in the US trustee in bankruptcy available for distribution in the US proceedings: but otherwise to take no further action until such became necessary in aid of the US proceedings. Again, it can only be that the court of the domicile of the company was prepared to grant recognition to the foreign (American) liquidation – otherwise Canadian assets would not have been transferred to America.

Similar arguments arise upon a consideration of the court's jurisdiction to wind up foreign companies under Part V of the Insolvency Act 1986. It is plain that the English court is not bound to exercise its jurisdiction to wind up a foreign corporation; the matter is one of discretion. In the exercise of such discretion the English court will 'consider whether any other jurisdiction is more appropriate for the winding up'.[12] It would seem that the identification of a more appropriate jurisdiction is not restricted to a liquidation in the place of incorporation. In *Re a Company (No. 00359 of 1987)*[13] a Liberian one-ship company had factual connections with England and Greece. Peter Gibson J, having determined that the English court had jurisdiction to make a winding up order, turned to consider whether there was any more appropriate foreign jurisdiction. On the facts his Lordship held that neither Liberia nor Greece could be said to be more appropriate.[14] Although not addressing any question concerning recognition of a foreign liquidation, Peter Gibson J envisaged that the English court might decline jurisdiction in favour of a foreign liquidation other than in the place of incorporation. So too, it is suggested, a foreign liquidation other than in the place of incorporation may be recognised in England.

Thus, in summary, there is a sufficient measure of authority[15] that the law of the place of incorporation does not occupy an exclusive position;

---

[12] *Re a Company (No. 00359 of 1987)* [1988] Ch. 210 at 226.

[13] [1988] Ch. 210, p. 101, *ante.*

[14] *Ibid.* at 226–227.

[15] Reference may also be made to *Slavenburg's Bank N.V.* v. *Intercontinental Natural Resources Ltd.* [1980] 1 W.L.R. 1076 in which Lloyd J, when dealing with the interpretation of the word 'liquidator' in s. 95 of the Companies Act 1948 (see now Companies Act 1985, s. 395), stated (at 1087) '. . . it means either an English liquidator or the foreign equivalent (*whether in the place of incorporation or elsewhere*) as the case may be.' (Emphasis added.)

other foreign liquidations may be granted recognition in the English court. However, the actual bases of recognition, and consequences thereof, remain to be particularised.

B. Carrying on Business

It will be recalled that on the facts of the cases discussed above business was generally carried on within the jurisdiction of the foreign courts concerned. Moreover, in *Queensland Mercantile and Agency Co. Ltd.* v. *Australasian Investment Co. Ltd.* the Lord President specifically identified the carrying on of business as a jurisdictional basis. A foreign liquidation may be recognised in England if the corporation (wherever incorporated) has carried on business within the jurisdiction of the relevant foreign court.

The cases reveal that recognition is possible even if there has been a principal liquidation in England or elsewhere (*Queensland Mercantile and Agency Co. Ltd.* v. *Australasian Investment Co. Ltd.*[16]) as well as when no principal liquidation has occurred (*Re Russo-Asiatic Bank*). However, the scope and consequences of such recognition will not be identical to those which flow from but one liquidation under the law of the place of incorporation.[17]

C. Submission

With reference to bankruptcy it is clearly established that foreign proceedings may be recognised in England if the debtor submitted to the jurisdiction of the foreign court.[18] However, submission by a corporation to the insolvency jurisdiction of a foreign court has but lightly been touched upon. In *Queensland Mercantile and Agency Co. Ltd.* v. *Australasian Investment Co. Ltd.*, it will be recalled, a company incorporated in Queensland had carried on business in England. The Queensland liquidator had sought assistance from the English court which ordered an ancillary winding up. That order was recognised in Scotland, the Lord President observing:[19]

> 'although there is a winding up in the colony which would enable the liquidator there to ingather the whole assets of the company, if he can reach them, it may aid him very much in the performance of that duty that there should be another liquidation in England or elsewhere where also the company has been carrying on business. There seems to me to be nothing incompatible in the coexistence of the two.'

[16] See also *BCCI (Overseas) Ltd.* v. *BCCI (Overseas) Ltd. (Macau Branch)* and *Re Lee Wah Bank Ltd.*, above. Note also the discussion in relation to the Bank of Credit and Commerce International S.A., p. 362, *infra.*

[17] The limits of recognition where there are two or more foreign liquidations are discussed at p. 178, *post.*

[18] *Re Davidson's Settlement Trusts* (1873) L.R. 15 Eq. 383 chapter 5, *ante.* The court may recognise and assist a foreign receiver if a defendant has submitted to the foreign court: *Houlditch* v. *Donegal* (1834) 8 Bli. N.S. 301 as explained in *Schemmer* v. *Property Resources Ltd.* [1975] Ch. 273 at 285–286.

[19] (1888) 15 R. 935 at 939.

It may well be that the Lord President considered carrying on business or submission as alternative bases for the recognition of the English proceedings. Certainly, if a liquidator or the company itself acting consistently with the law of the place of incorporation petitions for a winding up or administration in another court, then the validity of the proceedings in that other court should not later be open to question, and in particular not by the liquidator or the company. In *Re International Power Industries NV*[20] a Netherlands Antilles corporation had submitted to the bankruptcy jurisdiction of the US courts and was in Chapter 11 reorganisation there. The US court issued letters rogatory requesting the assistance of the courts in England. The US trustee was represented before Woolf J, whose judgment contains no suggestion that the US court lacked jurisdiction. Similarly in *Barclays Bank plc* v. *Homan* the English court recognised the US Chapter 11 proceedings: MCC having filed a petition in New York.[1]

Cases involving insolvency proceedings in two or more jurisdictions have sometimes arisen before the courts in relation to schemes of arrangement.[2] Let us say that an English company has creditors in, *inter alia*, England, New Zealand and Australia. A scheme of arrangement sanctioned by the English court cannot of itself bind the New Zealand or Australian courts. (The same is true in respect of an administration being conducted in England.) Indeed, even in the days of Empire, United Kingdom companies legislation did not extend to the colonies. Thus in *New Zealand Loan and Mercantile Agency Co. Ltd.* v. *Morrison*[3] the Privy Council held that an English scheme under the Joint Stock Companies Arrangement Act 1870 was not binding in Victoria and did not discharge a contract governed by the law of Victoria. Hence, in the above example, the English liquidator should consider obtaining approval of the scheme in accordance with the insolvency laws of New Zealand and of Australia. The English court would surely recognise proceedings in those courts with reference to the scheme of arrangement. Where a scheme of arrangement is to be approved in several countries it has been suggested by Vaughan Williams J that a territorial approach should in practice be adopted,[4] the creditors in each country being heard at a meeting to be held in that particular jurisdiction. His Lordship's suggestion (which cannot be said to be a rule of law)[5] is in line with the view that where there are principal and ancillary liquidations, the ancillary proceedings should be limited in their scope but may be recognised by the English court as effective within the territory in which they have been conducted.

In summary, where a corporation invokes the insolvency jurisdiction of a foreign court, or otherwise validly submits thereto, the proceedings may be accorded recognition by the English court.

---

[20] [1985] B.C.L.C. 128, p. 403, *infra*.

[1] [1993] B.C.L.C. 680, *supra*, p. 169.

[2] For example, *Re Queensland National Bank* [1893] W.N. 129, *Re Australian Joint Stock Bank* [1897] W.N. 48 and, more recently, *Re Kailis Groote Eylandt Fisheries Pty. Ltd.* (1977) 2 A.C.L.R. 479 (N.S.W.), (1977) 2 A.C.L.R. 510 (Vic.) and (1977) 2 A.C.L.R. 574 (S.A.).

[3] [1898] A.C. 349.

[4] *Re Queensland National Bank* [1893] W.N. 129, distinguishing his Lordship's earlier decision in *Re English, Scottish and Australian Chartered Bank* [1893] 3 Ch. 385 (the earlier case involving but one liquidation, in England, of an English company).

[5] In particular, there is no territorial restriction on the place at which a meeting may be held to consider a scheme of arrangement: *Re Sandhurst Mining NL* (1991) 9 A.C.L.C. 62 and *Re RCMA Reinsurance Ltd.* [1994] B.C.C. 378, see further p. 17, *supra*.

D. Comity

It might be advocated on the basis of international comity that a foreign liquidation should be recognised in England where *mutatis mutandis* the English court would itself have jurisdiction to make a winding up order. Although comity was held in *Travers* v. *Holley*[6] to constitute a basis for the recognition of foreign decrees of divorce, the doctrine has twice been rejected in the context of company insolvency: first by the Court of Appeal in *Re Trepca Mines Ltd.* and more recently by Hirst J in *Felixstowe Dock and Rly Co.* v. *United States Lines Inc.*[7] The authorities are discussed in chapter 5 with reference to the recognition of foreign bankruptcies. In conclusion, comity is not a sufficient basis for the recognition of foreign insolvency proceedings.

E. Presence of Assets

The English court will probably not accord recognition to a foreign liquidation based upon nothing more than the presence of assets within the jurisdiction of the foreign court. Nevertheless, even though such a foreign liquidation may not be recognised by the English court, the foreign law may yet have some effect as the *lex situs* governing the transfer of title to movable property in that foreign country. The matter is considered further in chapter 5 with reference to foreign bankruptcies. In addition, although jurisdiction may exist under a foreign law (as for instance in the US) on the basis of the presence of assets, if the company then submits to the foreign jurisdiction there will be no doubt that such submission will be sufficient for recognition under English law.

5. FOREIGN REORGANISATIONS

The English courts appear to have been quite happy to recognise a foreign reorganisation (rather than liquidation) conducted in accordance with the law of the place of incorporation. Thus, speaking with reference to a Texan corporation, Hoffmann J has stated:[8]

> 'This court . . . will do its utmost to co-operate with the United States Bankruptcy Court to avoid any action that might disturb the orderly administration of [the corporation] in Texas under Chapter 11.'

Whether the court may recognise a reorganisation being conducted otherwise than in accordance with the law of the corporate domicile, is not a question that has been much debated by the courts in England. If, for example, a BVI company has carried on all its business in the United States

---

[6] [1953] P. 246.

[7] [1960] 1 W.L.R. 1273 and [1989] Q.B. 360, respectively.

[8] *Banque Indosuez S.A.* v. *Ferromet Resources Inc.* [1993] B.C.L.C. 112 at 117. Note also *Felixstowe Dock and Rly Co.* v. *United States Lines Inc.* [1989] Q.B. 360, *Mithras Management Ltd.* v. *New Visions Entertainment Corpn.* (1992) 90 D.L.R. (4th) 726, as well as *Grupo Torras* v. *Al-Sabah* [1996] 1 Lloyd's Rep. 7 at 11, *Fournier* v. *Margaret Z* [1997] 1 N.Z.L.R. 629 and *Holt Cargo Systems Inc.* v. *ABC Containerline NV* (1997) 146 D.L.R. (4th) 736.

and is put into Chapter 11 there, it is difficult to conceive of any compelling reason why those proceedings may not be recognised in England. Moreover, in reality, any reorganisation will involve the submission of the relevant corporation to the foreign procedure; and we know from the Maxwell case that submission must surely be a sufficient basis for recognition.[9]

6. THE BOUNDARIES OF RECOGNITION

If a liquidation in accordance with the law of the place of incorporation were the only foreign liquidation that might be recognised in England then, of course, there would be no scope for conflict between two or more foreign liquidators. But as has been seen, recognition is not so limited and cases may therefore arise in which foreign liquidators assert inconsistent and even contrary claims. The manner in which the English court should resolve any conflicts between two or more foreign liquidators must now be discussed.

A. Liquidation in the Place of Incorporation

If there be but one foreign liquidation, in accordance with the law of the place of incorporation, no particular difficulty arises. Where a foreign corporation is already in liquidation in the place of incorporation any English winding up will, as a general rule, be ancillary to the principal liquidation abroad. Thus it might fairly be said that a liquidation in the place of incorporation has a degree of paramountcy.

Cases may arise, however, which present two (or more) foreign liquidations, one in the place of incorporation and another (or others) elsewhere. In *Re Federal Bank of Australia Ltd.* a Victorian company was in voluntary liquidation in Victoria and a compulsory winding up had also been ordered in South Australia. The company had a branch office and assets in England. Vaughan Williams J ordered a winding up in England, limiting the power of the Official Receiver to getting in the English assets and settling a list of English creditors. His Lordship did not specifically address the effect of the proceedings in South Australia, but merely stated:[10]

> 'I assume the principal liquidation will have to go on in Australia, and I assume that the duties of the English liquidator will be ancillary only to the action of the persons who have the conduct of the liquidation in Australia.'

The reference to 'principal liquidation' must mean the liquidation in Victoria rather than in South Australia. Accordingly, *Re Federal Bank of Australia Ltd.* suggests that where there are two foreign liquidations (one in the place of incorporation and an ancillary liquidation elsewhere) the English court is not obliged to deny recognition to the foreign ancillary liquidation but will be guided by the court conducting the principal

[9] See p. 170 *supra* and *Re International Power Industries NV*, p. 176, *supra*.
[10] (1893) 62 L.J. Ch. 561 at 563.

liquidation. Thus if, for example, the Victorian court had requested that the English court transfer any surplus assets to the proceedings in South Australia, such a request would have been acted upon in England. In *Re Alfred Shaw and Co. Ltd.*[11] a Victorian company which had also carried on business in Queensland and England was in liquidation in all three jurisdictions. The Queensland court regarded its own proceedings and those in England as ancillary to the principal liquidation in Victoria. Griffith CJ was willing to order a transfer of Queensland assets to the liquidator in England, provided the consent of the Victorian liquidators was obtained.

Both these cases were cited with approval in *Re Bank of Credit and Commerce International S.A. (No. 10)*;[12] and the complex arrangements made in the BCCI saga[13] are perhaps the very best illustration of how the English court (conducting an ancillary winding up) will strive as far as possible to co-operate with the court conducting the principal liquidation to ensure a proper distribution of assets on a global basis. Reference may also be made – the other side of the coin – to the Maxwell case: where English administrators (of an English incorporated company) fully co-operated with the US examiner and the US courts.[14]

The position is somewhat more complex where two foreign liquidators are not working in harmony but assert conflicting claims. It is plain that the English court cannot simply ignore the liquidation in the place of incorporation. However nor should the English court regard itself as merely an agent of the court conducting the principal liquidation and accede automatically to any requests made by the liquidator appointed in the principal liquidation.[15] Let us say that a company incorporated in Bermuda has carried on business at offices in Sweden and England. The company is in liquidation in Bermuda and a liquidator has also been appointed by the Swedish court. The company has considerable assets in England and a small number of creditors. The Bermudan liquidator and the Swedish liquidator each seek possession of the English assets. In such a case the English court should first secure the English assets: normally this may be done by making a winding up order (assuming that a petition is presented by a creditor or a request is received from the court in Bermuda under section 426 of the Insolvency Act 1986),[16] the English liquidator gathering in the English assets and settling a list of English creditors. Thereafter, provided the English court is satisfied that the English and Swedish creditors would not be discriminated against in the Bermudan court, the English court may remit assets to the Bermudan liquidator. But if the facts disclose that foreign creditors could not claim *pari passu* with local creditors in Bermuda, then the English court will

---

[11] (1897) 8 Q.L.J. 93, in particular at 97: see also *Queensland Mercantile and Agency Co. Ltd. v. Australasian Investment Co. Ltd.* (1888) 15 R. 935 at 939.

[12] [1997] Ch. 213 at 242–246, *per* Sir Richard Scott V-C.

[13] See also p. 362, *infra*. B.C.C.I. S.A. itself had some 47 branches (24 of which were in the United Kingdom, though not all in England) in 13 different countries: see n. 12, *supra*, at 224.

[14] See p. 169, *supra*.

[15] *Re Queensland Mercantile and Agency Co. Ltd.* (1888) 58 L.T. 878 at 879 and *Re Lee Wah Bank Ltd.*, above p. 171.

[16] Or, where appropriate, an undertaking that the assets will remain *in statu quo* may be accepted: *Re Matheson Bros Ltd.* (1884) 27 Ch. D. 225 at 231.

conduct its own winding up. Any creditors (Swedish or Bermudan) might claim in the English winding up, the English court taking into account the dividends received in either of the two sets of proceedings abroad.[17] A situation might also arise where there were simply assets in England being claimed by two competing liquidators and no winding up in England was being sought. In such a case the English court will, if satisfied that all creditors can claim *pari passu* in the liquidation in the corporate domicile, favour the claim of the principal liquidator.[18] (Although it may be noted that an order from the English court is not a prerequisite to a bank or other third party handing over assets to the principal liquidator in such circumstances.)

B. No Liquidation in the Place of Incorporation

It will only be in most unusual cases that there is no likelihood of a liquidation in the place of incorporation. Take the following example. A Swiss corporation has carried on business worldwide but with offices in several European cities. The corporation is seemingly insolvent but has a credit balance in an English bank account. Insolvency proceedings have not yet been commenced in Switzerland but a liquidator has been appointed by the French courts. Obviously the English court will not permit the French liquidator successfully to claim the English assets: the English court will await the outcome of proceedings in Switzerland and act accordingly.[19]

In the rare instances where there is indeed no likelihood of a liquidation in the place of incorporation different considerations must apply. Such cases fall to be divided into two categories. First, if there is only one foreign liquidation it may be recognised in England.[20] But recognition of a foreign liquidation does not deprive the English court of power to appoint a liquidator entitled exclusively to represent the corporation in England.[1] Secondly, there may be two or even more foreign liquidations. If two foreign liquidators are acting in harmony then the English court may assist them, provided to do so does not result in discrimination against any of the creditors. But where the foreign liquidators advance conflicting claims to assets in England, the English court will conduct its own winding up, although attempting so far as possible to ensure a fair distribution of the English assets.[2]

---

[17] *Selkrig v. Davies* (1814) 2 Rose 291, *Banco de Portugal v. Waddell* (1880) 5 App. Cas. 161 and generally chapter 10, *post*.

[18] See *Bank of Credit and Commerce International (Overseas) Ltd. v. Bank of Credit and Commerce International (Overseas) Ltd. (Macau Branch)* [1997] H.K.L.R.D. 304, *supra*.

[19] See *Re Alfred Shaw and Co. Ltd.* (1897) 8 Q.L.J. 93, *passim*.

[20] This is seemingly accepted in *Dicey and Morris*, p. 1138; cited with apparent approval in *Felixstowe Dock and Rly Co. v. United States Lines Inc.* [1989] Q.B. 360 at 374–375.

[1] *North Australian Territory Co. Ltd. v. Goldsbrough, Mort and Co. Ltd.* (1889) 61 L.T. 716, *Re Mid East Trading Ltd.* [1997] 3 All E.R. 481 at 491.

[2] The question of the equalisation of dividends was not apparently raised in *Re Russo-Asiatic Bank* (1930) 24 H.K.L.R. 16.

7. STATUTORY BASES OF RECOGNITION

A. Insolvency Act 1986, Section 426

Section 426(4) of the Insolvency Act 1986 provides:

'The courts having jurisdiction in relation to insolvency law in any part of the United Kingdom shall assist the courts having corresponding jurisdiction in any other part of the United Kingdom or any other relevant country or territory.'

It may well be that a liquidation in a relevant foreign court, which has requested the assistance of the English court under section 426(4), would be entitled to recognition in England under the existing common law rules. But if the requesting court's jurisdiction fell outside the common law rules, there is nothing in section 426 which necessarily prevents the English court from lending its assistance. The section is not seemingly restricted to cases where recognition is in any event available at common law.[3]

B. Civil Jurisdiction and Judgments Act 1982

The Civil Jurisdiction and Judgments Act 1982, which brought into force the provisions of the Brussels Convention 1968, is not generally relevant to cross-border insolvency. For the Brussels Convention and its 'partner' the Lugano Convention (brought into force by the Civil Jurisdiction and Judgments Act 1991) do not seek to apply in matters of bankruptcy or the winding up of insolvent companies.[4] In respect of the winding up of *solvent* companies Article 16(2) of the Conventions confer exclusive jurisdiction upon the courts of the Contracting State in which a company has its seat. A judgment of a court of a Contracting State acting under Article 16(2) is entitled to recognition in England.

Section 43 of the Civil Jurisdiction and Judgments Act 1982 identifies the seat of a corporation for the purposes of Article 16(2). It must first be noted that a company incorporated in the United Kingdom cannot have its seat in another Contracting State.[5] A foreign company will have its seat in a Contracting State other than the United Kingdom if (i) it was incorporated under the law of that State or its central management and control is exercised in that State; and (ii) the courts of that State would regard the company as having its seat in that State for the purposes of Article 16(2).[6] For example, assume that a Swiss corporation has its central management and control in Ireland and under Irish law the corporation has its seat in Ireland for the purposes of Article 16(2). The corporation is solvent. The Irish court would have exclusive jurisdiction under Article 16(2) and its proceedings would be recognised in England. However, the impact of the Conventions on the recognition of foreign liquidations is somewhat marginal. The Conventions do not apply in an insolvency.

---

[3] See p. 417, *post*.
[4] Civil Jurisdiction and Judgments Act 1982 (as amended), Sch. 1, Art. 1(2): see p. 12, *ante*.
[5] *Ibid.*, s. 43(2) and (7)(a).
[6] *Ibid.*, s. 43(6) and (7): see p. 121, *ante*.

8. SUMMARY

A liquidation or reorganisation in Scotland or Northern Ireland will be recognised in England. Other foreign liquidations or reorganisations will be entitled to recognition in England as follows:[7]

(i)   where the liquidation or reorganisation is conducted under, or recognised by, the law of the place of incorporation;

(ii)   where the corporation submitted to the jurisdiction of the foreign court;

(iii)   where the corporation has carried on business within the foreign jurisdiction.

It must be noted, however, that the effect of a foreign liquidation or reorganisation under (ii) or (iii) above is not necessarily identical to a liquidation or reorganisation falling within (i) above.[8]

9. LIQUIDATION OR BANKRUPTCY

In the majority of instances it will be readily apparent whether the recognition of foreign insolvency proceedings should be determined by reference to the rules on foreign liquidations (and reorganisations) or the rules on foreign bankruptcies. Moreover, it has been shown that domicile, submission and the carrying on of business constitute bases of recognition in respect of both foreign liquidations and foreign bankruptcies.[9] Nevertheless, it is obvious that any distinction between winding up and bankruptcy may be quite unknown in a particular foreign legal system. Equally, legal entities and associations may exist under a foreign law but be without parallel in English law. Hence situations may easily be envisaged in which it is open to question which set of recognition rules (liquidation or bankruptcy) should be applied.

In *Modern Terminals (Berth 5) Ltd.* v. *States SS Co.*[10] a Nevada corporation had petitioned under Chapter 11 of the US Federal bankruptcy legislation. The Hong Kong court applied the English cases[11] on bankruptcy, recognising the US proceedings. In *Felixstowe Dock and Rly Co.* v. *United States Lines Inc.*[12] a Delaware corporation had filed for reorganisation under Chapter 11 of the US Code. Hirst J treated the facts as involving the recognition of a foreign liquidation. The

---

[7]   Recognition, but only in respect of solvent companies, may be available under the Civil Jurisdiction and Judgments Act 1982, *supra.*

[8]   The effect of a liquidation other than in the place of incorporation, as well as the consequences of two or more liquidations, has been considered above. In respect of reorganisations commonsense indicates that it would be most unlikely to find conflicting approaches being taken in two or more jurisdictions.

[9]   See also chapter 5, *ante.*

[10]   [1979] H.K.L.R. 512, note *Mobil Sales and Supply Corpn* v. *Owners of Pacific Bear* [1979] H.K.L.R. 125 and *Pitts* v. *Hill* (1987) 66 C.B.R. (N.S.) 273, *passim.*

[11]   Such as *Re Blithman* (1866) L.R. 2 Eq. 23 and *Re Davidson's Settlement Trusts* (1873) L.R. 15 Eq. 383.

[12]   [1989] Q.B. 360 at 374–375. See also *New Hampshire Ins. Co.* v. *Rush & Tomkins Group plc*, *supra*, p. 129.

approach of Hirst J is to be preferred. That a foreign procedure is entitled 'bankruptcy' cannot be decisive; the US Federal Bankruptcy Code knows no distinction between bankruptcy and winding up. It must rather be a matter for the English court, taking into account evidence as to the nature and content of the foreign law, to determine whether a particular case falls within the category of foreign liquidation or of foreign bankruptcy.

Lord Davey in delivering the opinion of the Privy Council in *New Zealand Loan and Mercantile Agency Co. Ltd.* v. *Morrison* identified a 'material distinction' between bankruptcy and winding up:[13]

> 'In the former case the whole property of the bankrupt is taken out of him, whilst in the latter case the property remains vested in title and in fact in the company, subject only to its being administered for the purposes of the winding up. . . .'

However, his Lordship was only speaking with reference to English law. The vesting or otherwise of property by virtue of foreign proceedings does not determine the choice between bankruptcy and liquidation. In each case evidence as to the effect of the relevant foreign law must be considered. In *Re ITT*[14] the applicants had been appointed liquidators by a Luxembourg court of an 'indivision', a mutual investment fund existing under the law of Luxembourg (albeit a form of legal entity unknown to English law). The authority of the liquidators was recognised in the High Court of Ontario. *Re ITT* is an interesting example of the recognition of a foreign liquidation, for the evidence revealed that ITT's assets had actually been vested in the foreign liquidators under the law of Luxembourg.[15] The Luxembourg liquidators, as we have seen, were also recognised in England in *Baden, Delvaux and Lecuit* v. *Société Générale pour Favoriser le Développement du Commerce et de l'Industrie en France S.A.*, wherein it was noted that ITT was not a corporate entity, although it was 'a body that under Luxembourg law could be dissolved'.[16]

Accordingly, foreign insolvency proceedings may be classified as a liquidation even though those proceedings do not relate to a corporate entity and actually vest assets in the foreign representatives. It is, perhaps, unwise to seek to identify any hard and fast rules: the issue is inevitably one of fact and degree. Nevertheless, the greater the extent of separate legal personality conferred on an entity by the foreign law, the more readily the foreign proceedings may be considered as a liquidation. However, it must be noted that the lack of a clear boundary between bankruptcy and liquidation emphasises the need, as a matter of principle, for similar recognition rules applicable to both foreign bankruptcies and foreign liquidations.[17]

---

[13] [1898] A.C. 349 at 358. Note also *Primary Producers Bank of Australia Ltd.* v. *Hughes* (1931) 32 S.R.N.S.W. 14 and *Re African Farms Ltd.* 1906 T.S. 373 at 378–379.

[14] (1975) 58 D.L.R. (3d) 55.

[15] *Ibid.*, at 57.

[16] [1983] B.C.L.C. 325 at 333.

[17] Such rules being founded upon (corporate) domicile, submission and carrying on business in the foreign jurisdiction.

10. EUROPEAN CONVENTION ON INSOLVENCY PROCEEDINGS

When a corporation has its centre of main interests in a Contracting State that is the place where, in principle, insolvency proceedings should be opened; and those proceedings are entitled to recognition in all Contracting States.[18] Other insolvency proceedings may only be opened in a Contracting State in which the debtor has an establishment. In theory, such proceedings will be recognised in other Contracting States[19] but, as a practical matter, because such proceedings are restricted territorially questions of recognition are unlikely to arise.[20] Accordingly, under the Convention the centre of a debtor's main interests is the essential basis of recognition.

A situation might arise where, for example, a Delaware corporation had its centre of main interests in Luxembourg and insolvency proceedings had been commenced in both jurisdictions. The Convention impliedly requires the English court to recognise the proceedings in Luxembourg in preference to those in the place of incorporation. But if the place of incorporation were Bermuda and the court in Bermuda had submitted a section 426 request seeking recognition and assistance (such as the handing over of assets in England to the Bermudan liquidator), the Convention does not require the English court to refuse assistance. For Article 48(3) provides that the Convention shall not apply:

> 'in the United Kingdom of Great Britain and Northern Ireland, to the extent that it is irreconcilable with the obligations arising in relation to bankruptcy and the winding up of insolvent companies from any arrangements with the Commonwealth existing at the time this Convention enters into force.'

11. ILLUSTRATIONS

(1) Q is a Nevada corporation. Q is insolvent and proceedings have been commenced in the United States District Court for the Southern District of New York (in Bankruptcy) under the US Federal Bankruptcy Code. The US proceedings will be recognised in England.[1]

(2) I is an 'indivision', a legal entity existing under the law of Luxembourg. The courts in Luxembourg have appointed liquidators. The English court will recognise the liquidation in Luxembourg and the authority of the liquidators to bring proceedings in England.[2]

(3) The Hong Kong court has made a winding up order in respect of an insolvent company incorporated in New Zealand. The Hong Kong court

---

[18] See Arts. 3(1) and 16. See also pp. 9–12, *supra.*
[19] See Arts. 3(2) and 16.
[20] See Art. 3(2).
[1] See *Banque Indosuez S.A.* v. *Ferromet Resources Inc.* [1993] B.C.L.C. 112 and *Felixstowe Dock and Rly Co.* v. *United States Lines Inc.* [1989] Q.B. 360.
[2] *Baden, Delvaux and Lecuit* v. *Société Générale pour Favoriser le Développement du Commerce et de l'Industrie en France S.A.* [1983] B.C.L.C. 325; *Re ITT* (1975) 58 D.L.R. (3d) 55.

founded its jurisdiction upon the presence of assets in Hong Kong. The Hong Kong liquidation will not be recognised in England at common law.[3]

(4) In 1980 N was incorporated in the British Virgin Islands. In 1986 N reincorporated in Barbados. Such reincorporation is permitted under the law of the British Virgin Islands and of Barbados. A liquidator has recently been appointed in insolvency proceedings in Barbados. The proceedings in Barbados are entitled to recognition in England.[4]

(5) S is a New Zealand registered company which has a branch office in Scotland. A liquidator has been appointed in Scotland. The Scottish liquidation will be recognised in England.

(6) X is a Swedish corporation that has carried on much of its business in Ireland. X is insolvent and in liquidation in Sweden. The Swedish liquidator has petitioned the court in Ireland, seeking the appointment of a liquidator in Ireland. The Irish proceedings may be recognised in England.[5]

(7) An English registered company has a branch office in Queensland. The company is insolvent and liquidators have been appointed by the courts in England and in Queensland. The Queensland liquidator cannot (without the English liquidator's approval) represent the company in proceedings in England.[6]

(8) P is a company incorporated in Hong Kong. T and U are wholly owned subsidiaries of P. T is incorporated in Hong Kong, U is incorporated in the Philippines. The companies have operated as a group, carrying on closely linked businesses in Hong Kong and elsewhere in the Far East. The companies are insolvent. No proceedings have been commenced in the Philippines. All three companies are in liquidation in Hong Kong. The Hong Kong liquidators may be recognised by the English court.

---

[3] The result would, it is submitted, be the same if the Hong Kong court made a request pursuant to s. 426 of the Insolvency Act 1986, unless it were established that no disadvantage would be occasioned to creditors in New Zealand or elsewhere.

[4] Multiple incorporation is considered further in chapter 13.

[5] See *Barclays Bank plc* v. *Homan* [1993] B.C.L.C. 680, above, English company petitioning for US Chapter 11.

[6] *North Australian Territory Co. Ltd.* v. *Goldsbrough, Mort and Co. Ltd.* (1889) 61 L.T. 716.

Chapter 7

Bars to Recognition

1. INTRODUCTION

The circumstances in which the English court will recognise a foreign bankruptcy, liquidation or reorganisation have been considered in chapter 5 and chapter 6. Even though a foreign insolvency falls within one of the relevant bases of recognition, the English court may yet deny effect to the foreign proceedings. It may be said that there is a discretion to refuse recognition.[1] However, such discretion is not exercised capriciously, upon the particular whim of an individual judge.[2] For the discretion to deny recognition to a foreign insolvency is a judicial discretion and founded upon specific grounds.

The English court may refuse to give effect to foreign insolvency proceedings if to do so would be contrary to English public policy; if the foreign proceedings constitute a fraud or are in breach of natural justice; or, additionally, where there is an attempt to enforce a foreign penal or revenue law in England.

It must be noted at the outset that recognition will not be denied on the ground that the foreign insolvency has been conducted out of court. *Dulaney* v. *Merry and Sons*[3] concerned the vesting of property in a trustee appointed under a deed of assignment executed in accordance with the law of Maryland, the domicile of the debtors. Some time after the execution of the deed, the trustee had petitioned the courts in Maryland for confirmation of his authority. Channell J made it plain that recognition was accorded to the deed itself, regardless of subsequent court intervention:[4]

> 'It was proved before me by the evidence of experts that the deed was good according to the law of Maryland and that the property became duly vested in [the trustee]; that this was effected by the operation of the deed – that is, by the act of the parties, and not of the court. . . .'

---

[1] *Re African Farms Ltd.* 1906 T.S. 373 at 381–382 *per* Innes CJ.

[2] As Carey JA observed in *Canadian Arab Financial Corpn.* v. *Player* (with reference to a foreign receiver): 'I am not to be taken as suggesting for one moment that the court has not the power to refuse to confirm or recognise the appointment of a foreign receiver, but there must exist *strong and compelling restraints against such recognition*' ([1984] Cayman Islands L.R. 63 at 122, emphasis added).

[3] [1901] 1 K.B. 536.

[4] *Ibid.*, at 539, approved by Romer LJ in *Metliss* v. *National Bank of Greece and Athens* [1957] 2 Q.B. 33 at 49.

Similarly, a voluntary liquidation (or equivalent) of a company in accordance with its domiciliary law would undoubtedly be recognised in England.[5]

2. PUBLIC POLICY

It is a settled doctrine of English private international law that recognition must be refused if a foreign law, or its application, offends English public policy. Hence in *Re a Debtor, ex p Viscount of the Royal Court of Jersey* Goulding J accepted that the English court would not lend its assistance to any foreign insolvency proceedings which 'offended against some overriding principle of English public policy'.[6] Public policy, it may be noted, has a purely negative operation: it denies effect to the otherwise applicable foreign law. The application of public policy cannot be exactly defined, but it is plain that the doctrine may only be successfully invoked in the clearest of cases. The foreign insolvency, or more likely its consequences in England, must be manifestly offensive to some basic, fundamental principle of morality or justice.

In the Court of Appeal in *Metliss* v. *National Bank of Greece and Athens*[7] Romer LJ cited *Dulaney* v. *Merry and Sons*[8] as authority for the proposition that a foreign trustee's title to property in England will prevail over the claims of a later execution creditor. However, it was also made clear that this principle depended upon the English creditors not being discriminated against in the foreign proceedings.[9] In other words, where foreign proceedings did discriminate against English (and other) creditors, it was not that no recognition whatsoever could be given to those proceedings, but rather that consequences prejudicial to English (and other) creditors would not be accepted. The proceedings could, for example, be recognised as being effective within the territory of the foreign country concerned, but would not operate as an assignment of property in England.

That the English court rarely resorts to public policy is evidenced by the fact that there is not one reported instance of the court denying recognition to foreign insolvency proceedings on account of the public policy of the forum. Certainly recognition cannot be denied simply because the foreign

---

[5] A liquidation by the Economic Security Committee of Jordan in relation to a Jordanian bank was recognised by the Court of Appeal in *Firswood Ltd.* v. *Petra Bank* [1996] C.L.C. 608. Note also *Re Dominion Reefs (Klerksdorp) Ltd.* 1965 (4) S.A. 75 (recognition in South Africa of voluntary winding up in England) and *Bank of Credit and Commerce International (Overseas) Ltd.* v. *Bank of Credit and Commerce International (Overseas) Ltd. (Macau Branch)* [1997] H.K.L.R.D. 304 (recognition of liquidation of branch by executive order of the Governor of Macau).

[6] [1981] Ch. 384 at 402.

[7] [1957] 2 Q.B. 33 at 49, on appeal, [1958] A.C. 509.

[8] [1901] 1 K.B. 536, *supra*.

[9] As Parker LJ put it (at 54): 'This is, however, subject to the proviso that the foreign law enables the English creditors to share all the assets equally with the foreign creditors.' The reference here to 'English creditors' should not be taken literally so as to lead to the conclusion that discrimination against some other foreign creditors will be ignored by the English court. English law sets its face against discrimination against any creditors: see *per* Scott V-C in *Re Bank of Credit and Commerce International S.A. (No. 10)* [1997] Ch. 213 at 242.

law is strikingly different from English law;[10] nor where the foreign court has merely misapprehended the bankruptcy law of England.[11] In short, whilst public policy should always be borne in mind, in commercial matters generally it will only be in the most extreme circumstances that the doctrine will apply.[12]

Let us say that a Delaware bank is in liquidation in the United States pursuant to the US Federal Bankruptcy Code. The bank has assets and creditors in England. However, the English creditors will suffer discrimination in the US proceedings, in that the US assets are ring-fenced.[13] Were such a situation to arise, nevertheless reference to public policy would be inappropriate. Rather, the English court should conduct a winding up in respect of the English assets, allowing English, American and any other creditors to participate therein. In the conduct of its own winding up the English court would still be able to recognise the US proceedings.[14] For instance, although not allowing the US trustee to gather in English assets, the English court would take into account the level of dividends in the two sets of proceedings. Thus if it became apparent that creditors in the English winding up were likely to recover twice the dividend available in the US proceedings, the English court would remit relevant assets to the US court.[15] Accordingly, even where the foreign insolvency law discriminates against English creditors, it may be quite unnecessary to invoke the doctrine of public policy so as completely to deny recognition. The flexibility inherent in the English law rules relating to cross-border insolvency should enable the English court to find an alternative to reliance upon public policy. The doctrine of public policy must be seen as very much a last resort, only prayed in aid to prevent an otherwise unavoidable and gross injustice.

3. FRAUD, NATURAL JUSTICE AND RECIPROCITY

A. Fraud

It is beyond question that the English court may deny recognition to a foreign decree of insolvency obtained as a result of fraud.

If proceedings in the foreign court are not yet concluded it may be more convenient to raise the issue of fraud before the foreign court, with a view to obtaining the rescission, recall or annulment of the foreign proceedings. In *Re McCulloch* bankruptcy proceedings were under way in England when the debtor himself petitioned the Irish court. Bacon CJ felt that in the

---

[10] See, for instance, *Re ITT* (1975) 58 D.L.R. (3d) 55 and *Baden, Delvaux and Lecuit* v. *Société Générale pour Favoriser le Développement du Commerce et de l'Industrie en France S.A.* [1983] B.C.L.C. 325, *Burr* v. *Anglo-French Banking Corpn. Ltd.* (1933) 149 L.T. 282.

[11] *Ellis* v. *M'Henry* (1871) L.R. 6 C.P. 228: a Canadian judgment given effect in England even though the Canadian court had not properly applied the Bankruptcy Act 1861.

[12] For a much criticised application of public policy in the context of the recognition of foreign judgments see *Vervaeke* v. *Smith* [1983] 1 A.C. 145; Carter (1982) 53 B.Y.I.L. 302, Jaffey (1983) 32 I.C.L.Q. 500, Smart (1983) 99 L.Q.R. 24 and Jaffey (1986) 5 C.J.Q. 35, *passim.*

[13] See *Re Bank of Credit and Commerce International S.A. (No. 10)* [1997] Ch. 213 at 227.

[14] See *Felixstowe Dock and Rly Co.* v. *United States Lines Inc.* [1989] Q.B. 360.

[15] The sending of assets to a foreign court is discussed generally in chapter 12.

circumstances there was 'more or less of suspicion' attaching to the debtor's petition.[16] However, the issue was specifically left to the court in Ireland. That fraud has been raised in and rejected by the foreign court does not necessarily preclude the English court from reconsidering the matter.[17] Nevertheless, the party opposing recognition must clearly establish the alleged fraud. In *Foster* v. *Taylor*[18] the plaintiff brought an action in Canada on a US promissory note. The defendant pleaded his discharge under a US bankruptcy. The plaintiff argued that the defendant had in the US proceedings deliberately and fraudulently omitted to reveal the plaintiff's claim, with the consequence that the plaintiff received no notice and had no opportunity to take part in the US proceedings. The defendant's uncontradicted evidence was that, at the relevant time, he believed that the plaintiff's debt had already been paid. It was held that the plaintiff had failed to make out the alleged fraud.

Fraud will generally connote some grave wrongdoing on the part of the debtor in the foreign court, such as suppressing relevant evidence or bribing court officials. However there is some authority which casts the net of fraud a little more widely. It may in rare instances be argued that foreign insolvency proceedings, although regularly conducted according to the foreign law,[19] are a fraud upon the general body of creditors. In *Re Henry Hooman*[20] the insolvent, who had traded in New York, made an assignment of all his property to a trustee to pay off in the first instance one American banker and one English creditor. Thereafter, any residue was to be divided equally amongst the remaining creditors. Such an assignment was valid, at the time, according to the law of New York. The relevant assets were exhausted upon payment of the American banker in full and of a considerable sum to the English creditor. The English court was reluctant to give full effect to the New York assignment:[1]

'Had the assignment in New York been for the general benefit of creditors, American and English . . . this court would accept the assignment as a creditable document. But it cannot be supported by law that a person who has the opportunity in America of making a rateable distribution for the benefit of all his creditors shall confine his assignment to two, and because such an instrument is valid by the law of the State there, shall say it is devoid of bad faith as regards English creditors.'

The English court considered the New York assignment a fraudulent preference within the Judgments Act 1838 and made an adverse adjudication against the insolvent.

Re Henry Hooman appears never to have been the subject of judicial comment. However the above passage with its reference to 'bad faith' does lend support to the proposition that the very nature of a foreign insolvency may raise an inference of fraud. Certainly *Re Henry Hooman* establishes that the English court may refuse to give full effect to foreign insolvency

---

[16] (1880) 14 Ch. D. 716 at 720.

[17] See *Jet Holdings Inc.* v. *Patel* [1990] 1 Q.B. 335 and *Owens Bank* v. *Etoile Commercial S.A.* [1995] 1 W.L.R. 44.

[18] (1871) 31 U.C.R. 24.

[19] Cf. the observations of Staughton LJ in *Jet Holdings Inc.* v. *Patel* [1990] 1 Q.B. 335 at 345 in respect of natural justice.

[20] (1859) 1 L.T. 46.

[1] *Ibid.*

proceedings even though such proceedings may be unimpeachable under the relevant foreign law.[2]

It is perhaps unlikely that such an obviously preferential assignment as in *Re Henry Hooman* would be permitted under any modern insolvency law. However, it is interesting to speculate upon the action which the English court would be likely to take in response to such a situation. Let us say that X Corporation, incorporated in Panonia, has two directors and shareholders, A and B. X Corporation is insolvent and owes substantial sums to A and B in respect of directors' fees and other services. X Corporation enters into a similar assignment to that in *Re Henry Hooman*: X Corporation assigns its assets worldwide to a trustee to pay in the first instance the debts of A and B in full, any remaining assets being held for other creditors. The assignment is perfectly valid according to the laws of Panonia and, moreover, discharges any contractual debts of X Corporation governed by the law of Panonia. X Corporation has assets in England. Panonian and English creditors have begun actions in England, coupled with Mareva injunctions, seeking ultimately to lay their hands on the English assets. The ordinary creditors have no chance of recovering anything under the Panonian assignment. X Corporation and the trustee raise two arguments in the English proceedings. First, X Corporation seeks to strike out those proceedings relating to Panonian contracts, for the assignment purports to discharge all contracts governed by Panonian law; and, secondly, the Panonian trustee claims to be entitled to have the Mareva injunctions lifted so that the corporation's assets may be remitted to the Panonian proceedings. Having regard to the blatantly preferential nature of the assignment, and in the light of *Re Henry Hooman*, the English court would refuse to recognise the Panonian assignment as an effective discharge of contracts governed by Panonian law.[3] So too, in the exercise of the court's discretion, the Mareva injunctions would not be discharged. Instead the proceedings in England would be permitted to continue to judgment, although in such a case English assets may not be distributed without the intervention of winding up proceedings in England.[4]

Accordingly it may be that a foreign insolvency, though validly conducted under the relevant foreign law, may be denied recognition and effect as a fraud upon the general body of creditors. This is the more likely where, as in *Re Henry Hooman*, a debtor on the eve of insolvency deliberately chooses not to make 'a rateable distribution for the benefit of all his creditors'.[5] But it must not be thought that the English court may classify foreign proceedings as a fraud simply because the English court considers itself the only appropriate forum for the conduct of insolvency proceedings. *Geddes* v. *Mowat*[6] (a Scottish appeal before the House of Lords) concerned a debtor domiciled, resident and carrying on business in Scotland. On 4th January 1820 a commission of bankruptcy issued in England. A week later the debtor's estate was sequestrated in Scotland. Subsequently the English commission was found to be invalid and, in

---

[2] Cf. *Jet Holdings Inc.* v. *Patel* [1990] 1 Q.B. 335.
[3] The mere *appointment* of the Panonian trustee, and with it the right to represent X Corporation, might be recognised, as the appointment of the trustee was not in 'bad faith as regards English creditors': *Re Henry Hooman* (1859) 1 L.T. 46.
[4] *Felixstowe Dock and Rly Co.* v. *United States Lines Inc.* [1989] Q.B. 360 at 389.
[5] (1859) 1 L.T. 46.
[6] (1824) 1 Gl. & J. 414.

March 1820, a new commission issued. This second commission was founded upon the original act of bankruptcy (January 1820). The English assignees petitioned the Scottish court, claiming that the sequestration had been superseded by the English commission. That claim was rejected in the Court of Session. The House of Lords held that, as the initial English commission was a nullity, the sequestration had been first in time and was unaffected by the subsequent (valid) English commission. Yet Lord Gifford, very much *obiter*, also touched upon the legal position had the initial commission in England been valid:[7]

> 'There is another point to be observed upon; the bankrupt, as has already been stated, was a domiciled Scotsman . . . It is strongly to be suspected, that finding himself in difficulties in Scotland, and foreseeing a sequestration, he removed to England, in order to commit an act of bankruptcy, and upon that the English commission was founded; . . . and I think it might admit of a serious question, independently of the point of priority, whether this commission of bankruptcy in England, under these circumstances, might not be considered as having been issued in fraud of the law of Scotland; issued as it was against a party, native of Scotland, then resident in Scotland, domiciled in Scotland for years, going to England, in December, and on the 4th of January committing an act of bankruptcy . . . .'

The observation of Lord Gifford that foreign (in this case English) bankruptcy proceedings might have issued 'in fraud of the law of Scotland' must be considered in its proper context.

At the time of *Geddes* v. *Mowat* Scots law (founded upon *Stein's Case*[8]) was that a prior English bankruptcy rendered the Scottish court incompetent: that is, no subsequent Scottish sequestration could be maintained. Hence a Scottish debtor might easily arrange with certain of his creditors (particularly English creditors) that proceedings be first commenced in England. Thereby it might seem that the jurisdiction of the Scottish courts would be ousted as Lord Gifford put it 'in fraud of the law of Scotland'. But the exercise of bankruptcy jurisdiction in England has always been a question of discretion, as indeed it now is in Scotland.[9] That there is a prior foreign bankruptcy or liquidation certainly does not preclude the exercise of jurisdiction by the English court. Thus there will be no fraud against English creditors in the type of case envisaged by Lord Gifford in *Geddes* v. *Mowat*. His Lordship's observations most definitely should not be taken as suggesting that where the English court considers itself the natural forum for insolvency proceedings, then any foreign insolvency constitutes some attempted fraud.

In summary, the English court may refuse to recognise a foreign insolvency obtained in fraudulent circumstances. In this regard fraud refers to some grossly unfair and prejudicial or dishonest conduct. It is not necessary that such conduct be on the part of the insolvent.[10] Where the English court finds that the burden of establishing fraud has been satisfied, it is irrelevant that the guilty party may show that the conduct in question was permissible under a foreign legal system.

---

[7] *Ibid.*, at 423.
[8] *Royal Bank of Scotland* v. *Cuthbert* (*Stein's Case*) (1813) 1 Rose 462, p. 65, *ante.*
[9] Chapter 3, *ante.*
[10] It is not difficult to imagine a situation in which a petitioning creditor has deliberately concealed facts: see *McCormack* v. *Carmen* (1919) 17 O.W.N. 241 at 242, *passim.*

B. Natural Justice

Under the general principles of English private international law a foreign judgment may be denied recognition if it has been obtained in breach of the rules of natural justice.[11] In *Bergerem* v. *Marsh*[12] natural justice was considered applicable to the recognition of a foreign insolvency. The defendant had been a partner in a Belgian *société en nom collectif*. That firm had been declared bankrupt, along with the defendant personally, by the Belgian court acting of its own motion. The defendant did receive notice of the determination in Belgium and there pursued an unsuccessful appeal. Bailhache J recognised the Belgian insolvency, commenting:[13]

> 'the decree is more in the nature of *ex parte* proceedings, and that great care is taken that the person affected shall have full notice of the proceedings. Although this is a different method from ours it does not seem so contrary to natural justice that I ought to refuse to recognise it as a valid method of procedure. Notice was duly served on the defendant and he instructed counsel on his behalf to oppose the decree.'

Certainly, as a general proposition, the debtor should receive notice and have some opportunity to take part in the foreign proceedings.

The position is quite bluntly stated in Wolff as follows:[14]

> 'But the foreign administrator (trustee, curator, syndic etc.) must have been appointed in proceedings to which the debtor was a party, i.e. which were not made in his absence.'

However, it would surely be no breach of natural justice were a debtor to receive notice of proceedings but choose not to participate therein, with the consequence that a decree is made in his absence. *Re a Debtor, ex p Viscount of the Royal Court of Jersey*[15] may here be mentioned. The Royal Court had commenced *en désastre* proceedings for the sequestration of the debtor's movable estate. Some days before the commencement of those proceedings, the debtor had left Jersey and did not thereafter return. In due course the Royal Court requested the assistance of the English court pursuant to section 122 of the Bankruptcy Act 1914. The debtor objected to the request, *inter alia*, as being 'obtained *ex parte* at chambers, without any public hearing'.[16] Nevertheless, the English court lent its assistance. So too circumstances may arise in which the debtor flees the jurisdiction of the foreign court, thereby preventing the foreign court from giving the debtor actual notice. Reference may be made to *Re Behrends*.[17] The debtor had carried on business in Hamburg since 1852. In 1863 the debtor left

---

[11] *Dicey and Morris*, chapter 14 and Cheshire and North, *Private International Law* (12th ed., 1993) chapter 15.

[12] (1921) 91 L.J.K.B. 80.

[13] *Ibid.*, at 81.

[14] *Private International Law* (2nd ed., 1950), p. 564 (footnotes omitted). In *Re Anderson* [1911] 1 K.B. 896 Phillimore J recognised a New Zealand bankruptcy in which the debtor had participated, commenting (at 902): 'If he had not been a party to the adjudication, if it had been made against him in his absence, other considerations might very well have applied.'

[15] [1981] Ch. 384.

[16] *Ibid.*, at 402. Cf. *Larkins* v. *National Union of Mineworkers* [1985] I.R. 671 and *Bond Brewing Holding Ltd.* v. *Crawford* (1989) 92 A.L.R. 154 (*ex parte* foreign receiver).

[17] (1865) 12 L.T. 149. In *Strike* v. *Gleich* (1879) O.B. & F. 50 at 60 the New Zealand Court of Appeal recognised a South Australian insolvency although the debtor had fled South Australia and thus had not received notice of, nor participated in, the South Australian proceedings.

Hamburg, thereafter spending time in New York and England. In 1864 the debtor learnt that he had been made bankrupt in Hamburg 'from reading a notice of it in a New York newspaper'.[18] The debtor was not, as the report has it, *en contumace* as to his bankruptcy in Hamburg. Assignees or *curatores bonorum* were appointed in the Hamburg proceedings. Subsequently the debtor presented a petition before the Court of Bankruptcy in England. The vast majority of creditors resided in Hamburg, where the debtor's books of account and property were left. The Court of Bankruptcy held that the English proceedings would be adjourned *sine die* with liberty to the debtor to apply for his discharge after termination of the proceedings abroad. Far from denying recognition to the *in absentia* insolvency decree pronounced in Hamburg, the English court recognised that the *curatores bonorum* had recovered the debtor's assets in England[19] and, generally, that Hamburg was the proper place for the investigation of the insolvency.

In short, a foreign insolvency may be denied recognition on account of a breach of the rules of natural justice. But natural justice must always be assessed in the light of the particular facts of the case and having regard to the conduct of the debtor. Thus, in appropriate circumstances, that a decree is pronounced in the absence of the debtor may be irrelevant. Perhaps more obviously, there can be no basis for asserting that each and every creditor must have received notice and had an opportunity of participating in the foreign insolvency proceedings.[20]

C. Reciprocity

A foreign court cannot be obliged to give effect to an English bankruptcy or liquidation. One may note *Re Blakes*: the American courts had denied recognition to English assignees, which prompted Thurlow LC to observe: 'I had no idea of any country refusing to take notice of the rights of assignees under our laws. . . .'[1] But there is no merit in maintaining that the English court should deny recognition unless it is shown that the relevant foreign court would give reciprocal treatment and recognise an English insolvency. Reciprocity is not a basis for the recognition of foreign insolvencies;[2] so too, where a foreign insolvency does fall within an established basis of recognition, the absence of reciprocity is not sufficient justification for denying recognition. It is, perhaps, because of the inherent weakness of reciprocity that there is little authority upon this point.[3]

---

[18] *Ibid.*

[19] The Court of Bankruptcy recognised and appeared to have accepted the validity of payment of a debt by one Bamberger to the Hamburg assignees: see (1865) 12 L.T. 149 at 150.

[20] See, for example, the facts in *Foster* v. *Taylor* (1871) 31 U.C.R. 24, *ante.*

[1] (1787) 1 Cox Eq Cas 398.

[2] See p. 158, *supra.*

[3] Although it is interesting to note that in *Re Vocalion (Foreign) Ltd.* [1932] 2 Ch. 196 at 207 Maugham J said: 'This court no doubt holds that in the winding up here all creditors, whether British or foreign, who can prove their debts have equal rights; but it would seem that foreign courts do not always take the same view (see *Employers' Liability Assurance Corpn* v. *Sedgwick, Collins & Co.* [1927] A.C. 95, where the liquidation of the company in Russia was treated as valid in the House of Lords, though no provision had been made for English claims).'

However, in *Williams* v. *Rice* the Manitoba court rejected restricting recognition of a foreign insolvency on account of a lack of reciprocity.[4]

4. FINALITY

In relation to the enforcement at common law of a foreign judgment it is well-settled that the judgment must ·be: (i) final and conclusive and (ii) for a definite sum of money.[5] A foreign insolvency is not, of course, the same thing as a foreign judgment[6] and it is clear that (ii) above cannot conceivably be relevant in this context. Nevertheless, it has been expressly stated by a learned author that recognition will be denied if 'the foreign insolvency proceedings are not final'.[7] This opinion has, moreover, been quoted with apparent approval in a recent decision in New Zealand.[8]

It is readily apparent why a foreign judgment needs to be final and conclusive: for it is only once the case has been determined (subject to potential appeals) that a legal obligation to satisfy a judgment arises on the part of the defendant.[9] Yet in respect of foreign insolvency proceedings no such 'obligation' on the part of a specified defendant can be said to be created. More importantly, the making of a decree or the appointment of a trustee will only be the beginning of the relevant process under the foreign law – rather than its end. Accordingly it is difficult, at least in this author's view, to comprehend what is meant by the word 'final' in the particular context of foreign insolvency proceedings. It might perhaps be taken to mean that the appointment of a trustee or liquidator by the foreign court must not be merely provisional or on an interim (rather than final) basis. The cases, however, are against such a contention. In *Macaulay* v. *Guaranty Trust Co of New York[10]* the plaintiffs had on 13 June 1927 been appointed by a court in Delaware as receivers of an insolvent Delaware corporation. Subsequently the order of 13 June was vacated and an order was made 're-appointing the plaintiffs *pendente lite*'.[11] This fact was drawn specifically to the attention of Clauson J by counsel. Clauson J, although not commenting on the nature of the appointment, recognised the interim receivers. Similarly in *Pélégrin* v. *Coutts & Co.[12]* Sargant J recognised the right of an *administrateur*

---

[4] [1926] 3 D.L.R. 225 at 250–251. See also *Adams* v. *Cape Industries plc* [1990] Ch. 433 at 552, *passim.*

[5] *Dicey and Morris*, p. 461.

[6] See p. 141, *supra.*

[7] Wood, *Principles of International Insolvency* (1995) para. 15–13.

[8] *The Cornelis Verolme* [1997] 2 N.Z.L.R. 110 at 119. The question was, however, *obiter* as the facts had nothing to do with whether the Belgian bankruptcy was 'final'.

[9] See the discussion in *Dicey and Morris*, pp. 455–456.

[10] (1927) 44 T.L.R. 99.

[11] *Ibid.* It will also be noted that in *Hughes* v. *Hannover Rückversicherungs-Aktiengesellschaft* [1997] 1 B.C.L.C. 497 at first instance (see at 500) Knox J entertained a request for assistance where the facts involved provisional liquidators appointed in Bermuda. By the time the case came before the Court of Appeal a winding up order had been made in Bermuda and liquidators appointed. Nothing in the case suggests that no assistance could be given to provisional liquidators.

[12] [1915] 1 Ch. 696.

provisoire appointed by the French courts to recover assets in England. Although the facts concerned a Frenchman who had become of unsound mind, Sargant J decided the case by analogy with the situation that would have arisen had the Frenchman instead been adjudicated bankrupt in France.[13] More recently, reference may also be made to the collapse of the Bank of Credit and Commerce International S.A. When BCCI closed its doors in July 1991 provisional liquidators or the foreign equivalents were appointed in various jurisdictions[14] and it was only in January 1992 that BCCI actually went into liquidation in the place of its incorporation (Luxembourg) and elsewhere. Yet it was never suggested that foreign proceedings prior to January 1992 could not be recognised in England.[15] In short, it is submitted that the common law rule of finality that applies to foreign judgments has no place when it comes to foreign insolvency proceedings.

5. PENAL LAW

It is no part of the function of the English court to enforce the criminal law of a foreign country. Let us say that, arising out of a New York bankruptcy, the debtor and an associate are each fined US $10,000. The fines cannot be recovered by proceedings in an English court, either by attempting to bring an action on a foreign judgment or with reference to New York bankruptcy proceedings entitled to recognition in England.[16]

However, it must be stressed that the rule against foreign penal laws is strictly limited. Recognition will not be denied merely because there is a penal element involved in or relating to the foreign insolvency. A useful modern illustration may be found in *Re ITT*.[17] ITT was a mutual investment fund established in 1960 under the laws of Luxembourg as an 'indivision'–a legal entity unknown to English law. In 1972 a Grand Duchal regulation was passed in Luxembourg requiring investment funds such as ITT to register with the Banking Control Commissioner for Luxembourg. Registration was refused and the Commissioner was required to seek the liquidation of ITT. Thereafter ITT was declared bankrupt by the District Court in Luxembourg and liquidators appointed. The Luxembourg liquidation was recognised in Ontario, Houlden JA rejecting the submission that the Grand Duchal regulation was penal in nature:[18]

---

[13] *Ibid.* at 701–702.

[14] In Luxembourg a *commissaire de surveillance* was appointed, followed by liquidators in January 1992: see [1997] Ch. at 224–225.

[15] For a review of the history, see *Re Bank of Credit and Commerce International S.A. (No. 10)* [1997] Ch. 213 at 224–226.

[16] The rule against the enforcement of foreign penal and revenue laws also extends to foreign 'public' laws: see *Camdex International Ltd.* v. *Bank of Zambia (No 2)* [1997] C.L.C. 714.

[17] (1975) 58 D.L.R. (3d) 55.

[18] *Ibid.*, at 56. For a further illustration see *Pickles v China Mutual Insurance Co.* (1913) 10 D.L.R. 323 – Massachusetts incorporated insurance company put into receivership at the instance of public official in Massachusetts, recognised in Canada.

'I have given careful consideration to the decree and while it contains penal provisions, I do not think it is penal in nature in the sense in which that term has been interpreted in the conflict of laws.'

For foreign proceedings to come within the scope of the rule against penal laws, those proceedings must be in the nature of a suit in favour of the State whose law has been infringed[19] – often a penalty recoverable at the instance of the State or its duly authorised official.

Schemmer v. *Property Resources Ltd.*[20] is an example wherein foreign proceedings, although not designed to enforce a fine or other penalty, had been brought by a foreign governmental body to give effect to the criminal law of that country. The US District Court had appointed a receiver of a Bahaman company in proceedings instituted by the Securities and Exchange Commission under the Securities Exchange Act 1934 of the United States. Goulding J denied recognition to the US receivership as being founded upon a foreign penal law. The US receiver was not to be equated with a private plaintiff who had recovered a civil judgment under the US legislation. The US receiver was a 'public officer' charged to reduce the company's assets in England into possession 'in order to prevent the commission or continuation of offences against Federal law'.[1]

It is clear, however, that the rule against foreign penal laws only applies where the sole purpose of any action brought in England is to enforce that foreign penal law (in England).[2] The rule would not operate in the following situation. A US corporation, engaged in the oil refining business, has been fined several million dollars by a US court for breaching environmental protection laws.[3] The corporation was already in financial difficulty and the fines have pushed it into bankruptcy. A trustee has been appointed in the US proceedings and it has been revealed that, whilst there are large amounts owing to the corporation's bankers and trade creditors, the claims of the Federal authorities make up more than 50% of all the corporation's debts and liabilities.[4] There is no bar to the recognition of the US bankruptcy proceedings in England, nor to allowing the US trustee to recover assets in England. Moreover, if an ancillary winding up were conducted in England, the English court would (in appropriate circumstances) remit English assets to the US court for distribution on a global basis to all the creditors.[5]

---

[19] *Huntington* v. *Attrill* [1893] A.C. 150 at 157 *per* Lord Watson: 'A proceedings, in order to come within the scope of the rule, must be in the nature of a suit in favour of the State whose law has been infringed.'

[20] [1975] Ch. 273: see also *Larkins* v. *National Union of Mineworkers* [1985] I.R. 671.

[1] [1975] Ch. 273 at 288.

[2] See the discussion which immediately follows in respect of foreign revenue laws.

[3] Claims might also arise because, under the foreign law, a company had to re-imburse governmental authorities for the cost of environmental clean up operations. Such claims are not fines, but whether they would fall within foreign 'public' laws is in some doubt: see *United States* v. *Ivey* (1995) 130 D.L.R. (4th) 674; affd (1996) 139 D.L.R. (4th) 570 and compare *Camdex International Ltd.* v. *Bank of Zambia (No 2)* [1997] C.L.C. 714.

[4] See *Ayres* v. *Evans* (1981) 39 A.L.R. 129 below; more than 50% of claims in the bankruptcy owing to a foreign revenue.

[5] See chapter 14 for an analysis of ancillary winding up.

6. REVENUE LAW

A. The General Rule

Of doubtless greater significance than the exception in respect of foreign penal laws is the prohibition against the enforcement of foreign revenue laws. The prohibition was firmly established as part of English law in *Government of India* v. *Taylor.*[6] An English company had carried on its undertaking in India and had there incurred certain tax liabilities. The company was put into voluntary liquidation in England and the Government of India sought to recover unpaid taxes in the liquidation in England. The House of Lords unanimously held that a claim by or on behalf of a foreign state to recover taxes was unenforceable in the English courts, Lord Keith of Avenholm observing that 'in no circumstances will the courts directly or indirectly enforce the revenue laws of another country'.[7] It was further held that the foreign tax claim, being unenforceable in England, did not fall within the 'company's liabilities' under section 302 of the Companies Act 1948;[8] and accordingly such claim was not to be satisfied in the liquidation out of the company's property. Viscount Simonds stated:[9]

'I conceive that it is the duty of the liquidator to discharge out of the assets in his hands those claims which are legally enforceable, and to hand over any surplus to the contributories. I find no words which vest in him a discretion to meet claims which are not legally enforceable.'

It may also be noted (as it was in their Lordships' House[10]) that the rule against foreign revenue laws has been judicially upheld in foreign legal systems.[11]

The term foreign revenue law is widely construed and refers not merely to income and capital taxes – other non-contractual payments to the state or a governmental body will be included. Thus estate, customs, stamp and gambling duties, as well as local rates and state health insurance schemes, are all examples of foreign revenue laws.[12]

The rule, of course, is against the enforcement of foreign revenue laws: there is no obstacle to simple recognition. Thus the English court will not enforce a contract which is illegal according to its proper law, including any

---

[6] [1955] A.C. 491.

[7] *Ibid.*, at 510. The difficult question is quite what is considered indirect enforcement, see Smart (1986) 35 I.C.L.Q. 704, *passim.*

[8] Lord Keith adopted a somewhat different approach to that of the majority, see [1955] A.C. 491 at 512–513. Section 302 of the 1948 Act was re-enacted as s. 597 of the 1985 Act, now s. 107 of the Insolvency Act 1986 (for compulsory winding up see Insolvency Act 1986, s. 148(1)) see also, p. 203, *infra.*

[9] [1955] A.C. 491 at 509. Note also the discussion of *Re Oygevault International B.V.* (1994) 12 A.C.L.C. 708, p. 204, *infra.*

[10] Lord Somervell of Harrow referred to *Pillet's Traité de Droit International Privé* ([1955] A.C. 491 at 515), whilst Lord Keith relied (at 510) upon the 'admirable judgment' of Kingsmill Moore J in the High Court of Eire in *Peter Buchanan Ltd.* v. *McVey*, [1955] A.C. 516n [1954] I.R. 89.

[11] See, e.g., *United States* v. *Harden* (1963) 41 D.L.R. (2d) 721, *Jones* v. *Borland* 1969 (4) S.A. 29, *Bath* v. *British and Malayan Trustee Ltd.* [1969] 2 N.S.W.L.R. 114.

[12] *A-G for Canada* v. *Schulze* (1910) 9 S.L.T. 4, *Municipal Council of Sydney* v. *Bull* [1909] 1 K.B. 7, *Re Visser* [1928] Ch. 877, *Metal Industries (Salvage) Ltd.* v. *Owners of S.T. Harle* 1962 S.L.T. 114, *passim*: foreign exchange control legislation may be seen as foreign 'public' law; *Camdex International Ltd.* v. *Bank of Zambia (No 2)* [1997] C.L.C. 714.

relevant tax laws. Likewise it was accepted by Slade J in *Re Cable*[13] that English trustees of a settlement governed by the law of India would not be prevented from paying Indian estate duty out of assets in England. The operation of the decision in *Re Cable* in relation to insolvency is discussed below.[14]

B. The International Insolvency Context

In a cross-border insolvency case the fundamental question may be simply put: can the English court give assistance to a foreign assignee if the facts reveal that the foreign revenue authorities have entered a claim in the foreign insolvency proceedings? The significance of this inquiry is only increased when one considers that a modern insolvency case will almost inevitably involve a demand by revenue authorities for unpaid taxes.[15]

Let us say that a debtor carrying on business in Holland has been adjudicated insolvent by the Dutch courts. The debtor has assets in England which the Dutch assignee wishes to remit to the foreign insolvency proceedings. Generally speaking, there is no doubt that the English court will recognise the authority of a foreign assignee to deal with movables in England. However, let us further assume that the Dutch revenue authorities have entered a claim abroad. From *Government of India* v. *Taylor* it inevitably follows that the Dutch revenue could not pursue that claim before the English courts. If the rule against foreign revenue laws were strictly applied, it might be said that to assist the Dutch assignee would result in English assets being used in part ultimately to satisfy the Dutch revenue debt – a debt which could not directly be enforced in England. However, both commonsense and authority are against a strict interpretation of the revenue rule in the context of cross-border insolvency. The English court will not deny recognition to a foreign insolvency unless the foreign proceedings amount in substance to nothing more than an attempt to enforce a foreign tax debt.

An analysis of the cases must commence with *Peter Buchanan Ltd.* v. *McVey*,[16] a decision of the courts in Ireland but very much relied upon by Lord Keith of Avenholm in *Government of India* v. *Taylor*.[17] A Scottish company was put into liquidation in Scotland at the instance of the Scottish revenue. The liquidator was chosen by the Scottish authorities and worked 'in every respect hand in glove with the authorities'. The liquidator brought an action in Ireland to recover certain assets of the company. However, it was shown that after payment of costs of the liquida-

---

[13] [1976] 3 All E.R. 416 at 436; see also *Brokaw* v. *Seatrain UK Ltd.* [1971] 2 All E.R. 98 at 99.
[14] See, particularly, *Re Oygevault International B.V.* (1994) 12 A.C.L.C. 708 p. 204, *infra*.
[15] Forsyth J in the Alberta case *Re Sefel Geophysical Ltd.* [1989] 1 W.W.R. 251, 260 has gone so far as not to follow *Government of India* v. *Taylor*, stating: 'However, given the present trends in international comity in the recognition of foreign bankruptcy proceedings, I am not certain that the *India (Govt. of)* case is compatible with the current judicial climate. If the goal is to deal with liquidations in an orderly fashion in one country by virtue of deference shown by competing nations, surely some claims should be recognised.' Whatever the possible merit of the views of Forsyth J, *Government of India* v. *Taylor* binds the English court.
[16] [1955] A.C. 516n. [1954] I.R. 89.
[17] [1955] A.C. 491 at 510.

tion any money recovered would go to the Scottish revenue. Kingsmill Moore J held that the action was in substance an attempt to enforce the revenue law of Scotland and could not be maintained before an Irish court:[18]

> 'For the purpose of this case it is sufficient to say that when it appears to the court that the whole object of the suit is to collect tax for a foreign revenue, and that this will be the sole result of a decision in favour of the plaintiff, then a court is entitled to reject the claim by refusing jurisdiction.'

Such reasoning was upheld on appeal to the Supreme Court: the sole object and only purpose of the liquidation, and of the proceedings in Ireland, was to recover taxes.

However the Supreme Court also offered some guidance on the proper approach to a normal foreign liquidation, in which revenue as well as ordinary debts were present. Maguire CJ observed:[19]

> 'I agree that if the payment of a revenue claim was only incidental and there had been other claims to be met, it would be difficult for our courts to refuse to lend assistance to bring assets of the company under the control of the liquidator.'

In summary, the court must look at the substance of a foreign liquidation. If the sole object of the foreign proceedings is the enforcement of a revenue debt then the English court will refuse to assist the foreign liquidator.[20] However, in a typical case, where there are revenue and non-revenue claims, the revenue rule cannot be invoked to deny recognition. This proposition, derived from *Peter Buchanan Ltd.* v. *McVey*, becomes irresistible in the light of the weight of subsequent authority.[1]

The decision of the Court of Session in *Scottish National Orchestra Ltd.* v. *Thomson's Executors*[2] concerned a deceased, having died domiciled in Sweden, with assets in Scotland. The Swedish administrators sought to appropriate those assets to pay, *inter alia*, Swedish inheritance duty. Lord Robertson said that the administrators' claim would have failed if the only purpose had been to pay Swedish tax. However the facts were that, after the tax had been paid, the remaining assets would be held for the beneficiaries in Sweden. As it was not the sole or only purpose of the action to enforce a foreign revenue debt, the claim of the Swedish administrators was upheld. Like reasoning found favour in the Federal Court of Australia in *Ayres* v. *Evans.*[3] Ayres was adjudicated bankrupt in New Zealand and the High Court issued letters rogatory requesting the assistance of the Australian court as the bankrupt had assets in Australia. In the New Zealand bankruptcy proceedings the revenue debts, some of which were preferred, totalled more than 60% of all claims. At first instance Lockhart J held that the substance of the application was not the enforcement of a

---

[18] [1955] A.C. 516 at 529.

[19] *Ibid.*, at 533.

[20] At least to the extent that enforcement of the foreign revenue law *in England* is involved: *Re State of Norway's Applications (Nos. 1 and 2)* [1990] I A.C. 723 at 809. Note also *Re Gibbons, ex p. Walter* [1960] Ir. Jur. Rep. 60 and compare the remarkable decision in *Bullen* v. *HM Government 533* So. 2d 1344 (Fla. App. 4 Dist. 1989).

[1] In addition to the cases discussed below, the analysis of Maguire CJ seems to have been approved by Lord Mackay of Clashfern in *Williams & Humbert Ltd.* v. *W and H Trade Marks (Jersey) Ltd.* [1986] A.C. 368 at 440.

[2] 1969 S.L.T. 325.

[3] (1981) 34 A.L.R. 582; on appeal 39 A.L.R. 129.

foreign revenue debt and rejected counsel's argument that assistance should not be given where the 'greater part' of claims were by a foreign revenue authority.[4] That decision was upheld on appeal, Fox J stating:[5]

> 'I am of the opinion that the rule does not apply where a liquidator or an official assignee seeks to get in property which will in a due course of administration benefit ordinary creditors as well as the revenue.'

McGregor J added:[6]

> 'the leading authorities are really concerned with an action which sought recovery of revenue funds only. We are not concerned with such a situation. Here the action is by one whose function is to implement the laws of bankruptcy in New Zealand to get in the bankrupt's estate . . . for distribution amongst creditors, and not to enforce revenue laws; even if in the process the revenue should benefit.'

Ayres v. *Evans* was itself applied in *Priestley* v. *Clegg*,[7] wherein a South African court lent assistance to an English trustee in bankrutpcy even though UK revenue debts were estimated at 94% of all claims in the English proceedings.

C. Recent United Kingdom Authority

It cannot be suggested that *Scottish National Orchestra Ltd.* v. *Thomson's Executors, Ayres* v. *Evans* and *Priestley* v. *Clegg*[8] are binding on an English court. But the relevant principle, that a court will not deny recognition to a foreign insolvency provided it is not in substance an attempt to enforce a foreign revenue debt, has been approved in recent cases within the United Kingdom.

In *Re Tucker*[9] the High Court in England had sought the assistance of the High Court in the Isle of Man, pursuant to section 122 of the Bankruptcy Act 1914. The English court was requesting examination of witnesses (the 'noticed parties') and the production of certain documents in the Isle of Man. For the noticed parties it was argued, *inter alia*, that the Manx court should not lend its assistance as the only real creditor in the English bankruptcy was the UK Revenue. Deemster Luft found that the English proceedings were not a tax bankruptcy as the Revenue was not the only creditor, nor had the bankruptcy been instituted by the Revenue.[10] The Deemster made an order granting assistance. That order was upheld on appeal, *Ayres* v. *Evans* and *Priestley* v. *Clegg* being approved.[11]

In *Re Tucker (Application of Trustee in Bankruptcy)*[12] the Royal Court of Jersey was faced with a like request for assistance, except that the UK Revenue was by that stage the only creditor in the English bankruptcy

---

[4] (1981) 34 A.L.R. 582 at 589.
[5] (1981) 39 A.L.R. 129 at 131.
[6] *Ibid.*, at 144.
[7] 1985 (3) S.A. 955.
[8] 1969 S.L.T. 325, (1981) 39 A.L.R. 129 and 1985 (3) S.A. 955 respectively.
[9] [1988] F.L.R. 154. For an interesting and detailed account of the background to the litigation see Fidler (1989) 5 J. of Int. Bank. & Fin. Law 19.
[10] *Ibid.*, at 163–164.
[11] [1988] F.L.R. 323 at 337.
[12] *Ibid.*, at 378.

proceedings. The Jersey court, in light of the fact that there was no creditor other than the Revenue, refused to lend its assistance. It should be noted that the Jersey court would have been likely to have followed the course adopted in the Isle of Man High Court had there been non-revenue as well as revenue creditors.[13]

It is unnecessary to dwell upon the two decisions in the Tucker litigation. For the particular issue involved, a request by a foreign court to obtain information, has recently been ruled upon by the House of Lords. In *Re State of Norway's Applications (Nos. 1 and 2)*[14] a Norwegian court issued letters of request to the High Court in England seeking the examination of two witnesses in England. The evidence of the witnesses was to be used in a tax case in Norway. The letters of request were supported by both the State of Norway and the taxpayer's estate. In their Lordships' House it was held[15] that the Norwegian proceedings were a 'civil or commercial' matter within the Evidence (Proceedings in Other Jurisdictions) Act 1975. More significantly for present purposes, the granting of assistance did not involve the direct or indirect enforcement of the tax laws of Norway. Lord Goff of Chieveley put it as follows:[16]

> 'I return to the rule in the *Government of India* case . . . It is stated in *Dicey and Morris* p. 103 that indirect enforcement occurs (1) where the foreign state (or its nominee) in form seeks a remedy which in substance is designed to give the foreign law extra-territorial effect or (2) where a private party raises a defence based on the foreign law in order to vindicate or assert the right of the foreign state . . . I have to consider whether a case such as the present should nevertheless be held to fall foul of the rule. For my part, I cannot see that it should. I cannot see any extra-territorial exercise of sovereign authority in seeking the assistance of the courts of this country in obtaining evidence which will be used for the enforcement of the revenue laws of Norway in Norway itself.'

Thus it may be said that in *Re State of Norway's Applications (Nos. 1 and 2)* the foreign tax proceedings were recognised in England; additionally, the English court could properly assist the obtaining of evidence in England as to do so did not go beyond the enforcement of the foreign revenue law within the territory of the foreign state.

Helping a foreign state or its nominee to obtain *evidence* in England does not constitute indirect enforcement[17] – that evidence will be used for the enforcement of the revenue laws of the foreign state in the foreign state itself. So too it might be suggested that helping a foreign state or its nominee to recover *assets* in England should not be considered indirect enforcement of the foreign revenue law – those assets would be used for the enforcement of the revenue laws of the foreign state in the foreign state itself. Unfortunately, Lord Goff's speech in *Re State of Norway's Applications (Nos. 1 and 2)* does not reveal whether a distinction was intended between evidence on the one hand and assets on the other. However, Lord

---

[13] *Ibid.*, at 402. Note *passim* a judgment of the Guernsey Court of Appeal (*Re Tucker; Bird* v. *Meader* (6 February 1989, unreported) referred to in Fidler, n. 9, *supra*, in which the court lent assistance although the case was effectively a 'tax-bankruptcy': see *Muir Hunker on Personal Insolvency*, para. 3-481/3.

[14] [1990] 1 A.C. 723. The speech of Lord Goff of Chieveley was concurred in by the rest of the House.

[15] *Ibid.*, at 806. The issue is fully considered in Lipstein (1990) 39 I.C.L.Q. 120.

[16] *Ibid.*, at 809.

[17] *Re State of Norway's Applications (Nos. 1 and 2)* at 809.

Goff cast no doubt on the correctness of cases such as *Peter Buchanan Ltd.* v. *McVey*. Accordingly under the current authorities a foreign assignee, when indeed acting as the nominee of a foreign tax gathering authority, may receive assistance from the English court in obtaining evidence in England but remains precluded from suing or otherwise recovering assets in England.

It is this author's opinion, however, that there is no good reason why assets should not be handed over to a foreign trustee or liquidator even when acting as a nominee of a foreign revenue authority. It is to be hoped that, at some stage in the future, *Government of India* v. *Taylor* will be confined to its facts and held not to apply where the English court is asked to act in aid of *foreign* insolvency proceedings. That point, it would appear, has not yet been reached.[18]

D. Summary of Principles

Of course, *Re State of Norway's Applications (Nos. 1 and 2)* did not involve foreign insolvency proceedings. Nevertheless, the liberal approach to the foreign revenue rule adopted by Lord Goff is in keeping with the trend of the cross-border insolvency cases. In short, the foreign revenue rule will only operate to preclude recognition where two factors are both present: firstly, a foreign assignee is the nominee of the foreign revenue; and, secondly, enforcement of the foreign revenue law in England is contemplated. Thus it may be stated:

(i)   If there are revenue and non-revenue claims in the foreign insolvency, a foreign assignee is not to be regarded as the nominee of the foreign State, hence there is no obstacle to prevent the assignee bringing an action in England or otherwise recovering the insolvent's assets in England.

(ii) Where a foreign assignee merely seeks the assistance of the English court in obtaining evidence, there is no direct or indirect enforcement of the foreign revenue law in England; thus it is irrelevant whether the foreign assignee is a nominee of the foreign taxing authority. Such assistance may be granted.

E. Recognition and Rescue

It will be recalled that the relevant rule is one against the enforcement in England of a foreign tax law; hence the discussion above has focused on the circumstances in which there arises an exception to that rule or, more precisely, when that rule does not seek to apply: namely, where there are revenue and non-revenue claims in the foreign proceedings. Yet, additionally, one must not lose sight of the fact that there is no prohibition at all against the *recognition* of a foreign revenue law. A convenient starting point

---

[18]   In *Re Bank of Credit and Commerce International S.A. (No. 9)* [1994] 3 All E.R. 764 at 785, Rattee J referred to the rule in its 'traditional' form: assistance would not be given 'where the request is such that to comply with it would infringe the rule [against] enforcing another country's tax claims'. See also p. 203, *infra*.

is *Re Cable*[19] wherein Slade J held that English trustees of a settlement governed by Indian law would not be prevented from paying Indian estate duty out of assets in England. Likewise, the directors of an English company which has carried on business abroad could not, whilst it was a going concern, be prevented from paying foreign taxes. But the legal position becomes complex when that company is put into administration under the Insolvency Act 1986 having, let us say (in addition to English creditors) creditors in Ireland – one of which is the Irish Revenue. The plan proposed by the administrator, to restructure the company's business in England and in Ireland, may not involve any attempted enforcement of the Irish Revenue debt. For example, certain of the creditors as well as the Irish Revenue may be willing to grant the company a moratorium, to cancel a portion of their debts or to exchange debt for equity. In such a case it is strongly suggested that the foreign revenue rule cannot apply, because recognition rather than enforcement in England is all that is involved. The difficulty, however, is to determine in what manner the Irish Revenue can participate in the administration.

Pursuant to s. 24(1) of the Insolvency Act 1986 a meeting of 'creditors' must be summoned to decide whether to approve a proposed plan. The question is whether the Irish Revenue is a 'creditor'. If one applies the reasoning which found favour in *Government of India* v. *Taylor*[20] then the Irish Revenue is not a 'creditor'. For a majority of their Lordships accepted that 'liabilities' (which the liquidator was bound to discharge) meant 'only those obligations which are enforceable in an English court' and did not include obligations which might properly be enforced in a foreign court.[1] If, in our example, there is no 'liability' to the Irish Revenue, then it is a very short step to conclude that the Irish Revenue is not a 'creditor'. (Such a step was taken recently in the Australian case of *Re Oygevault International B.V.*, discussed below.) Precisely the same problem (the meaning of 'creditor') arises in relation to a scheme of arrangement under section 425 of the Companies Act 1985. Although it is interesting to note that in *Re RMCA Reinsurance Ltd.*[2] Morritt J, when dealing with a scheme of arrangement in relation to two Singaporean insurance companies, ordered a class meeting for the class of 'Singapore preferential creditor' to be held (in Singapore), even though the only such preferential creditor was the Inland Revenue in Singapore.[3] The question of whether the Revenue in Singapore was a 'creditor' for the purposes of section 425 was apparently overlooked. Returning to the example above, it is obvious that an attempt to conclude a rescue plan, but without including the Irish Revenue, would be almost bound to fail; not least because trade creditors will be reluctant to give up their rights if they know that the Irish Revenue can sit back and do nothing, wait until any plan is implemented and then take action to recover the whole of the tax debt by attaching the company's assets in Ireland, thereby effectively putting the company out of business.

It is fair to say that the majority in *Government of India* v. *Taylor* went further than the facts of the case strictly required. Rather than a blanket

[19] [1976] 3 All E.R. 417 at 436.
[20] [1955] A.C. 491, *supra* p. 197.
[1] *Ibid.* at 508.
[2] [1994] B.C.C. 378.
[3] *Ibid.*

ruling that a foreign tax debt can never be a 'liability', their Lordships could have decided the case on a narrower basis; namely that even if a foreign tax debt could be or was a 'liability', it was not a liability that the liquidator was bound to pay. (This was, in fact, the view expressed by Lord Keith of Avenholm.)[4] As a matter of strict precedent, therefore, an English judge – without departing from the *ratio* in *Government of India* v. *Taylor*, could hold that a foreign revenue authority may be a 'creditor' under the Insolvency Act or the Companies Act, even though the relevant debt may not be enforceable in an English bankruptcy or winding up. (In this manner the ruling in *Re RMCA Reinsurance Ltd.* could be reconciled with the earlier House of Lords' decision.)

In the meantime, however, practical solutions can be found. Firstly, two sets of proceedings may be initiated: one in England (in relation to English creditors) and one in Ireland (in relation to Irish creditors). The Irish Revenue would be a creditor for the purposes of the legislation in Ireland and (assuming the appropriate procedures were followed under Irish law) would be bound as a creditor.[5] Second, particularly if the amount due to the Irish Revenue is not large, the English administrator might simply pay off the Irish Revenue. The powers of an administrator are set out in the First Schedule to the Insolvency Act 1986 and include power to make 'any payment which is necessary or incidental to the performance of his functions' (para. 13). Such payment is not limited to payment to a 'creditor' and can be said to be necessary in order to formulate an acceptable proposal in a cost-efficient manner. An administrator could seek approval from the court before making such payment.[6]

The type of problem discussed above is less likely to arise where a company goes into liquidation: because the company will not be continuing its business after the termination of the English insolvency proceeding. Yet, even in a winding up, it may be in the interests of the creditors to pay off a foreign revenue debt even though that debt is not enforceable in the English winding up. In *Re Oygevault International B.V.*[7] the courts in Australia were winding up a group of companies. Most of the companies involved were Australian, but Oygevault ('the company') was incorporated in Holland. The company had massive liabilities but owed a small amount (A\$6,000) to the Dutch revenue authorities. There had been no liquidation in Holland but the Australian liquidators believed that if the Dutch authorities were not paid, winding up proceedings would be commenced there. The liquidators also expressed the view, which the court accepted, that the cost of paying the foreign revenue debt in full was insignificant compared to the expenses that would follow were the company to go into liquidation in its country of incorporation.[8] The liquidators, accordingly, sought leave to pay the foreign tax debt in full. The court took the view that

---

[4] [1955] A.C. 491 at 513.

[5] This type of approach, or at least something similar, seems to have been taken in *Re Business City Express Ltd.*, Rattee J, [1997] B.C.C. 826 (see p. 414, *infra*), a case involving an Irish company – in examinership in Ireland – that owed money to various creditors in England including the Commissioners of Customs and Excise.

[6] Insolvency Act 1986, s. 14(3).

[7] (1994) 12 A.C.L.C. 708.

[8] The Australian liquidation might then be seen as ancillary to the Dutch proceedings and considerable complexity and duplication of effort was envisaged: see *ibid.*, at 709.

the statutory power[9] to 'pay any class of creditors in full' could not be relied upon, as the Dutch Revenue was not a creditor. Nevertheless, it was held that the court had power to authorise a liquidator to make payments which he was not otherwise entitled or bound to make, where the payment was necessary for the purpose of preserving the assets of the company, or where payment was expedient in the interests of those interested in the liquidation. It is submitted that this eminently practical solution could be applied in England were like facts to arise.[10]

F. Local and Foreign Revenue Claims

Let us assume that a debtor has carried on business in New York and to a lesser extent in England. The vast majority of creditors and assets are in New York. There are but few creditors, together with a small amount of assets, in England. Bankruptcy proceedings have been commenced in both jurisdictions and the revenue authorities of each country have entered claims in the relevant local proceedings. Expert opinion reveals that the general body of English creditors will not be discriminated against in the New York proceedings. In this type of situation the English court has a discretion to stay its own bankruptcy proceedings in favour of the New York court as the clearly more appropriate forum.[11] English assets would then be remitted to the New York court, which would thus be in a position to deal with all the assets and all the creditors. That there are US revenue claims in the foreign proceedings makes no odds.[12] But the question remains as to how the UK revenue debts should be handled, for it is most unlikely that a US court will enforce a UK revenue debt in a bankruptcy taking place in New York.[13]

If the UK tax debt is preferred under English law it will have to be satisfied out of the English assets before such are remitted to the American assignee; however, where the UK Revenue is an ordinary creditor, the English court must make provision for a specified amount to be paid out of the English assets to the UK Revenue as a condition to handing over the English assets.[14] The calculation of this specified amount requires careful consideration, for there is no case law to provide direct assistance.[15] The specified amount to be held back by the English court should not be calculated with reference to the English bankruptcy alone. It would not be consistent with principle to work out the dividend an ordinary creditor

[9] See, in England, Insolvency Act 1986, Sch. 4, para. 1.

[10] Power to authorise such a payment might also be found under the Insolvency Act 1986 in para. 3(b) of Sch. 4.

[11] Chapter 3, *ante.*

[12] The New York bankruptcy is not in substance an attempt to enforce a foreign tax debt in England.

[13] Cf. the approach of Forsyth J in *Re Sefel Geophysical Ltd.* [1989] 1 W.W.R. 251. It was held that if a foreign court hands over assets, the courts of the forum may give effect to foreign revenue claims in respect of such assets. Forsyth J considered himself, as a matter of precedent, free to depart from *Government of India* v. *Taylor* [1955] A.C. 491, p. 198, n. 15, *supra.*

[14] See *Re Bank of Credit and Commerce International S. A. (No. 4)* [1995] B.C.C. 453 at 457 and *(No. 10)* [1997] Ch. 213 for the general position in respect of the retention of funds.

[15] The solution proposed in *Re Sefel Geophysical Ltd.* [1989] 1 W.W.R. 251, *supra,* is not available in England.

would be likely to receive in the English bankruptcy, having regard to the amount of English assets and the claims of English creditors, for English assets are not in any way reserved or earmarked for English creditors;[16] in general, any and all creditors may claim in English proceedings.[17] Instead a broader view must be taken. The specified amount reserved for the UK Revenue is to be calculated in accordance with the dividend an ordinary creditor would notionally receive in New York – the New York court dealing with all the debtor's assets and both sets of creditors, American and English.[18]

Of course, the figures required to calculate this specified amount may not be immediately available. Indeed, it could be many months before an accurate picture of the level of dividend can be obtained. In such circumstances the English court should limit the scope of its proceedings, instructing the English trustee only to ingather English assets, settle a list of English creditors and satisfy the preferred creditors.[19] The remaining English assets (or such portion thereof as appears appropriate) may then be held in England pending the determination of the specified amount as indicated above.[20]

7. COMPANIES ACT 1989, SECTION 183

Section 183 of the Companies Act 1989 ('the 1989 Act') should not actually be seen as a bar to recognition of foreign insolvency proceedings, but rather as imposing a specific restriction upon the *effect* to be given to such proceedings. Part VII of the 1989 Act is expressed (see s. 154(a)) to safeguard the operation of certain financial markets where a person party to market transactions becomes insolvent. Section 183 is designed to ensure that no foreign insolvency interferes with the proper operation of the markets. Section 183(1) enlarges the definition of 'insolvency law' for the purposes of section 426 of the Insolvency Act 1986:[1]

> 'The references to insolvency law in section 426 . . . include, in relation to a part of the United Kingdom, the provisions made by or under this Part and, in relation to a relevant country or territory . . . so much of the law of that country or territory as corresponds to any provisions made by or under this Part.'

This is combined with section 183(2), which restricts the effect that may be given under English law to a foreign insolvency:

> 'A court shall not, in pursuance of that section [i.e. s. 426] or any other enactment or rule of law, recognise or give effect to:

---

[16] *Re Bank of Credit and Commerce International S.A. (No. 10)* [1997] Ch. 213 at 242.

[17] Where creditors claim in English and in foreign proceedings see chapter 10.

[18] See Illustration 6, *post*.

[19] As in *Re National Benefit Assurance Co.* [1927] 3 D.L.R. 289, see also *Re Commercial Bank of South Australia* (1886) 33 Ch. D. 174 and cases discussed in chapter 14.

[20] When remitting assets to the more appropriate forum there is a general discretion to retain such amounts as the court may approve: see *Re National Benefit Assurance Co.* [1927] 3 D.L.R. 289 at 302 and *Re Bank of Credit and Commerce International S.A. (No. 10)*, *supra*.

[1] This section is, of course, the international assistance provision and is analysed in chapter 15.

(a) any order of a court exercising jurisdiction in relation to insolvency law in a country or territory outside the United Kingdom . . .

in so far as the making of the order . . . would be prohibited in the case of a court in the United Kingdom . . . by provision made by or under this Part.'

It will be noted that the restriction imposed by section 183(2) is in the broadest terms and applies not merely to section 426 assistance but also to recognition under any other enactment or rule of law: this must include recognition at common law.

8. NON-RECOGNITION OF A FOREIGN TERRITORY

In rare instances it may be that giving effect to a foreign insolvency is complicated by the fact that the territory in which the proceedings have been conducted is not recognised by Her Majesty's Government as a State. The argument being, in simplistic terms, that if the foreign territory is not recognised by Her Majesty's Government as a State, then Her Majesty's courts cannot give effect to any of its laws.[2] Fortunately, there are very few 'unrecognised States': Taiwan and, in Europe, the so-called Turkish Republic of Northern Cyprus are perhaps the best known contemporary illustrations.

In relation to corporate insolvency it is suggested that the Foreign Corporations Act 1991 has rendered State recognition irrelevant. Section 1 of the Act provides that any issue in respect of corporate status or 'any other material question' that arises in relation to a body that appears to have corporate status under the laws of a territory that is not recognised by Her Majesty's Government as a State, shall be determined as if the territory in question were a recognised State, provided the laws of that territory are applied by a settled court system established in that territory. A 'material question' is defined in section 1(2) as:

'A question (whether as to capacity, constitution or otherwise) which, in the case of a body corporate, falls to be determined by reference to the laws of the territory under which the body is incorporated.'

Thus whether a liquidator appointed in Taiwan in respect of a Taiwanese corporation has authority to sue in England to recover debts should, it is submitted, be regarded as a material question; for that question should be referred to the law of Taiwan as the law of the place of incorporation. Accordingly, the fact that Taiwan is not recognised as a State is not relevant.[3]

Turning to personal insolvency, where the 1991 Act obviously has no application, there is a well-known *dictum* of Lord Wilberforce[4] that 'where private rights, or acts of everyday occurrence . . . are concerned . . . the courts may, in the interests of justice and commonsense, where no

---

[2] See generally, *Dicey and Morris*, pp. 992–993. Recognition of a State is a quite different question from recognition of a government, *ibid.*

[3] There seems to be no English case law on the Act, but identical legislation was applied to recognise the status of a Taiwanese corporation in Hong Kong in *Taiwan Via Versand Ltd.* v. *Commodore Electronics Ltd.* [1993] 2 H.K.C. 650.

[4] *Carl Zeiss Stiftung* v. *Rayner & Keeler Ltd. (No. 2)* [1967] 1 A.C. 853 at 954.

consideration of public policy to the contrary has to prevail, give recognition to the actual acts or realities found to exist in the territory in question.' As Donaldson MR once commented, non-recognition does not require that the territory's inhabitants are treated as 'outlaws', who 'cannot marry, beget legitimate children, purchase goods on credit or undertake countless day-to-day activities having legal consequences'.[5] The question of the recognition of a Taiwanese bankruptcy recently arose before the courts in Hong Kong (in a judgment delivered when Hong Kong was under British administration). In *Ting Lei Miao* v. *Chen Li Hung*[6] Ting was, in October 1990, declared bankrupt by a court in Taiwan, which at the same time appointed trustees in bankruptcy. The following year an action was commenced in Hong Kong in the name of Ting against certain defendants. In 1995 the Taiwanese trustees in bankruptcy applied for leave to intervene in the action and be given conduct of the case. When the matter came before the Hong Kong court it was accepted that Taiwan was not recognised as a State by Her Majesty's Government, but that the *dictum* of Lord Wilberforce was good law. Nevertheless, the judge ruled that no effect could be given to the Taiwanese proceedings because to do so would require the court 'specifically to recognise the acts of a court of law' of an unrecognised territory:[7]

> 'There is . . . a distinction between approving the internal effectiveness of a system on which the parties rely to conduct their private affairs on the one hand and of expressly accepting the validity of the judicial acts of an unrecognised system on the other. The applicants' case falls within the latter. . . .'

With respect, however, it is difficult to understand why such a distinction must be drawn. Moreover, the English cases in no way support such a distinction. It is unfortunate the Hong Kong court was not referred to *Re James (an insolvent)*[8] in which Scarman LJ observed:[9]

> 'I do think that in an appropriate case our courts will recognise the validity of judicial acts, even though they be the acts of a judge not lawfully appointed or derive their authority from an unlawful government.'

In short, that a trustee was appointed by a court in a territory not recognised as a State does not of itself mean that such appointment can never be given any effect under English law.

9. EUROPEAN CONVENTION ON INSOLVENCY PROCEEDINGS

As one would expect, under the terms of the Convention (Article 26) recognition may be denied where the consequences of such recognition would be contrary to public policy:

---

[5] *Gur Corpn* v. *Trust Bank of Africa Ltd.* [1987] Q.B. 599 at 622.

[6] [1997] H.K.L.R.D. 841.

[7] *Ibid.*, at 853.

[8] [1977] Ch. 41. The actual decision in this case was whether a court in what had been the colony of Southern Rhodesia was a 'British court', for the purposes of the Bankruptcy Act 1914, after a 'Unilateral Declaration of Independence' in 1965 had been promulgated and an illegal regime had been established in what was termed 'Rhodesia'.

[9] *Ibid.*, at 70.

'Any Contracting State may refuse to recognise insolvency proceedings opened in another Contracting State or to enforce a judgment handed down in the context of such proceedings where the effects of such recognition or enforcement would be manifestly contrary to that State's public policy, in particular its fundamental principles or the constitutional rights and liberties of the individual.'

What is more noteworthy is that the Convention would do away with the rule against foreign revenue laws. The Convention in Article 39 in effect reverses the decision in *Government of India* v. *Taylor*[10] when dealing with claims by the revenue authorities in other Contracting States:

'Any creditor who has his habitual residence, domicile or registered office in a Contracting State other than the State of the opening of proceedings, including the tax authorities and social security authorities of Contracting States, shall have the right to lodge claims in the insolvency proceedings in writing.'

Although the matter is not spelt out in the Convention, it inevitably follows that a court in England would permit a foreign liquidator to recover assets in England even though the only creditor in the foreign proceedings was the revenue authorities in the relevant Contracting State.[11]

10. ILLUSTRATIONS

(1) On the eve of insolvency P, a German businessman, quits Germany and does not thereafter return. Insolvency proceedings are conducted in Germany and an assignee appointed. The assignee brings an action in England to recover a debt owing to P. The defendant in England argues that the German proceedings should be denied recognition as the insolvent was not a party to those proceedings. The assignee's title will be recognised in England.[12]

(2) The debtor, domiciled and ordinarily resident in England, is a wholesaler based in Manchester. In the course of business the debtor regularly visits and orders goods from suppliers in Ireland. The debtor, in dire financial straits, decides not to return from a business trip to Ireland but stays on with relatives there. A bankruptcy petition has been presented by creditors in England and, at roughly the same time, bankruptcy proceedings are also commenced in Ireland. The English proceedings will not be stayed in favour of the Irish courts.[13]

(3) X carried on business in Panonia and France. Last year X entered into an arrangement with his creditors in Panonia, such arrangement subsequently being ratified by the Panonian courts; thereafter X was declared bankrupt and a Panonian trustee appointed. However X, the Panonian creditors and the trustee deliberately concealed from the Panonian court that X had creditors in France. The French creditors have commenced

---

[10] [1955] A.C. 491, *supra.* It is hoped the Convention will be resurrected soon.
[11] The decision in *Peter Buchanan Ltd.* v. *McVey* [1955] A.C. 516n., *supra* is reversed.
[12] *Re Behrends* (1865) 12 L.T. 149.
[13] There is no fraud involved in the commencement of the Irish proceedings. However, as the Irish court is not clearly more appropriate no stay of English proceedings will be granted.

proceedings in France. Meanwhile the Panonian trustee has sought to take possession of X's assets in England. The English court will (*semble*) not recognise the title of the Panonian trustee, it having been obtained by fraud.[14]

(4) M T Inc., a Mondavian corporation, has been put into liquidation in Mondavia. The Mondavian liquidator wishes to bring an action in England against one of the corporation's English directors to recover certain secret profits. Under the law of Mondavia a Mondavian liquidator is entitled to deal with a corporation's property anywhere in the world. But, under Mondavian law, the English liquidator of an English company would not be permitted to represent the company in Mondavia. The authority of the Mondavian liquidator will be recognised in England, a lack of reciprocity under Mondavian law being no obstacle.

(5) P Ltd., incorporated in Ireland, has been put into liquidation in Ireland. P Ltd. has assets in England. In the liquidation Irish revenue claims amount to some 60% of all debts. The English court will permit the Irish liquidator to recover the assets of P Ltd. in England. The Irish liquidation is not in substance an attempt to enforce Irish tax law in England.[15]

(6) N is domiciled in England but resident in New York. For several years N has carried on business in New York but also undertook certain speculative ventures in the United Kingdom. N has been declared bankrupt, upon his own petition, in New York. Most of N's creditors are in New York together with the bulk of N's assets. N has a small number of creditors as well as some assets in England. The English creditors have commenced bankruptcy proceedings in England. The New York proceedings are already quite advanced and expert evidence reveals that English creditors may claim *pari passu* with American creditors in the US proceedings. However, the UK revenue authorities have entered claims (some of which are preferred) in the English proceedings – such claims will not be enforced by the US court. Once it is shown that the proceedings in New York are clearly more appropriate, the English court will stay its own proceedings with a view to sending the assets in England to the New York court. The stay will be on condition that any preferred creditors (including the UK revenue) are first paid off and, in addition, that a specified amount is reserved in respect of the non-preferred revenue debt due to the UK authorities.

The calculation of this 'specified amount' is shown by reference to the following figures. (These figures are obviously and grossly simplified with, *inter alia*, secured and preferred creditors as well as costs being ignored.) US assets total 580,000. US creditors total 2,800,000. English assets total 20,000. English creditors' claims amount to 190,000 to which must be added a UK revenue debt of 10,000.

---

[14] The position might be different if it were established that the French creditors might yet claim, *pari passu* with other creditors, in the Panonian proceedings.
[15] See *Peter Buchanan Ltd.* v. *McVey* [1955] A.C. 516n. and *Ayres* v. *Evans* (1981) 39 A.L.R. 129, *ante*.

Hence the worldwide assets amount to 600,000 and worldwide creditors total 3,000,000. Accordingly 2,000 will be kept in England in respect of the UK revenue debt (10,000 × $-'''\%$), the remaining English assets being remitted to the New York court.

(7) Majestic is a company incorporated in Israel. Majestic is insolvent and provisional liquidators have been appointed by the Israeli court. The Israeli court has authorised the provisional liquidators to take steps to secure the company's assets in England. The authority of the provisional liquidators will be recognised in England.[16]

(8) The facts are as in (7) above; however, the company is a Taiwanese company and the appointment of the provisional liquidators was made in Taiwan. The authority of the Taiwanese provisional liquidators to represent the company in England may be recognised.[17]

---

[16] See *Macaulay* v. *Guaranty Trust Co. of New York* (1927) 44 T.L.R. 99, *supra*.
[17] Foreign Corporations Act 1991, s. 1, *supra*.

Chapter 8

Consequences of Recognition

1. INTRODUCTION

That a foreign insolvency is recognised by the English court involves more than mere acknowledgment of the existence of the foreign proceedings. As a matter of principle, recognition 'carries with it the active assistance of the court'.[1] This approach was specifically approved in a recent New Zealand decision.[2] As long ago as the eighteenth century it was established that a foreign assignee might sue in the English courts and that foreign bankruptcy proceedings may vest the bankrupt's movable property in the foreign assignee.[3] Similarly, there is no doubt that a foreign liquidator may enforce a corporation's rights in England. In addition, whilst actual title is not usually transferred by a liquidation, a foreign liquidator may have authority to administer the corporation's assets in England.[4]

Foreign trustees or liquidators have been allowed to institute civil proceedings in England,[5] take over litigation already commenced by the debtor prior to the onset of insolvency,[6] seek declarations as to the effect of foreign insolvency proceedings,[7] and recover debts[8] as well as deal with

---

[1] *Re African Farms Ltd.* 1906 T.S. 373 at 377 *per* Innes CJ.

[2] *The Cornelis Verolme* [1997] 2 N.Z.L.R. 110 at 120, citing the relevant passage in the first edition of this work.

[3] *Richards* v. *Hudson* (1762) 4 Term Rep 187n., *Solomons* v. *Ross* (1764) 1 Hy. Bl. 131n., *Jollet* v. *Deponthieu* (1764) 1 Hy. Bl. 132n., *Neale* v. *Cottingham* (1770) Wallis 54.

[4] See, generally, *Baden, Delvaux and Lecuit* v. *Société Générale pour Favoriser le Développement du Commerce et de l'Industrie en France S.A.* [1983] B.C.L.C. 325, p. 166 *supra*. Should, however, the foreign liquidator of a foreign corporation seek to prove in the winding up in England of an English company, he must do so in accordance with the law of England: see *Re Kowloon Container Warehouse Co. Ltd.* [1981] H.K.L.R. 210.

[5] Many examples may be found in cases during the last century (such as *Copin* v. *Adamson* (1875) 1 Ex. D. 17, *Re Davidson's Settlement Trusts* (1873) L.R. 15 Eq. 383 or *Semphill* v. *Queensland Sheep Investment Co. Ltd.* (1873) 29 L.T. 737); for a more modern illustration see *Bank of Credit and Commerce Hong Kong Ltd.* v. *Sonali Bank* [1995] 1 Lloyd's Rep. 227 at 229.

[6] See, for example, *Goldsbrough, Mort & Co. Ltd.* v. *Doyle* (1893) 6 Q.L.J. 1 for an early illustration.

[7] *Bergerem* v *Marsh* (1921) 91 L.J.K.B. 80.

[8] *Smith* v. *Buchanan* (1800) 1 East 6 at 11, *Alivon* v. *Furnival* (1834) 1 Cr. M. & R. 277 at 296, *Re Behrends* (1865) 12 L.T. 149 at 150, *Macaulay* v. *Guaranty Trust Co of New York* (1927) 44 T.L.R. 99 at 100, *Barned's Banking Co. Ltd.* v. *Reynolds* (1875) 36 U.C.R. 256 (enforcement of call). Cf. *Jeffery* v. *M'Taggart* (1817) 6 M. & S. 126.

movable[9] and immovable assets,[10] including after-acquired property,[11] in England.

2. UNITED KINGDOM INSOLVENCIES

A. Insolvency Act 1986, Section 426(1)

As has been seen, the court in England will not question the jurisdiction of the courts in Scotland or Northern Ireland to commence insolvency proceedings against a debtor (corporate or individual).[12] As a practical matter an English judge will seek to give the fullest effect to a Scottish or Northern Irish insolvency. The precise legal framework in which recognition occurs is, however, somewhat complex and must depend upon the interpretation of section 426(1) and (2) of the Insolvency Act 1986:[13]

> '(1) An order made by a court in any part of the United Kingdom in the exercise of jurisdiction in relation to insolvency law shall be enforced in any other part of the United Kingdom as if it were made by a court exercising the corresponding jurisdiction in that other part.
> (2) However . . . nothing in subsection (1) requires a court in any part of the United Kingdom to enforce, in relation to property situated in that part, any order made by a court in any other part of the United Kingdom.'

The question is whether section 426(1) should be viewed as providing a comprehensive[14] statement as to recognition (and its consequences) or, in the alternative, whether it is part of a broader framework. In other words, does section 426(1) 'stand alone'?

Leaving to one side (for the time being) the predecessors of section 426(1), one must first determine how it was intended that the subsection should operate, in particular, whether section 426(1) should operate 'automatically': that is, once any order has been made, for instance in Scotland, whether such order immediately and automatically, and without any intervention by the English court, has the same effect in England as if it had been made by the court in England. It is suggested that section 426(1) does not have automatic effect, but is drafted with a view to the *court* in England *enforcing* orders made in any other part of the United Kingdom.[15] To take an example, let us say that three years prior to his sequestration in Scotland, the bankrupt made a gift of a house in England to a relative. The court in Scotland has set aside that gift as a gratuitous alienation and ordered that the property be restored to the debtor's estate. For that order to be carried into effect, or 'enforced' to use the word in subsection (1), the Scottish trustee must apply to the court in England (for the order to be made an order of the English court); and, in our example, subsection (2)

---

[9] Movables may likely vest in a foreign trustee but subject, of course, to prior attachments and charges: *Galbraith* v. *Grimshaw* [1910] A.C. 508, *infra*.
[10] Here the assistance of the English court will be required: *Re Kooperman* [1928] W.N. 101, *Re Osborn* [1931–32] 15 B. & C.R. 189, *infra*.
[11] See, for example, *Re a Debtor, ex p Royal Court of Jersey* [1981] Ch. 384, *infra*.
[12] See pp. 142 and 165, *supra*.
[13] See also p. 405, *infra*.
[14] See, generally, Fletcher, *The Law of Insolvency* (2nd ed., 1996) p. 703.
[15] These are the words used in s. 426(1) itself.

expressly confers upon the English court a discretion not to enforce the Scottish order. If it were the case that section 426(1) operated automatically (without the need to make the Scottish order an order of the English court), the discretion in subsection (2) would be meaningless: because there would simply be no need to go before the English court in the first place. In short, section 426(1) operates where there has been an order made in any part of the United Kingdom and an application is made to enforce that order in any other part of the United Kingdom.

If it is correct that section 426(1) contemplates that the enforcement of an order of the Scottish or Northern Irish court requires that such order is made an order of the court in England, it almost inevitably follows that section 426(1) does not stand alone but is part of a broader framework. For otherwise the liquidator of a Scottish company could do nothing in England without first having the Scottish winding up order made an order of the English court. Moreover, to continue with the example of a Scottish liquidator, it may very often be the case, even where a winding up order has been made by the court in Scotland, that the liquidator is appointed by the creditors without any court order. When the Scottish liquidator takes steps to recover assets in England he is seeking not the enforcement of an *order* of the court in Scotland, but rather recognition of his appointment by the creditors and of his authority under the legislation to gather in the relevant assets. Likewise, where the Scottish liquidator (even if appointed by the court) is given authority by the liquidation committee[16] to bring or defend an action in England, it is recognition of the authority conferred on the liquidator, not enforcement of any order of the Scottish court, that is the issue. Indeed, perhaps the strongest point is that section 426(1) must be intended to operate alongside general principles of recognition, rather than stand alone, because otherwise a Scottish voluntary liquidation (no court order) would be denied any effect in England, and vice versa.[17]

It is this author's view that section 426(1) does not exclude, but instead operates alongside, the general principle of recognition, namely that where insolvency proceedings are being conducted in accordance with legislation in force in one part of the United Kingdom those proceedings must be recognised in any other part of the United Kingdom. Thus, for example, a bankrupt's property in England will vest in a Scottish trustee because that is quite simply what the Bankruptcy (Scotland) Act 1985 requires;[18] and a liquidator appointed in Scotland (whether in a voluntary or compulsory liquidation, and whether or not appointed by the court) must be recognised as having full authority to represent the company in England.

---

[16] See Insolvency Act 1986, s. 167(1)(a).

[17] It also seems that s. 426(1) operates in respect of 'insolvency law'; but not all powers that may be exercised (or orders made) by the court in the course of a bankruptcy or winding up (or administration) are part of 'insolvency law' as defined in s. 426(10): see *Hughes* v. *Hannover Rückversicherungs-Aktiengesellschaft* [1997] 1 B.C.L.C. 497 and p. 411 *infra*. Thus s. 426(1) is not comprehensive and may have to be supplemented by the provisions of the Civil Jurisdiction and Judgments Act 1982 (as amended).

[18] The Act defines the estate of the debtor as 'his whole estate at the date of sequestration, wherever situated . . .' (s. 31(8)).

This view is strongly supported by reference to the predecessors of section 426(1) found in the Companies Acts[19] and the Bankruptcy Acts. For example, section 117 of the Bankruptcy Act 1883 stated:

'Any order made by a court having jurisdiction in bankruptcy in England under this Act shall be enforced in Scotland or Ireland in the courts having jurisdiction in bankruptcy in those parts of the United Kingdom respectively, in the same manner in all respects as if the order had been made by the court hereby required to enforce it . . . .'

Yet it was beyond doubt that the courts in Scotland accepted that property in Scotland vested in an English trustee on account of the expansive definition of property in the 1883 Act, rather than due to the operation of section 117.[20] Similarly, where a liquidator was appointed in Scotland, his authority to recover assets or commence litigation in England could not be questioned – as it flowed directly from the Companies Acts. But if the Scottish court in the course of a winding up made an order requiring a director resident in England to go to Scotland for examination (and that director failed to comply), that order could be made an order of the English court and then enforced through use of English procedures and personnel.[1] So too where the court in Scotland made a call, it had to be made an order of the English court before steps could be taken to enforce the call against recalcitrant English contributories.[2] The same view was once expressed by Jessel MR when dealing with the enforcement of an English injunction restraining actions commenced by creditors in Ireland.[3] An example can also be found where the court in Scotland made an order restraining creditors from proceeding with an action in California and that order was then enforced by Chitty J in relation to a creditor resident in England.[4]

B. Summary

The position, it is suggested, is that section 426(1) has not actually changed the general approach that prevailed prior to 1985.[5] A liquidator

---

[19] The Companies Act 1862 provided in s. 122: 'Any order made by the court in England for or in the course of the winding up of a company under this Act shall be enforced in Scotland and Ireland in the courts that would respectively have had jurisdiction in respect of such company if the registered office of the company had been situate in Scotland or Ireland, and in the same manner in all respects as if such order had been made by the courts that are hereby required to enforce the same. . . .' Like provision was also made, in s. 122, for the enforcement of Scottish and Irish orders in England.

[20] *Salaman* v. *Tod* 1911 S.C. 1214; Lord Kinnear did not even refer to s. 117, whilst Lord Mckenzie referred to the section only in passing and only then as one of many sections in the 1883 Act that expressly referred to Scotland.

[1] As in *Vegetable Oil Products Co. Ltd. (in liquidation)* 1923 S.L.T. 114.

[2] *Re City of Glasgow Bank* (1880) 14 Ch.D. 628, applying *Re Hollyford Copper Mining Co.* (1869) 5 Ch. App. 93. Note also *Re Western Bank of Scotland* (1859) 1 De G.F. & J. 1. When dealing with the enforcement of an English order against a Scottish contributory, Lord Fraser in *Johnstone's Trustee* v. *Roose* (1884) 12 R. 1 observed (at 2) that: 'The order of the court in England which is here founded on needs to be "backed" in Scotland'.

[3] *Re International Pulp and Paper Co.* (1876) 3 Ch.D. 594 at 599: '. . . this court can enforce its order in Ireland, that is, the person getting the order can record it in an Irish court, and then enforce it in Ireland.'

[4] *Pacific Coast Mining Co. Ltd.* v. *Walker* (1886) 13 R. 816 and (in England) [1886] W.N. 63.

[5] Dicey & Morris, *The Conflict of Laws* (10th ed. 1980) pp. 713–5.

or administrator currently appointed (by whatever procedures) in Scotland or Northern Ireland has full authority to represent the company in England on account of the basic principles of recognition of United Kingdom legislation. Where, in addition, the appropriate court has made an order (such as to set aside a preference) that order can be made an order of the English court under section 426(1) and enforced accordingly. However, if that order concerns property in England (and that may be property belonging to the company or to third parties) then section 426(2) applies; and nothing in section 426(1) requires the English court to enforce that order.

Turning to bankruptcy, real and personal property located in England[6] will vest in a Scottish trustee, for that is what the Bankruptcy (Scotland) Act 1985 requires. But such vesting of the debtor's property in England does not operate to defeat the interests of third parties. So that a Scottish trustee will take a subject to charges and liabilities existing at the date of the sequestration. Hence in *Galbraith* v. *Grimshaw* the House of Lords held that a Scottish trustee could only claim the 'free' assets of the debtor in England. (It is at common law that the Scottish trustee takes subject to English liabilities. Thus section 426(2) is not relevant, simply because the Scottish trustee's claim is not being considered under section 426(1).)

C. *Galbraith* v. *Grimshaw* 'reversed'

In *Galbraith* v. *Grimshaw*[7] the respondents had obtained judgment in Scotland for a sum of money and, relying on that judgment, had in October 1908 obtained a garnishee order *nisi* attaching a debt owed by a third party to the debtor in England. In the following month the debtor's estate was sequestrated in Scotland and a trustee appointed. (There was no bankruptcy in England.) The House of Lords, upholding the decision of the Court of Appeal,[8] ruled that the assets of the debtor vested in the Scottish trustee subject to all liabilities which were in existence at the date of the sequestration: the prior English attachment, although incomplete, was not defeated by the claim of the Scottish trustee.[9]

Two points must be noted. First, if the facts were to re-occur, the court in Scotland might (assuming it had jurisdiction over the attaching creditor)[10] make an order requiring the attaching creditor to hand over the proceeds of the attachment to the Scottish trustee: that order might then be enforced

---

[6] As far as an English court is concerned, property in Denmark or Thailand will likewise vest in the Scottish trustee: subject to charges under the *lex situs*, see *Callendar, Sykes & Co.* v. *Colonial Secretary of Lagos* [1891] A.C. 460.

[7] [1910] A.C. 508.

[8] [1910] 1 K.B. 339.

[9] Nothing in s. 117 of the Bankruptcy Act 1883 changed this proposition (*per* Lord Loreburn [1910] A.C. 508 at 511). As Farewell LJ pointed out in the Court of Appeal (at 343) the only 'order' that had been made by the Scottish court was the order vesting the property of the bankrupt in the trustee – no order had been made concerning the attachment in England – and s. 117 did 'not mean that an order of the Scotch bankruptcy court is to be read and enforced in this court in England irrespectively of the English law so as to affect adversely charges on property in England.'

[10] There would be jurisdiction if the creditor were resident in Scotland or had claimed in the Scottish bankruptcy, see p. 271 *infra*.

in England pursuant to section 426(1).[11] Secondly, and far more importantly, any claim by the Scottish trustee to assets in England would now trigger the operation of section 426(6):[12]

'Where a person who is a trustee . . . under the insolvency law of any part of the United Kingdom claims property situated in any other part of the United Kingdom (whether by virtue of an order under subsection (3) or otherwise), the submission of that claim to the court exercising jurisdiction in relation to insolvency law in that other part shall be treated in the same manner as a request made by a court for the purpose of subsection (4).'

It follows from the reference to subsection (4), which in its turn refers to subsection (5), that in a *Galbraith* v. *Grimshaw* situation the English court would now have a discretion to apply either English 'insolvency law' or Scottish 'insolvency law' to determine the competing claims of the trustee and the attaching creditor.[13] (Obviously, this discretion arises directly from section 426(6) and in no way relates to whether an order has been made in Scotland for the attaching creditor to disgorge the proceeds of the attachment.) Thus the English court is free to apply section 346 of the Insolvency Act 1986 (part of English 'insolvency law') and prevent the attaching creditor from retaining the proceeds of the attachment. There is little doubt, at least in this author's mind, that relying upon section 426(6) the English court would apply section 346 and find in favour of the Scottish trustee. For there is no merit in an approach that leaves a trustee to fall 'between two stools'[14] and allows a creditor to obtain a benefit not available to the general body of creditors. In addition, it hardly lies in the mouth of the attaching creditor to complain if English insolvency law is applied, since the creditor has availed himself of English law in order to put the attachment into operation in the first place. The creditor in *Galbraith* v. *Grimshaw* got an undeserved windfall and, moreover, a windfall that he had no reasonable expectation of acquiring. The loophole revealed in *Galbraith* v. *Grimshaw* has been closed (at least when one is dealing with a trustee appointed in Scotland or Northern Ireland).[15]

Of course, section 426(6) also operates in the reverse situation. So that a claim made by an English trustee in a Scottish court in relation to movables that have been attached in Scotland, or heritable estate subject to

---

[11] Although s. 426(2) might apply.

[12] It will be noted that s. 426(6) refers to s. 426(3); subsection (3) permits the making of statutory instruments to make provision for securing that a trustee appointed in one part of the United Kingdom has the same rights to property in another part of the United Kingdom as a trustee appointed in that other part of the United Kingdom would have. No regulations under s. 426(3) have yet been put in place. However, s. 426(6) applies when a UK trustee claims property 'under subsection (3) *or otherwise*'.

[13] For analysis of s. 426(4) and (5) see p. 405 *infra*. The subsections state:
'(4) The courts having jurisdiction in relation to insolvency law in any part of the United Kingdom shall assist the courts having the corresponding jurisdiction in any other part of the United Kingdom or any relevant country or territory.
(5) For the purposes of subsection (4) a request made to a court in any part of the United Kingdom by a court in any other part of the United Kingdom or in a relevant country or territory is authority for the court to which the request is made to apply, in relation to any matters specified in the request, the insolvency law which is applicable by either court in relation to comparable matters falling within its jurisdiction. . . .'

[14] [1910] A.C. 508 at 510 *per* Lord Loreburn.

[15] Clearly, by its terms, s. 426(6) does not apply to a truly 'foreign' trustee; although a foreign court could make a s. 426(4) request, in appropriate circumstances, asking that the English court apply English insolvency law to determine the rights of an attaching creditor in England.

inhibitions,[16] would enable the Scottish court to apply the relevant provisions of the Bankruptcy (Scotland) Act 1985[17] and favour the cause of the English trustee.

D. Winding up, Attachment and Restraint of Proceedings

Moving on from general principles of recognition and section 426, note must be taken of the effect of sections 130 and 128 in England where there is a winding up in Scotland.[18] Section 128 deals with the avoidance of attachments put into force against a company subsequent to the commencement of a winding up:

'(1) Where a company registered in England and Wales is being wound up by the court, any attachment, sequestration, distress or execution put in force against the estate or effects of the company after the commencement of the winding up is void.
(2) This section, so far as relates to any estate or effects of the company situated in England and Wales, applies in the case of a company registered in Scotland as it applies in the case of a company registered in England and Wales. '

Hence section 128 will operate where a winding up of a Scottish company is already under way in Scotland and a creditor then attempts to attach property in England. Although section 128(2) refers to a company 'registered in Scotland', by virtue of the reasoning in *Re Lineas Navieras Bolivianas S.A.M.*,[19] it must be taken that the provision also applies where the Scottish court is winding up a foreign company under Part V.

Although there is no binding English authority upon the point, it would seem that section 130(2) of the Insolvency Act 1986 may also affect English actions when a winding up order has been made in Scotland. Section 130(2) provides:

'When a winding up order has been made or a provisional liquidator has been appointed no action or proceeding shall be proceeded with or commenced against the company or its property, except by leave of the court and subject to such terms as the court may impose.'

The 'court' referred to is the court conducting the winding up. *Re International Pulp and Paper Co.*[20] illustrates the normal section 130(2) type of case. In May 1875 a creditor had commenced proceedings in Ireland against an English company. The creditor obtained judgment, acquired a charge on the company's property and, in November 1875, obtained from the Landed Estate Court in Ireland an order for sale of the company's Irish property. In December 1875 a winding up order was made in England. Acting under what was then section 87 of the Companies Act 1862, Jessel MR made an order restraining the creditor from proceeding with the action in Ireland. In *Re International Pulp and Paper Co.* the court making the restraining order was the court conducting the winding

---

[16] See *Morely's Trustee* v. *Aitken* 1982 S.C. 73, *passim*.
[17] Such as s. 37 of the Scottish Act.
[18] The result of s. 441 of the 1986 Act is that ss. 128 and 130 will not apply where there is a winding up in Northern Ireland.
[19] [1995] B.C.C. 666, see p. 111, *supra*.
[20] (1876) 3 Ch. D. 594, see further chapter 10, with particular reference to a secured creditor.

up; similarly in *Re Hermann Loog Ltd.*,[1] and *Re Thurso New Gas Co.*,[2] the English court, having jurisdiction in the winding up, restricted proceedings under way in Scotland.[3] Yet section 130(2) also operates *directly* upon any action commenced against a company which is subsequently wound up. In *Martin v. Port of Manchester Insurance Co. Ltd.*[4] the pursuer had brought an action in Scotland against an English company. The company was thereafter ordered to be wound up in England. The Court of Session restrained its own proceedings pursuant to section 177 of the Companies Act 1929 (identical in all material regards to section 130(2) of the Insolvency Act 1986), the Lord Justice-Clerk observing:[5]

> 'The result may appear anomalous, as the effect of it is to deprive the Supreme Court of Scotland of jurisdiction to proceed with this case which is properly before it except with leave of the High Court of Justice in England. That, however, is, I think, the clear result of the statute; and of course the same rule would be applicable in the converse case where an action was pending in the High Court of Justice in England against a company which was domiciled in Scotland and whose winding up was therefore under the jurisdiction of the Court of Session.'

Martin v. Port of Manchester Insurance Co. Ltd. would, it is submitted, be followed in England.[6] For as Dillon LJ observed in *Re Bank of Credit and Commerce International S.A. (No. 3)* it is 'highly desirable' in matter of company and insolvency law 'that the English court and the Scottish court should adopt the same construction and act in the same way in relation to the same sections.'[7] Accordingly, where a winding up has been made or a provisional liquidator appointed in Scotland, section 130(2) operates so that no action in the English courts may be commenced or proceeded with against the company or its property. The English court must stay the English action, leaving the plaintiff to seek permission from the Scottish court to continue the action. Section 130(2) of course also applies, *mutatis mutandis*, to stay an action in Scotland against a company being wound up by the court in England.

It will also be noted that section 130(2) specifically refers to proceedings against the company *or its property*. Thus in *Re International Pulp and Paper Co.* the English court restrained proceedings in Ireland even though the creditor had there obtained a charge over the company's Irish assets;[8] and in *Martin v. Port of Manchester Insurance Co. Ltd.* the Court of Session stayed its own action, the pursuer having already arrested the company's assets in Scotland.[9] Thus if a creditor has attached assets in England but not completed the attachment by the time a winding up order is made (or a provisional liquidator appointed) in Scotland, the English court will not allow the attachment to be completed. In relation to the time period before

---

[1] (1887) 36 Ch. D. 502.
[2] (1889) 42 Ch. D. 486.
[3] As far as the effect of diligence in Scotland in respect of assets of a company being wound up in England is concerned, the matter is governed by Insolvency Act 1986, s. 185; see in particular s. 185(4).
[4] 1934 S.C. 143.
[5] *Ibid.*, at 147. Note also *Stevenson & Co. v. Radford and Bright Ltd.* 1902 S.L.T. 82.
[6] As it was in Northern Ireland in *Boyd v. Lee Guinness Ltd.* [1963] N.I. 49.
[7] [1993] B.C.L.C. 1490 at 1509.
[8] (1876) 3 Ch. D. 594 at 595, leave to continue the action would now be given, see p. 283, *post*.
[9] 1934 S.C. 143 at 144–145.

a winding up order is made (or a provisional liquidator appointed) in Scotland – but after the presentation of a winding up petition – section 126 of the Insolvency Act 1986 will apply: (1) an action pending in the High Court or Court of Appeal in England may be stayed by those courts; and (2) any other action may be stayed by the court having jurisdiction to wind up the company, i.e. the Scottish court. Section 426 of the Insolvency Act, in particular subsection (2) thereof, does not affect the operation of sections 130(2) and 126.

3. FOREIGN INSOLVENCIES

The willingness of the English court to give effect to foreign insolvencies once prompted Sir George Rose to state: 'I entertain no doubt, that the effect of a sequestration abroad is precisely the same as a commission here.'[10] This comment requires very considerable qualification. In particular, foreign proceedings will not cause the provisions of the Insolvency Act 1986 to come into operation. Thus, for example, section 128 cannot be prayed in aid by a foreign liquidator to avoid attachments, nor may section 126 or section 285 be relied upon to restrain proceedings in England. A foreign bankruptcy will not vest English immovable property in the foreign assignee. Nor will foreign proceedings necessarily discharge an English contract.[11] It must also be borne in mind that the existence of a foreign insolvency does not prevent the English court from conducting its own proceedings; and in some cases it may well be that the foreign insolvency representative favours insolvency proceedings in England.[12] Nevertheless, that a foreign assignee or liquidator may gain effective control of assets in England (and represent the insolvent in the English courts) is itself of considerable practical importance. (As discussed in chapter 7, no assistance may be given to a foreign insolvency representative that would conflict with s. 183(2) of the Companies Act 1989.)

A. Role of the Foreign Law

One must be wary in formulating general rules as to the consequences of recognition, for the content of the particular foreign law involved must always be taken into consideration. Two early cases involving French law may usefully be contrasted. In *Tenon* v. *Mars*[13] the plaintiff brought proceedings in England in his own name as liquidator of a French partnership. The English court considered the case defective as the evidence did not show that, by the law of France, the liquidator had

---

[10] *Re Vanzeller* (1832) 2 L.J. Bk. 18 at 20.
[11] See further chapter 9.
[12] For an analysis of when a foreign representative may commence a bankruptcy or winding up in England, see p. 228 below.
[13] (1828) 3 Man. & Ry. KB 38. Note also *Gulf Consolidated Co.* v. *Credit Suisse First Boston Ltd.* [1992] 2 Lloyd's Rep. 301 (evidence did not establish authority of liquidator of company incorporated in Bahrain).

authority to sue in his own name. In *Alivon* v. *Furnival*[14] an action was brought in England upon a French judgment by syndics of a merchant bankrupt according to French law. The defendant questioned the right of the syndics to maintain the action for, in particular, although three syndics had been appointed in France only two of them were plaintiffs in the English suit. The Court of Exchequer recognised the rights of the syndics:[15]

'The property in the effects of the bankrupt does not appear to be absolutely transferred to these syndics in the way that those of a bankrupt are in this country; but it should seem that the syndics act as mandatories or agents for the creditors; the whole three or any two or one of them having the power to sue for and recover the debts in their own names. This is a peculiar right of action, created by the law of that country; and we think it may by the comity of nations be enforced in this, as much as the right of foreign assignees or curators, or foreign corporations, appointed or created in a different way from that which the law of this country requires. '

In short, the authority of the foreign trustee, assignee, liquidator, syndic or curator must be satisfactorily proved. This will involve establishing, obviously by expert evidence, that the foreign law is extraterritorial: that is, the foreign law applies to property in England and permits the representative to take action outside the country of appointment. Examples can be found in which certain US, Japanese and Taiwanese insolvency proceedings were held not to operate extraterritorially.[16] Once it is established that the foreign law permits its representative to bring proceedings to recover the insolvent's property abroad, then such will be given effect in England.

Alivon v. *Furnival* serves also as a reminder that recognition is not precluded or limited on account of differences between the foreign law and English law. The English court cannot itself appoint syndics, but their authority may be recognised as part of the relevant foreign insolvency law. Brief reference may also be made to *Re ITT*.[17] The courts in Ontario recognised the liquidation in Luxembourg of a legal entity known as an 'indivision', a type of mutual investment fund created according to the law of Luxembourg, and the effect of the Luxembourg liquidation was to vest the Ontario assets of ITT in the liquidators.

However, it is readily apparent that the English court may not give effect to those parts of a foreign insolvency law which are procedural in nature. Hence in *Wryghte* v. *Lindsay* Lord Cranworth considered that, although the courts of Scotland would assist the recovery of a call made in an English winding up, the machinery of English law whereby that is to be enforced could not be imported into Scotland.[18]

---

[14] (1834) 1 Cr. M. & R. 277.
[15] *Ibid.*, at 296 *per* Parke B, citing *Solomons* v. *Ross* (1764) 1 Hy. Bl. 131n.
[16] *Re Penn Central Transportation Co.* [1981] 2 F.C. 307 (US reorganisation), *Orient Leasing Co. Ltd.* v. *The Ship Kosei Maru* (1978) 94 D.L.R. (3d) 658 (Japanese reorganisation) and *Ting Lei Miao* v. *Chen Li Hung* [1997] H.K.L.R.D. 841 (Taiwanese bankruptcy).
[17] (1975) 58 D.L.R. (3d) 55, p. 183, *ante*.
[18] (1860) 2 L.T. 63 at 65: see now s. 81 of the Insolvency Act 1986.

B. Movables and Immovables

Provided it is established that the foreign law extends to movables in England, the English court will consider title thereto vested in the foreign assignee. As vesting is 'consequential and instantaneous'[19] upon the making of the foreign order, no confirmation or execution by the English court is required.[20] (Although if there is real difficulty as to the validity of foreign proceedings it may be appropriate to seek a declaration in England.[1]) In any event, following the decision of the House of Lords in *Galbraith* v. *Grimshaw*,[2] a foreign trustee[3] can only claim the free assets of the bankrupt: thus a foreign trustee's title will not of itself prevail where there has been a prior attachment in England. This principle will be applied, with appropriate modifications, where for example a foreign company has been put into liquidation abroad at a time when one of its ships has been arrested in England. If the ship is sold, the proceeds will be handed over to the foreign trustee or liquidator after satisfying *in rem* claims against the ship; alternatively, provided sufficient security is provided to satisfy the *in rem* claims, the ship may be released to the foreign trustee or liquidator.[4]

A foreign bankruptcy confers upon the foreign assignee no title to immovables in England.[5] Whether property in England is immovable or movable is a matter for English law as the *lex situs*. But there is sufficient authority to maintain that the English court may appoint the foreign trustee as receiver with authority to sell land in England and, after satisfaction of encumbrancers, the proceeds of sale may be remitted into the foreign insolvency. In *Re Fogarty*[6] the New South Wales court made an application (pursuant to section 118 of the Bankruptcy Act 1883) for the assistance of the courts in Queensland, seeking an order vesting the bankrupt's land in Queensland in the New South Wales assignee. The Chief Justice of Queensland made such an order. In *Re Kooperman*[7] the debtor, a Russian national resident in France, had submitted to the bankruptcy jurisdiction of the courts in Belgium. Astbury J, acting under the inherent jurisdiction of the court, appointed the Belgian curator as receiver of certain leasehold properties in England with authority to sell the same. Whilst in *Re Osborn*,[8] decided with reference to section 122 of the

---

[19] *Neale* v. *Cottingham* (1770) Wallis 54 at 75 *per* Lord Lifford.

[20] *Araya* v. *Coghill* 1921 S.C. 462. Unreasonably refusing to transfer property to the foreign trustee and insisting upon the foreign trustee bringing an action in England may be penalised in costs: see *Pélégrin* v. *Coutts & Co.* [1915] 1 Ch. 696 at 702.

[1] As in, for example, *Bergerem* v. *Marsh* (1921) 91 L.J.K.B. 80.

[2] [1910] A.C. 508. Note also *Singer & Co.* v. *Fry* (1915) 84 L.J.K.B. 2025, *Anantapadmanab-haswami* v. *Official Receiver of Secunderabad* [1933] A.C. 394, *Morley's Trustee* v. *Aitken* 1982 S.C. 73.

[3] The law is now different in respect of a United Kingdom bankruptcy, see p. 217, *supra*.

[4] See *The Cornelis Verolme* [1997] 2 N.Z.L.R. 110 and compare *Holt Cargo Systems Inc.* v. *ABC Containerline N.V. (Trustees of)* (1997) 146 D.L.R. (4th) 736.

[5] *Waite* v. *Bingley* (1882) 21 Ch. D. 674. Note, *passim, Macdonald* v. *Georgian Bay Lumber Co.* (1878) 2 S.C.R. 364, *Ex p Bettle* (1895) 14 N.Z.L.R. 129, *Ex p Stegmann* 1902 T.S. 40, *Australian Mutual Provident Society* v. *Gregory* (1908) 5 C.L.R. 615. Cf. *Re Aylwin's Trusts* (1873) L.R. 16 Eq. 585 and *Re Levy's Trusts* (1885) 30 Ch. D. 119 (foreign insolvency operating as a forfeiture of a life interest in English immovables under the terms of a will).

[6] [1904] Q.W.N. 67. See also *Re Greenaway* (1910) 27 W.N.N.S.W. 112.

[7] [1928] W.N. 101.

[8] [1931–32] 15 B. & C.R. 189, approved in *Hughes* v. *Hannover Rückversicherungs-Aktiengesellschaft* [1997] 1 B.C.L.C. 497 at 508.

Bankruptcy Act 1914, Farwell J also appointed a foreign trustee as receiver of English immovables.[9] Courts in Scotland, Ireland and elsewhere have similarly assisted foreign trustees to gain control of local immovable property.[10]

As far as foreign liquidations are concerned, title is likely to remain vested in the corporation. Yet the English court, provided it is established that the foreign law is extraterritorial, will recognise the authority of a foreign liquidator to represent the corporation and, accordingly, deal with assets in England – this would always be subject to charges existing over the land in question. Despite the absence of relevant English authority, there is no objection to allowing a foreign liquidator's authority to extend to immovables[11] although, it will be noted, the presence of assets within the jurisdiction constitutes a sufficient forensic connection for the English court to make its own winding up order. It is not difficult to see why, both in principle and as a matter of practice, a foreign liquidator must be permitted to deal with movables and immovables in England. Let us say that a French corporation has gone into liquidation in France and that the liquidator has, under French law, superseded the directors and exercises all relevant managerial powers. Quite simply, there is no one apart from the liquidator who (under the law of the place of incorporation) has relevant authority to act on behalf of the corporation.

C. After-Acquired Property

Re a Debtor, ex p Viscount of the Royal Court of Jersey[12] concerned a request by the Jersey court for an order in aid pursuant to section 122 of the Bankruptcy Act 1914. Goulding J reaffirmed the general rule as to movables in the following terms:[13]

> 'It is well-settled that bankruptcy proceedings outside the United Kingdom will be recognised as affecting the debtor's movables in England if the jurisdiction of the foreign court is recognised by English law and the foreign law itself extends to such assets.'

His Lordship further held that after-acquired property in England fell within the scope of the foreign proceedings. [14]

There are sound practical reasons why the title of a foreign assignee may be considered as extending to after-acquired property. For if it were otherwise the after-acquired property might not become available for distribution to the general body of creditors. Presence of assets in England does not enable the English court to commence its own bankruptcy proceedings

---

[9] As to whether a vesting order could be made under the Bankruptcy Acts 1883 and 1914, compare *Re Osborn* [1931–32] 15 B. & C.R. 189 with *Re Fogarty* [1904] Q.W.N. 67 and *Re Jackson* [1973] N.I. 67 and *Re Greenaway* (1910) 27 W.N.N.S.W. 112.

[10] See *Araya* v. *Coghill* 1921 S.C. 462, *Re Bolton* [1920] 2 I.R. 324, *Re Zeederberg* (1867) 5 S. 307, *Re Free State Colliery Co. Ltd.* (1895) 12 Cape L.J. 309 and *Ex p Stegmann* 1902 T.S. 40. See also p. 406, *infra*, in relation to s. 426 of the Insolvency Act 1986.

[11] Foreign liquidators were expressly permitted to deal with immovables in *Re Free State Colliery Co. Ltd.* (1895) 12 Cape L.J. 309, see also *Re African Farms Ltd.* 1906 T.S. 373.

[12] [1981] Ch. 384.

[13] *Ibid.*, at 401.

[14] *Ibid.*, at 404.

by which the after-acquired property could be secured. Moreover, it might not be competent for the foreign court to make a second (later) adjudication. Allowing a foreign trustee to recover after-acquired property tends towards a more comprehensive system of cross-border insolvency rules, reducing the possibility of individual creditors gaining an unfair advantage over their fellows.

In *Re Davidson's Settlement Trusts*[15] it was confirmed that the grounds of recognition were not restricted to the domicile of the bankrupt. There is, accordingly, no inherent reason to suppose that after-acquired property may only be claimed by a trustee appointed in the debtor's domicile. Indeed, in *Re Lawson's Trusts*[16] the debtor had petitioned the foreign court several years prior to the date on which the relevant property devolved upon him. North J, applying *Re Davidson's Settlement Trusts*, upheld the claim of the foreign assignee, albeit without making any particular reference to the circumstance that the case involved after-acquired property. So too, as recognition is not restricted to domicile, then whether the debtor has changed his domicile between the date of the foreign adjudication and the time at which the relevant property devolves upon the debtor (or is acquired by the debtor) should be of no particular significance.[17] It is submitted that if the foreign court was of competent jurisdiction (according to English law), and the foreign law extends to after-acquired property in England, it should follow that the such property falls within the foreign bankruptcy regardless of any changes in the domicile of the debtor.[18]

The situation becomes very much more complex where there have been bankruptcy proceedings in England and abroad, both trustees claiming the after-acquired property. Two issues at once arise: one as to jurisdiction, the other substantive. First, which court (foreign or English) should determine the question of title?; second, how does English law resolve the claims of competing trustees?

(i) *Jurisdiction*

In *Mein (Brown's Trustee)* v. *Turner*[19] a sequestration had issued in Scotland in 1846. Thereafter the bankrupt, still undischarged, had traded

---

[15] (1873) L.R. 15 Eq. 383, p. 146, *supra*. *Re Davidson's Settlement Trusts* was applied in *Bergerem* v. *Marsh* (1921) 91 L.J.K.B. 80, itself approved by the Court of Appeal in *Metliss* v. *National Bank of Greece and Athens S.A.* [1957] 2 Q.B. 33.

[16] [1896] 1 Ch. 175.

[17] It would only be of importance if one applies the (out-dated) maxim *mobilia sequuntur personam*. The decision in *Hall* v. *Woolf* (1908) 7 C.L.R. 207 (applied in *Re Eades' Estate* [1917] 2 W.W.R. 65) is against the statement in the text; however, *Hall* v. *Woolf* has attracted considerable criticism and it appears clear that the courts in Australia would depart from the decision if they were not bound by the doctrine of precedent: see *Radich* v. *Bank of New Zealand* (1993) 116 A.L.R. 676. Fortunately, the English courts have no such difficulty.

[18] 'Once it is accepted that a foreign sequestration order is entitled to local recognition as an assignment to the trustee of the bankrupt's movables owned by him at the date of that order, wherever they are situate, even though the bankrupt is not domiciled in that foreign country at that time, there seems to me no justification for saying that the foreign order should not be accorded full local recognition as applying also to after-acquired property, irrespective of any question as to the bankrupt's then domicile.' (*Per* Drummond J in *Radich* v. *Bank of New Zealand* (1993) 116 A.L.R. 676 at 691–692.)

[19] (1855) 17 D. 435.

at Liverpool. In 1854 an adjudication was made in England. The Scottish trustee petitioned the Court of Session for a declaration that the property acquired by the bankrupt in England since the sequestration was vested in the Scottish trustee. The Scottish court did not consider itself the proper forum, leaving the matter to the courts in England:[20]

> 'If a man had been a bankrupt in England and then come here, entered into trade, acquired property, and was sequestrated, then I think the Scotch would be the proper courts to judge the effect to be given to a claim by the English assignees, and I must pronounce a similar judgment here. This party here carried on a trade in Liverpool, and became bankrupt in England. The ground of the claim of the Scotch trustee is, that he was sequestrated ten years ago here. Well, he ought to go to England and claim there; and if the claim be good, the English courts will give effect to it.'

In *Mein (Brown's Trustee)* v. *Turner* the after-acquired property was in England and the English court had made the later adjudication. However, the crucial factor must have been that the property was in England: it was for the English court to determine the vesting of after-acquired property situate in England. Thus understood, *Mein (Brown's Trustee)* v. *Turner* should be followed in England. As a general rule, the English court should give way to a foreign court where after-acquired property is situate in that foreign jurisdiction. In any event, if the after-acquired property is in, let us say, New Zealand and the New Zealand law favours the New Zealand trustee, then a decision of the English court to the contrary may well be a *brutum fulmen*.

(ii) *Title*

When after-acquired property is located in England the English court will be properly seized of the question of title. An initial and most relevant inquiry is whether expert evidence shows that the foreign law seeks to apply to after-acquired property situate in England. If not, *cadit quaestio*: the after-acquired property is vested in the English trustee. For section 307(1) of the Insolvency Act 1986 states that the trustee may by notice in writing claim for the bankrupt's estate any property which has been acquired by, or has devolved upon, the bankrupt since the commencement of the bankruptcy. Section 307(3) makes provision for the vesting of after-acquired property as follows:

> '. . . upon the service on the bankrupt of a notice under this section the property to which the notice relates shall vest in the trustee as part of the bankrupt's estate; and the trustee's title to that property has relation back to the time at which the property was acquired by, or devolved upon, the bankrupt.'

In short, if there be no conflict in the operation of the foreign law and English law, then after-acquired property must vest in the English trustee pursuant to section 307.

Even where the foreign law does seek to extend to after-acquired property in England, such property will fall to the English trustee.[1] In

---

[20] *Ibid.*, at 442 *per* Lord Murray.
[1] Insolvency Act 1986, ss. 334 and 335 do not apply where a second bankruptcy has occurred abroad: *Re Temple* [1947] Ch. 345 (decided with reference to Bankruptcy Act 1914, s. 39).

Re Temple[2] an English adjudication had been made in 1927, an Indian decree pronounced in 1942 and, in the following year, certain movable property had devolved upon the bankrupt. Romer J (Roxburgh J concurring) held that the after-acquired property was to be administered in the English bankruptcy. His Lordship cited (but did not much rely upon)[3] the then rule 125 in *Dicey's Conflict of Laws*:[4]

> 'Where a debtor has been made bankrupt in more countries than one, and, under the bankruptcy law of each of such countries, there has been an assignment of the bankrupt's property . . . effect will be given in England to that assignment which is earliest in date.'

Thus it might be supposed that after-acquired property will fall to be administered in whichever of two proceedings is the earlier. But closer analysis reveals such a supposition as unsupportable. Compliance with section 307 of the Insolvency Act 1986 confers title upon the English trustee relating back to the very time the after-acquired property was acquired by or devolved upon the bankrupt. Hence the potential operation of a prior assignment by reason of a foreign bankruptcy is excluded. Here the relevant principle is that a foreign trustee takes only the free assets of the bankrupt. Further, quite apart from the clear words of section 307, there is authority that the (old) doctrine of relation back in English bankruptcy legislation could operate where there had been a prior foreign insolvency.[5] Accordingly, whether the English bankruptcy is antecedent or subsequent to the foreign proceedings, after-acquired property in England vests in the English trustee.

In *Re Temple* the property devolved upon the bankrupt in 1943 after both the English (1927) and Indian (1942) bankruptcies. But different scenarios may arise. For example, in Year 1 there is an English bankruptcy; in Year 2 property is acquired; and in Year 3 the foreign court makes an adjudication. Here the property is after-acquired property within section 307 of the Insolvency Act and the title of the English trustee will prevail. But the following situation requires a different analysis. In Year 1 there is a foreign bankruptcy; in Year 2 property devolves upon the bankrupt; and in Year 3 a bankruptcy order is made in England. Here the property is not after-acquired property for the purposes of section 307 of the Insolvency Act, for it has not devolved upon the bankrupt since the commencement of the English bankruptcy proceedings. Prior to the English bankruptcy the property would have vested (in Year 2) in the foreign trustee: the property thereafter forms no part of the bankrupt's estate for the purposes of the later English proceedings.[6]

---

[2] [1947] Ch. 345.
[3] *Ibid.*, at 349.
[4] Found as rule 171 in the 12th ed.
[5] *Banco de Portugal* v. *Waddell* (1880) 5 App. Cas. 161 at 169–170 *per* Lord Selborne.
[6] Nothing in *Re Kidd* (1861) 4 L.T. 344 denies giving effect to foreign proceedings in relation to after-acquired property: see p. 144 of the first edition of this work.

(iii) *Summary*

   (i)   Absent English bankruptcy proceedings, after-acquired property in England may vest in a foreign assignee, provided expert evidence establishes that the foreign law extends to such property.

  (ii) Where both English and foreign trustees claim after-acquired property, title will be determined by the *lex situs*. Accordingly, the English court should normally only entertain the question of title where the after-acquired property is situate in England.

 (iii) Subject to (iv) below, after-acquired property in England is governed by section 307 of the Insolvency Act 1986. Pursuant to section 307, after-acquired property vests in the English trustee from the time such property is acquired by or devolves upon the bankrupt. Thus there is no scope for a prior assignment by way of a foreign bankruptcy decree.

 (iv) Where property is acquired by or devolves upon the bankrupt after a foreign adjudication has been made, but prior to the commencement of English proceedings, such property does not fall within section 307 of the Insolvency Act 1986. The assignment under the foreign bankruptcy takes effect, so as to vest the property in the foreign trustee before the English proceedings have got under way.

Finally, it should be noted that after-acquired property presents little difficulty in respect of a foreign liquidation. Assets do not generally vest in a foreign liquidator; however, the liquidator's authority to represent the corporation and deal with its assets is recognised in England. It is irrelevant whether such assets include after-acquired property. Should an English winding up be ordered in respect of a foreign corporation, the corporation is thereafter represented in England by the English liquidator; and the foreign liquidator cannot deal with any of the corporation's assets in England without the consent of the English liquidator.

D. Relation Back

Whereas the title of a foreign trustee may extend to after-acquired property, the English court will not at common law[7] allow the trustee the benefit of any period of relation back under the foreign law. In *Union Bank* v. *Tuttle*[8] the plaintiffs in Victoria had seized the debtor's goods under executions upon Victorian judgments. Thereafter the debtor's estate was sequestrated in New South Wales. Under the law of New South Wales the sequestration had retrospective effect and prevailed over execution creditors. The Victorian court refused to confer upon the New South Wales insolvency any retrospective operation, preferring the claims of the local execution creditors. The House of Lords reached a like conclusion in *Galbraith* v. *Grimshaw*.[9] The respondents had obtained judgment for a sum of money in Scotland, such judgment being then extended to England pursuant to the Judgments Extension Act 1868. In October 1908 the

---

[7] It would seem a foreign relation back provision cannot be applied pursuant to a s. 426 request, as there is no corresponding provision under English 'insolvency law': see p. 417, *infra*.

[8] (1889) 15 V.L.R. 258, citing *Geddes* v. *Mowat* (1824) 1 Gl. & J. 414.

[9] [1910] A.C. 508, approved in *Re Jogia* [1988] 2 All E.R. 328 at 338.

respondents obtained a garnishee order *nisi* attaching a debt owing to the bankrupt in England. In November 1908 the bankrupt's estate was sequestrated in Scotland. It was held that a Scottish sequestration could not interfere with a prior local attachment, Lord Loreburn LC commenting:[10]

> 'the reason is that a foreign law making the title of the trustee relate back to transactions which the debtor himself could not have disturbed has no operation in England, while the English law as to relation back applies only to cases of English bankruptcy, and therefore the trustee may find himself (as in this case) falling between two stools. '

Of course should the property in question be located in, let us say, Germany then the operation of any doctrine of relation back under another foreign law must be a matter for German law as the *lex situs*.

4. FOREIGN REPRESENTATIVE COMMENCING INSOLVENCY PROCEEDINGS

There is no doubt that, upon proof of the relevant foreign law, a foreign trustee or liquidator (or administrator) may institute a civil action in England.[11] (On the other hand, the fact that a defendant to civil proceedings in England has been put into liquidation or bankruptcy abroad will not produce an automatic stay of the action in England.[12]) If the foreign law requires that, for instance, the liquidator must obtain the authority of the foreign court or the creditors' committee before commencing an action in England,[13] then such authority must be established – a retrospective ratification of proceedings commenced without authority will be valid, provided the foreign law is to that effect. A foreign insolvency representative, as one would expect,[14] may also take over the control of litigation in England which the debtor had begun as plaintiff prior to the insolvency. Similarly, there is no difficulty in a foreign company in liquidation abroad presenting a petition as creditor to have another company wound up in England.[15]

The situation is somewhat more complex where the foreign insolvency representative wishes to commence bankruptcy or winding up proceedings in England in respect of the insolvent.

---

[10] *Ibid.*, at 510, the actual decision in this case would now be different on account of s. 426(6) of the Insolvency Act 1986, see p. 216, *supra*.

[11] In addition to the cases cited above at p. 212, n. 5, see *Kamouh* v. *Associated Electrical Industries International Ltd.* [1980] Q.B. 199 at 206 (foreign trustee), *Manger* v. *Cash* (1889) 5 T.L.R. 271 (French syndics), *Bank of Ethiopia* v. *National Bank of Egypt and Ligouri* [1937] Ch. 513 and *Onassis* v. *H.P. Drewry S.a.r.l.* (1950) 83 Ll. L.R. 249 at 256, 260 (foreign liquidators).

[12] See the discussion at p. 231, *infra*. The position is otherwise where there is a winding up in Scotland, see p. 219, *supra*.

[13] See, for example, *Bank of Credit and Commerce Hong Kong Ltd. (in liquidation)* v. *Sonali Bank* [1995] 1 Lloyd's Rep. 227 at 229.

[14] See *Goldsborough, Mort & Co. Ltd.* v. *Doyle* (1893) 6 Q.L.J. 1.

[15] As in *Re a Company (No. 0013734 of 1991)* [1993] B.C.L.C. 59.

A. Foreign Liquidator

Let us say that an insolvent Spanish company, which carried on some business in England, has been put into liquidation in Spain and that the Spanish liquidator wants there also to be a winding up in England – this may be in order to seek to take advantage of broader avoidance powers under the English legislation or because Spanish law is not extraterritorial, or for any number of other reasons.[16] In practical terms no doubt the easiest option is that for arrangements to be made so that a creditor presents a petition in England, which the company does not oppose. Of course the Spanish liquidator, although he may be owed fees and so on, is not a creditor. Nevertheless, it is necessary to examine the circumstances in which the foreign liquidator may petition; and certainly there are reports[17] in which it is stated that the foreign company or liquidator has petitioned, although no explanation has as far as this author is aware ever been provided explaining the relevant mechanism.

A foreign company may be wound up under Part V of the Insolvency Act 1986.[18] The grounds for winding up are laid down in section 221(5):

'(a) if the company is dissolved, or has ceased to carry on business, or is carrying on business only for the purpose of winding up its affairs;
(b) if the company is unable to pay its debts;
(c) if the court is of the opinion that it is just and equitable that the company should be wound up.'

Inability to pay debts is defined in sections 222–224 and is slightly different from the explanation of inability to pay debts found in section 123 (applicable to English companies). But nothing in Part V identifies by whom a petition may be presented. Accordingly, one must look to section 221(1):

'Subject to the provisions of this Part, any unregistered company may be wound up under this Act: and all the provisions of this Act and the Companies Act about winding up apply to an unregistered company with the exceptions and additions mentioned in the following subsections. '

Thus although one finds in section 122 the circumstances in which a company may be wound up, that section will not apply to an unregistered company under Part V because section 221(5) specifically sets out (and in a more restricted way) the circumstances in which an unregistered company may be wound up. For example, an unregistered company cannot be put into compulsory liquidation[19] by the passing of a special resolution within section 122(1)(a).[20] But as there is nothing in Part V which deals with by whom a petition may be presented, sections 124 and 124A will apply to an

---

[16] *Queensland Mercantile and Agency Co. Ltd.* v. *Australasian Investment Co. Ltd.* (1888) 15 R. 935 at 939 *per* the Lord President in reference to an Australian liquidator who had sought an ancillary winding up in England (see p. 169, *supra*).

[17] *Ibid.*, other examples being *Re Kowloon Container Warehouse Co. Ltd.* [1981] H.K.C. 222 at 226, Japanese company, already in liquidation in Japan, petitioned in Hong Kong and *Re Irish Shipping Ltd.* [1985] H.K.L.R. 437 (Irish liquidator).

[18] See chapter 4, *supra*.

[19] Of course, an unregistered company can never be put into voluntary liquidation: s. 221(4).

[20] In *Orri* v. *Moundreas*, [1981] Com LR 168, LEXIS (transcript: Barnett, Lenton), Mustill J expressed the view that a resolution was not a ground for liquidating a foreign registered company under what was then s. 399 of the Companies Act 1948 (the equivalent of s. 221 of the 1986 Act). The relevant passage does not appear in the truncated report at [1981] Com. L.R. 168.

unregistered company.[1] Section 124, of course, allows 'the company' to present a petition; and therefore, returning to the example of the insolvent Spanish company, provided it is in accordance with the law of Spain, the Spanish liquidator may cause the company to present a petition on the ground that (see section 221(5)) the company has ceased to carry on its business or is unable to pay its debts.

B. Foreign Trustee

Whether a bankruptcy petition may be presented by a foreign trustee is more difficult and has resulted in differing judicial opinions. Section 264(1) determines by whom a petition may be presented and includes:

> '(a) by one of the individual's creditors or jointly by more than one of them,
> (b) by the individual himself. . . . '

It is difficult to see how a foreign trustee can rely upon subsection (1)(b) – the trustee is not the 'individual himself'. The matter, therefore, comes down to whether the foreign trustee can be considered a 'creditor' for the purposes of section 264(1)(a). A judge in a Canadian court has stated that a foreign trustee is not a creditor,[2] whilst the opposite view was advanced by Lord Morison in the Court of Session in *Hutcheson & Co.'s Administrator* v. *Taylor's Executrix*.[3] His Lordship stated that where a debtor had been made bankrupt abroad any 'qualified creditor' might apply for a sequestration under the Bankruptcy (Scotland) Act 1913, moreover, 'a foreign trustee with the necessary qualification' might himself apply under the Act.[4] Yet, with respect, this rather leaves open how it is that a foreign trustee has the 'necessary qualification'. The Act allowed a petition to be presented by 'a creditor or creditors qualified as hereinafter mentioned' (see section 11); the qualification (see section 12) was that there was a debt, other than a contingent debt, of 'not less than fifty pounds'. Although Lord Morison did not clearly articulate his views on the question, it can only be that his Lordship saw a foreign trustee in one way or another as a creditor. But it is less than obvious how it is that a trustee is a creditor. One possible solution is to regard foreign trustees as acting as 'mandatories or agents for the creditors',[5] so that the presentation of a petition by the foreign trustee is not an act *qua* trustee but *qua* agent of the creditors in the foreign proceedings. However, such an argument only begins to get off the ground where it is established that, under the relevant foreign law, the trustee is indeed acting as the agent of the creditors.

As a practical matter it might well be more advisable for a foreign trustee to arrange for a creditor to present the petition, or to use whatever power he may have under the foreign law to compel the debtor himself to petition in England.

---

[1] That s. 124A (petition by Secretary of State) applies to an unregistered company is revealed by *Re Senator Hanseatische Verwaltungsgesellschaft mbH* [1996] 2 B.C.L.C. 562.
[2] *Re Eades Estate* [1917] 2 W.W.R. 65 at 90.
[3] 1931 S.C. 484 at 494.
[4] *Ibid.*
[5] To use the words of Parke B in *Alivon* v. *Furnival* (1834) 1 Cr. M. & R. 277 at 296 when describing syndics appointed in France.

5. THE REGULATION OF ENGLISH PROCEEDINGS

A. General

That an insolvency is already on foot abroad does not prevent the English court from conducting its own bankruptcy or winding up, although, the existence of a foreign insolvency is a factor relevant to the exercise of the discretion, in the English court, whether to commence and continue its own insolvency proceedings.[6] In a like fashion, as discussed above, the fact that a defendant has been adjudicated abroad cannot of itself preclude a plaintiff in England from continuing his suit. A foreign insolvency will most definitely not result in an automatic stay of English actions brought against the insolvent. However the doctrine of the convenient or appropriate forum may assist an insolvent defendant in this context.[7] Moreover, leaving to one side the matter of a stay, the English court in the exercise of its inherent jurisdiction to regulate its own proceedings may take into account the foreign insolvency of a defendant and conduct its own proceedings accordingly. In particular, the English court may curtail the remedies that would otherwise be available to a plaintiff in a civil suit in England.

A recent example is to be found in the well-known case of *Felixstowe Dock and Rly Co.* v. *United States Lines Inc.*[8] The defendant corporation (U.S.L.) had been incorporated in Delaware and was undergoing reorganisation in the US District Court pursuant to Chapter 11 of the US Federal Bankruptcy Code. Although no winding up had been initiated in England, the plaintiff creditors had served writs and obtained Mareva injunctions. The Chapter 11 petition had been presented in the US District Court on 24th November 1986. On the same day that court made a restraining order, purporting automatically to stay and enjoin the commencement or continuation of any 'judicial, administrative or other action or proceeding' against U.S.L. worldwide.[9] The English writs were served, and the Marevas obtained, subsequent to the US restraining order. Before Hirst J it was contended on behalf of U.S.L. that, broadly speaking, the English court should not interfere in the Chapter 11 process by tying up assets in England with Mareva injunctions. His Lordship dismissed the application to discharge the Mareva injunctions, noting that England was the appropriate forum for the resolution of the plaintiffs' claims and, moreover, that the Chapter 11 process was limited to a reorganisation of U.S.L. as a going concern only in North America and thus would confer no benefit upon those creditors, such as the plaintiffs, in Europe:[10]

'If these were ordinary winding up proceedings under which U.S.L.'s assets would be collected together and distributed totally and rateably amongst all their creditors, U.S.L.'s argument under this head would have substantial force. But it is nothing of the kind. This is a scheme to reorganise the company as a

---

[6] See, generally, chapter 3 (bankruptcy) and chapter 4 (winding up). As Sir Peter Millett has recently put it: 'The English court will renounce jurisdiction if it considers that the interests of justice and convenience require the liquidation to be conducted solely abroad.' *Cross-Border Insolvency: The Judicial Approach* (1997) 6 I.I.R. 99 at 103.

[7] See pp. 245 and 395, *infra*.

[8] [1989] Q.B. 360.

[9] *Ibid.*, at 370.

[10] *Ibid.*, at 386.

going concern, but on a much narrower commercial basis limited to North America. No doubt this will be of great benefit both to U.S.L. themselves, and to their North American creditors . . . But the position of the plaintiffs is entirely different . . . there could be no possible benefit to them in seeing the Mareva funds repatriated to the United States. . . .'

The decision of Hirst J has often been criticised; and it has been noted that the ruling 'did great harm to the relations between the courts of the two countries, and seriously damaged the esteem in which UK courts had previously been held by insolvency practitioners and judges abroad.'[11] Yet the facts as presented before the English court – namely that the US proceedings were discriminatory – were so unusual that the refusal to give effect fully to the Chapter 11 proceedings can only be regarded as an exception rather than the rule. (Whether on the facts the US proceedings were indeed discriminatory, or whether the court misunderstood the US law, is not really something that can be usefully pursued.) In any event, however, in *Banque Indosuez S.A.* v. *Ferromet Resources Inc.*[12] which involved a Texan corporation in Chapter 11, Hoffmann J discharged injunctions obtained by the bank observing that, whilst the English court was not bound by the US worldwide stay, the court would 'do its utmost' to co-operate with the US Bankruptcy Court and would avoid any action which might disturb the Chapter 11 administration.[13] Recently, speaking extra-judicially, Lord Hoffmann has tried to put matters into perspective:[14]

'Hirst J has been accused of insularity, not showing due comity to a foreign court and not understanding Chapter 11 . . . I do not think these criticisms are fair . . . Not long after *Felixstowe* I heard a case myself in which a US creditor of a US corporation in Chapter 11 in Texas wanted a Mareva injunction against assets of the corporation in England. I refused the injunction, saying that fairness to all creditors required that he should participate in the reorganisation in Texas. But this was not the case in *Felixstowe*. The proposed scheme of reorganisation was that the assets removed from England would be used to keep U.S. Lines going in the United States but that it would withdraw from the European market. This meant that the Felixstowe Dock company would gain nothing from the reorganisation.'

Upon the facts in *Felixstowe Dock and Rly Co.* v. *United States Lines Inc.* it would have been harsh indeed had the English court discharged the Mareva injunctions, thereby leaving the plaintiffs with no hope of real redress. In addition, instead of ring-fencing English assets for English creditors, Hirst J made it plain that the plaintiffs would not be left entirely free to carve up the Mareva funds amongst themselves. His Lordship stated that the plaintiffs would not later be permitted to gain a priority over other creditors by way of a garnishee order.[15] Equally, the Mareva funds would not be distributed without the intervention of ancillary winding up proceedings in England.[16]

---

[11] Sir Peter Millett 'Cross-Border Insolvency: The Judicial Approach' (1997) 6 I.I.R. 99 at 108.
[12] [1993] B.C.L.C. 112.
[13] *Ibid.* at 117.
[14] 'Cross-Border Insolvency', *The 1996 Denning Lecture* (Bar Association for Commerce, Finance and Industry) 18 April 1996 (unpublished) p. 16.
[15] [1989] Q.B. 360.
[16] *Ibid.*, at 389.

In short, Hirst J sought to strike a balance. The plaintiff creditors could not be expected to prove in the foreign court which was conducting not a process of universal distribution but a process of deliberately preferential distribution.[17] On the other hand, the plaintiffs would not be allowed to proceed to execution as in a usual civil action. To prevent the plaintiffs gaining an unfair advantage over other creditors, an ancillary winding up in England would be conducted.

Finally, in *Felixstowe Dock* the judge was presented at an interlocutory stage with an 'all or nothing' situation: either the assets stayed in England (thereby at least to a certain extent frustrating the reorganisation) or they went to America (and apparently the plaintiffs would as a result be excluded from any sort of recovery). There was no room for manoeuvre. It is quite plain, particularly since the *Maxwell case*,[18] that an altogether different approach might now be taken. Where there is a real danger that a foreign reorganisation plan might discriminate against English or other creditors (or there is some other major difficulty – such as preferential debts in England that would not have such status abroad) a petition for winding up in England may be presented.[19] Thereafter a provisional liquidator could if necessary be appointed so as to stay any actions against the company. Negotiations could then take place between the liquidator in England and the foreign administrator with a view to reaching an agreement whereunder the English creditors would get a fair crack of the whip, without frustrating the reorganisation plan as a whole. Such agreement would then be submitted to the courts of both jurisdictions for approval.[20]

B. Attachments in England

One need look no further than *Felixstowe Dock and Rly Co.* v. *United States Lines Inc.* and *Banque Indosuez S.A.* v. *Ferromet Resources Inc.* for the point that a plaintiff is ultimately concerned with whether the insolvent has assets in England which may go towards satisfying any judgment. If there are no assets in England, or if all English assets have already vested in a foreign trustee or come under the control of a foreign liquidator, a creditor will be likely to have little enthusiasm for pursuing an English action to judgment. Not surprisingly, therefore, many cases may be found in which an unsecured creditor has sought to attach local assets in order possibly to gain some advantage not available in the foreign insolvency.

---

[17] *Per* Cons J in *Mobil Sales and Supply Corpn* v. *Owners of Pacific Bear* [1979] H.K.L.R. 125 at 134, quoted by Hirst J at [1989] Q.B. 387.

[18] See, generally, *Re Maxwell Communications Corpn. plc (No 2)* [1993] 1 W.L.R. 1402 at 1406 and *Barclays Bank plc* v. *Homan* [1993] B.C.L.C. 680 at 684, 696 (p. 332, *infra*).

[19] A petition may be presented by the company itself, see p. 230 above. A foreign company cannot generally be put into administration in England, see p. 136, *supra*.

[20] This is similar to what took place in *Re Business City Express Ltd.* [1997] B.C.C. 826 – although in this case an Irish rescue plan was extended to English creditors by Rattee J pursuant to a request from the Irish court under s. 426 of the Insolvency Act 1986: see p. 414, *infra*.

(i) *Bankruptcy*

One important consequence of the recognition of a foreign bankruptcy is the vesting of movable property in the foreign assignee. This has led the English court (when dealing with a foreign bankruptcy) to view attachments from the basis of title alone.[1] We have the authority of the House of Lords, in *Galbraith* v. *Grimshaw*, that the date of attachment is the critical factor:[2]

> 'The attachment in England will not prevail against a claim of a foreign trustee in bankruptcy which is prior in date, provided that the effect of the bankruptcy is to vest in the trustee the assets in question. If the attachment is prior in date, then I do not think it will be affected by the title of the trustee in a foreign bankruptcy. . . .'

Hence it is not that a foreign bankruptcy stays any English action, but simply that there may be very little purpose in an unsecured creditor continuing an English action if no attachment (or security) has been obtained prior to the vesting of assets in the foreign trustee or assignee. It is not enough that a writ was served prior to foreign bankruptcy, for the House of Lords clearly saw the issue as determined by title. Only a prior attachment (albeit uncompleted at the date of the foreign adjudication) will remain unaffected by the title of the foreign trustee. In *Neale* v. *Cottingham*[3] the defendant had brought an action in Ireland against the debtor on 27 October 1763. On the following day an English commission issued and the debtor's assets vested in the English assignees. On 31 October 1763 the defendant, still in Ireland, attached a debt owing to the bankrupt. The Lord Chancellor of Ireland (Lord Lifford), after consulting with Robinson J and Clayton CJ, held in favour of the assignees: the assets had already vested prior to the attachment. So too in *Dulaney* v. *Merry and Sons*[4] foreign trustees (appointed in Maryland in December 1899) were preferred to creditors levying execution (in March 1990) in England.

(ii) *Liquidation*

The position is similar in respect of a foreign liquidation, even though the corporation's assets may not vest in the foreign liquidator. In *Levasseur* v. *Mason & Barry Ltd.*[5] the defendant had obtained judgment in England against a French company and on 8 April 1889 obtained an order

---

[1] Actually the issue is far better analysed from the point of view of the attaching creditor, the question being not whether the property has vested in the foreign trustee, but rather whether the creditor had sufficient rights in respect of the relevant property prior to the commencement of the foreign proceedings.

[2] [1910] A.C. 508 at 510 *per* Lord Loreburn LC; cf. *Brown* v. *Carbery* (1864) 16 C.B.N.S. 2, attachment in England subsequent to Indian insolvency. See also the cases cited at p. 222, n. 2, *ante*. Prior attachments were preferred in *Norden* v. *Solomon* (1847) 2 M. 375 (Cape Colony), *Bruce* v. *Anderson* (1818) Stuart K.B. 127 and *Defa* v. *Bayless* [1964] B.R. 205 (Quebec).

[3] (1770) Wallis 54. Prior insolvencies prevented subsequent attachment in *Jollet* v. *Deponthieu* (1769) 1 Hy. Bl. 132n. and *Strothers* v. *Read* (1803) Mor. Appx. No. 4 (*forum competens*).

[4] [1901] 1 K.B. 536, p. 186, *supra*: approved by Romer LJ in *Metliss* v. *National Bank of Greece and Athens S.A.* [1957] 2 Q.B. 33 at 49.

[5] [1891] 2 Q.B. 73.

appointing a receiver of certain copper in England belonging to the French company. The copper was at the relevant time in the hands of a third party who had a lien thereon. The order provided for the receivership to take immediate effect but without prejudice to the rights of the third party. On 15 April the French company went into liquidation in France and the plaintiffs were appointed liquidators. The copper in question having been sold, and the third party's lien satisfied, a dispute arose as to whether the liquidators or the defendant were entitled to the balance remaining.[6] Subsequently, the defendant entered a proof in the French proceedings. For the liquidators two points upon the law of France were put forward. First, it was said that under French law the liquidation related back ten days, so that the liquidation was to be considered as prior to the English receiving order. Second, the liquidators maintained that under French law should a creditor prove in the liquidation (as the defendant had done) such a creditor was precluded from thereafter enforcing any security he may hold. Day J found that on the evidence the contentions of the liquidators as to the law of France were not made out.[7] His Lordship recognised the French liquidation[8] but held in favour of the rights of the defendant under the prior receivership. The judgment of Day J was upheld on appeal, Lord Coleridge CJ observing:[9]

'Here the receivership order was made before the liquidation in France took place . . . If no question with respect to the liquidation in France had arisen, it is perfectly clear that the receiving order, on the lien being discharged by payment, would operate . . . If so, it follows that, at the date of the receivership order, the present defendants had a right to execution upon the copper . . . The defendants' right to the copper is ascertained to have been complete at the date of the receivership order, and it follows the judgment of Day J must be affirmed.'

In short, as the receivership order took immediate effect and was prior to the foreign liquidation, the 'complete' or 'absolute'[10] rights of the English judgment creditor were not affected by the subsequent foreign liquidation.

The references in *Levasseur* v. *Mason & Barry Ltd.* to the 'complete' or 'absolute' rights of the judgment creditor suggest that the French liquidators might have prevailed had the liquidation pre-dated the English receivership order. There is, surprisingly, little English authority directly on the point; however, it seems that (as with a foreign bankruptcy) the date of any attachment is crucial. In related proceedings Lindley LJ had commented that:[11]

---

[6] Related proceedings are reported at (1889) 5 T.L.R. 533 and 582.
[7] (1891) 63 L.T. 700 at 703.
[8] *Ibid.*, at 702: 'The law of France would undoubtedly be applicable to, and would control, this liquidation; and whether it be considered as a liquidation, or as a bankruptcy of individuals, there can be no question that, by comity, all other civilised countries would recognise this bankruptcy or liquidation, and would recognise that this bankruptcy or liquidation transferred from the liquidating company to the liquidator all the estate and all the interest of the liquidating company wherever situate.'
[9] [1891] 2 Q.B. 73 at 77–78. Note also *Central Queensland Meat Preserving Co. Ltd.* v. *Bury* (1876) 4 Q.S.C.R. 168 (execution by Queensland judgment creditor two days prior to English winding up).
[10] [1891] 2 Q.B. 73 at 78 (*per* Lord Coleridge CJ) and at 79 (*per* Lord Esher MR).
[11] In the course of argument in *Mason and Barry Ltd.* v. *La Société Industrielle et Commerciale Des Métaux* (1889) 5 T.L.R. 582 at 583.

'If the liquidator had been appointed on 5 April [i.e. prior to the appointment of the receiver in England] the interest of the judgment creditor would have vested in him.'

It may be noted that in *Re Oriental Inland Steam Co.* Mallins V-C observed that 'whenever an execution is taken out, after the winding up order is obtained, the proceeds of that execution become part of the general assets of the company, and no creditor can avail himself of his diligence to the detriment of the other creditors'.[12] In *Brand* v. *Green*[13] the New York courts had on 14 April 1898 appointed a receiver of an insolvent New York corporation. On 22 April 1898 the plaintiffs had commenced actions in Manitoba and attached debts owing to the New York corporation. The Full Court in Manitoba likened the position of the insolvent corporation after the order of 14 April 1898 to that of an English company when it had been ordered to be wound up.[14] Killam CJ referred to *Levasseur* v. *Mason & Barry Ltd.* as decided on the basis that the English receivership was prior in time to the liquidation proceedings in France.[15] The Manitoba court held that the prior insolvency in New York precluded the later attachment of assets in Manitoba. In *Allen & Shaw Ltd.* v. *King*[16] an English company had been put into voluntary liquidation in England when a creditor issued a writ of execution attaching assets in South Africa. The English liquidator sought recognition in the South African court and an order staying the writ of execution. The South African court recognised the voluntary liquidation in England and stayed the execution, leaving the creditor to claim in the English liquidation.[17]

Of course, there was in *Allen & Shaw Ltd.* v. *King* no fear that a South African creditor would be discriminated against in an English liquidation. By contrast, it will be recalled that apparently in *Felixstowe Dock and Rly Co.* v. *United States Lines Inc.*[18] the English plaintiffs would not receive equal treatment with North American creditors in the context of that particular scheme of reorganisation under Chapter 11 of the US Federal Bankruptcy Code. The plaintiffs had begun proceedings by writ in England and obtained Mareva injunctions after the commencement of the US proceedings. Hirst J did not discharge the Marevas in light of the prejudice that would be occasioned should the plaintiffs be left merely with a claim in the Chapter 11 process. However, his Lordship pointed out that the plaintiffs would not later, as judgment creditors, be permitted to obtain

---

[12] (1874) 30 L.T. 317 at 319; affd (1874) L.R. 9 Ch. App. 557.

[13] (1900) 13 Man. R. 101. *Brand* v. *Green* was distinguished in *Bank of Nova Scotia* v. *Booth* (1909) 19 Man. R. 471 which was itself distinguished in *Pitts* v. *Hill* (1987) 66 C.B.R. (N.S.) 273, the Alberta court observing (at 279): 'It is one thing if a local creditor has a charge against local assets of a foreign debtor and that debtor then goes into bankruptcy in the foreign jurisdiction. One can readily see why the *subsequent* foreign bankruptcy should not deprive the local creditor of his charge. However, it is totally different if the foreign debtor goes into bankruptcy and subsequently a local unsecured creditor takes local judicial process to bolster his position. It is not offensive to say that the principle of comity should apply to make the *prior* bankruptcy effective.'

[14] (1900) 13 Man. R. 101 at 122.

[15] *Ibid.*, at 117. In *Pickford* v. *Atlantic Transportation Co.* (1899) 40 N.S.R. 237 the Nova Scotia court, applying an unreported decision of the Privy Council (*Hill* v. *Goodall* 3 Murd Epit 148n.), did not permit the attachment of the company's property after receivers had been appointed in winding up proceedings in New Jersey.

[16] [1912] C.P.D. 115.

[17] *Ibid.*, at 120.

[18] [1989] Q.B. 360, above.

priority over other creditors by garnishing debts in England: the assets (that is, the Mareva funds) would remain in England and would not be distributed without the intervention of an ancillary winding up.[19] Thus *Felixstowe Dock and Rly Co.* v *United States Lines Inc.* supports the proposition that an English plaintiff will not be permitted to gain a priority by an attachment subsequent to a foreign liquidation. It is also worthy of brief mention that courts of first instance in Hong Kong and Alberta have stayed execution upon judgments where plaintiffs have sought execution against US corporations already undergoing Chapter 11 reorganisations.[20]

(iii) *Foreign Injunctions and Restraining Orders*

Once an English bankruptcy or winding up has been commenced the court has jurisdiction, independent of any statutory provision, to restrain a creditor resident in England or who has claimed in England from continuing proceedings against the insolvent in a foreign court. In *Re Distin*[1] a debtor had filed a petition under the 1869 Act; meanwhile certain English creditors had brought actions against the debtor in Antwerp. The Court of Bankruptcy granted an injunction restraining the English creditors. Similarly, a foreign court conducting an insolvency may seek to exercise control over proceedings in England by means of an injunction against an English plaintiff or by a worldwide restraining order. But it is plain that the English court is not obliged to give effect to such an interim order pronounced in a foreign court.[2] Thus, in *Felixstowe Dock and Rly Co.* v *United States Lines Inc.* it was held that comity did not oblige the English court to treat a US restraining order as an overriding or paramount consideration, by itself binding the English court to discharge Mareva injunctions granted in favour of English plaintiffs against a US corporation which had filed a plan of reorganisation in the US Bankruptcy Court.[3]

On the other hand, in *Banque Indosuez S.A.* v. *Ferromet Resources Inc.* Hoffmann J exercised his discretion to discharge injunctions, leaving the bank to claim in the US Chapter 11:[4]

---

[19] *Ibid.*, at 389. Cf. *Primary Producers Bank of Australia Ltd.* v. *Hughes* (1931) 32 S.R.N.S.W. 14 at 20, the Australian case being simply wrong on this point.

[20] *Modern Terminals (Berth 5) Ltd.* v. *States SS Co.* [1979] H.K.L.R. 512 and *Pitts* v. *Hill* (1987) 66 C.B.R. (N.S.) 273.

[1] (1871) 24 L.T. 197, considered further in chapter 10.

[2] As long ago as 1823 Sir John Leach V-C had considered the matter in the following terms: 'It has been insisted that this court ought to follow the court of equity in Ireland, by granting the injunction which is sought for by the plaintiff, without entering into the merits of the case. I cannot entertain that opinion. An interlocutory order from the Court of Chancery in Ireland, can only be regarded here, as an authority, and not as binding . . .' (*Ball* v. *Storie* (1823) 1 Sim. & St. 210 at 214.) Note also the decisions of the Irish court in *Browne* v. *Roberts* (1870) 19 W.R. 115, the British Columbian court in *Nemaha Energy Inc.* v. *Wood & Locker Inc.* (1985) 68 B.C.L.R. 187 and the New Zealand court in *The Margaret Z* [1997] 1 N.Z.L.R. 629.

[3] [1989] Q.B. 360 That a US stay does not of itself bind creditors from pursuing actions in England was confirmed in *Barclay's Bank plc* v. *Homan* [1993] B.C.L.C. 680 at 684 (Hoffmann J) and 695 (Glidewell LJ).

[4] [1993] B.C.L.C. 112 at 117, see also the discussion p. 232, *supra*.

'This court is not of course bound by the stay under United States law but will
do its utmost to co-operate with the United States Bankruptcy Court and avoid
any action which might disturb the orderly administration of [the corporation]
in Texas under Chapter 11.'

In *Ferromet* there was no allegation that the US proceedings discriminated
against the bank and, moreover, the bank had been one of the parties who
filed in the US. The decision of Hoffmann J is particularly notable in that
the bank was a secured creditor and its claim fell (at least in part) under a
general security agreement and charge.[5] Yet as the bank had dealt with a
Texan corporation and the relevant indebtedness was secured by a charge
under Texan law, it is perhaps not altogether surprising that the bank was
left to pursue its case in Texas. The question whether a Mareva obtained by
a bank which had a charge governed English law, and which had not
participated in the US proceedings, would similarly be discharged must
be in some doubt. Certainly, when exercising its discretion the court will
surely attach some importance to participation in the foreign reorganisation proceedings. [6] Although it would be totally incorrect to suggest that an
English plaintiff can just ignore the foreign proceedings and by doing so
will be sure to obtain a Mareva. Obviously it would be quite contrary to
the current rescue culture for the courts to give the impression that English
plaintiffs will be better off if they ignore any reorganisation and attempt to
pursue their own remedies, than if they actively participate in trying to
facilitate a rescue. Returning to the facts in *Ferromet*, it is conceivable that
a bank in similar circumstances might prefer that there were a winding up
in England. For the appointment of an English liquidator would prevent
the foreign corporation sending its assets abroad and the bank could then
seek to enforce its security (at least to the extent that assets, within the
purview of the charge, were in England).

Although *Felixstowe Dock* was not referred to in the judgment of
Hoffmann J, Lord Hoffmann has rejected criticism of the earlier decision;[7]
and it may still be in appropriate circumstances that Marevas are granted
despite the existence of foreign insolvency proceedings. In *Rowland* v.
Gulfpac Ltd.[8] Rowland had in 1989 obtained control of Gulf USA (an
American corporation) and its various subsidiaries worldwide – including
Gulfpac which was an English company. Rowland and the other plaintiffs
were duly appointed as directors of the various companies and were in
control of the group's operations until 1991 when Rowland sold his
controlling shareholding. In late 1993 Gulf USA and various US subsidiaries went into Chapter 11 in Idaho. Gulfpac was not subject to Chapter 11
proceedings. A plan for reorganisation was eventually formulated and
confirmed by the Idaho court in 1995. Part of that plan involved the
transfer of the main asset of Gulfpac, namely a block of shares in a New
Zealand subsidiary ('GRP'), to Gulf USA for $1. The GRP shares were
worth at least several million dollars. Meanwhile, proceedings had been
brought in Idaho by a trustee appointed in the US Bankruptcy Court
against the plaintiffs claiming that between 1989 and 1991, when they
were in control of Gulf USA, various acts involving fraud, breach of

---

[5] Although Hoffmann J did not focus on this issue at all.
[6] See also *Rowland* v. *Gulfpac Ltd. per* Rix J, *infra*.
[7] See p. 232, *supra*.
[8] (24 July 1995, unreported) , QBD, LEXIS (transcript: Nunnery).

duty and conversion had been committed. The plaintiffs did not submit to the jurisdiction of the Idaho court, but instead brought proceedings in England in the form of what were termed (i) the indemnity action and (ii) the declaratory action. (The declaratory action is considered at p. 246 below.) In the indemnity action, which was brought only against Gulfpac, the plaintiffs were seeking a ruling that pursuant to Gulfpac's articles of association they were entitled to an indemnity in respect of any liability that they might be under to Gulf USA in the Idaho proceedings. In support of the indemnity claim the plaintiffs applied for a Mareva to prevent Gulfpac disposing of its shareholding in GRP to Gulf USA in accordance with the reorganisation plan.[9] Rix J noted that the continuation of the Mareva would prevent the implementation of the reorganisation plan. On the facts Rix J held that the plaintiffs did not have a good arguable case that the indemnity in Gulfpac's articles covered the potential liability of the plaintiffs in relation to their actions as directors not of Gulfpac but of Gulf USA. Accordingly, the Mareva was discharged. His Lordship also briefly considered what the position would have been had the plaintiffs established a good arguable case; and stated, after reviewing the decisions in *Felixstowe Dock* and *Ferromet*, that a Mareva would have issued. Rix J noted that Gulfpac was not subject to Chapter 11 and that there was a conflict in the expert evidence of US lawyers as to whether the automatic stay in the US proceedings applied to the action against Gulfpac. The crucial point seems, however, to have been that had the plaintiffs been entitled to an indemnity from Gulfpac, that indemnity would have been useless if all Gulfpac's assets were disposed of not for their true value but for $1:[10]

> 'It is obviously right that I should pay the highest regard to the orders of the Idaho court as well as to the basic fact that Gulf USA is in Chapter 11 bankruptcy proceedings before that court . . . Nevertheless, unlike Hoffmann J in the *Banque Indosuez case*, I am dealing with plaintiffs who were not parties to and had not initiated the bankruptcy proceedings in the United States and with a defendant, Gulfpac, which is itself not part of those bankruptcy proceedings, although it could have been, and whose only involvement in those proceedings is that its principal valuable asset will, under the reorganisation plan, be sold not at its value but for $1 to its parent company.'

The tenor of the judgment suggests that (assuming always that there was a good arguable case) the Mareva might have been continued even if Gulfpac had been in Chapter 11 and the US stay was established to extend to the indemnity action in England. But it must be stressed that the facts were highly unusual; and the situation was not one, as would normally be the case, where English creditors would be claiming on an equal footing with others in the US proceedings. Rather, the implementation of the plan would completely destroy the (alleged) indemnity rights of the plaintiffs: just as in *Felixstowe Dock* the plaintiffs would have got nothing out of the US reorganisation. In this sort of highly prejudicial, but very unusual, situation the judicial discretion may still be exercised in favour of the plaintiff.

[9] Rix J also held that the transfer of Gulfpac's assets for an admitted undervalue would not fall under s. 423 of the Insolvency Act 1986, since the purpose behind the transfer was to further the reorganisation rather than to defeat any rights of creditors or the directors' rights to an indemnity.

[10] It would be taking this comment totally out of context to suggest that Rix J felt that *Ferromet* would *only* apply where the creditor initiated the foreign proceedings.

Nevertheless, of course the actual decision in *Rowland* v. *Gulfpac Ltd.* was in favour of the US proceedings. Moreover, Rix J also held (and the Court of Appeal later agreed)[11] that in relation to the declaratory action the appropriate forum was the Idaho bankruptcy court. The plaintiffs could, as Rix J noted, pursue their claims in the Idaho court – but there was no real possibility of that ever happening because they were anxious not to submit to the jurisdiction of the Idaho court. In addition, whilst the discharge of the Mareva did not prevent the plaintiffs continuing with the indemnity action in England, to proceed would probably be a complete waste of time and money – since the reorganisation plan left Gulfpac without any assets. *Rowland* v. *Gulfpac Ltd.*, it is submitted, is definitely a decision in which comity prevailed.

In summary, and whilst it must be acknowledged that the case law is developing in this area, it is fair to say that the English court will pay the 'highest regard' to the existence of foreign rescue proceedings; and that means, in the absence of a highly prejudicial fact situation, that an English creditor should not expect to obtain Mareva relief.

(iv) *Summary*

A foreign insolvency does not automatically stay actions brought in England against the insolvent. But the English court, in the exercise of its inherent jurisdiction, will regulate English proceedings to prevent a creditor gaining an unfair advantage over the general body of creditors or unreasonably frustrating a foreign rescue plan. Thus an English attachment will not secure a priority where the foreign bankruptcy or liquidation commenced prior to the date of the attachment. On the other hand, rights acquired by means of an attachment in England prior to a foreign insolvency will not be prejudiced merely on account of subsequent foreign insolvency proceedings.

C. Prior Attachments and English Insolvency Proceedings

Although a foreign bankruptcy or liquidation may be recognised in England, its effect will not be to oust creditors' rights acquired through attachments prior to the foreign insolvency. But such rights are not inviolable. It must remain possible for the English court to intervene by means of its own bankruptcy or winding up proceedings. Let us say that a financially weak New York corporation has a number of English creditors and one substantial asset in England, an account in credit with a London bank. From *Levasseur* v. *Mason & Barry Ltd.* and *Galbraith* v. *Grimshaw* it follows that a creditor would be well-advised to move as swiftly as possible to attach those funds prior to any US insolvency. Let us further assume that a creditor does indeed attach the funds two weeks prior to the commencement of proceedings in New York. The rights under the attachment (even though not yet completed) will not be set aside by reason of the defendant's subsequent insolvency in a foreign court. However, the

---

[11] See further p. 246, *infra*.

corporation (or a creditor) may still petition the English court to commence its own winding up;[12] and, of course, in an English winding up a judgment creditor generally loses the benefit of any uncompleted execution or attachment pursuant to section 183(1) of the Insolvency Act 1986. Section 183(2)(c), however, permits the court to set aside the rights of the liquidator under section 183(1) on such terms as the court thinks fit. (In the reverse situation – where an English creditor has attached assets abroad and that attachment cannot be set aside in the English winding up – the English court will not normally prevent the liquidator from having the attachment set aside pursuant to the relevant provisions applicable in the *lex situs*.[13])

That section 183 may be used to supplement or rather bypass the common law rules as to attachments against a foreign corporation appears from *Re Suidair International Airways Ltd*.[14] The applicants had brought an action in England against a South African company in November 1949. In December 1949 a winding up petition was presented in South Africa and, on 18 January 1950, a provisional winding up order was there made. On 14 January 1950 the applicants signed judgment in default of defence. The applicants, having already received notice of the South African proceedings, thereafter on 31 January issued two writs of *fieri facias* and goods belonging to the company were seized. In March 1950 a winding up petition was presented in England and, the following month, a compulsory winding up order was made. Wynn-Parry J held that, on the particular facts involved, the court would exercise its statutory power to permit the applicants to retain the benefit of the execution, even though such was not complete at the commencement of the English winding up. Unfortunately, Wynn-Parry J was not asked to consider the fact situation in the light of *Levasseur* v. *Mason & Barry Ltd.* or *Galbraith* v. *Grimshaw*. But *Re Suidair International Airways Ltd.* actually involved an English judgment creditor who had in January 1950 issued execution not only after, but also with knowledge of, the defendant's prior insolvency in South Africa. Had there been no English winding up the applicants would not have been permitted, having regard to the existing foreign insolvency, to proceed with the execution and gain a priority over the general body of unsecured creditors. When some months later an English winding up commenced, the equivalent of section 183 of the Insolvency Act came into play, the statutory discretion superseding the common law position. But the actual exercise of the discretion by Wynn-Parry J was clearly flawed: in that the discretion should have been exercised having regard to the circumstance that, even at the time the applicants first seized the company's goods, they were already too late – there was a prior foreign insolvency already on foot. In short, Wynn-Parry J rather missed the point. Whether the discretion would today be exercised the same way must be open to some doubt.[15]

---

[12] The presence of assets in England being a sufficient (but not a necessary) jurisdictional basis: see chapter 4.

[13] The point seems to have been first decided in *American Express International Banking Corpn.* v. *Johnson* [1984] H.K.L.R. 372, but see now *Barclays Bank plc* v. *Homan* [1993] B.C.L.C. 680.

[14] [1951] Ch. 165 decided with reference to s. 325 of the Companies Act 1948. For an analysis of this decision in the context of ancillary winding up see chapter 14.

[15] See also the observations of Sir Peter Millett in 'Cross-Border Insolvency: The Judicial Approach' (1997) 6 I.I.R. 99 at 105 in relation to *Suidair*.

The decision of the Tasmanian court in *Re Songvaar Salvaging Co. Ltd.*[16] may also be mentioned as an example. A Victorian company which carried on business in Tasmania was put into voluntary liquidation in Victoria by a resolution of 12 September 1918. Previously two Tasmanian judgment creditors had caused execution to be levied on the company's Tasmanian assets. On 23 September 1918 a winding up petition was presented in Tasmania by one Strong, both a shareholder and director as well as a creditor of the company. Immediately after presentation of the petition, an *ex parte* order was obtained restraining the execution creditors from proceeding with the execution. Upon application by the execution creditors it was held that the court had jurisdiction to wind up the Victorian company, 'though it may be that the winding up should be ancillary to the winding up in Victoria';[17] in addition, the restraining order would stand upon terms that the execution creditors would be permitted to prove in the winding up.[18] So too it may be that an English judgment creditor has attached an individual's assets in England prior to the appointment of a foreign trustee, thereby being able to defeat the assertion that the relevant assets vested in the foreign trustee. Nevertheless, should a bankruptcy petition be presented in England (the presence of assets is not, however, an adequate forensic connection), the judgment creditor might be restrained under section 285 of the Insolvency Act 1986 from proceeding against the property of the bankrupt.

Accordingly, the consequences of a foreign insolvency upon attachments in England are to a large degree determined by the timing of the relevant proceedings in each jurisdiction. But those advising a foreign insolvent, or indeed an English creditor, should not overlook the possibility of advancing their client's position by resort to the discretion vested in an English court when conducting its own bankruptcy or winding up.

D. Attaching Creditor Entering Proof Abroad

As we have seen, a foreign insolvency will not of itself deprive an English creditor of 'the fruits of his diligence',[19] where that creditor has attached property in England prior to the foreign proceedings. It is now necessary to consider the position of the attaching creditor who also seeks to prove in the foreign insolvency. Of course, it may well be that the foreign court will not permit such a proof, or will so permit only upon terms (for instance, that the creditor bring into account any amount that may be received by virtue of the attachment in England). These, however, are questions for the foreign law to determine. The issue, as a matter of English law, may be put as follows: is an attaching creditor who has entered a proof in the foreign insolvency proceedings to be denied the benefit of the (prior) attachment in England as against the foreign assignee or liquidator?

---

[16] (1918) 14 Tas. L.R. 92.

[17] *Ibid.*, at 93–94. The making of an ancillary winding up order in such circumstances had been suggested in *Sack* v. *Lord Aldenham* (1911) 7 Tas. L.R. 84 at 89.

[18] It was subsequently *by consent* ordered that the execution creditors would rank as secured creditors in the winding up: (1918) 14 Tas. L.R. 92 at 96.

[19] *Galbraith* v. *Grimshaw* [1910] A.C. 508 at 511 *per* Lord Macnaghten.

If the foreign law permits a creditor at one time to attach property in England and also to prove without any qualification in the foreign proceedings, then there is no reason for the English court to deny the creditor the benefit of a prior attachment.[20] But, having regard to the decision of the House of Lords in *Selkrig* v. *Davies*,[1] it seems otherwise should the foreign law restrict the rights of a creditor who enters a proof. In *Selkrig* v. *Davies* an English commission issued in 1782. The appellant came in under the commission but later abandoned his claims without receiving any dividend.[2] In 1798 the appellant arrested certain shares standing in the bankrupt's name in Scotland. The question of preference as between the arrester and the English assignees having been resolved by the Court of Session in favour of the assignees, an appeal was brought before the House of Lords. Lord Eldon LC first considered that, as a matter of Scots law, the English bankruptcy vested movables in Scotland in the English assignees so as to prevent any subsequent diligence by a creditor in Scotland. But equally, leaving to one side the question of vesting, the appellant could not rely upon the arrestment because a claim had been entered in the English commission. The Lord Chancellor looked at the position specifically on the basis that the property in question *had not vested* in the assignees:[3]

'If, my Lords, he has got property which did not pass under the commission before he came in, whatever Chancellors may have said on the subject, they had no more right to call into the common fund, that which he had got by law, and which was kept out of the common fund than any other part of his property. It could only be therefore because the law did not pass the property of the individual coming within your jurisdiction, that you say to him, if you claim any thing under this commission, you shall not hold in your hands the property which you have got by force of the law of another country. If a man choose to say, I will not bring into the common fund that sum which I have received, then let him retire. Now, with reference to this view of the case, a claim has been made under this commission, and the claim has been admitted, and I have stated the importance of that, in the administration of the effects of the bankrupts. '

It must be stressed that *Selkrig* v. *Davies* was a decision upon a Scottish appeal. The law of England, which required a creditor who entered a claim to account for benefits received abroad, was a completely foreign law. There was a local attachment by a creditor who had participated in the foreign insolvency. Hence the importance of *Selkrig* v. *Davies* lies not so much in the statement of English law,[4] but rather that the House of Lords was willing to give effect to a foreign law as against a local attaching creditor who had claimed in the foreign bankruptcy, even though the property had not vested in the foreign assignee prior to the attachment. There are certain difficulties arising out of *Selkrig* v. *Davies*. First, Lord Eldon LC does not offer an explanation as to the theory underlying the

---

[20] *Levasseur* v. *Mason & Barry Ltd.* [1891] 2 Q.B. 73, p. 234, *ante*.

[1] (1814) 2 Rose 291.

[2] '[H]e resolved to abandon them, and did abandon them, without having received anything under the commission: that, in my opinion, makes no difference as to the effect of the proceedings he adopted.' (*Per* Lord Eldon LC (1814) 2 Rose 291 at 310.)

[3] *Ibid.*, at 318.

[4] 'It has been decided, that a person cannot come in under an English commission without bringing into the common fund what he has received abroad.' ((1814) 2 Rose 291 at 318.)

decision.[5] The case is, perhaps, satisfactorily explained on the broad basis of 'fraud'. It would be a 'fraud' for a creditor to claim in the foreign (English) bankruptcy and yet maintain rights under a local (Scottish) attachment in defiance of the foreign law. A fraud-based explanation has the advantage of requiring consideration of the particular facts that are presented by any given case.[6] The doctrine of *forum conveniens* might also be invoked: a foreign assignee, or liquidator, might now contend that the rights of the attaching creditor should in the interests of justice be determined in the foreign proceedings – proceedings, moreover, of which the creditor has sought to take advantage. Secondly, *Selkrig* v. *Davies* being a Scottish appeal is not binding on an English court. Although the Lord Chancellor's statement of the English law has been approved by the highest authority,[7] no English court has actually tackled the problem of an attaching creditor who claims in the foreign insolvency.[8] Nevertheless, cases decided by Lord Eldon have always been held in the highest regard: moreover, in other areas of cross-border insolvency, English courts have observed that creditors who prove in a foreign insolvency are not permitted to escape the application of the foreign law.[9]

Hence, in short, it may be ill-advised for a creditor who has attached property in England prior to a foreign insolvency later to claim in the foreign proceedings. At the very least it can be said that a creditor who has so acted will be required to put forward compelling reasons why the benefit of the attachment should not be given up. The English court should not assist a creditor, who has entered a proof in the foreign insolvency, to act in defiance of that law to the prejudice of the general body of creditors. This author's view, it is submitted, can be supported by reference to the recent decision in *Firswood Ltd.* v. *Petra Bank*;[10] and although the facts did not involve an attachment in England, the following remark of Schiemann LJ will be noted:[11]

> '. . . the creditor has chosen to contract with a company whose domicile is Jordan and therefore has to take Jordanian law as governing the priorities in the distribution of the company's assets; the system of priorities contains nothing surprising or at odds with English public policy; the creditor has in fact claimed in the liquidation in Jordan and that claim has been accepted in the liquidation

---

[5] Of course, the attachment in *Selkrig* v. *Davies* was many years after the English commission had issued. But Lord Eldon's observations were made on the basis that under Scots law there had been no vesting: 'if intimation was not given, it appears to me, that under the circumstances of this case, the English commission might have been applied to, and has been applied to, and that the appellant has thereby consented to bring his foreign debt under its distribution. . . .' (*Ibid.*, at 319.)

[6] For instance, there would be no fraud should it be revealed that the attaching creditor be discriminated against in the foreign proceedings. Although, in such an instance, it might well be appropriate to follow the advice in *Felixstowe Dock and Rly Co.* v. *United States Lines Inc.* [1989] Q.B. 360 at 389 and conduct English insolvency proceedings.

[7] *Banco de Portugal* v. *Waddell* (1880) 5 App. Cas. 161 at 167 *per* Earl Cairns LC.

[8] In *Pitts* v. *Hill* (1987) 66 C.B.R. (N.S.) 273 at 279 it was observed by the Alberta court: 'the plaintiff took advantage of Texas laws and the United States Bankruptcy Code. He cannot take the benefit of foreign laws in a foreign state and, in the next breath, say they do not apply to him . . . He must accept its burdens, one of which is that he cannot take any proceedings against the defendant.'

[9] See *Seligman* v. *Huth* (1875) Bitt. Prac. Cas. 64; on appeal, (1877) 37 L.T. 488, p. 264, *post*, and *Banque Indosuez S.A.* v. *Ferromet Resources Inc.*, *supra*.

[10] [1996] C.L.C. 608.

[11] *Ibid.*, at 618.

proceedings; . . . and it would be wrong to permit separate parallel proceedings in England whose only substantial purpose would be to obtain an English judgment with the aid of which it is hoped to deprive the liquidator of assets for distribution to the general body of creditors.'

E. Staying Actions

As has been shown, that a defendant has been adjudicated insolvent in a foreign court does not result in an automatic stay of any actions brought by creditors in England. In the past the English cases have tended to concentrate upon a single issue – whether a plaintiff has attached property prior to the commencement of the foreign insolvency proceedings. But, particularly since the decision of the House of Lords in *Spiliada Maritime Corpn.* v. *Cansulex Ltd.*,[12] there is another principle to be taken into consideration: the doctrine of the convenient or appropriate forum. For it is established as a general proposition that the English court may stay its own proceedings if:[13]

'there is some other available forum, having competent jurisdiction, which is the appropriate forum for the trial of the action, i.e. in which the case may be tried more suitably for the interests of all the parties and the ends of justice.'

The operation of this doctrine may be illustrated by means of an example.[14] A Canadian corporation has been put into liquidation in Canada. At the time of the liquidation two actions were already on foot in England. In the first, the plaintiff had already got judgment and attached assets in England. Such a prior attachment is not affected by the Canadian liquidation,[15] and it is plainly far too late for the Canadian liquidator to argue *forum non conveniens.*[16] (However, it will be recalled, the rights of the attaching creditor may be in jeopardy should the English court at once commence its own winding up.) On the other hand, the writ in the second action was only served a few months prior to the commencement of the liquidation in Canada. In this action the English plaintiff will not be permitted to gain any advantage over other creditors by a subsequent attachment of the corporation's assets.[17] Additionally, provided the relevant factual basis is made out, the Canadian liquidator may seek to have the English action stayed on the basis that the courts of Canada are clearly more appropriate for the determination of the plaintiff's claim. Of course, the Canadian liquidator may have no wish to raise the matter of the convenient forum; and, even if the question is raised, it can only be resolved in the light of the particular circumstances surrounding the action.[18]

[12] [1987] A.C. 460.
[13] *Spiliada Maritime Corpn.* v. *Cansulex Ltd.* [1987] A.C. 460 at 476 *per* Lord Goff of Chieveley. See also *Okell* v. *Foden* (1884) 11 R. 906 (bankruptcy) and *Edinburgh & Glasgow Bank* v. *Ewan* (1852) 14 D. 547 (winding up) and *Re Harrods (Buenos Aires) Ltd.* [1991] 4 All E.R. 348.
[14] For the situation where a foreign court requests the English court to stay proceedings, under s. 426 of the Insolvency Act 1986, see p. 406, *infra.*
[15] *Galbraith* v. *Grimshaw* [1910] A.C. 508, *Levasseur* v. *Mason & Barry Ltd.* [1891] 2 Q.B. 73, *ante.* Unless the attaching creditor claims in the Canadian proceedings, *supra.*
[16] Note *Nemaha Energy Inc.* v. *Wood & Locker Inc.* (1985) 68 B.C.L.R. 187, *passim.*
[17] *Felixstowe Dock and Rly Co.* v. *United States Lines Inc.* [1989] Q.B. 360 at 386 and 389.
[18] In other words there is no automatic stay, rather the burden is on the party seeking the stay to show that the foreign court is clearly more appropriate in the interests of all the parties and for the ends of justice.

Two recent cases, both of which came before the Court of Appeal, require consideration. The factual background in *Rowland* v. *Gulfpac Ltd.* has already been discussed.[19] It will, however, be recalled that in addition to the 'indemnity action' the plaintiffs had also commenced a 'declaratory action' in England. When Rowland sold his controlling interest in Gulf USA, in 1991, a settlement agreement had been entered into. The settlement agreement was governed by English law. The central feature of the settlement agreement was that Gulf USA agreed to release Rowland and his fellow directors from any liability arising out of their stewardship of Gulf USA during 1989 to 1991. In light of the fact that, on the face of it, the settlement agreement appeared to absolve Rowland and the other directors from any liability, the US trustee and other relevant parties in the Idaho proceedings against the directors (commenced in January 1994) were alleging that the settlement agreement was (i) void for fraud or (ii) voidable as a fraudulent transfer under the US Bankruptcy Code. The plaintiffs, who did not want to submit to the Idaho court,[20] began the declaratory action in England, seeking declarations that the settlement agreement was valid and that the claims brought in Idaho fell within the ambit of the settlement agreement and were extinguished by the settlement agreement. In substance, negative declarations were being sought. The defendants, Gulf USA, the US trustee and others (Gulfpac was not a defendant in the declaratory action), were not present in England, accordingly, the plaintiffs relied upon RSC Order 11. Hence the plaintiffs had to show, *inter alia*, that England was clearly the appropriate forum in which the case ought to be tried – in the interests of all parties and for the ends of justice. Rix J noted that although the settlement agreement was governed by English law, one essential issue in dispute was whether Gulf USA was insolvent when the settlement agreement was made:

> 'It follows that not only do questions of United States insolvency law arise but they arise in the context of the bankruptcy proceedings already being administered in Idaho, and also in the context of other complaints made in the Idaho proceedings, all of which are . . . complaints made by Gulf USA against the directors of Gulf USA in their conduct of the stewardship of that American company.
>
> In these circumstances, it seems to me . . . that the directors failed to discharge the *Spiliada* burden that faces them.'

That determination was upheld on appeal, Staughton LJ observing:[1]

> 'The truth of the matter is that if [the plaintiffs] wish, as they profess to do, that one court should be able to resolve the whole dispute, they have only to submit to the jurisdiction of the Idaho court. In that event, if they win or lose, the judgment will be recognised here. There are very powerful arguments, which we need not enter upon, that . . . the Idaho court is the most suitable.'

---

[19] At p. 238, *supra*.

[20] Because if the directors submitted then, pursuant to the common law rules of private international law, any Idaho judgment could be enforced against them in England.

[1] *Sub nom. Inoco plc* v. *Gulf USA Corpn.* (24 January 1997, unreported LEXIS (transcript: Smith Bernal).

Thus, at the end of the day, in the indemnity action the Mareva was discharged and, in the declaratory action, the directors failed to get leave to serve the Idaho defendants.[2]

Firswood Ltd. v. *Petra Bank*[3] concerned a Jordanian bank that was put into liquidation in Jordan in July 1990 following a decision of the Economic Security Committee of Jordan.[4] In 1987 the bank had guaranteed the indebtedness of a principal debtor to a Swiss corporation, Monaval Finanz AG. The guarantee contained a jurisdiction clause in favour of the English courts. The primary debt was repayable by ten instalments and a number of such instalments were duly paid by the principal debtor prior to July 1990. In November 1990, long before the last instalment was due, Monaval made a claim in the Jordanian liquidation in respect of the whole of the then outstanding primary debt. In September 1991 the liquidation committee of the bank in Jordan made a decision ('the capitalisation decision') acknowledging the indebtedness to Monaval in the sum of approximately SF4.8 million. In December 1992 Monaval assigned all its relevant rights and interests in the claim to Firswood. In March 1993, after a letter before action,[5] Firswood issued a writ in England against the bank claiming SF4.8 million and interest. Firswood argued that its claim against the bank came within the Civil Jurisdiction and Judgments Act 1982 (as amended) and, therefore, leave to serve the bank out of the jurisdiction was not required. The Court of Appeal held that the plaintiff's claim was based not on the guarantee but on the capitalisation decision in the liquidation; accordingly, the claim was taken out of the scope of the Civil Jurisdiction and Judgments Act by the 'bankruptcy exception' under the Conventions.[6] Hence leave to serve the bank pursuant to RSC Order 11 was required.[7] Schiemann LJ, agreeing with the judge at first instance, considered that the Order 11 discretion would be exercised against the plaintiff. (Schiemann LJ also said that, even if the claim fell within the 1982 Act, the court had a discretion to stay the English proceedings in favour of Jordan; and again the discretion would be exercised against the plaintiff and in favour of a stay.)[8] His Lordship relied upon the following facts: that the bank was being wound up in its country of incorporation; that the creditor (Monaval) had claimed in the foreign liquidation; that Monaval's claim had been accepted in the liquidation; that Monaval had assigned its claim to Firswood, which had knowledge of the

---

[2] Costs had naturally been awarded against the plaintiffs. Subsequently, the plaintiffs sought (under RSC Order 47 rule 1) a stay of the order for costs on the basis that any costs paid would immediately be sent to the Chapter 11 proceedings in Idaho, with the result that should the plaintiffs ever get a judgment in the indemnity or declaratory actions, there would be no funds in England against which any such judgment could be enforced. Rix J dismissed the plaintiffs' applications: unreported, 12 May 1997.

[3] [1996] C.L.C. 608.

[4] An interesting account of the life and death of the very same Petra Bank can be found in the judgment of Judge Lifland in *Re Hourani* 180 B.R. 58 (Bkrtcy. S.D.N.Y. 1995).

[5] The plaintiffs in the letter made it plain that it was their intention to get judgment in England and then to seek to have that judgment enforced, making use of the Brussels or Lugano Conventions, in any European country where there might be assets of the bank.

[6] Art. 1(2) of the Brussels Convention states that the Convention does not apply to '. . . bankruptcy, proceedings relating to the winding up of insolvent companies or other legal persons, judicial arrangements, compositions and analogous proceedings'. See, generally, the discussion at p. 13, *supra.*

[7] [1996] C.L.C. 608 at 614.

[8] *Ibid.,* at 618.

liquidation abroad; and that the action brought by Firswood relied upon the acceptance by the liquidation committee in Jordan (in its capitalisation decision) of Monaval's claim:[9]

> 'The assignee can have no higher claim to priority than the creditor; the creditor has chosen to contract with a company whose domicile is Jordan and therefore has to take Jordanian law as governing the priorities in the distribution of the company's assets; the system of priorities contains nothing very surprising or at odds with English public policy; the creditor has in fact claimed in the liquidation in Jordan and that claim has been accepted in the liquidation proceedings; the creditor has then assigned that claim and it would be wrong to permit separate parallel proceedings in England whose only substantial purpose would be to obtain an English judgment with the aid of which it is hoped to deprive the liquidator of assets for distribution to the general body of creditors. '

Although England might be a suitable forum for resolution of the dispute, it had not been shown by the plaintiff to be a more suitable forum than that available in Jordan.

One might also do well to bear in mind the observations of the judge in *Re Olympia & York Developments Ltd.*:[10]

> 'In the context of multi-jurisdictional insolvencies the courts of different jurisdictions should strive – to the extent that they can within the parameters of their own fundamental precepts of justice – to ensure that matters are adjudicated in the proper forum with the closest connection to the subject matter. Principles of international comity, including those incorporated in the *forum non conveniens* test, provide the touchstones to assist them in doing so . . . .'

The justice and convenience of a case is the governing principle where the insolvent, as defendant, raises the *forum conveniens* issue, or where the plaintiff (creditor) seeks leave under RSC Order 11. It is perhaps fair to say that there is something of a judicial tide in favour of the *forum conveniens* approach in international insolvency cases. Yet this is scarcely surprising as one of the major objectives of the doctrine is to save unnecessary expense; and international insolvencies have something of a reputation for involving very substantial costs.

(Of course, the Brussels and Lugano Conventions, as part of the Civil Jurisdiction and Judgments Act 1982 (as amended), are relevant to the question of *forum conveniens* not least because the Conventions cut down, at least in some degree, the circumstances in which the English court may exercise its discretion. Where the proceedings are within the scope of the Conventions – as is most likely the case where a *creditor* is suing the insolvent debtor[11] – but the English court's jurisdiction does not derive from any of the bases of jurisdiction under the Conventions, then the discretion to stay English proceedings undoubtedly exists. Thus, for example, where an English creditor sues a New York debtor in England on

---

[9] *Ibid.*

[10] (1996) 29 O.R. (3d) 626 at 633. Blair J cited, inter alia, *Re a Company (No. 00359 of 1987)* [1988] Ch. 210 in support of his opinion. See also p. 331, *infra* for more on the Canadian decision in the context of concurrent insolvencies.

[11] *Firswood Ltd.* v. *Petra Bank*, above, is unusual in that the action was not being brought on a contract, or other obligation entered into prior to the insolvency of the bank, but on a decision of the Jordanian liquidation committee. For more on the 'bankruptcy exception' to the Conventions see p. 13, *supra.*

the basis of the debtor's presence in England,[12] the court may stay the action if it considers that the Bankruptcy Court in New York is a clearly more appropriate forum.[13] Where one of the bases of jurisdiction under the Conventions does apply, then the English court may yet stay its own proceedings, provided that the more appropriate foreign court is not in a Contracting State.[14] Thus should an English creditor sue a New York debtor in England, relying upon an English jurisdiction clause,[15] the court may stay the action in favour of New York. But there can be no discretion to stay where the allegedly more appropriate foreign forum is, for instance, in France or Greece.[16] Nevertheless, it must always be borne in mind that in many instances the Conventions will work to the advantage of the insolvent French businessman or Greek corporation. For the primary rule under the Conventions is that, in the absence of exclusive or special jurisdiction, the defendant can in any event only be sued in the courts of the domicile. Nothing in the Conventions prevents a court in one part of the United Kingdom staying an action in favour of the courts in another part of the United Kingdom.[17])

Whenever the discretion to stay is being considered, decisions of the Scottish courts may be useful illustrations, since the *forum conveniens* doctrine was imported into English law directly from Scotland. In *Okell v. Foden*[18] an English debtor's affairs were being liquidated by arrangement under the Bankruptcy Act 1869 and competing claims were being advanced to a fund of money that had been brought from Canada into Scotland – the debtor had also carried on another business with a partner in Canada and the Canadian creditors wanted to prevent the money being removed to England, as they feared it might be distributed to the separate creditors of the debtor. The funds were arrested in Scotland, which gave the court there jurisdiction. The Court of Session declined jurisdiction, leaving the Canadian creditors to make their case in the English bankruptcy proceedings:[19]

> 'It seems to me that this is clearly a case for applying the rule that, where bankruptcy proceedings are once instituted, no matter in what country, everyone interested in the estate must go there to have their claims settled . . . I do not say that this court has no jurisdiction – that would be putting the case too high. We have jurisdiction . . . but I think that clearly this is a case for the application of the rule of *forum non conveniens*.'

It may be noted that the Scottish proceedings were being used to prevent the court conducting the insolvency from gaining control of assets: just as creditors today seek to use Mareva injunctions in England.

---

[12] In relation to a corporation that presence would be a branch office in England, at which the debtor may be served.

[13] For the impact of the Conventions generally upon the discretion to stay, see *Dicey and Morris*, pp. 400–402.

[14] *Re Harrods (Buenos Aires) Ltd.* [1992] Ch. 72.

[15] See *Firswood Ltd.* v. *Petra Bank, supra*, where the debtor was a Jordanian rather than New York bank.

[16] See *Re Harrods (Buenos Aires) Ltd., supra*.

[17] *Dicey and Morris*, p. 400–401.

[18] (1884) 11 R. 906, see also *Edinburgh & Glasgow Bank* v. *Ewan* (1852) 14 D. 547 in relation to an English winding up at a time when, as was the case prior to the Companies Act 1862, the Winding Up Acts did not apply in Scotland.

[19] *Ibid.*, at 911.

6. *SOLOMONS* V. *ROSS*

In *Galbraith* v. *Grimshaw*[20] it was ruled that the rights of an attaching creditor in England would not be prejudiced by a subsequent foreign bankruptcy. The House of Lords declined to follow *Solomons* v. *Ross*[1] in which Bathurst J had, apparently, reached a different conclusion. Lord Loreburn LC contented himself with the comment that he was not prepared to act upon the earlier scantily reported case.[2] In *Solomons* v. *Ross* merchants in Amsterdam had stopped payment on 18 December 1759. Two days later Ross, an English creditor, by a foreign attachment in the Lord Mayor's Court garnished a debt owing to the bankrupts. On 2 January 1760 the Chamber of Desolate Estates in Amsterdam appointed curators of the bankrupt's property. In March 1760 Ross obtained judgment in the Lord Mayor's Court. It was determined that Ross would give up the benefit of the attachment to the curators, but without prejudice to the defendant Ross coming in as a creditor of the bankrupt.[3]

In *Galbraith* v. *Grimshaw* no explanation of the decision of Bathurst J was offered, and even a most extensive academic analysis has led to no firm conclusion.[4] However, it may be suggested that *Solomons* v. *Ross* was decided on the basis of previous authority. In *Mackintosh* v. *Ogilvie*[5] the defendant, an English creditor, had prior to the commission in England arrested debts owing to the bankrupt in Scotland. Only after the English commission had issued did the creditor recover judgment in Scotland. (There was also evidence that the defendant had fraudulently misled the courts in Scotland.) Lord Hardwicke prevented the defendant leaving England by a writ *ne exeat regno*. But, more interestingly, the Lord Chancellor commented upon the right of a creditor who although having previously attached property in England, by the custom of London, only recovered judgment after the bankruptcy:[6]

> 'The defendant had not obtained sentence before the bankruptcy; it is then like a subsequent foreign attachment by the custom of London. Would this court suffer a creditor to obtain a priority by such an attachment only, if no sentence was pronounced before the bankruptcy? Certainly not.'

Their Lordships in *Galbraith* v. *Grimshaw* might well have been a little more forthcoming in their analysis of *Solomons* v. *Ross* had the opinion of Lord Hardwicke also been put before the House.

Nevertheless, the authority of *Galbraith* v. *Grimshaw* cannot now seriously be questioned.[7] However, *Galbraith* v. *Grimshaw* lays down but a general rule. Thus a creditor with a prior attachment in England may yet be affected by a foreign insolvency if, the attachment not being complete, a

---

[20] [1910] A.C. 508, *supra*.
[1] (1764) 1 Hy. Bl. 131n. and, more fully, (1764) Wallis 59n.
[2] [1910] A.C. 508 at 511.
[3] (1764) Wallis 59n. at 61.
[4] See Nadelmann (1946) 9 M.L.R. 154 at 160: 'By what reasoning the court reached its decision remains a matter of conjecture.' The facts in *Solomons* v. *Ross* are not entirely free from doubt, see n.7, *infra*.
[5] (1747) 1 Dick 119, more fully, (1747) 3 Swan. 380n. For the restraint of English creditors from attaching assets abroad see, generally, chapter 10.
[6] (1747) 3 Swan. 380n.
[7] It may be noted that the report of *Solomons* v. *Ross* at (1764) Wallis 59n. does not actually reveal that the attachment was prior to the bankruptcy at Amsterdam.

claim is entered in the foreign insolvency[8] or the creditor's very debt is discharged under its governing law.[9]

7. CONCURRENT ENGLISH AND FOREIGN BANKRUPTCIES

Specific problems arise with regard to the vesting of movable property where bankruptcy proceedings are at one time on foot both in England and abroad. The effect of concurrent bankruptcies is examined in chapter 12.

8. EUROPEAN CONVENTION ON INSOLVENCY PROCEEDINGS

It is fair to say that in outline the Convention sets certain minimum standards as to the consequences of recognition and that such minimum standards are in broad agreement with the current common law rules. The major consequences of recognition are dealt with in three separate provisions. First, Article 17 states that the judgment opening the main proceedings 'shall, with no further formalities, produce the same effects in any other Contracting State as under the law of the State of the opening of the proceedings, unless the Convention provides otherwise and as long as no proceedings referred to in Article 3(2) [secondary proceedings in respect of an establishment] are opened in that other Contracting State.' The Convention, as one might expect, 'provides otherwise' in a number of specific areas. The effect of the insolvency upon lawsuits pending in another Contracting State is governed by the law of that other State (Article 15). Contracts of employment are treated in a correspondingly similar way (Article 10), as are contracts relating to the acquisition or use of immovable property (Article 8). Rights *in rem* (Article 5) are likewise not prejudiced by the opening of insolvency proceedings in another Contracting State.

Secondly, Article 18 allows the liquidator appointed in the main proceedings to 'exercise all the powers conferred on him by the law of the State of the opening of proceedings in another Contracting State, as long as no other insolvency proceedings have been opened there nor any preservation measure to the contrary has been taken there. . . .' Article 18 goes on to say that the liquidator may remove the debtor's assets to the main proceedings, subject to rights *in rem* and reservation of title (Articles 5 and 7). In exercising his powers in another Contacting State the liquidator must comply with the law of that State, in particular with regard to the procedures for the realisation of assets. In addition, Article 29 gives the liquidator appointed in the main proceedings the right to request the opening of secondary proceedings in another Contracting State.

---

[8] *Selkrig* v. *Davies* (1814) 2 Rose 291, *supra*.
[9] See, further, p. 268, *post*.

Thirdly, having already dealt in Article 17 with the judgment opening the main proceedings, the Convention also deals with other judgments and rulings that are given during the course of the main insolvency proceedings. Article 25(1) provides:

'Judgments handed down . . . and which concern the course and closure of insolvency proceedings . . . shall also be recognised with no further formalities. Such judgments shall be enforced in accordance with Article 31 to 51 of the Convention on Jurisdiction and the Enforcement of Judgments in Civil and Commercial Matters. . . .'

This provision also applies in respect of preservation measures taken after the request for the opening of insolvency proceedings.

9. ILLUSTRATIONS

(1) P was recently appointed in Thailand assignee of an insolvent firm carrying on business in Thailand. P wishes to bring an action in England to recover property belonging to the firm. The English court will recognise P's extraterritorial authority provided such is satisfactorily established by expert evidence as to the law of Thailand.[10]

(2) MN Ltd., registered in Scotland, is in liquidation in Scotland. The Scottish court has made an order against a defendant director, resident in England, setting aside a gift of property in England as a gratuitous alienation (Insolvency Act 1986, section 242). That order will be enforced in England.[11]

(3) X Ltd. is a Bermudan company in respect of which a winding up order has been made in Scotland. Prior to the winding up order C had filed a writ, and obtained Mareva injunctions, against X Ltd. in England. Once the Scottish winding up order is brought to the attention of the English court,[12] the English action must be stayed.[13]

(4) T, domiciled in England, has been adjudicated insolvent upon his own petition in Hong Kong and a trustee there appointed. Under the law of Hong Kong all the bankrupt's estate, real and personal, wheresoever situate vests in the trustee. T owns movable and immovable property in England. The English court will recognise the title of the Hong Kong trustee over movables in England and, in addition, may appoint the trustee as receiver of T's immovable property in England with authority to sell the same.[14]

[10] *Alivon* v. *Furnival* (1834) 1 Cr. M. & R. 277, cf. the cases referred to at p. 221, n. 16, *supra.*
[11] Insolvency Act 1986, s. 426(1), subject to s. 426(2) above.
[12] See *Martin* v. *Port of Manchester Authority* 1934 S.C. 143.
[13] Insolvency Act 1986, s. 130(2) as explained in *Martin* v. *Port of Manchester Authority* 1934 S.C. 143, *supra.*
[14] *Re Kooperman* [1928] W.N. 101. The court in Hong Kong might also request the assistance of the English court pursuant to Insolvency Act 1986, s. 426.

(5) On 1 August 1996 B was adjudicated insolvent by the courts of New Zealand, in whose jurisdiction B carried on business. Under New Zealand law all B's property wherever situate, including any after-acquired property, is considered as vested in the New Zealand trustee. On 31st December 1996 certain funds in England devolved upon B. The English courts will assist the New Zealand trustee in the recovery of the after-acquired funds in England.[15] (Such assistance may be given under the inherent jurisdiction of the court or, a request having been made by the New Zealand courts, pursuant to section 426 of the Insolvency Act 1986.)

(6) As in Illustration 5 above; however, on 1 September 1996 a bankruptcy order was made in England against B and, later that month, a trustee was appointed in England. The English trustee has by notice in writing, pursuant to section 307 of the Insolvency Act 1986, claimed the after-acquired property which devolved upon the bankrupt on 31st December 1996. The title of the English trustee relates back to the time the after-acquired property devolved upon B. Accordingly, a claim by the New Zealand trustee to the after-acquired property must be rejected.

(7) As in Illustration 5 above; however, on 31 January 1997 a bankruptcy order is made in England and a trustee subsequently appointed. Here the funds which devolved upon B on 31 December 1996 are not after-acquired property within section 307 of the 1986 Act, and the claim of the New Zealand trustee will prevail, for the funds had vested in the New Zealand trustee prior to the commencement of the English proceedings.

(8) V Inc., a New York corporation, was declared bankrupt in the US District Court in November 1997. Prior to the US proceedings, a creditor had obtained judgment in England and attached property belonging to V Inc. in England. The US court has made a restraining order which seeks to prevent creditors from commencing or continuing any proceedings of whatever nature, anywhere in the world, against the corporation. Neither the US bankruptcy,[16] nor the restraining order,[17] will affect the attaching creditor's rights in England.

(9) As in Illustration 8 above; however, in December 1997 a winding up order was made, upon a petition presented by the US trustee acting on behalf of V Inc., by the English court in respect of V Inc. Pursuant to section 183(1) of the Insolvency Act 1986, the attaching creditor will, *prima facie*,[18] not be entitled to retain the benefit of the attachment as against the English liquidator, unless the creditor had completed the attachment (by receipt of the debt) prior to the commencement of the English winding up.

(10) As in Illustration 8 above; however, the attaching creditor has made a claim in the US bankruptcy proceedings. The English court (*semble*) will

---

[15] *Re a Debtor, ex p Royal Court of Jersey* [1981] Ch. 384.
[16] *Galbraith* v. *Grimshaw* [1910] A.C. 508, *Levasseur* v. *Mason & Barry Ltd.* [1891] 2 Q.B. 73.
[17] *Felixstowe Dock and Rly Co.* v. *United States Lines Inc.* [1989] Q.B. 360 and *Banque Indosuez S.A.* v. *Ferromet Resources Inc.* [1993] B.C.L.C. 112.
[18] See *Re Suidair International Airways Ltd.* [1951] Ch. 165.

not allow the creditor to proceed with attachment should the property in question be claimed by the US trustee.[19]

(11) M, a Japanese businessman, has been declared insolvent by judicial process in Japan. Shortly before the commencement of the Japanese insolvency, an English creditor had commenced proceedings by writ against M seeking to recover a debt alleged to have arisen under a contract governed by Japanese law. Leave to serve out of the jurisdiction pursuant to R.S.C. Order 11 will be denied; and the creditor will be left to pursue the case in Japan.[20]

(12) Incorporated is a Nevada corporation but registered as an oversea company under the Companies Act 1985. Incorporated has carried on business in North America and Europe. On 1 November 1997 Incorporated presented a petition for reorganisation under Chapter 11 of the US Bankruptcy Code in the US District Court. The plan envisages a scaling down of Incorporated's activities in North America and Europe. In September 1997 P, an English creditor, began an action against Incorporated in England and obtained a Mareva injunction. P's claim arises out of Incorporated's business activities in Europe. The evidence does not suggest that P would be treated unfairly in the Chapter 11 proceedings. The Mareva will be discharged.[1]

(13) As in Illustration 12 above; however, on 2 November 1997 P presented a winding up petition in England based upon an undisputed debt. An ancillary winding up may be conducted in England.[2]

---

[19] *Selkrig* v. *Davies* (1814) 2 Rose 291, as explained above.
[20] On the basis the Japanese court would be the clearly more appropriate forum, assuming it is established that the creditor would not be discriminated against in Japan.
[1] See *Banque Indosuez S.A.* v. *Ferromet Resources Inc.* [1993] B.C.L.C. 112, *supra.*
[2] If it is plain that the creditors' interests would be satisfactorily and fairly dealt with in the US proceedings, then the court might decline to make a winding up order. If an order is made it will be with a view to agreeing a scheme which does not undermine the reorganisation being conducted in America.

Chapter 9

Discharge

1. INTRODUCTION

The cases, stretching back for more than two centuries, established that whether the discharge of a debt in the course of foreign insolvency proceedings was accepted as effective in England was, as a general rule, a matter for the proper law of the contract pursuant to which the debt was incurred. However, the common law concerning the scope and operation of the proper law of a contract has largely been replaced by the rules laid down in the Rome Convention – brought into English law as from April 1991 by the Contracts (Applicable Law) Act 1990. Unfortunately, the Rome Convention does not deal comprehensively (still less clearly) with discharge by way of foreign insolvency proceedings; and it appears that insolvency practitioners and their advisers must accordingly be aware of both the common law and statutory rules.

A. Common Law

There are many reported cases in which the English court has been called upon to consider whether a foreign insolvency has the effect of discharging an insolvent's contractual obligations.[1] Leaving to one side United Kingdom bankruptcies, the judges have with but few exceptions approached the issue not as pertaining to the consequences of recognition, but rather as a matter governed by the proper law of the contract.[2] As a general rule, leaving to one side United Kingdom bankruptcies, a foreign insolvency operates as a discharge of a debt only to the extent permitted by the proper law of the particular contract concerned.[3] Of course, it is trite that should a foreign bankruptcy be recognised it may vest movable property in England in the foreign trustee. Hence, as long ago as 1814, it was judicially suggested that discharge should follow upon the vesting of property;[4] indeed, Patteson J

---

[1] A discharge from tortious liability under the insolvency law of the place where the tort was committed is effective in England: see *Phillips* v. *Eyre* (1870) L.R. 6 Q.B. 1, 28 and generally Part III of the Private International Law (Miscellaneous Provisions) Act 1995.

[2] In relation to the common law rules see, generally, *Dicey and Morris* (11th ed. 1987), chapter 32; and *Cheshire and North* (11th ed. 1987), chapter 18.

[3] *Ellis* v. *M'Henry* (1871) L.R. 6 C.P. 228 at 234 and cases there cited.

[4] *Per* Jabez Henry, President of the Court at Demerara, in *Odwin* v. *Forbes* (1814–17) Buck. 57 at 64 affirmed by the Privy Council, *ibid*.

once declared it 'monstrous' to suppose that a bankrupt might be deprived of his English property yet not also be discharged from his debts.[5] But such views have not prevailed in England.[6] When dealing with the effect of a foreign insolvency upon the debts and liabilities of the insolvent, the rules governing the recognition of foreign insolvencies fall away and it is to the proper law of the contract that regard must be paid.

Nevertheless, there has been established a significant gloss upon the proper law approach. A creditor who has assented to the foreign insolvency, by entering a proof, is bound by a discharge granted in the course of the foreign proceedings. A creditor is not permitted to participate in a foreign insolvency and subsequently, in England, seek to enforce a debt in defiance of a foreign discharge.[7]

B. Rome Convention

In relation to contracts entered into after 1 April 1991,[8] the Convention (i) lays down rules for determining the governing law of any particular contract and (ii) specifies which matters fall within the scope of that governing law.[9] It is in this latter regard that Article 10(1)(d) provides that the law selected by applying the rules under the Convention shall govern 'the various ways of extinguishing obligations'. Article 10(1)(d) has been taken by commentators to include the discharge of contract debts by way of bankruptcy.[10] Yet discharge of a debt following a *corporate re-organisation* appears not to fall within Article 10(1)(d), because Article 1 of the Convention ('Scope of the Convention') provides that the rules under the Convention do not apply to:

'(2)(e) questions governed by the law of companies . . . such as the creation . . . internal organisation or winding up of companies and other bodies corporate. . . .'

Whilst Article 1(2)(e) is not as patently clear as the excluding provision found in Article 1 of the Brussels Convention ('bankruptcy, proceedings relating to the winding up of insolvent companies or other legal persons, judicial arrangements, compositions and analogous proceedings'),[11] it is submitted that the effect of a foreign scheme of arrangement (or other equivalent re-

---

[5] In *Shepherd* v. *Beresford* (1851) 1 Mac. & H. 251 at 254: 'The just principle . . . was, that a man should be protected to the extent to which his property vested; and if his property in this country vested for the benefit of all his creditors, he ought certainly to be protected here.'

[6] For a decision of the German court abandoning the proper law approach, see *Re French Insolvency Proceedings* [1991] I.L.Pr. 459.

[7] *Phillips* v. *Allan* (1828) 8 B. & C. 477, *Seligman* v. *Huth* (1875) Bitt. Prac. Cas. 64, on appeal, (1877) 37 L.T. 488, *Glass* v. *Keogh* (1867) 4 W.W. & A'B. (L) 189 and *Nicholson* v. *Binks* (1832) 11 S. 153, discussed *infra*.

[8] The Contracts (Applicable Law) Act 1990 came into operation in the United Kingdom on this date: S.I. 1991/707.

[9] For a general discussion, see *Dicey & Morris* (12th ed. 1993) chapter 32 and *Cheshire & North* (12th ed. 1993) chapter 18.

[10] See *Cheshire & North* (12th ed. 1993) p. 517 and Kaye, *The New Private International Law of Contract of the European Community* (1993) pp. 308–309. *Dicey & Morris* in Rule 172 (discharge by bankruptcy) refers to Rule 180 and the latter Rule reflects Article 10(1)(d).

[11] See p. 13, *supra*.

organisation procedure) should be considered to be 'governed by the law of companies'. Accordingly, the extinction by such a scheme of a contractual obligation falls outwith the Rome Convention and continues to come under the common law rules. (A discharge in the winding up of a company is expressly outside the Rome Convention.)[12] Unlike the Brussels Convention, however, 'bankruptcy' is not excluded by Article 1 of the Rome Convention.[13]

2. UNITED KINGDOM INSOLVENCIES

A discharge from debts or liabilities following an English insolvency is valid irrespective of the proper law of the contract.[14] It was at one time considered that a discharge upon a *cessio bonorum* in Scotland or under an Act of the Irish Parliament could not affect a contract governed by English law.[15] But such is now only of historical interest. For a discharge in a bankruptcy in Scotland or Northern Ireland pursuant to legislation of the United Kingdom Parliament must be given full effect in England, irrespective of the proper law of the contract.[16] The English court will not allow an action to be maintained upon a contract (whether the proper law be English, French or whatever) against a bankrupt who has been discharged under a Scottish or Northern Irish bankruptcy. The strength of this rule is brought out not least by the decision in *Longbottom* v. *Stokes*.[17] Both plaintiff and defendant were resident in England when the plaintiff recovered judgment upon an English contract. The defendant later went to Ireland and was discharged from his debts pursuant to the Irish Insolvent Debtors Act 1840. The English court gave effect to the Irish discharge, being made under an Act of the Imperial Parliament, even though the parties and their contract had no real connection to Ireland. A discharge of debts pursuant to a scheme of arrangement (or other appropriate insolvency procedure) pursuant to legislation in force in Scotland or Northern Ireland would likewise be given full effect in England – regardless of the governing law of the contract.

---

[12] Of course, if a company has been wound up (in the place of incorporation) it is almost inevitable that the company will cease to carry on its business and be dissolved. Accordingly, the company will have ceased to exist and whether or not its debts have been discharged is unlikely to be of much, if any, practical relevance.

[13] See further, p.267, *infra*.

[14] *Ellis* v. *M'Henry* (1871) L.R. 6 C.P. 228 at 235–236.

[15] *Phillips* v. *Allan* (1828) 8 B. & C. 477, *Lewis* v. *Owen* (1821) 4 B. & Ald. 654 and *Shallcross* v. *Dysart* (1826) 2 Gl. & J. 87.

[16] *Ellis* v. *M'Henry* (1871) L.R. 6 C.P. 228 at 237, see also Bankruptcy (Scotland) Act 1985, s.55(1), *Sidaway* v. *Hay* (1824) 3 B. & C. 12, *Ferguson* v. *Spencer* (1840) 1 Man. & G. 987 and *Simpson* v. *Mirabita* (1869) L.R. 4 Q.B. 257. Note, however, *Re Nelson* [1918] 1 K.B. 459 where it was held that the (old) provisions in the Irish Acts of 1857 and 1872 in respect of compositions did not, on their true construction, operate outside Ireland.

[17] (1851) 1 Mac. & H. 259. Where the Rome Convention is applicable, this rule would be maintained as a mandatory rule of the forum: see p. 267, *infra*.

3. FOREIGN INSOLVENCIES (COMMON LAW)

A. Application of the Proper Law

(i) *Discharge under Proper Law*

A discharge in accordance with the proper law will be effective in England. This rule, which is imperative, is so well-established that it cannot admit of any doubt. In 1724 the Scottish court held that a debt under an English bond was regulated by English law and discharged upon the defender's bankruptcy in England.[18] Two years later Lord King, in the Court of Chancery, granted a perpetual injunction to prevent a party from suing upon a bill drawn at Leghorn and discharged by that foreign law.[19] A discharge under the proper law was also given effect by Lord Mansfield in *Ballantine* v. *Golding* and by Lord Ellenborough in *Potter* v. *Brown*.[20] In a somewhat more recent example,[1] the Privy Council has given effect to a discharge under the proper law in pursuance of a scheme of arrangement.

(ii) *Mere Suspension of Remedy*

However, expert evidence must be produced to show that the foreign proper law does indeed bring about the discharge of the debt in question. Should a defendant fail to prove the content of the foreign insolvency law,[2] or if that law amounts to merely a restriction upon the remedies available to a plaintiff in the foreign court, then an action on the debt may be pursued in the English court (assuming always that there is jurisdiction). In *Frith* v. *Wollaston* the plaintiff brought an action in England upon a judgment obtained in the Cape Colony. The defendant pleaded that his estate had been sequestrated there and that under Cape law any action or execution against the insolvent was stayed. The Court of Exchequer held that the defendant's plea afforded no defence – the foreign law created but a 'suspension of the execution upon the judgment', not the discharge of that obligation.[3]

(iii) *Discharge other than under Proper Law*

With the exception of United Kingdom bankruptcies, a discharge which is not obtained under the proper law is ineffective. This is so even though the bankruptcy itself may be recognised as vesting a debtor's movable estate in

---

[18] *Rochead* v. *Scot* (1724) Mor. 4566.

[19] *Burrows* v. *Jemino* (1726) 2 Stra. 733.

[20] (1784) Cooke, *Bankrupt Laws* (8th ed.), p. 487 and (1804) 5 East 124, respectively. Note also *Gardiner* v. *Houghton* (1862) 2 B. & S. 743 and *Ohlemacher* v. *Brown* (1879) 44 U.C.Q.B. 366, *passim*.

[1] *State Aided Bank of Travancore Ltd.* v. *Dhrit Ram* (1941) L.R. 69 Ind. App. 1. Note also *Re Banque Des Marchands De Moscou (Koupetschesky)* [1952] 1 All E.R. 1269.

[2] See, for example, *Anon.* v. *Anon.* (1810) 1 Anst. 80 or *Faure Electric Accumulator Co. Ltd.* v. *Phillipart* (1888) 58 L.T. 525 at 529.

[3] (1852) 7 Exch. 194 at 198. Note *Newman* v. *Fleetwood* (1870) 9 S.C.R. (N.S.W.) 166 and *Brown* v. *Hudson* (1826) Taylor 390, *passim*. Merely because a debt is not discharged does not mean a plaintiff creditor may attach English assets where there has been a prior foreign insolvency, *infra*.

the foreign assignee. The point is well illustrated by *Smith* v. *Buchanan.*[4] The defendants, resident in Maryland, had been declared insolvent in Maryland and a trustee appointed. The plaintiffs, who had not claimed in the foreign proceedings, obtained judgment in England upon an English contract. Lord Kenyon CJ did not deny recognition to the foreign insolvency proceedings. But the foreign insolvency, to which the plaintiffs had given 'no assent either express or implied',[5] was simply no answer to an action upon a contract governed by English law. The same rule is applicable upon the insolvency of a foreign corporation. In *Gibbs* v. *Société Industrielle des Métaux*[6] the plaintiffs had recovered judgment under a contract governed by English law against the defendant, a French company in judicial liquidation in France. The defendants appealed on the basis, *inter alia*, that a discharge under French law (the law of the company's domicile) was a good defence to the English action. The Court of Appeal rejected the defendant's contention as suggesting 'a principle for which there is no foundation in law or reason',[7] their Lordships affirming the doctrine in *Smith* v. *Buchanan*. In short, it is not enough that a discharge be obtained under the law of the domicile,[8] the 'seat' of a corporation,[9] a defendant's residence[10] or place of business.[11]

Nevertheless, in some instances it is relevant to broaden the inquiry and consider issues that arise even though a discharge has not been granted in accordance with the proper law. Let us say that a trader carrying on business mainly in New York and Ontario has been declared bankrupt in the US courts. Most of the creditors and assets are in New York or Ontario, but there are some assets in England. As far as English law is concerned, any discharge in the US proceedings will only be effective in respect of contracts governed by American law (that is, the law of the State of New York, Oregon etc): a US bankruptcy will not discharge a contract the proper law of which is the law of Ontario. Yet, of course, a creditor under an Ontario contract can only bring an action in England once the jurisdictional requirements of English law are satisfied. Much more significantly, even if a creditor has got judgment in England he may not be allowed to levy execution upon the debtor's assets in England. For if a foreign insolvency is recognised in England and is shown to extend to assets situated in England, then no individual creditor may gain a priority over the general body of creditors by an attachment in England subsequent to the commencement of the foreign insolvency proceedings.[12]

In conclusion, where a debt has been discharged under the proper law that is an end of the matter: the plaintiff will no longer have a valid cause of

---

[4] (1800) 1 East 6. There appears to be a potential exception as a result of the abolition of the non-merger rule, p. 260, *infra*.

[5] *Ibid.*, at 11. The importance of assent is considered in detail below.

[6] (1890) 25 Q.B.D. 399 (approved in *New Zealand Loan and Mercantile Agency Co. Ltd.* v. *Morrison* [1898] A.C. 349, 359).

[7] *Ibid.*, at 406. See also *Cape Copper Co. Ltd.* v. *Comptoir D'Escompte* (1890) 6 T.L.R. 454.

[8] *Gibbs* v. *Société Industrielle des Métaux* (1890) 25 Q.B.D. 399.

[9] *Tharsis Sulphur and Copper Co. Ltd.* v. *Société des Métaux* (1889) 58 L.J.Q.B. 435.

[10] *Smith* v. *Buchanan* (1800) 1 East 6, *Lewis* v. *Owen* (1821) 4 B. & Ald. 654.

[11] *Shallcross* v. *Dysart* (1826) 2 GL. & J. 87.

[12] *Galbraith* v. *Grimshaw* [1910] A.C. 508 at 510, chapter 8, *ante*. The question of a stay of execution arose in *Gibbs* v. *Société Industrielle des Métaux* (1890) 25 Q.B.D. 399 but was not then decided, see *ibid.*, 409, 410 and 411.

action. But if there has been no discharge, under the proper law or at all,[13] it simply means the plaintiff's claim cannot be struck out as non-existent. Such a plaintiff may take advantage of an attachment put in force in England prior to a foreign bankruptcy (*Galbraith* v. *Grimshaw*) or liquidation (*Levasseur* v. *Mason & Barry Ltd.*[14]); however, subsequent attachments will not be effective. A convenient illustration may be found in *Cape of Good Hope Bank* v. *Mellé*,[15] a decision in the Cape Colony. In 1891 the defendant's estate had been sequestrated in the Transvaal and a trustee appointed. Subsequently, the Bank brought an action in the Cape to recover a debt. The debt had been incurred and was payable in the Transvaal (i.e. the law of the Transvaal was the proper law). The law of the Transvaal was to the effect that a sequestration did not extinguish the debt but merely restricted the remedies of a plaintiff. De Villiers CJ, following the decision of the Court of Exchequer in *Frith* v. *Wollaston*, held that the Transvaal sequestration was not a discharge and could not therefore preclude an action in the local courts. However, in the light of the prior foreign insolvency, the Bank could not levy execution against any of the insolvent defendant's estate in the Cape which might be claimed by the foreign trustee.

B. Abolition of Non-Merger Rule

As has been seen above, the English courts often maintained that (in the absence of assent) a foreign insolvency could not discharge an English contract. The position was unaltered even if the creditor concerned had obtained a judgment on the contract in the foreign court prior to the foreign insolvency – because at common law an English cause of action did not merge with, and hence be extinguished by, a foreign judgment.[16] To take an example, let us say that C obtained judgment against D in New York on an English contract, but some time afterwards D was made bankrupt in New York and eventually obtained his discharge. At common law there was nothing to prevent C subsequently bringing an action in England on the original cause of action and, of course, the New York bankruptcy would not discharge the English contract. However, the non-merger rule has been abolished by section 34 of the Civil Jurisdiction and Judgments Act 1982, which provides:

> 'No proceedings may be brought by a person in England and Wales . . . on a cause of action in respect of which a judgment has been given in his favour in proceedings between the same parties or their privies, in a court in another part of the United Kingdom or in a court of an overseas country, unless the judgment is not enforceable or entitled to recognition in England and Wales.'

---

[13] There may merely have been a stay of proceedings.

[14] [1891] 2 Q.B. 73, p. 234, *ante*. For the effect of a discharge upon a prior attachment see p. 268.

[15] (1893) 10 J. 280.

[16] For the background to s. 34 see *Dicey & Morris*, p. 466. The effect of s. 34 in the context of discharge by foreign insolvency proceedings has not, as far as this author is aware, been explored in any judgments or academic writings.

(Section 34 applies in respect of all foreign judgments, not just those delivered in an EU country.) Thus returning to the example given above, C would be barred (irrespective of any question as to the governing law of the contract) from subsequently bringing an action on the original English contract. Although the New York judgment would not be 'enforceable' in England – since the bankruptcy in New York would presumably be the equivalent of satisfaction of that judgment – the judgment would nevertheless be 'entitled to recognition' in England.

Accordingly, the practical result of the abolition of the non-merger rule may in appropriate circumstances be to give a fuller effect to a foreign discharge than used to be the case.

C. Extended Proper Law

The question has been raised as to whether an extended operation may be given to the proper law rule.[17] To take an example: let us say that, as a matter of English private international law, the proper law of a particular contract is German law, and that upon insolvency in Germany the debtor received a discharge. The German discharge will be acted upon in England. Now let us modify the facts and assume that the insolvency and discharge have taken place in France but, further, that French discharge would be recognised as effective under German law.[18] It would seem sensible for the English court to give effect to such a discharge. Thus it may be said that a foreign discharge will operate in England if either granted in accordance with the proper law of the contract, or recognised as effective under the proper law. However, of course, it will be for the defendant to prove that the proper law does indeed recognise the discharge. It may be safely assumed that such cases will be rare. (In addition, this approach may not be permissible in bankruptcy cases where the Rome Convention applies.[19])

4. PLAINTIFF PARTICIPATING IN FOREIGN INSOLVENCY (COMMON LAW)

In *Smith* v. *Buchanan*, it will be recalled, an English contract was held not to be discharged by a bankruptcy in the State of Maryland, Lord Kenyon observing that the plaintiffs had given 'no assent either express or implied' to the foreign proceedings. It is of significance that, where a party has come in under a foreign insolvency, the proper law rule may simply not apply. It may not always have been noticed, but there is a body of authority which deals with the effect of a foreign discharge (not under the proper law) upon the rights of a party who has participated in foreign insolvency proceedings.

---

[17] See *Dicey and Morris*, p. 1182.
[18] Which is precisely what took place in *Re French Insolvency Proceedings* [1991] I.L.Pr. 459.
[19] See the discussion of Art. 15, *infra*.

A. Scottish Jurisprudence

The Court of Session has firmly set its face against a creditor seeking to avoid the consequences of a foreign insolvency to which that creditor has assented. In *Rhones* v. *Parish*[20] a merchant had been made bankrupt under the law of Bremen. Thereafter the creditors, including the respondents, elected a certain number of the members of the Senate of Bremen as trustees. The respondents meanwhile arrested movables in Scotland belonging to the bankrupt and also entered a proof in the proceedings in Bremen. The Lord Ordinary pronounced an interlocutor against the respondents:

> 'the respondents having given their vote for the choice of trustees, or having proved their debts before the trustees, and made a demand for payment, is sufficient evidence of their having acceded to the trust right, which it seems by the law of Bremen is vested in certain members of the Senate, chosen by the creditors, and that accession precludes them from taking separate measures in this country in order to obtain a preference over the rest of the creditors.'

That interlocutor was adhered to by the court. Then upon another petition being presented 'after a hearing in presence upon the effect of the accession, the court adhered to their former judgment'. A like determination was made in *Glover* v. *Vasie*[1] with reference to an English bankruptcy. Vasie, an English creditor, had received a dividend under an English commission but later arrested assets in Scotland. After extensive argument, the court's interlocutor barred Vasie from competing with the English assignees:

> 'Robert Vasie of Hexham, an Englishman, claiming under an English debt, and having already drawn a dividend of the bankrupt's effects on account of said debt, under the said commission, is barred from competing with the assignees, or claiming preference on his arrestments. . . . '

That interlocutor was also subsequently adhered to by the court. As in *Rhones* v. *Parish*, the creditor could not obtain any priority by reason of the attachment nor, in addition, might Vasie compete with the assignees.[2] Subsequent Scots case law is also most helpful. In *Rose* v. *M'Leod*[3] a commission issued in England against a bankrupt who had traded at Berbice. A dispute ensued between the English assignees and Rose as to whether the bankrupt had been truly indebted to Rose. An arbitrator in London decided that a certain sum was due to Rose. That debt had been contracted and was payable in Berbice. But instead of proving in England, Rose brought an action in Scotland.[4] The Court of Session considered that the debt, arising in Berbice, was not discharged by a certificate under an

---

[20] (1776) Mor. 4593 and App. No. 2 (Foreign). Note also *Cathcart* v. *Blackwood* (1765) 2 Paton 150, *passim*.

[1] (1776) Mor. 4562 and App. No. 3 (Foreign).

[2] The court had earlier reached the opposite conclusion in *Ogilvie* v. *Aberdein* (1747) Mor. 4556, but in that case the attachment was prior to the English commission; and it must be noted that *Ogilvie* v. *Aberdein* was not applied in the landmark decision of *Strothers* v. *Read* (1803) Mor. App. No. 4 (*forum competens*).

[3] (1825) 4 S. 311.

[4] Proceedings were also brought in Berbice which went to the Privy Council: see (1825) 4 S. 311 at 312, *passim*.

English commission.[5] More importantly in this context, it was held that the reference to the arbitrator was not equivalent to entering a proof in England so as to prevent Rose from disputing the validity of the English discharge.

If *Rose* v. *M'Leod* assumes that a foreign discharge will be effective against a creditor who has entered a proof, it was so held in *Nicholson* v. *Binks*.[6] Nicholson was indebted to Binks under a Scottish contract when the former petitioned for relief under the Irish Insolvent Debtors Act 1821. Binks not only claimed in the Irish proceedings but was also appointed as the assignee. After Nicholson had obtained his discharge in Ireland, Binks brought proceedings in Scotland. It was held that, whether or not the Irish discharge was good against all Scottish creditors,[7] Binks' participation in the foreign insolvency barred him from objecting to the foreign discharge.

B. Common Law Authorities

Lord Kenyon's reference in *Smith* v. *Buchanan* to 'assent either express or implied' was taken up by the Court of King's Bench in *Phillips* v. *Allan*.[8] The plaintiff brought an action in England upon an English debt. The defendant pleaded that he had been discharged upon a *cessio bonorum* in Scotland and, moreover, the plaintiff had appeared before the Court of Session to oppose the defendant's release from custody. Judgment was given for the plaintiff. As stated above, a *cessio bonorum*, not being under an Act of Parliament, did not discharge an English debt. In addition, the plaintiff's appearance before the Scottish Court was not a consent to the *cessio bonorum*:[9]

> 'The plea does not show that the plaintiff sought to take a distributive share of the defendant's property (which he might have done by the law of Scotland), but only that he endeavoured to prevent the defendant's being free from restraint in Scotland in respect of his debt.'

Although the plaintiff had participated in the foreign proceedings, he had not 'sought to have the benefit of the law of Scotland by taking a share of the defendant's property'.[10]

---

[5] This part of the decision would now be reversed: see *Ellis* v. *M'Henry* (1871) L.R. 6 C.P. 228 at 236.

[6] (1832) 11 S. 153.

[7] In *Lewis* v. *Owen* (1821) 4 B. & Ald. 654 and *Shallcross* v. *Dysart* (1826) 2 GL. & J. 87 the English courts had recently held that the Irish Acts did not bind English creditors.

[8] (1828) 8 B. & C. 477. It seems the plaintiffs in *Potter* v. *Brown* (1804) 5 East 124 may have proved in the foreign bankruptcy (*ibid.*, at 128); however, the point was not raised and the defendant was in any case discharged under the proper law. (See also *Quelin* v. *Moisson* (1828) 1 Knapp 265n.)

[9] (1828) 8 B. & C. 477 at 483 *per* Bayley J. In *Tharsis Sulphur and Copper Co. Ltd.* v. *La Société des Métaux* (1889) 58 L.J.Q.B. 435 at 439 Field J quoted with approval from the judgment of Bayley J, and appeared to accept that if a creditor sought relief from the foreign court then the creditor would be bound (although on the facts before Field J no proof had been entered in the foreign proceedings): See also *Re Mottet* (1887) 84 L.T.Jo. 188 at 190: 'creditors . . . can, if they like, prove in the bankruptcy, and then would probably be bound by the discharge in a foreign court of law'.

[10] *Ibid.*, at 484–485 *per* Holroyd J.

In reliance upon the *dicta* in the Court of King's Bench, the Victorian court in *Glass* v. *Keogh*[11] held that a creditor who proves and receives a dividend in a foreign insolvency is bound by a discharge thereunder, irrespective of the proper law.[12] Moreover, Quain J in *Seligman* v *Huth* is reported to have put the matter in the following terms:[13]

> 'It was decided in *Phillips* v. *Allan* that proving for an English debt under bankruptcy proceedings abroad operated as a discharge.'

The plaintiffs were assignees under a US bankruptcy of a firm ('K and Co.') carrying on business in New York. K and Co. had an agreement with the defendants, bankers in London, whereby the latter would accept drafts upon themselves drawn by K and Co. Prior to K and Co. stopping payment, two bills of exchange were forwarded to the defendants to be held upon certain conditions. At the time K and Co. stopped payment they were indebted to the defendants to a considerable sum and, rather than holding the bills in question upon the specified terms, the defendants appropriated the bills. The defendants proved in the US bankruptcy in respect of their debt and received a dividend. The plaintiff assignees then brought an action in trover in England in respect of the appropriation of the two bills. The defendants argued, *inter alia*, that the balance owing to them by K and Co., pursuant to the parties' agreement, had to be taken into account by way of counterclaim or set off. Quain J, as we have seen, considered the defendants' debt (although an English debt) was barred, since the defendants had proved in the US insolvency.[14] His Lordship referred the question of set off to the court. The Common Pleas Division (the judgment is not reported) held in favour of the assignees and that determination was affirmed by the Court of Appeal.[15] Unfortunately, whether proof under the US proceedings barred the defendants' debt was not pursued before the Lords Justices. The view was taken that the plaintiffs (suing as assignees) sought to recover the bills as property of the bankrupts, hence the agreement (and any debt) between K and Co. and the defendants was irrelevant.[16] Brett LJ, however, seems to have contemplated giving effect to the US bankruptcy:[17]

> 'There can be no counterclaim, because a counterclaim under the Judicature Act has no existence except where an action could be brought by the person setting up the counterclaim. In this case it would be against the plaintiffs as assignees, and against them no counterclaim in respect of the balance, as balance, could be maintained by the present defendants: no independent action could be brought against the present plaintiffs by the present

[11] (1867) 4 W.W. & A'B. (L) 189.

[12] The plaintiffs in *Gibbs* v. *Société Industrielle des Métaux* (1890) 25 Q.B.D. 399 had entered a claim in the French liquidation. The majority of the Court of Appeal (Lindley and Lopes LJJ) did not mention the point. Lord Esher MR stated (at 406–407) that the defendant's contentions as to a discharge under the law of France had not been made out.

[13] (1875) Bitt. Prac. Cas. 64, also reported at 60 L.T. Jo. 122. Note also, *passim*, *Phelps* v. *Borland 103* N.Y. 406 (Court of Appeals of New York, 1888) (US creditor bound by English discharge on account of receiving a dividend under an English composition).

[14] His Lordship's statement assumes, of course, that the discharge under the foreign bankruptcy law is satisfactorily established by expert evidence or the parties' agreement.

[15] (1877) 37 L.T. 488.

[16] *Ibid.*, at 493.

[17] *Ibid.* (emphasis added).

defendants. *The latter would be bound to go into the Bankruptcy Court in America and prove for their dividend.'*

At the very least, there is nothing to suggest that the Court of Appeal took exception to the proposition put forward by Quain J.

Phillips v. *Allan* and *Seligman* v. *Huth* are consistent with the decision reached in *Taylor* v. *Hollard*,[18] although the earlier cases were not there cited. The defendant had borrowed money in England from the plaintiff under a contract governed by English law. The plaintiff in 1884 recovered judgment in England for £15,067 9s. 11d. In 1886 the plaintiff brought an action on the English judgment in the Transvaal. The South African court gave judgment for the plaintiff, but only for the sum of £9,635 4s. 6d. Thereafter the plaintiff sequestrated the defendant's estate in South Africa and, in due course, was paid by the curators the full amount previously awarded in the South African court. The defendant was eventually discharged and, according to the law in the Transvaal, was released from all debts claimable against his estate. In 1900 the plaintiff brought an action in England to recover the balance (the difference between the English and South African judgments). Jelf J, having held that the plaintiff's case was in any event statute-barred,[19] also considered the effect of the foreign insolvency. It does not appear to have been put to Jelf J that participation in the foreign proceedings might of itself bind the plaintiff and it seems *Phillips* v. *Allan* was not cited. Nevertheless, whilst repeating the orthodox view that a 'release in the foreign country could not per se get rid of a cause of action arising out of a contract' governed by English law,[20] his Lordship also stated:[1]

'If the plaintiff had merely obtained judgment in the Transvaal and . . . had not taken any steps to realise that judgment, he could, I think, have sued afterwards in this country for the original debt.[2] But, in my opinion, when he accepted the judgment . . . and proceeded to sequestration . . . I think he had elected to take the judgment of the foreign country to which he had appealed in discharge of the whole cause of action, and could not afterwards sue for the residue of the debt in England.'

Although the facts in *Taylor* v. *Hollard* were unusual and, moreover, the general proposition derived from *Phillips* v. *Allan*[3] was not put before the court, the judgment tends to support a commonsense approach to a plaintiff's participation in foreign insolvency proceedings: the plaintiff should not be allowed to blow hot and cold.[4]

---

[18] [1902] 1 K.B. 676.

[19] It may be noted that a foreign insolvency does not suspend the running of time for the purposes of limitation, see *Re Kidd* (1861) 4 L.T. 344 and cf. Bankruptcy (Scotland) Act 1985, s.78 referring to ss.8(5) and 22(8) as well as para. 3 of the Fifth Schedule.

[20] [1902] 1 K.B. 676 at 682, citing the first edition of *Dicey's Conflict of Laws* (1896).

[1] *Ibid.*, at 681.

[2] This was because of the non-merger rule, now repealed, see *supra*.

[3] Namely, that real participation in the foreign insolvency binds the plaintiff, regardless of the fact that his contract is governed by English law.

[4] To use the expression of Jelf J in *Taylor* v. *Hollard* at 681. The courts seem generally to be adopting a tough stance towards creditors who claim in the foreign insolvency and then try to get some advantage by way of English proceedings: see *Firswood Ltd.* v. *Petra Bank* [1996] C.L.C. 608, p. 247, *supra*.

C. Conclusion

The entering of an appearance by a creditor in a foreign insolvency will not of itself prevent that creditor subsequently bringing an action in England to enforce his debt. But the situation is different where the debt has been discharged under the foreign proceedings and the creditor has given assent to those proceedings by taking,[5] or even seeking to take,[6] a distributive share of the insolvent's assets thereunder, or otherwise fully participating in the foreign process.

This author would suggest that policy reasons are very much in favour of binding the creditor who has actively participated in foreign insolvency proceedings. This may perhaps best be illustrated by an example. A foreign company in financial difficulty has undergone a rescue procedure in its country of incorporation. P, an unsecured creditor whose debt arose under an English contract, participated in those foreign proceedings and voted at creditors' meetings.[7] The rescue plan, which was approved by the requisite majorities under the foreign law, involved additional funding being provided by a third party investor on the basis that 50% of all the debts owing, *inter alia*, to the unsecured creditors would be discharged.[8] Some months after the plan is put into operation (P having already received 50% of the initial debt), P brings an action in England against the company for the balance, claiming that no foreign proceedings can discharge an English debt. Allowing P's claim would frustrate the 'rescue culture' that is an integral part of the framework of modern insolvency laws in the United Kingdom. Moreover, if P had voted in favour of the plan, then simple justice dictates that P should be bound; yet even if P voted against the plan, there is no good reason why P should be given a second chance to try to defeat the plan – the more so in that P is seeking to recover something that is not available to the majority of the other unsecured creditors.

In short, there is a rule of English law that, irrespective of any question of the law governing a contract, a creditor who fully participates in the foreign insolvency process will be bound by any discharge granted thereunder.

5. SUMMARY

A discharge under an insolvency in any part of the United Kingdom is, as a matter of English law, a valid discharge regardless of the proper law of the contract.[9] A foreign discharge will only be acted upon by the English court:

---

[5]   *Seligman* v. *Huth* (1877) 37 L.T. 488, *Glass* v. *Keogh* (1867) 4 W.W. & A'B. (L) 189, *Nicholson* v. *Binks* (1832) 11 S. 153, *Glover* v. *Vasie* (1776) Mor. 4593.

[6]   *Seligman* v. *Huth* (1875) Bitt. Prac. Cas. 64 applying *dicta* in *Phillips* v. *Allan* (1828) 8 B. & C. 477. (There was no discharge in *Frith* v. *Wollaston* (1852) 7 Exch. 194, 198 *per* Parke B.)

[7]   The creditor should be bound whether voting in favour of or against the plan.

[8]   Of course, if the unsecured creditors received some equity or security pursuant to the plan, then under normal English contract law principles there would be sufficient consideration for those creditors to be bound.

[9]   *Ellis* v. *M'Henry* (1871) L.R. 6 C.P. 228 at 234–235 and cases *supra*.

(i)   if the discharge is effective under the proper law of the contract;[10] or

(ii)   as against a party to English proceedings, where that party has assented to the foreign insolvency.[11]

6. ROME CONVENTION

As mentioned above, commentators have taken the view that discharge by way of bankruptcy falls within the Rome Convention.[12] It is here proposed to examine to what extent the Convention departs from the common law approach already outlined.

First, the effect of Article 10(1)(d) is that the discharge of contractual obligations is a matter for the governing law, as determined by the application of the Convention rules.[13] The general approach mirrors the common law. (Whether the governing law of the contract may be given an 'extended meaning' – so as to include discharges not granted by but recognised under the governing law – is doubtful:[14] for Article 15 states that the governing law of a particular country means 'the rules of law in force in that country other than its rules of private international law'.)[15]

Secondly, the substance of the common law rule that a United Kingdom discharge takes effect regardless of the proper law is maintained. According to Article 7(2), nothing in the Convention restricts the application of any mandatory rules of the forum: a mandatory rule is one which applies 'irrespective of the law otherwise applicable to the contract'.[16]

Thirdly, it is submitted that the common law rule that binds a creditor who assents to the foreign proceedings is not affected by the Convention. The common law rule is nothing to do with (and does not seek to determine) which law governs the contract in question or the issue of discharge – it is not a choice of law rule. This is significant because the very scope of the Rome Convention itself is expressed in Article 1(1) as follows:

> 'The rules of this Convention shall apply to contractual obligations in any situation involving a choice between the laws of different countries.'

Cases such as *Nicholson* v. *Binks*, *Glass* v. *Keogh* and *Seligman* v. *Huth* do not involve a 'choice between the laws of different countries': these cases involve the recognition of the consequences of a foreign insolvency in the particular circumstances where a creditor has actively and fully participated in those proceedings.

---

[10] *Ibid.*, at 234.

[11] *Phillips* v. *Allan*, *Nicholson* v. *Binks*, *Glass* v. *Keogh* and *Seligman* v. *Huth*, all *supra*.

[12] See p. 256, *supra*. This author has some difficulty with that view. However, since the practical application of the Convention produces very similar results to the common law rules, there is little reason to debate the issue here.

[13] See p. 256, *supra*.

[14] See p. 261, *supra*.

[15] Article 15 is entitled 'Exclusion of renvoi', but the actual wording used in the text is far broader than just renvoi.

[16] Article 7(1) (foreign mandatory rules) does not apply in England: see s.2(2) of the Contracts (Applicable Law) Act 1990.

Finally, the abolition of the non-merger rule[17] is unaffected by the implementation of the Convention, since again there is no choice of law issue involved.

7. INSOLVENCY ACT 1986, SECTION 426

An insolvency representative from a relevant country or territory may find resort to section 426 of the Insolvency Act 1986 most helpful when seeking to ensure that English creditors are bound by a foreign discharge (or even a foreign stay). In *Re Business City Express Ltd.*[18] Rattee J acted pursuant to a request from the Irish court to extend an Irish scheme of composition to England and thereby make the arrangement binding on all relevant English creditors. A foreign moratorium or stay pending the formulation and approval of a rescue plan could likewise be the subject of a section 426 request.

8. THE EFFECT OF A DISCHARGE UPON A PRIOR ATTACHMENT

The House of Lords held in *Galbraith* v. *Grimshaw*[19] that once an attachment has been put into force in England, such attachment (though uncompleted) will not be affected by the subsequent vesting of the bankrupt's property in a trustee under a foreign insolvency. The question in each case, said Lord Loreburn, was 'whether the bankrupt could have assigned to the trustee, at the date when the trustee's title accrued, the debt or assets in question situated in England'.[20] But, of course, their Lordships were only concerned with title to assets attached in England. On the facts no issue arose as to the validity of the very debt owing to the attaching creditor. There had been no discharge under the foreign insolvency in *Galbraith* v. *Grimshaw*.

However, it is possible that after the English court has made a garnishee order *nisi*, yet prior to the order being made absolute, a defendant is not merely adjudicated bankrupt but also discharged from his debts and liabilities by the foreign court. If that discharge is effective in England (i.e. as part of the governing law of the contract[1]) it extinguishes the debt owing to the attaching creditor. Accordingly, the garnishee order *nisi* can no longer be made absolute: there is simply no debt owing to the attaching creditor. That a foreign discharge may operate even after a plaintiff

---

[17] See p. 260, *supra*.
[18] [1997] B.C.C. 826. See also *Re Goodman International* (1990) 5 B.J.I.B. & F.L. 530, p. 406, *infra* where all civil actions, attachments and winding up proceedings in England were prohibited pursuant to a s. 426 request from the Irish court.
[19] [1910] A.C. 508, discussed in detail in chapter 8.
[20] *Ibid.*, at 510.
[1] Should the attaching creditor prove in the foreign proceedings, he cannot rely upon the attachment in defiance of the foreign law; see *Selkrig* v. *Davies* (1814) 2 Rose 291 at 318–319, p. 243, *ante*.

creditor has obtained judgment in England is confirmed by *Simpson* v. *Mirabita*.[2] The plaintiff's action was commenced in England on 2nd October 1868. In the following month the defendant was adjudicated bankrupt in Ireland. On 10 December 1868 judgment was entered for the plaintiff in England. It was only in January 1869 (even after costs had been taxed in the English action) that the defendant obtained his discharge in Ireland. Nevertheless, that discharge was given effect by the English court.

9. ILLUSTRATIONS

(1) P has recently commenced an action in England against D in respect of a debt arising under a contract governed by French law. That debt has been discharged in bankruptcy proceedings in Northern Ireland. The Northern Irish discharge is a good defence to P's action in the English court.[3]

(2) In January 1997 T, a New Zealand businessman, presented a bankruptcy petition in New Zealand and an assignee was there appointed. The New Zealand assignee has, in accordance with New Zealand law, claimed T's assets in England. Prior to the commencement of the proceedings in New Zealand, R had begun an English action against T for breach of a contract governed by New Zealand law; and in March 1997 T's liability was admitted and judgment entered for R. T has not yet been discharged in New Zealand but, under New Zealand law, all actions against a bankrupt are stayed pending the bankruptcy proceedings. R has recently sought to levy execution upon T's English assets. The English court will not give effect to the stay (not being a discharge) under New Zealand bankruptcy law. However, by reason of the prior foreign insolvency, R may not attach T's assets in England.[4]

(3) As in Illustration 2 above; however, R's action is brought upon a contract governed by English law. The result is as in Illustration 2: R will not be permitted to attach T's English assets.

(4) X is a corporation registered in the State of Euphoria. X is in judicial liquidation under the insolvency law of Euphoria. As a result of the liquidation, according to expert evidence on Euphorian law, all debts and liabilities of X have been discharged. The Euphorian discharge is valid in England with reference to contracts governed by the law of the State of Euphoria.

(5) K, a New York businessman, has for many years conducted business with H, an English broker. K has been made bankrupt in the US courts. At the time of his bankruptcy K was considerably indebted to H. H made a claim in the US bankruptcy and received a certain dividend. H has now

---

[2] (1869) L.R. 4 Q.B. 257 (the case did not involve an attachment). A like decision had also been reached in *Shepherd* v. *Beresford* (1851) 1 Mac. & H. 251.
[3] See *Simpson* v. *Mirabita* (1869) L.R. 4 Q.B. 257 and p. 267, *supra*.
[4] See *Cape of Good Hope Bank* v. *Mellé*, p. 260 *ante*.

brought an action in England against K. K's debt has been discharged according to US law. Irrespective of the proper law, H is bound by the discharge in the US bankruptcy proceedings.[5]

(6) As in Illustration 5 above; however, H appeared before the US courts merely to argue (unsuccessfully in the result) that the US bankruptcy should be rescinded because of fraud on the part of K. H, having failed to have the bankruptcy rescinded, withdrew and entered no claim in the US proceedings.[6] K's discharge will be effective in England only in respect of those contracts governed by American law.

(7) On 31 January 1998 M was adjudicated insolvent in accordance with the law of the State of Euphoria and a trustee there appointed. M has assets in England. Prior to the Euphorian insolvency, G obtained judgment in England against M and, in January 1998, a garnishee order *nisi* was served on M. G's English action concerned a contract governed by Euphorian law. Under the provisions of the insolvency law of Euphoria, 60 days after making an adjudication all debts and liabilities of an insolvent are automatically extinguished.[7] The garnishee order *nisi* will not, after 1 April 1998, be made absolute.[8]

---

[5] See *Seligman* v. *Huth, supra.* For an example involving a foreign rescue of an ailing corporation, see p. 266, *supra.*

[6] See *Phillips* v. *Allan* (1828) 8 B. & C. 477 at 485 *per* Holroyd J.

[7] There is no objection to a foreign discharge operating against a creditor who has already obtained judgment against the bankrupt in England: indeed, that is exactly what took place in *Simpson* v. *Mirabita, supra,* text to n. 2.

[8] For, thereafter, the foreign discharge has extinguished the debt owed to G.

Chapter 10

Hotchpot and Attachments

1. INTRODUCTION

Since 1764 and the landmark decision of Bathurst J in *Solomons* v. *Ross*,[1] the competing rights of foreign assignees and English creditors have been a central issue in the English private international law of bankruptcy. Yet nearly two decades beforehand, Lord Hardwicke had considered the position of *English* assignees where a creditor had sought satisfaction of his debt by attaching the bankrupt's assets abroad. In *Mackintosh* v. *Ogilvie* an English creditor, who had arrested the bankrupt's effects in Scotland, was restrained at the instance of English assignees by a writ of *ne exeat regno*, the Lord Chancellor observing:[2]

> 'I cannot grant an injunction or prohibition to the Court of Session, but I will certainly restrain the party. I will not permit a creditor here to gain such a priority, to pass by the commission of bankruptcy, go into Scotland or Holland, where arrestments are suffered, and arrest debts there, etc., to obtain a preference, and evade the laws of bankruptcy here. That is the nature of the present case. The defendant endeavours to procure an entire satisfaction by another law of effects there. If I discharged the writ, he might go out of the Kingdom, and evade all account here.'

In modern commerce (no less than two and a half centuries ago) a creditor may be well-advised to explore whatever opportunities are available for the recovery of debts; and to a creditor who has attached assets abroad, insolvency proceedings in England may not seem a particularly attractive option. Hence it should be no surprise to learn that there is a body of case law which identifies, over a range of different circumstances, whether or not a creditor may properly proceed against an insolvent's assets situate outside the jurisdiction of the English court.

In outline, three propositions may be advanced. First, there is the 'hotchpot' rule: a creditor who not only obtains payment in respect of a debt in a foreign court but also claims in an English bankruptcy or winding up must, in general, bring 'into the common fund' any sum recovered abroad. Secondly, the English court may restrain an English creditor, or a foreign creditor who has made a claim in the English insolvency proceedings, from

[1] (1764) 1 Hy Bl. 131n., chapter 8, *ante.*
[2] (1747) 3 Swan. 380n. The evidence also suggested that the English creditor had fraudulently misled the courts in Scotland.

continuing an action brought against the insolvent in a foreign court.[3] Lastly, the English court may require an English creditor to surrender moneys obtained by legal process in a foreign court.[4] However, it must be stressed that the operation of these propositions is subject to not inconsiderable exceptions and qualifications. Hence there may, in practice, be some room for a creditor (foreign or English) to strengthen his position through use of proceedings both in the English and a foreign court.

Further, whatever may be the position in respect of creditors, under section 291(2) of the Insolvency Act 1986 the bankrupt may be compelled to do all such things (either in the United Kingdom or elsewhere) as may reasonably be required by the official receiver for the protection of any property that may be claimed for the bankrupt's estate by the trustee: this will include abandoning proceedings in a foreign court to enable the trustee to sell such property.[5]

2. HOTCHPOT

A. General Rule

In *Banco de Portugal* v. *Waddell*[6] insolvency proceedings were being conducted in England and in Portugal with reference to a firm that traded in London and Oporto. The appellants, holders of certain bills of exchange, received a dividend in Portugal and sought afterwards to tender a proof upon the bills in the English bankruptcy. The House of Lords, approving the decision in *Ex p Wilson*[7] and the words of Lord Eldon in *Selkrig* v. *Davies*,[8] held that the proof could be admitted, but on condition that the appellants would not receive any dividend thereon until after the other creditors in England had received a dividend equal to that which the appellants had obtained by means of the Portuguese proceedings:[9]

> 'Every creditor coming in to prove under, and to take the benefit of, the English liquidation, must do so on the terms of the English law of bankruptcy: he cannot be permitted to approbate and reprobate, to claim the benefit of that law, and at the same time insist on retaining as against it, any preferential right

---

[3] The restrain of foreign proceedings will only be required should the foreign court itself refuse to respect the English insolvency: see *per* Millett LJ in *Mitchell* v. *Carter* [1997] 1 B.C.L.C. 673 at 687.

[4] A foreign creditor who has entered a claim in England before recovering assets abroad may similarly be required to account, *infra*.

[5] See *Re Harris* (1896) 74 L.T. 221, cf. *Ferguson's Trustee* v. *Ferguson* 1990 S.L.T. (Sh. Ct.) 73, p. 308 *post*. Note also *Re Maguire* (1922) 2 C.B.R. 543 where the Ontario court, applying *Re Harris*, ordered the bankrupt to execute a transfer of shares in a foreign company.

[6] (1880) 5 App. Cas. 161. Note also *Re Pim* (1881) 7 L.R. Ir. 458 and *Clydesdale Bank* v. *Anderson* (1890) 27 S.L.R. 492, *passim*.

[7] (1872) 7 Ch. App. 490 (see p. 339, *infra*); see also *Stewart* v. *Auld* (1851) 13 D. 1337 (equalising dividend in Scotland after insolvency in New South Wales).

[8] (1814) 2 Rose 291 at 318: 'It has been decided, that a person cannot come in under an English commission without bringing into the common fund what he has received abroad.'

[9] (1880) 5 App. Cas. 161 at 169 (*per* Lord Selborne); see also the order drawn up in *Ex p Wilson* (1872) 7 Ch. App. 490 at 494.

inconsistent with the equality of distribution intended by that law, which he may have obtained either by the use of legal process in a foreign country, or otherwise.'

The hotchpot rule will be relevant whether moneys have been recovered outside England through foreign insolvency proceedings[10] or by the more direct method of attaching the insolvent's assets.[11]

The basis of the hotchpot rule requires some analysis. Two considerations make it abundantly clear that the rule is quite independent of (even inconsistent with) the vesting of property in the English trustee and the maxim *mobilia sequuntur personam*. Let us say that bankruptcy proceedings are commenced under the laws of Brazil and an assignee appointed in January 1997. Six months later, by which time a dividend has been paid in Brazil, the bankruptcy jurisdiction of the English court is invoked. Assets in Brazil cannot possibly vest in the English trustee. Yet the English court will not close its eyes to the fact that a Brazilian creditor who proves in England has already received a dividend. There is authority on this point,[12] but it is hardly necessary. In addition, of course, the hotchpot rule is not excluded in every winding up, even though the assets of the company do not vest in the English liquidator. Rather it seems the hotchpot rule developed, as a matter of practical justice, in an effort to prevent foreign creditors gaining too great an advantage over their English counterparts. Thus Lord Eldon opined that a foreign creditor claiming in an English bankruptcy must be considered 'to all intents and purposes an English creditor'.[13] His Lordship's observation despite the passage of more than 175 years remains a useful signpost, though not an inflexible rule of law.[14]

B. Secured Interests and Attachments

(i) *Secured Interests*

In a purely domestic English insolvency a secured creditor may, as a general rule, realise his security and prove for any outstanding balance as an ordinary, unsecured creditor. The cases present a slightly unclear picture where it is a foreign creditor who proves in England after realising his security abroad. The starting point must be *Captain Wilson's Case*[15] before Lord Hardwicke. The case is not fully reported but an account is to be found in the judgment of Lord Loughborough in *Sill* v. *Worswick*.[16] A commission of bankruptcy issued in England in respect of Captain Wilson,

---

[10] As in *Banco de Portugal* v. *Waddell* itself. Note also *Re Northland Services Pty. Ltd.* (1978) 18 A.L.R. 684.

[11] As suggested by Lord Eldon LC in *Selkrig* v. *Davies*, n. 8, *supra*.

[12] In *Banco de Portugal* v. *Waddell* (1880) 5 App. Cas. 161 the doctrine of relation back operated so that title first vested in the English trustee, but Lord Selborne (at 170) made it clear that it would not have made any difference had the action of the Portuguese court been earlier.

[13] *Selkrig* v. *Davies* (1814) 2 Rose 291 at 318.

[14] A foreign creditor may recover under an attachment abroad and then prove in England, subject to the hotchpot rule: an English creditor may be restrained from attaching the insolvent's assets abroad once insolvency proceedings have commenced in England, *infra*.

[15] 1 H. Bl. 691n., for other proceedings see (1752) 1 Atk. 128, *passim*.

[16] (1791) 1 H. Bl. 665.

who had considerable debts due to him in Scotland. Meanwhile various English creditors had instituted proceedings in Scotland,[17] and one particular group had obtained assignments of specific debts notified to the relevant debtors, a process known as an intimation. The intimation took place prior to the English bankruptcy. These creditors were considered by Lord Hardwicke 'to stand in the same situation as creditors claiming by mortgage', i.e. secured creditors. The report continues:[18]

> 'All therefore he would do with respect to them was, that if they recovered under that decree, they could not come in under the commission without accounting to the other creditors for what they had taken under their specific security.'

To say that a secured creditor must account is somewhat ambiguous.[19] However, another report makes the matter quite plain:[20]

> 'Lord Hardwicke went so far as to refuse to permit the Scotch creditors to come in under the commission, on the same footing as those in this country, unless they would abandon the priorities which they had obtained by the law of Scotland, as to the effects there.'

From the little explanation of Lord Hardwicke's judgment now available it is impossible to ascertain whether his Lordship was seeking to lay down a rule applicable to all creditors (foreign or English) who enter a proof, or whether a solution was merely being proposed in respect of English creditors who proceeded abroad with notice of the English bankruptcy. But, certainly, any suggestion that every creditor who proves in England must give up money recovered abroad under a foreign security cannot be correct. Whatever may have been intended by Lord Hardwicke, *Captain Wilson's Case* has been overtaken by subsequent authority and has now no value as a precedent in English law.

Of rather more use is the decision of Vaughan Williams J in *Re Somes, Ex p De Lemos*.[1] The bankrupt owned a mine upon which, as a matter of Venezuelan law, De Lemos had acquired a lien or charge for working expenses. De Lemos realised his security by means of a judicial sale in Venezuela. He was thereafter permitted to prove in England for the outstanding balance without bringing into hotchpot the sum already recovered abroad. Vaughan Williams J considered the appropriate test was whether the creditor's right was 'in the nature of a mortgage or charge or security held independently of any proceedings taken to realise it'.[2] In summary, the hotchpot rule will not apply to sums recovered in a foreign court, either before or after the commencement of insolvency proceedings

---

[17] See *Wilson's Assignees* v. *Wilson's Creditors* (1755) Mor. 4556 *sub nom. Bradshaw and Ross* v. *Fairholm (Wilson's Creditors)* (1755–58) Kilkerran 280. The reports in Scotland reveal that the claim of the English assignees prevailed, so it would appear that Lord Hardwicke's comments were made prior to the determination in Scotland and are, therefore, *obiter*.

[18] Note 15, *supra*.

[19] There is an obvious difference between giving credit for what has been received abroad and actually giving up what has been received abroad.

[20] As a note to *Le Chevalier* v. *Lynch* (1779) 1 Doug. KB 170.

[1] (1896) 3 Mans. 131. See also *Callender Sykes & Co.* v. *Lagos Colonial Secretary* [1891] A.C. 460. As to what property vests in an English trustee, see p. 341, *infra*.

[2] *Ibid.*, at 135. In *Selkrig* v. *Davies* Lord Eldon is reported in 2 Dow. 231 at 249 to have said: 'if a Scotch creditor thought proper to come in under an English commission, he . . . must deliver up . . . all securities for his debt before he could be permitted to prove'. No such comment appears in the report at 2 Rose 291 and *Selkrig* v. *Davies* in fact concerned only an attachment put into force after the bankruptcy. The report in *Rose* is to be preferred.

in England, by virtue of a property interest vested in the creditor under the foreign law.

(ii) *Attachments*

It appears to follow from the reasoning of Vaughan Williams J in *Re Somes, Ex p De Lemos* that the hotchpot rule should apply to a creditor who has obtained payment in a foreign court by means of an attachment, rather than under a particular security. Indeed his Lordship made reference as an example to the right of arrestment of assets in Scotland[3] and, in *Selkrig* v. *Davies*,[4] Lord Eldon was dealing with an arrestment in Scotland put into force after a commission had issued in England. There can be no question that the rule will apply where a foreign creditor,[5] subsequent to the commencement of an insolvency in England, has attached property abroad. However, a creditor who has completed an attachment *prior* to the debtor's insolvency in England may be likened to a secured creditor.[6] For the attached assets may vest in the creditor upon completion of the relevant judicial act in the foreign court. Moreover, as far as authority is concerned, it should not be forgotten that in *Ex p D'Obree* Lord Eldon himself said in respect of completed prior foreign attachments that 'the creditors attaching are entitled to hold such property or the value thereof in diminution of their debts, *and to prove the residue*'.[7] Absent from the Lord Chancellor's judgment in *Ex p D'Obree* is any reference to proving the residue upon condition that the creditors bring into the common fund what has been recovered abroad. Yet despite the apparent inconsistency in the judgments,[8] the appropriate principle cannot be in much doubt. A foreign creditor who proves in England having recovered assets abroad should, at least in this regard, be treated no less favourably than the equivalent English creditor. In a wholly domestic insolvency in England a creditor who has completed execution prior to the bankruptcy or winding up is not constrained by the hotchpot rule.[9] There is, accordingly, a compelling reason for conferring the same freedom upon a foreign creditor who has recovered under a prior foreign attachment.

(iii) *Summary*

The doctrine of hotchpot has no operation in respect of a creditor who recovers money or property abroad (i) by virtue of a mortgage, charge, lien

---

[3] (1896) 3 Mans. 131 at 133, *arguendo*.

[4] (1814) 2 Rose 291.

[5] An English creditor will not be allowed to attach property abroad after insolvency proceedings have commenced in England, *infra*.

[6] Vaughan Williams J had himself expressly so held in *Re West Cumberland Iron and Steel Co.* [1893] 1 Ch. 713 at 723.

[7] (1803) 8 Ves. 82 at 83 (emphasis added).

[8] *Ex p D'Obree* was not cited in *Re Somes, ex p De Lemos*, nor did Vaughan Williams J refer to his earlier decision in *Re West Cumberland Iron and Steel Co.* [1893] 1 Ch. 713. A completed prior attachment would explain why the hotchpot rule did not apply in *Re Bowes* [1889] W.N. 53 (administration).

[9] See, generally, Insolvency Act 1986, ss. 346 and 183.

or other secured interest under the foreign law, or (*semble*) (ii) under a foreign attachment completed prior to the commencement of insolvency proceedings in England.

C. The Creditor's Undertaking

It may be recalled that upon the facts in *Banco de Portugal* v. *Waddell* the foreign dividend was already in the hands of the proving creditor; that a dividend had been received as well as the amount thereof was not an issue. But in some instances it may be that the English proceedings are well in advance of the foreign insolvency. No dividend may have been determined abroad; indeed, the creditor may have yet to decide whether or not to enter a claim in the foreign proceedings. In such circumstances it will be appropriate for the English court to allow a claim by a foreign creditor, but only upon the creditor giving an undertaking to hand over to the trustee or liquidator any dividends which may thereafter be received under the foreign insolvency. (If such undertaking has not expressly been given, it is almost inevitable that the English court would regard it as inferred as a condition of entering a proof.)

At first blush it might appear that the weight of authority, in particular *Ex p Black* and *Re Deane and Youle*,[10] is against requiring such an undertaking. In the former, Dutton, Pierce and Jefferies carried on business in London (under the style Jefferies, Pierce & Co.) and in Rio (as Dutton, Pierce & Co.). The firm stopped payment in Rio, and Jefferies, the only partner resident in England, had been made bankrupt in England and assignees appointed. A creditor who held two bills of exchange, drawn by the Rio house upon and accepted by the London house, sought to prove in the English bankruptcy. The assignees raised an objection on the basis that the creditor would also be able, should he so wish, to prove and receive a dividend in the insolvency proceedings in Rio. The Court of Bankruptcy considered the creditor entitled to prove in England without the imposition of 'a condition the effect of which would be to withhold the dividend'.[11] A similar, perhaps even clearer, reluctance to qualify the rights of the creditor may be found in *Re Deane and Youle*. The bankrupts had carried on business in common in Liverpool and, with a third person, in Pernambuco. An adjudication was made in England in 1854. In April 1855 Mellor (a creditor who had proved upon a bill of exchange, drawn by the Brazilian firm upon and accepted by the Liverpool firm) received a dividend in England. Subsequently, the Pernambuco firm entered into a *concordata* as a result of which Mellor received far larger dividends in Brazil. Knight Bruce LJ expressed himself quite plainly:[12]

> 'If the law of Brazil does in effect give a creditor who has received a dividend in this country a right to receive a dividend there also, there can be no pretence for taking it from him by the intervention of an English Court of Justice.'

Thus Mellor kept both English and Brazilian dividends.

[10] (1856) 28 L.T.O.S. 53 and (1862) 3 De G.F. & J. 760, respectively.
[11] (1856) 28 L.T.O.S. 53.
[12] (1862) 3 De G.F. & J. 760 at 765.

However, *Ex p Black* and *Re Deane and Youle* are no longer relevant authorities. For the judgments, even if correct at the time they were delivered,[13] concerned the old rules as to double proof. That is, where there were two commissions of bankruptcy taking place in England, or a commission in England and a sequestration abroad, a bill holder was not permitted to prove in both proceedings but was put to an election. In contrast, the doctrine of hotchpot is based on the premise that a creditor does indeed claim a debt[14] both in England and abroad, but the creditor is, at the same time, accountable for sums received or receivable in the foreign proceedings. An illustration may be found in *Re Kidd*. A Scottish firm (Gilmour & Co.) sought to prove in an English bankruptcy after it had already received a dividend under an earlier sequestration in Scotland. Mr Commissioner Fonblanque admitted the proof whilst making provision for the dividend received *and any future dividends*:[15]

'That the proof of Messrs. Gilmour & Co. be admitted for the amount of the original debt and interest . . . after giving credit for all dividends receivable under the said sequestration, the said Messrs. Gilmour & Co. undertaking to hand over to the estate any future dividends which they might receive under the said sequestration.'

No criticism of the commissioner's order was made in the Court of Appeal in Chancery. The order in *Re Kidd* must be correct for English judges have repeatedly maintained that, once a foreign creditor has proved in England, he may be restrained *in personam* from commencing or continuing proceedings abroad.[16] If the court will restrain a foreign creditor, similarly there must be jurisdiction to require that creditor to give up assets or money recovered abroad after a proof has been entered in England.

Reference may also here be made to *Re Bank of Credit and Commerce International S.A. (No. 10)*. Sir Richard Scott V-C, when dealing with the retention of funds by the English liquidators in order to pay a dividend to net creditors (who would have been disadvantaged if their dividend had been paid in Luxembourg because of the rules on set off in force in Luxembourg), commented:[17]

'The creditor would, of course, as a condition of being paid the sum by the English liquidators, have to confirm that he had not received and would withdraw any claim to a dividend from the Luxembourg liquidators.'

Whilst the Vice-Chancellor did not refer to any authority, his Lordship's approach strongly supports *Re Kidd*.

Taking a broader perspective, a practical point of some relevance to the foreign creditor emerges. By entering a proof in England a foreign creditor may thereafter risk losing the whole benefit of any action and execution under way in the foreign court. Whereas, if the foreign creditor receives money in a foreign court and only then enters a proof in England, the foreign creditor actually retains the benefit derived from the foreign

---

[13] The contrary opinion had been expressed in *Re Vanzeller* (1832) 2 L.J. Bcy. 18 at 20: 'he might receive a dividend in this country, and then go abroad, and receive a dividend there, if this court did not interpose and prevent it'.

[14] Of course any debt, not merely under a bill of exchange.

[15] (1861) 4 L.T. 344. Note also *Re Pim* (1881) 7 L.R. Ir. 458.

[16] *Ex p Tait* (1872) L.R. 13 Eq. 311, *Carron Iron Co.* v. *Maclaren* (1855) 5 H.L. Cas. 416 at 442–443; see also *Cockerell* v. *Dickens* (1840) 3 Moo. P.C.C. 98 at 134–135, *passim*.

[17] [1997] Ch. 213 at 252. For a general discussion of this important case, see p. 362, *infra*.

proceedings and is restricted merely by the hotchpot rule. Thus a foreign creditor may, at times, be well-advised to delay entering a proof in an English insolvency until any proceedings in a foreign court have been successfully concluded.

D. Summary

A creditor may claim in an English insolvency upon bringing into the common fund any money or assets recovered by virtue of a foreign insolvency or other proceedings against the insolvent. Accordingly, the creditor will not be paid any dividend in England until the other creditors in England have received dividends equivalent to that which has been obtained in the foreign court. However, a creditor will not be so restrained in respect of money or assets recovered abroad under:

(i)   a mortgage, charge, lien or other security, or (*semble*)
(ii)   an attachment abroad completed prior to the commencement of insolvency proceedings in England.

In addition, should a creditor prove in England and subsequently receive money or assets by way of foreign proceedings (other than in respect of a mortgage, charge, lien or other security) the English court may order that such money or assets be handed over to the English trustee or liquidator.

3. RESTRAINING FOREIGN ACTIONS

English insolvency law has as one of its broad objectives the equitable distribution of assets. Thus, once insolvency proceedings are under way, there is a need for some power to restrain an individual creditor from instituting proceedings at his own will and pleasure against the insolvent. (Of course, this problem is in no way unique to English law and practitioners will be all too familiar with the worldwide stay frequently imposed under US bankruptcy law.) There is no inherent difficulty where the English court seeks to regulate actions brought in England. However, restraining foreign actions is somewhat more complex. For, as a matter of principle and commonsense, no order of an English judge will compel a foreign court to abandon its own proceedings. Thus an English trustee or liquidator may often be well-advised first to petition the foreign court to stay or dismiss an individual creditor's attempt to seize assets there.[18] Nevertheless, the English court possesses jurisdiction to restrain a creditor from carrying on an action abroad. In *Re Distin*[19] the Court of Bankruptcy granted injunctions restraining English creditors from maintaining actions brought against the debtor at Antwerp in respect of

---

[18] *Per* Millett LJ in *Mitchell* v. *Carter* [1997] 1 B.C.L.C. 673 at 687.
[19] (1871) 24 L.T. 197, approved in *Bank of Tokyo Ltd.* v. *Karoon* [1987] A.C. 45n. and *Re Paramount Airways Ltd.* [1993] Ch. 223.

English debts. Similarly, in *Re North Carolina Estate Co.*[20] an English creditor, who had proved in an English winding up, was restrained by Chitty J from continuing an action in North Carolina. Such *in personam* jurisdiction is reinforced, in the case of a winding up,[1] by section 130(2) of the Insolvency Act 1986 which applies where an action has been brought by a creditor in any part of the United Kingdom.

A. Insolvency Act 1986, section 130(2)

(i) *Outline*

Section 130(2) of the Act states:

> 'When a winding up order has been made or a provisional liquidator has been appointed, no action or proceedings shall be proceeded with or commenced against the company or its property, except by leave of the court and subject to such terms as the court may impose.'

The subsection reproduces legislation previously found in the Companies Acts and in particular derived from section 87 of the Companies Act 1862. The 1862 provision was interpreted by Jessel MR in *Re International Pulp and Paper Co.*[2] as applying to actions or proceedings in any part of the United Kingdom. Thus the Master of the Rolls restrained an Irish creditor (who had not proved in England) from continuing a suit brought in Ireland in respect of the company's Irish property. The provision has also been employed to restrain Scottish proceedings. In *Re Middlesborough Firebrick Co. Ltd.*[3] Pearson J restrained creditors whose actions in Scotland had been commenced prior to the English winding up order; and in *Re Hermann Loog Ltd.* a creditor who had obtained arrestments in Scotland, but only subsequent to the English winding up order, was similarly restrained by North J.[4]

It is important to note that the statutory jurisdiction to restrain a creditor may be invoked irrespective of whether the creditor in question resides in England, is a British citizen or has made a claim in the winding up. Section 130(2) has been interpreted as simply allowing the English court to restrain a creditor from proceeding with an action in any part of the United Kingdom. But the subsection cannot be prayed in aid where

[20] (1889) 5 T.L.R. 328, approved in *Bank of Tokyo Ltd.* v. *Karoon* [1987] A.C. 45n. and *Mitchell* v. *Carter* [1997] 1 B.C.L.C. 673. For the position in respect of a receiver appointed by debenture holders see *Re Maudslay, Sons & Field* [1900] 1 Ch. 602 and *Re Derwent Rolling Mills Ltd.* (1904) 21 T.L.R. 81, 701.

[1] In *Re Spalding* (1889) 61 L.T. 83 Cave J (*obiter*) considered that the provisions of the Bankruptcy Act 1883 could be used to restrain a creditor from proceeding with an action in Victoria. The better view was that the statutory powers under the bankruptcy legislation are territorial and apply only to actions begun in the jurisdiction: *Re Newton, ex p Bankrupt* v. *Aldergate Films* [1956] C.L.Y. 6984.

[2] (1876) 3 Ch. D. 594: applied with reference to what is now Insolvency Act 1986, s. 126 in *Re Dynamics Corpn of America* [1972] 3 All E.R. 1046 (Templeman J). Section 130(2) also operates to stay action under way in England when a winding up order is made, or a provisional liquidator is appointed, in Scotland: see p. 218, *ante.*

[3] (1885) 52 L.T. 98.

[4] (1887) 36 Ch. D. 502. For the position after the presentation of a winding up petition but before an order has been made see Insolvency Act 1986, s. 126 and *Re Dynamics Corpn of America* [1972] 3 All E.R. 1046.

the creditor sues in Turkey, France or the People's Republic of China.[5]
(The operation of section 130(2) in respect of actions under way in
England, when a winding up order has been made in Scotland, has been
described in chapter 8.)

(ii) *Security and Attachments*

The court at the request of a secured creditor will generally grant leave
under section 130(2) to proceed with an action to enforce a security. Hence
in *Re Wanzer Ltd.*[6] a Scottish landlord was permitted to enforce a right of
hypothec, such being a secured interest according to the law of Scotland. It
was no obstacle to the granting of leave that the landlord had brought
proceedings in Scotland to enforce the hypothec only after the making of
the winding up order.[7]

Yet, whether leave will be obtained by a creditor who relies upon an
arrestment in Scotland (or an attachment in Northern Ireland) very much
depends upon the timing of such arrestment. It will be recalled that in *Re
Hermann Loog Ltd.* the English court issued an injunction preventing a
creditor from gaining any benefit by means of an arrestment issued after
a winding up order had been made. In addition, section 128(1) provides
that where an English company[8] is being wound up by the court any
attachment or execution against the effects of the company put into force
after the commencement of the winding up is void. There is every reason
to suppose that the 'effects of the company' referred to in section 128(1)
encompass property belonging to the company in Scotland.[9] Whereas in
Re West Cumberland Iron and Steel Co.[10] the creditor's action in Scotland
was not restrained, letters of arrestment having issued some months prior
to the commencement of the winding up in England. Swinfen Eady J
reached a like conclusion in *Re National Provincial Insurance Corpn.
Ltd.*[11] Creditors obtained arrestments in Scotland on 1st June and 1st
July 1911. On 17th July 1911 a petition was presented in England to
wind up the corporation, a compulsory order being made on 9th August
1911. The creditors obtained judgment in Scotland on 26th July 1911 and,
in February 1912, sought leave to bring an action of 'furthcoming' in
Scotland. Initially, in chambers, his Lordship refused leave. However,
upon evidence being presented as to Scottish law, namely that an action

---

[5] See *Re Vocalion (Foreign) Ltd.* [1932] 2 Ch. 196 at 204 *per* Maugham J. An extraterritorial
   application to the provision, as in *Re South-Eastern of Portugal Rly Co.* (1869) 17 W.R.
   982 or *Pacific Coast Mining Co.* v. *Walker* (1886) 13 R. 816, is contrary to authority.
[6] [1891] Ch. 305.
[7] North J felt the landlord had been 'entirely in the wrong' in bringing an action without
   leave and ordered the landlord to pay the costs the liquidator had up to that time incurred:
   see [1891] 1 Ch. 305 at 314. Note also the apportionment of costs in *Re Boustead, ex p
   Rogers* (1881) 16 Ch. D. 665.
[8] This provision also applies where a foreign company is being wound up in England: see
   p. 111, *supra*.
[9] The situation is analogous with that under s. 130(2). Where the English court is conducting
   a winding up the 'property' of the company referred to in s. 130(2) includes property in
   Scotland (see *Martin* v. *Port of Manchester Insurance Co. Ltd.* 1934 S.C. 143, p. 218, *supra*)
   and vice versa.
[10] [1893] 1 Ch. 713.
[11] (1912) 56 Sol. Jo. 290.

of furthcoming was the means by which a creditor realised the benefit of earlier arrestments, leave was given to bring proceedings in Scotland. But it is important to note that although the English court may give leave to a creditor with a prior arrestment to proceed in Scotland, the Scottish court may (acting under section 185(4) of the Insolvency Act 1986) cut down a diligence executed within 60 days of the winding up order. (The relationship between the English court granting leave and the Scottish court's exercise of its powers to cut down a diligence is considered below.)

In *Re West Cumberland Iron and Steel Co.* and *Re National Provincial Insurance Corpn. Ltd.* the arrestments were prior to the winding up petition. However, in some instances, the presence of yet earlier voluntary winding up proceedings may necessitate a somewhat more particular analysis. Section 128(1) of the Insolvency Act 1986 provides that where an English company is being wound up by the court 'any attachment, sequestration, distress or execution put into force against the estate or effects of the company after the commencement of the winding up is void'.[12] Despite use of the word 'void', it is well-established that the court has a discretion to permit such attachments and grant leave under section 130(1) for a creditor to proceed.[13] The 'commencement of the winding up' referred to in section 128(1) is further elaborated in section 129, as follows:

> '(1) If, before the presentation of a petition for the winding up of a company by the court, a resolution has been passed by the company for voluntary winding up, the winding up of the company is deemed to have commenced at the time of the passing of the resolution . . .
> (2) In any other case, the winding up of a company by the court is deemed to commence at the time of the presentation of the petition for winding up.'

Accordingly, if an English company passes a resolution for a voluntary winding up and subsequently a creditor obtains letters of arrestment in Scotland, such arrestment may be rendered ineffective pursuant to section 128(1) and section 130(2). The relevant authority on this point is *Re New Thurso Gas Co.*[14] The company passed a resolution for a voluntary winding up in August 1887. In November 1887 creditors obtained judgment against the company in Scotland and, in April 1888, letters of arrestment were issued. In June 1888 a petition was presented for winding up the company and the relevant order made. Kay J, noting that the winding up commenced in August 1887, refused to permit the creditors to gain any priority by reason of the later arrestment in Scotland. His Lordship did not injunct the creditors, but ordered that they 'do all in their power to enable the liquidators to get in the assets of the company in Scotland'.[15] In addition, it is to be stressed that even if there is no winding up by the court, a creditor will not be permitted to gain an advantage by an arrestment of assets in Scotland after the passing of the resolution for a voluntary winding up. For section 112(1) of the Insolvency Act 1986 gives the court power in a voluntary winding up to make any order which would be available in a compulsory winding up.

---

[12] See also n. 8, *supra*.
[13] *Re New Thurso Gas Co.* (1889) 42 Ch. D. 486 and *Re Lineas Navieras Bolivianas S.A.M.* [1995] B.C.C. 666.
[14] (1889) 42 Ch. D. 486.
[15] *Ibid.*, at 493.

In short, a secured creditor will be granted leave under section 130(2). Leave will also be granted to a creditor who has arrested assets prior to the presentation of the winding up petition and, where relevant, the passing of a resolution for a voluntary winding up.

It is important to recognise, however, that whether or not the English court restrains a creditor is not necessarily the end of the matter.[16] For although the English court will not prevent a creditor with a prior arrestment from proceeding in Scotland, under Scottish law the creditor (even if he establishes his case against the company) may not be allowed to retain the benefit of that arrestment if it was put into effect within the period of 60 days prior to the winding up order. Section 185 of the Insolvency Act 1986 applies; in the case of a company registered in Scotland, relevant parts of section 37 of the Bankruptcy (Scotland) Act 1985. In particular, section 37(2) and (4) of the 1985 Act (as modified in its application to winding up)[17] cuts down an inhibition, arrestment or poinding on the estate of the company within the period of 60 days before the date of the commencement of the winding up. Interestingly, and perhaps a little surprisingly to an English lawyer, where the winding up is by the court the date of commencement is deemed by section 185(3) to mean the day on which the winding up order is made.[18] The relevance of these provisions to English law is clarified by section 185(4) which provides:

> 'This section, so far as relating to any estate or effects of the company situated in Scotland, applies in the case of a company registered in England and Wales as in the case of one registered in Scotland.'

The combined effect of sections 128(1), 130(2) and 185(4), together with the relevant case law from both sides of the border,[19] may be illustrated by way of an example.[20] Let us say that a creditor obtains an arrestment in Scotland on 1 July 1998. Two weeks later a winding up petition is presented in England and on 11 August 1998 a winding up order is made. Firstly, the Scottish court must at once stay any proceedings in Scotland on account of the direct operation of section 130(2).[1] The Scottish court will await a decision from the court conducting the winding up in England as to whether the creditor may proceed in Scotland. Second, the English court, assuming that it follows existing authority, will not restrain the creditor in our example because the attachment is prior to the commencement of the English winding up (and therefore also falls outside section 128(1)). Third, when the creditor returns to the Scottish court he will be disappointed to learn that Scottish law cuts down diligence within the period of 60 days prior to the making of the winding up order (see section 185(3) above).

---

[16] An example can be found in *Radford & Bright Ltd.* v. *Stevenson & Co.* (1904) 6 F. 429, 11 S.L.T. 695: proceedings stayed in Scotland pending decision from English court conducting the winding up (see *Stevenson & Co.* v. *Radford & Bright Ltd.* 1902 10 S.L.T. 82), the English court allowing the action to proceed and the Scottish court ultimately finding in favour of the liquidator and recalling arrestments.

[17] See s. 185(2) of the Insolvency Act 1986.

[18] For details see *Palmer's Company Insolvency in Scotland* (1993), Bennett (ed.) pp. 217–218.

[19] *Martin* v. *Port of Manchester Insurance Co. Ltd.* 1934 S.C. 143, p. 218, *supra* and *Re Hermann Loog Ltd.* (1887) 36 Ch.D. 502. It will also be noted that, applying *Re Lineas Navieras Bolivianas S.A.M.* [1995] B.C.C. 666, see p. 111 above, that s.185(4) will also apply when a foreign company is being wound up in England.

[20] Cf. *Re National Provincial Insurance Corpn. Ltd.* (1912) 56 Sol. Jo. 290, *supra*.

[1] *Martin* v. *Port of Manchester Insurance Co. Ltd.*, *supra*.

In more general terms, it is relevant to observe that the legislation allows a liquidator to get, as it were, 'two bites of the cherry'. If the attachment in Scotland is after the *presentation of the petition* in England then the English court will restrain the arresting creditor (and that decision will of course be respected in Scotland). The English court may restrain a creditor even though under Scottish law the arrestment would not be set aside – because it occurred more than 60 days prior to the making of the *winding up order*. Yet if the arrestment is prior to the presentation of the petition (i.e. the English court will not restrain the creditor), but nevertheless within 60 days of the making of the winding up order, then the liquidator can have the Scottish court set aside the arrestment.[2]

As a matter of general principle, therefore, it emerges that there is no objection to an English liquidator applying to a foreign court to set aside an attachment (or other transaction) even though under English law that attachment (or other transaction) may be unimpeachable. This author would suggest that this principle is useful not only in relation to Anglo-Scottish liquidations, but also when it comes to putting cases such as *Barclays Bank plc* v. *Homan*[3] into a broader conceptual framework.

Finally, there remain two cases which require some comment, not least because they appear inconsistent with the above analysis. In *Re International Pulp and Paper Co.* Jessel MR, it will be recalled, restrained an Irish creditor from proceeding with an action in Ireland. However, the report reveals that a month before the winding up commenced in England the creditor had registered judgment in Ireland against the company 'and had thus a charge on the company's Irish property'.[4] Accordingly, prior to the English winding up the creditor had obtained security. The significance of such a charge under Irish law was not mentioned by counsel or the Master of the Rolls, nor has the issue been picked up in later authorities. Nevertheless, if facts similar to those in *Re International Pulp and Paper Co.* were to occur today, a secured creditor would undoubtedly be given leave under section 130(2) of the Insolvency Act 1986.[5] Whereas, if the facts of *Re Field Ltd.*[6] were to reoccur, an injunction would most certainly issue. A winding up petition was presented on 20th June 1900 and, two days later, a provisional liquidator was appointed. The winding up order was made on 10th July 1900. On 18th July 1900 the creditor obtained judgment in Scotland. On 13th August 1900 execution was issued, it being proposed that the company's assets in Scotland would be sold. Farwell J is very briefly reported as having refused an injunction, which might be 'an interference with the Scotch courts'.[7] To the extent that *Re Field Ltd.* suggests that a creditor will be allowed the benefit of execution put into force after the making of a winding up order, or the appointment of a provisional

---

[2] Unless the company has already paid the claim of the creditor, whereupon the diligence lapses: see *Palmer, supra* n.18, at 218.
[3] [1993] B.C.L.C. 680, p. 332, *infra*.
[4] (1876) 3 Ch. D. 594 at 595.
[5] *Re Wanzer Ltd.* [1891] 1 Ch. 305, *Re West Cumberland Iron and Steel Co.* [1893] 1 Ch. 713 and *Re National Provincial Insurance Corpn. Ltd.* (1912) 56 Sol. Jo. 290.
[6] (1900) 44 Sol. Jo. 689.
[7] *Ibid.*

liquidator, the decision is inconsistent with both prior and subsequent authority[8] and should not be followed.

(iii) *Northern Irish Proceedings*

The Companies Act 1862 made provision for the establishment of companies in the United Kingdom. Accordingly, it was considered in *Re International Pulp and Paper Co.* that section 87 should be construed as conferring, upon the court conducting the winding up, jurisdiction to restrain actions in any part of the United Kingdom: that is, in Scotland or in Ireland. However, since 1932 Northern Ireland has had its own companies legislation.[9] Thus there is some question[10] whether the power to restrain proceedings should now be interpreted in a different manner, particularly as section 130(2) of the Insolvency Act 1986 is not one of those provisions (by section 441) extended to Northern Ireland.

Section 130(2) gives the court power to restrain an 'action or proceeding'. Section 87 of the Act of 1862, which referred to an 'action, suit or proceeding', was interpreted as encompassing an action, suit or proceeding in any part of the United Kingdom. In the Companies (Consolidation) Act 1908, in force prior to the division of Ireland, the current wording was used;[11] and must have meant an action or proceeding in any part of the United Kingdom. Certainly, this view has been taken by the Court of Appeal in Northern Ireland.[12] That section 130(2) of the Insolvency Act 1986 does not extend to Northern Ireland may affect the content of the law of Northern Ireland, but it does not prevent the English court from exercising its jurisdiction founded upon the general words of the subsection and restraining a creditor's action in Northern Ireland.

B. *In Personam* Jurisdiction

(i) *Outline*

Leaving aside statutory provisions, the English court has a broad power when conducting bankruptcy or winding up proceedings to restrain a creditor amenable to the jurisdiction[13] from prosecuting a foreign action. (The position in relation to administration is considered separately, below.) Of course, the English court would not attempt directly to halt an action under way in New York or Hong Kong, instead the court may act *in personam* and restrain a creditor by injunction from proceeding with a foreign action – although in many instances it may be more appropriate for

---

[8]   *Re West Cumberland Iron and Steel Co.* [1893] 1 Ch. 713, *Re National Provincial Insurance Corpn. Ltd.* (1912) 56 Sol. Jo. 290 and *Re Hermann Loog Ltd.* (1887) 36 Ch. D. 502.

[9]   See, generally, *Boyd* v. *Lee Guinness Ltd.* [1963] N.I. 49.

[10] See also Insolvency Act 1986, s. 126(1)(a).

[11] Section 142 of the 1908 Act provided: 'When a winding up order has been made, no action or proceeding shall be proceeded with or commenced against the company except by leave of the court. . . .'

[12] *Boyd* v. *Lee Guinness Ltd.* [1963] N.I. 49 (Lord MacDermott CJ dissenting).

[13] That is, generally speaking, a creditor resident in England or a foreign creditor who has proved in the English insolvency.

an English trustee or liquidator first to seek relevant relief from the foreign court itself (this will particularly be the case where there are foreign creditors who do not participate in the English insolvency). The circumstances in which such inherent power is likely to be invoked are revealed by the following illustrations. In *Re Distin*[14] injunctions issued to prevent English creditors from maintaining actions in Belgium. In *Re Tait*[15] an Irish creditor, who had entered a claim in the English bankruptcy, was restrained from pursuing an action in Ireland. Whilst in *Re North Carolina Estate Co.*[16] a creditor, who was resident in England and had entered a proof in the English winding up, was to be restrained from continuing an action in the courts of North Carolina. Whereas an injunction will not issue in respect of a foreign creditor who enters no claim in the English insolvency proceedings.[17] The nature of the jurisdiction was considered by Robert Goff LJ in *Bank of Tokyo Ltd.* v. *Karoon* in the following terms:[18]

'In the course of the 19th century, there developed a line of cases in which assets were being administered by the English court, and one interested person sought to gain an advantage over other interested persons by prosecuting proceedings in a foreign country where part of the assets were situated. In such cases, for example, where a person sought in this way to gain the benefit of foreign assets . . . of a bankrupt after his petition in bankruptcy (see, e.g., *In re Distin*), or of a company after winding up proceedings had been commenced (see, e.g. *In re North Carolina Estate Co. Ltd.*), such a person has been restrained by injunction from pursuing foreign proceedings, but only if he were a domiciled Englishman or otherwise amenable to the jurisdiction of the English court.'

It scarcely needs to be highlighted that an injunction does not issue as of right. Thus a most significant distinction has been drawn, not least in the early cases, between the existence of the jurisdiction to restrain a creditor and the exercise thereof. However, it is worthy of note that restraining an English creditor will in no way prevent foreign creditors from attaching and dividing up the insolvent's property abroad,[19] at least where the foreign creditors have entered no proof in the English proceedings. (Although in such a case the English court would readily allow an English creditor to proceed abroad upon an undertaking to hand over any realisations to the English trustee or liquidator;[20] it would also be within the court's power to grant leave to proceed abroad upon the (less stringent) condition that the hotchpot rule apply to whatever the creditor recovered abroad[1] – but this would only be done where it was quite clear that there was no possibility of the English trustee or liquidator being able in one way or another to recover the assets in question for the benefit of all the creditors.)

---

[14] (1871) 24 L.T. 197, approved in *Re Paramount Airways Ltd.* [1993] Ch. 223.
[15] (1872) L.R. 13 Eq. 311.
[16] (1889) 5 T.L.R. 328, approved most recently in *Mitchell* v. *Carter* [1997] 1 B.C.L.C. 673.
[17] *Re Chapman* (1872) L.R. 15 Eq. 75, *Re Vocalion (Foreign) Ltd.* [1932] 2 Ch. 196 at 209–210 *per* Maugham J. See also *Carron Iron Co.* v. *Maclaren* (1855) 5 H.L. Cas. 416 wherein the House of Lords (by a majority), in the context of an administration, held against restraining a Scottish company, but with an office and assets in England, from carrying on proceedings in Scotland.
[18] [1987] 1 A.C. 45n. at 60.
[19] See *per* Maugham J in *Re Vocalion (Foreign) Ltd.* [1932] 2 Ch. 196 at 205.
[20] This was accepted by Lord St. Leonards in *Carron Iron Co.* v. *Maclaren* (1855) 5 H.L. Cas. 416 at 458.
[1] So that the creditor could retain the moneys recovered but not claim any dividend in England until an equivalent level of distribution had occurred, see *supra*.

(ii) *Existence of Jurisdiction*

In *Pennell* v. *Roy*[2] a creditor resident in England had brought an action in the courts of Scotland against assignees of an English bankrupt. Kindersley V-C granted an injunction but that determination was reversed on appeal, Knight Bruce LJ commenting:[3]

> 'A creditor who has not proved or claimed, nor seeks to prove or claim under an English bankruptcy, is under no more obligation, nor owes any more duty to the assignees or the other creditors, than he would if he were no creditor at all, and consequently, if he enters into a foolish and perverse litigation with the assignees, they must defend themselves as other men do. . . .'

The observation of the learned Lord Justice must, however, now be wholly disregarded. For whereas it is certain that the court will not restrain a creditor resident abroad who has entered no claim,[4] the authorities establish that residence in England is in itself sufficient to found jurisdiction against a creditor who institutes a foreign suit.[5]

Any creditor, irrespective of residence, who claims in English insolvency proceedings may also be restrained.[6] It is submitted (though the Scottish court has apparently held otherwise[7]) that nothing short of coming in under an English bankruptcy or winding up will suffice. In *Pacific Coast Mining Co. Ltd.* v. *Walker*[8] the respondents had brought two sets of proceedings against the company: one in San Francisco and another (upon a different cause of action[9]) in the Court of Session. The company was being wound up in Scotland and the liquidators sought an order restraining the respondents from carrying on with the proceedings in San Francisco. The respondents were not resident in Scotland, nor had they entered a claim in the winding up. But the respondents had, after commencement of the winding up, sought leave to continue their Scottish action. The Scottish court held that jurisdiction had been made out and restrained the respondents. The Lord President opined that 'the fact of the dependence of these actions is sufficient to bring them within the jurisdiction of this court'.[10] No English authority has gone so far as *Pacific Coast Mining Co. Ltd.* v. *Walker*, and the decision should not be followed in England. For the respondents had not sought to take a 'distributive share'[11] under the

---

[2] (1853) 3 De G.M. & G. 126.

[3] *Ibid.*, at 134. The Scottish court ultimately left the dispute to be decided in the Court of Bankruptcy in England: *Roy* v. *Campbell* (1850) 12 D. 1028 and (1853) 16 D. 51.

[4] See *Re Chapman* (1872) L.R. 15 Eq. 75. In *Re Boyse* (1880) 15 Ch. D. 591 (administration of an estate) it seems to have been overlooked that the claimants, although foreigners resident abroad, had entered a claim in England.

[5] *Re Distin* (1871) 24 L.T. 197. The creditors in *Jones* v. *Geddes* (1845) 1 Ph. 724 and *Re Central Sugar Factories of Brazil* [1894] 1 Ch. 369 were resident in England.

[6] *Carron Iron Co.* v. *Maclaren* (1855) 5 H.L. Cas. 416 at 442–443, *Re Vocalion (Foreign) Ltd.* [1932] 2 Ch. 196 at 210 and *Re Tait* (1872) L.R. 13 Eq. 311. See also *Re Belfast Shipowners Co.* [1894] 1 I.R. 321.

[7] *Pacific Coast Mining Co. Ltd.* v. *Walker, infra.*

[8] (1886) 13 R. 816.

[9] Of course, if a creditor has brought the same action in England and abroad an injunction may issue under the general rules of private international law: see *Société Nationale Industrielle Aérospatiale* v. *Lee Kui Jak* [1987] A.C. 871 and the discussion of *Barclays Bank plc* v. *Homan* [1993] B.C.L.C. 680, p. 332 *infra.*

[10] (1886) 13 R. 816 at 818; see also [1886] W.N. 63.

[11] To use the words of Bayley J in *Phillips* v. *Allan* (1828) 8 B. & C. 477 at 483 in the context of participation by an English creditor in a foreign insolvency.

insolvency; no claim whatsoever had been made in the winding up. More-over, that the respondents were parties to an *action* in Scotland was simply irrelevant, for the order restraining the respondents was not made in the course of that action but under the winding up. If such a fact situation were to occur in England, the court could properly go no further than discontinuing the English action or allowing it to continue on terms (see sections 130(2) and 285(1)), but the English court cannot injunct a creditor resident abroad who has not entered a claim in the English insolvency.

(iii) *Theoretical Considerations*

Although it is easily stated that the English court may restrain a creditor if that creditor is (a) resident in England or (b) has entered a proof in the English insolvency, the precise basis of this jurisdiction is far from certain.[12] In particular it must be asked whether the insolvency cases are just illustrations of the exercise by the English court of the more general jurisdiction, applicable in ordinary civil litigation, to injunct a party from commencing or continuing proceedings as a plaintiff in a foreign court. Certainly, cases such as *Re Distin* and *Re North Carolina Estate Co. Ltd.* have been cited more than once in recent years by judges dealing with ordinary civil litigation,[13] in which context it is now clear that an injunction will only be granted if it is established that the foreign proceedings are 'vexatious or oppressive'.[14]

On the other hand, the language of vexation and oppression does not always appear in the insolvency cases; and some of the cases[15] might be read as suggesting that when the English court is administering assets its power to injunct is independent of any question of vexation. In addition, an injunction may issue regardless of whether the foreign action was begun prior to the commencement of the insolvency in England: in other words, when the foreign action was begun in no way could it be regarded as improper or vexatious – the 'trigger' for the injunction was not the nature or character of the action itself but rather the making in England of the bankruptcy or winding up order. Moreover, in the context of ordinary civil litigation (in the form of a *lis inter partes*) it is always stressed that the English court exercises its power to injunct only with very great caution; yet if an English creditor commences an action abroad against a company in liquidation in England, one *prima facie* expects an injunction to issue.

Nevertheless, this author would suggest that it is not helpful to regard the insolvency cases as in some way cut off or segregated from the more general jurisdiction to restrain foreign proceedings. The power to injunct

---

[12] Although it is clear enough that the mere fact that an injunction (if granted) could be enforced in England, e.g. against property of the creditor, is not sufficient to found jurisdiction: *Carron Iron Co.* v. *Maclaren* (1855) 5 H.L. Cas. 416.

[13] See *Bank of Tokyo Ltd.* v. *Karoon*, p. 285, *supra* and *Société Nationale Industrielle Aérospatielle* v. *Lee Kui Jak* [1987] A.C. 871 at 892, as well as *Barclays Bank plc* v. *Homan* [1993] B.C.L.C. 680 at 686 (although the facts here involved an administration, it was not a case of restraining a creditor) and *Mitchell* v. *Carter* [1997] 1 B.C.L.C. 673, see further p. 334, *infra*.

[14] *Société Nationale Industrielle Aérospatielle* v. *Lee Kui Jak*, *supra* and *Airbus Industrie GIE* v. *Patel* [1998] 2 All E.R. 257.

[15] See, for example, the speech of the Lord Chancellor in *Carron Iron Co.* v. *Maclaren* (1855) 5 H.L. Cas. 416 at 438–429.

where there is an insolvency in England does not 'stand alone'. The language of vexation and oppression is unobjectionable once it is accepted that for an unsecured creditor subject to English insolvency law[16] to commence or continue an action abroad[17] is by its very nature vexatious or oppressive in (at least) two distinct regards. Firstly, the English liquidator or trustee is put in a position where he must spend time and money defending the action abroad and trying to prevent the creditor from taking foreign assets for himself: this will delay the administration by the liquidator or trustee and the costs incurred[18] will deplete the fund ultimately for distribution to the available creditors. Second, and more importantly, other (unsecured) creditors are put in an intolerable position: if there is no injunction, they must either stand by and watch the plaintiff in the foreign action sweep off the foreign assets or themselves start proceedings in the foreign court to try to get a share of those assets. If vexation and oppression are viewed in this light, it is suggested that the insolvency cases should be seen as part of a broader and more comprehensive jurisdiction.[19] The most recent judicial pronouncement seems to take this approach, treating the insolvency jurisdiction as simply an example of when an anti-suit injunction may be granted.[20] Indeed, there is one very definite advantage to taking such an approach (see the discussion below in relation to administration orders.)

(iv) *Exercise of Jurisdiction*

Although the general purpose in restraining a creditor is to protect and enforce the authority of the English court over assets of the insolvent, an injunction will not issue automatically. The matter requires an exercise of discretion by the court. Thus an injunction will be refused should convenience favour the continuation of the foreign action. It may be noted that Lord Cranworth LC in *Carron Iron Co.* v. *Maclaren*, an administration case, observed that the court would not interfere 'if from any cause it appears likely to be more conducive to substantial justice that the foreign proceedings should be left to take their course'.[1] For example, if the debtor altogether denies liability under a contract governed by the law of New York and an action is already under way in New York, it is likely to be more convenient for the question of liability to be determined in New York,

---

[16] Particularly, a creditor who has entered a claim or is resident in England.

[17] It being intended that assets abroad will be seized to satisfy any judgment obtained in the action.

[18] Even if the liquidator is successful abroad, it is unlikely that all the costs would be recouped.

[19] A case might arise where a non-resident creditor, who had not entered a claim, were present in England and thus could be served in England. Such a creditor might be said to be 'amenable to the jurisdiction of the English court' (to use the words of Robert Goff LJ in *Bank of Tokyo Ltd.* v. *Karoon*, set out at p. 285, *supra*). Nevertheless, there can be no doubt that the court would in the exercise of its discretion decline to issue an injunction, even if it could be argued that in strict theory there might be jurisdiction in such a case: see *Mitchell* v. *Carter* [1997] 1 B.C.L.C. 673 at 687, stressing *residence* in England.

[20] *Per* Millett LJ in *Mitchell* v. *Carter* [1997] 1 B.C.L.C. 673 at 687, see further p. 334, *infra*.

[1] *Ibid.*, at 439; or as Lord Lyndhurst LC had earlier put it (in *Jones* v. *Geddes* (1845) 1 Ph. 724 at 727): 'Upon the whole, then, after weighing the conveniences and inconveniences of the different courses to be adopted, I think it is not advisable to interfere . . . and that the injunction ought, therefore, to be dissolved.'

the plaintiff in New York, if judgment is recovered, thereafter entering a claim in the English insolvency (but not attaching assets in New York).[2] Similarly, undertakings given by a creditor may make an injunction simply unnecessary. Hence in *Re Newton, ex p Bankrupt* v. *Aldergate Films*[3] Dankwerts J refused to restrain the creditor (an English company) from proceeding with an action against the bankrupt in California, upon the creditor undertaking to bring into the English bankruptcy any assets that might be recovered in the courts of California.

Nor will an injunction issue if the consequences thereof would be unfair to the creditor. This is of particular relevance when turning to consider the position of secured creditors.

(a) *Secured and attaching creditors.* A secured creditor will not be restrained from enforcing his security in a foreign court, although it has been suggested[4] that the creditor ought properly to obtain permission from the English court before proceeding abroad. Thus in *Moor* v. *Anglo-Italian Bank*[5] Jessel MR declined to restrain mortgage creditors under Italian law, over whom the English court had jurisdiction, from realising their security by means of a judicial sale of property in Florence. More generally, only in rare cases would the court restrain a creditor who has brought an action abroad to establish rights in respect of foreign immovable property. That a secured creditor will not normally be restrained mirrors the application of the hotchpot rule. For just as a secured creditor may realise his security abroad and claim for any balance in the English insolvency without bringing into the common fund sums recovered abroad, that creditor obviously will not be prevented from bringing proceedings in the foreign court to enforce his security.

So too an attaching creditor who has, prior to the commencement of the English insolvency, obtained security over movable property abroad should not be restrained. In *Re Vocalion (Foreign) Ltd.* Maugham J, with reference to English winding up proceedings, observed:[6]

'it seems that a creditor who has obtained in a foreign country security on personal property ought not in equity to be deprived of his rights because of a supervening statutable trust for creditors of a debtor.'

His Lordship might, perhaps, have put the proposition yet more strongly had he been referred to *Re West Cumberland Iron and Steel Co.*[7] For there the court declined to injunct an English creditor who had attached assets in Scotland, thereby obtaining security under Scots law, prior to the commencement of insolvency proceedings in England. But, as a matter of principle, a creditor will not be allowed to acquire security by an

---

[2] In *Re Queensland Mercantile Agency Co. Ltd.* (1888) 58 L.T. 878 North J, acting pursuant to the provisions of the Companies Act 1862, determined that proceedings under way in Scotland were to be stayed and the matter be investigated *de novo* in the courts of Queensland: see further chapter 14.

[3] [1956] C.L.Y. 6984.

[4] *Per* Jessel MR in *Re Boustead, ex p Rogers* (1881) 16 Ch. D. 665 at 667.

[5] (1879) 10 Ch. D. 681. Note also *Ferguson's Trustee* v. *Ferguson* 1990 S.L.T. (Sh. Ct.) 73, discussed p. 308, *post.*

[6] [1932] 2 Ch. 196 at 206.

[7] [1893] 1 Ch. 713, *supra.* An injunction may nevertheless issue if the attaching creditor has committed fraud: *Mackintosh* v. *Ogilvie* (1747) 3 Swan. 380 n.

attachment in a foreign court *subsequent* to the commencement of the English insolvency.[8]

(b) *Actions in rem.* A judgment of a foreign court pronounced *in rem* has traditionally been regarded by the English court as good against all the world. In *Minna Craig SS Co.* v. *Chartered Mercantile Bank of India, London and China*[9] a winding up order was made in England in respect of an English company, the owner of the *Minna Craig*. Immediately thereafter a court in Germany pronounced a judgment *in rem* in favour of the defendants. Subsequently, the English liquidator brought proceedings in England in an attempt to force the defendants to disgorge the amount of money recovered under the German judgment. The Court of Appeal held in favour of the defendants as holders of a lien: 'an authoritative and final declaration of right under a judgment *in rem*'.[10] Lord Esher MR commented:[11]

> 'They received the money which was paid to them by order of the German Court, but as being persons declared by the decree of the Court to have a lien on the ship, and to be therefore interested in the proceeds of her sale to the extent of that lien.'

However, it is pertinent to observe that nothing in the judgments delivered in the Court of Appeal touches upon the power of the court to restrain a creditor amenable to the jurisdiction. At the time the English winding up order was made, it would appear that the defendants had no lien whatsoever under German law and were not secured creditors. Thus, in accordance with established authority, the English court could at that time have restrained the defendants as creditors who had not then any lien or security, but were seeking to gain such a priority by the institution of proceedings in a foreign court after the making of the winding up order. Perhaps surprisingly, no argument on the restraining of creditors was addressed to their Lordships.

Minna Craig Steamship Co. v. *Chartered Mercantile Bank of India, London and China* must, of course, be followed in the Supreme Court.[12] However, it would be most unfortunate should the judgment of the Court of Appeal be taken as in any way restricting the power to injunct a creditor. It would be unsatisfactory indeed if English creditors, perhaps even with notice of a winding up or bankruptcy, were considered free to institute proceedings *in rem* abroad in order to obtain a lien or security not in existence at the time of the commencement of English insolvency proceedings. In *Re Jenkins and Co. Ltd.*[13] a company, owners of the *Denbighshire*, was being wound up in England when the respondents arrested the ship in

---

[8] The point emerges clearly in *Re West Cumberland Iron and Steel Co.*, *supra*, but relevant authority dates back to *Hunter* v. *Potts* (1791) 4 Term Rep 182. In *Re Central Sugar Factories of Brazil; Flack's Case* [1894] 1 Ch. 369 it may have been overlooked that, at the time the winding up order was made in England, Flack was not a secured creditor under the law of Brazil.

[9] [1897] 1 Q.B. 460.

[10] *Ibid.*, at 470 *per* Chitty LJ.

[11] *Ibid.*, at 465–466.

[12] A German court (*semble*) would not now generally have jurisdiction to pronounce a judgment *in rem* against a defendant domiciled in England, on account of the Brussels Convention: see *The Deichland* [1990] 1 Q.B. 361, *passim*.

[13] (1907) 51 Sol. Jo. 715. Note also *Re Belfast Shipowners Co. Ltd.* [1894] 1 I.R. 321.

Germany. The respondents had made a claim in the English winding up; and the question was whether the respondents, assuming they would obtain a lien by German law, ought to be restrained. Pickford J granted an injunction, relying upon section 85 of the Companies Act 1862:[14]

> 'It was said that because German law did give this advantage he ought not to interfere. He did not agree with that contention. Section 85 gave him the power to prevent this advantage accruing to these particular creditors, and the case of *North Carolina Estate Co.* shewed that the fact that proceedings were taking place in a foreign court did not deprive him of that power. There were no special circumstances to induce him to restrain from granting the application, for it was admitted by the respondents that if the ship had been arrested in England they could not have resisted an injunction.'

Unfortunately, the report does not indicate whether the decision of the Court of Appeal was cited before Pickford J. (In addition Pickford J did not clearly distinguish the statutory power to restrain actions and the broader *in personam* jurisdiction.) Nevertheless, *Re Jenkins and Co. Ltd.* is in line with earlier authority. To conclude, whatever may be the position when a judgment *in rem* has actually been recovered abroad, the English court may restrain a creditor (who is not already in the position of a secured creditor) from instituting *in rem* proceedings in a foreign court subsequent to the commencement of an English bankruptcy or winding up.

(c) *Foreign partnerships.* That one member of a foreign partnership is resident in England and has been declared bankrupt here, does not enable the English court to restrain creditors from bringing an action against the partnership in a foreign court. For the cases, both English and Scottish, reveal a distinction between the individual partner and the rights of the firm as a whole. The point may be illustrated by the decision of the Master of the Rolls in *Brickwood* v. *Miller.*[15] The bankrupt, a partner in two firms established in the West Indies, conducted the business of the English branch of the two firms. The defendant, resident in England, had attached property belonging to the two firms in the West Indies, and the English assignees sought to compel the defendant to account for what had been received under the attachments. It was held that the bankruptcy in England of one of the members of a foreign partnership did not prevent the foreign partners from paying partnership debts abroad. So too, a partnership creditor was not obliged to refund money received or recovered abroad:[16]

> 'How are the West Indian partners to be controlled in the management of their trade, or restrained, by any proceedings here, from paying and applying the partnership assets as they think fit? Equality of distribution cannot possibly be attained. Are we then to tell a creditor, that, because he happens to reside in England, and his debt has been contracted there, he shall not be allowed to take such remedies against his foreign debtor as the laws of their country may

---

[14] *Ibid.* Section 85 (although Pickford J may have meant s. 87) provided: 'The court may, at any time after the presentation of a petition for winding up a company under this Act, and before making an order for winding up . . . restrain further proceedings in any action, suit or proceeding against the company. . . .' Pickford J apparently did not appreciate that the provisions of the Companies Act were limited to the United Kingdom. His Lordship should have relied upon the court's *in personam* jurisdiction.

[15] (1817) 3 Mer. 279.

[16] *Ibid.*, at 283–284.

permit? . . . [the court] cannot, in this case, reach the West Indian property, or bind the West Indian partners. Then you would take from the partnership creditor one remedy, without substituting any other in the place of it. This would be to say, that the West Indian property must be left for any creditors but English creditors.

Then, if English creditors are not to be restrained from suing, it would be incongruous to force them to refund what they have recovered abroad.'

Thus the defendant, an English resident creditor, was allowed to retain money recovered in the West Indies in respect of debts owing to him by the West Indian firms. Sir William Grant made it quite plain that the decision would have gone the other way had the bankrupt been a sole trader in England or a member of an insolvent English partnership.

Reference may also be made to *California Redwood Co. Ltd.* v. *Walker*[17] (the reverse situation). The liquidator of a Scottish company applied for an interdict restraining proceedings brought in California by a Californian partnership. For the liquidator it was argued that, as one of the partners of the Californian firm was amenable to the jurisdiction of the Scottish courts, an order might issue. The liquidator's application was refused. The court considered 'nothing could be more inexpedient or unjust' than to seek to restrain a partnership suit brought in a foreign court to enforce a partnership debt, when the court had no jurisdiction whatsoever over one of the partners thereof.[18] An injunction would, however, issue in respect of such a suit should the foreign partnership in question enter a claim in the local liquidation.

(d) *Ex p Tait.* The distinction between an individual partner and the firm drawn in *Brickwood* v. *Miller* and *California Redwood Co. Ltd.* v. *Walker* was, perhaps, somewhat blurred in the judgment of the Chief Judge in *Ex p Tait.*[19] The case is often given as an example of the (undoubted) proposition that the English court may restrain a foreign creditor who enters a proof in an English insolvency. However, the actual facts were a little more complex than might first appear. The insolvent, Sir Peter Tait, was a member of two firms, Tait & Co. and Tait, Abraham & Co. Tait & Co., which had entered into a deed of inspectorship in England, was indebted to Lynch, an Irish creditor, in the sum of £698; Sir Peter Tait was separately indebted to Lynch in the sum of £1548; as against these two sums there was a set off of £545. In addition, the firm of Tait, Abraham & Co. was owed £450 by Lynch. Lynch made a claim for £698 under the deed of inspectorship, which claim was rejected. But Lynch did not claim for the money owed by Sir Peter Tait personally. Thereafter, Lynch brought an action in Ireland against Sir Peter Tait, whose estate was also being administered under the deed of inspectorship in England, for the whole of the joint and separate debts (less the set off). Sir James Bacon would not permit the Irish action to continue:[20]

'The right I have to restrain is a right against Lynch personally, because he has claimed under this deed and sues in respect of a claim under this deed; and

[17] (1886) 13 R. 810.
[18] *Ibid.*, at 815.
[19] (1872) L.R. 13 Eq. 311.
[20] *Ibid.*, at 313.

whatever may be the nature of the claim said to exist, it is clear that he claims to be a creditor under the deed.'

The Chief Judge also required that an action by Tait, Abraham & Co. against Lynch be stayed, although in subsequent proceedings that action was allowed to continue on the basis 'that there was no kind of connection between the circumstances under which the two actions respectively were brought'.[1] On the facts in *Ex p Tait* the Irish creditor was properly restrained, for the Irish action included the very debt which had already been claimed in the English insolvency of Tait & Co. However, the position would surely have been different had the foreign creditor brought an action in Ireland merely in respect of the separate debt of Sir Peter Tait. In such a case there would be no overlap between the English claim (against the partnership for a joint debt) and the Irish action (against Sir Peter Tait for a separate debt).

(e) *English and oversea companies.* That the court may injunct a creditor resident in England requires some elaboration in respect of corporate creditors. A company registered in England plainly falls within the jurisdiction. It would seem that a foreign corporation with a branch or representative office in England (whether or not registered as an oversea company under the Companies Act 1985) is resident in England in this context. However, the English court is reluctant in the exercise of jurisdiction over such a corporation. *Re Vocalion (Foreign) Ltd.*[2] concerned an English company, being wound up in England, which had carried on business in Australia. Prior to the liquidation, the Bank of New South Wales, registered in England as an oversea company,[3] had brought proceedings against the company in Melbourne, Victoria. Maugham J granted leave for the Bank to carry on with the proceedings in Victoria:[4]

> 'the court ought *prima facie* not to exercise the equitable jurisdiction which, as I have held, exists, for the reason that in general it will be more conducive in such a case to substantial justice that the foreign proceedings should be allowed to proceed . . . In considering this question I must assume that the Supreme Court in Melbourne will properly deal with the matter, and will not disregard so far as may be material the legal effects of the liquidation of the company. . . .'

In comparison, it may be noted that the English court has restricted individual creditors resident in England from pursuing actions abroad, even where such actions were already on foot prior to the English insolvency.[5] *Re Vocalion (Foreign) Ltd.*, however, should not be seen as providing a blanket exception for foreign companies with a branch in England. For on the facts the Bank appeared to be a secured creditor and, in any event, Maugham J seemed to accept (as must have been the case) that under the law of Victoria an unsecured creditor (if the Bank was indeed unsecured) would not be allowed to obtain the benefit of an attachment or execution after the commencement of the winding up in England.

---

[1] (1872) 52 L.T. Jo. 293.
[2] [1932] 2 Ch. 196, approved recently in *Mitchell* v. *Carter* [1997] 1 B.C.L.C. 673.
[3] That the Bank had registered as an oversea company meant the Bank was subject to the ordinary civil jurisdiction of the court, but it did not follow that an injunction would issue: [1932] 2 Ch. 196 at 210.
[4] *Ibid.*, at 210–211: it also appeared that the Bank was a secured creditor in Victoria.
[5] As, for example, in *Re Distin* (1871) 24 L.T. 197.

If a similar situation were to arise today and it was made clear that the foreign corporation (with a branch in England) was an unsecured creditor and was trying to put into effect a subsequent attachment in the foreign proceedings, this author would suggest that an injunction would likely issue. Certainly, if the foreign corporation entered a proof in England, *Re Vocalion (Foreign) Ltd.* would be readily distinguishable.[6]

(v) *Summary*

The English court may act *in personam* against a creditor to restrain an action brought in a foreign court, provided the creditor is resident in England or has entered a claim in the English insolvency. (Note also the operation of section 426 of the Insolvency Act 1986, below.) The exercise of the *in personam* jurisdiction is a matter of discretion. In general, an injunction will not issue where substantial justice favours the continuation of the foreign action, or where the creditor has obtained security in the foreign court prior to the commencement of the English insolvency proceedings. But, once the English insolvency is under way, an unsecured creditor amenable to the jurisdiction will be prevented from taking steps in a foreign court to gain a priority over the general body of creditors.

The *in personam* jurisdiction operates in conjunction with the hotchpot rule. As we have seen, an injunction will not normally issue to restrain a secured creditor. Similarly, a secured creditor may realise his security abroad and claim for any outstanding balance unrestricted by the hotchpot rule. Whereas if a foreign unsecured creditor claims in England and also then brings an action abroad, the court may act *in personam* to restrain the creditor or, in the alternative, require an undertaking that the creditor hand over money recovered abroad to the English trustee or liquidator. Lastly, if a foreign creditor has already recovered money in a foreign action, and only then proves in England, it will be too late to restrain the foreign action: here the hotchpot rule will apply. The foreign creditor will receive no dividend in England until the other creditors have received dividends equivalent to the amount recovered in the foreign action.

It must be noted that the *in personam* jurisdiction is used to restrain foreign actions. There is not one reported instance wherein the English court has prevented a creditor, foreign or English, from entering a claim in a foreign insolvency.[7] No doubt this is, at least in part, because a creditor

---

[6] Note also *Carron Iron Co.* v. *Maclaren* (1855) 5 H.L. Cas. 416 wherein it was held that there was no jurisdiction (in the context of an administration) to restrain a Scottish company from proceeding against the deceased's estate in Scotland. The company had rented offices in England for its agents, who were paid a salary and had contractual authority to bind the company. The Master of the Rolls (see 22 L.J. Ch. 274) had held that there was jurisdiction as the company (to the extent that a company might be said to be resident anywhere) was 'resident in all the offices where in point of fact it has an agent carrying on business on behalf and in the name of the company' (*ibid.* at 278). Lord St. Leonards agreed with the Master of the Rolls, but Lord Cranworth LC and Lord Brougham did not. The majority felt that the company was not 'so established, or represented, in this country, as to justify the courts in treating them as parties within their jurisdiction' (5 H.L. Cas. at 441). There can be no doubt, however, that now such a company, if for instance it were incorporated in New York, would be required to register under the Companies Act 1985; and, as in *Re Vocalion (Foreign) Ltd.*, there would be jurisdiction to restrain the company from proceeding abroad.

[7] The matter is considered further at p. 307, *post*.

who claims in a foreign insolvency is not seeking to gain a priority over the general body of creditors, but rather to share with other creditors in the insolvent's assets. (The same will generally be true in relation to an English creditor who presents a bankruptcy or winding up petition (or equivalent) in a foreign court.) Indeed, it might seem inconsistent for the English court to restrain a creditor from entering a claim in a foreign insolvency, as the policy of English insolvency law is to permit all creditors, foreign or English, to claim in England. Where a creditor claims in both an English and a foreign insolvency, the hotchpot rule is normally quite sufficient to prevent any prejudice to the general body of creditors in England.

(vi) *Failure to Obey Injunction and Foreign Default Judgments*

The failure of a creditor to comply with an injunction will amount to contempt and be punished accordingly. But it is possible that a creditor might, in breach of an injunction, obtain (default) judgment in the foreign court and then enter a claim in the English insolvency for the amount of the foreign judgment. Leaving aside the penalty for contempt, it is clear that in such a situation the English liquidator or trustee will be entitled to disregard the foreign judgment – even though the foreign court might generally be regarded as being of competent jurisdiction according to principles of English private international law. The creditor may enter a claim in the insolvency, but must establish the basis of that claim (and the amount thereof) without reference to the foreign judgment, obtained as it was in breach of the English injunction.[8]

It is also worthwhile to consider the law applicable in a related situation. There may well be cases where a foreign creditor has begun an action against the debtor in a foreign court (this may or may not be prior to the commencement of the English insolvency). Let us assume that there is no jurisdiction to injunct the creditor and that the foreign court allows the action to continue. The creditor in due course obtains (default) judgment abroad. Subsequently the creditor submits a proof in England in the amount of the foreign judgment. Sir Richard Scott V-C has recently affirmed the long-established practice that a trustee or liquidator is not bound by such a judgment, but can look behind it in order to ascertain the real amount of any indebtedness for the purposes of admission to proof.[9]

(vii) *Ancillary Winding up and Injunctions*

The corporate insolvency cases where the English court has issued injunctions to restrain foreign proceedings have generally involved English companies. The court, however, has an extensive jurisdiction to wind up foreign companies – in particular those which have assets in England or

---

[8] For a Canadian ruling to such effect, see *Re Pittsburgh Cobalt Co.* (1911) 19 O.W.R. 535 (creditor obtaining judgment in Pennsylvania after the making of a winding up order in Ontario and in breach of an injunction issued by the Ontario court, then seeking to enter a proof relying on the foreign judgment).
[9] See *Re Focus Insurance Co. Ltd.* [1996] B.C.C. 659 at 662. This practice is by no means restricted to foreign *default* judgments.

have at some time carried on business in England.[10] In one instance the court, when conducting the winding up of a foreign company, restrained an action under way in Scotland.[11] Although in that case the order was made under a statutory power,[12] rather than the court's *in personam* jurisdiction, it must be that truly foreign proceedings can be restrained under the court's equitable jurisdiction.[13] Indeed, such a course of action was contemplated in the Ontario court in *Re Lake Superior Native Copper Co. Ltd.*[14] An English company, in liquidation in England, was also later put into liquidation in Ontario. After the making of the order in Ontario, Plummer – who was resident in Ontario – brought an action in the United States against the company and attached a ship owned by the company. The judge in Ontario held that there was jurisdiction to restrain Plummer, but decided on the facts that such jurisdiction would not be exercised.

(viii) *Insolvency Act 1986, Section 426*

As has been seen, when a bankruptcy or winding up is being conducted in England the court may restrain a creditor resident in England from continuing proceedings in, for example, Brazil. As a matter of principle, as well as authority, there is no jurisdiction to injunct if the creditor resides in Scotland or Northern Ireland. But in such a case the English court may in effect 'extend' its powers by making a section 426 request to the courts in Scotland or Northern Ireland, as appropriate, asking that that court restrain the creditor in question. The making of an order under section 426 is not obligatory, but there is every reason to believe that a court in Scotland or Northern Ireland would make the order sought – provided the facts would support the making of such an order were the requested court the one conducting the bankruptcy or winding up proceedings. The English court could certainly act, in appropriate circumstances, were it to receive a request from a court in another part of the United Kingdom or a relevant country or territory.[15]

4. ADMINISTRATION PROCEEDINGS

Contained within Part II of the Insolvency Act 1986 are provisions which prevent creditors from bringing proceedings against a company in administration both (a) once an administration order has been made and (b) during the period between the presentation of a petition and the making of

---

[10] See chapter 4, *supra*.

[11] *Re Queensland Mercantile and Agency Co. Ltd.* (1888) 58 L.T. 878, p. 377, *infra*.

[12] See now Insolvency Act 1986, s. 130(2), *supra*.

[13] Note also *Hughes v. Hannover Rückversicherungs-Aktiengesellschaft* [1997] 1 B.C.L.C. 497: section 426 request from a court in Bermuda (winding up a Bermudan company) to injunct a party, who was subject to the jurisdiction of the English court, from commencing proceedings in the United States. The injunction was refused on the facts as a matter of discretion, rather than on the basis that the court had no jurisdiction to injunct because it was not conducting the principal liquidation.

[14] (1885) 9 O.R. 277.

[15] For the operation of s. 426, p. 405, *infra*.

an order.[16] Such provisions, obviously, will be used to restrain proceedings in Great Britain.[17] It has been suggested that the relevant provisions ought to be construed extraterritorially, so as to confer jurisdiction on the English (or Scottish) court to restrain proceedings anywhere in the world.[18] The major difficulty, however, with this argument is that the Part II provisions closely resemble sections 126(1) and 130(2) – applicable in a winding up – and these sections have been consistently (at least in the last hundred years) interpreted as being purely territorial in reach.[19] Moreover, if Parliament had intended to depart from the long-established territorial approach to the statutory restrain of proceedings, it would surely have done so expressly. What then of the court's *in personam* or equitable jurisdiction?

The question whether the court may, acting *in personam*, restrain an English creditor (or a foreign creditor who has entered a claim) from commencing an action abroad has yet to be judicially tested. But it has been stated in a leading work that the situation in respect of an administration cannot be equated with that which prevails in a winding up, since only in the latter does a statutory trust in favour of the creditors come into existence:[20]

'. . . there would appear to be no scope for the exercise of the equitable jurisdiction, since there is, in the case of an administration order, no vested right on the part of unsecured creditors. Administration is a collective procedure in the interests of all creditors . . . but no trust arises and the company does not cease to be beneficial owner of its assets. . . .'

This author would argue, however, that the equitable jurisdiction may yet be invoked (although this may not be necessary where the administrator successfully raises the matter before the foreign court).

First, that an administration order does not create a statutory trust, and therefore the creditors have no 'vested right', cannot be conclusive. For although an injunction may generally only be granted in aid of some legal or equitable right, it has recently been confirmed that such is no longer essential in relation to an anti-suit injunction.[1] Secondly, whilst it cannot be suggested that administration falls within the category of bankruptcy or winding up, we have the authority of the House of Lords that 'the width and flexibility of equity are not to be undermined by categorisation'.[2] Indeed, one may go back to the first case before their Lordships' and recall the words of Lord Cranworth LC:[3]

---

[16] See Insolvency Act 1986, ss. 10(1)(c) and 11(3)(d).

[17] Whether ss. 10 and 11 would be construed as covering actions in Northern Ireland is open to a little doubt but, in any event, the best practical solution would probably be to act under s. 426 (see above) and request that the court in Northern Ireland exercise its own power to stay any actions there.

[18] Lightman and Moss, *The Law of Receivers of Companies* (1994, 2nd ed.) pp. 407–408. The authority of this suggestion is only increased by the fact that the relevant chapter was contributed by Professor Morse – one of the editors of *Dicey and Morris*.

[19] See pp. 279–280, *supra*.

[20] *Lightman and Moss*, n. 18 *supra*, at p. 408.

[1] *Airbus Industrie GIE* v. *Patel* [1997] 2 Lloyd's Rep. 8 at 19, referring to *South Carolina Insurance Co.* v. *Assurantie Maatschappij De Zeven Provincien N.V.* [1987] A.C.24. Nothing in the House of Lords in *Airbus* (see [1998] 2 All E.R. 257) suggests otherwise.

[2] *Castanho* v. *Brown* [1981] A.C. 557 at 573.

[3] (1855) 5 H.L. Cas. 416 at 439.

'But even when there is no question as to the foreign litigation being or not being necessary, or being or not being likely to be so effectual as litigation in this country, still if a person within the jurisdiction of the Court of Chancery is instituting proceedings in a foreign court, the instituting of which is contrary to equity and good conscience, the Court will . . . restrain the prosecution of such foreign suit, just as if it had been a suit in this country.'

It is suggested that it is plain that, to take an example, if a foreign creditor enters a claim in the administration and then commences litigation abroad with the intention of attaching assets there, such conduct may be seen as offending against 'equity and good conscience' – even if it be permitted under that foreign law.[4] Thirdly, and taking a somewhat broader perspective, recent cases[5] have highlighted a willingness on the part of the English court (when exercising a discretion[6] arising in the context of civil litigation) to recognise and actively assist US Chapter 11 proceedings – including worldwide stays granted by the US Bankruptcy Court. Generally in cross-border insolvency situations (as is the case in other areas of private international law) the English court claims for itself and exercises a wider jurisdiction than it is prepared to recognise on the part of a foreign court.[7] It would be most odd if, in relation to reorganisation proceedings, the court might act in such a way as to take cognisance of extraterritorial foreign stays and yet deny itself the very same jurisdiction.

In short, it is suggested that the equitable jurisdiction is not excluded simply because one is dealing with an administration. An administrator may seek an injunction from the English court to restrain an English creditor (or any other creditor who has claimed) from continuing foreign proceedings – although it may often make practical sense for the administrator to plead his case (for a stay) before the foreign court before seeking an anti-suit injunction in England.[8]

5. DISGORGING ASSETS RECOVERED ABROAD

A. Outline

Just as the English court may injunct a creditor resident in England from carrying on an action against the insolvent in a foreign court, so too such a creditor may be required in certain circumstances to surrender money or property recovered by means of legal process abroad. (Should assets be recovered abroad other than by means of legal process it has been held[9] that the English court may compel an English creditor, or a foreign creditor

---

[4] Certainly, if the action had been a suit in this country, to recall the words of Lord Cranworth, it would be restrained.

[5] See for example *Banque Indosuez S.A.* v. *Ferromet Resources Inc.* [1993] B.C.L.C. 112, p. 237, *supra*, and *Rowland* v. *Gulfpac Ltd.*, p. 238, *supra*.

[6] Such as to discharge a Mareva injunction or not to give leave to serve out of the jurisdiction, see the cases cited in n. 5, *supra*.

[7] Thus, for instance, an English discharge is effective whatever the governing law of the contract but this is not the case in respect of a foreign discharge, see p. 258, *supra*.

[8] See the general observations of Millett LJ in *Mitchell* v. *Carter* [1997] 1 B.C.L.C. 673 at 687 in relation to anti-suit injunctions.

[9] *Re Morton, ex p Robertson*, (1875) L.R. 20 Eq. 733 at 737–738. For another example, see *Re Rawang Tin Mining Co. Ltd.* (1890) 4 S.S.L.R. 570.

who has entered a proof, to account for such benefit.) As with the exercise of the *in personam* or anti-suit jurisdiction, there is no reported instance wherein the English court has forced a creditor to give up a dividend previously received in a foreign insolvency.[10] The type of case in-which a creditor will be compelled to account may be illustrated by reference to *Re Oriental Inland Steam Co.*[11] The company, registered in England, carried on business in India. The creditor, likewise incorporated in England, obtained judgment in India in May 1867. In November that year the company was ordered to be wound up in England. Thereafter, the creditor both proved in the English liquidation and attached property belonging to the company in India. Malins V-C held that the creditor was obliged to refund the proceeds of the attachments to the English liquidator: for creditors were not allowed to avail themselves of proceedings in a foreign court, after the date of the winding up, in order to gain a priority over the general body of creditors. That determination was upheld on appeal: the benefit obtained abroad had to be given up, for 'assets must be distributed in England upon the footing of equality'.[12] In short, once an English insolvency has commenced, English creditors are not at liberty to attach the insolvent's assets abroad. It is one thing to respect the authority of a foreign court over assets within its jurisdiction, it is quite another matter, once an insolvency is under way in England, to allow English creditors to seek to avoid the consequences of that insolvency and recover debts by attaching the insolvent's assets abroad. (Although where a creditor is compelled to refund money recovered abroad, that money may be something of a windfall for the general body of creditors in England.)

The basis upon which the court may oblige a creditor to give up assets requires some consideration. It must be stressed that, despite certain judicial observations,[13] the matter cannot simply be determined by the vesting of property and an application of the maxim *mobilia sequuntur personam*. If there is a bankruptcy in England the debtor's property, whether it is in England or abroad, vests in the English trustee.[14] Should the debtor then be adjudicated by a foreign court, English law will indeed recognise the right of the foreign court to deal with assets within its own jurisdiction.[15] Hence if a foreign creditor recovers property in a foreign court, that creditor is entitled to hold on to that property.[16] (Of course, if the foreign creditor then chooses to prove in the English insolvency, the hotchpot rule will apply.) The inadequacy of the maxim *mobilia sequuntur personam* is starkly revealed by the decision of the House of Lords in *Banco de Portugal*

---

[10] The matter is considered further at p. 306, *infra*.

[11] (1874) 9 Ch. App. 557 affirming (1874) 30 L.T. 317. (Note also the decision upon the facts in *Re Robinson* (1860) 11 Ir. Ch. R. 385: Irish company attaching bankrupt's assets in New York after an adjudication had been made in Ireland.)

[12] *Ibid.*, at 559 *per* James LJ.

[13] Much of the judgments in, for example, *Hunter* v. *Potts* (1791) 4 Term Rep 182 and *Sill* v. *Worswick* (1791) 1 Hy. Bl. 665 is devoted to the maxim.

[14] Insolvency Act 1986, s. 436: see *Callender Sykes & Co.* v. *Lagos* [1891] A.C. 460 as to charges under the *lex situs* and, generally, p. 341, *infra*.

[15] The *lex situs* also governs the validity of a security created over immovables (*Moor* v. *Anglo-Italian Bank* (1879) 10 Ch. D. 681) or movables (*Re West Cumberland Iron and Steel Co.* [1893] 1 Ch. 713); *Callender Sykes & Co.* v. *Lagos Colonial Secretary*, n. 14, *supra*.

[16] See, for example, *per* Lord Eldon in *Selkrig* v. *Davies* (1814) 2 Rose 291 at 318 or *per* Cairns LC in *Banco de Portugal* v. *Waddell* (1880) 5 App. Cas. 161 at 167.

v. *Waddell*.[17] Bankruptcy proceedings were commenced in England and in Portugal, although the title of the English trustee to the bankrupts' assets was prior to that derived from the foreign insolvency. Portuguese creditors, the appellants before their Lordships' House, received a dividend in Portugal and thereafter sought to prove in England. The appellants were admitted to prove, upon condition that they would not be entitled to dividends until the English creditors had received a dividend equivalent to that which the appellants had already obtained by means of the Portuguese proceedings. Lord Blackburn drew a clear distinction between the vesting of property and the position of foreign creditors:[18]

> 'the Court of Bankruptcy in England had the right to administer all the personal property of these bankrupts, wherever that personal property was, whether in Portugal or in England; that when a Portuguese subject in any way got hold of part of that property, under Portuguese law he was entitled to hold it; but when he had so got hold of part of the property, and he came to England to take advantage of the proceedings under the Bankruptcy Act, he could only do so upon appropriating that which he had received under the Portuguese law in payment of the dividends, and taking no dividends until that sum was exhausted.'

Because the Portuguese creditors had claimed in England, the hotchpot rule applied; whereas the maxim *mobilia sequuntur personam*, as title had first vested in the English trustee, would have rendered every creditor automatically liable to give up the assets recovered abroad and which were already regarded as vested in the English trustee. The maxim cannot stand with the reasoning and the decision in *Banco de Portugal* v. *Waddell*.

The power to compel a creditor to account for assets recovered is, both in practical terms and as a matter of principle, connected to the jurisdiction to restrain a creditor from carrying on an action in a foreign court.[19] A foreign creditor will not be restrained from bringing an action in a foreign court; neither will such a creditor be obliged by the English court to give up any property recovered by means of that action. But an injunction may issue to restrain an English creditor and, in cases where an English creditor might have been restrained, the court may require the creditor to account. In these circumstances it is the creditor's residence in England upon which jurisdiction is founded. This view has recently received support (albeit *obiter*) from Millett LJ who, when speaking of the possibility of an unsecured creditor gaining an unfair advantage by using an attachment abroad, has said:[20]

> 'To prevent this, the English court has jurisdiction to restrain creditors from bringing or continuing the foreign execution process (see, for example, *Re Oriental Inland Steam Co., ex p Scinde Rly Co.* and *Re North Carolina Estate Co.*). In all the cases in which the court has hitherto exercised this jurisdiction, the creditors in question were resident in England.'

---

[17] (1880) 5 App. Cas. 161.

[18] *Ibid.*, at 175.

[19] See *Brickwood* v. *Miller* (1817) 3 Mer. 279 at 284 *per* Grant MR: 'Then, if English creditors are not to be restrained from suing, it would be incongruous to force them to refund what they have recovered.' Note also the undertaking in *Re Oriental Inland Steam Co.* (1874) 30 L.T. 317.

[20] *Mitchell* v. *Carter* [1997] 1 B.C.L.C. 673 at 687 (citations omitted). For further discussion of the case, see p. 334, *infra*. The question of the basis of this jurisdiction had been raised in *Re Paramount Airways Ltd.* [1993] Ch. 223 at 238, but was left undecided.

B. Historical Development

(i) *Eighteenth Century Authorities*

Prior to 1791 the weight of authority was against compelling a creditor, English or otherwise, to give up money or property recovered by means of an attachment abroad. The view was taken, most notably by Lord Mansfield (e.g. in *Waring* v. *Knight*), that 'if a man uses legal diligence in a foreign country and obtains a preference, it cannot be helped'.[1] Lord Mansfield's opinion was evidently founded to a considerable extent upon the circumstance that an English commission was then thought not to vest foreign property in the assignees, but only gave the assignees a right to sue for it. However, in *Hunter* v. *Potts* Lord Kenyon CJ did allow assignees to recover from a creditor resident in England (and who knew of the commission) money obtained by means of an attachment in Rhode Island:[2]

> 'For it must be remembered, that during the progress of this business all these parties resided in England; that the defendant, knowing of the commission and of the assignment, in order to gain a priority, transmitted an affidavit to Rhode Island to obtain an attachment of the bankrupt's property there, in violation of the rights of the rest of the creditors, which were then vested: but such an attempt cannot be sanctioned in a court of law.'

Later the same year Lord Loughborough in *Sill* v. *Worswick*[3] expressed similar sentiments and, in particular, declined to apply the earlier decision of Lord Mansfield in *Waring* v. *Knight*. In *Sill* v. *Worswick* the defendant was resident in England and had notice of the English commission prior to the attachment. However, the defendant had also sworn an affidavit of his debt before the Mayor of Lancaster in order to institute proceedings in the foreign court. The *ratio* in *Sill* v. *Worswick* is therefore confined to a situation in which the defendant's attachment is[4] 'a process which he has commenced in England'; and the greater part of the judgment is devoted to showing simply that, by reference to the fiction that movables follow the person, an English bankruptcy might operate in respect of movable property abroad. Nevertheless, Lord Loughborough considered Lord Kenyon's opinion in *Hunter* v. *Potts* as 'founded upon the clearest and most evident principles of justice'.[5] Further, Lord Loughborough qualified his judgment as relating to English creditors: his Lordship distanced himself from any suggestion that a foreign creditor who recovered assets by means of an attachment abroad could be held liable to account.[6]

That an English creditor could be required to account was finally established in *Phillips* v. *Hunter*.[7] The bankrupts carried on business in England and were indebted to Phillips and Co., a trading firm in England. The partners in Phillips and Co. resided in England, with the exception of one Crammond who had gone to America to conduct the firm's business there. After the commission had issued in England, and with knowledge that the bankrupts had stopped payment, Crammond on behalf of the firm

---

[1] See *Phillips* v. *Hunter* (1795) 2 Hy. Bl. 402 at 413, citing *Waring* v. *Knight* (1795) 2 Hy. Bl. 413n., 1 H. Bi. 693n.
[2] (1791) 4 Term Rep 182 at 194.
[3] (1791) 1 Hy. Bl. 665.
[4] *Ibid.*, at 694.
[5] *Ibid.*, at 693.
[6] *Ibid.*
[7] (1795) 2 Hy. Bl. 402.

attached property belonging to the bankrupts in Pennsylvania. The majority in the Exchequer Chamber (Lord Eyre CJ dissenting) held that the English assignees had the right, by way of an action for moneys had and received, to recover the proceeds of the attachment:[8]

> 'It must be remembered, in discussing this question, that . . . the bankrupts were English traders, that the defendants were partners in an English house, that the debt from the bankrupts to the defendants was contracted in England, that the bankrupts as well as the defendants were resident in England, and that Crammond, who on this verdict must also be taken to be an English subject, went from this kingdom to America, for the special and temporary purpose of transacting business for the English house . . . All these facts appearing on the record, this case must be argued as arising between English subjects upon English property. . . The great principle of the bankrupt laws is justice founded on equality. No creditor shall be permitted to acquire an undue preference, and by so doing, prevent an equal distribution among all the creditors . . . No creditor whose debt was contracted within the sphere of operation of those laws, and who has notice of the insolvency of the debtor, can recover any part of the common fund for his own particular advantage. . . .'

Lord Eyre, for his part, dissented on the ground, *inter alia*, that the rights of English assignees to property in Pennsylvania were exclusively governed by the law of Pennsylvania, and a determination under the law of Pennsylvania could not be upset in England by an action for moneys had and received.

(ii) *Later Cases*

Subsequent authority adds a little by way of explanation. Lord Eldon LC once observed that 'a creditor, living in England, and subject to the bankrupt laws, having attached the estate of the bankrupt abroad, must restore it.'[9] In *Hovil* v. *Browning* Le Blanc J is reported to have said of *Hunter* v. *Potts* and *Sill* v. *Worswick*:[10]

> 'Both those were cases of creditors who were cognizant of the bankruptcy, and who proceeded against the bankrupt's property abroad in order to get a preference, in fraud of the bankrupt laws, by which they were bound.'

In comparison, there is a decision of Sir William Grant in which the Master of the Rolls distinguished *Hunter* v. *Potts* and *Sill* v. *Worswick* and allowed a creditor resident in England to hold on to the proceeds of an attachment abroad. In *Brickwood* v. *Miller*[11] the bankrupt, a partner in two firms established in the West Indies, conducted the business of the English branch of the two firms. The defendant, who was resident in England and whose debt was contracted in England, had attached property belonging to the two firms in the West Indies. Grant MR considered that the two firms were 'at least as much West Indian as English establishments';

---

[8] *Ibid.*, at 404–405.
[9] *Benfield* v. *Solomons* (1803) 9 Ves. 77 at 80, *arguendo*. See also *per* Bayley J in *Cazenove* v. *Prevost* (1821) 5 B. & Ald. 70 at 74, n. 14, *infra* and *per* Collins J in *Minna Craig* SS Co. v. *Chartered Mercantile Bank of India London and China* [1897] 1 Q.B. 55 at 63, text to n. 3, p. 305 *post*.
[10] (1806) 7 East 154 at 158, *arguendo*.
[11] (1817) 3 Mer. 279.

that the bankruptcy in England of one of the members of a foreign partner-ship did not prevent the foreign partners from paying partnership debts abroad; and that a partnership creditor would not be restrained from bringing an action in a foreign court nor obliged to refund money recovered thereby. *Hunter* v. *Potts* and *Sill* v. *Worswick* were limited to a sole trader in England or the bankruptcy of a member of an English partnership. The especial significance of *Brickwood* v. *Miller* is the connection drawn between the jurisdiction to restrain a creditor and the power to compel a creditor to refund property recovered under an attach-ment abroad.[12] This connection is also expressed in a recent judgment of Millett LJ.[13]

(iii) *Analysis*

It can fairly be said that no English court has ever fully tackled the relevant theoretical considerations. The development of the case law divides into two stages. First, it was thought that a creditor could not be made to give up property recovered abroad (nor restrained from instituting an action in a foreign court) because the English bankrupt laws did not apply abroad: *Waring* v. *Knight* is, perhaps, the strongest example of this line of reason-ing. But, secondly, the field of operation of the law of bankruptcy was extended to movables abroad by the fiction *mobilia sequuntur personam* as, for example, illustrated in *Sill* v. *Worswick*. However, where there has been an attachment in a foreign court it is accepted (notably in *Sill* v. *Worswick* itself) that a foreign creditor can retain the benefit of such attachment whereas an English creditor may not.

In short, there is real difficulty in producing a theoretical analysis consistent with both the somewhat ancient cases and modern principles of English private international law. The following might be suggested. An English bankruptcy operates in respect of property abroad belonging to the bankrupt[14] because the statute so dictates (see the definition in section 436). Where property belonging to the bankrupt is, after the appointment of the English trustee, attached abroad and the property or proceeds thereof is given by the foreign court to the attaching creditor, the English court recognises (with one exception) that title to the property or the proceeds thereof has vested in the creditor. The one exception concerns a creditor resident in England who attaches property abroad – such a creditor may, at the discretion of the court, be required to refund the benefit of the attachment abroad. The problem, as far as theory is concerned, is that this is a unique jurisdiction. To state that an English creditor cannot act 'in fraud of the bankrupt laws'[15] or acquire an 'undue preference' in 'defiance

---

[12] 'Then, if English creditors are not to be restrained from suing, it would be incongruous to force them to refund what they have recovered abroad': (1817) 3 Mer. 279 at 284.

[13] *Mitchell* v. *Carter* [1997] 1 B.C.L.C. 673 at 687, p. 300, *supra*.

[14] 'The assignees are unquestionably entitled to all the property that belonged to the bankrupt at the time of his act of bankruptcy: and there can be no doubt, also, that if a subject of this country, by means of legal process abroad, gets into his hands, after the bankruptcy, money belonging to the bankrupt, he is liable to refund it to the assignees': *Cazenove* v. *Prevost* (1821) 5 B. & Ald. 70 at 74 *per* Bayley J. *Cazenove* v. *Prevost* establishes that whether property does indeed belong to the bankrupt at the time of the bankruptcy is determined by the *lex situs*.

[15] *Per* Le Blanc J, n. 10, *supra*.

of those laws to which he owes submission'[16] carries the matter no further, particularly when it is observed that a general doctrine of *fraude à la loi* forms no part of English private international law.

Perhaps the most that can be said, from the theoretical point of view, to support the old cases is that they are consistent with a broad principle of cross-border insolvency law in respect of attachments. A creditor should not be permitted to gain an advantage by instituting or continuing an action against the insolvent or his property once insolvency proceedings have been commenced, either in England or abroad. The English court should give effect to this principle not only when property is attached in England and an insolvency is on foot abroad,[17] but also when property is attached in a foreign court – at least in the latter instance to the extent that the attaching creditor is (on account of residence in England or because of submitting a proof) subject to the jurisdiction of the English court.

C. Exercise of Discretion and Secured Creditors

Although a creditor may be resident in England it does not inevitably follow that the creditor must be required to refund money recovered abroad. That the creditor brought proceedings in the foreign court with knowledge of the prior English insolvency is a most relevant consideration, but not of itself decisive one way or the other. Should the creditor (prior to the commencement of the English insolvency) obtain security[18] in accordance with the foreign law, that creditor will not be restrained from prosecuting a foreign action to realise such security, nor will there be any obligation to account.[19] More generally, the English court will consider the relative connections of the insolvent and the creditor to England and the prejudice to the general body of creditors and, in particular, if the foreign action would not have been restrained by an exercise of the court's *in personam* jurisdiction, the creditor will not be required to give up the benefits of such an action. For example, let us say, a company incorporated in Singapore has a branch in England. Liquidations have been commenced in both Singapore and England, the English proceedings being ancillary to the principal liquidation abroad. A creditor, resident in England, has brought an action against the company in Singapore, which action has been allowed to proceed by the court in Singapore. It cannot be suggested that the English court would restrain the creditor: so too the creditor, although resident in England and having notice of the liquidations, would not be called upon to account by the English court.

The connection between restraining a creditor by injunction and compelling a creditor to give up money recovered abroad requires particular emphasis. For, as a practical matter, once it is known that an

---

[16] *Phillips* v. *Hunter* (1795) 2 Hy. Bl. 402 at 409.

[17] See pp. 233–237, *ante*.

[18] Be it a mortgage, charge, lien or by way of attachment abroad.

[19] As Malins V-C remarked in *Re Oriental Inland Steam Co. Ltd.* (1874) 30 L.T. 317 at 318: 'In this case, if the Scinde Company had had a lien on any property of the Oriental Company in India, in existence before the commencement of the winding up, the court would not interfere with that.' A like opinion was expressed by Mellish LJ: (1874) L.R. 9 Ch. App. 557 at 560. Note also *Sill* v. *Worswick* (1791) 1 Hy. Bl. 665 at 689.

unsecured English creditor has commenced a suit in a foreign court, the English liquidator or trustee should take action. Instead of waiting for the creditor to recover judgment and issue execution abroad, the English liquidator, administrator or trustee will be better advised immediately to bring those proceedings to the attention of the English court. The court may then injunct the creditor, or allow the creditor to carry on with the foreign suit upon undertaking to abide by any order the court may subsequently make in respect of money or property recovered abroad.[20] (The costs of obtaining an injunction or undertaking are likely to be significantly less than those incurred in arguments over the intricacies of a series of eighteenth century authorities.) Another option available to the English liquidator, administrator or trustee is, of course, to bring the English proceedings to the attention of the foreign court – with a view to obtaining an order from the foreign court which prevents the creditor from attaching assets. But whilst the 'normal assumption', as Millett LJ has put it 'is that the foreign judge is the person best qualified to decide if the proceedings in his court should be allowed to continue',[1] it cannot be that the fact that the foreign court refuses to stay its proceedings will prevent the English court from issuing an injunction (or requiring a creditor to disgorge). Indeed, in those countries which adopt a strictly territorial approach to bankruptcy, it is almost inevitable that without any consideration of the merits the foreign court will in effect ignore the English proceedings.[2]

Moreover, the general body of creditors may suffer a disadvantage should the English liquidator or trustee fail to seek an injunction against an English creditor who brings proceedings *in rem* in a foreign court. In *Minna Craig SS Co.* v. *Chartered Mercantile Bank* it was accepted, as a general principle, that 'where an English creditor by process of law in a foreign country gets hold of assets which from the English standpoint would be divisible among the general body of creditors, he cannot retain the proceeds as against the trustee'.[3] However, it was further held that this principle did not apply where an English creditor had recovered a judgment *in rem* in a foreign court. Thus the Court of Appeal did not allow an English liquidator to recover money received by an English creditor pursuant to a foreign judgment *in rem*, even though the foreign action had been commenced only after a winding up order was made in England. Nevertheless, nothing in the judgments of the Court of Appeal touched upon the power of the court to injunct an English creditor who has no lien or charge at the time a winding up order is made. There is authority that the court may indeed restrain such a creditor should an attempt be made to obtain a judgment *in rem* after the commencement of English insolvency proceedings.[4]

---

[20] Such an undertaking was required from the attaching creditor in *Re Oriental Inland Steam Co. Ltd.* (1874) 30 L.T. 317.
[1] *Mitchell* v. *Carter* [1997] 1 B.C.L.C. 673 at 687.
[2] It is, of course, in exactly this type of situation that an injunction may be most needed. The remarks of Millett LJ, *supra*, n. 1 should not be taken to suggest that the English court will leave the matter entirely to the foreign court.
[3] [1897] 1 Q.B. 55 at 63 *per* Collins J, affirmed *ibid.*, at 460.
[4] *Re Jenkins and Co. Ltd.* (1907) 51 Sol. Jo. 715, p. 290, *ante*. See also *Re Belfast Shipowners Co. Ltd.* [1894] 1 I.R. 321.

D. Debtor in the Foreign Court

If an English creditor attaches a debt due to the insolvent in a foreign court, that creditor may be required to give up the proceeds of such attachment. The debtor in the foreign court, however, cannot be later sued in England by the English trustee or liquidator for the debt originally owed to the insolvent:[5] payment made to a creditor who has attached the debt in a foreign court relieves the debtor from further liability. In general, as Lord Selborne once remarked, the English court may sometimes injunct the plaintiff in the foreign proceedings:[6]

> 'But there is neither principle nor precedent (that I am aware of) for restraining a defendant, sued in a foreign court . . . from obeying, while within the foreign jurisdiction, the orders, lawful according to the *lex loci*, of that foreign court.'

More particularly, in *Le Chevalier* v. *Lynch*[7] it was held that an English trustee could not maintain an action against a debtor whose debt had been attached, although after the bankruptcy, in accordance with the law of St. Christopher.

6. CREDITOR RECOVERING DIVIDEND ABROAD

There is no reported instance wherein the court has restrained a creditor resident in England from participating in a foreign insolvency. For the 'golden thread', as Robert Goff LJ has put it, running through the cases where an injunction has been granted is that it has been 'considered necessary and proper for the protection of the exercise of the jurisdiction of the English court'.[8] Should an English creditor bring an action abroad and attach assets, such assets may be prevented thereby from being gathered in by the English trustee, administrator or liquidator. But, if a foreign court is actually conducting its own insolvency, any assets in that country will not in any event[9] fall to be administered in English proceedings. Accordingly, whereas jurisdiction exists to restrain an English creditor from claiming in a foreign insolvency, that jurisdiction will rarely be exercised.[10] Indeed, if an English creditor chooses to seek a dividend abroad, rather than in the English insolvency, that may redound to the benefit of those creditors who do claim in England.[11]

The following general propositions may be advanced. An English creditor may ignore the English insolvency and claim and recover a dividend in foreign insolvency proceedings. Should a creditor, English or

---

[5] *Le Chevalier* v. *Lynch* (1779) 1 Doug. 170, *Mawdesley* v. *Parke* (1770) 1 Hy. Bl. 680n.
[6] *Ewing* v. *Orr Ewing* (1885) 10 App. Cas. 453 at 501.
[7] (1779) 1 Doug. 170.
[8] In *Bank of Tokyo Ltd.* v. *Karoon* [1987] 1 A.C. 45n. at 60.
[9] At least, not unless the foreign court decides to limit the scope of its own insolvency proceedings and remit assets to England.
[10] The jurisdiction would be exercised if the foreign insolvency proceedings did not envisage a ratable distribution amongst the creditors, but allowed the bankrupt to give all his assets to one or two particular creditors: see, for example, the foreign insolvency proceedings described in *Re Hooman* (1859) 1 L.T. 46, p. 189, *ante*.
[11] Where a dividend is sought in two sets of proceedings, the hotchpot doctrine applies, see p. 272, *supra*.

foreign, recover a dividend in foreign insolvency proceedings and then claim in England, the hotchpot rule will apply: the creditor will not receive any dividend in England until the other creditors in England have received a dividend equal to that which the creditor has already obtained in the foreign insolvency. Thus in *Stewart* v. *Auld*[12] the appellant's refusal to bring into hotchpot the dividend recovered in the foreign insolvency meant that no claim would be entertained in the local (Scottish) bankruptcy proceedings – there was no suggestion that the appellant should be ordered to give up the dividend already recovered abroad. Finally, if a creditor, English or foreign, enters a proof in England and thereafter also seeks to receive a dividend abroad, that creditor must undertake to give up any dividend which may be recovered abroad:[13] if such undertaking is not forthcoming, the English court will stay receipt of dividends in the English insolvency or, if practical, may require the creditor to give up the foreign dividend.

7. ENGLISH CREDITOR COMMENCING FOREIGN INSOLVENCY PROCEEDINGS

Where insolvency proceedings are already on foot in England, there can be no general rule against an English creditor seeking to open insolvency proceedings in foreign jurisdiction – just as such a creditor may enter a claim and recover a dividend in any foreign insolvency, although naturally the hotchpot rule will apply in such circumstances. A foreign insolvency process (involving a ratable distribution) cannot be equated with a foreign attachment (where the creditor seeks to sweep away assets for himself). Nevertheless, there is Australian authority – although not involving an insolvent company – to the effect that the court may restrain a party subject to the jurisdiction from presenting a winding up petition in a foreign court, where that petition is solely a 'vexatious harassing' of the company in question.[14] Where a debt is owed to a creditor and the company is insolvent it will be highly unusual for the presentation of a petition (in a foreign court) to be vexatious, even though the company is being wound up in England, because such a creditor is not driven by an improper motive or trying to steal an advantage unavailable to the general body of creditors. Moreover, there is much force in the view that in such a case the foreign court can best deal with whether there is something irregular or improper about the petition presented by the creditor.[15] But it is possible to imagine a situation in which the English court might grant an injunction. Let us say that a company is in administration[16] in England and that a particular creditor ('the creditor') has entered a claim and expressed strong views against the proposed rescue plan. Knowing that he will be outvoted and in an attempt to scupper the plan, or at least make life more difficult for the

---

[12] (1851) 13 D. 1337: *Ex p Wilson*, as reported at 26 L.T. 489, concerned *English* creditors.

[13] *Re Kidd* (1861) 4 L.T. 344, text to n. 15, p. 277, *ante*.

[14] *Murphy Corpn. Ltd.* v. *Pembroke Securities Ltd.* (1989) 7 A.C.L.C. 1016 at 1028, note Smart (1995) 4 I.I.R. 199 at 202–203.

[15] See the general observations of Millett LJ in *Mitchell* v. *Carter* [1997] 1 B.C.L.C. 673 at 687.

[16] That the *in personam* jurisdiction applies to administration is discussed, p. 296, *supra*.

administrator, the creditor presents a winding up petition abroad – in a jurisdiction which takes a strict territorial approach and will totally ignore the English proceedings and the creditor's participation therein.[17] Here the level of vexation is sufficiently high to warrant interference by the English court.

8. CIVIL JURISDICTION AND JUDGMENTS ACT 1982

The power of the English court to restrain a creditor from bringing proceedings against the insolvent in a foreign court must, albeit briefly, be considered in the light of the Civil Jurisdiction and Judgments Act 1982. The Act (as amended) gives effect in the United Kingdom to the Brussels and Lugano Conventions. Broadly speaking, the Conventions provide a detailed set of rules as to when a court in a Contracting State will have jurisdiction in civil and commercial matters and the consequences thereof.[18] Should the Conventions apply in respect of the jurisdiction of the English court to restrain a creditor it is quite obvious that much of the established case law would have to be re-examined. The potential application of the Convention to the *in personam* jurisdiction of the court when conducting insolvency proceedings is not considered in the leading text-books on private international law, insolvency law or indeed the Convention itself. However, the issue has been the subject of a decision in the courts of Scotland.

Ferguson's Trustee v. *Ferguson*[19] concerned an action by a Scottish trustee to interdict the bankrupt from dealing with and in particular selling certain immovable property in Spain. It was held that there was no jurisdiction to restrain the bankrupt. Much of the judgment of the Sheriff Principal concerns the domestic law of Scotland, but the court also relied upon Article 16(1) of the Convention as conferring exclusive jurisdiction on the Spanish courts:[20]

> 'Turning to the 1982 Act, I accept the solicitor for the pursuer's submission that art. 16(1) does not create an exclusive jurisdiction in all issues relating to heritage in the *forum rei sitae*. The question is whether this interdict raises questions relating to a right *in rem* . . . it seems to me that the pursuer is seeking to prevent the defender from exercising a right *in rem* by selling the property and is raising a question as to whether the defender has such a right. For these reasons, I consider that . . . the court had no jurisdiction in these proceedings.'

If the approach of the Sheriff Principal to the 1982 Act be correct, then the English court might wholly lack jurisdiction to restrain not only (as on the facts) the insolvent but also any creditor who brings an action in the courts of a Contracting State, even though the creditor has entered a claim in the English insolvency.

Ferguson's Trustee v. *Ferguson* cannot be followed. The ruling is plainly wrong in two important regards: one relating to Article 16(1) itself, the

---

[17] This example assumes that the foreign court has jurisdiction under its own law on the basis, for instance, of assets (albeit of no great value) in the foreign country.
[18] See the discussion, p. 12, *supra*.
[19] 1990 S.L.T. (Sh. Ct.) 73.
[20] *Ibid.*, at 75.

other concerning the operation and applicability of the Conventions where a debtor is insolvent. In respect of Article 16(1) a number of cases have emphasised that to fall within the Article it is not enough that the dispute is ultimately concerned with who controls certain immovable property: the plaintiff must be bringing an action specifically to determine the 'extent, content, ownership or possession of immovable property'.[1] Thus the European Court has ruled that an action for a declaration that a defendant held land on trust, and for an order requiring the execution of appropriate documents to effect a transfer of legal ownership, was based upon a right *in personam* and, accordingly, fell outside Article 16(1).[2] Rights asserted in the course of an English insolvency against a bankrupt (e.g. to convey foreign land into the name of the trustee) or a creditor (e.g. to force the abandonment of an attachment over foreign land) must inevitably fall outside Article 16(1). More generally, in relation to the Conventions as a whole, Article 1 of the Brussels Convention should have been drawn to the attention of the court in *Ferguson's Trustee* v. *Ferguson*. In Article 1 it is stated that the Convention does not apply to 'bankruptcy, proceedings relating to the winding up of insolvent companies or other legal persons, judicial arrangements, compositions and analogous proceedings'.[3] Article 1 covers not only the insolvency process itself but also any proceedings derived directly from and closely connected to the bankruptcy, composition or winding up.[4] Proceedings brought to restrain a creditor, it is submitted, satisfy this test. For, as already pointed out,[5] prior to the commencement of the insolvency there is nothing objectionable about an unsecured creditor seeking to attach assets abroad: but once an insolvency is under way in England, such conduct becomes an unacceptable attempt to steal a march on the general body of creditors and on that basis may be restrained.[6] It is submitted that, in such a case, the connection between an injunction and the insolvency being conducted in England is immediate indeed.

In relation to section 130(2) of the Insolvency Act 1986, and its operation within the United Kingdom,[7] it may be noted that all proceedings under provisions of the Insolvency Act (i.e. all types of winding up, even a members' voluntary liquidation) are excluded from the Modified Convention.[8] Thus nothing under the Conventions alters the operation of section 130(2).

In summary, the Civil Jurisdiction and Judgments Act 1982 in no way restricts the power of the English court to restrain proceedings under

---

[1] *Reichert* v. *Dresdner Bank*: 115/88 [1990] E.C.R. I-27, see also p. 16, *supra*.

[2] See *Webb* v. *Webb*: C-294/92 [1994] E.C.R. I-1717, [1994] Q.B. 696.

[3] The same provision also appears, of course, in the Lugano Convention.

[4] *Gourdain* v. *Nadler*: 133/78 [1979] E.C.R. 733, p. 13, *supra*.

[5] See p. 287, *supra*.

[6] Cf. *Re Hayward* [1997] Ch. 45; an action, brought by a trustee in bankruptcy to recover property said to belong to the bankrupt, fell outside Article 1 and thus within the Convention rules. But in *Re Hayward* the same action (to recover the property) could have been brought by Hayward prior to his bankruptcy. Clearly, this is not the case where an injunction is sought to restrain a creditor – the creditor's resort to foreign proceedings is only restrained because the intervention of insolvency proceedings has fundamentally altered the rights of the creditor to enforce any debts.

[7] See p. 279, *supra*.

[8] Civil Jurisdiction and Judgments Act 1982, Sch. 5, para. 1, as amended by Sch. 14 of the Insolvency Act 1986.

section 130(2) of the Insolvency Act, or in the exercise of its *in personam* jurisdiction. Also if the facts of *Ferguson's Trustee* v. *Ferguson* were to occur before the English courts, the bankrupt would not be allowed (by virtue of section 291(2) of the 1986 Act) to interfere with the property abroad and, moreover, could be compelled to convey the property to the trustee or execute a power of attorney to enable the trustee to effect a sale thereof.[9]

9. ILLUSTRATIONS

(1) R, a businesswoman with extensive trading interests in several Scandinavian cities, has been made bankrupt in England. Q, a creditor resident in Sweden, after the commencement of the English bankruptcy brought an action against R in Sweden and recovered a certain sum. Q will be permitted also to prove in the English bankruptcy. However, the hotchpot rule will apply: Q will receive nothing in England until the other creditors have received a dividend equivalent to the amount which Q recovered in Sweden.

(2) As in Illustration 1, *supra*; however, Q was a secured creditor under the law of Sweden. Q may prove in England for the outstanding balance of the debt without bringing into hotchpot the money recovered in Sweden.[10]

(3) As in Illustration 1, *supra*; however, subsequent to entering a proof in England, Q brought a further action against R in the Swedish courts. The English court may restrain Q by injunction from carrying on with the second action.

(4) MT Ltd., an English company, was ordered to be wound up in England in February 1998. Several months earlier T, resident in England, had brought proceedings against MT Ltd. in Argentina and attached property belonging to MT Ltd. T had thereby become a secured creditor in accordance with the law of Argentina. T will not be restrained from carrying on the action in Argentina. Moreover, T may thereafter prove in the English liquidation without bringing into hotchpot the money recovered by way of the security in Argentina.[11]

(5) D, an English creditor, had commenced proceedings against the debtor in New South Wales when a bankruptcy order was made in England. D may be restrained from carrying on with the action in New South Wales. But no injunction will be necessary should D undertake to give up to the English trustee any money recovered abroad if subsequently so ordered by the English court.[12]

---

[9] See *Re Harris* (1896) 74 L.T. 221: bankrupt required to execute power of attorney in respect of land in Guatemala on pain of contempt.

[10] See *Re Somes, ex p De Lemos* (1896) 3 Mans. 131.

[11] See *Ex p D'Obree* (1803) 8 Ves. 82 and *Re West Cumberland Iron and Steel Co.* [1893] 1 Ch. 713 at 723, *supra*.

[12] *Re Newton, ex p Bankrupt* v. *Aldergate Films* [1956] C.L.Y. 6984.

(6) EMP is an English company in respect of which an administration order under Part II of the Insolvency Act 1986 was made in May 1998. Z, an unsecured creditor resident in England, in June 1998 began actions against EMP in New York and Taiwan with a view to attaching assets in those jurisdictions. The English court may injunct Z from continuing with the action in Taiwan;[13] and the administrator will be authorised to take appropriate steps in the US Bankruptcy Court to prevent Z proceeding with any attachment in New York.[14]

(7) PCM is an English company in respect of which a winding up order has been made in England. W and H are partners in a firm formed and carrying on business in the State of California. At the time the winding up order was made, W and H were plaintiffs in an English action against PCM. Since the making of the winding up order, W and H have brought a (different) action against PCM in California and attached PCM's assets there. W and H will not be permitted to continue the English action; however, the English court has no jurisdiction to restrain W and H from carrying on with the proceedings in California. (Although PCM's liquidator will be authorised to seek relief under section 304 of the US Bankruptcy Code.[15])

(8) As in Illustration 7 above; however, W and H after learning of the English liquidation brought a suit in California upon the same cause of action in respect of which W and H were already suing in England. The English court has jurisdiction, under the general rules of private international law,[16] to restrain W and H from carrying on with the action in the courts of California. (Although, as a practical matter, the liquidator would be expected, and well-advised, to rely upon section 304 of the US Bankruptcy Code.)

(9) Bankruptcy proceedings have been commenced against the insolvent both in England and New Zealand. B, a creditor resident in England, has entered no claim in the English bankruptcy but has proved in the New Zealand proceedings. The English court (*semble*) will not restrain B from claiming in New Zealand.

(10) As in Illustration 9, *supra*; however, B after receiving a dividend in New Zealand seeks to claim in England. B's claim may be admitted but the hotchpot rule must apply. (Thus B's claim in the English bankruptcy will not give B any dividend which is not also available to the English creditors generally.)

(11) BT Inc. is a Liberian corporation which has carried on business in the United Kingdom and in North America. Bankruptcy proceedings have been commenced in New York; and BT Inc. has been put into liquidation in England. X, a creditor resident in the United States, has sought to participate in the English liquidation and, at the same time, to claim in

---

[13] As Taiwan adopts a strictly territorial approach to insolvency, the Taiwanese courts will ignore the English administration. For questions of recognition involving Taiwanese bankruptcies, see p. 207, *supra*.

[14] See *Mitchell* v. *Carter* [1997] 1 B.C.L.C. 673, *supra*.

[15] *Ibid.*

[16] See, generally, *Société Nationale Industrielle Aérospatiale* v. *Lee Kui Jak* [1987] A.C. 871.

New York. X may claim in England upon undertaking to hand over to the English liquidator, if so ordered by the English court, any sums that may thereafter be received by virtue of the foreign insolvency. (For, it will be recalled, if X were to receive a dividend in New York and then prove in England the hotchpot rule would apply; accordingly, X will not be left completely free to receive a dividend in England and then receive further sums abroad.)

(12) The debtor, who carried on business in England and India, has been made bankrupt in England. S Ltd., an English company, after the making of the bankruptcy order recovered judgment against the debtor in India and attached the debtor's assets there. Absent evidence establishing that S Ltd. was a secured creditor under the law of India, the English court will require S Ltd. to give up the proceeds of the attachment in India.[17]

(13) A winding up order has recently been made in England in respect of an English company, SS Co. Ltd. Shortly after the making of the winding up order C arrested a ship belonging to SS Co. Ltd. in an Indonesian port. C is a creditor resident in England. C has recovered a judgment *in rem* from an Indonesian court. The English liquidator now seeks an order in England requiring C to give up the proceeds received by virtue of the Indonesian judgment. No such order will be made.[18]

(14) As in Illustration 13, *supra*; however, as soon as the ship is arrested by C in Indonesia, the liquidator applies to the court in England for an injunction restraining C from carrying on with the proceedings in Indonesia. If C were not, prior to the arrest, a secured creditor under Indonesian law (*semble*) an injunction will issue to restrain C.[19]

---

[17] *Re Oriental Inland Steam Co. Ltd.* (1874) 9 Ch. App. 557.
[18] *Minna Craig SS Co.* v. *Chartered Mercantile Bank of India, London and China* [1897] 1 Q.B. 460, *supra*.
[19] *Re Jenkins and Co. Ltd.* (1907) 51 Sol. Jo. 715, *supra*.

Chapter 11

Priority, Set-Off and Foreign Currency Debts

1. PRIORITIES

A. *Lex Fori*

In general, the English court has in an insolvency approached the question of priorities from a purely domestic standpoint. Thus it has been said that 'the proper order and priority of distribution of assets is always a matter for the *lex fori*'.[1] Attention may be called to *ex p Melbourn*[2] which reveals the rigour of the *lex fori* approach. The bankrupt and the appellant had, several years prior to the adjudication in England, entered into a marriage settlement at Batavia in accordance with the Dutch Indian Civil Law. The settlement was not registered in Batavia, the effect of which under the Dutch Indian Civil Law was that the appellant's debt would be postponed to claims of third parties. The English court held that in an English bankruptcy the appellant was not to be postponed but could claim *pari passu* with other creditors. Non-registration in Batavia did not relate to the validity of the appellant's claim, merely its enforcement; and that enforcement was governed solely by English law:[3]

> 'Now, there seems no doubt at all that in the case of bankruptcy the question of priority of the different creditors *inter se* must be governed by the law of the country where the bankruptcy takes place, and where the assets of the company are being administered.'

It will be noted that in *ex p Melbourn* the *lex fori* was applied in a wholly rigid manner (and to the disadvantage of the general body of the English creditors). It is one thing to say that a creditor who wishes to prove in England must take English law as he or she finds it and cannot claim some advantage which exists only under a foreign procedural rule, but it is somewhat arbitrary to allow a foreign creditor, perhaps with no connection at all to England, to claim *pari passu* with English creditors in respect of a debt which would be effectively worthless everywhere other than in an English insolvency. A greater encouragement to forum shopping in the

---

[1] *Thurburn* v. *Steward* (1871) L.R. 3 P.C. 478 at 513 *per* Lord Cairns. Note also *Bankers Trust International Ltd.* v. *Todd Shipyards Corpn.*, *The Halcyon Isle* [1981] A.C. 221.

[2] (1870) 6 Ch. App. 64; note also *Re Sibeth* (1885) 14 Q.B.D. 417, *Re Wiskeman* (1923) 92 L.J.K.B. 349, *Lusk* v. *Elder* (1843) 5 D. 1271, *Re Kloebe* (1884) 28 Ch. D. 175, *Re Doetsch* [1896] 2 Ch. 836 and *Canada Deposit Insurance Corpn.* v. *Canadian Commercial Bank* [1993] 3 W.W.R. 302.

[3] *Ibid.*, at 69. The opposite conclusion, upon indistinguishable facts, was reached in Scotland in *Williamson* v. *Taylor* (1845) 8 D. 157.

context of cross-border insolvency can scarcely be imagined (although, as recent case law has demonstrated, the rules on set-off also encourage forum shopping by creditors).

B. *Lex Situs*

The case law reveals, however, that the *lex fori* rule is not without exception. Where foreign assets come to be distributed in an English insolvency the English court may refer to foreign law to determine priorities, at least in certain circumstances.

Reference may be made to the litigation that arose out of the winding up of the Queensland Mercantile and Agency Co. Ltd. ('QMA').[4] QMA was incorporated in Queensland where it acted as agent for a Scottish company ('AIC'). In October 1887 QMA was ordered to be wound up in the courts of Queensland. In January 1888 an ancillary winding up order was made in England by North J. However, prior to the orders of the Queensland and English courts, AIC had commenced proceedings against QMA in Scotland. In the Scottish proceedings AIC had arrested certain of QMA's assets (unpaid share capital) in Scotland thereby becoming, so it was said, a secured creditor under Scots law on the assets so arrested. The first issue that arose before North J was whether, acting under the provisions of the then companies legislation (see now Insolvency Act 1986, section 130(2)), the English court would restrain AIC from proceeding with the suit in Scotland.[5] North J stayed the Scottish proceedings but expressly reserved to AIC the full benefit of the security, if any, it had already obtained under Scots law.[6] Subsequently, the Court of Session gave effect to the order of North J and the unpaid share capital was handed over to the English liquidator.[7]

Thus it had been resolved that (after the question of liability of QMA to AIC was determined[8]) the security of AIC would be determined in the English court but according to Scots law. As Lindley LJ later put it:[9]

> 'the whole was done . . . in order that the money might come into this country and be subject to the orders of this court, so that this court should decide the claims of [AIC] as they would have been decided in Scotland if the Scotch proceedings had gone on.'

Indeed, the funds having been received in England (and the question of liability between QMA and AIC having been decided in Queensland in favour of AIC), further litigation ensued. For the Union Bank of Australia had in 1886, that is, prior to the arrestment of the unpaid share capital, obtained debentures being a first charge on the uncalled capital of QMA. Thus the English court, in *Re Queensland Mercantile and Agency Co., ex p*

---

[4] *Re Queensland Mercantile Agency Co. Ltd.* (1888) 58 L.T. 878 and *Re Queensland Mercantile and Agency Co., ex p Australasian Investment Co.* [1892] 1 Ch. 219, affirming [1891] 1 Ch. 536. See also the discussion at p. 377, *post*.
[5] *Re Queensland Mercantile Agency Co. Ltd* (1888) 58 L.T. 878.
[6] *Ibid.*, at 879.
[7] *Queensland Mercantile and Agency Co. Ltd.* v. *Australasian Investment Co.* (1888) 15 R. 935.
[8] North J ordered that the question of *liability* be determined in Queensland, see p. 378, *infra*.
[9] [1892] 1 Ch. 219 at 225.

Australasian Investment Co.,[10] was called upon to determine the competing rights of the Union Bank (claiming by virtue of its earlier debentures) and of AIC (claiming by virtue of its later arrest of assets in Scotland).[11] The evidence as to the law of Scotland was that 'the said arrestments will have priority over the assignment of the debentures'.[12] That evidence was acted upon in the Court of Appeal: the question of priority, although arising in the context of a winding up in England, being determined as it would have been decided in Scotland had the Scottish proceedings gone on.[13]

The litigation concerning the Queensland Mercantile and Agency Co. Ltd. must be seen in the light of the English rules on attachment. It is plain that a creditor who attaches an insolvent's assets in a foreign court will be permitted to retain the benefit thereof, provided the attachment is prior to the commencement of the English insolvency. Thus in *Re West Cumberland Iron and Steel Co.*[14] the English court declined to injunct an English creditor who had attached the company's assets in Scotland (thereby obtaining security under Scots law) prior to the winding up in England. In *Re Queensland Mercantile Agency Co. Ltd.* North J departed from the normal rule and did restrain a creditor (AIC) which had a prior attachment in Scotland, but only upon condition that the full benefit of the security under Scots law be reserved to the creditor. Thus when, in the course of the winding up in England, a question of priority arose between AIC and another secured creditor (the debenture holder) that issue was decided in England as it would have been determined in the Scottish court. In summary, the following propositions may be advanced. Where the English court restrains a creditor who has a prior attachment in a foreign court, and the attached assets are subsequently transmitted to the English insolvency proceedings, the creditor will be entitled to the benefit of his security under the foreign law. Accordingly, if in the English insolvency another creditor claims priority in respect of the relevant assets, the English court will determine that question by applying the foreign law and its rules as to priority, so that the attaching creditor will be put into the same position as if the attachment in the foreign court had not been restrained.

---

[10] Note 4, *supra*.

[11] It is important to stress that *Re Queensland Mercantile and Agency Co., ex p Australasian Investment Co.* cannot be explained away as based upon any undertaking. For, whatever may have been agreed between QMA and AIC, the Union Bank entered the proceedings (to claim priority over AIC's arrestment) only after the Scottish proceedings had been stayed and it had already been ruled that Scottish law would be applicable when the assets were remitted to the English liquidator.

[12] [1892] 1 Ch. 219 at 223.

[13] The judgment of North J ([1891] 1 Ch. 536) seems to consider the facts as involving an assignment governed by Scottish law as the *lex situs*. The Court of Appeal ([1892] 1 Ch. 219) simply applied Scottish law, without reference to an assignment. It is submitted that the reasoning of North J is a little misleading. For his Lordship had ruled, *before* evidence was given as to the effect of Scottish law, that Scottish law would determine the question of the security, if any, of AIC – thus Scottish law was applicable prior to the validity of any assignment according to the *lex situs* being raised. The approach of the Court of Appeal is to be preferred: quite simply, Scottish law governed because the initial order of North J (preserving AIC's security) meant that the English court was bound to determine the claims of AIC 'as they would have been decided in Scotland if the Scotch proceedings had gone on' (*per* Lindley LJ, n. 9, *supra*).

[14] [1893] 1 Ch. 713, see p. 280, *supra*.

A further situation in which foreign rules as to priority will be applied in England is derived from the law relating to simultaneous administrations. In *Cook* v. *Gregson*[15] the deceased had died domiciled in Ireland leaving assets in both Ireland and England. The same persons were executors in Ireland and in England. Normally an administration (unlike an insolvency) is wholly territorial, governed by the law of the country in which the personal representatives have obtained their grant. Thus debts must be paid according to the *lex fori*, with only surplus assets being transmitted to the court of the domicile.[16] However, in *Cook* v. *Gregson* the Irish assets were sent to England without the Irish debts being paid off. The question for the English court, having received the proceeds of the Irish assets, was whether priorities should be determined according to English or Irish law. Kindersley V-C was in no doubt that Irish law governed the question of priorities, his Lordship giving an Irish judgment creditor a priority which did not exist under the English rules.[17] Moreover, the Vice-Chancellor's decision was approved in *Carron Iron Co.* v. *Maclaren* by Lord St Leonards, who considered that the English court would give effect to 'any priority to which, from the nature of his security, a creditor in Scotland or Ireland is entitled against the assets in either country according to the law of the country, although they may come to be distributed here'.[18] A like rule should be adopted where a foreign court has transmitted assets to an English insolvency. Although the assets eventually come to be administered in England, a creditor's claim for priority according to the foreign law may be given effect in respect of the transferred assets.[19] There is further authority that the proceeds of foreign land will remain subject to the original *lex situs* even though brought into an English insolvency.[20]

C. Summary

As a general rule, in an English insolvency questions of priority are determined by English law, *qua lex fori*. However, this rule admits of an exception: where foreign assets are transmitted to England, priorities in respect of such assets may be governed by the foreign law, as the original *lex situs* thereof. An exception so formulated serves the ends of justice and favours a more comprehensive system of cross-border insolvency rules.[1]

---

[15] (1854) 2 Drew. 286.

[16] *Dicey and Morris*, pp. 1015–1016.

[17] (1854) 2 Drew. 286 at 288.

[18] (1855) 5 H.L. Cas. 416 at 455.

[19] A similar result was reached by the court in Alberta in *Re Sefel Geophysical Ltd.* [1989] 1 W.W.R. 251 but by reference to a constructive trust: *Cook* v. *Gregson* was not cited. It is submitted that the approach in *Cook* v. *Gregson* is very much to be preferred.

[20] *Waterhouse* v. *Stansfield* (1851) 9 Hare 234 at 239: 'The interest in the proceeds is in substance and effect an interest in the estate itself; and no rule is more universal than that the *lex loci rei sitae* governs the disposition of the estate.' See also *Norton* v. *Florence Land and Public Works Co.* (1877) 7 Ch. D. 332 and *Ex p Stegmann* 1902 T.S. 40 at 54.

[1] See also pp. 385–387, *post*.

2. THE INCIDENTAL QUESTION

The dominant role of the *lex fori* in respect of priorities has never been judicially examined with reference to the incidental question. The doctrine of the incidental question is accepted, at least by the leading authors, as a part of English private international law.[2] The doctrine is said to have three elements. Firstly, there must be an issue governed under English private international law rules by a foreign law (the main question). Secondly, there must be a subsidiary issue capable of arising independently of the main question and which has its own choice of law rule. Thirdly, the application of this latter choice of law rule would lead to a conclusion different from that which would follow should the law governing the main question be applied. Where a true incidental question does arise it is said that the law governing the main question also determines the incidental question.[3] Examples of incidental questions given by Wolff may be cited:[4]

'(a) The legitimacy of a child depends on the validity of a marriage between its parents. If under the conflict rule of the English forum the legitimacy is governed by the law of country X, it is the conflict rule of country X which will decide what law governs the question of the validity of the marriage.

(b) Under many laws (for example, French and German law) an adoption (of C by A) is valid only if the adopter A has no legitimate issue of his own. Suppose the English court has to adjudicate on the validity of an adoption. Then the incidental question may be: is a given person B the legitimate child of the adopter A? The answer is to be found through the conflict rule of the legal system that governs the adoption, and not through the English conflict rule.

(c) The validity of a marriage between A and B, which under the conflict rule of the English forum is subject to the domiciliary law of country X, may depend on the nullity of a previous marriage concluded between A and C. Again, the conflict rule of X will decide under which municipal law the marriage A-C is to be examined.'

In other words, the incidental question is consumed by the law governing the main question.

With this explanation of the incidental question let us re-examine *ex p Melbourn*. In *ex p Melbourn* the provisions of the Dutch Indian Civil Law had not been complied with and thus the dispute was as to whether the appellant could yet claim *pari passu* with other creditors in an English bankruptcy. Mellish LJ addressed the problem thus:[5]

'Now, I do not think there is any dispute as to the general principle of law which should govern this case . . . In the construction of a contract the question whether there has been a contract made at all is to be decided by the law where the contract was made, but the remedy is to be according to the law here.'

The Lord Justice concluded, firstly, that under the foreign law there was a valid contract but, secondly, that priority was determined by English law. Hence it might be suggested that *ex p Melbourn* raised an incidental question – the main question being the validity of the contract (governed by a foreign law), the issue of priority being the incidental question – and

---

[2] *Dicey and Morris*, pp. 48–55, *Cheshire and North*, pp. 53–56.
[3] The law governing the main question will include the relevant conflict of laws rules.
[4] Wolff *Private International Law* (2nd ed., 1950), p. 207 (footnotes omitted).
[5] (1870) 6 Ch. App. 64 at 69.

that the law governing the main question (Dutch Indian Civil Law) should likewise have determined the question of priorities.

However, whatever the possibilities in theory of the *lex causae* over-reaching the *lex fori*, it cannot seriously be suggested that the English court should depart from the *lex fori* where an incidental question has arisen. For, quite simply, reference to the incidental question in the context of insolvency might require the court at one time to apply several different and incompatible foreign laws as to priority.[6]

3. SET-OFF

Questions concerning set-off in cross-border insolvency cases have very much been brought to the fore by the judgment of Sir Richard Scott V-C in *Re Bank of Credit and Commerce International S. A. (No. 10).*[7] The English court was conducting an ancillary winding up, whilst the main liquidation was in Luxembourg. The English liquidators were proposing to transfer funds to Luxembourg to enable the Luxembourg liquidators to make distributions to creditors on a worldwide basis. However, the set-off rules which would have to be applied by the Luxembourg liquidators were very restrictive, in comparison to the English rules, and when compared to the English rules would work to the disadvantage of those creditors who had claimed in England.[8] The result of the ruling of Scott V-C is clear enough: if there is a winding up in England, even an ancillary winding up, the provisions on set-off found in rule 4.90 of the Insolvency Rules must always be applied – quite irrespective of the governing law of the debts concerned or the residence of the creditors who have entered proofs in England.[9] So that, before transferring assets to be distributed in the principal liquidation abroad, the English liquidators were required to retain sufficient funds to ensure that net creditors could be 'compensated' for any disadvantage that they might suffer by an application of the set-off rules applicable under the law governing the foreign liquidation.[10] (It inevitably follows that the same approach would be taken to the set-off provision applicable in bankruptcy, see Insolvency Act 1986, section 323: section 323 would also be regarded as mandatory.)

But *Re BCCI S. A. (No. 10)* has not gone uncriticised;[11] and, moreover, the judgment does not touch upon how the English court should deal with foreign set-off rules where there has been an insolvency abroad but no bankruptcy or winding up in England.

---

[6] There are, however, passages in the judgments in *Williamson* v. *Taylor* (1845) 8 D. 156 which could be used to support the application of the incidental question doctrine.

[7] [1997] Ch. 213, see also p. 363, *infra*.

[8] *Ibid.*, at 236–237.

[9] Scott V-C was of the opinion that there was no discretion to disapply rule 4.90, but that even if there was such a discretion it would not be exercised: *ibid.*, at 247–249.

[10] The Vice-Chancellor illustrated the application of the ruling by an illustration, see *ibid.* at 252.

[11] See Fletcher (1997) 10 Insol. Int. 68–70, *infra*.

A. Insolvency in England

Perhaps the first issue that must be addressed concerns the nature of the English set-off rules: are they substantive or procedural? In *Re BCCI S.A. (No. 10)* Scott V-C stated:[12]

'The set-off brought about by rule 4.90 applies, under English law, to every creditor and every debtor whether or not the proper law of the debt is English law.'

On the face of it, therefore, it might appear that rule 4.90 is procedural – just as the rules on priorities (discussed above) are procedural – since it applies in all cases where there is a winding up in England regardless of the governing law of the debts involved. But on the very same page, the Vice-Chancellor also quotes from the speech of Lord Hoffmann in *Stein* v. *Blake*, that bankruptcy set-off is 'mandatory and self-executing', and that:[13]

'Bankruptcy set-off . . . affects the substantive rights of the parties by enabling the bankrupt's creditor to use his indebtedness to the bankrupt as a form of security'.

This passage obviously points towards a substantive approach. Scott V-C also opined that, in relation to debts governed by English law, rule 4.90 formed part of the proper law; so that, if the question of the discharge of an English debt were to arise before a foreign court, and the foreign court were to regard that question as governed by the proper law, then the foreign court should apply rule 4.90.[14] This clearly shows that rule 4.90 was thought by Scott V-C to be substantive in nature.

Yet if rule 4.90 is substantive (rather than procedural) the question inevitably arises as to the theoretical basis on which the English court, as Scott V-C expressly held, must apply rule 4.90 whatever the proper law of the debts concerned. Although the judgment of the Vice-Chancellor is silent on this point, it is this author's view that rule 4.90 (and also section 323) has to be seen as what in private international law is referred to as an 'overriding statute' or, to use a perhaps more fashionable expression, a 'mandatory rule of the forum'. Of course, the words 'overriding statute' are nowhere to be found in rule 4.90; the term is merely a convenient label. *Dicey and Morris* describes overriding statutes as being the expression of 'crystallised rules of public policy, because they lay down mandatory rules that the parties cannot contract out of, directly or indirectly'.[15] This seems to fit English insolvency set-off rules to a tee; and it will be noted that Scott V-C held that rule 4.90 applied to *all* creditors who had claimed in the English liquidation (regardless of their residence or the proper law of their debts) and that the better view was that there was no discretion to disapply rule 4.90 in relation to any particular group of creditors.[16]

Even though there is a conceptual framework into which *Re BCCI S.A. (No. 10)* can readily be fitted, the consequences of the mandatory application

---

[12] [1997] Ch. 213 at 236.
[13] *Stein* v. *Blake* [1996] A.C. 243, 251 and 255. Scott V-C also stated (at 246): 'Rule 4.90 . . . is a substantive rule of English law. *Stein* v. *Blake* [1996] A.C. 243 establishes that that is so.'
[14] [1997] Ch. 213 at 248–249.
[15] *Dicey and Morris*, at p. 24. The expression mandatory rule of the forum is now found in the Rome Convention and the Contracts (Applicable Law) Act 1990, see also p. 267, *supra*.
[16] *Supra*, n. 7, at 247–249.

of rule 4.90 are not altogether satisfactory. The application of rule 4.90 to net creditors who resided in England, and whose dealings were governed by English law, may be contrasted with applying rule 4.90 to, let us say, creditors who had throughout resided and dealt with BCCI in Luxembourg. Any such (Luxembourg resident) creditor who had proved in England (and of course English law allows all creditors to prove without discrimination in an English insolvency) would be getting an unexpected and perhaps undeserved advantage and, moreover, an advantage that would no longer be available to their fellow creditors in Luxembourg:[17] Scott V-C did not require the liquidators to make any provision for creditors who had not by that stage submitted a proof in the English proceedings.[18] The Vice-Chancellor made it clear that rule 4.90 applied to all relevant proofs that had been lodged with the English liquidators, regardless of residence or the place at which accounts with BCCI had been held. In other words, rule 4.90 was applied wholly rigidly: either a proof had been submitted in England or it had not; and it is fair to say that whether a proof had in fact been submitted might in some instances be almost a matter of accident – influenced perhaps, as Professor Fletcher has recently put it 'by whatever advice a particular creditor happened to receive at a past time before the present judgment purported to settle the law'.[19]

In response, as it were, to this undeniably correct criticism three points may be made. First, if, as has been suggested by this author, rule 4.90 is a *mandatory* rule of the forum then as a matter of principle it is not a rule which can be easily disapplied or restricted, particularly if there is nothing in the rule itself which gives guidance as to the basis on which it is to be restricted.[20] Secondly, in relation to net creditors who claimed in England, it is perhaps not unreasonable to assume that there was a greater number of such creditors who were resident in England, or had dealt with branches in England, than the number of such creditors who were resident in Luxembourg and had dealt exclusively with BCCI in Luxembourg.[1] To this extent it may well be that, although not precise, rough and ready justice was done by Scott V-C (and what could have been extensive litigation to decide whether an individual foreign creditor could reasonably expect the benefit of rule 4.90 was avoided[2]). Thirdly, whilst the Vice-Chancellor's ruling conferred an unexpected benefit on some foreign creditors (whose accounts were not held in the United Kingdom),[3] this would be by no means a unique situation. The rules on priority, as described above, have precisely the same effect and are a clear endorsement of and encouragement to foreign shopping in international insolvency cases.[4] Moreover, the well-advised foreign creditor can in other areas

---

[17] See Fletcher, *supra*, n. 11. See also the discussion at p. 365, *infra*.
[18] [1997] Ch. 213 at 253.
[19] *Supra*, n. 11, at p. 70.
[20] Cf. the situation where s. 426 of the Insolvency Act 1986 has been invoked, see *infra*.
[1] Commonsense indicates that creditors resident in England (or resident in Asia and having accounts in England) would likely claim in England; certainly far more banking business was done by BCCI in England than in Luxembourg, see generally [1997] Ch. 213 at 224.
[2] Although if a rigid approach had been taken, such as only extending rule 4.90 to creditors with accounts in the United Kingdom, the amount of litigation might not have been great.
[3] Although, in theory, it could have been that the foreign court would not allow individuals subject to its jurisdiction to retain the benefit of the English set-off provision, requiring those creditors within its reach to disgorge.
[4] See *ex p Melbourn, supra*.

manipulate the rules to gain maximum advantage: for example, the foreign creditor should make sure he completes his execution on the debtor's assets abroad *before* entering a proof in the English bankruptcy or winding up.[5]

In any event, the ruling in *Re BCCI S.A. (No. 10)* will only apply where the English court is conducting winding up proceedings. Let us say that a foreign corporation, in liquidation abroad, has not carried on business in England but does have assets in England – so there is undoubted jurisdiction to wind up the company. A foreign creditor presents a winding up petition and, in response to the argument by the foreign liquidator that the petition should be dismissed on the ground of *forum non conveniens*,[6] asserts that if there were a winding up rule 4.90 would operate in a way that was more advantageous (to him) than the foreign set-off rules. In such a case rule 4.90 will not prevent the English court from dismissing the petition (or staying the proceedings) if it is appropriate to do so having regard to all the circumstances. It is not that the court 'disapplies' rule 4.90 but rather that, if no winding up in England is being conducted, rule 4.90 simply does not apply.[7]

B. Set-Off and Section 426

In *Re BCCI S.A. (No. 10)* the co-operation between the liquidators in England and Luxembourg was on the basis of specifically tailored agreements[8] and did not involve section 426 of the Insolvency Act 1986. But a case might arise in similar circumstances where a foreign court falling within section 426 were to submit a request to the English court to apply the foreign set-off rules. The matter is not entirely free from authority. In *Re Bell Lines Ltd.*[9] the Irish court had appointed an interim examiner in respect of an Irish company and made a request to the English court that the examiner's powers be extended to England. It was pointed out by counsel for the examiner that under Irish law, in contrast to English law, there was no set-off between separate bank accounts of the company, except with the consent of the examiner. Jacob J noted that, referring to *Hughes* v. *Hannover*,[10] he had power generally to apply Irish insolvency law and ruled that on the facts it would not be contrary to English public policy to give effect to the Irish set-off provision:[11]

> 'It is clear that different countries have different laws in relation to set-off and it is not self-evident that one law is so right that any other law is repugnant.'

---

[5] See p. 278, *supra.*

[6] See p. 127, *supra.*

[7] For an analogy, see *Radich* v. *Bank of New Zealand* (1993) 116 A.L.R. 676, where the Australian court exercised its discretion to decline jurisdiction in a bankruptcy case and thereby avoided having to apply the (unsatisfactory) rule laid down by the High Court of Australia in *Hall* v. *Woolf* (1908) 7 C.L.R. 207.

[8] The factual background to the 'pooling agreement' and the 'costs and recoveries agreement' is set out at [1997] Ch. 213 at 227–230.

[9] Chancery Division, 6th and 7th February 1997, unreported, Jacob J. The author is grateful to Gordon Stewart of Allen & Overy, London, for making available copies of the (two) judgments.

[10] See now [1997] 1 B.C.L.C. 497 and p. 407, *infra.*

[11] Judgment, 7 February 1997, p. 3.

Jacob J's order was *ex parte* and his Lordship stated that any third party should be able to apply for variation thereof. In addition, it is not certain from the judgment that the earlier decision of the Vice-Chancellor was cited. Nevertheless, and even if as this author has suggested rule 4.90 was perceived by Scott V-C to be a mandatory rule of the forum, it is suggested that there is no inconsistency between *Re BCCI S.A. (No. 10)* and *Re Bell Lines Ltd.*: because in the latter case there was no winding up in England, so rule 4.90 had simply not been brought into operation. However, if the same facts as in *Re BCCI S.A. (No. 10)* were to re-occur, except that the bank were an Irish bank and the Irish court were to request pursuant to section 426 that assets be transferred to Ireland without any deductions in respect of English set-off rules, this author would suggest that the English court would not comply with such a request. For creditors with accounts at English branches must be entitled to assume that, even though section 426 allows the application of the foreign insolvency law, English set-off rules will apply to their accounts.[12] Yet if the Irish court were to re-formulate its request so as specifically to undertake that creditors who held accounts at English branches would be given the benefit of the English set-off rules, it is suggested that the English court would accede to such a request. Section 426 gives the court the power not to apply rule 4.90 in those cases where the English court applies the relevant foreign rules; and it hardly lies in the mouth of creditors with accounts in Ireland to argue that they would be prejudiced by the application of the Irish set-off rule.[13]

C. No Insolvency in England

Even though no insolvency is commenced in England, set-off may yet be relevant in the context (for example) of a civil action brought by or against a foreign trustee or liquidator.

Whether a party to English litigation may raise a set-off, or counter-claim, has been regarded as a matter of procedure and accordingly governed by English law.[14] However, foreign rules of set-off will not be disregarded where their effect is to extinguish, in whole or in part, the relevant debt.[15] In *MacFarlane* v. *Norris*[16] the plaintiff had been appointed in a Scottish sequestration trustee of the bankrupt's estate. The plaintiff brought an action in England to which the defendant pleaded a Scottish set-off in the nature of mutual credits. The Court of Queen's Bench accepted that set-off was generally a matter of procedure. Nevertheless the judges were prepared to give effect to Scots law. Blackburn J put it thus:[17]

> 'The plaintiff sues as trustee of a trader in Scotland, who became bankrupt; and the question, what passed under the transfer of the bankrupt's goods and chattels to the trustee must be settled by the Scotch law, which must be averred

---

[12] The clear prejudice to English creditors with accounts in England would be a good reason to decline such assistance.

[13] It is suggested that the views expressed by Scott V-C in *Re BCCI S.A. (No. 10)* were in no way directed to how the court might exercise its discretion in a s. 426 case.

[14] *Meyer* v. *Dresser* (1864) 16 C.B.N.S. 646.

[15] See *Dicey and Morris*, pp. 181–182 and Wolff, p. 317, n. 4, *supra*, at pp. 233–234.

[16] (1862) 2 B. & S. 783.

[17] *Ibid.*, at 794.

on the pleadings . . . And I cannot read the averment at the end of the plea otherwise than as averring that the property of the bankrupt, under such circumstances, came to the trustee with a right to deduct cross claims; in other words, that the transfer in the Scotch law is a transfer of the balance of account after allowing for mutual credits.'

Cockburn CJ opined:[18]

'It is true the pleader has adopted the form of the English plea of set-off and mutual credit; but we must take the plea as substantially amounting to this; here are mutual credits, the effect of which, by Scotch law, is the discharge of the debtor from all excepting the balance.'

In short, the law of Scotland discharged or extinguished part of the debt and thus only vested in the plaintiff trustee the outstanding balance. Whereas such a set-off according to foreign law may be acted upon in England, it is of course for the party relying thereon to prove that the foreign set-off is substantive in its operation.

4. FOREIGN CURRENCY DEBTS

The Insolvency Rules 1986 make express provision for the conversion into sterling of debts in foreign currencies. In rule 4.91 it is stated that:

'For the purpose of proving a debt incurred or payable in a currency other than sterling the amount of the debt shall be converted into sterling at the official exchange rate prevailing on the date when the company went into liquidation.'

The date when a company goes into liquidation (rather than the date the winding up commences) is when the winding up order is made or when the resolution for voluntary liquidation is passed.[19] Like provision is made in rule 6.111 for bankruptcy – the relevant date being the date of the bankruptcy order.[20] Despite such express provision, there is one problem that remains: a problem that was quite recently brought to the attention of the Supreme Court in Ireland.

In *Re Don Bluth Entertainment Ltd.*[1] an examiner (roughly equivalent to an English administrator) had been appointed over an Irish company and, pursuant to authority granted by the Irish court, had borrowed US$1,050,000 as part of a rescue plan. It subsequently became apparent that the company could not be saved and it was accordingly put into liquidation in October 1992.[2] Under the Companies (Amendment) Act 1990 of Ireland the borrowing was treated as an 'expense' properly incurred by the examiner. Section 29(3) provided that such expenses:

'. . . shall be paid in full and shall be paid before any other claim, secured or unsecured, under any . . . winding up of the company. . . .'

---

[18] *Ibid.*, at 793.
[19] See s. 247(2) and *Re Dynamics Corpn. of America (No. 2)* [1976] 1 W.L.R. 757.
[20] Conversion into sterling is not required when making a statutory demand: *Re a Debtor (No. 51/SD/1991)* [1992] 1 W.L.R. 1294.
[1] [1994] 2 I.L.R.M. 436, [1994] 3 I.R. 155.
[2] There was only a short period between when the petition was presented and when the winding up order was made, thus on the facts it seems it did not matter which date was taken.

Owing to a significant loss in value of the Irish pound in the 18 months after the company went into liquidation, the question arose as to whether the date of the liquidation should be taken as the conversion date. The High Court, applying the common law authorities,[3] favoured October 1992 and the lender appealed. The Supreme Court unanimously held that the case fell outside the common law rules: unless the liquidator paid over to the lender sufficient Irish pounds to enable the lender, on the date of payment, to purchase US$1,050,000 the debt would not be 'paid in full' within section 29(3). Moreover, the decision in the court below went against the policy behind the legislation, namely to encourage third parties to lend in order to promote the survival of companies in difficulty.

Precisely the same problem might arise in England when an administration has ended in a liquidation (although the legislative provisions are not identical on either side of the water). Where an administration order is discharged and a company is put into liquidation, section 19(4) and (5) will operate.[4] Subsection (4) confers upon the administrator in respect of his expenses and remuneration a charge over any property of the company at that time in his custody or under his control. Subsection (5) states that:

> 'Any sums payable in respect of debts or liabilities incurred, while he was an administrator, under contracts entered into by him . . . in the carrying out of his . . . functions shall be charged on and paid out of any such property as is mentioned in subsection (4) in priority to any charge arising under that subsection.'

The key words in section 19(5) are, it is submitted, any 'sums payable'. Where a company is put into liquidation in England in circumstances similar to *Re Don Bluth Entertainment Ltd.* there is no doubt that the lender will be entitled to what is sometimes referred to as 'super-priority'. But the fact that the lender has priority is only part of the answer. Such priority is in relation to any sums payable when the administrator is discharged – which will be before even the winding up petition is presented. Yet whatever that sum is in US dollars, it still has to be converted into sterling in order to be proved as a debt in the subsequent winding up.[5] It is at this stage that rule 4.91 must operate.

This author would respectfully submit that the decision of the Supreme Court in Ireland makes good sense. For although a well-advised lender can always hedge against a fall in the value of sterling, to place that obligation on the lender will only increase the final cost of borrowing to a company already in severe financial difficulty. Nevertheless, rule 4.91 does not seem to permit of any exception and nothing in section 19, it is submitted, can reasonably be interpreted as creating any such exception.

Finally, although this particular issue does not seem to have caught the attention of commentators on English insolvency law, it is plain that amendment to rule 4.91 should be made as soon as possible.

---

[3] In particular, *Re Lines Bros Ltd.* [1983] Ch. 1.

[4] See Fletcher, *The Law of Insolvency* (2nd ed., 1996) pp. 469–471 and Rajani, *Corporate Insolvency* (2nd ed., 1994) p. 105: the s. 19 charge has priority over any floating charges.

[5] Unless it is suggested that s. 19(5) be read as conferring authority on a liquidator to pay a debt which is *not* proved in the winding up, thereby avoiding rule 4.91 altogether. But this author would suggest that such a construction is totally to re-write the subsection.

5. EUROPEAN CONVENTION ON INSOLVENCY PROCEEDINGS

Article 4(1) lays down as a basic proposition that, unless otherwise provided in the Convention, the law applicable to insolvency proceedings will be the law of the Contracting State where such proceedings have been commenced. That law is to govern, in particular:[6]

'(a) against which debtors insolvency proceedings may be brought on account of their capacity;

(b) the assets which form part of the estate and the treatment of assets acquired by or devolving on the debtor after the opening of the insolvency proceedings;

(c) the respective powers of the debtor and the liquidator;

(d) the conditions under which set-offs may be invoked;

(e) the effects of insolvency proceedings on current contracts to which the debtor is party;

(f) the effects of the insolvency proceedings on proceedings brought by individual creditors, with the exception of lawsuits pending;

(g) the claims which are to be lodged against the debtor's estate and the treatment of claims arising after the opening of insolvency proceedings;

(h) the rules governing the lodging, verification and admission of claims;

(i) the rules governing the distribution of proceeds from the realization of assets, the ranking of claims and the rights of creditors who have obtained partial satisfaction after the opening of insolvency proceedings by virtue of a right *in rem* or through a set-off;

(j) the conditions for and the effects of closure of insolvency proceedings, in particular by composition;

(k) creditors' rights after the closure of insolvency proceedings;

(l) who is to bear the costs and expenses of the insolvency proceedings;

(m) the rules relating to the voidness, voidability or unenforceability of legal acts detrimental to all creditors.'

Thus sub-paragraphs (h) and (i) would permit the English court to continue to apply the *lex fori* to questions of priority, as well as to the conversion of foreign currency debts into pounds sterling. Sub-paragraph (d) also allows the application of English law to questions of set-off. However, Article 6(1) must be taken into account:

'The opening of insolvency proceedings shall not affect the right of creditors to demand the set-off of their claims against the claims of the debtor, where such a set-off is permitted by the law applicable to the insolvent debtor's claim.'

The relationship between Articles 4(2)(d) and 6(1) is explained in the *Explanatory Report on Insolvency Proceedings*:[7]

'If the *lex concursus* allows for set-off, no problem shall arise, and Article 4 should be applied in order to claim the set-off. On the other hand, if the *lex concursus* does not allow for set-off, then Article 6 constitutes an exception to the general application of that law in this respect, by permitting, *ex jure*

---

[6] See Art. 4(2).

[7] Para. 90, the Report (although not in its final version) is contained in *EC Convention on Insolvency Proceedings: A Consultative Document* (The Insolvency Service, DTI, February 1996).

conventionis, the set-off according to the law applicable to the insolvent debtor's claim. In this respect, the set-off becomes a guarantee.'

As the insolvency set-off provisions of Engish law are relatively liberal, compared to those applicable in civil law jurisdictions, it is probable that most set-offs in an English bankruptcy or winding up could be brought within Article 4(2)(d). In practical terms, Article 6(1) would be more likely to be relevant when no insolvency proceedings are opened in England, but a creditor wants in the foreign insolvency to raise a set-off arising under an agreement governed by English law.[8]

6. ILLUSTRATIONS

(1) A Co. Ltd. is an English company in liquidation in England. C wishes to claim in the winding up upon a contract governed by the law of France. French law determines the validity of C's claim; however, any question as to priority must be decided according to English law.

(2) M Co. Ltd. is an English company in respect of which a winding up order has been made in England. Prior to the commencement of the winding up S, an English creditor, had attached property belonging to the company in New York, and under New York law S had obtained security upon the property so attached. The English court has jurisdiction to restrain S from proceeding with the New York attachment and to require S to abandon the attachment so as to allow the English liquidator to gather in the relevant property. However, if the English court so acts,[9] it will reserve to S the 'full benefit' of any security under New York law.[10] Thus if the assets are subsequently also claimed by another creditor in the English liquidation, the question of priority will be decided in accordance with the law of New York.[11]

(3) W carried on business in England and South Africa. W has been made bankrupt in England and a trustee appointed. The trustee has brought an action in England against R upon a contract governed by the law of South Africa. R wishes to bring a counterclaim. The availability of a counterclaim is a matter for English law *qua lex fori*.

(4) Exco Ltd., incorporated in Jordan, has carried on business in England through a branch office. The company is in liquidation in Jordan and an ancillary winding up has been ordered in England. The intention is that ultimately assets collected in England will be transferred to be distributed in the principal liquidation in Jordan. Creditors who have submitted proofs in England have established that Jordanian set-off rules

---

[8] The applicable law being the law governing the insolvent debtor's claim: see Segal (1997) 23 Brook. J. Int'l. L. 57 at 66–67.

[9] The English liquidator may, however, prefer to be free to apply to the foreign court to have the attachment set aside: see *Barclays Bank plc* v. *Homan* [1993] B.C.L.C. 680, p. 332, *infra*.

[10] *Re Queensland Mercantile Agency Co. Ltd.*, *supra*.

[11] *Re Queensland Mercantile and Agency Co., ex p Australasian Investment Co.* [1892] 1 Ch. 219.

will deny them set-off rights that they would have in an English winding up. The English liquidators must make appropriate arrangements,[12] by way of retention of funds in England, to ensure that the creditors will not be prejudiced by an application of the Jordanian rules.

---

[12] See *Re B.C.C.I. S.A. (No. 10)* [1997] Ch. 213 at 252.

Chapter 12

Concurrent Insolvencies

1. GENERAL

Since the time of Lord Eldon[1] English judges have been aware of the complexities which may flow from concurrent insolvencies. In recent years the lack of an international convention dealing with cross-border insolvencies, and the 'crying need' for such a convention,[2] has been high-lighted in a number of high-profile cases: most notably involving the Bank of Credit and Commerce International S.A. and Maxwell Communications Corporation plc.[3] But as Millett LJ has observed (with specific reference to cross-border insolvency):[4]

> '. . . commercial necessity has encouraged national courts to provide assistance to each other without waiting for such co-operation to be sanctioned by inter-national convention . . . It is becoming widely accepted that comity between the courts of different countries requires mutual respect for the territorial integrity of each other's jurisdiction, but that this should not inhibit a court in one jurisdiction from rendering whatever assistance it properly can to a court in another in respect of assets located or persons resident within the territory of the former.'

The sort of assistance and co-operation referred to by the learned Lord Justice may occur either when the English court is conducting its own insolvency proceedings, or when no such proceedings have been com-menced in England. Examples of the latter situation have been discussed earlier in this work[5] and include the recognition of the authority of a foreign insolvency representative to deal with movable property in England

---

[1] See *ex p Cridland* (1814) 3 Ves. & B. 95 at 101–102.
[2] *Per* Nicholls V-C in *Re Paramount Airways Ltd* [1993] Ch. 223 at 239.
[3] See, for example, the comments of Browne-Wilkinson V-C in *Re Bank of Credit and Commerce International S.A.* [1992] B.C.L.C. 570 at 577. Note also the following observa-tion of Hoffmann J in *Barclays Bank plc* v. *Homan* [1993] B.C.L.C. 680 at 691–692: 'As the Vice-Chancellor said in *Paramount Airways*, the only satisfactory solution to the possibility of jurisdictional conflicts in cross-border insolvencies would be an international convention. In the absence of such a convention, the only way forward is by the discretionary exercise of judicial self-restraint.' See also, generally, Grierson 'Issues in Concurrent Insolvency Jurisdiction: English Perspectives' Chapter 24 in Ziegel (ed.) *Current Developments in International and Comparative Corporate Insolvency Law* (1994).
[4] *Crédit Suisse Fides Trust S.A.* v. *Cuoghi* [1997] 3 All E.R. 724 at 730: the case on its facts did not involve insolvency but rather a worldwide Mareva injunction.
[5] See generally chapter 8, *supra.*

and the regulation (such as by the discharge of Mareva injunctions[6] or the exercise of discretion[7] under RSC Order 11) of civil actions commenced in England against an insolvent foreign defendant. Yet the English court will be just as willing to co-operate, and perhaps even more so,[8] where insolvency proceedings *have* been commenced in England – although no amount of goodwill on the part of the English courts and English insolvency representatives can prevent their foreign counterparts from adopting a nationalistic and unco-operative stance.[9] Thus, it must always be borne in mind that when dealing with concurrent insolvencies each case must be approached in the light of its particular facts: hence, although in certain instances two or more sets of insolvency proceedings may cause great difficulty to the insolvent and creditors (not to mention trustees, liquidators and the like), other examples may be found in which English and foreign insolvency representatives have – with the approval of their respective courts – co-operated to the benefit of all concerned.[10]

In the first edition of this work it was stated that the guiding principle for the English court must be the desire to adopt the most appropriate means of ensuring substantial equality between creditors in different countries;[11] and judicial comments to this effect are not difficult to find.[12] However, it is perhaps worth stressing that avoiding unnecessary costs should always be an objective to which more than just lip-service is paid.

A. Staying Proceedings: The Exercise of Discretion

(i) *Bankruptcy and Winding Up Proceedings*

A bankruptcy or winding up order will not follow automatically upon the presentation of the relevant creditor's petition. The English court, in the exercise of its discretion, determines whether it is appropriate for insolvency proceedings to be opened in England. The existence and conduct of a foreign bankruptcy or winding up is, of course, a matter relevant to the exercise of such discretion; and the acceptance of a suitably modified doctrine of the convenient forum has now become a reality.[13] In addition, when dealing with a foreign corporation, the English court has recently re-affirmed its willingness to conduct a winding up ancillary or auxiliary to the main liquidation in the country of incorporation.[14] In short, in many

---

[6] As in *Banque Indosuez S.A. v. Ferromet Resources Inc.* [1993] B.C.L.C. 112, p. 237, *supra*.

[7] See *Firswood Ltd. v. Petra Bank* [1996] C.L.C. 608, p. 246, *supra*.

[8] Lord Hoffmann in *'Cross-Border Insolvency': The 1996 Denning Lecture*, 18 April 1996, at p. 21 has stated; 'English courts have always felt more comfortable about co-operation with foreign insolvency proceedings when there were already proceedings on foot in this country.'

[9] A good example being the attitude of German insolvency representatives in the Lancer Boss plc insolvency: see Turing [1994] I.C.C.L.R. c-146 note.

[10] See *Re Macfadyen & Co.* [1908] 1 K.B. 675, *infra*. When the English court is conducting an ancillary winding up, it will obviously be seeking to co-operate with the foreign process. Ancillary winding up is considered fully in chapter 14.

[11] See the first edition of this work, at p. 213.

[12] See, e.g., *per* Browne-Wilkinson V-C in *Re Bank of Credit and Commerce International S.A. (No. 2)* [1992] B.C.L.C. 579 at 581.

[13] See chapter 3, *supra*.

[14] *Re Bank of Credit and Commerce International S.A. (No. 10)* [1997] Ch. 213, discussed p. 363, *infra*.

instances the best way to promote equality (and to lessen costs) is to avoid conducting concurrent insolvencies, or at least to limit the scope of English proceedings to an ancillary character.

One practical difficulty, however, which may face an English judge is that there is currently no general requirement under the Insolvency Act 1986 that the existence of prior foreign insolvency proceedings must be revealed by a petitioning creditor or the insolvent. By virtue of the Oversea Companies and Credit and Financial Institutions (Bank Disclosure) Regulations 1992, which added ss. 703P–703R to the Companies Act 1985, where a foreign limited liability company has a branch office in England the company must, within a specified time period, deliver a return to the Registrar of Companies containing relevant particulars of any winding up of that company abroad. (Disclosure is required both by the foreign company and the foreign liquidator.) Particulars are also required where such a company becomes subject to insolvency proceedings abroad other than winding up.[15] But, in relation to an individual, English law contains no such disclosure provisions. The position is far better in Scotland where section 10 of the Bankrupcy (Scotland) Act 1985, following upon recommendations of the Scottish Law Commission,[16] requires that if, during the course of a sequestration, the petitioner (or a concurring creditor) or the debtor becomes aware of bankruptcy or analogous proceedings being pursued elsewhere in the United Kingdom or in a foreign country, then that fact must be brought to the attention of the Scottish court as soon as possible. There can be no reason why such a provision should not be enacted in England – and indeed extended to cover corporate insolvencies.[17]

(ii) *Staying English Litigation*

Where insolvency proceedings are on foot in England and abroad, the English court may restrict the scope of its own proceedings where a particular issue can more appropriately be dealt with in the foreign court. As Hoffmann J has put it: '[i]n the absence of [an intentional] convention, the only way forward is by the discretionary exercise of judicial self-restraint'.[18] The point may be illustrated by way of an example. A debtor with homes and substantial business interests in England and Hong Kong has been made bankrupt in both jurisdictions. In 1997 the debtor made a payment to a creditor in the Philippines, the money being transferred from a bank account in Hong Kong to the creditor's bank in Manila. The English trustee wishes to attack the payment as a preference under section 340 of the Insolvency Act 1986. Whilst undoubtedly the English court could take jurisdiction in such a case,[19] it is suggested that the court should

---

[15] For further details, see p. 135, *supra*.

[16] *Report on Bankruptcy and Related Aspects of Insolvency and Liquidation*, Scottish Law Commission No. 68, 1982, pp. 98–101.

[17] The Branch Disclosure Regulations obviously only relate to foreign companies with a branch in England, yet the winding up jurisdiction under Part V of the Insolvency Act 1986 is far more extensive.

[18] *Supra*, n. 3.

[19] It is inevitable that 'any person' in s. 340(1) would include a creditor in the Philippines: the provision operates extraterritorially, see *Re Paramount Airways Ltd.* [1993] Ch. 223 and p. 19, *supra*.

decline jurisdiction[20] once it is established that the Hong Kong trustee is able to bring the (roughly) equivalent proceedings in Hong Kong. The fact that, were the transaction to be challenged in England, the trustee could rely upon the presumption found in section 340(5) – and no such presumption existed under the bankruptcy legislation in force at the relevant time in Hong Kong – would not be enough to prevent the English court from declining jurisdiction (in favour of Hong Kong).[1] As Blair J put it in *Re Olympia and York Developments Ltd.*:[2]

> 'In the context of multi-jurisdictional insolvencies the courts of different jurisdictions should strive – to the extent that they can within the parameters of their own fundamental precepts of justice – to ensure that matters are adjudicated in the proper forum with the closest connection to the subject-matter. Principles of international comity, including those incorporated in the *forum non conveniens* test, provide the touchstones to assist them in doing so: see *Re Maxwell Communications Corpn.* 170 B.R. 800 (Bankr., S.D.N.Y., 1994) . . .'

The judgment (of Judge Brozman) in the Maxwell insolvency[3] and the approach of the appellate courts[4] may be seen as something of a classic example of a court declining jurisdiction in a preference action where the facts showed that a foreign forum (namely England) was clearly more suitable. Moreover, the Maxwell insolvency shows that a court will not be swayed from declining jurisdiction merely because there is a far smaller chance (or even no chance at all)[5] of having an alleged preference set aside under the more closely connected foreign law. For if a transaction has its centre of gravity abroad, then there is nothing inherently unreasonable in deferring to the foreign law: even if the foreign law regards that transaction as unimpeachable and the application of English law might have led to a different result.

(iii) *Restraining Foreign Proceedings*

The jurisdiction of the English court, once an insolvency is underway, to restrain a creditor who commences or continues an action abroad has

---

[20] Thus, for example, leave would not be granted to serve the creditor in the Philippines: see *Re Paramount Airways Ltd.*, *ibid.*, at 240–241 in relation to leave to serve s. 238 proceedings abroad.

[1] Throughout 1997 Hong Kong retained the 'old' law of fraudulent preference: see Booth (1997) 6 I.I.R. 183, *passim*.

[2] (1996) 29 O.R. (3d) 626 at 633. The case concerned a claim by the administrator of four Canadian corporations within the Olympia and York group for payment of fees etc (by the four Canadian corporations). Some $7 million of the claim related to work done and expenses incurred in the United States in re-organisation proceedings under the US Bankruptcy Code. Having regard to the circumstance that the assessment of this part of the claim (which was disputed) would involve 'an appreciation of complex matters of US tax, corporate and real estate law' (at 631), the Canadian court stayed the proceedings as far as relating to the US restructuring expenses and left the administrator to pursue the matter in the Bankruptcy Court in New York.

[3] 170 B.R. 800 (Bankr., S.D.N.Y. 1994) also reported as *Re Maxwell Communications Corpn. plc* [1995] I.L.Pr. 226.

[4] 186 B.R. 807 (S.D.N.Y. 1995) (Judge Scheindlin in the District Court), *Re Maxwell Communications Corpn. plc* 93 F.3d 1036 (2d Cir. 1996): see particularly 93 F.3d 1036 at 1051, 1053 *per* Judge Cardamone.

[5] Which is why, of course, the creditor bank tried (unsuccessfully) to prevent the administrators from pursuing a preference action in the United States in the first place: see *Barclays Bank plc* v. *Homan* [1993] B.C.L.C. 680, *infra*.

already been discussed.[6] In the particular context of concurrent insolvencies, the hotchpot rule will be applied to creditors who enter proofs in both the English and foreign insolvencies. Even if an English-resident creditor seeks a 'preferential dividend'[7] or some other enhanced priority[8] – to which that creditor would not be entitled under English domestic insolvency law – the English court will not restrain that creditor from claiming abroad, nor will the court require the creditor later to disgorge any such preferential dividend (although the hotchpot rule will be applied if a proof is also entered in the English proceedings).

Thus perhaps the more likely situation[9] involving concurrent insolvencies in which the English court might be asked to restrain foreign proceedings is where the English liquidator, administrator or trustee is seeking to take advantage of provisions of the foreign insolvency law. Of course, the English court cannot restrain foreign proceedings themselves, but rather acts *in personam* to injunct a party subject to the jurisdiction of the English court. Hence, for example, if there is an English company with a branch in Paris, and liquidations are under way in both countries, the English court will simply have no jurisdiction to restrain the French liquidator from taking whatever action he feels is appropriate in France, even though there might in theory be jurisdiction to restrain the English liquidator from doing the act in question. Moreover, as the court will not act in vain, as a matter of general principle the English liquidator will not be restrained if the act in question may in any event be carried out by the French liquidator.[10] Any complaint will simply have to be brought in the French court.

The leading authority in this area is, of course, *Barclays Bank plc* v. *Homan*.[11] Maxwell Communications Corporation plc ('MCC') was an English company which had substantial interests – particularly through its US subsidiaries – in the United States. MCC had been put into administration in England and was also under Chapter 11 reorganisation in New York. Shortly before MCC filed for administration it had repaid an overdraft of some US$30 million to Barclays, Barclays having put considerable pressure on Kevin Maxwell in particular for MCC to make the repayment. The money came from the sale by MCC of a US subsidiary as a going concern. The subsidiary was sold for US$157.5 million which was paid initially to the Nat West branch in New York. The following day that sum was transferred to MCC's US dollar account with Nat West in London; and a few days later US$30 million was paid to Barclays in New York, which sum was thereafter credited to MCC's overdrawn account with Barclays in London. Barclays was confident that, as it had received payment only after putting considerable commercial pressure on MCC, it could successfully resist any claim brought by the administrators that the repayment was a preference for the purposes of section 239 of the Insolvency Act 1986. The administrators, who had been recognised by the US Bankruptcy Court as the corporate governance of MCC,[12] were

---

[6] See p. 278, *supra*.

[7] Note *ex p Wilson, Re Douglas* (1872) 7 Ch. App. 490, discussed p. 339, *infra*.

[8] One is not here referring to an attachment abroad.

[9] Although it will be very highly unusual for the court to restrain such proceedings.

[10] Note the comment of Hoffmann J in *Barclays Bank plc* v. *Homan* [1993] B.C.L.C. 680 at 693.

[11] [1993] B.C.L.C. 680 (Hoffmann J. and C.A.), *sub nom. Re Maxwell Communications Corpn. (No 2) plc* [1992] B.C.C. 757.

[12] *Ibid.*, at 684 – although an examiner had also been appointed in the US court.

however considering applying in the US under section 547 of the Bankruptcy Code; and under the US provision, subject to certain defences, any payments made within 90 days of the filing of the Chapter 11 petition might be avoided.

Hoffmann J declined to injunct the administrators from proceeding in the US court and did not consider that such proceedings could be described as 'unconscionable' or categorised as 'vexatious or oppressive'. Whilst it might be said that England was the natural forum for any avoidance action, that was by itself insufficient to justify an anti-suit injunction; and 'the normal assumption' as Hoffmann J put it[13] 'is that the foreign judge is the best person to decide whether an action in his own court should proceed.' (Of course, the US Bankruptcy Court in turn decided that, having regard to the 'Englishness' of the case, any preference action ought to be brought in England.[14]) Hoffmann J also pointed out that he had no power to restrain the examiner appointed in the Chapter 11 proceedings and that 'this court has in the end no real control over what is done in the name of MCC in New York'.[15] The determination of Hoffmann J was upheld on appeal. Their Lordships essentially agreed with the judge that, on the facts, proceedings in the US Bankruptcy Court could not be said to be vexatious or oppressive. But Leggatt LJ also made a point of more general importance in cases where the English court and a foreign court are seeking to co-ordinate their (concurrent) insolvency proceedings:[16]

'Hoffmann J recognised the jurisdiction of the United States Bankruptcy Court when he made his order of 31 December 1991. This court having recognised the United States court in relation to this insolvency, it would, in my judgment, offend against comity for this court now to decree which claims the administrators can, and which they cannot, allege in the United States court are preferences'.

In other words, in concurrent insolvency cases the court will be particularly reluctant to interfere (even indirectly) with proceedings in the foreign court, as any such interference may undermine the broader co-operation necessary to conduct an effective multi-jurisdictional rescue or liquidation.[17]

Barclays Bank plc v. *Homan* was, of course, decided upon its facts and concerned an attempt to prevent the administrators taking steps abroad. Nevertheless, the decision is consistent with, and it is submitted supports, a

---

[13] *Ibid.*, at 691, see also the comments of Glidewell LJ at 703.

[14] *Supra*, n. 4.

[15] [1993] B.C.L.C. 680 at 693.

[16] *Ibid.*, at 706. The reference to the order of 31 December 1991 is explained in the judgment of Hoffmann J (at 684): 'On 31 December 1991 I authorised the administrators to consent to an order of the United States court in New York which would enable the administrators and examiner to harmonise their work and eliminate unnecessary duplication and expense . . . But the order was expressed not to affect the jurisdiction of this court and the United States court under their respective laws or to preclude a party in interest from seeking an expansion or reduction of the examiner's powers.'

[17] This same principle will, of course, be applicable where the forum decides to stay its own proceedings in deference to a more appropriate foreign court. As Judge Cardamone put it in *Re Maxwell Communications Corp. plc*, *supra* n. 4, at 1053: 'where a dispute involving conflicting avoidance laws arises in the context of parallel bankruptcy proceedings that have already achieved substantial reconciliation between the two sets of laws, comity argues decidedly against the risk of derailing that co-operation by the selfish application of our law to circumstances touching more directly upon the interests of another forum.'

general principle of English law applicable in cross-border insolvencies and which can be expressed in a positive form. English insolvency representatives (when gathering in the debtor's estate, setting aside attachments and avoiding transactions) are entitled to go before a foreign court and seek to rely upon (more advantageous)[18] provisions of foreign law; particularly where, as will normally be the case, the foreign law is the *lex situs*. This general principle finds support in Parliament's expressed intention when dealing with the consequences of attachments in Anglo-Scottish liquidations.[19]

(iv) *Declarations and Injunctions*

In *Barclays Bank plc* v. *Homan* the plaintiff, in addition to an injunction, also sought a declaration that the administrators could only bring proceedings for repayment of the US$30 million in the English courts. Such declaratory relief was refused by reference to the very same grounds as applied in respect of the plaintiff's claim for an injunction.[20] In *Mitchell* v. *Carter*; *Re Buckingham International plc* the applicants tried a slightly different tack.[1]

In 1994 the applicants obtained judgment in England against the company. In 1995 the company's bankers appointed administrative receivers. In May 1996 the applicants obtained recognition of the English judgment in Florida and began a process of attachment there. (The US attachment was said to be roughly equivalent to a garnishee order nisi.[2]) Before completion of the US attachment, a winding up petition was presented in England; and Knox J authorised the provisional liquidators to apply to the US Bankruptcy Court to prevent the applicants from completing their attachment.[3] The provisional liquidators obtained a temporary restraining order from the US court. In the meantime, a winding up order was duly made in England. The applicants – having no doubt carefully considered the decision in *Barclays Bank plc* v. *Homan* – did not try to convince the English court to injunct the liquidators from seeking to have the attachment set aside by the US court. Any such attempt would have been bound to have failed. Instead the applicants sought an order from the English court in substance that, in the event the liquidators were successful in having the attachment vacated by the US court, the applicants

---

[18] More advantageous to the insolvency representative, that is, than the equivalent English provisions.

[19] See the analysis of s. 185(4) of the Insolvency Act 1986 at p. 283, *supra*.

[20] [1993] B.C.L.C. 680 at 693.

[1] [1997] 1 B.C.L.C. 673 (Blackburne J and C.A.). Further proceedings on the substantive issue are reported as *Re Buckingham International plc (No. 2)*, (1997) Times, 20 November (Harman J), *infra*; on appeal (16 February 1998 unreported).

[2] *Ibid.*, at 676.

[3] In other words (see *ibid.*, at 677) the liquidators had two choices: (1) to invoke the *in personam* jurisdiction of the English court to restrain the applicants from continuing with their incomplete foreign attachment (see p. 284, *supra*); or (2) to apply to the US court (pursuant to s. 304 of the US Bankruptcy Code) to prevent the incomplete attachment from proceeding. The liquidators chose the latter course of action which, *per* Millett LJ, was in accordance with the 'normal assumption' that the foreign court is best qualified to determine if proceedings in that court should be allowed to proceed (see [1997] 1 B.C.L.C. 673 at 687).

would nevertheless be allowed to retain the benefit of the attachment as against the liquidators.

On account of the way the case progressed procedurally, the first question (by way of a preliminary issue) to come before the English court was whether the court had *jurisdiction* to determine whether the applicants might be entitled to retain the benefit of the attachment. The Court of Appeal held that, as the question arose in the course of an English winding up, the court had jurisdiction to direct the liquidators either to intervene in foreign attachment proceedings or not to so intervene. The question as to whether the applicants would be allowed to retain the fruits of their execution was regarded by their Lordships as inextricably intertwined with whether or not the liquidators should be allowed to continue with their proceedings in the United States:[4]

> 'The court does, in my view, have jurisdiction to decide whether the fruits of those garnishment proceedings, if successful, should be retained by the appellants. If they should, then it would not be appropriate for the liquidators to continue with their proceedings in the USA.'

An additional, and it is submitted more compelling, reason why the English court was required to exercise jurisdiction was that 'in the modern spirit of co-operation in cross-border insolvency proceedings', as Millett LJ put it, 'the judge in the court in Florida has deferred to the decision of this court, being the court seized of the liquidation'.[5] In any event, when the hearing on the merits came before Harman J,[6] it was ruled that there was no justification for allowing the applicants to obtain payment of their debt in priority to the rest of the unsecured creditors.[7]

There are perhaps two lessons to be drawn from *Re Buckingham International plc*. First, the approach adopted – of dealing with a jurisdictional question as a preliminary issue – does not serve any useful purpose and only increases costs. Secondly, where English creditors find themselves in the position the applicants were in when the winding up commenced, their interests may often be best served by agreeing with the liquidator that any attachments will be abandoned, so that the money may be remitted to England,[8] and the English court will be left to decide whether the facts merit a departure from the *pari passu* principle.

B. Protocols and Other Arrangements

The co-operation between the English and US courts – and more importantly between the administrators and the examiner – in the Maxwell insolvency has been judicially described as a 'remarkable sequence of events leading to perhaps the first world-wide plan of orderly liquidation ever achieved.'[9] Yet it cannot be said that the Maxwell insolvency

[4] [1997] 1 B.C.L.C. 673 at 686 *per* Aldous LJ.
[5] *Ibid.*, at 687: oddly this fact is not mentioned in the judgment of Aldous LJ.
[6] *Sub nom. Re Buckingham International plc (No. 2)*, (1997) Times, 20 November. See also n. 1, *supra*.
[7] An appeal was subsequently dismissed: 16 February 1998 (Lord Bingham CJ, Judge and Robert Walker LJJ) unreported.
[8] See also p. 289, *supra*.
[9] *Per* Judge Cardamone in *Re Maxwell Communications Corpn. plc* 93 F. 3d 1036 at 1042, quoting Westbrook (1996) 64 Fordham L. Rev. 2531 at 2535.

represents a typical cross-border insolvency scenario, indeed one may fairly question whether there are really any 'typical' cases. Moreover, the Protocol[10] agreed upon by the administrators and the examiner, and subsequently approved by their respective courts, was drawn up with one eye on the specific issues raised or likely to become relevant under the laws of the two jurisdictions involved: if, for instance, the facts had involved an English company with subsidiaries in Spain, no doubt some quite different issues would have been brought up for consideration. Nevertheless, the case illustrates just how much can be achieved through co-operation, even without an international convention.[11] The Maxwell insolvency also highlights the oft-made point that the case-law and statutes in this field tend to mark boundaries rather than lay down rigid rules to be applied in all situations; and within those broad boundaries practitioners have very considerable scope to put together appropriate solutions. Lord Hoffmann himself has spoken extra-judicially of the limited role the courts have to play in supervising any plan the respective insolvency representatives have agreed upon:[12]

> 'The Protocol was brought before me for approval. I think it took me about 20 minutes to read and approve it. I checked to see whether it contained anything which looked like an obvious mistake. Otherwise the chances are I would have approved of whatever it said. I had appointed administrators and it was their duty to take charge of the business and collect the assets according to their professional judgment. They were eminent insolvency accountants who had an experience in the management of insolvent businesses which I certainly did not share. I would ordinarily therefore accept their judgment of the best way to go forward . . . they felt that the interests of creditors were best served by agreeing to the Protocol. In those circumstances, it is hardly surprising that I approved. It involved no conflict between the interests of English creditors and any principle of comity or internationalism.'

These comments obviously do not for one moment, however, suggest that the court is merely a rubber-stamp; and a relatively recent example can be found where a court in the United Kingdom required modification of an agreed scheme of arrangement.

Re ABP Holdings Ltd.[13] arose out of the rescue of the Goodman International group of companies.[14] The High Court in Dublin had appointed an examiner to the companies in the Goodman group in the Republic of Ireland and subsequently approved a scheme of arrangement ('the Irish scheme') put forward by the examiner. ABP Holdings Ltd. ('ABP') was incorporated in Northern Ireland and, although beneficially owned by Goodman International, fell outside the Irish scheme. A winding up petition had been presented in respect of ABP, but it was proposed that a scheme of arrangement be approved and the petition dismissed. The scheme of arrangement in relation to ABP was, in substance, a satellite scheme – for it and its terms revolved around the overall Irish scheme

---

[10] For an illuminating discussion of the Protocol and the Maxwell insolvency generally, see Westbrook (1996) 64 Fordham L. Rev. 2531; note also Flaschen and Silverman in Ziegel (ed.) *Current Developments in International and Comparative Corporate Insolvency Law* (1994) pp. 709–727 and Fletcher (1993) 6 Ins. Int. 10–13.

[11] See the comment of Millett LJ in *Crédit Suisse Fides Trust S.A.* v. *Cuoghi*, set out at p. 328, *supra*.

[12] *Supra*, p. 329, n. 8 at pp. 19–20.

[13] [1991] N.I. 17.

[14] Other proceedings are noted as *Re Goodman International* (1990) 5 B.J.I.B. F.L. 530.

applicable to Goodman International. The ABP scheme required certain creditors ('the banking creditors') to partake in and be bound by the Irish scheme. The necessary majority of the banking creditors approved the ABP scheme. But a clause in the Irish scheme amounted to a waiver of any liability which, *inter alios*, a director of any company in the group might be under for breach of duty to his company. Campbell J in the Chancery Division in Northern Ireland refused (without modification) to confirm this part of the scheme in relation to ABP. His Lordship considered that the clause offended against the statutory rule[15] (also applicable in England)[16] which prohibits 'any provision, whether contained in a company's articles or any contract with the company or otherwise, for exempting any officer of the company . . . from . . . any liability . . . in respect of any negligence, default, breach of duty or breach of trust of which he may be guilty in relation to the company.'[17]

ABP Holdings Ltd., it is submitted, is a pertinent illustration of the point that the court will not simply approve of whatever is placed before it without the exercise of its own discretion.[18] This author would, however, respectfully disagree with the judge's interpretation of (the equivalent in Northern Ireland of) section 310 of the Companies Act 1985. Although section 310 does refer to 'any provision', whether contained in the articles or any contract with the company or otherwise, there is no good reason to suppose that Parliament (when the section was first introduced in 1928)[19] intended to limit the court's power when approving a scheme of arrangement. It is suggested that 'any provision' should be interpreted as meaning any provision contained in the articles or a contract or any other like private arrangement – but not to include a provision in a scheme of arrangement, protocol or other agreement which depends upon court approval for its very validity. The mischief behind section 310 supports this interpretation.[20] Moreover, if section 310 were applied to court-sanctioned schemes an anomaly would result. Section 310(1) refers to the liability of an 'officer of the company'; and the word 'company' must mean a company registered under the Act in Great Britain, rather than a foreign company.[1] But the court's power to sanction a scheme of arrangement undoubtedly (see section 425(6)(a)) includes both British and foreign companies. It would be somewhat ridiculous to conclude that the court might approve a scheme of arrangement which relieved a director of (potential) liability where the company concerned is a foreign company,

---

[15] Article 318(1) of the Companies (Northern Ireland) Order 1986, identical to s. 310(1) of the Companies Act 1985 (as amended).

[16] For a general discussion of s. 310, although not dealing with the issue raised here, see *Gower's Principles of Modern Company Law* (6th ed., 1997) pp. 623–625.

[17] Campbell J ([1991] N.I. 17 at 32) was prepared to approve the scheme subject to appropriate modifications (see also, at 31, in relation to modification to deal with the situation in the event the companies in the Goodman International group could not be rescued and were forced into liquidation).

[18] For earlier illustrations of multi-jurisdictional schemes of arrangement see *Re Australian Joint Stock Bank* [1897] W.N. 48, *Re Queensland National Bank* [1893] W.N. 129, *Re Commercial Bank of Australia Ltd.* (1893) 19 V.L.R. 333 (and note at [1894] 1 Q.B. 57), as well as *Re Kailis Groote Eylandt Fisheries Pty. Ltd.* (1977) 2 A.C.L.R. 479 (N.S.W.), 510 (Vic.) and 3 A.C.L.R. 288 (S.A.) and the commentary by Bennett (1978) 52 A.L.J. 320.

[19] Companies Act 1928, s. 78.

[20] Namely, to prevent directors being able to contract out of liability for breaches of duty: see *Re City Equitable Fire Insurance Co. Ltd.* [1925] Ch. 407.

[1] See Companies Act 1985, s. 735(1).

but cannot do so in relation to an English company. In short, it is suggested that the application of section 310 in *Re ABP Holdings Ltd.* to schemes of arrangement should not be followed.[2] Whether the court approves a scheme, protocol or other arrangement will be decided upon its merits[3] and is not restricted by section 310 of the Companies Act 1985.

Turning now to personal insolvency, a well-known example of concurrent proceedings can be found in *Re Macfadyen & Co.*[4] A partnership had carried on business in England and in India and insolvency proceedings were commenced, more or less simultaneously, in both jurisdictions. The English trustee and the official assignee in India came to an agreement for the ratable distribution of the firm's assets amongst all the creditors, in particular:[5]

> 'in order to ensure a ratable distribution of all assets among the creditors, neither the official assignee nor the trustee shall distribute a dividend without first ascertaining that the other of them has in his hands, available for dividend, sufficient to enable him to distribute a dividend at the like rate. Eventually the official assignee or the trustee, as the case may require, shall remit to the other such balance as may be necessary in order to ensure such ratable distribution. . . .'

The English court considered the arrangement 'manifestly for the benefit of all parties interested' and gave its approval thereto. One issue that was apparently not raised in *Re Macfadyen & Co.* is quite where the statutory authority to transfer assets (to a foreign assignee) is to be found.[6] Nevertheless, despite the absence of any clear statutory provision,[7] the case has been followed and has received the approval of Sir Peter Millett – albeit extra-judicially.[8]

Although not cited in *Re Macfadyen & Co.*, it may be noted that a broadly similar but less formal arrangement arose before the Court of Session in *Stewart* v. *Auld.*[9] A firm had carried on business in Scotland and in New South Wales. The firm was made bankrupt in New South Wales and in the following month a sequestration had issued in Scotland. The Australian assignee administered those assets in Australia and the Scottish trustee the estate in Scotland.[10] The appellant had received a

---

[2] It is submitted that this author's view finds indirect support in *Re Bank of Credit and Commerce International S.A. (No 4)* [1995] B.C.C. 453 at 460, where Scott V-C deals with the release of claims against certain directors of BCCI – although the s. 310 issue was not expressly raised.

[3] Obviously, the court would be unlikely to approve a scheme which provided a director with an indemnity for an outright fraud he has committed against the company, but the situation may well be different in relation to other (non-fraudulent) breaches or potential or alleged breaches.

[4] [1908] 1 K.B. 675.

[5] *Ibid.*, at 677.

[6] In *Re Fenton & Sons* (1900) 26 V.L.R. 88 the Full Court in Victoria had held that, in the absence of statutory authority, a trustee had no power to transfer assets to a foreign trustee to enable the latter to pay an equalising dividend abroad. Section 324(1) of the Insolvency Act 1986 if read literally would support this view.

[7] The same issue arises in relation to ancillary winding up: see p. 362, *infra*.

[8] 'Cross-Border Insolvency: The Judicial Approach' (1997) 6 I.I.R. 99 at 112: Millett LJ refers to *Re Commodore Business Machines Inc.*, December 1995, Supreme Court of the Bahamas in which *Macfadyen* was approved.

[9] (1851) 13 D. 1337.

[10] The Australian assignee specifically refrained from asserting his right to the bankrupt's movable estate in Scotland, which otherwise would have been regarded as vested in the Australian assignee on account of the prior Australian insolvency.

dividend of 7s. 6d. in the pound in Australia when the Scottish trustee declared an equalising dividend, from which creditors (including the appellant) who had recovered in Australia were excluded. The Scottish court, with reference to the principle of equal distribution amongst creditors, confirmed the course of action taken by the trustee.

C. No Discrimination

Where English and foreign courts are not acting in close co-operation it is perhaps most important that the principle of equality amongst creditors be observed, at least in the English court. That a foreign law may confer an advantage upon its own creditors in no way allows, still less requires, the English court to discriminate against those foreign creditors. As has been seen, if a creditor receives a dividend in a foreign insolvency that creditor will be permitted also to claim in England but will not receive anything until other creditors in England have been paid dividends equivalent to that received from the foreign court. The hotchpot doctrine, as it is commonly known, will apply even though the foreign court has ring-fenced the local assets and thereby given priority to its own creditors: equality rather than tit for tat is the relevant objective.

In *ex p Wilson*[11] the bankrupt had traded in England (as D & Co.) and in Brazil (as D, L & Co.). Insolvencies were under way in both jurisdictions. The respondents, resident in England[12] and holders of bills of exchange drawn by D, L & Co. upon and accepted by D & Co., received a dividend in Brazil and sought further to prove in England. Brazilian law had given what was described as a preference to Brazilian creditors.[13] Nevertheless, the respondents were permitted to prove in England subject to the hotchpot rule:[14]

> 'The Brazilian law lays hold of those assets which are within the reach of the Brazilian courts, and in administering them gives a preference to particular creditors; . . . if a particular creditor who is able to lay hold of assets of the bankrupt abroad comes here to share with the other creditors, he must bring into the estate here that which the law of the foreign country has given him over the other creditors. I am of the opinion that the order ought to be varied by allowing the respondents to prove, but not to receive dividends until the English creditors have received equal dividends with them.'

A quite different approach to preferences under a foreign law was apparently once taken by the Scottish courts. In *Bennet (Trustee for Crawford & Co.'s Creditors)* v. *Johnson*[15] a firm carried on business in Scotland and Newfoundland. Certain creditors received a preference in the Newfoundland insolvency[16] in accordance with the Newfoundland Act 1809, section 7 (49 Geo. III, c.27). In an action brought in Scotland

---

[11] *Ex p Wilson, Re Douglas* (1872) 7 Ch. App. 490. Hotchpot is considered in detail in chapter 10.

[12] As appears from the report at (1872) 26 L.T. 489.

[13] (1872) 7 Ch. App. 490 at 492; the Brazilian business being regarded under Brazilian law as a distinct body, and creditors thereof being entitled to preference.

[14] *Ibid.*

[15] (1819) 2 Bell's Com. 686n.

[16] Note *Re Crawford & Co.* (1818) Nfld. 100 and 242, *passim.*

by the Scottish trustee it was ordered that the creditors preferred in Newfoundland 'communicate to the trustee, for general distribution, the funds which they had received abroad'.[17] Leaving to one side the question whether the courts in Scotland could properly ignore the consequences of an insolvency under an Act of the Imperial Parliament, the approach to foreign preferences in *Bennet* v. *Johnson* should not be adopted in England. The hotchpot rule, as illustrated in *ex p Wilson*, is to be applied[18] (even though the creditor is resident in England).

D. Remitting Assets

One means by which the efficient and equitable distribution of assets may be advanced is the handing over of English assets to a foreign trustee or liquidator. Such a course of action was expressly contemplated in *Re Macfadyen & Co.*[19] So too, when it comes to winding up, there are clear illustrations of the willingness to remit assets abroad for the payment of an equalising dividend.[20] More generally, assets realised in an ancillary winding up may be sent to the court conducting the principal liquidation for distribution. The point was made beyond doubt in the various BCCI cases.[1] Should the English court stay its own bankruptcy proceedings in favour of a foreign forum, a similar approach would be appropriate.[2] But attention may be drawn to the consideration that the sending of assets to a foreign court is, in all instances, a matter of discretion.

Reference must be made to *Re Lorillard*: if only to make it absolutely clear that the decision is not relevant to insolvency cases.[3] A testator died domiciled in New York with assets in both England and America. In accordance with the normal rules of private international law in respect of administrations,[4] the estate in England was administered, leaving a surplus after payment of creditors. However, the American estate was insufficient to discharge the claims of certain creditors whose debts, although enforceable in the American courts, were statute-barred under English domestic law. A summons was issued by the American administrator seeking an order that the surplus assets be transferred to him for distribution to creditors in the American administration. Eve J refused so to order; and that determination was upheld on appeal. But *Re Lorillard* in no way prevents the transfer of English assets to a foreign court conducting an insolvency. For the judgments in the Court of Appeal were based wholly upon an exercise of discretion in the court below; as Warrington LJ stated 'there being no authority conflicting with what the learned judge has done

---

[17] Above, n. 15.

[18] This was the view taken, correctly it is submitted, by the English liquidators in *Re National Employers' Mutual General Insurance Association Ltd.* (1995) 15 A.C.S.R. 624 at 626.

[19] Text to n. 4, *supra*. See also *Re O'Reardon* (1873) 9 Ch. App. 74 and *Ayres* v. *Evans* (1981) 39 A.L.R. 129.

[20] See, for example, *Re Standard Insurance Co. Ltd.* [1968] Qd. R. 118, *Re Alfred Shaw & Co. Ltd.* (1897) 8 Q.L.J. 93, discussed in chapter 14.

[1] See p. 362, *infra*.

[2] Chapter 3, *ante*. The jurisdiction to send assets abroad was recognised, but not exercised, in *Re O'Reardon* (1873) 9 Ch. App. 74.

[3] [1922] 2 Ch. 638.

[4] See *Dicey and Morris*, chapter 26.

in the exercise of his discretion, I am of the opinion that we ought not to interfere with that exercise'.[5] Quite plainly, therefore, *Re Lorillard* cannot be said to support any contention that there is no discretion to sanction the transfer of assets abroad. Moreover, recalling Warrington LJ's words, there is of course relevant authority relating to the transfer of assets in a cross-border insolvency, for such was approved in *Re Macfadyen & Co.* and in several cases involving ancillary windings up, most recently *Re BCCI S.A. (No. 10)*.[6] Further, *Re Lorillard* did not concern an equalising dividend. Finally, as a matter of principle, *Re Lorillard* has no relevance to the remitting of assets upon a bankruptcy or winding up on account of the fundamental differences between administration and insolvency. Following the death of a testator, English assets must be administered in England. The foreign personal representative, even if appointed in accordance with the domiciliary law, is not permitted simply to act in England – an English grant must be obtained. Whereas a foreign bankruptcy may vest title to movables in England in a foreign assignee, similarly, a foreign liquidator's authority to represent the corporation in England does not depend upon any English grant or *exequatur*.[7] Thus there is an undoubted discretion in the English court to stay its own bankruptcy or winding up proceedings, or even to decline to make a bankruptcy or winding up order and, in either case, assets may be given over to the foreign trustee or liquidator. Such a situation simply cannot arise in an English administration.

2. VESTING OF ASSETS

A. 'Property'

The Insolvency Act 1986 provides that the 'bankrupt's estate' vests in the trustee immediately upon his appointment;[8] and that the bankrupt's estate comprises of 'all property belonging to or vested in the bankrupt at the commencement of the bankruptcy'.[9] The word 'property' is defined in section 436, for the purposes of the whole Act, as including:

'money, goods, things in action, land and every description of property wherever situate . . .'

This definition is also relevant in liquidations and administrations since these procedures are also extraterritorial in scope, extending to property of the company outside England.[10] The issue that requires some consideration is the relationship in English law between the section 436 definition of property (i.e. property wherever situate) and the *lex situs*; although it goes without saying that whether an English trustee, administrator or liquidator can actually exercise control over assets abroad will to a considerable

---

[5] [1922] 2 Ch. 638 at 646.
[6] [1997] Ch. 213, p. 363, *infra*.
[7] Chapter 8, *ante*. See also *Re Kooperman* [1928] W.N. 101, p. 222, *supra*.
[8] Insolvency Act 1986, s. 306(1).
[9] Insolvency Act 1986, s. 283(1)(a).
[10] For recent authority, see *per* Scott V-C in *Re BCCI S.A. (No. 10)* [1997] Ch. 213 at 241–242: 'The English statutory insolvency scheme purports to have worldwide, not merely territorial, effect . . . The liquidators must get in and realise the company's assets as best they may whatever may be the country in which the assets are situated.'

extent[11] depend upon the content of, and recognition under, the relevant foreign law.

The statutory provisions outlined above have the effect that all property – anywhere in the world – which was vested in the bankrupt at the date of the commencement of the bankruptcy must be regarded as vesting in an English trustee. Yet it is *lex situs* which determines what property was vested in the bankrupt at the relevant time.[12] To take an illustration, let us say that the debtor owned a lorry in Greenland and had contracted to sell the lorry to a purchaser. Let us further assume that under the law of Greenland, unlike under English law, the title to (and legal and beneficial ownership of)[13] a lorry only passes to a purchaser upon registration with the relevant authority in Greenland. In addition, at the date of the commencement of the bankruptcy the sale of the lorry had not been registered, although the purchaser had paid the contract price and taken delivery, and under the law of Greenland ownership remained vested in the debtor: the purchaser having only personal rights, for return of the contract price, against the debtor. Under the *lex situs* the lorry at the relevant date belonged to the debtor. Accordingly, the provisions of the Insolvency Act 1986 will operate to vest the lorry, as a matter of English law,[14] in the trustee. If, however, the facts were that under the *lex situs* the purchaser had acquired a lien or charge over the lorry, then title to the lorry would vest in the English trustee subject to such lien or charge. This is also the position where a lien or charge has been acquired over foreign immovable property.[15]

B. Concurrent Bankruptcies

Just as the vesting of assets in an English trustee is extra-territorial, it is also clearly established that movable property in England may vest in a foreign trustee.[16] Thus, upon concurrent bankruptcies, assets may be claimed by both the English and foreign trustees. If those assets are in France, it must be the courts of France which determine whose title is the better. The following only addresses the situation where there are assets in England being claimed by both trustees. The basic approach seems to be that the first in time will prevail. (It will also be noted that concurrent

---

[11] A bankrupt can be required to convey foreign property to the trustee (see Insolvency Act 1986, s. 291(2) and *Re Harris* (1896) 74 L.T. 221) and the English court will in certain circumstances have *in personam* jurisdiction over creditors (see chapter 10) and officers of an insolvent company and any other persons who are in possession of the company's property: see s. 234(2).

[12] See *Cazenove* v. *Prevost* (1821) 5 B. & Ald. 70, especially at 80 *per* Best J: ownership of French bank shares dealt with by French court in accordance with French law.

[13] Assuming that there is any distinction between legal and beneficial ownership under the *lex situs*.

[14] As far as the theoretical position under English law is concerned, it does not matter whether the courts in Greenland would recognise the English trustee's title.

[15] See *Callendar, Sykes & Co.* v. *Lagos Colonial Secretary* [1891] A.C. 460 and note *Canada* v. *Curragh Inc.* (1994) 114 D.L.R. (4th) 176: insolvency in Ontario but creditors asserting lien on company's mine in Yukon – Ontario court leaving the courts in the Yukon to determine the amount of any lien.

[16] See p. 212, *supra*.

liquidations or administrations[17] do not present such problems, since (i) assets do not normally vest in the liquidator or administrator and (ii) the English representative will have complete authority to deal with the company's assets in England.)

If bankruptcy proceedings have been commenced in England and a bankruptcy order made, no subsequent foreign adjudication will divest the English trustee of title to property in England,[18] although the English court will in such circumstances recognise the authority of the foreign assignee to deal with and distribute those assets within the jurisdiction of the foreign court.[19] The problematic situation, however, is where the foreign adjudication[20] precedes the English bankruptcy: for it may be suggested, and not without authority, that movables in England will already have vested in the foreign assignee and cannot thereafter vest in the English trustee. Title and jurisdiction must at once be distinguished. That there is a prior foreign adjudication (entitled to recognition in England) does not deprive the English court of jurisdiction to make a bankruptcy order. Equally, the existence of a prior foreign adjudication cannot require the English court to stay its own proceedings.[1] Accordingly, cases dealing with the existence and exercise of bankruptcy jurisdiction are of little assistance in this regard, likewise the basis of recognition of foreign bankruptcies.[2] We are here concerned solely with movables in England claimed by a foreign assignee. (There may, of course, be immovable property in England or movables not falling within the scope of the foreign proceedings.[3])

The vesting of property upon concurrent bankruptcies is by no means a novel issue. In *Stein's Case*,[4] twice subsequently approved by the House of Lords,[5] the Court of Session held that movable estate in Scotland would pass under an English commission which preceded a Scottish sequestration.[6] Similar determinations have been reached in New Zealand and South Africa.[7] The English cases also favour the claim of a prior foreign assignee. In *Re Anderson*[8] the debtor had been adjudicated bankrupt both in New Zealand and, six years later, in England. At the time of the New Zealand bankruptcy, as well as thereafter, the bankrupt was entitled to a reversionary interest in a fund of personalty in England. Such reversionary interest

---

[17] As occurred in the Maxwell insolvency, see p. 335, *supra*.
[18] *Re O'Reardon* (1873) 9 Ch. App. 74, *ex p Young* (1862) 7 L.T. 534 (and cf. *Young* v. *Buckel* (1864) 2 M. 1077).
[19] *Banco de Portugal* v. *Waddell* (1880) 5 App. Cas. 161 at 169 (Lord Selborne) and 175 (Lord Blackburn).
[20] The situation in relation to the vesting of property where there is a bankruptcy in Scotland or Northern Ireland is considered above at p. 215. Note also s. 426 discussed below.
[1] Chapter 3, *ante*.
[2] In particular, *Re Artola Hermanos* (1890) 24 Q.B.D. 640, p. 70, *ante*.
[3] After-acquired property has been considered at pp. 223–227, *supra*.
[4] (1813) 1 Rose 462, p. 65, *ante*.
[5] *Selkrig* v. *Davies* (1814) 2 Rose 291 and *Geddes* v. *Mowat* (1824) 1 Gl. & J. 414 (both being Scottish appeals), see also *Stewart* v. *Auld* (1851) 13 D. 1337 at 1342, *Young* v. *Buckel* (1864) 2 M. 1077, *Goetze* v. *Aders* (1874) 2 R. 150 and *Araya* v. *Coghill* 1921 S.C. 462, *passim*.
[6] Note the observations of Lord Eldon LC in *ex p Cridland* (1814) 3 Ves & B. 94 at 99–100.
[7] *Cleve* v. *Jacomb* (1864) Mac. 171, *Howse, Sons & Co. (Trustee)* v. *Howse, Sons & Co. (Trustees)* (1884) 3 J. 14.
[8] [1911] 1 K.B. 896. (*Re Blithman* (1866) L.R. 2 Eq. 23, *Re Davidson's Settlement Trusts* (1873) L.R. 15 Eq. 383, *Re Lawson's Trusts* [1896] 1 Ch. 175, *Re Hayward* [1897] 1 Ch. 905 and *Re Craig* (1916) 86 L.J. Ch. 62 did not involve concurrent bankruptcies.)

was not disclosed by the bankrupt in either set of proceedings, but was discovered by the official receiver in the English bankruptcy. Phillimore J held that title to the fund had vested in the New Zealand assignee and thereupon ceased to belong to the bankrupt: accordingly, the fund formed no part of the bankrupt's property when the later bankruptcy (in England) was pronounced.[9] *Re Anderson* did not on its facts involve contemporaneous proceedings, yet such did arise on at least three occasions[10] before the old Court of Bankruptcy, perhaps the best illustration being *Re Hughes*. The bankrupt had carried on business as a shoemaker in London and Londonderry. An adjudication was made (upon the debtor's own petition) in Ireland and three days later a creditor's petition was presented in England, under which an adjudication was subsequently made. A dispute arose concerning the proceeds of property in England:[11]

> 'The only question is as to assets. By law all the property of the bankrupt, wherever situate, passes to the court which first acquires title to it. I do not think I ought to interfere in the matter. So far as I can understand it, the money must be paid over to the assignee in Ireland; and if the party complaining have any objection to make, he must oppose the bankrupt in the Court of Bankruptcy there.'

Thus property in England had vested in the Irish assignee by reason of the prior Irish bankruptcy. Similar conclusions were reached in *Re Parker* and *Re Wilson and Armstrong*, concerning sequestrations under the Bankruptcy (Scotland) Act 1856.

Re Hughes, *Re Parker* and *Re Wilson and Armstrong*, taken together with *Re Anderson*, illustrate that a foreign bankruptcy may vest assets in England in a foreign assignee regardless of subsequent English bankruptcy proceedings. In the past, under the Bankruptcy Acts, the doctrine of relation back could by reference to the date of the act of bankruptcy overreach the title that a foreign assignee would otherwise acquire by virtue of a prior foreign adjudication.[12] But now the matter will be resolved simply by reference to the date on which title is said to have vested in the foreign assignee. It is by no means immediately apparent if, in the context of concurrent bankruptcies, the draftsman of the Insolvency Act intended to increase the scope of operation of foreign bankruptcies.[13] It remains possible, of course, for the English court to deny recognition altogether to a foreign bankruptcy – but the circumstance that foreign bankruptcy proceedings were commenced a few days prior to a bankruptcy order being made in England does not establish fraud.[14]

Where there are two bankruptcies within the United Kingdom, section 426 of the Insolvency Act 1986 becomes relevant. If, for example, assets have vested in an English trustee shortly before a trustee was appointed in Scotland, the Scottish trustee may nevertheless plead his case before the English court. In such circumstances, even though there has been no request from the Scottish court, section 426(6) allows the English court

---

[9] *Ibid.*, at 902–903.

[10] *Re Hughes* (1858) 31 L.T.O.S. 207 and *Re Wilson and Armstrong* (1876) 60 L.T. Jo. 434; on appeal (1876) 3 Ch. D. 455, noted at p. 66, *ante*, as well as *Re Parker* (1859) 1 L.T. 15.

[11] (1858) 31 L.T.O.S. 207.

[12] See, for example, *per* Lord Selborne in *Banco de Portugal* v. *Waddell* (1880) 5 App. Cas. 161 at 170.

[13] By removing the doctrine of relation back.

[14] See *Geddes* v. *Mowat* (1824) 1 Gl. & J. 414 and the analysis thereof at p. 190, *ante*.

to exercise its powers under section 426(4) and (5).[15] Hence, if the facts revealed a closer connection in Scotland, the English court would likely stay the English bankruptcy and order the English trustee to transfer assets to the Scottish trustee. In an appropriate case an English trustee could make a similar request to a court in Scotland or Northern Ireland.[16]

3. EUROPEAN CONVENTION ON INSOLVENCY PROCEEDINGS

The Convention only seeks to deal with the infra-Community effects of insolvency. Thus, if there are concurrent bankruptcies involving the courts in England and the United States, the Convention simply would not apply. In an infra-Community situation – such as where a company with its head office in England has an establishment[17] in Germany – the Convention provides a basic framework for the conduct of concurrent insolvencies. Article 3(1) determines that the Contracting State where the debtor has its centre of main interests will conduct the main proceedings; proceedings opened in another Contracting State (in which there is an establishment) are referred to as secondary proceedings and are territorial in scope (Article 3(2)).[18] Returning to the example given above, any proceedings in Germany would be territorial and the English liquidator would be entitled to recognition (and could recover assets) in all other Contracting States: clearly, the scope of potential conflict between the English and German proceedings would be greatly reduced compared to the current common law position. In Chapter 3 of the Convention further detail is provided as to the relationship between main and secondary proceedings. There is, for example, in Article 31 a duty upon the two liquidators to co-operate with each other and immediately to exchange any relevant information. The primary role of the main proceedings is emphasised by Article 33, which allows the liquidator in the main proceedings to request a stay of the secondary proceedings – which request may be rejected 'only if it is manifestly of no interest to the creditors in the main proceedings' (Article 33(2)). Such a stay may be ordered for up to three months and is renewable.

More generally, the Convention cuts down the circumstances in which the English court can exercise insolvency jurisdiction: the idea being that there can be only one set of main proceedings and any secondary proceedings are only justified if there is an establishment in the relevant country.

---

[15] In s. 426(6) it is stated: 'Where a person who is a trustee or assignee under the insolvency law of any part of the United Kingdom claims property situated in another part of the United Kingdom (whether by virtue of an order under subsection (3) or otherwise), the submission of that claim to the court exercising jurisdiction in relation to insolvency law in that other part shall be treated in the same manner as a request made by a court for the purpose of subsection (4).'

[16] See also p. 213, *supra*, for the operation of s. 426(1) generally. A court in any relevant country or territory could similarly make a s. 426 request, where there were concurrent proceedings in that country and England, with a view to co-ordinating the two sets of proceedings.

[17] Where an English company has a subsidiary in Germany, the Convention will not be relevant since the parent and subsidiary are separate legal entities and their insolvencies are also regarded as separate for the purposes of the Convention.

[18] For a more detailed discussion, see pp. 9–12, *supra*.

Winding up jurisdiction, for example, could no longer be based on the presence of assets in, or other (lesser) connections to, England. Hence, at least in theory, one major advantage of the Convention would be that it would reduce the potential number of situations in which concurrent insolvencies could be conducted.

4. ILLUSTRATIONS

(1) RMG is a New Zealand corporation which has a branch office in England. RMG is insolvent and a liquidator has been appointed in New Zealand. A winding up petition has also been presented in England. An English winding up may be ordered to be ancillary to the New Zealand proceedings, the English liquidator acting in co-operation with the principal liquidator abroad.[19]

(2) A firm has carried on business in England and in India. The firm has assets and creditors in each country. Insolvency proceedings have been commenced in both jurisdictions. The English court may give its approval to a scheme, agreed upon by the English trustee and foreign assignee, for pooling the firm's assets and distributing them ratably amongst both sets of creditors.[20]

(3) Y is a sole trader who has carried on business in England and in Brazil. Insolvency proceedings have been conducted in Brazil as a result of which C received a certain dividend. A bankruptcy order has been made in England and C has sought to prove in the English proceedings. C will be permitted to participate in the English bankruptcy but must bring into hotchpot the sum recovered abroad: C will receive no dividend in England until the other creditors have been paid dividends equal to that which C received in Brazil.[1]

(4) A was made bankrupt in New Zealand in January 1998 and an assignee appointed. Under the law of New Zealand all the bankrupt's property, wherever situate, vests in the New Zealand trustee. In March 1998 a bankruptcy petition was presented in England and, in April 1998, an order was made. Provided the New Zealand bankruptcy proceedings are recognised in England, the New Zealand assignee will have title to the bankrupt's movable property in England by virtue of the prior foreign assignment.[2]

(5) B, although domiciled in England, has for the last few years been ordinarily resident and has carried on most of her business activities in New Zealand. In May 1998 B was made bankrupt in New Zealand; however, in the previous month a bankruptcy order had been made in England and a trustee appointed. The New Zealand court has made a section 426

[19] See, generally, chapter 14.
[20] *Re Macfadyen & Co.* [1908] 1 K.B. 675.
[1] *Ex p Wilson* (1872) 7 Ch. App. 490: hotchpot is considered further in chapter 10.
[2] See *Re Hughes* (1858) 31 L.T.O.S. 207 and *Re Anderson* [1911] 1 K.B. 896, *supra*.

request to the High Court in England, requesting that the English proceedings be stayed and assets transferred to the New Zealand trustee. The English court may accede to the request.

(6) MCC is an English company with extensive business interests and assets in the United States. Administrators have been appointed in England and the company has also been put into Chapter 11 re-organisation under the United States Bankruptcy Code. The US Bankruptcy Court has also appointed an examiner. The English administrators and the US examiner have agreed upon a Protocol – setting out the basis of co-operation between the two sets of proceedings – and it is proposed that the Protocol be submitted for approval before the English and US courts. The English court has jurisdiction to authorise and approve the Protocol.[3]

[3] See pp. 335–336, *supra.*

Chapter 13

Corporate Domicile

1. INTRODUCTION

Although in English company law it is fundamental that a corporation has its own legal personality, such personality is by no means identical to that of an individual. Thus, rules of law initially developed for the individual may at times only be appropriate to the corporation after substantial modification: the attribution of a *mens rea* to a company may serve as an example.[1] So too in private international law, that one is dealing with a corporation may affect the principles to be applied. This becomes at once apparent upon considering the domicile of a corporation.[2] A corporation, be it English or foreign, is unlike an individual in that its existence derives from a legal system. In English private international law[3] the personal law (or domicile) of a corporation is closely bound to the place in which incorporation has occurred and, as a general rule, a corporation is simply domiciled in the place in which it has been incorporated[4] and (it was often said[5]) that domicile cannot be changed.[6] The personal law of a corporation (corporate domicile) governs a variety of issues: corporate capacity, internal management, the rights and liabilities of the corporators, not to mention the very existence of the corporation. More particularly, with reference to cross-border insolvency, the English court not only grants recognition to a liquidation under the law of the place of incorporation, but may also regard its own winding

---

[1] See, generally, *Gower's Principles of Modern Company Law*, Davies (ed.) (6th ed., 1997) pp. 229–230.

[2] Farnsworth *The Residence and Domicile of Corporations* (1939), p. 201 *et seq.*; *Dicey and Morris*, pp. 1103–1105 and *Cheshire and North*, pp. 174 and 897–899.

[3] For a comparative analysis note Wolff *Private International Law* (2nd ed., 1950), pp. 297–301.

[4] 'The domicile of a corporation is in the country under whose laws it is incorporated.' (*Dicey and Morris*, rule 154 (1).)

[5] See, however, the discussion of multiple incorporation, below.

[6] 'The domicile of origin, or the domicile of birth, using with respect to a company a familiar metaphor, clings to it throughout its existence': *Gasque* v. *IRC* [1940] 2 K.B. 80 at 84. It has been suggested (in the judgment of Buckley J in *Carl-Zeiss Stiftung* v. *Rayner and Keeler (No. 3)* [1970] Ch. 506 at 544) that the law of the place in which the corporation was incorporated might substitute another system of law 'as the proper law of the corporation'. For the position of the so-called 'refugee corporation' see Mann (1962) 11 I.C.L.Q. 471 and Nygh (1976) 12 U.W.A.L.R. 467.

up proceedings as ancillary or auxiliary thereto. As Vaughan Williams J once put it:[7]

> 'One knows that where there is a liquidation of one concern the general principle is ascertain what is the domicile of the company in liquidation; let the court of the country of domicile act as the principal court to govern the liquidation; and let the other courts act as ancillary, as far as they can, to the principal liquidation.'

Ancillary winding up is considered in detail in chapter 14, below.

However, the traditional approach to corporate domicile requires some modification where a corporation has been incorporated in not just one but two or more different jurisdictions.[8] Such multiple incorporation could occur at a state level (that is, in two states or provinces within a federal country) or transnationally: it is well known that in recent years a number of national legal systems[9] (in particular several tax havens) have introduced legislation allowing corporations formed abroad to reincorporate locally, and *vice versa*.

At the outset multiple incorporation must be distinguished from simple registration. A corporation which carries on business in several countries will most likely be incorporated in only one jurisdiction but registered, as a foreign or 'oversea company',[10] in the other countries. Registration does not create the corporation, it merely subjects that corporation, which has been brought into existence in the place of its incorporation, to relevant provisions of the law of the place of registration. A French corporation registered under section 690A of the Companies Act as an oversea company remains a French corporation. But multiple incorporation occurs where a corporation is actually created under two legal systems. In English law the domicile and with it the very status flowing from multiple incorporation has been little discussed,[11] but two propositions may be advanced. Firstly, a foreign corporation cannot reincorporate in England, nor may a United Kingdom company reincorporate abroad: for the Companies Act creates a separate legal entity and one which cannot be reproduced in any form in any other jurisdiction. Secondly, where both the law of the place of incorporation and of reincorporation permit, a corporation may incorporate in two different jurisdictions and hence be regarded, in English law, as having two domiciles.

---

[7] *Re English, Scottish and Australian Chartered Bank* [1893] 3 Ch. 385 at 394.

[8] The question is discussed more fully by the author in 'Corporate Domicile and Multiple Incorporation in English Private International Law' [1990] J.B.L. 126, upon which this chapter draws heavily.

[9] See [1990] J.B.L. 126 at 135 for details. Note also *Hughes* v. *Hannover Rückversicherungs-Aktiengesellschaft* [1997] 1 B.C.L.C. 497 – insurance company re-locating its domicile from Massachusetts to Bermuda – discussed, *infra*.

[10] Pursuant to s. 690A or s. 691 of the Companies Act 1985.

[11] Although *Dicey and Morris* does state, with reference to this author's views, (at p. 1104, footnotes omitted): '. . . a corporation incorporated in two countries (or more) may be recognised as so incorporated, if, under the law of each such country, this situation is recognised as having come about. Accordingly, an English court should recognise such a corporation as having a domicile in each of those countries by virtue of being incorporated there.'

2. ROLE OF CORPORATE DOMICILE

A. General

The principles of domicile developed in English law with reference to the individual; and it is not putting it too highly to state that such principles can be applied to a corporation only with a 'certain sense of strain'.[12] Domicile in respect of an individual is divided into domicile of origin, of dependency and of choice. Yet none of these can be readily applied to a corporation. Of course, a corporation is ascribed a domicile upon its creation – it is perhaps for this reason that judges have spoken of such domicile as a domicile of origin.[13] However, an individual's domicile of origin is determined by the father's (or mother's) domicile at the date of birth, whereas a corporation is domiciled in the place in which it is incorporated and, in particular, without reference to the domiciles of its corporators. At first glance it might seem that the irrelevance of the corporators' domiciles flows from the principle in *Salomon* v. *A. Salomon and Co. Ltd.*[14] that a company is a person separate from its shareholders. However *Salomon* v. *A. Salomon and Co. Ltd.* embodies a rule of English company law and does not necessarily apply to a foreign corporation.[15] That the domicile of a corporation is not determined by reference to its corporators' domiciles is rather a matter of practicality. For although an individual has only one father (or mother) there may be hundreds of corporators having between them a multitude of domiciles. Further, whilst a corporation may have a minority (of shareholders, that is), it has no infancy and therefore domicile of dependency has no application. More-over, any suggestion that a corporation may acquire a domicile of choice in the same manner as an individual (by a combination of residence and intention to remain permanently) is simply untenable.

When dealing with an individual it is clearly established that in the English court domicile is determined solely according to English law.[16] Thus an individual may be domiciled in New York quite irrespective of the content of New York law. Where a foreign corporation is involved, English law is not the only law to be considered. If the corporation has not been properly incorporated under the foreign law, domicile becomes irrelevant, for there is simply no corporation.[17] Thus recognition of a corporate entity, when duly created under the law of the place where it is formed, is the foundation upon which corporate domicile in English private international law is built.

The role of the law of the place of incorporation must not be misunder-stood: it does not determine the corporation's domicile but is limited to the existence of the corporation. To take an example, provided a corporation has been properly incorporated in New York, that is, according to New

---

[12] Morris *The Conflict of Laws* (4th ed., 1993) p. 29.

[13] *Gasque* v. *I.R.C.*, n. 6, *supra*.

[14] [1897] A.C. 22.

[15] See *Multinational Gas and Petrochemical Co.* v. *Multinational Gas and Petrochemical Services Ltd.* [1983] Ch. 258 at 269, *Johnson Matthey & Wallace Ltd.* v. *Ahmad Alloush* (1984) 135 N.L.J. 1012 and *Rayner (Mincing Lane) Ltd.* v. *Department of Trade and Industry* [1990] 2 A.C. 418 at 509. For the situation as to international organisations, see *Westland Helicopters Ltd.* v. *Arab Organisation for Industrialisation* [1995] Q.B. 282.

[16] *Dicey and Morris*, rule 8.

[17] *Re Imperial Anglo-German Bank* (1872) 26 L.T. 229, *infra*.

York law, it will under English rules of private international law be domiciled in New York – that under New York law the corporation might not even have a 'domicile', or might be domiciled elsewhere, is irrelevant.

A corporation may come into being as the result of a formal process of incorporation, as indeed under the Companies Act 1985. Yet it should not be overlooked that, in many legal systems, corporate personality may be conferred without such a formal process. An English court will recognise a corporate entity whether or not created through a formal act of incorporation.[18]

B. Existence and Dissolution

The law of the place of incorporation determines whether, and at what time,[19] a corporation has been brought into existence, as well as the dissolution thereof.[20] However, that a foreign corporation has been dissolved abroad does not, with one exception, prevent the English court from winding up the corporation as an unregistered company under provisions now to be found in Part V of the Insolvency Act 1986. In such circumstances, following the decision of the House of Lords in *Russian and English Bank* v. *Baring Bros & Co.*,[1] the corporation is regarded as having been brought back to life and is wound up 'as if it had not been dissolved'.[2]

The one exception is where a foreign corporation is not merely dissolved abroad, but rather the effect of the law of the place of incorporation is that the alleged corporation has never existed as a legal entity. This is the combined effect of *Re Imperial Anglo-German Bank* and *Burr* v. *Anglo-French Banking Corpn. Ltd.*[3] In the former, it was proposed to form a company in Germany to be known as the Imperial Anglo-German Bank. However, the requirements of German law were not satisfied and there was no valid incorporation. It was held (*per* James and Mellish LJJ) that the court had no jurisdiction to make a winding up order: the failure to comply with German law meant the entity which had been intended to be formed had 'never come into existence at all'.[4] In the latter case, the Compania de Salitre de Chile had been formed in 1931 under two decrees of the Chilean legislature. But in 1933, by Presidential decree, the two earlier decrees were repealed and 'left without effect'.[5] Thereafter an action was brought

---

[18] *Von Hellfeld* v. *Rechnitzer* [1914] 1 Ch. 748, *Dreyfus* v. *IRC* (1929) 14 T.C. 560, see also *Bumper Development Corpn.* v. *Metropolitan Police Comr* [1991] 4 All E.R. 638 and *Oxnard Financing S.A.* v. *Rahn* [1998] 3 All ER 19, CA.

[19] See *The Saudi Prince* [1982] 2 Lloyd's Rep. 255 at 260.

[20] *Russian Commercial and Industrial Bank* v. *Comptoir D'Escompte de Mulhouse* [1925] A.C. 112, *Employers' Liability Assurance Corpn. Ltd.* v. *Sedgwick, Collins & Co. Ltd.* [1927] A.C. 95, *Dairen Kisen Kabushiki Kaisha* v. *Shiang Kee* [1941] A.C. 373 at 376. Note also *National Bank of Greece and Athens S.A.* v. *Metliss* [1958] A.C. 509 and *The Kommunar (No. 2)* [1997] 1 Lloyd's Rep. 8.

[1] [1936] A.C. 405. See further M. Mann (1954) 3 I.C.L.Q. 689 and (1955) 18 M.L.R. 8.

[2] *Ibid.*, at 427. But whether a creditor may prove in England for debts contracted after the date of the dissolution has not been finally decided: see *Re Russian Commercial and Industrial Bank* [1955] Ch. 148 and contrast *Re Banque des Marchands de Moscou* [1952] 1 All E.R. 1269 and *Re Russian Commercial and Industrial Bank* (1963) 107 Sol. Jo. 415.

[3] (1872) 26 L.T. 229 and (1933) 149 L.T. 282 respectively.

[4] (1872) 26 L.T. 229 at 230. Cf. *Re Vanilla Accumulation Ltd.* (1998) Times, 24 February.

[5] (1933) 149 L.T. 282.

against the Compania de Salitre de Chile in England. Swift J considered that the effect of the Presidential decree was not merely that the corporation ceased to exist but that, according to the law of Chile, there had never been such a corporation brought into existence. If the effect of the foreign dissolution is that the corporation never existed (*Burr* v. *Anglo-French Banking Corp. Ltd.*) then there is no entity in respect of which the English court can then make a winding up order (*Re Imperial Anglo-German Bank*). In such circumstances a creditor's remedy is likely to be against the person who purported to act as agent for the non-existent corporation. However, should a winding up order be made in England at a time when the foreign corporation is in existence (according to the law of the place of incorporation at that time), the English liquidation must be allowed to continue despite subsequent retrospective legislation in the place of incorporation rendering the original incorporation a nullity and of no effect.[6]

C. Corporate Capacity

It is generally said that the capacity of a corporation to enter into a transaction is governed by both the constitution of the corporation and the proper law of the contract.[7] In other words, the constitution determines whether a transaction *can* be entered into at all, whereas the proper law governs whether (provided there is no lack of capacity) a valid transaction has been entered into. Thus a lack of capacity under the constitution of a corporation will be fatal. (The common law position has it would appear not be altered by the introduction of the Contracts (Applicable Law) Act 1990.[8]) Perhaps the clearest example of a conflict between a corporation's constitution and the proper law of the contract is *Cape Copper Co. Ltd.* v. *Comptoir D'Escompte*.[9] Two actions were brought in England by the plaintiffs: one against the Société des Métaux, the other against the Comptoir D'Escompte. In 1887 various persons interested in the copper market came to an arrangement in France designed specifically to limit the production, and thereby increase the price, of copper. Such an agreement was undoubtedly illegal in France but not in England. In the following year the plaintiffs joined the scheme. The plaintiffs entered into one contract with the Société des Métaux and another, a contract of guarantee, with the Comptoir D'Escompte (a French discount company). Both contracts were governed by English law. Subsequently the Société des Métaux was put into liquidation in France. Day J rejected defences based upon illegality and further held that the liquidation in France of the Société des Métaux did not affect the validity of contracts governed by English law.[10] Nevertheless, his Lordship gave judgment in favour of the Comptoir D'Escompte on the

---

[6] For a discussion of retrospective changes in the *lex causae* generally, see *Dicey and Morris*, pp. 60–69.

[7] *Dicey and Morris*, rule 156(1); *Janred Properties Ltd.* v. *Ente Nazionale Italiano per il Turismo* [1989] 2 All E.R. 444.

[8] See *Dicey and Morris*, pp. 1113–1114.

[9] (1890) 6 T.L.R. 454.

[10] For discharge see chapter 9.

basis that a contract of guarantee was *ultra vires* the relevant clauses in the corporation's statutes:[11]

'The Comptoir was an incorporated body. In France the powers of companies were limited by their statutes, and it had been urged that the Comptoir had power under its statutes to give guarantees.'

After referring to the relevant clauses, Day J is reported as follows:[12]

'These transactions were utterly without the power of a discount concern, such as the Comptoir . . . Transactions such as these were not within the business of a discount house, and were certainly not within its statutes. He held, therefore, that the transactions were utterly beyond all powers of the Comptoir, and were *ultra vires*, and, therefore, he gave judgment for the Comptoir D'Escompte, with costs.'

Although *Cape Copper Co. Ltd.* v. *Comptoir D'Escompte* was decided with reference to a written constitution, the same principle would doubtless apply if the corporation in question had come into existence without a formal process of incorporation and the lack of capacity stemmed from specific provisions under the law of the place of incorporation.

D. Liability of Corporators

Whether corporators have the benefit of limited liability is governed by the law of the place of incorporation.[13] Thus the liability of shareholders in an English company for the debts of the company will be limited (in accordance with the Companies Act), regardless of the law of the country in which business has been conducted. Of course, it may be otherwise if the shareholders have used the company as their agent and are themselves liable as principals.

Under section 24 of the Companies Act 1985 (as amended) a member of a company (other than a private company limited by shares or guarantee) may become liable for payment of the company's debts if the company carries on business without having at least two members, does so for more than six months and the member knows that there is only one member. Section 24, both from its content and its place in the 1985 Act (Chapter 1 Company Formation), obviously relates only to companies registered under the Companies Acts. In comparison, liability for fraudulent and wrongful trading may arise in respect of both English and foreign corporations which are being wound up in England.[14] Section 213 of the Insolvency Act 1986 provides:[15]

---

[11] (1890) 6 T.L.R. 454 at 455.

[12] *Ibid.*

[13] *Risdon Iron and Locomotive Works* v. *Furness* [1906] 1 K.B. 49, *General Steam Navigation Co.* v. *Guillou* (1843) 11 M. & W. 877, *Rayner (Mincing Lane) Ltd.* v. *Department of Trade and Industry* [1990] 2 A.C. 418 at 509. For the liability of directors see *Bower* v. *Société des Affréteurs du Great Eastern* (1867) 17 L.T. 490, *passim*.

[14] *Re a Company (No. 00359 of 1987)* [1988] Ch. 210 and *Re Howard Holdings Inc.*, *supra* p. 26.

[15] The provisions of the Brussels Convention will not apply to s. 213: note Case 133/78 *Gourdain* v. *Nadler* [1979] E.C.R. 733 and p. 13, *supra*.

'(1) If in the course of winding up a company it appears that any business has been carried on with intent to defraud creditors of the company or creditors of any other person, or for any fraudulent purpose, the following has effect.

(2) The court, on the application of the liquidator, may declare that any persons who were knowingly parties to the carrying on of the business in the manner above-mentioned are to be liable to make such contributions (if any) to the company's assets as the court thinks proper.'

A foreign corporation may be wound up in England as an unregistered company under Part V of the Insolvency Act 1986, and thereupon 'all the provisions of this Act and the Companies Act about winding up apply to an unregistered company'.[16] Section 213 refers to 'persons who were knowingly parties' to the fraudulent trading, thus avoiding possible linguistic difficulties which might arise (particularly in respect of a foreign corporation) had reference been made to the directors or shareholders thereof. (But, in any event, wrongful trading applies to a foreign company in liquidation under Part V.)

E. Internal Management

Matters such as the raising and maintenance of capital, the issue and forfeiture of shares, the exercise of voting rights, payments of dividends and directors' powers and duties, fall to be determined according to the law of the place of incorporation.[17] Moreover, when a foreign corporation is involved the English court is most unlikely to interfere in the above-mentioned matters. For although the English court is not generally precluded from resolving questions as to the internal management of a foreign corporation, it is in practice almost inevitable that the foreign court will be a clearly more appropriate forum. Thus several cases may be found where English judges have declined to intervene in the internal affairs of a foreign corporation.[18] But since the coming into force of the Civil Jurisdiction and Judgments Act 1982 it must be noted that questions of internal management may fall within Article 16(2) of the Brussels Convention, conferring exclusive jurisdiction on the courts of the Contracting State in which the company has its seat.[19]

3. MULTIPLE INCORPORATION

A company formed under the Companies Act 1985 is not domiciled in both England and Scotland; it will have but one domicile according to the place

---

[16] Insolvency Act 1986, s. 221(1), see also pp. 110–111, *supra*.

[17] For example, *Sudlow* v. *Dutch Rhenish Rly Co.* (1855) 21 Beav. 43 (forfeiture of shares), *Bill* v. *Sierra Nevada Lake Water and Mining Co.* (1859) 1 L.T. 256 (increasing capital), *Pickering* v. *Stephenson* (1872) L.R. 14 Eq. 322 (improper purpose), *Pergamon Press Ltd.* v. *Maxwell* [1970] 1 W.L.R. 1167 (fiduciary power) and *Mills* v. *Mills* (1938) 60 C.L.R. 150 at 180–181. Note *International Credit and Investment Co. (Overseas) Ltd.* v. *Adham* [1994] 1 B.C.L.C. 66 at 71. See also the discussion at p. 371, *post*.

[18] *Sudlow* v. *Dutch Rhenish Rly Co.*, *Bill* v. *Sierra Nevada Lake Water and Mining Co.* and *Pergamon Press Ltd.* v. *Maxwell*, all *supra*.

[19] See *Dicey and Morris*, pp. 383–384, and note *Grupo Torras S.A.* v. *Sheikh Fahad Mohammed al Sabah* [1996] 1 Lloyd's Rep. 7.

of its registered office.[20] However, under the domestic law of certain federal countries it may be that a corporation can be formally incorporated in more than one state within the federal unit. Such a corporation may be called a 'multi-state corporation'. In addition, it is possible that multiple incorporation may occur not only within a single political unit but at a transnational level: that is, when a corporation is created under each of two national (rather than state) legal systems. If a corporation is created under, and has legal personality conferred by, two state or national legal systems, its personal law or domicile cannot be determined simply by reference to the usual rule and looking to the law of the place of incorporation – there will be two such places. As *Dicey and Morris* notes, the English court has not yet given detailed consideration to cases involving multi-state corporations (or indeed any element of multiple incorporation).[1] In cross-border insolvency multiple incorporation may present some difficulty in respect of the recognition of foreign liquidations. Let us say that in 1985 a company was incorporated in Nauru; in 1993 the company was reincorporated in the British Virgin Islands and was thereafter dissolved in Nauru. In 1997 the company goes into liquidation in the British Virgin Islands and the liquidator wishes to recover assets belonging to the company in England. Such a company should be regarded as domiciled in the British Virgin Islands and the liquidator recognised accordingly.[2]

A. United Kingdom Companies

Multiple incorporation can only occur in accordance with the two legal systems involved – both legal systems must allow a corporation created under its own law to exist under, and be created by, the law of another country. Multiple incorporation cannot occur in respect of a company brought into existence under the companies legislation of the United Kingdom. A corporation created abroad cannot subsequently be incorporated in the United Kingdom, since the Companies Act creates a new legal entity, one that did not exist prior to incorporation. The consequences of two such incorporations will be two corporations: one created abroad and one created under the Companies Acts. So too a company created under the Companies Act cannot (in the absence of an Act of Parliament) later be reincorporated in any foreign country. If the shareholders of an English company wish to form a *société anonyme* in France they can do so but, as a matter of English law, the English company and French corporation are two distinct legal persons.[3] In *Tayside Floorcloth Co. Ltd. (Petitioners)* a company domiciled in Scotland sought to amend its memorandum of association 'to procure the company to be incorporated, registered or recognised in any foreign country'.[4] The Lord

---

[20] See *Re Baby Moon (U.K.) Ltd.* [1985] P.C.C. 103.

[1] See, however, p. 1104, n. 12: 'In the United States a corporation may be reincorporated in another state and thus may have more than one domicile.'

[2] This appears to be accepted by the Court of Appeal in *Hughes* v. *Hannover* [1997] 1 B.C.L.C. 497, discussed *infra*.

[3] As in *Re Irrigation Co of France Ltd., ex p Fox* (1871) 6 Ch. App. 176: note also *Bank of Otago Ltd.* v. *Commercial Bank of New Zealand Ltd.* (1867) Mac. 233.

[4] 1923 S.C. 590 at 591.

President, disallowing the amendment in respect of incorporation in any foreign country, stated:[5]

> 'The difficulty arises on the word "incorporated". There is, of course, nothing which gives rise to criticism in the company desiring to be "registered" or "recognised" in any foreign country or colony, so as to push its business or promote its interests there; but a proposal to authorise the company to be "incorporated" elsewhere than in its own domicile may involve risk of change of status, and may expose it, however unintentionally, to alterations in its constitution which might be inconsistent with its establishment as a British limited liability company.'

Indeed, even if the constitution of a United Kingdom company purported to give the company power to incorporate abroad, such incorporation could only be regarded as creating a second and completely different corporation, it could not alter the status of the United Kingdom company. However, it must be possible for an English company to transfer its domicile to a foreign country, or from England to Scotland, if Parliament has passed specific legislation to that effect. Private Acts of Parliament have been employed for this purpose.[6]

B. Foreign Corporations

There are, however, legal systems which do permit a corporation at one time to be incorporated locally as well as in some other foreign jurisdiction.[7] Thus, for instance, in 1968 the Companies (Transfer of Domicile) Act was enacted in New South Wales, and upon satisfying certain conditions, a foreign corporation will be deemed to be a company incorporated under the companies legislation of New South Wales.[8] More recent provision can be found in the British Virgin Islands. By virtue of sections 84 to 88 of the International Business Companies Ordinance 1984 a foreign company may reincorporate in the British Virgin Islands, and a company incorporated under the Ordinance may itself reincorporate under the law of a foreign jurisdiction in such manner as provided for under the laws of that foreign jurisdiction.[9]

The very existence of a corporation is governed by the law of the place of incorporation. Similarly, whether a corporation may exist under more than one legal system is a matter of status and must be referred to the law of the places in which incorporation is said to have occurred. If a corporation is duly and validly created under the law of the place of incorporation its existence will be recognised in England: multiple incorporation must be approached in the same manner. For English law gives complete freedom to foreign legal systems to create corporations in their own way and in their

---

[5] *Ibid.*, at 592.

[6] See Mayson, French and Ryan, *Company Law*, (14th ed., 1997) at p. 71, referring to the British Olivetti Limited Act 1980 as an example.

[7] Details can be found at [1990] J.B.L. 126 at 134–135 and references therein.

[8] See now in Australia s. 133 of the Corporations Law 1989 and Nygh, *Conflict of Laws in Australia* (6th ed., 1996) at p. 544.

[9] See also, for example, the legislation in Anguilla: in 1995 the Companies Ordinance, the International Business Companies Ordinance and the Limited Liability Company Ordinance were passed; each Ordinance allows for re-domiciliation into and out of Anguilla.

own forms. It is likely to serve only to defeat the intentions of the corporators (and the interests of creditors) should English law deny effect to multiple incorporation where the requirements of both legal systems involved have been satisfied.[10]

This author would suggest that any lingering doubt as to the validity of multiple incorporation and 're-domiciliation' in English private international law has been removed by *Hughes* v. *Hannover Rückversicherungs-Aktiengesellschaft*.[11] The actual decision involved a section 426 request made by the court in Bermuda, which court had appointed liquidators in respect of an insolvent insurance company. The company had been incorporated in 1927 in Massachusetts but, in 1985, had relocated to Bermuda, after complying with the requirements specified under the laws of Massachusetts and of Bermuda. A short time after the re-domiciliation the company was put into compulsory liquidation in Bermuda. The facts are fully rehearsed in the judgment of Morritt LJ and, although his Lordship did not explicitly state that the re-domiciliation to Bermuda was valid, the judgment can only be seen as based upon the assumption that the company was, at the relevant time, a Bermudan company.[12]

C. Summary

Whether a corporation may exist under more than one legal system is a question of status and must be referred to the law of the places in which incorporation is said to have taken place. The English court cannot recognise a corporation as incorporated in two places if, according to the law of either place, the corporation cannot exist at one time under both legal systems. Where multiple incorporation is permitted under two state or national legal systems, the corporation will be domiciled in each place of incorporation, and acts validly performed according to the law of either domicile may be recognised in England. So too, where such a company ceases to exist in its first place of incorporation it will have effectively transferred its domicile to the second place of incorporation.[13]

4. ILLUSTRATIONS

(1) A Ltd., incorporated in Euphoria, carries on business in England. Under the law of Euphoria corporations have no capacity to hold land. A Ltd. is domiciled in Euphoria and its capacity to own land in England must be tested with reference to Euphorian law.[14]

(2) SNL, incorporated in California and carrying on business throughout North America, has a number of shareholders who reside in England. The

---

[10] For the resolution of conflicts as to the content of the laws of the two corporate domiciles, see [1990] J.B.L. 126 at 129–133.
[11] [1997] 1 B.C.L.C. 497, discussed generally at p. 407 *infra*.
[12] *Ibid.*, 501–502.
[13] As in *Hughes* v. *Hannover* itself.
[14] Page 352, n. 7, *supra*.

English shareholders object to a scheme to raise SNL's capital in accordance with the provisions of Californian law. The validity of the scheme is governed by Californian law and the English court is not an appropriate forum for the determination of the shareholders' rights.[15]

(3) In 1995 a group of business interests in London, Hong Kong and Singapore came to an arrangement to co-ordinate their respective trading activities in the three jurisdictions. It was proposed, *inter alia*, that a company (to be known as the 'SBJD Co. Ltd.') would be incorporated in Hong Kong to further the arrangements of the parties. In 1997 initial steps were taken in Hong Kong to incorporate the company. However, later that year the understanding between the parties fell through, as a result of which the company was not incorporated under the law of Hong Kong. The English court has no jurisdiction to make a winding up order in respect of SBJD Co. Ltd., no such corporation having been brought into existence.[16]

(4) Z Corp. was incorporated in Barbados and, shortly thereafter, re-incorporated in the British Virgin Islands. The laws of Barbados and of the British Virgin Islands make provision for the multiple incorporation of a corporation in such a manner. Z Corp. was later dissolved in accordance with the law of Barbados. Recently Z Corp. has been put into liquidation in the British Virgin Islands and a liquidator appointed. The liquidator wishes to recover Z Corp.'s assets in England. The English court will regard Z Corp. as domiciled in the British Virgin Islands and recognise the authority of the liquidator there appointed to deal with assets in England.[17]

(5) As in Illustration 4, *supra*; however, there has been no dissolution of Z Corp. in Barbados. Moreover, liquidators have been appointed in both Barbados and the British Virgin Islands, and each of the liquidators is seeking to gain control of Z Corp.'s assets in England. Z Corp. is insolvent and has assets and creditors in England. The English court, upon a petition being presented, will conduct its own winding up in respect of the English assets and allow all creditors (foreign and English) to enter a claim after bringing into hotchpot any dividend received abroad.[18]

---

[15] *Bill* v. *Sierra Nevada Lake Water and Mining Co.*, *supra*.
[16] *Re Imperial Anglo-German Bank*, *supra*.
[17] *Hughes* v. *Hannover*, *supra*. The consequences of recognition are discussed more fully in chapter 8.
[18] For the doctrine of hotchpot, see chapter 10.

Chapter 14

Ancillary Winding Up

1. INTRODUCTION TO THEORY AND PRACTICE

A. Overview

It is a general principle of private international law, as illustrated in the preceding chapter, that matters affecting the status of a corporation are determined by the law of the state of incorporation. Thus even a doctrine as fundamental to English company law as separate corporate identity and *Salomon* v. *A. Salomon and Co. Ltd.*[1] may find no equivalent under the governing law of a foreign corporation.[2] Nevertheless, there is no doubt that a foreign corporation may be wound up in England as an unregistered company under Part V of the Insolvency Act 1986.[3] Moreover, that a foreign corporation is in liquidation under the law of the place of its incorporation does not preclude the English court from exercising its winding up jurisdiction. In such circumstances, however, there is authority for the proposition that the English court may regard its own proceedings as ancillary to the main liquidation, that is, the liquidation taking place under the law of the state of incorporation.[4] As Vaughan Williams J put it in *Re English, Scottish and Australian Chartered Bank*:[5]

> 'One knows that where there is a liquidation of one concern the general principle is ascertain what is the domicile of the company in liquidation; let the court of the country of domicile act as the principal court to govern the liquidation; and let the other courts act as ancillary, as far as they can, to the principal liquidation.'

---

[1] [1897] A.C. 22.
[2] See *Rayner (Mincing Lane) Ltd.* v. *Department of Trade and Industry* [1990] 2 A.C. 418 at 509 *per* Lord Oliver.
[3] See chapter 4, *supra*.
[4] See, for example, *Re Commercial Bank of South Australia* (1886) 33 Ch. D. 174, 178, *Re English, Scottish and Australian Chartered Bank* [1893] 3 Ch. 385, 394, *Re Federal Bank of Australia Ltd.* (1893) 62 L.J. Ch. 561, *Re Victoria Date Co. Ltd.* (1898) 42 Sol. Jo. 755, *Sedgwick, Collins and Co. Ltd.* v. *Rossia Insurance Co. of Petrograd* [1926] 1 K.B. 1 at 16, *Re Vocalion (Foreign) Ltd.* [1932] 2 Ch. 196, 206, *Re International Tin Council* [1987] Ch. 419 at 447, *Felixstowe Dock and Rly Co.* v. *United States Lines Inc.* [1989] Q.B. 360 at 376–377; see also *Re Federal Bank of Australia Ltd. (No 2)* (1893) 3 B.C. (N.S.W.) 80 and (1898) 8 B.C. (N.S.W.) 35, *Re Alfred Shaw and Co. Ltd.* (1897) 8 Q.L.J. 93 and *Re Standard Insurance Co. Ltd.* [1968] Qd.R. 118.
[5] Note 4, *supra*.

This comment, although made in a case dealing with the winding up of an English company, has been repeatedly approved and applied: most notably, of course, in *Re Bank of Credit and Commerce International S.A. (No.10)* (discussed *infra*). The theoretical reason for the English court to treat its own liquidation as merely ancillary is, as stated above, that the law of the country of incorporation governs the status of a corporation, and that includes its dissolution.[6] But, from a more practical point of view, two 'full' liquidations (rather than one main and one ancillary liquidation) are likely to result in not only increased costs but also disparity between the creditors in each country.

The making of a winding up order in relation to a foreign corporation must be placed in the broader context of the recognition of foreign liquidations. The English court will recognise the authority of a foreign liquidator (appointed in accordance with the law of the place of incorporation) to recover the corporation's assets in England,[7] to institute proceedings to enforce the rights of the corporation and generally to represent the corporation in England: indeed, the English court may even regard the corporation's assets as vested in the foreign liquidator if that be the effect of the foreign insolvency law.[8] But a creditor, English or foreign, may yet petition for a winding up in England; and it may often be the case that the foreign liquidator is himself anxious that winding up proceedings are commenced in England (not least because of the immediate stay of actions against the corporation by virtue of section 130(2) of the Insolvency Act 1986).[9] However, the making of a winding up order, together with the consequences of such an order, is a matter requiring an exercise of discretion by the court. A winding up order does not have to be made.[10]

That a winding up is declared by the court to be ancillary to the main liquidation abroad means that the scope of the English proceedings should be restricted or, as Scrutton LJ once said, 'carefully limited in effect'.[11] An ancillary winding up is, at least *prima facie*, territorial and envisages that the English liquidator will only act within the jurisdiction. More significantly, as the terminology suggests, an ancillary winding up of a foreign corporation should not follow the same course as the usual, full-scale liquidation of an English registered company. The English liquidator's role has been broadly described as that of the 'assistant' of the principal liquidator abroad,[12] the former seeking to work in conjunction with the latter because the resolution of claims and the distribution of assets in a

---

[6] See *Lazard Bros* v. *Midland Bank* [1933] A.C. 289 at 297 *per* Lord Wright; for an example involving the liability of shareholders see *Re Federal Bank of Australia* (1898) 8 B.C. (N.S.W.) 35.

[7] Provided the foreign law so extends, chapter 8, *ante*.

[8] See *Levasseur* v. *Mason & Barry Ltd.* (1891) 63 L.T. 700 at 702 *per* Day J, *Re ITT* (1975) 58 D.L.R. (3d) 55.

[9] Actions in Scotland may also be stayed: *Re Queensland Mercantile Agency Co. Ltd.* (1888) 58 L.T. 878, *infra*. See also p. 314, *supra*.

[10] See *Re Wallace Smith & Co. Ltd.* [1992] B.C.L.C. 970, *infra*.

[11] 'I desire to add . . . that the operations of the winding up in this country here should be very carefully limited. There is already a liquidation in the country of origin, Russia. As far as I can find, such winding up orders here have hitherto been treated only as ancillary and carefully limited in effect': *Sedgwick, Collins and Co. Ltd.* v. *Rossia Insurance Co. of Petrograd* [1926] 1 K.B. 1 at 13. Cited with approval by Scott V-C in *Re BCCI S.A. (No. 10)* [1997] Ch. 213 at 243.

[12] *Re Federal Bank of Australia Ltd.* (1893) 62 L.J. Ch. 561 at 563 *per* Vaughan Williams J.

single set of proceedings (in the foreign, more appropriate, court) should promote greater equality between creditors from different countries, as well as leading to a saving in costs (although use of the word 'assistant' does not mean that the English liquidator is merely an agent of the foreign liquidator, or in any way expected or required to comply with the instructions of the foreign liquidator).[13] Where an ancillary winding up is ordered it may be convenient for the powers of the English liquidator to be restricted to collecting the English assets and settling a list of creditors in England.[14] Such assets, after satisfying preferred creditors in England and other approved payments,[15] are to be remitted to the foreign court conducting the main liquidation.

Perhaps the best illustration of an ancillary winding up is *Re National Benefit Assurance Co.*[16] The company was incorporated in England but also carried on business in Canada. The liabilities in Canada were a fractional amount of those in England. The company had been put into liquidation in England and a liquidator had also been appointed in an ancillary winding up in Manitoba. The Canadian liquidator had collected in the assets of the company in Canada. The Manitoba Court of Appeal, after considering relevant English authorities,[17] held that the duties of the Canadian liquidator were ancillary to the English winding up proceedings and, accordingly, ordered the assets to be given over to the English liquidator, after payment of preferred creditors in Canada and the costs of the liquidation. Thus, the majority of creditors in Canada were left to seek satisfaction of their claims in the main liquidation in England:[18]

'If, in the present liquidation, the Canadian assets were retained here it would only be for the purpose of paying the Canadian creditors *pari passu* with the English and other creditors . . . As there can be no apprehension that the Canadian creditors will not have equal treatment with all other creditors, there is no reason why the assets in the hands of the Canadian liquidator should not now be remitted to the English liquidator, less amounts required to pay Canadian preferred creditors, and other amounts either approved by the court or by the English liquidator, and costs of the liquidation.'

Thus understood, the power of the English court to direct that a winding up be ancillary to the principal liquidation abroad represents a useful means to advance co-operation and reduce conflict between courts when cross-border insolvency problems have arisen. However, despite the significant number of occasions on which the courts have endorsed the concept of the ancillary winding up, fundamental questions remain unanswered as to both the basis and conduct of such a winding up.

---

[13] See the remarks of North J in *Re Queensland Mercantile Agency Co. Ltd.* (1888) 58 L.T. 878, approved by Scott V-C in *Re BCCI S.A. (No. 10)*, *supra*.
[14] *Re Commercial Bank of South Australia* (1886) 33 Ch. D. 174, as explained in *Re BCCI S.A. (No. 10)*.
[15] Payments for preferred, secured and other creditors are discussed below.
[16] [1927] 3 D.L.R. 289.
[17] *Re Matheson Bros Ltd.* (1884) 27 Ch. D. 225, *Re Commercial Bank of South Australia*, *Re Federal Bank of Australia Ltd.*, *Sedgwick, Collins and Co. Ltd.* v. *Rossia Insurance Co. of Petrograd*, all n. 4, *supra*, and *North Australian Territory Co. Ltd.* v. *Goldsbrough, Mort & Co. Ltd.* (1889) 61 L.T. 716.
[18] [1927] 3 D.L.R. 289 at 301–302 *per* Trueman JA.

B. Re Bank of Credit and Commerce International S.A.

(i) *Introduction*

In *Re BCCI S.A. (No. 10)*[19] Sir Richard Scott V-C subjected the cases on ancillary winding up to a rigorous analysis and, whilst not dissenting from anything decided in the earlier authorities, revealed a number of difficulties, not to mention the odd inconsistency. Moreover, it is fair to say that the problems highlighted in the judgment of the Vice-Chancellor stem, to a very considerable degree, from the failure of the legislature sensibly to tackle this issue at any time in the last hundred years.

The provisions relied upon to wind up foreign companies in England have changed little (and only then in relatively minor detail) since the Companies Act 1862. As noted earlier in this work,[20] the relevant provisions (now found in Part V of the Insolvency Act 1986) give absolutely no guidance as to the jurisdictional criteria which must be satisfied before a winding up petition can be presented in relation to a foreign company. Indeed there is only one section that actually mentions foreign companies and that provision is seemingly never relied upon and has long been regarded as otiose.[1] It will be no surprise, therefore, to discover, that the words 'ancillary winding up' appear nowhere in the Insolvency Act (or indeed the Insolvency Rules). Rather the expression was coined by the judges a little over a hundred years ago; and there is no reason to suppose that North, Kay and Vaughan Williams JJ and the other judges sitting at first instance in the Chancery Division in the 1880s and 1890s (let alone the judges in, for example, Australia) had a uniform notion of quite what was meant by 'ancillary' winding up.[2] Nevertheless, it was always readily apparent that if, for example, a New Zealand company had a branch office in London, the English court could never realistically expect to wind up *the company*; and it was beyond question that a branch in London was not an entity capable of being separately wound up under English law.[3] It is perhaps fair to say that the 'ancillary' winding up was little more than an *ad hoc* solution to this particular problem – a convenient mechanism to preserve the company's assets *in statu quo* and 'warn off' any predatory creditors.[4] Yet, despite any clear statutory basis,[5] the mantra of ancillary winding up has over the years been repeated a sufficient number of times that, as Scott V-C has noted, it is probably too late for any judge except in the House of Lords to reject the very notion of an 'ancillary' liquidation:[6]

---

[19] [1997] Ch. 213.

[20] See p. 93, *supra*.

[1] Note the discussion of s.225, *supra*, p. 112.

[2] See, for example, the very active role played by North J in *Re Queensland Mercantile Agency Co. Ltd.* (1888) 58 L.T. 878, p. 377, *infra*.

[3] Note the comments of Browne-Wilkinson V-C in *Re BCCI S.A.* [1992] B.C.L.C. 570 at 574.

[4] It is probably no coincidence that most of the cases which touch on ancillary winding up concern the earliest stages of the insolvency process. The longer the local insolvency goes on, the less ancillary it seems to become.

[5] See *per* Scott V-C in *Re BCCI S.A. (No. 10)* [1997] Ch. 213 at 239–240 and 245–246. One may note here that there is no statutory basis for the transfer of assets by an English trustee to a foreign trustee in order to equalise dividends, as was sanctioned in *Re Macfadyen & Co.* [1908] 1 K.B. 675, p. 338, *supra*.

[6] *Ibid.*, at 246.

'The accumulation of judicial endorsements of the concept of ancillary liquidations have [*sic*], in my judgment, produced a situation in which it has become established that in an "ancillary" liquidation the courts do have power to direct liquidators to transmit funds to the principal liquidators in order to enable a pari passu distribution to worldwide creditors to be achieved. The House of Lords could declare such a direction to be ultra vires. But a first instance judge could not do so and I doubt whether the Court of Appeal could now do so.'

(ii) *Re BCCI S.A. (No. 10)*

Before further consideration of *Re BCCI S.A. (No. 10)*, certain observations of one of Sir Richard Scott V-C's predecessors may be noted. In July 1991, when dealing with an application to adjourn the hearing on the Bank of England's winding up petition in respect of BCCI, Sir Nicolas Browne-Wilkinson V-C at once emphasised that – if it came to a winding up in England – such proceedings could not be seen as merely relating to English branches of BCCI.[7] In the following month his Lordship, although without referring to the cases, more than hinted at the auxiliary nature of any winding up that might occur in England.[8] In *Re BCCI S.A. (No. 3)* it was left to the Court of Appeal to note the ancillary status of the English liquidation, Dillon LJ adding that:[9]

'. . . the English liquidators of S.A. have no authority to collect or administer the assets of S.A. in other jurisdictions. That is a matter for local liquidations or banking regulatory authorities in each separate country.'

(The authority of liquidators in an ancillary winding up is discussed further below.)[10]

Re BCCI S.A. (No. 3) concerned the approval by Nicholls V-C, and the Court of Appeal, of the 'pooling agreement' and 'contribution agreement' that had been negotiated between the various sets of liquidators. An essential element of the agreements was that the English liquidators might transfer funds, after making relevant deductions, to the liquidators in Luxembourg. However, the refusal of the appellate court in Luxembourg to approve the contribution agreement resulted in further negotiations and the eventual approval of the revised agreements, which in England was given by Scott V-C in *Re BCCI S.A. (No. 4)*.[11] In this judgment the court again noted that funds would be transferred to the Luxembourg liquidators ('Luxembourg being the principal liquidation centre, given that BCCI S.A. was incorporated in Luxembourg')[12] after the deduction of adequate funds to be retained by the English liquidators to pay, for example:

(i)   claims of creditors who would be prejudiced if forced to prove only in Luxembourg and

---

[7] *Re BCCI S.A.* [1992] B.C.L.C. 570 at 574.
[8] *Re BCCI S.A. (No. 2)* [1992] B.C.L.C. 579 at 581: 'BCCI is incorporated in Luxembourg which prima facie is the court where the prime winding up proceedings . . . will have to be conducted as being the law of the country of incorporation.'
[9] [1993] B.C.L.C. 1490 at 1496 (affirming [1993] B.C.L.C. 106).
[10] See p. 372 *et seq.*
[11] [1995] B.C.C. 453 (*sub nom. Re BCCI S.A. (No. 10)* [1995] 1 B.C.L.C. 362).
[12] [1995] B.C.C. 453 at 456–457.

(ii)   proprietary claims which might in due course be established against the liquidators in England.[13]

Some 18 months later the English liquidators were reaching the point where they were ready to transfer funds to Luxembourg, to be distributed by the Luxembourg liquidators amongst all the creditors worldwide on a *pari passu* basis. The concern of the English liquidators was, however, whether funds should be retained (and if so in what amount) in particular to take account of the fact that English set-off rules were of a far wider scope than the equivalent provisions of the law of Luxembourg. Thus Scott V-C was required[14] to consider both the general nature of a so-called 'ancillary' winding up and, specifically, whether the court would authorise the liquidators to disregard English set-off rules, thereby leaving relevant creditors 'to their fate' as it were in Luxembourg liquidation. In *Re BCCI S.A. (No. 10)* the Vice-Chancellor held that the set-off provision of English law, namely rule 4.90 of the Insolvency Rules, was mandatory and could not be disapplied.[15] Moreover, even if the court had a discretion in this regard, rule 4.90 should not be disapplied. His Lordship's view was that, even though the winding up in England was ancillary to the principal liquidation abroad, the court had no 'inherent power' to ignore the statutory insolvency scheme laid down in the 1986 Act and, moreover, that no such power could be found in the Act itself.[16] The cases on ancillary winding up established the following propositions:[17]

'(1) Where a foreign company is in liquidation in its country of incorporation, a winding up order made in England will normally be regarded as giving rise to a winding up ancillary to that being conducted in the country of incorporation. (2) The winding up in England will be ancillary in the sense that it will not be within the power of the English liquidators to get in and realise all the assets of the company worldwide. They will necessarily have to concentrate on getting in and realising the English assets. (3) Since in order to achieve a pari passu distribution between all the company's creditors it will be necessary for there to be a pooling of the company's assets worldwide and for a dividend to be declared out of the assets comprised in that pool, the winding up in England will be ancillary in the sense, also, that it will be the liquidators in the principal liquidation who will be best placed to declare the dividend and to distribute the assets in the pool accordingly. (4) None the less, the ancillary character of an English winding up does not relieve an English court of the obligation to apply English law, including English insolvency law, to the resolution of any issue arising in the winding up which is brought before the court. It may be, of course, that English conflicts of law rules will lead to the application of some foreign law principle in order to resolve a particular issue.'

In particular, proposition (4), above, meant that the court would not relieve the liquidators of: (i) the obligation to determine which proofs of debt (of those that had actually been submitted in England) should or should not

---

[13] *Idem.* It was accepted throughout that deductions would have to be made in respect of preferential creditors under English law, see [1997] Ch. 213 at 235.
[14] In *Re BCCI S.A. (No. 10)* [1997] Ch. 213, see also p. 318, *supra* for more details on set-off.
[15] See pp. 320–321, *supra.*
[16] [1997] Ch. 213 at 239–240 and 247.
[17] *Ibid.*, at 246.

be admitted; nor (ii) the requirement that English set-off rules be applied to all proofs so admitted.[18]

(iii) *Practical Implications*

On the facts in *Re BCCI S.A. (No. 10)* the application of English set-off rules had a dramatic impact. About one in six of the 36,000 proof of debt forms received by the English liquidators were affected by rule 4.90 set-off.[19] (In addition, there were around 4,000 claims, of a value of some $300 million, which had been accepted by the English liquidators but which had been initially rejected on various procedural grounds by the liquidators in Luxembourg.[20]) Hence the amount of funds that had to be retained by the English liquidators was very considerable; and not really of a minor or ancillary nature. Nevertheless, the facts of the BCCI insolvency were very special indeed and the application of rule 4.90 set-off in a more unusual fact scenario should be noted.

Normally, of course, it is not the bank that goes insolvent but rather the customer. To take an illustration, let us say that a trading company incorporated in Luxembourg has carried on business throughout Europe and has a (relatively small) branch in England – most UK operations being conducted through an English subsidiary. A winding up order is made in relation to the company and the proceedings are declared to be ancillary to the principal liquidation in Luxembourg. The English liquidator, following the instructions laid down by the Vice-Chancellor, will collect the company's assets in England and must entertain proofs submitted by any creditor (not just English creditors).[1] Two points will be noted. First, when gathering in assets in England the liquidator will only claim the net amount owing after taking into account any rule 4.90 set-off. Whether any particular debtors, having paid a net sum to the English liquidator, might be sued in Luxembourg for any balance outstanding according to the law of Luxembourg is not a matter that English insolvency law could ever regulate.[2] Secondly, Luxembourg banks (to which the company owed money) are unlikely at the end of the day to receive a windfall from the application of rule 4.90 set-off. If, for example, the company had a deposit of $1 million with a bank in Luxembourg and a current account overdraft of $1,500,000, the situation would be as follows. The bank, although having no connection to England, may claim in the English liquidation and rule 4.90 must be applied, so that the bank will be a net creditor in the sum of $500,000. Assuming that the worldwide dividend is 20%, the bank will be entitled ultimately to receive $100,000 from the English liquidator. In Luxembourg, however, where no set-off is on the facts permitted, the bank will be liable to be sued for $1 million and, on the other hand, may enter a proof for $1,500,000. The dividend payable in Luxembourg would be $300,000, less the $100,000 which the bank has received (or may receive)

---

[18] *Ibid.*, at 247–248.
[19] *Ibid.*, at 236–237.
[20] *Idem.*
[1] It is not correct to suggest that a function of an ancillary winding up is to protect the interests of 'English' creditors: see [1997] Ch. at 242. All creditors who prove in England are treated equally.
[2] *Ibid.*, at 251.

in England. Yet, as the bank owes the Luxembourg liquidator $1 million, the bank at the end of the day will find itself in deficit in the sum of $700,000. In other words, whether the bank enters a proof in England or not, its liability in Luxembourg will be quite unaffected.[3] Thus, in a more usual type of insolvency, the application of rule 4.90 set-off will not drive a coach and horses through the ancillary nature of the English winding up.

(iv) *No Discretion to Disapply Statutory Scheme*

It is also important from a practical perspective not to mistake the impact of the ruling of the Vice-Chancellor that the court had no general power to authorise English liquidators to ignore the statutory insolvency scheme. For the making of an order for an 'ancillary' winding up is not mandatory.[4] It is not mandatory in the sense that any winding up in England *must* be ancillary; nor is it mandatory in the sense that, if a valid petition is presented, a winding up order must be made. *Re Matheson Bros Ltd.* and *Re Jarvis Conklin Mortgage Co.*[5] were both cited in argument before Scott V-C and if his Lordship had been uneasy about those decisions he would surely have said so. In both cases the English court declined to make any order in respect of a foreign company, with a branch in England, on the basis that the foreign liquidator could get in the assets in England and English creditors would not in any event be discriminated against in the foreign liquidation. Reference may also be made to the decision of the Queensland court in *Re New England Brewing Co. Ltd.*[6] The company, incorporated in New South Wales, had carried on business in Queensland and a creditor presented a petition in Queensland. At the date of the (adjourned) hearing, a winding up order had been made in New South Wales and a liquidator appointed. The petitioning creditor argued that the company's affairs required investigation by a Queensland liquidator, particularly in respect of an allotment of shares which may have involved breaches of the companies legislation. Apart from the question of the investigation of the company's affairs, Lucas J regarded the case as a simple winding up which did not justify the additional expense of a liquidation in Queensland. His Honour noted that there was every reason to suppose that the New South Wales liquidator would adequately carry out any investigation that might be required and, accordingly, exercised his discretion against making a winding up order.[7] Recently the Court of Appeal in England has likewise declined to make a winding up order in respect of a foreign company, being satisfied that the Dutch liquidator

---

[3] Thus, in the more normal type of situation, rule 4.90 set-off may in practice likely only benefit parties who are not amenable to the jurisdiction of the courts in Luxembourg.

[4] As Scott V-C undoubtedly accepted: see his Lordship's first proposition set out at p. 364, *supra*.

[5] (1884) 27 Ch.D. 225 and (1895) 11 T.L.R. 373 respectively: see further p. 373, *infra*.

[6] [1970] Q.W.N. 49. See also *Gavigan* v. *A.M.P.L.* (1997) 8 N.Z.C.L.C., 261, 449 at 261, 453.

[7] If Lucas J had been minded to make an order, he made it clear that (*idem.*) he would have appointed the New South Wales liquidator as liquidator in Queensland. The practice of appointing the foreign liquidator as the local liquidator (see for example *Re Irish Shipping Ltd.* [1985] H.K.L.R. 437) is really no longer available in England, since any English liquidator must be a qualified insolvency practitioner in England (although two liquidators from the same international firm of accountants is always an option).

would properly carry out his investigative duties.[8] In short, nothing in *Re BCCI S.A. (No. 10)* affects the court's jurisdiction to decline to make a winding up order or, where an order has already been made, to stay proceedings on the basis that all relevant matters can be satisfactorily dealt with in the more appropriate foreign forum.

In addition, even where there is an ancillary winding up in England, and no question of a stay arises, it does not follow that the winding up will unfold in the same manner as a 'normal' English winding up. Quite apart from the restriction inherent in an ancillary winding up (i.e. being limited to the collection of assets within the jurisdiction), many provisions of the statutory insolvency scheme confer a discretion on the liquidator or the court. Thus in an ancillary winding up, it is suggested, the court would normally start from the assumption that it would not exercise its avoidance powers extraterritorially.[9]

(v) *Theoretical Considerations: A Revised Framework*

The importance of *Re BCCI S.A. (No. 10)* in terms of theory is twofold. Firstly, Scott V-C gave the judicial seal of approval to the concept of an ancillary winding up – despite the absence of any apparent statutory basis for such a direction. Second, however, his Lordship was in substance prepared to go no further than the old English cases had indicated: in an 'ancillary' winding up the liquidator's role would *prima facie* be restricted to settling a list of creditors who proved in England and gathering English assets, with a view to transferring such assets to the principal liquidator for distribution on a worldwide basis; but the court had no further power to authorise the English liquidator to disregard his statutory obligations under the Insolvency Act 1986. Yet the judgment contains very little about when a winding up in England will be 'ancillary' and when it will not.

It is clear that there is no rule that, where a foreign company is already in liquidation abroad, a winding up conducted in England must be ancillary in nature. For a very recent example one need look no further than *Lehman Bros Inc. v. Phillips: Re Mid East Trading Ltd.*[10] The company was incorporated in the Lebanon and was already in liquidation there. A creditor presented a winding up petition in England and an order was made – the petition had the support of the Lebanese liquidator and a large number of Lebanese creditors. A significant amount of the company's investment advice activities had been conducted through accounts with the London office of Lehman Brothers, before that business was moved to Bear Stearns in New York. The English liquidators, again with the support of the Lebanese liquidator, commenced discovery proceedings in the US Bankruptcy Court against Lehman Brothers and subsequently also against Bear Stearns. The liquidators also applied before the English court for an order pursuant to section 236 of the Insolvency Act 1986 for Lehman Brothers to produce certain documents held at that time in New York. The Court of Appeal upheld the order of Evans-Lombe J that the

---

[8] *New Hampshire Insurance Co.* v. *Rush & Tomkins Group plc*, p. 129, *supra*.
[9] See further p. 383, *infra*.
[10] [1998] 1 All E.R. 577, affirming [1997] 3 All E.R. 481.

documents should be produced. The point this author is trying to make is that it is very difficult to detect anything 'ancillary' about the conduct of the English liquidation – except to the extent that the liquidators' actions had the support of their Lebanese counterpart.[11]

Where the English court declares that its proceedings will be ancillary to the principal liquidation abroad, no fixed or rigid course of conduct is thereby set in motion, still less a course of conduct that will be precisely duplicated in all other ancillary winding up cases. Rather 'ancillary' winding up should now be seen as part of a broader spectrum of available assistance in cross-border insolvency cases. This author would suggest that a number of points on the spectrum can be identified:

(1)   *winding up petition dismissed* – where the facts are relatively straight-forward it may be immediately apparent (upon the giving, if necessary, of suitable undertakings) that no winding up in England is required;

(2)   *winding up petition adjourned* – the facts are relatively simple as in (1) above; however, the foreign liquidator may wish to have the opportunity to consider whether English proceedings (such as the appointment of a provisional liquidator)[12] would be helpful, or there may be issues that can likely be resolved over the course of the adjournment and then the petition can be dismissed (or proceedings stayed);[13]

(3)   *winding up proceedings stayed* – the English court has made an order but, after a relatively short period of time, the difficult issues have been resolved and the proceedings can be stayed, the liquidation continuing in the more appropriate foreign forum;[14]

(4)   *'classic' ancillary winding up* – territorial proceedings (in respect of assets in England and creditors who choose to prove in England) are conducted with a view ultimately to sending assets to the principal liquidation abroad; avoidance powers and investigatory powers may at times be invoked (similarly on a territorial basis);

(5)   *'extended' ancillary winding up* – as in (4) above but with the English liquidator playing a greater role, for instance in relation to the investigation of the company's affairs and at times even seeking to exercise appropriate powers extraterritorially;

(6)   *mutual co-operation* – a more or less 'full-scale' English winding up including payment of dividends, subject to any protocol or other arrangement entered into with the foreign liquidator and allowing for assets to be transferred from one jurisdiction to another to ensure equality of dividends in the different liquidations.[15]

---

[11] See also *Re Queensland Mercantile Agency Co. Ltd.*, p. 377, *infra*.

[12] Once a petition has been presented, see s. 135 of the Insolvency Act 1986, a provisional liquidator may be appointed; and see p. 399, *infra*.

[13] It may often be useful to adjourn the hearing for a few weeks while waiting for a liquidator to be appointed in the country of incorporation – it will often depend upon creditors whether main or ancillary proceedings are started first: note *Mercantile Credits Ltd.* v. *Foster Clark (Australia) Ltd.* (1964) 112 C.L.R. 169.

[14] See also p. 366, *supra*. For the application of the *forum conveniens* doctrine to winding up, see *Re Wallace Smith & Co. Ltd.* [1992] B.C.L.C. 970. *Re Oriental Bank Corpn.* (1884) 10 V.L.R. (E.) 154 is an old example of a stay in favour of foreign proceedings.

[15] The type of scenario that arose in the context of personal insolvency in *Re Macfadyen & Co.* [1908] 1 K.B. 675, p. 338, *supra*.

These points are, of course, in no way rigidly fixed; and clearly they will merge one into the other as the role taken on by the English liquidator increases.[16]

It is also suggested that this 'sliding-scale' approach fits more easily with the decided cases than any assertion that an ancillary winding up has one, and only one, meaning. A passage in the judgment of Millett J in *Re International Tin Council* is illuminating.[17] His Lordship had explained that when the English court makes a winding up order in relation to a foreign company there will be practical limitations on the effectiveness of such an order outside the jurisdiction:[18]

> 'But in theory the effect of the order is worldwide. The statutory trusts which it brings into operation are imposed on all the company's assets wherever situate, within and beyond the jurisdiction. Where the company is simultaneously being wound up in the country of its incorporation, the English court will naturally seek to avoid unnecessary conflict, and so far as possible to ensure that the English winding up is conducted as ancillary to the principal liquidation. In a proper case, it may authorise the liquidator to refrain from seeking to recover assets situate beyond the jurisdiction, thereby protecting him from any complaint that he has been derelict in his duty.'

Hence the 'ancillaryness' of the winding up comes not from the order itself but from the way in which the liquidator's powers are restricted – or, more precisely, the way in which the court excuses the liquidator from exercising certain powers and carrying out certain duties that he would otherwise be bound to exercise or carry out.[19] This confers considerable freedom upon the court and, it is submitted, fits neatly with the 'sliding-scale' of assistance suggested above. For example, if the foreign liquidator wants the English liquidator to play a major investigatory role and to recover assets in the United States – but not for example in Latin America – the English court can so authorise the English liquidator. Or, if both liquidators agree that on the facts it would be best for each liquidator to distribute dividends to creditors, after equalising transfers of funds have been made, then such conduct can be authorised by the court. An ancillary winding up must be seen as an adaptable tool – within the limits laid down in *Re BCCI S.A. (No. 10)* – and in respect of which the views of the professional liquidators will be given due weight.[20]

(vi) *'Ancillary Winding Up Order'*

In the light of the above discussion it is perhaps worth emphasising that there are not two distinct types of winding up order that the court may make under section 125 of the Insolvency Act 1986: (i) a winding up order and (ii) an ancillary winding up order. There is only one type of order but, having made the winding up order, the judge may (prospectively) excuse the

---

[16] If the liquidator in England believes that a certain course of action involving co-operation with the foreign representative is desirable, the court will attach great weight to that view: see the comments of Lord Hoffmann, set out at p. 336, *supra*.

[17] [1987] Ch. 419.

[18] *Ibid.*, at 446–447.

[19] See the analysis of Scott V-C in *Re BCCI S.A. (No. 10)* [1997] Ch. 213 at 241–242 and 244–245.

[20] See n. 16, *supra*.

liquidator from acting extraterritorially and direct that (unless the facts otherwise require) the liquidator should be working towards ultimately sending funds abroad for distribution. But if it subsequently transpires that sending assets to the foreign liquidator might not be the most efficient method of distribution – for example, both liquidators would prefer an equalising dividend approach[1] – the view of the English liquidator will be given great weight by the court in authorising any agreement with the foreign liquidator.

2. THE DISCRETION OF THE ENGLISH COURT

As discussed above, merely because a petition to wind up a foreign corporation is presented in England, and the jurisdictional criteria have been established, does not mean that the court is obliged to make an ancillary order. A satisfactory approach to the winding up of foreign corporations must be flexible enough to take into account the different factual considerations which may present themselves in any particular instance. That incorporation has taken place abroad cannot of itself dictate that an English liquidation must be merely auxiliary or ancillary: the interests of justice may require otherwise. Equally, it may be that even an ancillary winding up in England is quite simply unnecessary, and that relevant issues can be solved by recognition of the foreign liquidator's authority to deal with the corporation's assets in England.

A. The Interests of Justice

It is plain that the English court will not direct a winding up to be ancillary to a liquidation abroad if to do so would be against the interests of justice. For example, a company may be incorporated in Panama or Liberia (or the Isle of Man) yet do all its business and have all, or nearly all, its creditors and corporators in England. If such a company were to become insolvent, there seems no compelling reason why an English liquidation should to a greater or lesser extent give way to proceedings in Panama or Liberia; rather, having regard to the location of creditors and shareholders and the availability of evidence, it would appear that the English court would be an appropriate forum for the liquidation. In comparison, if a foreign corporation has only a slight connection to England (for instance, relatively few creditors) and has conducted the most part of its business activities in the country of incorporation or elsewhere outside the United Kingdom then *prima facie* the English court will not be a suitable forum for a full-scale winding up: this may be particularly so where a foreign corporation has carried on business in several different countries, as only the courts in the country of incorporation can properly conduct the main liquidation and call upon the courts of other jurisdictions to act ancillary thereto.[2] In short,

---

[1] See n. 15, *supra*.
[2] See, generally, *Re Alfred Shaw & Co. Ltd.* (1897) 8 Q.L.J. 93, *infra*.

the English court should regard its own proceedings as ancillary where the corporation in question is in liquidation in the country of incorporation and that foreign court is the appropriate forum.

The doctrine of the natural or convenient forum (*forum conveniens*) is now undeniably part of English private international law. As Lord Goff put it in *Spiliada Maritime Corpn. v. Cansulex Ltd.*:[3]

'The basic principle is that a stay will only be granted on the ground of *forum non conveniens* where the court is satisfied that there is some other available forum, having competent jurisdiction, which is the appropriate forum for the trial of the action, i.e. in which the case may be tried more suitably for the interests of all the parties and the ends of justice.'

His Lordship was, of course, speaking in respect of international litigation generally, yet it may be noted that like considerations have influenced English judges hearing disputes concerning foreign companies for some time. In *Bill* v. *Sierra Nevada Lake, Water and Mining Co.*[4] the constitution of a company incorporated and carrying on business in the State of California, but whose affairs were principally managed in London, allowed for the increase of the capital of the company. A resolution having been carried which made provision for such increase, a shareholder sought an injunction in England. Stuart V-C granted the injunction, and the Lords Justices allowed the appeal, Knight Bruce LJ commenting:[5]

'The domicile, the purposes and the objects of the Sierra Nevada Company are such, in my opinion, that the court ought not to act against the defendants for the purpose of injunction, or by way of injunction in such a case as the present one. . . .'

In *Pergamon Press Ltd.* v. *Maxwell*[6] the members of a New York company ('Incorporated') sought an order from the English court, in effect, to supervise the exercise of a fiduciary power that arose in the internal management of Incorporated. Pennycuick J noted that 'other and much more extensive litigation between the same parties is pending in the United States' and declined to intervene, observing:[7]

'the court of New York is the only proper tribunal in which the members of Incorporated could seek to control the exercise of this discretionary power.'

More recently, *Re a Company (No. 00359 of 1987)*[8] tackled the question whether the English court would, in the absence of assets in England, wind up a Liberian company. Peter Gibson J held that, whilst there were no assets in England, the facts established a sufficiently close connection to the English jurisdiction to justify the making of a winding up order. Significantly, his Lordship was fortified in this conclusion by the consideration that there was 'no more appropriate jurisdiction for the winding up of the company'.[9]

---

[3] [1987] A.C. 460 at 476, see generally pp. 63–64, *supra*.
[4] (1860) 1 L.T. 256.
[5] *Ibid.*, at 257.
[6] [1970] 1 W.L.R. 1167.
[7] *Ibid.*, at 1172.
[8] [1988] Ch. 210, chapter 4, *supra*.
[9] *Ibid.*, at 227. See also *Tong Aik (Far East) Ltd.* v. *Eastern Minerals & Trading (1959) Ltd.* [1965] 2 M.L.J. 149 in which the Singapore court refused to order the winding up of a Malayan company, it being stressed that the Malayan court was the 'appropriate court' and the 'complete absence of any suggestion that the appropriate proceedings cannot be taken under the Malayan enactment'.

Further in *Re Wallace Smith & Co. Ltd.*[10] it was accepted that the *forum conveniens* doctrine was applicable to the winding up of a foreign company under Part V of the Insolvency Act 1986.

Thus, when dealing with the insolvency of a foreign corporation it is necessary to consider whether, in the interests of all the parties and for the ends of justice, the English court is the proper tribunal in which a liquidation should proceed. If the English court is the appropriate forum, then the English winding up need not be ancillary to any other liquidation. The facts of *Re a Company* may serve as an illustration. It will be recalled that Peter Gibson J concluded that there was a sufficient nexus between the Liberian company and England to permit the making of a winding up order and, moreover, that there was no other more appropriate jurisdiction in which the company could be wound up. His Lordship expressly ruled out Liberia as a more appropriate jurisdiction since: 'The company seems to have had nothing to do with Liberia after its incorporation.'[11] As a consequence, a winding up order was made. However, it is submitted that, even if the company had actually been put into liquidation in Liberia, the conduct of the English proceedings would not have been affected, for the English court would still have been a more appropriate jurisdiction than Liberia – although, of course, the English court would instruct the liquidator to act as far as possible to ensure that unsecured creditors received the same level of dividend in both the English and Liberian proceedings.[12]

B. Assisting the Principal Liquidation Abroad

It must be stressed that, in the majority of cases, the court of the state of incorporation is likely to be the appropriate forum in which to wind up a foreign corporation. In such circumstances the English court should undoubtedly regard those proceedings as the principal liquidation and lend its assistance thereto. Yet there remains an important question as to the form which such assistance should take. For, as discussed above, the court is not obliged to make a winding up order, ancillary or otherwise, in respect of a foreign corporation. Thus it has been stated that a foreign liquidation 'does not take away the right of the courts of this country to make a winding up order here, though it would no doubt exercise an influence upon this court in making the order'.[13] The cases make it plain that an exercise of discretion is required. In *Re Union Bank of Calcutta* a joint stock banking company established in India, with correspondents and liabilities in England, was in liquidation in India. A shareholder's petition for winding up was dismissed by Knight Bruce V-C who felt that 'much more mischief would arise from acting on this petition than declining now to interfere'.[14] Additionally, the court may refuse to make a winding up order if such an order is unnecessary. In *Re Jarvis Conklin Mortgage Co.*[15] a company had been incorporated in the State of Missouri to lend money

---

[10] [1992] B.C.L.C. 970, discussed at p. 127, *supra*.
[11] [1988] Ch. 210 at 227. See also *Re Syrian Ottoman Rly. Co.* (1904) 20 T.L.R. 217.
[12] See p. 340, *supra*.
[13] *Re Matheson Bros Ltd.* (1884) 27 Ch. D. 225 at 230 *per* Kay J.
[14] (1850) 3 De G. & S.M. 253 at 257.
[15] (1895) 11 T.L.R. 373.

on American lands. The company was in liquidation in America and had a certain amount of uncalled share capital in England. Romer J exercised his discretion against making a winding up order. His Lordship is reported as stating:[16]

> 'The company had only a branch office in this country. More than a year ago the company had been in liquidation in America, and the receivers there had got in the greater part of the assets. It was not suggested that the liquidation in America would not be efficient, or that the assets would not be properly got in. If a winding up order was made it would only be ancillary to the American one, and such a winding up was not needed.'

Although not specifically explained by Romer J, upon the facts of *Re Jarvis Conklin Mortgage Co.* no winding up order was required to gather in the uncalled share capital in England, because the English court might recognise the foreign liquidation and with it the authority of the foreign liquidator to deal with the movable property in England. (In *Tong Aik (Far East) Ltd.* v. *Eastern Minerals & Trading (1959) Ltd.*[17] the Singapore court refused to order the winding up of a Malayan company on the basis, *inter alia*, that the Malayan court was the 'appropriate court' for the liquidation and there was no reason why proceedings could not there be taken.)

Thus, instead of conducting an ancillary winding up, the English court may simply recognise the authority of a foreign liquidator to deal with assets in England. But it should always be remembered that the appointment of the liquidator under the law of the place of incorporation, as well as the powers of the liquidator according to that law, must be proved before the English court. (Further, recognition of a foreign liquidation does not confer the advantages available to a liquidator in England under the Insolvency Act 1986 or under other legislation.[18]) Pending the securing of assets in England by a foreign liquidator, the court may accept an undertaking, by those managing the corporation's affairs in England, that the assets will remain *in statu quo*. *Re Matheson Bros Ltd.*[19] concerned a creditor's petition to wind up a New Zealand company already in liquidation in New Zealand. Kay J, although having great regard to the proceedings in the New Zealand courts, felt that the company's assets in England had to be secured. His Lordship accepted an undertaking from the company's managing director and agent in England that the assets would remain undistributed until further order of the court:[20]

> 'I shall accordingly hold that the court has sufficient jurisdiction to sanction the acceptance of the undertaking . . . I consider that I am justified in taking steps to secure the English assets until I see that proceedings are taken on the New Zealand liquidation to make the English assets available for the English creditors *pari passu* with the creditors in New Zealand.'

---

[16] *Ibid.* The substantial reason for the petitioners seeking an English winding up was to obtain the sanction of the court to a scheme of arrangement but Romer J considered 'that was not a sufficient ground for ordering an ancillary winding up here'. The opposite view was taken in *Re Australian Joint Stock Bank* [1897] W.N. 48 and see now Companies Act 1985, s. 425(6)(a).

[17] [1965] 2 M.L.J. 149.

[18] Such as pursuant to s. 17A of the Drug Trafficking Offences Act 1986.

[19] (1884) 27 Ch. D. 225.

[20] *Ibid.*, at 231.

Of course, as intimated by Kay J, if the English (or other)[1] creditors would be discriminated against in the foreign liquidation, the English court would be unlikely to accept that assets should be given over to the foreign liquidator; instead a winding up order would be made in England, all creditors being allowed to claim in the English winding up provided they were prepared to bring into hotchpot[2] any dividend received in the foreign proceedings.[3]

In summary, once it is shown that a liquidation has begun under the law of the place of incorporation[4] and, moreover, that the foreign court is the relevant forum for the winding up of the foreign corporation, the English court has a discretion in respect of any assistance to be given to the foreign liquidation proceedings. The English court may order an ancillary winding up (restricting the powers of the liquidator) or the English court may simply recognise the authority of the foreign liquidator to gather in any English assets, leaving English creditors to bring their claims in the foreign insolvency proceedings.[5] Where a winding up order is made and the court indicates that its proceedings should as far as possible be ancillary to the principal liquidation abroad, the court may expressly limit the liquidator's initial role to getting in the English assets and setting a list of relevant creditors[6] – but where such a restriction is imposed, the liquidator will be at liberty to seek authorisation to exercise additional powers[7] and, in determining a liquidator's request, the court will be reluctant to depart from the liquidator's professional opinion as to how assets can be most effectively realised in co-operation with the foreign liquidation process.

3. THE CONDUCT OF AN ANCILLARY WINDING UP

A. Gathering and Remitting English Assets

If the English court exercises its discretion against making a winding up order, the position is quite clear: the foreign liquidator's authority to collect in English assets may be recognised, with the consequence that the English creditors will be left to bring their claims in the foreign proceedings. Such an approach has the benefit, firstly, of saving costs and, second, of ensuring equality between the different creditors, foreign and English.[8] Where the English court does order an ancillary winding up, it is apparent that it will be the *English* appointed liquidator who will

---

[1]   An ancillary winding up is not just to protect 'English' creditors: see [1997] Ch. 213 at 242.
[2]   See, generally, chapter 10 as to the hotchpot rule.
[3]   The making of an order, and directing that it be ancillary, was accepted by the Court of Appeal as a matter of discretion in *Re Federal Bank of Australia Ltd.* (1893) 62 L.J. Ch. 561.
[4]   If the liquidation has not yet begun abroad, the best course of action may often be to adjourn for a brief period to enable the foreign proceedings to 'catch up': for an illustration see *Re New England Brewing Co. Ltd.* [1970] Q.W.N. 49.
[5]   See also the discussion at p. 366, *supra*.
[6]   In *Re Victoria Date Co. Ltd.* (1898) 42 Sol. Jo. 755 the report refers merely to collecting assets in England, but this is not the view of Scott V-C in *Re BCCI S.A. (No. 10)* – although the earlier case was not cited. See the discussion *infra*, p. 375.
[7]   See the discussion of *Re Commercial Bank of South Australia Ltd.* (1886) 33 Ch. D. 174 and *Re Hibernian Merchants Ltd.* [1958] Ch. 76 in *Re BCCI S.A. (No. 10)* [1997] Ch. 213 at 243–244.
[8]   See the analysis above.

gather in the corporation's assets (and generally represent the corporation) in England:[9] for the most obvious and immediate purpose of an ancillary winding up is to secure assets within the jurisdiction of the English court, thereby protecting at least temporarily English creditors (and share-holders). In *Re Commercial Bank of South Australia*[10] the Bank, incorpo-rated in South Australia but with a branch in England, suspended payment in both Australia and England. The Bank had shareholders in England as well as a large number of creditors and considerable assets. North J held that, even though a winding up order had been made in Australia, the creditors were entitled to an order in England, stating:[11]

> 'I think that the winding up here will be ancillary to a winding up in Australia, and . . . I will take care that there shall be no conflict between the two courts, and I shall have regard to the interests of all the creditors and all the contribu-tories, and shall endeavour to keep down the expenses of the winding up so far as is possible.'

Accordingly, the English liquidator was instructed not to act 'except for the purpose of getting in the English assets and settling the list of English creditors'.[12] This comment has given rise to a certain degree of controversy, but it cannot be taken as preventing the liquidator – even if such a direc-tion is given – from being at liberty to apply to the court to exercise any of the powers under the Insolvency Act 1986.[13] Moreover, Scott V-C has held that there is no general power to disapply the insolvency scheme laid down in the Act.[14] Hence, in this author's view, such a restriction is now of no value and indeed only increases costs: for, if a particular duty is imposed on the liquidator by the Act, he will have to apply to the court to carry out that duty; and, according to *Re BCCI S.A. (No. 10)*, the court has no power to relieve the liquidator from the statutory obligation in question. Should the court wish to give some directions or guidance, the following might be considered useful:

(1) that the court relieve the liquidator of the obligation to seek to recover assets outside the United Kingdom;[15]
(2) that the realisation of assets within the jurisdiction be with a view ultimately, provided all creditors[16] may claim without discrimination in the foreign proceedings, to sending the proceeds abroad to be distributed on a worldwide basis by the foreign liquidator; and
(3) that the liquidator is encouraged to co-operate, as far as is practic-able, with the foreign liquidator.

---

[9] Although the foreign liquidator may appear in the English court, as in *Re B.C.C.I. S.A.* [1992] B.C.L.C. 570.
[10] (1886) 33 Ch. D. 174: for subsequent litigation in England see (1887) 36 Ch. D. 522.
[11] *Ibid.*, at 178. See also *Re Hibernian Merchants Ltd.* [1958] Ch. 76 at 79.
[12] *Ibid.*, at 178–179.
[13] See n. 7, *supra.*
[14] See p. 366, *supra.*
[15] *Re BCCI S.A. (No. 10)* [1997] Ch. 213 at 246, *Re International Tin Council* [1987] Ch. 419 at 447.
[16] Not just *English* creditors. The comment of Kay J in *North Australian Territory Co. Ltd.* v. *Goldsbrough, Mort & Co. Ltd.* (1889) 61 L.T. 716 at 717 that the 'only purpose' of an ancillary winding up was 'to protect the property . . . and the creditors in this country' was described in the first edition of this work (p. 241) as putting the matter 'too bluntly': see the observation of Scott V-C to like effect in *Re BCCI S.A. (No. 10)* [1997] Ch. 213 at 242.

In an appropriate case, the court might also wish to remind the liquidator that (particularly where creditors would not suffer any significant prejudice) the liquidator might in due course apply for a stay of the English winding up, on the basis that all remaining issues can be satisfactorily dealt with in the foreign forum.[17]

But it must never be thought that an ancillary winding up order creates a separate fund of assets reserved for, and to be divided up amongst, the English creditors. The ultimate objective of an ancillary winding up is to hand over the proceeds of the realisation of assets in England to the court conducting the main liquidation abroad. The desire, as far as possible, to have a single set of proceedings for distribution of assets is readily comprehensible. Let us say that an Ontario corporation is in liquidation in Canada. The greater part of the corporation's assets is in Canada but there are also a few creditors and some assets in England, where an ancillary order has been made. The English assets cannot in any way be earmarked for English creditors, as it is undeniable that any creditor (English or foreign) may claim in insolvency proceedings in England. Thus all the Canadian creditors might claim in the English winding up, thereby destroying any possible advantage to the English creditors.[18] It is far more sensible that the English court, once satisfied that English creditors will not be discriminated against in the Canadian proceedings, remit English assets to the courts in Canada.

In appropriate circumstances the English court may be willing to send English assets, or the proceeds thereof, to a liquidation taking place other than in the corporate domicile. *Re Alfred Shaw & Co. Ltd.*, a decision of the Chief Justice of Queensland, concerned a company incorporated in Victoria but which carried on business in Queensland and in England. The company was in voluntary liquidation in Victoria: winding up orders had also been made in Queensland and in England. The company's assets were principally in Queensland, although there were some assets in England. The company had no substantial assets in Victoria and all the Victorian creditors had proved in Queensland. The Queensland liquidator sought leave from the court to transmit to England such sum of money as would enable the English liquidator to pay in England a dividend equal to that intended to be paid in Queensland. Griffith CJ accepted that the proceedings in Queensland (as well as in England) were merely ancillary and that the local court would normally have transmitted the proceeds to the principal liquidation abroad. However, the local liquidator was seeking to send assets to another ancillary liquidation (in England). The Chief Justice was not prepared to make any order without hearing the Victorian liquidators, but stated:[19]

> 'If they appear and concur in the application, I think I shall be justified, acting in aid of the Victorian liquidation, in ordering the transmission of a proper sum to the official liquidator in England for the purpose of paying to the creditors who have proved there a dividend equal to that authorised to be paid the Queensland creditors.'

---

[17] See the analysis at p. 366, *supra*.
[18] A point brought out by Griffith CJ in *Re Alfred Shaw & Co. Ltd* (1897) 8 Q.L.J. 93 at 96.
[19] (1897) 8 Q.L.J. 93 at 97.

Where ancillary liquidations are under way in a number of jurisdictions, including England, *Re Alfred Shaw & Co. Ltd.* should be followed:[20] the English court sending assets to the principal liquidators, or such other court specified by the principal liquidators as is consistent with maintaining equality between English and foreign creditors.

B. Further Participation

The essence of an ancillary winding up is that the English proceedings should assist, rather than be in conflict with, the main liquidation abroad. Although, as Scott V-C put it in *Re BCCI S.A. (No. 10)*, 'the ancillary character of an English winding up does not relieve the English court of the obligation to apply English law, including English insolvency law, to the resolution of any issue arising in the winding up which is brought before the court.'[1] Such assistance may, at times, require quite active involvement on the part of the English court. Reference may here be made to the first stages in the insolvency of the Queensland Mercantile and Agency Co. Ltd.[2] The Queensland Mercantile and Agency Co. Ltd. ('QMA') was incorporated in Queensland where it acted as agent for the Australasian Investment Co. ('AIC'), a Scottish registered company. In October 1887 QMA was ordered to be wound up in the courts of Queensland. In January 1888 a winding up order in respect of QMA was made in England 'and the winding up here was directed to be ancillary to the proceedings in Australia'.[3] In February 1887, prior to the orders of the Australian and English courts, AIC had commenced proceedings against QMA in Scotland, alleging that QMA had misappropriated investments belonging to AIC. In the Scottish proceedings AIC arrested certain assets belonging to QMA in Scotland and thereby it was said became, under Scots law, a secured creditor on the funds so arrested. The first issue to arise before North J was whether, on a motion by the English liquidator of QMA, the English court would restrain AIC from proceeding with the Scottish action. His Lordship in *Re Queensland Mercantile Agency Co. Ltd.* considered the nature of the English liquidation, stating:[4]

> 'It is true that there is a liquidation of the company also going on in Queensland, where the head office of the company was situate. To a certain extent I treat the winding up here as ancillary to the winding up there, but not to such an extent as to make this court an agent for the courts in Queensland, and I must investigate the matter as far as I can here.'

Although not considering the English court a mere 'agent for the courts in Queensland', North J did attempt to co-ordinate the two liquidations and

---

[20] The judgment of Griffith CJ was cited with approval by Scott V-C in *Re BCCI S.A. (No. 10)*, *supra*, at 245–246.

[1] *Supra.*, at 246.

[2] *Re Queensland Mercantile Agency Co. Ltd.* (1888) 58 L.T. 878. Later proceedings *sub nom. Re Queensland Mercantile and Agency Co., ex p Australasian Investment Co.* [1891] 1 Ch. 536 are discussed in chapter 11. Scottish proceedings *Queensland Mercantile and Agency Co. Ltd.* v. *Australasian Investment Co.* are reported at (1888) 15 R. 935.

[3] (1888) 58 L.T. 878 at 879. See also *per* Scott V-C in *Re BCCI S.A. (No. 10)* [1997] Ch. 213 at 241.

[4] *Ibid.*

the Scottish proceedings. For his Lordship granted a stay of the Scottish proceedings and ordered that AIC's claim against QMA be determined in the latter's liquidation:[5]

> 'It is clear to me that as a matter of convenience it is far better for everyone that the matter should be investigated in the liquidation than in Scotland.'

In granting the stay, North J expressly reserved to AIC the benefit of the security it had obtained by the arrest of assets in Scotland.[6] Moreover, and significantly, it was ordered that the extent of liability of QMA to AIC be determined not in the English winding up but rather in the Queensland proceedings, for all the evidence relevant to AIC's claim was in Queensland and it 'would be far less expensive to all the parties to let the claims be investigated *de novo* in Queensland'.[7]

It must be noted that in *Re Queensland Mercantile Agency Co. Ltd.* the English court did not stay its own winding up in favour of the Queensland proceedings. North J ordered only that the question of liability between QMA and AIC be determined in Queensland. Once that liability had been ascertained, the English winding up continued and further litigation ensued as to the Scottish assets that came under the control of the English liquidator.[8] Nevertheless, the decision of North J is a most relevant example of co-operation between an English and a foreign court: the English court conducting what might be termed an 'extended' ancillary winding up.[9]

Re Queensland Mercantile Agency Co. Ltd. also serves to illustrate an important problem that may arise when the English court exercises its ancillary winding up jurisdiction. An English winding up order may be granted in respect of a foreign corporation, the English court stating that the local proceedings be 'ancillary' to the main liquidation. However, once the English liquidation is on foot there is a very real possibility that the English court will expand its role and fully investigate substantive issues arising in the liquidation. In such a manner the proceedings in England may lose any significant ancillary character. Indeed, in *Re Queensland Mercantile Agency Co. Ltd.* the English court used the proceedings in Queensland to determine the amount of a claim to be made in the English winding up. In such circumstances it can scarcely be said that the English winding up is in fact truly ancillary to the foreign proceedings.

However, no criticism of the approach of North J is intended. For it may be noted that the Queensland liquidator had himself sought a further winding up in England:[10]

> 'although there is a winding up in the colony which would enable the liquidator there to ingather the whole assets of the company, if he can reach them, it may aid him very much in the performance of that duty that there should be another

---

[5] *Ibid.*

[6] 'I propose to reserve to the plaintiffs in Scotland the full benefit of the security, and staying the action will not deprive them of any benefit they have got by having commenced it there': (1888) 58 L.T. 878 at 879. The question of priority that subsequently arose is discussed at p. 314, *supra*.

[7] *Ibid.*, at 880.

[8] See p. 314, *supra*.

[9] See p. 368, *supra*.

[10] (1888) 15 R. 935 at 936 *per* the Lord President. See also the analysis of this case in chapter 6.

liquidation in England or elsewhere where also the company has been carrying on business.'

One of the strengths of the ancillary winding up is its flexibility. Taking into consideration the working of the foreign liquidation, the English court may confine itself to what might loosely be described as an administrative role, or the English liquidator may co-operate on a more equal footing with the foreign liquidator. This author would refer to *Lehman Bros Inc.* v. *Phillips: Re Mid East Trading Ltd.*[11] as an example of the latter situation.

C. Summary

At this stage one can identify a number of basic principles, drawn from the decided cases, which should guide the English court when assisting the liquidation of a foreign corporation. Firstly, the English court must be satisfied that the foreign corporation is in liquidation under the law of the place of incorporation and that the relevant foreign court is, in the interests of justice, the appropriate forum for the liquidation. Secondly, the English court may lend assistance to the foreign liquidation proceedings if the creditors in England can bring their claims in the foreign proceedings *pari passu* with other creditors of the same class. Thirdly, it lies within the discretion of the English court either to order an 'ancillary' winding up or to recognise the authority of the liquidator[12] appointed by the foreign court to deal with assets in England. Fourthly, if an ancillary winding up is ordered, the powers of the liquidator may in practice be limited to collecting the English assets and settling a list of creditors. Finally, the assets so collected shall, after satisfying preferred creditors and other approved payments,[13] be remitted to the foreign liquidator so that the claims of the creditors can be dealt with on an equal footing in one single liquidation.[14]

D. *Re Suidair International Airways Ltd.*

In the light of the above principles the judgment of Wynn-Parry J in *Re Suidair International Airways Ltd.* may be examined.[15] A South African company with an office in England owed money to the applicants. Following delays in payment and generally evasive behaviour on the part of the South African company, the applicants commenced an action in England and obtained a default judgment against the company. In the meantime, a winding up petition had been presented in South Africa and a provisional liquidator there appointed. The applicants, with notice of the South African proceedings, issued two writs of *fieri facias* which resulted in the seizure of goods of the company. A winding up petition was then presented

---

[11] [1998] 1 All E.R. 577, p. 367, *supra.*
[12] See also p. 399, for the use to which a provisional liquidator may be put in such circumstances.
[13] Charges and other matters are dealt with below at p. 386.
[14] These last two sentences were quoted by Scott V-C in *Re BCCI S.A. (No. 10)* at 239–240, who commented: 'The good sense of the procedure outlined in this passage is evident. . . .'
[15] [1951] Ch. 165: see also p. 241, *ante,* for criticism of the judgment.

by a creditor in England and a winding up order was made in due course. The applicants sought an order that they might retain as against the Official Receiver the benefit of the writs of *fieri facias*.[16] Before Wynn-Parry J it was argued by the Official Receiver that, as the winding up in England was ancillary to the South African liquidation, the law of the main liquidation (South African law) should be applied in determining whether the applicants were to retain the benefit of the two writs. Such a contention was firmly rejected:[17]

> 'It appears to me that the simple principle is that this court sits to administer the assets of a South African company which are within its jurisdiction, and for that purpose it administers, and administers only, the relevant English law . . . If that principle be adhered to, no confusion will result. If it is departed from, then for myself I cannot see how any other result would follow than the utmost possible confusion. Who could lay down as a clear and exhaustive proposition where the court was to draw the line in any particular case between administering the English law and the law of the main liquidation?'

Accordingly the applicants were permitted, by reference to section 325(1)(c) of the Companies Act 1948, to retain the benefit of the two writs.

However, the 'simple principle' of Wynn-Parry J is perhaps too simple. Even accepting that in an English winding up the court applies English domestic law, his Lordship's comment confuses the nature of an ancillary winding up. If a winding up is ancillary it should not follow the course of an ordinary, full-scale winding up. An ancillary winding up is 'carefully limited in effect'.[18] The objective of an *ancillary* winding up is, having secured the company's assets in England, to remit those assets to the foreign liquidator, enabling the court of the main liquidation to deal with all the assets and the creditors. An ancillary winding up is not primarily a device by which assets in England may be gathered in and distributed in accordance with English domestic law: that, obviously, would be in no way ancillary to the main liquidation.[19] Rather, if a winding up is directed by the English court to be ancillary to the main liquidation abroad, the English court will be seeking to avoid distributing property according to English law, leaving the matter as far as possible to the court conducting the main liquidation.[20]

It is relevant to observe that the court in *Re Suidair International Airways Ltd.* was not referred to *Re Commercial Bank of South Australia, Re Federal Bank of Australia Ltd.* or *Sedgwick, Collins and Co. Ltd.* v. *Rossia Insurance Co. of Petrograd*,[1] which reveal the restricted scope of an ancillary winding up. Not one case actually dealing with the ancillary winding up of a foreign corporation was cited before Wynn-Parry J. (Nor is the analysis in *Re Suidair International Airways Ltd.* satisfactory from the

---

[16] Pursuant to s. 325(1) of the Companies Act 1948, see now Insolvency Act 1986, s. 183.

[17] [1951] Ch. 165 at 173–174: the passage was quoted with apparent approval in *Re BCCI S.A. (No. 10), supra,* at 244.

[18] *Per* Scrutton LJ in *Sedgwick, Collins & Co.* v. *Rossia Insurance Co. of Petrograd* [1926] 1 K.B. 1 at 13.

[19] Although it may be on certain facts that such an approach is indeed required, see p. 368, *supra.*

[20] Although some funds, as in *Re BCCI S.A. (No. 10)* itself, may have to be distributed in England to those creditors who would in one way or another be prejudiced in the foreign proceedings (see p. 385 *infra* for details).

[1] *Supra.*

general cross-border insolvency law aspect. For the issue on the facts, it will be recalled, was whether the applicants might retain the benefit of two writs of *fieri facias*. Prior to the issue of the writs the applicants knew of the South African liquidation. The general principle is that whereas a prior attachment in England is not prejudiced by a later foreign insolvency, an unsecured creditor is not permitted to gain a priority by an attachment subsequent to, and especially with notice of, a foreign insolvency. The judgment in *Re Suidair International Airways Ltd.* gives no consideration to the relationship between the rules on attachments and the then section 325 of the Companies Act 1948.[2]) If the facts of *Re Suidair International Airways Ltd.* were to re-occur the following approach would be appropriate having regard to the nature of an ancillary winding up. The English court would initially consider whether a winding up in England should be ancillary to the South African liquidation, paying due regard to whether the South African court was, in the interests of justice, the appropriate forum for the liquidation. Having ordered the English winding up to be ancillary to the South African proceedings, the English liquidator would collect in the company's assets in England, with a view ultimately to handing over those assets to the South African liquidator, and settle a list of creditors who proved in England. After gathering in the assets, the English liquidator might apply to the English court for authorisation to hand the proceeds over to the South African liquidator.[3] At this stage an application, as in *Re Suidair International Airways Ltd.*, could be made to permit judgment creditors to retain the benefit of their execution. The English court, acting under section 183 of the Insolvency Act 1986, might allow the judgment creditors to retain the benefit of their execution, and the balance of the proceeds of realisation of the English assets would be given over to the South African liquidator.

Thus, it is not suggested that the decision upon the facts of *Re Suidair International Airways Ltd.* is incorrect. However, instead of conducting a full-scale winding up, an ancillary winding up may be employed to institute proceedings of a limited scope, which prevent both unfairness to English judgment creditors as well as the increased costs which flow from two concurrent sets of proceedings. It must be noted, however, that speaking of the decision in *Re Suidair International Airways Ltd.* in the context of section 426 of the Insolvency Act 1986, Sir Peter Millett has stated that 'it should not be assumed that the outcome would be the same today.'[4]

E. Discrimination

In *Felixstowe Dock and Rly Co.* v. *United States Lines Inc.*[5] the defendant, a Delaware corporation, carried on business throughout the world and was registered in England as an oversea company under s. 691 of the Companies Act 1985. The defendant corporation was under

---

[2] This issue is discussed in chapter 8.
[3] Of course, if the proceedings in South Africa discriminated against English or other (non-South African) creditors, assets would not be remitted to the foreign liquidator.
[4] 'Cross-Border Insolvency: The Judicial Approach' (1997) 6 I.I.R. 99 at 105: for a s. 426 request would allow the English court to apply South African law.
[5] [1989] Q.B. 360. See also p. 231, *supra*.

reorganisation in the United States in accordance with Chapter 11 of the US Federal Bankruptcy Code. The reorganisation envisaged the continuation of the defendant's business in North America, but the cessation of operations in Europe. The plaintiffs commenced proceedings in England against the defendant and obtained Mareva injunctions, restraining the defendant from removing certain assets out of the jurisdiction. The defendant's applications to discharge the Mareva injunctions were dismissed by the English court. Hirst J considered, *inter alia*, that the balance of convenience favoured the continuation of the Mareva injunctions. For the US proceedings were to reorganise the defendant corporation in North America, a process which, it was apparently accepted on the facts, would not benefit creditors such as the plaintiffs in England. The decision of Hirst J rests upon this particular fact; and there is no doubt that in the normal US Chapter 11 situation – where all groups of creditors may benefit from the reorganisation, or at least are not in substance treated differently – Mareva injunctions will be discharged.[6]

Although upon its facts *Felixstowe Dock and Rly Co.* v. *United States Lines Inc.* did not involve any liquidation (ancillary or otherwise) in England, cases concerning ancillary winding up were raised before the English court. However, it must be noted that the judgment of Hirst J is not wholly free from confusion. Only two of the four cases[7] to which Hirst J referred actually concerned a foreign corporation; and it is quite incorrect to state that *Re English, Scottish and Australian Chartered Bank* dealt with a 'banking company incorporated in Australia'.[8] More interestingly, Hirst J accepted the submission that:[9]

> 'English practice is to regard the courts of the country of incorporation as the principal forum controlling the winding up of a company but that, in so far as that company has assets here, the usual practice is to carry out an ancillary winding up in England in accordance with our own rules, while working in harmony with the foreign courts.'

It is submitted that Hirst J, like Wynn-Parry J in *Re Suidair International Airways Ltd.*, has, to a certain degree, misunderstood the essential nature of an *ancillary* winding up. An ancillary winding up is not designed to be a means of distributing assets in England in accordance with English law. In an appropriate case, an ancillary winding up terminates when the English liquidator hands over English assets to the foreign liquidator, English creditors being left to claim *pari passu* with other creditors in the main liquidation. Thus, far from preventing the handing over of assets to a foreign liquidator by requiring a domestic liquidation,[10] an ancillary winding up envisages the court of the main liquidation having control of all the corporation's assets[11] and dealing with the claims of all the

---

[6] See the discussion of *Banque Indosuez S.A.* v. *Ferromet Resources Inc.* [1993] B.C.L.C. 112, at p. 237 *supra*.

[7] *Re Commercial Bank of South Australia, Re English, Scottish and Australian Chartered Bank, Re Vocalion (Foreign) Ltd., Re Suidair International Airways Ltd.*, all *supra*, which Hirst J described (at 376) as 'four cases involving foreign registered companies', but only the first and last-mentioned cases actually involved foreign companies.

[8] [1989] Q.B. 360 at 379: it was in fact an English bank.

[9] [1989] Q.B. 360 at 379.

[10] As Hirst J appeared to believe: [1989] Q.B. 360 at 379.

[11] After relevant amounts have been retained by the English liquidator in respect of costs and in relation to the claims of preferential creditors etc.

creditors.[12] In the context of *Felixstowe Dock and Rly Co.* v. *United States Lines Inc.*, however, it might have been noted that the principles of ancillary winding up require that English creditors are not discriminated against in the foreign liquidation, that English and foreign creditors may claim *pari passu*. In *Felixstowe Dock and Rly Co.* v. *United States Lines Inc.* the proceedings in the United States were limited to reorganising the corporation as a going concern in North America; and it was apparently the case[13] that creditors in Europe, such as the plaintiffs, would not benefit from the United States proceedings. In short, an ancillary winding up envisages the handing over of English assets to the principal liquidator abroad; but since the very first reported English decision on the subject it has been required that English creditors will not be discriminated against in the foreign proceedings.[14]

4. EXTRATERRITORIALITY

When an ancillary winding up is being conducted, the English liquidator will be seeking to gather in assets within the jurisdiction. However, this general approach derives from the cases, rather than from any restriction found in the legislation itself:[15]

> 'The statutory insolvency scheme purports to have worldwide, not merely territorial, effect . . . The liquidators must get in and realise the company's assets as best they may whatever may be the country in which the assets are situated. But, if the company is incorporated abroad, English liquidators' ability to get in and realise the company's foreign assets will be very limited. It follows that, if a foreign company has a winding up order made against it in England, the English liquidators' role is likely, perforce, to be limited to getting in, realising and distributing the English assets. It was in that sense, I think, that Kay J was describing the English liquidation as "merely . . . ancillary."'

As an ancillary winding up is *prima facie* limited to assets in England, it must follow that the liquidator's role as a whole is similarly restricted. Thus, although the court has extensive extraterritorial powers under the Act – such as to set aside preferences and transactions at an undervalue[16] – one would not expect such powers to be exercised extraterritorially in an ancillary winding up. Indeed, Sir Peter Millett has gone as far as stating that the 'courts should not allow any of the relevant sections to be invoked in an ancillary liquidation'.[17]

This author would respectfully agree with the general sentiment expressed by Sir Peter. Nevertheless, if, as has been argued,[18] a so-called 'ancillary'

---

[12] This point has now been made abundantly clear by Scott V-C in *Re BCCI S.A. (No. 10)*, *supra*, see also Sir Peter Millett, above, n. 4, at p. 100.

[13] See p. 232 *supra* for further details.

[14] See *Re Matheson Bros Ltd.*, *supra*.

[15] *Re BCCI S.A. (No. 10)* [1997] Ch. 213 at 241–242; the reference to the words of Kay J is a reference to *North Australian Territory Co. Ltd.* v. *Goldsbrough Mort & Co.* (1889) 61 L.T. 716 at 717.

[16] See *Re Paramount Airways Ltd.* [1993] Ch. 223, p. 19, *supra*.

[17] 'Cross-Border Insolvency; The Judicial Approach' (1997) 6 I.I.R. 99 at 103.

[18] See p. 368, *supra*.

winding up covers not a single situation but a range of situations, it cannot be said that powers with an extraterritorial element can *never* be exercised in relation to a foreign company that is also in liquidation in its country of incorporation. Reference may here be made to *Lehman Bros Inc.* v. *Phillips: Re Mid East Trading Ltd.*,[19] which arose out of the winding up of a Lebanese company already in liquidation in the Lebanon. For the Court of Appeal upheld the order of Evans-Lombe J, acting under section 236 of the Insolvency Act 1986, requiring a US party (with offices in England) to produce documents that had been generated and continued to be held in New York. Whilst *Lehman Brothers Inc.* v. *Phillips* contained an element of extraterritoriality, since the documents were in New York, the application had the support of the Lebanese liquidator;[20] and the case may be seen as an illustration of a more general principle, namely, that whilst 'comity between the courts of different countries requires mutual respect for the territorial integrity of each other's jurisdiction . . . this should not inhibit a court in one jurisdiction from rendering whatever assistance it properly can to a court in another in respect of assets located or persons resident within the territory of the former.'[1] The Lebanese liquidator had supported the commencement of a winding up in England, as well as the section 236 application, and Lehman Brothers could be regarded as being resident within the territory of the English court. In other words, the question is one of degree[2] – both as to the role the English liquidator is playing and the extent of extraterritoriality involved.[3]

A similar issue could arise concerning the court's *in personam* jurisdiction to restrain creditors. Let us say that a Lebanese company, in liquidation in the Lebanon, has had various dealings in England and a winding up order has been made, the judge directing that the proceedings be ancillary to those in the Lebanon. Creditors' actions underway in England, or elsewhere in the United Kingdom,[4] will be stayed pursuant to section 130(2) of the Insolvency Act 1986. But a creditor resident in England may also have brought an action in, for example, France. It would be going too far to say that the English court would never restrain the creditor from continuing with the action in France,[5] but a particularly strong case would have to be made out as to why an injunction should issue, rather than the Lebanese liquidator pleading his case before the French courts.

---

[19] [1998] 1 All E.R. 577, see p. 367, *supra.*
[20] *Ibid.*, at 580.
[1] *Crédit Suisse Fides Trust S.A.* v. *Cuoghi* [1997] 3 All E.R. 724 at 730 *per* Millett LJ.
[2] For the court has a discretion whether to exercise its statutory avoidance and investigatory powers: see p. 25, *supra.*
[3] It goes without saying that the English court would not allow its proceedings to be used, in effect, to make a second attempt at having a transaction set aside, where the foreign liquidator has already tried and failed before the court conducting the principal liquidation.
[4] As in *Re Queensland Mercantile Agency Co. Ltd.* (1888) 58 L.T. 878.
[5] Cf. *Re Lake Superior Native Copper Co. Ltd.* (1885) 9 O.R. 277 where, on the facts, an injunction was not issued (principal liquidation in England, ancillary liquidation in Ontario, creditor resident in Ontario pursuing action in Michigan: see p. 295, *supra*).

5. PREFERENTIAL DEBTS, SET-OFF AND CHARGES

A. Outline

Questions of priority are generally said to be governed by the *lex fori*.[6] Such an approach presents obvious difficulties where, as in an ancillary winding up, assets are to be transferred from one court to another. The two courts may well have quite different rules as to priority, not to mention set-off. In this regard two situations must be distinguished. First, where the English court is conducting the principal liquidation; and, secondly, where there is an ancillary winding up in England. In respect of the former, there is some authority that the English court can (in limited circumstances) have regard to the foreign rules on priority.

In *Cook* v. *Gregson*[7] (an administration case) the deceased had died domiciled in Ireland leaving assets in both Ireland and England. The same persons were executors in each jurisdiction. Normally, of course, an administration (unlike an insolvency) is wholly local, governed by the laws of the country in which the personal representatives have obtained their grant. Thus debts must be paid according to the *lex fori* and only surplus assets handed over to the court of the domicile.[8] However, in *Cook* v. *Gregson* the Irish assets were transferred to England before paying off the debts in Ireland. The question for the English court, accordingly, was whether the proceeds of the Irish assets should be administered in England under the English or Irish law as to priorities. Kindersley V-C had no doubt that Irish law had to govern the question of priorities.[9] The Vice-Chancellor's decision was approved in *Carron Iron Co.* v. *Maclaren* by Lord St. Leonards, who considered that the English court would give effect to 'any priority to which, from the nature of his security, a creditor in Scotland or Ireland is entitled against the assets in either country according to the law of the country, although they may come to be distributed here'.[10] Such a principle should also apply in cross-border insolvency cases. The foreign court when conducting an ancillary winding up may have transferred assets to the main liquidation in England but without paying off preferred creditors under the foreign law: the English court may apply the foreign assets in satisfaction of the foreign preferred creditors as if those assets were being distributed in the foreign court.[11]

However, although the English court has a measure of discretion to depart from a rigid *lex fori* approach to priority when it is conducting the principal liquidation, it does not follow that a foreign court (conducting the principal liquidation) would have any regard to English rules as to priorities. It is, accordingly, well-established that the English court will authorise an English liquidator to retain relevant sums before transferring assets to the principal liquidator abroad.[12]

---

[6] See, e.g., *Re Melbourn* (1870) 6 Ch. App. 64 and p. 313, *supra.*.
[7] (1854) 2 Drew. 286, discussed further in chapter 11.
[8] *Dicey and Morris*, p. 1014.
[9] (1854) 2 Drew. 286 at 288.
[10] (1855) 5 H.L. Cas. 416 at 455.
[11] See further *Re Sefel Geophysical Ltd.* [1989] 1 W.W.R. 251, p. 316, n. 18, *ante.*
[12] *Re BCCI S.A. (No. 10)* [1997] Ch 213, *supra.*

B. Preferred Creditors

It will be recalled from *Re National Benefit Assurance Co.* that, before transferring assets abroad, the court in control of an ancillary winding up may require payment of local preferred creditors, costs of the ancillary liquidation and any other approved payments.[13] Sir Richard Scott V-C has also held that the English liquidator must retain sufficient funds to ensure that creditors who have entered a proof in England and are entitled to the benefit of a set-off, under rule 4.90 of the Insolvency Rules 1986, will not be disadvantaged by the application in the foreign proceedings of the foreign set-off rules.[14] Of course, funds would not have to be retained should the foreign liquidator (after obtaining authorisation from the foreign court) be able to give a satisfactory undertaking that English set-off rules would be applied in the foreign proceedings in relation to assets handed over by the English liquidator.

One issue that might arise in an ancillary winding up is the extent of the preferential debts. In a winding up, section 175 of the Insolvency Act 1986 refers one to section 386 and thereby to the Sixth Schedule. One category of preferential debt is any amount owed to a person 'who is or has been an employee of the debtor'[15] and is owed in respect of remuneration due in the four months[16] before the date of the winding up order. The question is whether any employee, for example a clerk working exclusively at the head office abroad, may fall within the Sixth Schedule. This author would suggest that looking at the Sixth Schedule as a whole, with its frequent references to British legislation, Parliament must be taken to have intended that employees engaged by a foreign company abroad (and working abroad) are not included.[17]

Should the English court pay off preferred creditors under the Insolvency Act 1986 prior to transferring assets (if any assets remain)[18] to the main liquidation abroad, whether the English preferred creditors may then also claim for any outstanding amounts in the main liquidation (and upon what terms) will ultimately be determined in the principal liquidation in accordance with the foreign law.[19]

C. Secured Creditors

Just as the rights of preferential creditors may be protected in an ancillary winding up, so too can those of secured creditors. A creditor may have a charge valid under English law (including private international law[20]) but

---

[13] See p. 361, *supra*; and note also *Re Air Express Foods Pty. Ltd.* (1978) 2 A.C.L.R. 523.

[14] See p. 364, *supra*.

[15] Insolvency Act 1986, Sch 6, para. 9.

[16] The relevant date is defined in s 387; but the four month period must mean four months prior to the winding up order in England: see *Re Australian Federal Life and General Insurance Co. Ltd.* [1931] V.L.R. 94.

[17] This author would prefer *Re Australian Cycle and Motor Co. Ltd.* (1901) 7 Argus L.R. (C.N.) 53 to *Re Commonwealth Agricultural Service Engineers Ltd.* [1928] S.A.S.R. 342 at 351.

[18] All the assets may be used up in paying the expenses and the preferential creditors, as in *Re Union Theatres Ltd.* (1933) 35 W.A.L.R. 89.

[19] See *Re Standard Insurance Co. Ltd.* [1968] Qd. R. 118, *passim*.

[20] As to floating charges see, generally, Collins (1978) 27 I.C.L.Q. 691 and Lightman & Moss, *Law of Receivers of Companies* (2nd ed., 1994) pp. 423–427.

which would not be given effect in the main liquidation abroad. Here the English court may require that English assets subject to the charge be applied in satisfaction of the charge, the balance thereafter being transmitted to the foreign liquidator.

The converse situation presents a more difficult problem. A charge may be unenforceable against the liquidator appointed in an ancillary winding up in England, e.g. for failure to register the charge, yet constitute a perfectly valid security according to the law administered in the main liquidation abroad. (Of course, this will only occur where the foreign law ignores the *lex situs*.[1]) Should the English court remit assets to the foreign liquidator such assets may be applied, wholly or in part, in satisfaction of a charge invalid under English law (the *lex situs*) to the apparent prejudice of the unsecured creditors in England. In such circumstances the English court must, *prima facie*, distribute the English assets according to English law;[2] although seeking as far as possible to equalise the dividend available to unsecured creditors in the two sets of proceedings.[3] However an alternative course may at times be available.[4] The foreign liquidator may be willing to undertake that, if English assets are transmitted to the foreign court, such assets will not be used to satisfy any secured[5] claim by the holder of the charge (invalid as it is under English law, the *lex situs*). The foreign liquidator should generally be required to give security for such undertaking;[6] or, preferably, seek and obtain permission from the court conducting the main liquidation for such undertaking. However, if the foreign liquidator cannot or will not give the necessary undertaking,[7] the English assets must be distributed in the English winding up, wherein both English and foreign creditors may claim.[8]

6. SUMMARY

The cases clearly demonstrate that the English court may give assistance to a foreign liquidator. Yet, the form of such assistance very much depends upon the facts of each individual case: the number and circumstances of creditors in England; the nature of any assets in England; the process under way in the foreign court, together with the powers of the foreign liquidator; these are just a few matters which may have to be considered. It cannot be maintained that where a corporation is in liquidation under the law of its place of incorporation, an ancillary winding up must be conducted in England. For the making of a winding up order is a matter of discretion;

[1] Cf. *Re Anchor Line (Henderson Bros.) Ltd.* [1937] Ch. 483.
[2] As in *Re Northland Services Pty. Ltd.* (1978) 18 A.L.R. 684 (charge void under Northern Territories law, the *lex fori*, but valid in South Australia, the state of incorporation).
[3] By means of the hotchpot rule, for foreign creditors may also claim in an English winding up: *Re Azoff-Don Commercial Bank* [1954] Ch. 315.
[4] *Re Australian Federal Life and General Insurance Co. Ltd. (No. 2)* [1931] V.L.R. 317.
[5] The chargeholder may, however, claim as an unsecured creditor.
[6] As in *Re Australian Federal Life and General Insurance Co. Ltd. (No. 2)* [1931] V.L.R. 317.
[7] Or does not appear in the English proceedings: see *Re Northland Services Pty. Ltd.* (1978) 18 A.L.R. 684 at 687.
[8] Subject to the hotchpot rule. Any amount not claimed by creditors would be transmitted to the foreign liquidator.

an order need not be made. In some instances it may be appropriate simply to recognise the authority of the foreign liquidator to deal with both assets and creditors in England. In comparison, an English winding up should not be ancillary if the corporation in question, although incorporated abroad, has little connection to the place of incorporation and England is the proper forum for the liquidation.

Yet, where an ancillary winding up has been ordered, it is important to bear in mind the nature of such proceedings. It has been said that the English liquidator should be considered not a mere agent but rather the assistant of the principal liquidator.[9] This nomenclature is useful as a way of indicating that a full-scale liquidation in England should be avoided. But it must not be supposed that the English liquidator is obliged to obey instructions from the foreign liquidator or the court conducting the main liquidation. Nor does the circumstance that an English winding up is ancillary to the principal liquidation abroad relieve the court of the obligation to apply English insolvency law to the resolution of any relevant issue that arises in the course of the winding up[10] – although, of course, the fact that the winding up is ancillary will always be a weighty factor when the court is called upon to exercise its discretion (for example, to avoid a transaction carried out abroad).[11] The English liquidator seeks to work in conjunction with the foreign liquidator because the resolution of claims, and the distribution of assets, in a single set of proceedings should promote equality between creditors from different countries, as well as leading to a saving in costs. An ancillary winding up may be a convenient method of securing assets in England – such assets to be handed over ultimately to the liquidator appointed by the court conducting the main liquidation – but the English court must be satisfied that the English and other creditors will not be discriminated against in the foreign proceedings. In addition, prior to authorising the English liquidator to give the proceeds of sale of English assets to the foreign liquidator, the English court may insist upon certain payments to specified creditors in England who would be unduly prejudiced by being required to pursue their claims in the foreign proceedings.[12] In short, whilst concrete rules cannot be laid down, an ancillary winding up is by definition limited in scope, and the English court should be guided by the desire to achieve, as far as may be possible, equality between the different groups of creditors in various countries.

7. EUROPEAN CONVENTION ON INSOLVENCY PROCEEDINGS

The first point to note about the Convention is that, if it were to come into force in England, it would limit the circumstances in which a winding up might be ordered by the English court. If the corporation has its centre of main interests in another Contracting State, then the English court would only have winding up jurisdiction if there is an establishment

---

[9] Page 360, n. 12, *supra*.

[10] *Re BCCI S.A. (No. 10)* [1997] Ch, 213 at 246.

[11] See p. 383, *supra*.

[12] See the discussion at pp. 385–387, *supra*. For revenue debts falling outside Sch 6, see p. 205, *supra*.

in England.[13] Proceedings opened in respect of an establishment would, in many ways, broadly follow the English law concept of an ancillary winding up. Such proceedings are termed 'secondary proceedings' under the Convention; and would be restricted to assets in England (or more precisely, one would imagine, assets in the United Kingdom).[14] The law applicable to secondary proceedings would be – as at present in respect of an ancillary winding up – English law.[15] The Convention expects the liquidators in the main and any secondary proceedings to co-operate with each other and they would be duty bound to communicate information to each other.[16] Article 33 provides that the court conducting secondary proceedings must stay the liquidation upon receipt of a request from the liquidator in the main proceedings and, moreover, that such a request may only be rejected 'if it is manifestly of no interest to the creditors in the main proceedings'. Such a stay may be ordered for up to three months and would be renewable.

The Convention does not seem expressly to contemplate assets, once collected in the secondary proceedings, being sent to the main proceedings for distribution.[17] Article 35 states:

'If by liquidation of assets in the secondary proceedings it is possible to meet all claims allowed under those proceedings, the liquidator appointed in those proceedings shall immediately transfer any assets remaining to the liquidator in the main proceedings.'

However, there is nothing in the Convention that would in any way prevent the current practice from being followed: assets collected in England being handed over for distribution in the main proceedings abroad.[18]

8. ILLUSTRATIONS

(1) O Ltd., incorporated in the Isle of Man, has carried on business in England and to a lesser extent in Scotland. Nearly all the company's creditors and assets are in England, where the company has its principal place of business. O Ltd. is insolvent and a winding up petition has been presented in England. A winding up order will be made by the English court, and that winding up will not be ancillary to any liquidation that may subsequently be commenced in the Isle of Man.[19]

(2) MB Ltd. is a New Zealand company which has conducted a certain amount of business in England by means of an agent. MB Ltd. has assets

---

[13] See Art. 3(2).
[14] See Chapter III of the Convention and Article 27 in particular.
[15] Article 28.
[16] See Arts. 3(1) and (2).
[17] Note that Art. 32 allows the liquidators in the main and any secondary proceedings to lodge claims – on behalf of the creditors they respectively represent – in the other proceedings.
[18] For by Article 28 English law would govern any secondary winding up in England; and English law does allow assets to be sent, after appropriate deductions, to the principal liquidation.
[19] Although the court would seek generally to co-operate with the Manx court.

in England and a small number of English creditors. MB Ltd. is in liquidation in New Zealand, and a creditor's petition has been presented in England. If an acceptable undertaking is given that the company's assets will not be removed from the jurisdiction, the English court may order the petition to stand over. Provided it is then established that English creditors will not be unfairly disadvantaged by having to claim in the New Zealand liquidation, no winding up in England will be required.[20]

(3) Incorporated is a Delaware corporation which has traded in North America and to a far lesser extent in Europe, through a branch office in England. Incorporated has assets and creditors in England. Incorporated is insolvent and bankruptcy proceedings have been commenced in the US. A number of creditors, English and foreign, have recently brought actions against Incorporated in England. Upon a petition being presented, the English court may make a winding up order directing that its proceedings be ancillary to those in the US (provided English and other creditors will not be discriminated against in the US), and that the liquidator should restrict his activities in the first instance to gathering in English assets and settling a list of creditors who prove in England. Additionally, actions in England against Incorporated will be stayed pursuant to section 130(2) of the Insolvency Act 1986.[1]

(4) As in Illustration 3 above; however, it has become apparent that there are a number preferential debts under English law which will not be preferred in the US. It has also been established that other English creditors may claim *pari passu* with creditors of the same class in the US proceedings. The court may order that the proceeds of the English assets be transmitted to the US trustee upon satisfying the claims of the preferential creditors in England and the costs of the ancillary liquidation.[2]

(5) A Ltd. is a Hong Kong company in liquidation in Hong Kong. A Ltd. carried on the most part of its business in the Far East but also had an office in England. A Ltd. has assets and creditors in England. An ancillary winding up order has been made and it is proposed that, in due course, the proceeds of the English assets will be handed over to the Hong Kong liquidator. However, A Ltd. has granted a charge over the assets in England, which charge is void under English law for want of registration. There is some question as to whether the charge would be regarded as void in the Hong Kong liquidation. The English assets will be remitted to Hong Kong upon the Hong Kong liquidator giving an undertaking and security that the assets will not be employed to satisfy a secured claim by the chargeholder.[3]

---

[20] It will be different, of course, should the foreign liquidator favour an ancillary winding up order: see *Queensland Mercantile and Agency Co. Ltd.* v. *Australasian Investment Co.* (1888) 15 R. 935 at 936.

[1] Actions in Scotland or Northern Ireland may also be stayed under s. 130(2).

[2] See *Re BCCI S.A. (No. 10)* and *Re National Benefit Assurance Co., supra.*

[3] It is preferable that the Hong Kong liquidator seek approval from the court conducting the main liquidation for such undertakings.

Chapter 15

International Co-operation and Assistance

1. INTRODUCTION

Whenever a court is called upon to tackle any insolvency with international elements it is likely that a certain tension will be present. On the one hand, the English court can scarcely ignore the desirability, in general, of giving effect to a foreign law and the acts of a foreign court: judicial comity, reciprocity, predictability and the expectations of the parties, to name but a few factors, are relevant in this regard. On the other hand, the facts of a particular case may highlight an apparent need to protect parties, both the insolvent and creditors, who are linked to England and to English law. This is particularly so because insolvency, unlike ordinary civil litigation, tends to involve the quite deliberate preferential treatment of certain claimants. Of course, the existence of similar tensions throughout the field of private international law (e.g. contracts, torts, marriage or divorce) cannot be denied. However, the very scope of insolvency proceedings, the range of issues that may be raised, has profoundly influenced the approach of English law to questions of cross-border insolvency. Moreover, it should not be overlooked that the 'rescue culture' that has emerged in recent years – at both a national and transnational level – requires a flexible response from practitioners and courts alike.

Traditionally, rules of English private international law are fixed and specific, some might even say rigid. Thus the essential validity of a contract, of a marriage or of a transfer of title to property, does not lie within the discretion of the judge – rather such issues are governed by particular rules (or exceptions thereto). So too, in respect of cross-border insolvency. We have seen that there are various topics governed by more or less specific rules: for instance the existence of jurisdiction to make a bankruptcy or winding up order; the recognition of foreign insolvencies; the vesting of movables in a foreign trustee; the discharge of debts following United Kingdom and foreign bankruptcies; as well as questions of priority and set-off. Yet there are perhaps almost as many issues which fall to be determined by reference to judicial discretion: for instance, the exercise of jurisdiction in bankruptcy; the staying of bankruptcy or winding up proceedings;[1] the making of an 'ancillary' winding up order and the sending of assets abroad;[2]

---

[1] See *Re Wallace Smith & Co. Ltd* [1992] B.C.L.C. 970, p. 127, *supra*.
[2] See the analysis of *Re BCCI S.A. (No. 10)* [1997] Ch. 213, pp. 362–368, *supra*.

the appointment of a foreign trustee as receiver of immovable property in England;[3] remitting assets to a foreign trustee to pay an equalising dividend;[4] granting or discharging Mareva injunctions against a foreign trustee;[5] restraining civil actions brought abroad either by a creditor or by the English insolvency representative;[6] or the sanctioning of agreements between an English trustee, liquidator or administrator and his foreign counterpart upon concurrent insolvencies.[7]

It is suggested that the scope of insolvency proceedings, coupled with the vast range of different fact situations that may arise internationally, has required that so much emphasis has been placed upon judicial discretion. Intervention by Parliament has thus far not reduced but rather increased the scope for judicial discretion. Thus, whilst section 426 of the Insolvency Act 1986 lays down a general framework for international co-operation and assistance – although so far only some 19 countries or territories[8] have been designated for the purposes of section 426 – the court retains a broad discretion as to whether assistance, and what form of assistance, will be given. In addition, in an important development in 1997, Parliament has extended the power of the English court to grant interim relief so as to cover insolvency proceedings underway anywhere in the world.[9] Yet, again, whether interim relief will be granted in any particular insolvency case has been left very much at large.

Fortunately, in a series of high-profile cases, the judges have recently made plain a willingness to provide assistance (whenever possible) to foreign insolvency representatives and foreign courts.[10] Two comments by a Lord Justice of Appeal during the first half of 1997 are worth noting. First, in a journal article, Sir Peter Millett, whilst not shying away from the problematic cases as well as the general difficulties caused by the lack of an international convention in this field, summed up the position as follows:[11]

'. . . some consistency in the approach of the English judiciary to cross-border insolvency can be detected. Its watchwords are flexibility, co-operation and judicial restraint.'

Secondly, and this time wearing his judicial robes, Millett LJ observed:[12]

'In . . . areas of law, such as cross-border insolvency, commercial necessity has encouraged national courts to provide assistance to each other without waiting for such co-operation to be sanctioned by international convention . . . It is becoming widely accepted that comity between courts of different countries requires mutual respect for the territorial integrity of each other's jurisdiction, but that this should not inhibit a court in one jurisdiction from rendering

---

[3] *Re Kooperman* [1928] W.N. 101.

[4] *Re Macfadyen & Co.* [1908] 1 K.B. 675, p. 338, *supra*.

[5] Note *Banque Indosuez S.A.* v. *Ferromet Resources Inc.* [1993] B.C.L.C. 112, discussed p. 237, *supra*.

[6] *Barclays Bank plc* v. *Homan* [1993] B.C.L.C. 680, p. 332, *supra*.

[7] Discussed at pp. 335–336, *supra*.

[8] Together with the Channel Islands and the Isle of Man: the countries are listed on p. 405, *infra*.

[9] The Civil Jurisdiction and Judgments Act 1982 (Interim Relief) Order 1997, S.I. 1997/302, see the analysis, *infra*.

[10] One may refer here to the Maxwell insolvency, see p. 336, *supra*, or the collapse of BCCI, see p. 362, *supra*, as well as remarkable events involving Barings, see Rushworth (1995) 7: 1 Int. Insol. & Cred. Rights Rep. at pp. 13–15.

[11] 'Cross-Border Insolvency: The Judicial Approach' (1997) 6 I.I.R. 99 at 103.

[12] *Crédit Suisse Fides Trust S.A.* v. *Cuoghi* [1997] 3 All E.R. 724 at 730.

whatever assistance it properly can to a court in another in respect of assets located or persons resident within the territory of the former.'

This chapter focuses upon the giving of assistance by the English court to a foreign court or a foreign insolvency representative. Yet one must never lose sight of the fact that, when it comes to corporate rescue, pre-insolvency international co-operation by bankers and other professionals may often avert the need to involve the English court.[13]

2. ASSISTANCE UNDER THE GENERAL LAW

A. Proceedings and Property in England

The rules of English law relating to cross-border insolvency necessarily and directly express the extent to which a foreign insolvency is given effect in England. Let us take some examples. If a foreign bankruptcy, liquidation or re-organisation falls within the established bases of recognition at common law, the consequences of such recognition may be of great assistance to the foreign representative. For recognition, as a judge once put it, is not a mere acknowledgment of the existence of the foreign insolvency but rather 'carries with it the active assistance of the court'.[14] A view expressly endorsed in a recent decision of the court in New Zealand acting under the common law.[15] In particular, a foreign trustee or assignee may claim the bankrupt's movable property in England, as well as bring or defend civil proceedings to protect the rights of the bankrupt. It is a measure of the co-operative attitude of the common law that the effect of foreign insolvency proceedings may be 'automatic': in that, unlike for example in respect of a foreign judgment, no action, *exequatur* or other procedure must first be taken by the foreign insolvency representative in the English court.[16] More-over, whilst the vesting of assets only applies to movables, the court has given itself the discretion to appoint a foreign trustee or assignee as receiver of immovables in England with authority to sell the same and remit the proceeds to the foreign proceedings. Similarly, a foreign liquidator (in the absence of a winding up in England) may deal with all the corporation's assets and rights in England. But if the foreign liquidator favours the commencement of a winding up in England, then the foreign liquidator may cause the company to present a petition to initiate that process;[17] and, of course, once a petition has been presented a provisional liquidator may be appointed.[18] In constrast, however, there are other rules which adopt (at least *prima facie*) a more restrictive approach. The validity of a contract is, as a matter of general English private international law, determined by its governing law. A discharge upon a foreign insolvency is not given any enhanced status; and that the foreign insolvency is recognised in England does not displace the governing law approach – even though the bankrupt's property may have vested in the foreign assignee. Yet, in a series of

---

[13] One notable success has been the 'London Approach', see Blanden (1997) 147 *The Banker* 20.
[14] *Re African Farms Ltd.* 1906 T.S. 373 at 377 *per* Innes CJ.
[15] *The Cornelis Verolme* [1997] 2 N.Z.L.R. 110 at 120, citing the first edition of this book.
[16] See p. 141, *supra*.
[17] See p. 229, *supra*.
[18] See p. 399, *infra*.

cross-border insolvency cases, strict adherence to the governing law has been modified by an exception where a creditor suing in England has already sought a distributive share in insolvency proceedings abroad.[19]

Moreover, there are issues in respect of which no automatically applicable rule or exception can be laid down, other than in the most general terms, and which can only be decided in the light of the particular facts involved. In some instances the English court, acting in accordance with the interests of justice, may stay its own bankruptcy or winding up proceedings in favour of a foreign forum. Or, when a petition is heard, the court may simply decline jurisdiction on the ground of *forum non conveniens*.[20] There will be yet further instances where the English court is for some reason unwilling to give full effect to orders made in a foreign court but, nevertheless, modifies its own proceedings to prevent unfairness. In *Felixstowe Dock and Rly Co.* v. *United States Lines Inc.*[1] the defendant, a Delaware corporation, was under re-organisation in the United States in accordance with Chapter 11 of the US Bankruptcy Code. The re-organisation envisaged the continuation of the defendant's business in North America but the cessation of operations in Europe. The plaintiffs commenced proceedings in England against the defendant and obtained Mareva injunctions. The defendant's applications to discharge the Mareva injunctions were dismissed by the English court, even though the US Bankruptcy Court had previously made a worldwide restraining order. Hirst J considered that the balance of convenience lay against the defendant, for the US proceedings were to re-organise the defendant corporation in North America and that would provide no benefit for those creditors, such as the plaintiffs, in England. In effect, therefore, Hirst J considered that the US proceedings were discriminatory.[2] Although this finding on the facts that the US Chapter 11 was discriminatory has been criticised – and in a normal fact situation involving Chapter 11 there certainly will be no discrimination at all – two points will be noted. First, as a matter of principle, Hirst J plainly favoured co-operation with a foreign insolvency process, stating:[3]

> 'I wish however to stress that the court would in principle always wish to co-operate in every proper way with an order like the present one made by a court in a friendly jurisdication (of which the United States is a most conspicuous example). But whether this is appropriate in any given case, and if so the precise nature and extent of such co-operation, must depend upon the particular sphere of activity in question and the English law applicable thereto . . . together with the overall circumstances.'

Secondly, although the assets subject to the Mareva injunctions would not be sent to the United States, his Lordship made it quite clear that such assets were not in any way earmarked for the plaintiffs and would not be distributed without the intervention of winding up proceedings in England.[4]

---

[19] *Supra*, p. 266.

[20] *Supra*, p. 63.

[1] [1989] Q.B. 360 and p. 231, *supra*.

[2] US Chapter 11 proceedings will not normally be regarded as discriminatory, see *Banque Indosuez S.A.* v. *Ferromet Resources Inc.*, *supra*, n. 5, and *Felixstowe Docks* very much depends upon the particular findings of fact by the judge.

[3] [1989] Q.B. 360 at 376.

[4] The solution adopted by Hirst J might not work in respect of personal insolvency, since the presence of assets in England is not a sufficient jurisdictional basis for the presentation of a bankruptcy petition under s. 265 of the Insolvency Act 1986.

In other words, although the plaintiffs might be discriminated against in the foreign proceedings, the English court (taking into account the prior foreign insolvency) was anxious to ensure that assets in England would be available for distribution amongst all the creditors: for it will be recalled that any creditor, foreign or English, may claim in an English insolvency. Yet where, as in a normal case, the foreign proceedings do not discriminate, it must be stressed that the English court will readily discharge a Mareva injunction that would otherwise hamper the foreign court in the conduct of its insolvency proceedings.[5]

Additionally, whilst a foreign insolvency does not automatically stay civil actions underway in England, foreign proceedings will in appropriate circumstances preclude a plaintiff from any subsequent *attachment* of assets in England.[6] A foreign representative should also note that the English court, if called upon to exercise its discretion, will take into account that a debtor is undergoing insolvency proceedings abroad (provided the plaintiff may claim *pari passu* in those proceedings with other creditors of the same class). The question of the exercise of the court's discretion in this context arises in one of two main situations. First, a plaintiff may require leave to serve the debtor abroad under RSC Order 11: *Firswood Ltd.* v. *Petra Bank* is a recent relevant example at the appellate level of the refusal of leave to serve a foreign bank in liquidation abroad.[7] Secondly, the foreign insolvency representative may request that the court stays an action on the ground that the dispute can clearly be dealt with at substantially less inconvenience and expense in the foreign court. The courts in Scotland have had many decades of experience in dealing with the doctrine of *forum non conveniens*; and, although a somewhat old authority, the approach of the Court of Session in *Okell* v. *Foden* is worth mentioning.[8] The bankrupt had business interests in the United Kingdom and in Canada. In a liquidation by arrangement under the Bankruptcy Act 1869 in England two trustees were appointed. One of the trustees went to Canada and recovered a certain sum, which money was then lodged with a bank in Scotland. Creditors raised an action of multiplepoinding in Scotland, the effect of which was to prevent the trustee from dealing with the assets in the English bankruptcy. The Court of Session sustained a plea of *forum non conveniens*: whilst the Scottish courts had jurisdiction, it was more expedient that questions concerning entitlement to the money be determined in the English liquidation.[9]

The exercise of discretion (taking into account the foreign insolvency proceedings) is only relevant if there is indeed a discretion to be exercised. Here the Brussels and Lugano Conventions, as introduced into English law by the Civil Jurisdiction and Judgments Act 1982 (as amended) must be considered. Although pursuant to Article 1 the Conventions do not apply

---

[5] As Hoffmann J put it in *Banque Indosuez, supra* n. 5, at 117: 'This court is not of course bound by the stay under United States law but will do its utmost to co-operate with the United States Bankruptcy Court and avoid any action which might disturb the orderly administration of [the corporation] in Texas under Chapter 11.'

[6] *Supra* p. 234.

[7] [1996] C.L.C. 608, p. 247, *supra*.

[8] (1884) 11 R. 906 and note also *Edinburgh & Glasgow Bank* v. *Ewan* (1852) 14 D. 547, as well as *Bank of Otago Ltd.* v. *Commercial Bank of New Zealand* (1867) Mac. 223 and *Howell* v. *Dominion of Canada Oils Refinery Co. Ltd.* (1875) 37 U.C.Q.B. 484.

[9] *Ibid.*, at 911.

to bankruptcy and the winding up of insolvent companies (and judical arrangements, compositions and analogous proceedings),[10] a claim by a plaintiff *against* an insolvent company – for instance for damages for non-delivery of goods – will not come within the Article 1 exception.[11] Hence, where the Conventions confer jurisdiction on the courts in England there will be no general common law power to stay proceedings in favour of the courts in another Contracting State (e.g. France)[12] even though the defendant is in liquidation there. However, there is a discretion to stay an action in favour of the courts in Scotland or Northern Ireland[13] or of a non-Contracting State (e.g. Singapore or New York). But even if a stay (e.g. in favour of the French court) cannot be granted, a plaintiff will not be allowed to attach the company's assets in England after the foreign insolvency has commenced;[14] and, in any event, if there are assets in England, the winding up jurisdiction of the English court may be invoked[15] – with the result that an automatic stay under section 130(2) of the Insolvency Act 1986 will come into operation once the winding up order is made or a provisional liquidator appointed.

B. Interim Relief and Provisional Liquidators

(i) *Interim Relief*

The Civil Jurisdiction and Judgments Act ('the 1982 Act') implemented in the United Kingdom the Brussels Convention of 1968 on Jurisdiction and the Enforcement of Judgments in Civil and Commercial Matters ('the Convention'). Article 24 of the Convention allows the courts of a Contracting State to grant provisional, including protective, measures in aid of the courts of another Contracting State which has jurisdiction under the rules of the Convention as to the substantive matters in dispute.[16] In section 25 of the 1982 Act Parliament laid down when such provisional or protective measures – referred to in English law as 'interim relief' – would be available. (Since 1991 interim relief has also been available in relation to States party to the Lugano Convention.)[17] In particular, section 25(1) stated that interim relief was only available where the relevant foreign proceedings were: (i) commenced in another Contracting State; and (ii) within the scope of Article 1 of the Convention. Section 25 was of little use in international insolvency cases since Article 1 of the Convention specifically excludes bankruptcy, insolvent winding up, judicial arrangements, compositions and analogous proceedings. This exclusion covers not only insolvency proceedings themselves, but also any related proceedings directly derived from and closely connected to such bankruptcy, winding

---

[10] See the discussion at pp. 12–15, *supra*.
[11] See, as an example, *Contant v. Somers* [1993] I.L.Pr. 379.
[12] The matter is discussed in Dicey and Morris, *Private International Law* (12th ed., 1993) at pp. 400–402 (and Supplements).
[13] *Idem.* An example might be where the defendant's estate has been sequestrated in Scotland. The Scottish court might also request a stay of actions underway in England pursuant to s. 426 of the Insolvency Act 1986, *infra*.
[14] *Supra*, p. 234.
[15] Although bankruptcy jurisdiction, under s. 265, is a little more difficult to establish.
[16] See generally, Dicey and Morris, *The Conflict of Laws* (12th ed., 1993) at pp. 389–391.
[17] Pursuant to the Civil Jurisdiction and Judgments Act 1991.

up or arrangement.[18] Section 25(3) of the 1982 Act, however, expressly allowed the power to grant interim relief to be extended by Order in Council. The Civil Jurisdiction and Judgments Act 1982 (Interim Relief) Order 1997 ('the 1997 Order')[19] which came into force on 1 April 1997,[20] has done precisely that and provides that the court may now grant interim relief:[1]

'. . . in relation to proceedings of the following description, namely:
(a) proceedings commenced or to be commenced *otherwise than in a Brussels or Lugano Contracting State*;
(b) proceedings whose subject-matter is *not* within the scope of the 1968 Convention as determined by Article 1 thereof.'

Quite simply, a foreign insolvency representative from a Brussels or Lugano Contracting State or *any other* jurisdiction can now apply before the English court for interim relief in aid of foreign proceedings. Accordingly, the English court may, for example, be faced with an application for interim relief brought by a *syndic* who, having commenced proceedings in France to establish the personal liability of a defendant director for the debts of an insolvent company, seeks to prevent the disposal of the defendant's assets in England. Similarly, a US trustee might seek a Mareva injunction in aid of proceedings brought in the US Bankruptcy Court to recover assets which the debtor, on the eve of insolvency, had transferred to an associate resident in England.

The granting of interim relief lies within the discretion of the English court, but nothing in the 1997 Order extends the type of interim relief which may be granted. Quite clearly, the English court cannot use the 1997 Order to apply Part II of the Insolvency Act 1986 (administration) to a foreign company, to apply English avoidance powers or to order a stay of English proceedings pursuant to section 130(2) of the Insolvency Act 1986. In addition, section 25(7) of the 1982 Act specifically prevents interim relief being used as a means of obtaining evidence. Nevertheless, the most commonly sought type of interim relief, namely a Mareva injunction, will be available. Thus, for example, a Swiss trustee who has brought proceedings in Switzerland against the directors of an insolvent corporation and their associates in order to set aside illegal preferences, may apply in England for a Mareva injunction freezing the defendants' assets in England. In addition, there is nothing to prevent the English court from granting a worldwide Mareva injunction, together with an ancillary disclosure order, even if the Swiss court might not have had jurisdiction so to do.[2]

Indeed, it is possible to imagine a situation where, assuming that all the foreign representative requires is a Mareva injunction, the foreign representative might make an application pursuant to the 1997 Order rather than relying upon the more extensive powers under section 426 of the Insolvency Act 1986. Because an application for interim relief will be

---

[18] See *Gourdain* v. *Nadler* [1979] E.C.R. 733, p. 13, *supra*.

[19] S.I. 1997/302.

[20] Consequential amendments (notably to RSC Ord 11) have also been introduced: see S.I. 1997/415. For a general discussion, without reference to insolvency, see Scott (1997) 16 C.J.Q. 165.

[1] Article 2 of S.I. 1997/302, emphasis added.

[2] See *Crédit Suisse Fides Trust S.A.* v. *Cuoghi* [1997] 3 All E.R. 724 (although not an insolvency case).

made directly by the foreign representative, whereas section 426 requires that the insolvency representative applies to the foreign court and that the foreign court then submits a letter of request to the English court. In a straightforward case, the 1997 Order may be used to lessen the expense that would otherwise be involved if a section 426 application were to be pursued.[3] In any event, section 426 only applies to a small number of countries and territories, whilst the immediate attraction of the 1997 Order is that it covers an applicaton by a foreign trustee, liquidator or administrator from any jurisdiction.

The 1997 Order requires that there are 'proceedings' abroad – or that 'proceedings' are to be commenced there – before the English court can act in aid. Obviously the 1997 Order, and before that section 25 itself, was drafted with normal civil litigation[4] in mind. If a plaintiff is suing a defendant, there will necessarily be 'proceedings'. So too if a liquidator has brought an action abroad against a director in relation to improper conduct, or against a creditor to set aside a preference, these will constitute 'proceedings'. Yet whether the word 'proceedings' covers the foreign insolvency process itself (the collection and realisation of assets, the determination of creditors' claims, the distribution of assets and so on) is a different question.

Let us say that a debtor was recently made bankrupt in the US and the US trustee knows that there is considerable property (real and personal) in England which stands in the name of the debtor's spouse. The US trustee has some suspicion, but at this early stage nothing more than suspicion, that the property in England might once have belonged to the debtor and have been transferred to the spouse in questionable circumstances. It may be several weeks or months before the US trustee will be in a position to determine whether he will invoke his avoidance powers against the spouse and attempt to recover the property on behalf of the creditors.[5] In other words, the US trustee does not yet know whether any specific proceedings against the spouse will likely be pursued. Nevertheless, can the US trustee apply for a Mareva injunction in England, arguing that there are proceedings in aid of which the English court may act, namely, the overall insolvency process being conducted under the US Bankruptcy Code? This author would suggest that the answer, regrettably, is in the negative. For the word 'proceedings' in the 1997 Order must have the same meaning that it has in section 25; and it is beyond all doubt that section 25 was drafted with ordinary civil litigation in mind – plaintiff (A) against defendant (B). In short, an application for interim relief can only be entertained by the English court where there have been raised, in the course of the foreign insolvency process, issues which (at the time of the application) it is contemplated will be determined by some sort of trial.

Some support for this commentator's opinion can be found in *Re International Power Industries NV.*[6] The facts involved an application, by a US trustee in bankruptcy, under the Evidence (Proceedings in Other Jurisdic-

---

[3] Of course, if more intervention by the English court might be required, a section 426 application would likely be more appropriate.

[4] In the form of a *lis inter partes.*

[5] If it has been decided by the US trustee that an action will shortly be instituted against the bankrupt and spouse, then the requirement of proceedings (to be commenced) will plainly have been satisfied.

[6] [1985] B.C.L.C. 128; and see p. 403, *infra.*

tions) Act 1975. The trustee wished to examine certain individuals resident in England as to the affairs of a Netherland Antilles corporation that had submitted to the Chapter 11 jurisdiction of the US Bankruptcy Court. Section 1 of the 1975 Act provides that the High Court must be satisfied that:

> '. . . the evidence to which the application relates is to be obtained for the purpose of civil proceedings which either have been instituted before the [foreign] court or whose institution before that court is contemplated.'

It was held that the Act was not intended to be used as part of a general fact-finding exercise by the trustee when carrying out his investigatory functions under US bankruptcy law; and was only available where 'proceedings which will result in a trial' were contemplated.[7] It seems likely that a similar approach will be taken to the interpretation of 'proceedings' for the purposes of the 1997 Order. It will not be enough merely that a formal insolvency process has been initiated abroad (whether or not under the supervision of the foreign court). A foreign insolvency representative will, accordingly, have to be careful as to the timing of any application for interim relief.

Although the 1997 Order was obviously not designed with insolvency proceedings especially in mind – hence the ambiguity as to the meaning of 'proceedings' – the fact that interim relief may now be available in aid of a foreign insolvency is a welcome development. It is inevitable that the Mareva injunction will be the type of interim releif most often sought by a foreign representative; and this may be particularly useful in cases where the foreign representative is employing his avoidance powers or is pursuing directors for fraudulent or other irregular or unsatisfactory trading practices.[8]

(ii) *Provisional Liquidators*

The 1997 Order will likely come into play where a foreign representative is pursuing claims abroad against third parties who themselves have assets in England. The 1997 Order however, will have little role to play where it is the debtor who has assets in England and third parties are attempting by legal process in England to get hold of those assets. In this latter situation the foreign representative may sometimes be content to rely upon the common law rule that, if a foreign insolvency is already underway, individual creditors will not be permitted to gain an advantage by the subsequent attachment of the debtor's property in England.[9] But, particularly in the case of a foreign company which is being re-organised abroad – and which cannot[10] be put into administration under Part II of the Insolvency Act 1986 – the foreign representative may prefer to gain breathing space by

---

[7] *Ibid.* at 137 *per* Woolf J. The legislation should be amended, see p. 404, *infra*.
[8] Where a civil action is commenced *in England*, the court will be careful to exercise its interlocutory powers in such a way as not to frustrate the efficient conduct of any foreign insolvency process: see *Banque Indosuez S.A.* v. *Ferromet Resources Inc.* [1993] B.C.L.C. 112.
[9] See p. 234, *supra*.
[10] A foreign company cannot generally be put into Part II administration, see p. 130, *supra*, although this may occur pursuant to a s. 426 request: *Re Dallhold Estates (UK) Pty. Ltd.* [1992] B.C.L.C. 621.

arranging for a winding up petition to be presented in England and, at the same time, applying for the appointment of a provisional liquidator.[11] The appointment of a provisonal liquidator will, of course, bring into operation the automatic stay under section 130(2) of the Insolvency Act 1986.[12] Whilst creditors' actions in England are stayed, the company will be able to explore the possibility of re-negotiating its debt and concluding an informal workout, or proposing a scheme of arrangement under section 425 of the Companies Act 1985.[13] If such a solution can be achieved, the winding up petition may be dismissed and the provisional liquidator discharged.[14]

An application for the appointment of a provisional liquidator may be made, by a creditor, in altogether different circumstances.[15] For example, it may be that a foreign company, which would seem to have assets some-where in the world, has been run in a less than reputable fashion out of a hotel room in England.[16] A party ('the creditor') who has dealt with the company asserts that he is owed a debt; a claim which the company does not admit. Should the creditor present a winding up petition and seek the appointment of a provisional liquidator, the company would doubtless raise a flurry of arguments to back up the contention that the debt is disputed and, accordingly, the petition should be dismissed. Whilst as a matter of principle it is not appropriate to seek to determine disputed questions of fact at the hearing of a winding up petition, the Court of Appeal[17] has made it quite plain – in a case that happened to involve a foreign company[18] – that the courts will not be deflected by a 'put-up job';[19] and will not allow a company[20] 'to raise a cloud of objections on affidavits and then claim that, because a dispute of fact cannot be resolved without cross-examination, the petition should not be heard at all but the matter should be left to be determined in some other proceedings.'

C. Foreign Judgments

The circumstances in which foreign insolvency proceedings will be recog-nised in England have been discussed earlier in this work.[1] Thus it is clear

---

[11] Prior to the appointment of a provisional liquidator there will be no automatic stay, but the foreign company might still apply for a stay of a particular action under s. 126 of the Insolvency Act 1986; see *Re Dynamics Corpn. of America* [1972] 3 All E.R.1046 for an illustration.

[12] This provision, although extending to actions throughout the United Kingdom, is not truly extraterritorial: see p. 279, *supra*.

[13] Schemes of arrangement are applicable to foreign companies; Companies Act 185, s.425(6)(a).

[14] See Moss & Phillips (1993) 6 Ins. Int. 1, and note the earlier attempt in *Re Dynamics Corpn of America, supra* n. 11.

[15] See Smart (1996) 112 L.Q.R. 397, *passim*.

[16] There will be jurisdiction to wind up the company in such circumstances, see p. 102, *supra*.

[17] In *Re Claybridge Shipping Co. S.A.* [1981] Com. L.R. 107, and in full at [1997] 1 B.C.L.C. 572, applied in *Alipour* v. *Ary* [1997] 1 W.L.R. 534.

[18] Although it cannot really be suggested that the principles applicable to English and foreign companies are different in this regard.

[19] As Lord Denning MR put it; see [1981] Com. L.R. 107 at 108.

[20] *Per* Oliver LJ, *ibid.*, at 109.

[1] See chapters 5 and 6, *supra*.

that, for example, if a debtor files for bankruptcy in the United States, a US trustee will be entitled to recognition in England and can act accordingly. However, it is quite plain that, just because a foreign insolvency is entitled to recognition in England, it does not follow that *every* order made by the foreign court (when conducting that insolvency) will be enforceable in England.[2] The following paragraphs concern the enforcement in England of orders and judgments which a foreign court makes *against third parties* during the course of the foreign insolvency process.[3] A relevant illustration might be where the US trustee (months or years after his initial appointment) obtains a judgment against a creditor setting aside an unlawful preference and requiring the creditor to repay money to the trustee. At common law, provided the US court had jurisdiction over the defendant creditor, the US judgment may be enforced in England as a final and conclusive judgment for the payment of a sum of money.[4] In other words, a judgment of a foreign court arising out of an insolvency may be enforceable in England by the application of the very same rules as apply to any foreign judgment for a sum of money.

(i) *Civil Jurisdiction and Judgments Act 1982*

The first point to note is the limited role the Civil Jurisdiction and Judgments Act 1982 (as amended) has to play in this regard. For although the Brussels and Lugano Conventions apply to any judgment – not just a judgment for a sum of money – judgments which derive directly from and are closely connected to insolvency proceedings are completely excluded by Article 1.[5] Hence a judgment setting aside a preference or ordering a defendant director to pay 'damages' for wrongful or fraudulent trading cannot be brought within the Act. On the other hand, a cause of action against a director will not fall within the Article 1 exclusion merely because the proceedings have been brought by the liquidator. Thus, for instance, if the Irish court were to award damages against a director for breach of fiduciary duty or the director's common law duty of skill and care, such a judgment would be within the Convention, regardless of the fact that the company was in liquidation and the liquidator had made the decision to sue the director in question.[6]

---

[2] For example, a worldwide stay granted in US proceedings is not binding in England: *Banque Indosuez S.A.* v. *Ferromet Resources Inc.* [1993] B.C.L.C. 112 at 117, *supra*, p. 237.

[3] For an example of a judgment against the bankrupt arising out of foreign bankruptcy proceedings, see *Berliner Industriebank Aktiengesellschaft* v. *Jost* [1971] 2 Q.B. 463.

[4] Note *Green* v. *Paramount Capital Corpn.*, (20 December 1991, unreported), Ont. H.C., (LEXIS). US trustee bringing proceedings against the defendant in the US Bankruptcy Court to set aside a preference. The defendant contested the jurisdiction but then also argued as to the merits. Gotlib J regarded the defendant as having submitted to the foreign court's jurisdiction and enforced the US judgment (being for $500,000 plus interest): for related proceedings, see 14 O.R. (3d) 319. See also *Re Focus Insurance Co. Ltd.*, *infra* n. 6.

[5] See p. 13, *supra* for details.

[6] The same would be true in relation to the equivalent proceedings under Dutch, French or Norwegian law. For a common law illustration, see *Re Focus Insurance Co. Ltd.* [1996] B.C.C. 659 at 663: Bermudan judgment for US$19 million against a director for breach of fiduciary duty registered in England.

(ii) *Enforcement at Common Law and Under the Acts of 1920 and 1933*

If a Belgian court were to make a decree pursuant to the relevant provisions of Belgian insolvency law[7] setting aside a preference and ordering the defendant to pay 500,000 Belgian francs to the liquidator of an insolvent company, that order would not fall within the Brussels Convention. The judgment, however, could be enforced in England pursuant to the Foreign Judgments (Reciprocal Enforcement) Act 1933.[8] For the Act was made applicable to Belgian judgments in 1936[9] and, although very largely superseded by the Civil Jurisdiction and Judgments Act, remains applicable where proceedings fall outside the scope of the Brussels Convention.[10] The 1933 Act applies to any judgment (which is either final and conclusive or for an interim payment) for a sum of money given in 'civil proceedings':[11] 'civil proceedings' undoubtedly includes proceedings in connection with insolvency matters.[12] Proceedings taken in connection with bankruptcy or winding up are not regarded for the purposes of the 1933 Act as coming within the expression an 'action in personam' and, therefore, the jurisdiction of the foreign court is tested by reference to the rules of English private international law[13] – rather than section 4(2)(a) of the 1933 Act. Accordingly, in the example above, the Belgian judgment will be enforced in England if the defendant was present in Belgium at the time the proceedings were commenced or voluntarily submitted to the jurisdiction of the Belgian courts.[14]

In relation to those countries to which Part I of the 1933 Act has not been extended, a final and conclusive judgment for a sum of money (but not, for example, to set aside a gratuitous alienation of property)[15] may be enforced at common law, regardless of whether that judgment arises out of a bankruptcy, re-organisation or liquidation.[16] In addition, with reference to a number of designated Commonwealth jurisdictions, a final and conclusive judgment for a sum of money is enforceable under Part II of the Administration of Justice Act 1920.

---

[7] For the position in respect of the so-called *actio Pauliana*, see pp. 15–17, *supra.*

[8] At the time of writing the 1933 Act had been applied to some 14 countries as well as Guernsey, Jersey and the Isle of Man. A general discussion of the 1933 Act, although with no reference to insolvency-related judgments, is found in Dicey and Morris, *Private International Law* (12th ed., 1993) p. 523 *et seq.*

[9] S.R. & O. 1936/1169 and see *Halsbury's Statutory Instruments*, vol. 10, pp. 229–253 for further details of other countries and jurisdictions.

[10] See s. 9 of the 1982 Act and Art. 55 of the Convention.

[11] Foreign Judgments (Reciprocal Enforcement) Act 1933, ss. 1(2)(b) and 11(1).

[12] This becomes apparent upon reading s. 1(2) of the 1933 Act and looking at, for example, Art. 4(3)(c) of the Anglo-Belgian Convention set out in the Schedule to S.R. & O. 1936/1169, *infra*, n. 13.

[13] See ss. 4(2)(c) and 11(2). The matter is rather more adequately explained in Art. 4(3)(c) of the Anglo-Belgian Convention, above n. 12, as follows: 'In the case of judgments given in proceedings of the kind referred to in the present paragraph [i.e. "judgments in bankruptcy proceedings, or proceedings for the winding up of companies or other bodies corporate"], the jurisdiction of the original court shall be recognised in all cases where such recognition is in accordance with the rules of private international law observed by the court applied to.'

[14] See, further, *Dicey and Morris*, above n. 8, at pp. 472–473 for the common law rules.

[15] Cf. *Platt* v. *Platt* 1958 S.C. 95.

[16] As in *Green* v. *Paramount Capital Corpn.*, above n. 4. See also *Barned's Banking Co. Ltd.* v. *Reynolds* (1875) 36 U.C.R. 256 (enforcement of call) and cf. *Wryghte* v. *Lindsay* (1860) 2 L.T. 63.

Finally, although enforcement under the common law and the Acts of 1920 and 1933 is only possible in respect of a judgment for a sum of money, other judgments and orders given in insolvency related cases may have some effect in England: for example, giving rise to a plea of *res judicata*.[17]

D. Evidence

An order made by a foreign court that a party submit to examination obviously cannot in any way be likened to a judgment for a sum of money enforceable at common law. In ordinary civil proceedings, where plaintiff sues defendant, resort may be had to the Evidence (Proceedings in Other Jurisdictions) Act 1975, which was passed to enable the United Kingdom to comply with the Hague Convention on the Taking of Evidence Abroad in Civil and Commercial Matters 1970.[18] Section 1 of the 1975 Act provides that, where a request is received from a foreign court, the High Court must be satisfied that:

> '. . . the evidence to which the application relates is to be obtained for the purpose of civil proceedings which either have been instituted before the [foreign] court or whose institution before that court is contemplated.'

The question which has given rise to difficulty is whether a foreign bankruptcy, re-organisation or liquidation is of itself a proceeding for the purposes of section 1.

The English authority upon this point is *Re International Power Industries N.V.*[19] A Netherlands Antilles corporation had submitted to the Chapter 11 jurisdiction of the US Bankruptcy Court and a trustee had been appointed. The US trustee was investigating the corporation's affairs; and the US Bankruptcy Court issued letters rogatory requesting the assistance of the English court for the examination of two (unwilling) witnesses in England. Woolf J ruled against the US trustee, holding that the 1975 Act did not cover a preliminary fact finding exercise by a trustee at a stage when no civil proceedings, designed to result in some kind of trial between parties, were contemplated.[20] Accordingly, although a foreign representative can rely upon the 1975 Act when, for example, suing a defendant to recover the debtor's assets or set aside a preference, the 1975 Act is restricted to where there is some specific issue in dispute, which it is contemplated will be determined by something in the nature of a trial in the foreign court.[1]

---

[17] An example being *Deak Perera (Far East) Ltd.* v. *Deak* [1995] 1 H.K.L.R. 145 (noted (1995) 4 I.I.R. at 204), in which the Hong Kong Official Receiver was prevented by issue estoppel from re-arguing in Hong Kong the scope of a settlement agreement, when the US Bankruptcy Court had already ruled against the Official Receiver on the point in question.

[18] For a general discussion, without reference to insolvency, see Collins (1986) 35 I.C.L.Q. 765.

[19] [1985] B.C.L.C. 128. There was an appeal which was settled: see McRae and Kelley (1988) 64 C.B.R. 276 at p. 294.

[20] *Ibid.*, at 137. For a contrary Dutch decision, see McRae and Kelley at p. 305.

[1] In practical terms, a foreign representative may be able to gather enough information in the home state to enable some proceedings against a defendant to be commenced, and then the foreign representative will be able to rely in England upon the 1975 Act.

A number of observations must be made. Firstly, the courts often made orders for examination of witnesses under the mutual co-operation provisions of the old Bankruptcy Acts and there is no doubt that orders may now be made pursuant to section 426 of the Insolvency Act 1986, although only in respect of those countries and territories that have been designated.[2] Second, and this point applies particularly to a foreign corporation, a foreign representative may well be able to transfer assets to England and then arrange for a winding up petition to be presented.[3] In this way information and evidence can be gathered by an English liquidator (working, broadly speaking, in co-operation with his foreign counterpart). Third, the ruling of Woolf J was, of course, only at first instance and it will be noted that the United States Court of Appeals for the Second Circuit has recently arrived at the directly opposite conclusion.[4] Nevertheless, the Court of Appeal in England has referred to *Re International Power Industries N.V.* with apparent approval[5] and, in this author's opinion, it is unlikely that the decision of Woolf J would be overruled by an appellate tribunal. Nevertheless, the decision in *Re International Power Industries N.V.* reveals that the 1975 Act is out of step with the modern movement towards international co-operation in insolvency cases. Parliament should amend the 1975 Act accordingly.

Finally, in the first edition of this work it was argued that, despite *Re International Power Industries N.V.*, there might at common law be an inherent jurisdiction to provide assistance, in respect of the examination of witnesses, to a court conducting insolvency proceedings abroad.[6] For there are a number of cases establishing that examination of witnesses could be ordered under section 118 of the Bankruptcy Act 1883 (mutual co-operation between 'British' courts);[7] and there was authority that section 118 was concerned merely with procedures and did not create 'new rights' but rather 'new remedies for enforcing existing rights'.[8] However, there is no judicial guidance as to how such an inherent jurisdiction could be enforced against a reluctant witness;[9] and, moreover, albeit in a very different context and without reference to insolvency, the Court of Appeal has stated that there is no inherent jurisdiction outside the 1975 Act.[10] Such difficulties highlight the desirability of the statutory reversal of *Re International Power Industries N.V.* as soon as possible.

---

[2] See below, p. 419, *infra*.

[3] There does not seem to be anything objectionable in assets being transferred to England solely in order to give the English court winding up jurisdiction: see *Re Kailis Groote Eylandt Fisheries Pty. Ltd.* (1977) 2 A.C.L.R. 574 and (1977) 3 A.C.L.R. 288.

[4] In relation to Italian bankruptcy proceedings: see *Lancaster Factoring Co. Ltd.* v. *Mangone* 90 F. 3d 38 (1996) in respect of the equivalent US legislation (28 U.S.C. at 1782) bringing into force the Hague Convention. The judges specifically rejected the contention that the Italian bankruptcy was not a 'proceeding' the purposes of the US legislation. Note also *B.C.C.I.* v. *Haque* (1996) 42 C.B.R. (3d) 95 (Ont.).

[5] *Re Tucker* [1990] Ch. 148 at 161.

[6] At pp. 258–259 of the first edition.

[7] For example, *Re Nall* (1899) 20 L.R. (N.S.W.) B. & P. 25 and *Re Turnbull* (1886) 2 Q.L.J. 131.

[8] *Hall* v. *Woolf* (1908) 7 C.L.R. 207 at 212. Similar views were expressed in *Galbraith* v. *Grimshaw* [1910] A.C. 508 at 511.

[9] There is no difficulty, of course, if a witness agrees to give evidence or information in England.

[10] *Re Pan American World Airways Inc's Application* [1992] Q.B. 854 at 859, and see *per* Evans-Lombe J in *England* v. *Purves* (1998) Times, 29 January.

3. ASSISTANCE PURSUANT TO SECTION 426 OF THE INSOLVENCY ACT 1986

A. Introduction

In broad terms, section 426 of the Insolvency Act 1986 lays down a framework for international co-operation between courts exercising jurisdiction in relation to insolvency matters. It must be made clear at the outset, however, that section 426 deals with 'in-coming' requests for assistance, rather than 'out-going' requests.[11] Nothing in section 426 restricts the circumstances in which the English court may request assistance from a foreign court.

The section makes provision for the courts in one part of the United Kingdom to give assistance to the insolvency courts in (i) another part of the United Kingdom or (ii) relevant countries and territories. Thus section 426(4) states:

'(4) the courts having jurisdiction in relation to insolvency law in any part of the United Kingdom shall assist the courts having the corresponding jurisdiction in any other part of the United Kingdom or any relevant country or territory.'

The expression 'relevant country or territory'[12] encompasses any of the Channel Islands and the Isle of Man, as well as currently some 19 jurisdictions[13] (mainly within the Commonwealth) designated by statutory instrument.[14] Unfortunately, major trading partners such as the United States, France, Germany and Japan have not been so designated and therefore fall outside the scope of section 426 assistance.[15]

The bare bones of section 426(4) are fleshed out somewhat by section 426(5), which makes it plain that the assistance that may be given by the English court is not restricted to measures that are available under English insolvency law:

'(5) For the purposes of subsection (4) a request made to a court in any part of the United Kingdom by a court in any other part of the United Kingdom or in a relevant country or territory is authority for the court to which the request is made to apply, in relation to any matters specified in the request, the insolvency law which is applicable by either court in relation to comparable matters falling within its jurisdiction.

---

[11] A certain amount of confusion seems to have arisen in *Re McIsaac* [1994] B.C.C. 410, where it seems to have been thought that s. 426 was relevant to a (out-going) request to be made to a US court. The section simply does not apply to out-going requests (see, for example, *Moolman* v. *Builders & Developers Pty. Ltd.* 1990 (1) S.A. 954, where the English court requested assistance from the South African courts; at that time South Africa was not a s. 426 country); and, in any event, the United States is not a relevant country for s. 426 purposes: see Smart (1996) J.L.S. 141 at 142–143 for details.

[12] Which is defined in s. 426(11).

[13] Those jurisdictions are Anguilla, Australia, The Bahamas, Bermuda, Botswana, Canada, Cayman Islands, Falkland Islands, Gibraltar, Hong Kong, Ireland, Montserrat, New Zealand, St. Helena, Turk and Caicos Islands, Tuvalu and Virgin Islands (see the Co-operation of Insolvency Courts (Designation of Relevant Countries and Territories) Order 1986, S.I. 1986/2123), with Malaysia and South Africa being added by S.I. 1996/253.

[14] The Insolvency Act 1986 (Guernsey) Order 1989 (S.I. 1989/2409) makes s. 426 part of the law of Guernsey, *passim*. Section 426 applies to Northern Ireland, see s. 441(1)(a) of the Insolvency Act 1986.

[15] Although, of course, the English court will act under the general law to provide assistance to such representatives.

In exercising its discretion under this subsection, a court shall have regard in particular to the rules of private international law.'

It has recently been held by the Court of Appeal that,[16] where a request is received from a foreign court, the English court has three 'sources of law' from which appropriate assistance may be derived: (a) the English court's inherent jurisdiction and powers; (b) English 'insolvency law'; and (c) the foreign 'insolvency law'. For the purposes of section 426, 'insolvency law' is defined in subsection (10) as follows:

'In this section "insolvency law" means:
(a) in relation to England and Wales, provision made by or under this Act or sections 6 to 10, 12, 15 19(c) and 20 (with Schedule 1) of the Company Directors Disqualification Act 1986 and extending to England and Wales;
(b) [provision is made in relation to Scotland]
(c) [provision is made in relation to Northern Ireland]
(d) in relation to any relevant country or territory, so much of the law of that country or territory as corresponds to provisions falling within any of the foregoing paragraphs.'

Thus, for example, a request from a Malaysian court (made in relation to an alleged preference given to a creditor in England) might ask the English court to apply section 239 of the Insolvency Act 1986 or the corresponding provision under Malaysian law. But, in any event, although section 426(4) uses the word 'shall', the English court retains a discretion as to whether the requested assistance – or any other comparable assistance – may properly be granted.[17] (As it has now been settled that the English court does indeed have a discretion to refuse assistance, there is no good reason[18] why section 426 should remain applicable to only a relatively few foreign jurisdictions – all of which have an English common law heritage. Parliament may, quite safely, open up section 426 to all foreign countries; and, if a request from a court in Mexico or Japan is unreasonable or at odds with the policies underlying English insolvency law, the court may refuse to lend assistance.)

In any event, a search through the law reports (and relevant literature) reveals a broad range of assistance that has already been granted under section 426. The administration regime under Part II of the Insolvency Act 1986 has been applied to a foreign company.[19] A foreign re-organisation law has been extended to England with, *inter alia*, the English court making an order restraining creditors from presenting a winding up petition or commencing other civil proceedings in the English courts.[20] The English court has made an order restraining the commencement of actions against

---

[16] See *Hughes* v. *Hannover Rückversicherungs-Aktiengesellschaft* [1997] 1 B.C.L.C. 497, noted by Smart (1998) 114 L.Q.R. 46 and Fletcher [1997] J.B.L. 480, discussed in detail below.

[17] *Idem.*

[18] As far as this author is concerned. It is often said that s. 426 is reciprocal, but this is not strictly the case as, for example, there is no provision in Hong Kong statute law (and has not been since the repeal of s. 122 of the Bankruptcy Act 1914) for giving assistance to the English court.

[19] *Re Dallhold Estates (UK) Pty. Ltd.* [1992] B.C.L.C. 621. Note also *Re Nolisair International Inc.* (26 April 1993, unreported), Mummery J, referred to by Grierson in *Current Developments in International and Comparative Corporate Insolvency Law* (Ziegel, ed.) at p. 604, and see also in relation to the Barings collapse, Rushworth (1995) 7: 1 Int. Insol. & Cred. Rights Rep. at pp. 13–15.

[20] *Re Goodman International* (1990) 5 B.J.I.B. & F.L. 530 (note).

an insolvent corporation, save with leave of the foreign court conducting the winding up.[1] English avoidance powers have been invoked by a foreign representative.[2] A foreign scheme of arrangement has been extended to England so as to bind English creditors.[3] Documents held by parties in England have been ordered to be produced to a foreign liquidator.[4] The English court, where a foreign liquidator had commenced a civil action in the foreign court against a director for breach of duty, has issued a Mareva injunction freezing the director's assets in England[5] (although a Mareva injunction may now be obtained in such circumstances by any foreign representative – as interim relief[6] – without the need to invoke section 426). It is also apparent that witnesses may be examined in England;[7] that the court may exercise its *in personam* jurisdiction to restrain an English creditor from proceeding with litigation abroad;[8] that a bankruptcy order may be made in relation to an individual who is not otherwise subject to the English court's jurisdiction;[9] that assets, including after-acquired property, may be vested in a foreign representative;[10] and more generally that any of the court's powers under the 1986 Act may be invoked.

B. The Interpretation of Section 426

The leading authority on section 426 is the relatively recent decision in *Hughes* v. *Hannover Rückversicherungs-Aktiengesellschaft*,[11] the first case on the section to reach the Court of Appeal. The facts involved the winding up of the Electrical Mutual Liability Insurance Co. Ltd. in Bermuda. The company had originally been incorporated in 1927 in the State of Massachusetts but, in 1995, had re-located to Bermuda.[12] This transfer of corporate domicile was effected in accordance with the laws of Massachusetts and Bermuda. At this time, one of the re-insurers of the company was the

---

[1] See *Re a Company (No. 0013734 of 1991)* [1993] B.C.L.C. 59 at 69 referring to an order made in January 1989 restraining proceedings against an insurance company in liquidation in Bermuda.

[2] *Re BCCI S.A. (No. 9)* [1994] 3 All E.R. 764, on appeal (but not on this point) [1994] 1 W.L.R. 708.

[3] *Re Business City Express Ltd.* [1997] B.C.C. 826; but this issue now gives rise to some difficulty in the light of *Hughes* v. *Hannover*, see the analysis at p. 414, *infra*.

[4] See *Bell Group Finance (Pty.) Ltd.* v. *Bell Group (UK) Holdings Ltd.* [1996] 1 B.C.L.C. 304 at 308.

[5] See *Re Focus Insurance Co. Ltd.* [1996] B.C.C. 659 at 660–661 referring to a Mareva injunction granted by Mervyn Davies J in July 1991.

[6] See p. 396, *supra*.

[7] Although there may be reason to refuse to make an order see *England* v. *Purves*, (1998) Times, 29 January, *infra*.

[8] See *Hughes* v. *Hannover*, *infra*.

[9] For example, there are assets in England but the debtor is not domiciled, resident, present or carrying on business in England. This follows from *Re Dallhold Estates (UK) Pty. Ltd.* above, and note *Shaw and Mandatory (Petitioners)* (1868) 5 S.L.R. 171 where the Scottish court decided not to order a sequestration despite a request from an Australian assignee (a request from the foreign court was not required under s. 218 of the Bankruptcy Act 1861).

[10] *Re a Debtor, ex p Viscount of the Royal Court of Jersey* [1981] Ch. 384, decided under the 1914 Act but approved in *Hughes* v. *Hannover*.

[11] [1997] 1 B.C.L.C. 497.

[12] See also p. 357, *supra*, in relation to the transfer of corporate domicile.

respondent, referred to throughout as 'Hannover Re'. Hannover Re was incorporated in Germany but had a place of business in England – Hannover Re did not have any place of business in Bermuda. The company and Hannover Re had entered into treaties of re-insurance, which provided for arbitration to take place in accordance with the law of Massachusetts at a location agreed upon by the arbitrators and umpire. In October 1995 the company presented a petition in Bermuda for winding up on the ground it was insolvent and provisional liquidators were appointed.[13] In January 1996 Hannover Re demanded arbitration pursuant to the provisions of the re-insurance treaties, seeking to have those treaties rescinded. For obvious reasons the liquidators did not want the treaties rescinded.

As Hannover Re had no corporate presence in Bermuda, it was beyond the reach of any order that might emanate from the Bermudan court. Faced with the prospect of arbitration proceedings (which in all likelihood would take place in Massachusetts) the liquidators could simply have commenced an ancillary case under section 304 of the US Bankruptcy Code seeking an injunction from the Federal Court restraining the commencement of any arbitration in Massachusetts or elsewhere in the United States.[14] Instead, however, a less direct approach was taken. Shortly after Hannover Re demanded arbitration, the court in Bermuda issued a letter of request to the High Court in England, invoking section 426 of the Insolvency Act 1986 and requesting that the English court injunct Hannover Re from commencing or continuing any proceedings against the company not only in England but also 'in any and all jurisdictions'.[15] Hannover Re was undoubtedly amenable to the jurisdiction of the court and was served at its place of business in England. In substance, therefore, the underlying dispute had no factual connection to England and the injunctive relief sought was wholly extraterritorial: for although it was theoretically possible that the arbitrators and umpire would select England, it was not seriously disputed that the place of arbitration would be somewhere in the United States, probably Massachusetts.

At first instance[16] the liquidators contended that, a request for assistance having been received from a court in a relevant country or territory, the English court could grant a purely extraterritorial injunction. It was argued that the English court was empowered by section 426(5) to apply either the relevant foreign or English 'insolvency law'; and that within English 'insolvency law' fell not merely the Insolvency Act and Company Directors Disqualification Act 1986 provisions (and subordinate legislation) specifically identified in section 426(10)(a), but also any and all ancillary powers – such as the court's general equitable jurisdiction to grant injunctions. This broad interpretation of 'insolvency law' pursuant to section 426(10) – so as to include the court's general equitable jurisdiction – was accepted by Knox J. Nevertheless, the judge ruled against the liquidators on the basis that, even though section 426(4) used the words 'shall assist', the court retained a discretion as to whether or not assistance would be given; and having particular regard to the consideration that the parties' dispute was more

---

[13] The provisional liquidators were subsequently, after a winding up order had been made in Bermuda, appointed as the liquidators.
[14] *Supra*, n. 11, at 503.
[15] *Ibid.*, at 500.
[16] The judgment of Knox J is not reported, although available on LEXIS.

closely connected to the United States than to England, and that an appropriate remedy could be sought under section 304 of the US Bankruptcy Code, the court would not grant a purely extraterritorial injunction.

The liquidators' appeal was rejected by the Court of Appeal, although by way of a somewhat different line of reasoning than in the court below. Before looking at the reasoning of Morritt LJ it is worth noting that it is inherent in *Hughes* v. *Hannover* that, in appropriate circumstances, an extraterritorial injunction may issue against a party (specifically, a creditor) pursuant to a section 426 request.

In the Court of Appeal it was held that extraterritorial injunctive relief pursuant to the court's general equitable jurisdiction could not be granted under section 426(5). It was not doubted that section 426(5) allowed the court to apply either English 'insolvency law' or the 'insolvency law' of the requesting court,[17] however, the court rejected the broad interpretation of 'insolvency law' that had been favoured by Knox J. Morritt LJ (with whom Thorpe and Roch LJJ agreed) stressed that section 426(10) identified 'what the words "insolvency law" mean, not what they include' and that subsection (10) provided a 'complete definition' of that expression for the purposes of section 426.[18] Hence the court's power pursuant to section 426(5) to restrain proceedings against a company in liquidation was limited to those provisions identified as part of 'insolvency law' by subsection (10). The obstacle which confronted the liquidators in this regard was that under the Insolvency Act 1986 the power to restrain proceeding (see section 130(2)), is territorial and cannot be used to restrain proceedings abroad.[19] Nevertheless, although the relief sought did not come within section 426(5), Morritt LJ held that the court had jurisdiction to grant an extra-territorial injunction pursuant to subsection (4). For whilst the expression 'insolvency law' appeared in subsection (4), it did so merely to identify the appropriate courts upon which the obligation to assist was imposed.[20] Thus it is stated in subsection (4) that the 'courts *having jurisdiction in relation to insolvency law* in any part of the United Kingdom shall assist . . .'[1] Subsection (4) in contrast to subsection (5) does not require the requested court to apply 'insolvency law'. Moreover, Morritt LJ held that subsection (5) was in addition to rather than a restriction upon subsection (4).[2] (His Lordship was fortified in this conclusion by reference to cases[3] decided under a predecessor of section 426 (Bankruptcy Act 1914, section 122) wherein the English court had in the exercise of its general equitable jurisdiction appointed the foreign trustee as receiver of the debtor's property, including real property, in England. Morritt LJ considered it plain that it had not been the intention of Parliament that section 426 should cut down the 'jurisdiction or ability of the courts in England to

---

[17] See, for example, *Re BCCI S.A. (No. 9)* [1994] 3 All E.R. 764, application of Insolvency Act 1986 provisions at the request of the court in the Cayman Islands.

[18] [1997] 1 B.C.L.C. 497 at 516.

[19] See p. 279, *supra* (the same territorial restriction also existed under the law of Bermuda).

[20] *Supra*, n. 18.

[1] Emphasis added.

[2] *Supra*, n. 18, at 513.

[3] In particular, *Re Osborn* [1931–32] B. & C.R. 189 and *Re a Debtor, ex p Viscount of the Royal Court of Jersey* [1981] Ch. 384.

afford assistance'[4] that had previously existed under the Bankruptcy Act 1914.)

As a consequence of the ruling that section 426(5) was additional to and extended the court's jurisdiction under section 426(4), it followed that when dealing with any request there were three available options, or as Morritt LJ put it 'three sources of law'. The English court could: (a) relying upon subsection (4), invoke its own general jurisdiction and powers; (b) under subsection (5), apply English 'insolvency law', as exhaustively defined in section 426(10); and (c) under subsection (5), apply the foreign 'insolvency law', again as explained in section 426(10).[5] A request for an extraterritorial injunction could not be brought within (b) or (c), but it was within the court's power under (a).

Having ruled that there was power to grant the relief sought, Morritt LJ turned to consider whether the use of the expression 'shall assist' in section 426(4) required the court without more to accede to the request for assistance. Morritt LJ did not accept the notion that Parliament had intended the court to act as if it were an 'executive agency' rather than 'seeking to do justice in accordance with law'.[6] The contention that assistance would only be withheld on the ground of public policy was likewise rejected.[7] The appropriate test was for the court to consider whether the requested assistance, or any other comparable assistance, could 'properly be granted'.[8] In addition, in cases (such as *Hughes* v. *Hannover*) where the relief sought (for example, an injunction) was discretionary, the consideration that a foreign court had submitted a request was merely one factor to be taken into account – albeit a weighty factor – and would not be treated as conclusive.[9] On the facts Morritt LJ held that it was not a case where the assistance sought could properly be given. Hannover Re was not a *creditor* seeking to attach the company's assets in foreign proceedings, rather it was a debtor. Because the arbitration in Massachusetts would not interfere with the orderly administration of the liquidation, there would have been no good reason even if the company had been in liquidation in England for restraint of that arbitration.[10] Further, the underlying dispute was one with which the court in England had no connection but which was strongly connected to Massachusetts and there was no reason why, given the procedure available under section 304 of the US Bankruptcy Code, the Federal Court in the United States should not consider whether the arbitration ought to proceed.[11]

(i) *The Exercise of Discretion*

In *Hughes* v. *Hannover* the Court of Appeal approved three first instance decisions under section 426 in which it had been held that the English court

---

[4] [1997] 1 B.C.L.C. 497 at 515.

[5] *Ibid.*, at 517. When the English court is asked to exercise its powers under the section it does so on the basis of the hypothesis that 'the matters specified in the request fall within the jurisdiction of the court applying the insolvency law under consideration in so far as "comparable matters" would do so', *per* Morritt LJ (*idem.*).

[6] *Idem.*

[7] *Ibid.*, at 518: for more details on the refusal of assistance, see p. 417, *infra*.

[8] *Idem.*

[9] *Idem*, see also at 522.

[10] *Ibid*, at 523.

[11] *Idem.*

was not bound automatically to accede to a request from a foreign court.[12] Indeed, similar views were expressed as long ago as the 1860s, when the Lord President stated, in relation to a provision under the Bankruptcy Act 1861, that it 'would be too strict a construction of the statute' to hold that the court was 'under any obligation, without leave to exercise our discretion or enquire into the circumstances, to award . . . [assistance] . . . whenever anyone came . . . and demanded it'.[13]

Once, however, it is accepted that the court has a discretion, the question immediately arises as to basis of the exercise of that discretion. Morritt LJ, it will be recalled, stated that the question for the court was whether 'assistance may properly be granted' and, on the facts, concluded that it was not 'a proper case in which to grant the relief sought'.[14] It might be suggested that the use of such wording brings to mind Order 11 of the Rules of the Supreme Court: whether it is established that a case is a proper one for service of a writ out of the jurisdiction. Moreover, Morritt LJ relied upon the lack of factual connection to England as one of the reasons for refusing assistance. Nevertheless, it is suggested that trying to draw analogies with Order 11 is to read too much into the judgment of Morritt LJ. In this regard it will be noted that the decisions in *Re Dallhold Estates (UK) Pty. Ltd.* and *Re BCCI S.A. (No. 9)* were approved by Morritt LJ without any criticism.[15] In the former, Chadwick J stated that assistance ought to be granted 'unless there is some compelling reason why that should [not] be done'.[16] In the latter, Rattee J put it thus: 'this court should exercise its discretion in favour of giving the particular assistance requested . . . unless there is some good reason for not doing so'.[17] In addition, whereas in an Order 11 case questions of comity are against the exercise by the English court of an exorbitant jurisdiction, the situation is the very opposite under section 426: for the foreign court has requested assistance under a specific statutory framework (and normally such assistance would concern acts and parties within England). In short, nothing in *Hughes* v. *Hannover* should be taken as imposing upon an applicant any burden in respect of the exercise of the court's discretion.[18]

It is perhaps a fair summary of the ruling on the facts in *Hughes* v. *Hannover* to say that, whilst the English court is anxious to assist a requesting court under section 426, it will not act where to do so would constitute a quite unnecessary interference with the territorial integrity of *another* foreign court.[19]

---

[12] *Re Dallhold Estates (UK) Pty. Ltd.* [1992] B.C.L.C. 621, *Re BCCI S.A. (No. 9)* [1994] 3 All E.R. 764 and *Re Focus Insurance Co. Ltd.* [1996] B.C.C. 659.

[13] *Shaw and Mandatory (Petitioners)* (1868) 5 S.L.R. 171; under s. 218 of the 1861 Act a request from trustee or assignee appointed in a colony was of itself sufficient for courts in the United Kingdom to commence bankruptcy proceedings – no act of bankruptcy or other jurisdictional requirements had to be established.

[14] *Supra.*

[15] *Supra* n. 12.

[16] At 627.

[17] At 785.

[18] The circumstances in which assistance will be refused are considered further *infra*, p. 417.

[19] See the observation of Millett LJ in *Crédit Suisse Fides Trust S.A.* v. *Cuoghi* [1997] 3 All E.R. 724 at 730, set out at p. 392, *supra*.

(ii) *Enforcement Within the United Kingdom*

The narrow interpretation of 'insolvency law' adopted by the Court of Appeal in *Hughes* v. *Hannover* raises difficult questions as to the interaction between section 426(1) and section 18(3) of the Civil Jurisdiction and Judgments Act 1982 ('the 1982 Act'). For both provisions deal with the intra-United Kingdom enforcement of judgments and orders. Section 426(1) provides:[20]

> 'An order made by a court in any part of the United Kingdom in the exercise of jurisdiction in relation to insolvency law shall be enforced in any other part of the United Kingdom as if it were made by a court exercising the corresponding jurisdiction in that other part.'

Thus when, for example, a court in Scotland is winding up a company its orders will in general be enforceable in England as if they were orders from an English court. In such a case the orders of the Scottish court will not be enforceable in England under section 18 of the 1982 Act because, although that section operates in respect of any judgment or order given by a court in the United Kingdom, section 18(3)(ba) specifically excludes a judgment or order 'given in the exercise of jurisdiction in relation to insolvency law, within the meaning of section 426 of the Insolvency Act 1986'.[1] In *Hughes* v. *Hannover* Morritt LJ pointed out that whether a narrow or broad interpretation of 'insolvency law' were adopted under section 426(10), there was no risk of any 'gap' opening between section 426(1) and section 18(3) of the 1982 Act, because both sections made use of the same definition of 'insolvency law'.[2] In other words, if an order were made 'in the exercise of jurisdiction in relation to insolvency law' it would be enforceable under section 426(1); but if an order were made otherwise than pursuant to provisions identified as 'insolvency law' within section 426(10), that order would be enforceable under the 1982 Act.

Whilst this author would respectfully agree with Morritt LJ – that there can be no 'gap' between section 426(1) and section 18(3) – a narrow interpretation of 'insolvency law' gives rise to some very fine and surely unintended distinctions. To take an illustration, let us say that a company has been put into liquidation in Scotland. Should the Scottish court set aside a transaction as an unfair preference under section 243 of the Insolvency Act 1986, its order would be enforceable in England pursuant to section 426(1). This is on account of the definition of 'insolvency law' in relation to Scotland in section 426(10):

> 'In this section "insolvency law" means . . .
> (b) in relation to Scotland, provision extending to Scotland made by or under this Act . . . [specified sections] of the Company Directors Disqualification Act 1986, Part XVIII of the Companies Act 1985 or the Bankruptcy (Scotland) Act 1985. . . .'

However, should the Scottish court set aside a preference pursuant to its common law powers,[3] the order would not come within section 426(10)(b) and therefore could only be enforced in England under the Civil Jurisdic-

---

[20] Note also the discussion of s. 426(1) at p. 213, *supra* (in respect of the vesting of property).

[1] This provision was introduced in 1986.

[2] [1997] 1 B.C.L.C. 497 at 511.

[3] Which have survived the passing of the Insolvency Act 1986: see *Bank of Scotland* v. *Pacific Shelf (Sixty Two) Ltd.* (1988) 4 B.C.C. 457.

tion and Judgments Act 1982.[4] Like issues would arise where, for instance, the English court grants an extraterritorial injunction (not part of its 'insolvency law' jurisdiction) to restrain creditors from proceeding with an action in California and then seeks to have the order enforced in Scotland or Northern Ireland.[5]

Moreover, where an order of a court in Scotland falls to be enforced in England under section 426(1), such enforcement is expressly subject to section 426(2). Subsection (2) states that nothing in subsection (1) requires a court in any part of the United Kingdom 'to enforce, in relation to property situated in that part, any order made by a court in any other part of the United Kingdom'. There is, however, no similar restriction upon enforcement under the Civil Jurisdiction and Judgments Act 1982. Thus, whether the Scottish court sets aside a preference under its statutory or common law powers results in not only procedural but also substantive differences when it comes to the enforcement of such an order in England. Of course, the advantage of a broad interpretation of 'insolvency law' would be simplicity: all insolvency-related orders (whether or not actually stemming from a provision of the Insolvency Act 1986) would be enforceable pursuant to section 426(1). However, such a construction is no longer open to the courts – at least not unless the matter comes one day before the House of Lords.

(iii) *Companies Act 1989, Section 183*

In addition to section 18(3) of the Civil Jurisdiction and Judgments Act 1982, the interpretation of 'insolvency law' under section 426 impacts upon section 183 of the Companies Act 1989 (the '1989 Act') – although section 183 was apparently not considered in *Hughes* v. *Hannover*. Part VII of the 1989 Act is expressed to safeguard the operation of certain financial markets where a person party to market transactions becomes insolvent. Section 183 is designed to ensure that no foreign insolvency interferes with the proper operation of the markets.

Section 183(1) enlarges the definition of 'insolvency law' for the purposes of section 426:

> 'The references to insolvency law in section 426 . . . include, in relation to a part of the United Kingdom, the provisions made by or under this Part and, in relation to a relevant country or territory. . . so much of the law of that country or territory as corresponds to any provisions made by or under this Part.'

Of greater significance for present purposes is section 183(2), which restricts the effect that may be given under English law to any foreign insolvency:

> 'A court shall not, in pursuance of that section [i.e. s. 426] or any other enactment or rule of law, recognise or give effect to:
> (a) any order of a court exercising jurisdiction in relation to insolvency law in a country or territory outside the United Kingdom . . .

---

[4] For the position in relation to an action under s. 423 of the Insolvency Act 1986, see p. 15 *supra*.
[5] Cf. *Re Scottish Pacific Coast Mining Co.* [1886] W.N. 63.

in so far as the making of the order . . . would be prohibited in the case of a court in the United Kingdom . . . by provision made by or under this Part.'

It will at once be noted that the restriction imposed by section 183(2) is in the broadest terms and applies not merely to section 426 assistance but also to recognition under any other enactment or rule of law. The restriction, however, is expressed to apply to orders of a foreign court 'exercising jurisdiction in relation to insolvency law', a phrase clearly derived from section 426 itself. Yet if *Hughes* v. *Hannover* is correct (and 'insolvency law' is given a narrow meaning) it appears that there may be a gap in section 183(2). A foreign court might make an order under its own general equitable or equivalent jurisdiction (which is apparently not part of 'insolvency law'): the foreign court would therefore not be exercising jurisdiction in relation to 'insolvency law'; and its order would fall outside the section 183(2) restriction. It could be argued that Parliament would not have intended the operation of a significant restriction upon recognition of foreign insolvency proceedings to be cut down by a narrow construction of the words 'insolvency law', particularly as the whole tenor of section 183(2) is to impose the broadest of restrictions.

Of course, it is unlikely that a case will ever arise under section 183(2) where the difference between a narrow or broad interpretation of 'insolvency law' would actually affect the final result.[6] Nevertheless, to this author at least, it is slightly unfortunate that the Court of Appeal in *Hughes* v. *Hannover* did not give some guidance as to the operation of section 183(2).

(iv) *Foreign Schemes of Arrangement*

One difficulty that emerges in relation to the definition of 'insolvency law' in section 426(10) concerns quite how the English court can give effect to a foreign scheme of arrangement. For example, a company may have been put into liquidation in Hong Kong but thereafter a scheme of arrangement has been approved in accordance with the Hong Kong Companies Ordinance (which is identical in substance to the Companies Act 1985 in this regard). The Hong Kong court wants to ensure that creditors in England – whose debts arise under contracts governed by English law and who have not participated in the Hong Kong proceedings[7] – will be bound by the scheme. Accordingly, the foreign court submits a section 426 request. The English court, in light of the narrow definition of 'insolvency law', cannot apply section 425 of the Companies Act 1985 since that provision is not one of those listed in section 426(10). Nor is it readily apparent that the English court can apply the Hong Kong provision, for the Hong Kong provision corresponds to section 425 of the Companies Act 1985, rather than to anything found in the Insolvency Act 1986 (and section 425 is not listed in section 426(10)). It may well be correct that in some instances the relevant foreign composition provision can be said to correspond (roughly)

---

[6] Since the English court could, even if s. 183(2) were not applicable, invoke public policy to deny recognition to the foreign proceedings.

[7] Where a creditor has participated it seems that a scheme will be binding, see p. 266, *supra*.

to Part I of the Insolvency Act 1986 (Company Voluntary Arrangement),[8] but this is not really the case in the example given above.

The only authority on the point is *Re Business City Express Ltd.*,[9] which was decided very shortly before *Hughes* v. *Hannover* and therefore contains no discussion of the 'insolvency law' issue. A composition or scheme of arrangement had been entered into in Ireland, after a company had gone into examinership there, and the Irish court had issued a request that the English court make the scheme binding on English creditors. (In fact, the Irish court had made its own approval conditional on the success of a section 426 request.) In the course of his judgment, Rattee J noted that 'there is no provision of English law which would enable me to make the scheme binding on English creditors as the Irish court desires'.[10] But his Lordship was prepared to apply the Irish law to the creditors in England.[11] Whilst the perfect good sense of this ruling cannot be doubted, the judgment does not consider in what way the Irish law corresponded to provision made by or under the Insolvency Act 1986. It cannot really be said that the Irish scheme of arrangement corresponded to Part II administration in England, for administration may or may not lead eventually to a scheme of arrangement.[12] If the point were to arise today it might be possible (after receipt of expert evidence) to conclude that the Irish scheme corresponded to a company voluntary arrangement – but the point is in some doubt.

In short, there is now unwelcome (and even perhaps unnecessary) uncertainty on this point. In light of the difficulty raised by the narrow approach to 'insolvency law' adopted in *Hughes* v. *Hannover*, the addition of Part XIII of the Companies Act 1985 to section 426(10) should be urgently considered.

C. United Kingdom Insolvencies

Where an insolvency is being conducted in Scotland or Northern Ireland, the English court may be called upon to act in aid thereof either under section 426(1) or section 426(4) – depending upon the way in which the Scottish or Northern Irish representative has conducted the relevant proceedings.[13] But, in any event, it is important to make it clear that the decision and reasoning in *Galbraith* v. *Grimshaw* has no bearing upon mutual assistance under section 426.[14]

The relationship between subsection (1) and subsection (4) of section 426 may best be illustrated by way of an example. Let us say that a winding up is underway in Scotland and the liquidator believes that there is compelling evidence that 18 months ago the company gratuitously disposed of certain

---

[8] Which does, of course, come within s. 426(10).
[9] [1997] B.C.C. 826.
[10] *Ibid.*, at 828.
[11] *Idem.*
[12] It is undoubtedly the case that examinership in Ireland corresponds to administration in England, but that does not answer the question in relation to a scheme of arrangement which the examiner has proposed and to which the creditors and the court have given their consent.
[13] See also p. 213, *supra*.
[14] This is the case in relation to both United Kingdom and foreign requests under s. 426.

immovable property in England. The recipient of the alienation has at all relevant times been living in Spain and has ignored the liquidation. The Scottish liquidator has a range of options in such a situation. Firstly, the liquidator may (relying upon section 242 of the Insolvency Act 1986) obtain a decree of reduction in Scotland and thereafter apply to have the order of the Scottish court enforced in England by reference to section 426(1) – although the effect of section 426(2) is that the English court is not bound automatically to enforce the Scottish decree. Second, the liquidator could have the Scottish court formulate a section 426(4) request to the English court: for example, that the English court acting under section 426(5) apply English avoidance powers (i.e. section 238 of the Insolvency Act 1986) to the transaction. Third, a request from the Scottish court might ask the English court to apply the substantive law of Scotland, that is section 242.[15] Fourth, without reliance upon section 426 at all, the Scottish liquidator may directly seek an order in the High Court in England setting aside the transaction pursuant to section 423 of the Insolvency Act 1986 – provided the transaction was at an undervalue and designed to put assets out of the reach of creditors.[16] Section 423, of course, does not require that a winding up be commenced in England.[17] Section 424(1) permits an application under section 423 to be made, *inter alios*, by a 'liquidator' and there is every reason to believe that the term 'liquidator' is not restricted to a liquidator appointed by the court in England.[18] Support for this view can be found in a number of Commonwealth cases,[19] including one before the Supreme Court of Canada,[20] in which (under a predecessor of section 423) transactions were set aside at the suit of a foreign representative and without there being any local insolvency or a request from the foreign court.

Where the Scottish liquidator chooses to invoke section 426, the English court will grant assistance without regard to the decision in *Galbraith* v. *Grimshaw*.[1] In *Galbraith* v. *Grimshaw* the House of Lords allowed an English creditor to proceed with an attachment of property in England, despite the fact that the attachment was incomplete at the date of the sequestration of the bankrupt's estate in Scotland. The House of Lords declined to apply the retrospective provisions of Scottish bankruptcy law, which would have invalidated the attachment, and their Lordships also held that the then English doctrine of relation back could not operate, because no bankruptcy proceedings had been commenced in England. Nevertheless, the decision is irrelevant to the English court's exercise of discretion under section 426.[2] *Galbraith* v. *Grimshaw* did not involve any request for assistance by the Scottish court under the relevant Bankruptcy

---

[15] Although this would involve the additional complexities of proving the foreign (Scottish) law before the English court.

[16] Different time periods, of course, apply in relation to these various avoidance powers and this would no doubt influence the formulation of the Scottish request for assistance.

[17] In relation to s. 423 generally, see p. 15, *supra*.

[18] See *Slavenburg's Bank* v. *Intercontinental Ltd.* [1980] 1 W.L.R. 1076 at 1087 (p. 174, n. 15, *supra*).

[19] Such as *Niven* v. *Grant* (1903) 29 V.L.R. 102 and *Minot Grocery Co.* v. *Durick* (1913) 10 D.L.R. 126.

[20] *McNeil* v. *Sharpe* (1915) 70 D.L.R. 740.

[1] [1910] A.C. 508; and see also p. 216, *supra*.

[2] See *Re BCCI S.A. (No. 9)* [1994] 3 All E.R. 764 at 779–780 *per* Rattee J.

Act provision. Moreover, as was revealed in *Galbraith* v. *Grimshaw* itself,[3] the only order of the Scottish court was that vesting the bankrupt's estate in the trustee: there was no specific order concerning the attachment in England and still less any attempt to have such an order enforced in England under the mutual aid provision in the Bankruptcy Act 1883. Thus the only question actually determined by the House of Lords was what property vested in a foreign (including Scottish) trustee. Indeed, even if one considers the mutual aid provision under the Bankruptcy Act 1883, it was said merely to affect procedures:[4] whereas section 426 allows the very substance of the foreign law or English law to be applied.

D. Refusal of Assistance

It is clear from *Hughes* v. *Hannover* that there are limits upon the assistance that the English court may grant pursuant to section 426. It will be recalled that Morritt LJ identified three sources of law which were available when considering a request:

(a) the English court's inherent jurisdiction and powers,
(b) English 'insolvency law' and
(c) the corresponding foreign 'insolvency law'.

Hence if a request were to seek the application of the inherent jurisdiction of the foreign court, or an insolvency procedure that had no (rough) equivalent under the Insolvency Act 1986, the requested assistance could simply not be granted. It also goes without saying that if a request were to offend against English public policy, or to have no purpose other than the enforcement in England of a foreign revenue law,[5] assistance would likewise be refused. But assistance will also be refused if it is not a proper case in which to give the requested assistance, or other comparable assistance. The following seeks to identify some guidelines as to this 'proper case' requirement.

By way of a preliminary point, it seems fairly apparent that section 426 must be interpreted free of any restrictions applicable to the recognition of foreign insolvency proceedings under the common law rules. For example, the fact that the insolvency proceedings underway in the requesting court would not fall within the established bases of recognition at common law,[6] is no bar to the granting of assistance under section 426. Similarly, that the law of the requesting court is territorial, and does not purport to extend to assets or persons in England, will not prevent the English court from acceding to a request (to apply, for example, the avoidance powers under the Insolvency Act 1986 or under the foreign insolvency law).

Nevertheless, restrictions are implicit when it comes to the nature of the assistance sought. If, recalling the three 'sources of law,' the request seeks the application of the inherent powers of the English court, it must inevitably follow that such assistance will be refused if in corresponding circumstances (i.e. in an English insolvency case) that relief would not be

---

[3] See [1910] 1 K.B. 339 at 343.
[4] See [1910] A.C. 508 at 511.
[5] See *per* Rattee J in *Re BCCI S.A. (No. 9)* [1994] 3 All E.R. 764 and 785 and p. 197, *supra*.
[6] For example, based solely upon the presence of assets.

available. For example, bankruptcy proceedings are on foot in New Zealand and a creditor, resident in England but not amenable to the jurisdiction of the New Zealand court, after the commencement of those proceedings has attached the debtor's assets in Peru and recovered a sum of money. A section 426 request may ask the English court to exercise its equitable jurisdiction to require the attaching creditor to disgorge the money recovered in Peru. But the case law establishes (where the English court is conducting its own bankruptcy proceedings) that, if the attaching creditor were at all relevant times a secured creditor according to Peruvian law, the equitable jurisdiction will not be exercised.[7] The fact that a request is made under section 426 cannot cause the English court to exercise a jurisdiction that it would rule against exercising in an English insolvency. *Hughes* v. *Hannover* is, of course, an authority on exactly this point. The position is the same where the request seeks the application of English (statutory) insolvency law provisions. To take an illustration, an individual may be subject to the jurisdiction of the English court and a transaction may have been entered into which appears to have been at an undervalue. But if the facts show clearly that England is *forum non conveniens*, and that avoidance proceedings can readily be taken in the *forum conveniens*, the English court will decline to exercise its statutory powers – even though the court in South Africa or Hong Kong may have submitted a section 426 request. Thus one may state as a general guideline, in relation to the first two 'sources' of law, that assistance will not be granted under section 426 if the requested relief would not be ordered in the equivalent English insolvency proceedings.

Yet, this general guideline cannot be applied to cases involving the third 'source' of law identified by Morritt LJ – the foreign insolvency law. Of course, it is not difficult to imagine circumstances in which the relief sought, relying upon the foreign insolvency law, would also be available under English insolvency law.[8] It is suggested, however, that the very fact that section 426(5) expressly encompasses foreign insolvency law means that Parliament could not have intended that relief would only be available where the requirements of English law were made out. In other words, it must have been intended that the 'foreign insolvency law option' was additional to remedies and relief that were in any event available under English law. The point may be illustrated by way of an example. Let us say that the relevant time period under a foreign preference law is fixed in all cases at 12 months. Hence, in certain circumstances, the period may be longer than that under section 240 of the Insolvency Act 1986. Let us assume further that an alleged preference was given to a creditor, resident in England, 10 months before the onset of the insolvency proceedings abroad. Thus, assuming that the creditor was not an associate and that the transaction was not at an undervalue,[9] the transaction cannot be avoided as a preference under English insolvency law, although it does come within the scope of operation of the foreign law. In such circumstances, and always assuming that the transaction in question has its centre of gravity in the relevant foreign country, this author would strongly

---

[7] See p. 304, *supra*.
[8] For example, a person might be examinable under either s. 236 of the Insolvency Act 1986 or the corresponding provision of the foreign insolvency law.
[9] See Insolvency Act 1986, s. 240(1).

suggest that the English court ought to accede to a section 426 request to apply the foreign preference provision – even though no remedy would be available under English insolvency law. On the other hand, were the transaction to be more closely connected to England, it is suggested that (having regard to the principles of private international law) the English court would exercise its discretion against applying the foreign avoidance law.[10]

England v. *Purves*[11] concerned an application to apply the foreign insolvency law. An Australian company was in liquidation and the Australian court had made a section 426 request that certain witnesses be ordered to submit for examination in England. The difficulty was that, in Australia, a civil action had already been commenced by the liquidator against the witnesses in question. Evans-Lombe J ruled[12] that under section 236 of the Insolvency Act 1986 an order for examination would not have been made on account of the existence of the civil action. The request, however, sought the application of the Australian examination provision; and it was apparently the case that in Australia an order would have been made in the circumstances. Evans-Lombe J refused the request. The report contains the following passage:[13]

'Had the application been pursued by an English liquidator under section 236 it would have been dismissed. It followed that his Lordship should not accede to the letter of request and the liquidator's application.'

The actual decision on the facts in *England* v. *Purves* may be correct, in the light of the particular finding of the judge that examination would be oppressive.[14] However, to the extent that the report suggests that relief (by reliance upon the foreign insolvency law) must be refused if it is not also available under English insolvency provisions, the ruling is most unhelpful and should not be extended.

Finally, what may be referred to as 'cherry picking' should be mentioned. Normally, a section 426 request will seek either the application of English law or the relevant foreign law. But, for example, should the facts involve two transactions (one having its centre of gravity in England and the other being more closely connected to the foreign jurisdiction) there is no reason why the request cannot seek the application of English law to one transaction and the foreign law to the other.[15] That is not to say, however, that the requesting court can simply 'pick and choose'. It perhaps goes without saying that a request cannot validly ask that the court apply the whole of an English avoidance provision, except in relation to the relevant time period, where the (longer) foreign insolvency provision should be applied.

---

[10] It would not be a proper case for the requested assistance and no comparable assistance would be available under English insolvency law.

[11] (1998) Times, 29 January.

[12] Applying *Cloverbay Ltd.* v. *Bank of Credit and Commerce International S.A.* [1991] Ch. 90.

[13] *Supra*, n. 11.

[14] Although it is far from clear to this author why parties who were at the relevant time resident abroad, and had dealt with a foreign company, should be entitled to the protection of English law. A business party dealing with a South Australian company would (if any thought were given to the question) in all likelihood expect that the company, if it were subsequently and unfortunately to go into liquidation, would be liquidated in Australia and Australian law would apply.

[15] The alternative would simply be to have two separate letters of request.

4. EUROPEAN CONVENTION ON INSOLVENCY PROCEEDINGS

Where main proceedings are opened in a Contracting State, in accordance with Article 3 of the Convention, those proceedings are automatically entitled to recognition in any other Contracting State and, moreover, the liquidator will be able to exercise extensive powers throughout all Contracting States[16] – except where a local liquidator has been appointed in secondary (territorial) proceedings.[17] In addition, judgments and orders made by the court conducting the main proceedings will be enforceable in other Contracting States in the same way that ordinary (non-insolvency) judgments are enforceable, under specified[18] provisions of the Brussels Convention. This would apply to all judgments, not just those for a sum of money. Where the debtor's centre of main interests was not located in a Contracting State,[19] the common law rules on assistance would continue to apply unaffected by the Convention. The Convention is in effect expressly without prejudice to any obligation to provide assistance arising under section 426 of the Insolvency Act 1986.[20]

5. ILLUSTRATIONS

(1) IRL is a New Zealand corporation in liquidation in New Zealand. The New Zealand court has issued letters of request seeking the assistance of the High Court in England in relation to the examination of certain witnesses in England. The New Zealand liquidator is seeking to build up an accurate picture of IRL's financial dealings in England prior to liquidation. Although the Evidence (Proceedings in Other Jurisdictions) Act 1975 is not available,[1] the examinations may be ordered acting pursuant to section 426 of the Insolvency Act 1986.[2]

(2) CTJ is a Panamanian corporation that owns a ship. CTJ has been run by agents out of Hong Kong but does not have any place of business of its own anywhere in the world.[3] The Hong Kong court has put CTJ into liquidation, on the basis of a 'sufficient connection' to Hong Kong.[4] The Hong Kong court has issued letters of request for the examination of a

---

[16] See Arts. 16–18.

[17] But any such local liquidator, who may only be appointed if there is a local 'establishment', is under a duty to co-operate with the liquidator in the main proceedings: see Art. 31.

[18] See Art. 25.

[19] It is, for example, in New York or Moscow.

[20] See Art. 48(3).

[1] See *Re International Power Industries N.V.*, *supra* p. 403.

[2] It would be usual for the examinations to be ordered pursuant to s. 236 of the Insolvency Act 1986, rather than relying upon the equivalent New Zealand provision: see also *England v. Purves*, *supra*.

[3] The company has long since ceased to have any real connection to Panama.

[4] Applying *Re a Company (No. 00359 of 1987)* [1988] Ch. 210.

director who resides in England. Acting under section 426, the court may order the examination.[5]

(3) G Co. is an Irish corporation that has been put into examinership in Ireland. Having received a section 426 request from the Irish court, the court in England may apply the Irish examinership law in England. Thus a stay of civil actions or an order preventing the presentation of a winding up petition in England may be ordered.[6]

(4) The facts are as in Illustration (3) above; however, it has been requested that G Co. be put into administration under Part II of the Insolvency Act 1986. The English court has jurisdiction so to do.[7]

(5) Inc. is a Delaware corporation that has gone into Chapter 11 in the United States. In the US Bankruptcy Court an avoidance action has been commenced against D, a director of Inc. The English court has jurisdiction, in appropriate circumstances, to grant a Mareva injunction against D as interim relief in aid of the US proceedings.[8]

(6) The facts are as in Illustration (5) above; however, the US Bankruptcy Court has recently entered judgment against D for US$500,00. D appeared in the US proceedings and argued as to the merits before withdrawing. The judgment may be enforced at common law in England.[9]

(7) A has been made bankrupt in Scotland. Shortly before the date of the sequestration in Scotland, C attached A's assets in England and obtained a garnishee order nisi. The Scottish court has issued a request that the High Court, in relation to C's incomplete attachment, apply section 346 of the Insolvency Act 1986 and deny C the benefit of the incomplete attachment. The High Court will act pursuant to the request of the Scottish court.[10]

---

[5] In other words, assistance may be given regardless of whether the liquidation would be entitled to recognition under the common law rules.
[6] As in *Re Goodman International* (1990) 5 B.J.I.B. & F.L. 530 (note).
[7] *Re Dallhold Estates (UK) Pty. Ltd.* [1992] B.C.L.C. 621.
[8] See p. 396, *supra.*
[9] See *Green* v. *Paramount Capital Corpn.*, p. 401, n. 4, *supra.*
[10] Thus in substance reversing the ruling in *Galbraith* v. *Grimshaw* [1910] A.C. 508.

Index